ABOUT THE AUTHOR

The purpose of this section is, at least in part, to answer three questions that you, my dear reader, may have; "Who is this person, why should I read his writing and how can I trust him?"

As I hope reading this book will demonstrate, subjective (we all have personal reasons for d problems than it solves (see § 11.1 Why Can Serioı both multifaceted and must be earned (§ 53 Tru

CW01499215

What a brief biography might be able to do is by virtue of which you can apply your own criteria for value. In other words, how you evaluate my biography in relation to the need that has led you to start to read this book might be helped along by you having some kind of frame of reference. However, in the final analysis, this frame of reference is simply a heuristic crutch; something that allows us to take a shortcut without having to strain our little grey cells (§ 72.5 Cognitive Load and Heuristics).

THE BEGINNING

I was born in Tehran in 1964. My mother was a teacher of Philosophy and Logic and my father was an accountant. My maternal grandfather was a theologian (before he gave it up and became a railroad inspector) and my paternal grandfather was a vet who escaped from Baku, Azerbaijan and took refuge in Iran following the Bolshevik invasion.

I was a precocious child and, at school, I was difficult to control (my grade for 'discipline' was well below par). My primary school teacher suggested to my mother that, ideally, I should be accelerated a year because some academic pressure would help focus my energies more productively. There wasn't a mechanism for doing that within the Iranian education system, but my mother found a way. Nevertheless, I changed schools every year and, at one point, twice in one year. In 1975, she decided to continue her studies in Philosophy in England and took me with her. After a few months, she gained admittance to an MPhil programme in Philosophy of Religion at Kings College London and I started my secondary schooling (with kids of my own age for a change) in Barnsley, South Yorkshire. A year later, I was enrolled at Ackworth School, a long-standing (est. 1779) coeducational boarding school in West Yorkshire.

THE MIDDLE

In 1986, I obtained my bachelor's degree in Applied Chemistry at Cardiff University. After that, I was invited by our Toxicology lecturer (who turned out to be the head of the Pharmacology department) to begin a research program looking into the mechanisms of development of an interesting type of asthma (byssinosis) that is caused by the inhalation of cotton dust by cotton workers. During that time, I became interested in the placebo effect. A few years later, I embarked on a course in clinical hypnosis hoping to gain insights into the power of suggestion as it pertained to the placebo effect. Through our instructor, I became interested in biofeedback and neurofeedback. Meanwhile, I was also interested in becoming a teacher and embarked on a teacher training course at Bath University, specialising in teaching chemistry to 11 to 18 year olds.

In 1996, I went to visit my family in Iran. At border control, I was told that I would not be allowed to leave the country until I had completed a period of National Service, so I did.

When I returned to the UK in 1999, I became a volunteer researcher at Professor John Gruzelier's lab at the school of Behavioural Sciences at Imperial College, London where I learnt much about neurofeedback and psychology. In 2004, I decided to become a psychologist and, in 2006, I obtained a master's degree in Psychology of Education from the Institute of Education (IOE), University of London. For the next five years, I worked with Research teams at the IOE looking into factors that affect students' subject choices. In 2011, I set up my own business as a consultant and life coach, specialising in Emotion Management.

THE END

The end has yet to come.

THE MISSING BITS

You can read more about 'the author' at www.introducingaffinitology.com

Trexicon Publishing

is proud to present

Introducing

Affinitology

Towards a New Science of Connecting with People

by

Dr Beej

Bijan Riazi-Farzad

BSc (Hons), MSc, PhD, MBPsS

First Printing, 2024

ISBN: 978-1-4716-0481-2

Trexicon Publishing
www.trexiconpublishing.com

Trexicon Publishing, Talbot House, 204-226 Imperial Drive, Rayners Lane, Harrow,
Middlesex, England, United Kingdom, HA2 7HH

For more information about Affinitology and the author, please visit
www.introducingaffinitology.com

DEDICATION

To Poupak

who has been there to refuel my resolve whenever the fuel gauge was about to move into the red.

Please...

Before starting to read this book, I urge you to take a moment to answer the questions in the following link first (see § 10.2 *"How do you track progress?"* for an explanation).

introducingaffinitology.com/baseline_questionnaire/

Scan this

ACKNOWLEDGEMENTS

> **"Bernard of Chartres... pointed out that we see more and farther than our predecessors, not because we have keener vision or greater height, but because we are lifted up and borne aloft on their gigantic stature."** [†]
>
> - John of Salisbury, Metalogicon (1159)

† This is, apparently, the earliest recorded version of the adage, "standing on the shoulders of giants."

I am grateful to my teachers throughout the years (and the ages) beginning with **my mother** who taught me to question and to reason logically and **my father** who taught me about pragmatism. Also, to

- Ariana whose zest for life is evident in everything she does.
- Parsa whose compassion and sense of responsibility was evident from before he could talk and has not diminished.
- Bahman who has been a father to me.
- My maternal grandfather who taught me about consistency of action, perseverance and the value of corns and calluses.
- My cousin, Alireza, who has been my friend since we were children and who is a role model of acceptance; he has never asked me to explain any of my actions even when I have been clearly remiss.
- My paternal grandfather who taught me that it is never too late to start from scratch.
- Andrew Ward who showed me what benevolence and dedication look like in practice.
- Jacqui who demonstrated the difference between love and possessiveness in practice.
- Gengiz for introducing me to the works of Tony Robbins
- Professor Michael Reiss who has been a role model of leadership and tolerance. He taught me that "few things in life are disastrous" and helped me make decisions by saying, "do what only you can do."
- Noshad who helped me learn that every ending is a new beginning.

- Professor John Gruzelier who has no idea how positively instrumental he was in my life's trajectory.
- Yvonne Reynolds who saw in me what I couldn't see in myself.
- Anne (née) Lane who taught me more than she knows.
- Professor Shirley Simon who taught me not to bury the main point in the middle of the text.
- Andreas Tiliris who showed me what generosity of spirit looks like.
- Shiva and Dhiren who supported me when I needed it.
- Dr Masoud Ahmadi who taught me not to ask people if they need help but to simply give it when they clearly do.
- Dr Ali Rashidi who buffered me against life's onslaughts when I needed it.
- Mahvash who deserves more than I knew how to give.
- My cousin, Hamid Bagheri who has taught me more than he knows.
- Professor Paul Nichols who believed in me enough to invite me to do research with him in Pharmacology.
- My pupils throughout the decades who have taught me more than I have taught them.
- My clients whose trust, sincerity, willingness to share and courage in spite of life's blows have been a constant reminder of the robustness of the human spirit.
- The late Peter Avery (OBE) who demonstrated what I now consider to be some of the highest of human virtues.
- Arthur Bray who, as a role model, taught me much about management.
- The Persian sages, throughout the ages, especially Hafez, Sa'di and Rumi who have been my spiritual companions since I was in Primary School.

The list is, of course, endless and right now it feels to me like I am trying to thank all the cells in my body for being there to help me become more than I am. Thinking this reminded me of the following anecdote that my mother told me.

> *Once, when I was just a baby, a lady on a bus told my mother that pillows can be bad for babies' necks. In the almost six decades since then, I have slept without pillows. This experience has taught me how we can take off layers of dependence, one onion skin at a time.*

I am, therefore, also grateful to that stranger on the bus and the myriad of others whose positive influence I will never even be aware of, but who, nevertheless, have had a profound impact on my life, especially those who have made it possible for me to serve. **You all have your place in the mosaic and tapestry of my psyche and I am grateful to all of you for that.**

PROLOGUE

I started work on this book in 2017. It is now 2023. During this period, there have been staggering changes in technology and society. In my humble opinion, much of what we have gained in quantity (more 'friends', more products, more information), we have lost in quality - fewer truly intimate moments, planned obsolescence, less reliable information, shorter attention spans and less deep contemplation. We now seem to be living in a world where dopamine dominates and serotonin is medication. In some ways, I lament that I was not able to publish this work sooner since I feel that, now, more than ever, we need to reassess the nature of our psyche, our interactions and the nature of our humanity.

PREAMBLE TO 'ABOUT THE AUTHOR'

This book is about relationships and I believe that it would be somewhat hypocritical of me to talk about relationships with you in a cold and clinical manner. That's why I do not consider this book to be strictly a textbook. I prefer to think of it more as a (necessarily) one-way conversation or discourse. In conversation, we tend to reveal much about ourselves, not only through our tone and body language, but also through the things that interest us (and distract us) as well as our mannerisms. I suspect (nay; expect) that you will glean more about my personality, character and idiosyncratic tendencies through how and what I reveal about myself through the main text of this book than you will from reading a conventional 'About the Author' script.

Returning to a phrase that I used just now, it is lamentable that the words 'cold and clinical' are often used together to denote lack of emotion. In Persian, the equivalent to the word clinical is بالینی (*baaleeni*) which literally translates as, 'of the bedside'. Interestingly, in English, 'bedside manner' relates to the interpersonal (and emotional) aspects of clinical practice which is far from 'cold and clinical'. [This reminds me of the movie, Patch Adams, starring Robin Williams, which I recommend to anyone interested in clinical practice.]

Anyway, for the sake of completeness, there now follows an 'About the Author' section.

TABLE OF CONTENTS

PART 1 PRELIMINARIES

PART 2 UNDERSTANDING RELATIONSHIPS

PART 3 MEDICAL AFFINITOLOGY

PART 4 THE PHYSICS OF RELATIONSHIPS

PART 5 THE NEXT LEG OF THE JOURNEY

LIST OF FIGURES

LIST OF TABLES

LIST OF EXERCISES

Author's notes on first edition

One of the lifetime ambitions of my late friend, Sir Peter Avery, was to translate the 'Divan of Hafiz' from Persian into English. From time to time, I would ask him how far he had gotten and he would tell me that he was not quite happy with it and he needed to make slight adjustments. After several years of waiting, I told him that people were being denied his wisdom because he was focusing on the details too much. One day, I called upon him and inquired about the progress of his translation and he told me that he had handed over the manuscript to his publisher. A few months later, I asked him whether the work had been published or not and he told me that his publisher was having financial problems and that is why the publication of the book was delayed. I asked him why he didn't give his book to a different publisher and he said, "Because I don't know how the other publisher makes his money." Clearly, the way he was living his life reflected the Core Values and Principles of what he was studying and translating. [The book was published not long before he passed away. It is called 'The Collected Lyrics of Hafiz of Shiraz']

It recently occurred to me that I had fallen into a similar trap of perfectionism whilst depriving my audience of what I want to give them. I then remembered reading somewhere that Google considers itself to be in 'perpetual beta'. That helped to curb my perfectionist tendencies.

I have been working on this book for about 6 years and perhaps I should have taken this stance much earlier. Nevertheless, I have now decided to release the first version of this book, flaws and all, and to continue to develop it with the help of my readers.

This note serves several purposes:

- ☞ As an apology and a justification to my readers
- ☞ As an invitation for engagement and collaboration
- ☞ As an inspiration for other authors caught in the let-me-make-it-just-a-little-bit-better trap
- ☞ As a means of reassuring myself that I am doing the 'right' thing.

It is my privilege to be your guide

Depending on your travel style, you may be a 'Planner' and prefer to plan your journey in detail in advance or you may be an 'Improviser', preferring to just take a step in any direction and see where providence takes you.

Since you are reading this work, you have chosen a third alternative, which is to employ the services of a guide. I am grateful to you for giving me that privilege.

I have endeavoured to blend the structure of a planned journey with the excitement of an improvised one. I look forward to your feedback regarding the extent to which I have succeeded at this quest.

Gender pronoun

There is nothing in this book that cannot be applied equally to both men and women. My use of 'he' or 'she' [except when I am telling a story where the gender of the individual concerned is clear and/or relevant] simply reflects what I perceive to be a weakness in the English Language, i.e., a lack of gender-neutral pronouns for referring to persons. To appease the more sensitive amongst us, I have endeavoured to alternate my use of these pronouns between 'he' and 'she'.

A Brief Overview of This Book

An outline of a transformational journey

Although I originally conceived this work as a course, I invite you to think of it as a journey; a journey into the pendulous but enchanting, sometimes dangerous, often confusing, but always exciting land of interpersonal relationships. On this journey, we take our typical understandings of the nature of relationships and transform them in ways that enable us to create what I have called SMERs (Satisfying and Mutually Empowering Relationships).

In § 1.2 (The Seed), I explain how this book transformed itself from what was to be a simple book to accompany a course into becoming a full-blown textbook on a proposed new academic discipline. Any new field of human endeavour requires (and acquires) new concepts, necessitating the development of specialised vocabulary to convey those ideas. As such, you will be introduced to a few new words here.

My intention is that, through the use of this specialised vocabulary (jargon), we will be able to talk about interpersonal relationships much more precisely and in greater depth. Just as importantly, I hope that this specialised vocabulary will enable us to perceive relationships from various perspectives.

As I explain further in Unit 3 (The Power of Language), we tend to think of words as tools for communication. However, I suggest that communication, in spite of its enormous importance, is a secondary function of language (words).

Yes, you heard me correctly. Words do something much more important than to facilitate communication; words create; yes *create*, thoughts. And thoughts are the fundamental units of our sense of being, our understanding of our own existence. They don't merely allow us to *express* what we know and think, they *define* and characterise what and *how* we think. They literally 'program' our minds by providing the operators, the code, syntax, commands, arrays, loops, arguments, functions, variables and other units that are needed for developing and running our mental processes.

The following table and its annotations are a sketch of a roadmap, comparing the typical view of relationships with the view presented here. I hope that by the end of this journey, you will feel differently about yourself, other people and your relationships.

Table 1: Part 1

A comparison of (the expected changes in) our understanding of relationships after going on this journey together

Typical view	Affinitological view
Two people become involved because each of them wants[3] something.	Two Identities[1] interact[2] because they have common or complementary *elements*.[4]
They form a relationship.	A Nexus[5] emerges[6] from the interaction.
The quality of a relationship depends on how the two people involved treat each other.	The quality of the relationship depends on what the Identities focus on (pay attention[7] to).
How these two people treat each other depends on their personalities.	How Identities interact depends on the situation and how each Identity interprets the situation.[8]
How the relationship develops depends on the decisions that each person in the relationship makes. These decisions are based on priorities.	How the Nexus develops depends on the decisions that each Identity makes.[9] These decisions depend on the Identity's values [10] *in the specific situation.*

Table 1: Part 1 Notes

[1] Each of us, as individuals, have a number of Identities (§ 29.4 The Omniself). At any one moment one of the Identities within each individual forms a bond with an Identity within another individual. Here, we explore the nature and qualities of such bonds from various points of view (Unit 5: Classification of Relationships).

[2] The unit of a relationship is an interaction (or a memory of an interaction). Each interaction is like a LEGO™ brick. Relationships are built or deconstructed depending on the arrangement of these bricks (interactions) and their contexts (because context is the basis for deriving meaning).

[3] There are at least two problems with the idea of relationships being based on both parties wanting something; Firstly, wanting implies conscious choice (relationships are not always created consciously) and, secondly, in this context, wanting implies that the primary intention is to 'take' (any 'giving' being a means for taking).

[4] These common or complementary *elements* can be needs, wants, goals, values, skills, experiences, resources, the environment or something else. Although this theme runs throughout our discourse, we explore the concept of common and complementary elements in detail in § 47 (Common and Complementary Elements).

[5] A Nexus is a Third Entity (akin to a chemical bond) that is partly dependent upon, but separate from, the individuals who led to its emergence.

[6] Emergence is something from nothing through the principle that the whole is more than the sum of its parts.

[7] How we treat each other depends on what we pay attention to and what we pay attention to depends on our values (§ 34.1.2 Values).

[8] A pivotal concept along our journey is that the meaning of anything depends on its context. This context (or situation) also determines which of our Identities comes to the fore to interact with that particular situation. We explore this in more depth in § 29.4 (The Omniself).

[9] Different Identities within the same individual may make a different decision under the same circumstances.

[10] Each Identity's values sensitise it to different aspects of the environment.

Table 1: Part 2

Typical view	Affinitological view
Other people can interfere with a relationship.	Other Identities can influence the Nexus.[11]
Conflict disrupts relationships.	The effect of conflict on relationships can be empowering or disempowering depending on how each Identity reacts to the conflict situation.
Relationships are stable.	Relationships are in a constant state of flux.[12] Relationships that do not change are not healthy.[13]
Relationships are definable.	Relationships are living systems.[14]
The relationship between two people is nobody else's business.[15]	Relationships are not independent of their ecosystem.[16] This ecosystem consists of other individuals and their Identities.

Table 1: Part 2 Notes

11   The distinction between 'interfere' and 'influence' is that the former has negative connotations. In practice, influence can empower or disempower the Nexus to a lesser or greater extent depending on the quality of the Nexus. We explore this perspective in § 60.2 (Interference).

12   A stable relationship is not one where the relationship does not change; it is one where a bond is maintained between the Identities that form the relationship, *in spite of change* (§ 58.2 Good Vibrations).

13   A relationship that does not change does not grow. Relationships that do not grow tend to fade away; they get squeezed out by other relationships. Relationships that do not change and do not fade away become putrid, that is, encourage the growth of entities that feed on the stagnancy (i.e., that aspect of the psyche becomes vulnerable to exploitation). Putridity also discourages the growth of more empowering relationships - you can't farm on a quagmire or at least, it requires a great deal of expertise and the question becomes, "When is it worth it?". If a stagnant relationship does not become infested, it will become barren space; occupying a part of the psyche that is unproductive or underutilised, like an unoccupied building in a prime location that prevents others from making an empowering use of it because it has someone else's name on it; it is 'possessed' by someone who is not there (his spirit haunts the place by way of legal possession).

14   As yet, we cannot define life. However, relationships show all the characteristics that we consider to be the identifying features of living systems (§ 26.2 Characteristics of Living Systems). As such, they can make decisions that are independent of the Identities that led to their emergence. They use the same physical bodies that house them (§ 29.4 The Omniself) to manifest their decisions.

15   In legalese, this is called 'Privity of Contract'. In practice, other people make it their business, e.g., if you try to use the clause to keep government out of a contractual relationship, there is usually a clause that thwarts such an attempt.

16   Like all living systems, relationships are sustained through their interaction with their environment.

This page is left intentionally blank

Part 1
Preliminaries

> "Given the choice between… overcomplication and simplicity, I have thrown in with the 'people', tossing in a big word now and then as a sort of hamburger to distract the watchdogs of the academies, whilst I slip in through the basement doors and say hello to my friends."
>
> - Eric Berne, What do you say after you say hello?

Unit 1

Introduction

Image by Mohamed Hassan from Pixabay

"If you have an apple and I have an apple and we exchange
these apples then you and I will still each have one apple.
But if you have an idea and I have an idea and we exchange
these ideas, then each of us will have two ideas."

George Bernard Shaw

Chapter 1

The Evolution of an Idea

A few decades ago, I conceived of a book to write. I thought of calling it "In Search of Relationships." It was inspired by some work I did in pharmacology in the 1980s to help develop a better understanding of the relationship between the dose of a drug and how tissues responded to it. My intention was to help us to steer away from linear thinking. I wanted to show that, as scientists, we can explore different mathematical models, including exponential, sinusoidal, polynomial, etc. instead of relying on linear or logarithmic scales most of the time. The idea still remains to be realised. That was before I studied psychology.

* * *

It was our first day at university and we listened eagerly to the authority figure who strode into the lecture theatre confidently to introduce us to the department. He began by saying, "Forget everything that you have been taught at school about chemistry. You are going to be taught everything that you need to know about chemistry from scratch." I was quite relieved.

Don't worry, I'm not going to ask you to forget everything you know about relationships. We are, however, going to look at relationships from various different perspectives, some of which may be quite unfamiliar territory. All I ask is that you embrace each new perspective first (try it on for size) and then, if it doesn't feel comforting enough, look for a perspective that does.

On this journey, we are going to re-examine our notion of relationships by asking basic questions about the nature of relationships. So fundamental in fact, they will require us to rethink our concept of relationships. Here comes a taster.

As a father, my relationship with my son is different from my relationship with my son as his friend or his tutor (if I happen to be helping him with his school work, for example). Clearly, each of these 'relationships' requires a different 'me' to be present, otherwise there would be no point in having words like, father, friend and tutor. We can, therefore, be different 'people' at different times with even the same person. This means that our 'relationships' can change from moment to moment. To put it another way, what we see here is that I can have at least three different relationships with my son, as a father, as a friend and as a tutor. Each of these relationships has its own quality, dynamics and rules and involves different expectations. See § 92 (Relationship Frameworks) and § 33 (Atasinex Cluster).

For instance, having now become aware that what I call 'myself' and what I call 'my son' can have at least three different relationships with each other, I cannot say that, as his father, my relationship with my son, is made up of myself and my son. To do so would not allow us to distinguish between my relationship with him as his father and my relationship with him as his tutor.

It now becomes apparent that we need to 'split' each individual into different 'roles', or what I have called 'Identities' (my 'Father' Identity, my 'Friend Identity', my 'Tutor' Identity and his 'Son' Identity, his 'Pupil' Identity and his 'Friend' Identity) and we need to examine the characteristics (beliefs, values and expectations) of each of these Identities separately.

For example, what is expected of a 'father'? What is the 'complementary' expectation of a son for there to be a father-son relationship. Similarly, what is expected of a 'tutor' and what is the corresponding expectation of a 'pupil' for there to be a healthy tutor-pupil relationship.

Other questions also arise, such as, to what extent can (and does) my Father Identity interfere with my Tutor Identity? To what extent can these be kept separate? When my Tutor Identity is active or dominant, where does my 'Father' Identity go and vice versa?

These concepts can be applied to other types of relationship or what I have called, relationship frameworks (§ 92). At this stage, all I ask is that you allow your curiosity to do most of the work.

1.1
Relationships are what we live for

In my several decades of personal and professional life experience, I have yet to come across a case where my clients', friends' or colleagues' problems were not inextricably intertwined with their relationships. Indeed, relationships *are* what we live for. Without relationships we would die. And if we did survive, we would rather be dead [There are exceptions of course, but let's not go there]. Solitary confinement is considered to be one of the harshest punishments and many authorities on the subject consider long-term solitary confinement to be a form of torture.

If you look for the word 'relationship' in a search engine and take away the results that offer definitions only, you will find that most of the top results are about relationships where there is a sexual element. What you will also notice is that there is a plethora of advice about how to improve your love life. However, I believe that the vast majority of issues that we face regarding our romantic relationships stem from a lack of basic understanding of ourselves and the nature of **relationships in general**.

A romantic relationship is a relationship first.

If I don't have a firm grasp of what a 'relationship' is, how can I create a healthy 'romantic' one? Any advice that we get about romantic relationships that does not cover the basics (or which is not at least clear about assuming knowledge of the basics) is not likely to lead to lasting improvement in any of our relationships. Basics such as, "Who am I?", "What do I want?", "What is a relationship?", "What is a healthy relationship?", "Where do I want to be and why?".

In many ways, much of what I discuss with my clients (and teach in my courses), would have served me well had I known about them at a much younger age. But we need to accept this as the universal irony of life; much of what we learn through experience benefits future generations more than it does ourselves. That reminds me of this endearing soundbite that I saw written along the side of a hippie van back in the 1980s,

---

**"We do not inherit the world from our ancestors;
we borrow it from our children."**

1.2

The Seed
(How the Adventure Began)

After several decades of working within various fields of endeavour including, medical research, computing, chemistry, business, teaching, education research, psychology and counselling, I decided to launch a website dedicated to providing some of the much-needed information and skills that, on the whole, schools do not help us to acquire. Indeed, in spite of a minimum of 12 years of schooling, the education system not only fails to provide us with many of the basic skills we need for a prosperous life, it actively prevents us from acquiring some of those skills. For example, it gives us a distorted view of personal and social values.

When putting together content for the site, I decided to include a section consisting of online courses based on my own workshops and seminars. I planned to talk about decision-making, identity formation, happiness, self-confidence, spirituality, love and much more. The more content I thought of, the more it became apparent to me that the information will need to be organised into separate 'schools' and that I should begin with the single most important aspect of our lives that is not directly addressed within the education system; relationships. At this point, the seed of a 'Relationship School' was planted.

When I began to work on the content of the Relationships course, I thought all I needed to do was to gather material from my seminars and workshops, spice it up with some anecdotes from my personal and professional experiences and that would be it. But that's not what happened. When I set off on this journey, I had no idea that I would end up somewhere so completely different from what I had envisaged.

I started by putting together a simple course structure. As I began to fill out the various sections, it soon became apparent that this was going to turn out to be more than just a training manual to accompany a course; it was becoming a full-blown textbook on a topic that no one had treated in this way before. It began to grow and evolve in ways that I never anticipated when I conceived the project. Sometimes it felt like it had a life of its own and my mind and body were simply a medium for its expression.

What started off as a book intended to provide primarily practical advice supported by theory, has transformed itself into a more theoretical book which, I hope, will seed the development of new practical approaches for improving our interpersonal relationships.

In the end, it became what you see before you. I don't know what to call it; a textbook, a treatise, a discourse, a monograph, a proposal, a course, a manual or something else. So, my dear reader, I will let you be the judge of that. Meanwhile, in keeping with my original idea of what this was going to be, I am calling it a coursebook. As you read through this book, you will come across material that refers to that original idea of this being a book to accompany a course. I decided not to take these sections out. I regard them as something like a coccyx; a remnant of an evolutionary past.

In this volume, I also hope to present a bird's-eye view of the relationship terrain so as to allow us to perceive relationships in a more holistic way and to help make our relationships grow and endure. I hope that you will enjoy reading it as much as I have enjoyed researching, developing, writing and sharing it.

The following transcript from the movie "Lucy" condenses the essence of the spirit in which this course was developed.

> Lucy: "They're all exploding inside my brain, all this knowledge. I don't know what to do with it."

> Professor Norman: "If you're asking me what to do... You know, if you think about the very nature of life, I mean, from the very beginning, the development of the first cell that divided into two cells. The sole purpose of life has been to pass on what was learnt. There was no higher purpose. So, if you're asking me what to do with all this knowledge you're accumulating, I'd say pass it on. Just like any simple cell going through time."

If you have seen the movie, you will know that, in the end, Lucy 'downloads' all her knowledge in to a computer. I do not have the luxury of being able to do that and, therefore, whilst creating this work, I found myself struggling with another conflict; a conflict between quality, quantity and speed. The better I want this work to be, the later it will begin to help people and the longer it will be.

In my quest to resolve these conflicts I was guided by two experiences. The first was something that I was told by one of my mentors at a Toastmasters club. He said, "People will not know what you decided to leave out." This reminds me of an experience from my boarding school days.

> *When I was about 12 years old, one of my fellow schoolmates was assembling a model aircraft kit. It was about 25cm long. With a fine paintbrush, he was delicately painting the inside of the cabin of the aircraft. I said to him, "Why are you painting the inside? No one is going to see that." And his response was an enduring life lesson that has remained with me to this day. He said, "But I will know that I have painted the inside of it."*

This meant that, every time I began to worry that this work is not getting into the hands of the people who need it fast enough, a voice inside my head tried to console me by saying, "No one will know what you excluded" and another voice retorted, "But *I* will know." So, I just carried on writing and said to myself, I will know when it is time to publish when these two Identities (§ 29.4 The Omniself) resolve their conflict.

I hope that this work will not only help us improve the quality of our interpersonal relationships, but that it will also arouse interest in new approaches to research within this area. I also believe that it will inspire and further enable novelists and other storytellers in their creative endeavours.

1.3

How to Approach this Book

Think about how you might 'approach' someone that you find interesting or attractive. You wouldn't rush in and try to have a 'deep and meaningful' relationship with that person on your first encounter would you? First, we need to stand back and observe, assess the situation and work out a strategy for approaching the person in a way that is conducive to a satisfactory first interaction. An interaction that will interest and excite both of you. I suggest that you approach this book in a similar vein. Flick through it, get to know it superficially first and then probe for more depth.

I set many challenges for myself when embarking on this journey. One of these was to blur the distinction between a textbook and a self-help book. As such, this book is what you might call a hybrid, but I suggest that you don't start putting labels on it just yet.

This book is also an attempt to introduce a new scientific discipline, one that consolidates Individual Psychology and Social Psychology (§ 1.5 A Missing Link).

As you begin to read this book, you may find certain things about it strange. At times, it may be the words that I use. At other times it may be its structure and how it flows. At yet other times, you may start to ask yourself, "What has any of this got to do with relationships?" Let me suggest that at those moments, what you are doing is like holding a piece of a jigsaw puzzle in your hand and asking, "Where does this piece fit in?"

If jigsaw puzzles aren't your thing, then you can think of it like this: How do we feel when we first listen to a new genre of music? At first, it feels strange. After we listen to it a few times, depending on our environment and our mood, we either grow to like it or decide that we can't relate to that particular genre. Now, if a friend that we respect tells us that he or she likes that type of music, we will probably make a greater effort at trying to understand and to like it. Such is the power of empowering relationships. And that is what this book is about.

If you find a section of the book not to your liking, feel free to skip to a different section, perhaps one with more anecdotes or graphics or quotes. The book's sections are strongly interlinked so that you will be guided towards the section that you skip at some point, but this time, with some background information that will put the material that seemed unengaging at first into a more appealing context.

Throughout this book, you will see cross-references [there are over 1000 of them]. They look like this: (§ X). I suggest that on your first reading, you treat these as "Oh, I don't have to worry about not understanding this fully at this time because it will be clarified later" and not as an indication that you need to read that section first before you continue. Just keep on reading and trust that more explanation is forthcoming.

[Originally, I used the conventional notation that looks like this "(see § X)". But then I realised that I could shorten the book by the equivalent of three whole pages by removing the word 'see']

On subsequent readings, these in-line references act as reminders of what we have talked about in different sections of the course and will act as triggers to enrich our understanding. In other words, they become, "Oh, yes, I remember that. Wow, and it connects with this; it makes more sense now."

1.4

Affinitology

Here, I introduce the term 'affinitology' (§ 21 What is Affinitology?). It is part of my attempt to set into motion the development of a new science of interpersonal relationships modelled on the medical sciences.

This book draws from the growing knowledgebase in modern psychology, along with personal experience with thousands of students and clients as well as my own decades of research in physical, medical and social sciences, spiced with ancient wisdom gleaned from my life-long interest in Persian mysticism.

The whole concept of affinitology revolves around the three components that are needed for any kind of relationship to exist: The Self, The Other and what I have called, The Third Entity or The Nexus.

The Third Entity is the connection or the bond. It is as important as the people in the relationship, but it is often neglected because it is invisible; "It's about you and me, baby!" Well, actually, it is not just about you and me, it is also about the things that bring us together and hold us together physically, emotionally, financially, culturally, socially, spiritually, etc (Unit 11: Dimensions of Human Experience).

In this book, I use the words Connection, Bond, Relationship, The Nexus and The Third Entity interchangeably (to mean the same thing). However, as we progress through the course, you will notice that I begin to make certain distinctions between them. For example, in everyday language, we use the word relationship to refer to all three elements that comprise a relationship; The Self, The Other and the Nexus [Although we may not have thought of the last consciously before]. In § 35.1 (Embryology of Relationships), I propose the term Pactum with a view to eliminating the confusion between 'relationship' being the Nexus and 'relationship' being something that also includes the two Identities that comprise the relationship.

1.5
A Missing Link

Affinitology is a grey area. In fact, it's the grey area in the following diagram (Figure 1). But seriously, one of my objectives in this book is to demonstrate that there is a gap in our current classification of knowledge. Here, I argue for the need for a new discipline to bridge individual psychology and social psychology.

I hope one day, perhaps in the not-so-distant future, when we ask children, "What do you want to be when you grow up?", "I want to be an affinitologist" will be an option.

I also propose various approaches for addressing this gap. In doing so, I draw upon existing knowledge within various disciplines including physics, chemistry, biology, medicine, economics and mathematics.

Figure 1 Affinitology in Relation to Personal and Social Psychology

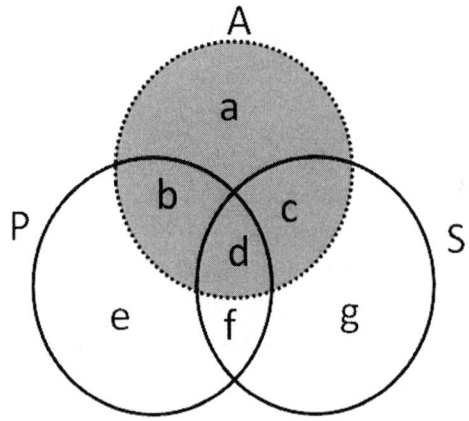

Circle P: Individual Psychology
Circle S: Social Psychology
Circle A: Affinitology

Region 'a' is about those aspects of interpersonal relationships that are independent of the individual characteristics of the two people that constitute the relationship and their social environment. For example, we can talk about many [though not all] aspects of 'love' or 'parenting' without needing to bring into the discussion those factors that are within the domain of Individual

Psychology (personality, etc) or Social Psychology (how people's thoughts and behaviours are affected by other people).

An example of a concept that would fall within region 'b' would be Agreeableness; an individual trait that has a direct impact on the quality of our relationships. In other words, we cannot study Agreeableness without considering its impact on a person's interpersonal relationships. However, this trait is relatively independent of who it is that we are interacting with; it is a personal trait.

[You might be wondering how a trait that is about how we perceive relationships be independent of the people with whom we are interacting. And that would be a commendable observation. We do this by one of two methods. The first is that we ask people (through interviews or questionnaires) to tell us what they do or like to do in different situations involving people. This takes out the specifics (assumes that when we are answering the questions, we are not thinking about a specific situation or a specific person). Secondly, we observe what people do in different situations and with different people and look into the thoughts and behaviours that remain relatively constant across the different situations and people. In other words, we generalise. Note that such generalisations are heuristics (§ 72.5 **Cognitive Load and Heuristics**) and do not always serve us well.]

Region 'c' represents those aspects of interpersonal relationships that affect, and are affected by, social factors such as social norms and social taboos.

Region 'd' is about those aspects of interpersonal relationships that cannot be studied (or even considered) without taking into account both the social environment and individual factors. An example could be the teacher-student relationship within a classroom.

Region 'e' represents those aspects of individual psychology that can be studied and interpreted without the need to collect data about the person's relationships or membership of groups. For example, where we lie on the introvert-extravert spectrum is not directly about how we interact with other people; introversion and extraversion are about whether a person prefers to process data that is coming in directly from the senses or to process data stored in memory. This means that we can study where someone lies on the introvert-extravert continuum without the need to look at how the person interacts with other people (although we often confuse the issue by doing so).

The influence of crowds on individual psychology and vice versa would be an example of a subject that would fall within region 'f' because our behaviour within a crowd situation depends more on the situation than on our specific interactions with individual Identities within the crowd. Indeed, I have argued (§ 32 **Extended Relationships**) that, in crowd situations, we create a separate Identity within ourselves that bonds with the specific or general 'crowd concept' and not with any of the Identities that constitute the crowd.

Region 'g' is where we can study the mechanisms and dynamics of social groups without the need to collect information about the personality characteristics of the individuals that constitute the group, such as the study of what it takes to generate a Mexican wave.

1.6

Relationship Science

A significant body of research carried out, by individual psychologists and social psychologists, is directly related to interpersonal relationships. The more I began to think through the various ideas that I have presented in this work, the more those ideas began to overlap, and perhaps even infringe upon, the work of many pioneers in the field. This has not been my intention; the ideas flowed out of my head as a natural progression from the previous thoughts. It was only later that I noticed the similarity between some of what I had written and what others have been working on.

Much of the previous work in this field has stemmed from interest in marriage, family relations and parenting and involves the study of these relationships in the context of existing theories such as Attachment Theory, Evolutionary Theories and Interdependence Theory.

Although this is not intended as a strictly academic work, old habits die hard and I hope and trust that what I have proposed here will complement the efforts of my academic and clinical colleagues by providing ideas and insights that will help us improve both the direction and quality of research and practice with a view to understanding and, more importantly, improving, our interpersonal relationships.

Chapter 2

Satisfying Relationships

2.1
What is a SMER?

Throughout this course, I refer to SMERs (satisfying and mutually empowering relationships). The meaning of each of the words that make up the acronym can be very subjective (they can mean different things to different people). Therefore, I feel that it is important to clarify what I mean by the words 'satisfying', 'empowering' and 'mutual'.

2.1.1
What is empowering?

When you empower someone or something you give it power that it didn't have before. But what is power? Or, more accurately, what do I mean by power in this context?

In physics, power is the rate at which energy is converted from one form to another. I propose that the affinitological equivalent to Newtonian Energy is 'Motivational Energy'. I expound on this in Unit 22 (Thermodynamics of Relationships).

When a relationship is empowered in some way, it is able to

  a) convert one type of Motivational Energy into a different kind of Motivational Energy; one that it did not have the potential to contemplate/conceive/perceive/achieve before,
  b) be more efficient in the conversion or
  c) sustain Motivational Energy for longer.

One of the main reasons that we enter into any kind of relationship is that we expect it to give us power that we would not have without the relationship. That power may be as simple as the power to give more.

A relationship can also empower us in other ways. Here are some examples:

- **Expand our comfort zone** so that we can pay more attention to phenomena that we used to avoid or selectively ignore.

- **Expand the range of perspectives from which we can view the world** so that we can switch between different types and qualities of motivational energy in different domains such as attraction, curiosity, caution, awe and wonder.

- **Amplify our emotions by heightening our attentional sensitivity**. Relationships can change what we pay attention to (focus on) by changing our value judgements.

2.1.2
What is Satisfying?

One moment, Wittecam was lying on the ground in the middle of a wet street and the next moment he was lounging on a bed in a beautiful garden surrounded by beautiful people who obeyed his every wish. He was about to get up when he was gently directed to stay lying down. "Just tell us what you want and we will bring it for you" came a gentle voice. "Ah! I'm in heaven" he thought as he reclined back into the soft mattress. Time passed and Wittecam continued to receive whatever he wished for except that, whenever he tried to get up, he was told, "You can ask for anything that you want but you are not allowed to do anything for yourself." Finally, in frustration, he shouted, "This place is hell" at which point, a young beauty gently ran her fingers through his hair and whispered in his ear, "Where did you think you were?"

Something is satisfying when it fulfils a need up to the point where we do not feel the need anymore. After that, we may 'want' more, but we do not 'need' more [at which point, the 'want' is a means of satisfying (or compensating for) a different need].

Having said that, 'satisfaction' is a slippery concept and a double-edged sword. It is slippery because, like happiness, we don't think about it when we are satisfied, therefore thinking about it means that we are dissatisfied [unless one is an academic ;-)]. Not only that, but, if we happen to be satisfied, that is, in the 'state of satisfaction', thinking about it brings us out of that state.

Satisfaction is a double-edged sword because the word implies an endpoint after which we don't feel the need to pursue it. Think for a moment about what that means. It means that complete satisfaction leads to stagnancy. When I'm completely satisfied, I have no reason to do anything and that is a very 'unsatisfactory' state to be in, once we become aware of being there.

I believe that most of us endeavour not to become vegetables [actually that's unfair to vegetables but that's a discussion for another time and place, suffice it to say that vegetables, being alive, are not stagnant (§ 26.2 Characteristics of Living Systems)]. Therefore, dissatisfaction is necessary for us to want to become a better person.

So, where does that leave us with regards to relationships? I define a satisfying relationship like this:

> **A satisfying relationship is one where the individuals involved don't feel that there is anything missing from the relationship.**

I can't leave it hanging in the air like that, so let us, you and I, explore this a little more together.

There is a theory of motivation known as the Two Factor theory or Herzberg's motivation-hygiene theory. I think it is relevant to our discussion about satisfaction because it helps us to resolve the above conflict between being satisfied and being stagnant.

Herzberg's research was primarily focused on job satisfaction. His two-factor model is based on the finding that there are some things that employees expect by default from a work environment. For example, at an interview one does not think to ask, "Do I get toilet facilities?" Herzberg called these hygiene factors. In other words, hygiene factors are those things that, if not present, are a deal breaker. There are other things, on the other hand, that are nice to have but, if not present, would only become a deal breaker if, all else being equal, are offered by another employer. Although Herzberg's work was focused on job satisfaction, it can be applied to motivation in all areas of life. Here are two, highly contrived, scenarios that I made up to help explain this more clearly.

Let's assume that you have arrived at a strange town and you walk into the only car rental place. You are offered (for the same price) a choice between a Lamborghini Aventador without a steering wheel and a Citroen 2CV with a steering wheel. Which would you choose?

For the second part of this exercise, let's assume that the car rental place offers you (for the same price) the 2CV with a Bluetooth media player and the Aventador with no media player. Which would you choose?

In the first scenario, the steering wheel is a hygiene Factor. In spite of all the positive associations that we may have with a Lamborghini, without a steering wheel, functionally, it is not a car.

In the second scenario, the absence of a media player is probably not enough to sway my decision in favour of the 2CV (note that this is in comparison with the Lamborghini Aventador [*with* a steering wheel] at the same price).

How can we apply these understandings to relationships?

We could talk about relationship hygiene factors. Factors that, if not present, are deal breakers. For example, can you imagine any kind of empowering and mutually satisfying relationship (SMER) without trust, communication or autonomy? If you have doubts about the last one, think back to the story of Wittecam at the beginning of this section.

2.1.3
What is Mutual

For the purposes of our discussion here, any aspect of the relationship that empowers and/or satisfies both The Self and The Other is 'mutual'; also known as a win-win scenario (§ 31.2 Types of Symbiosis).

2.2
What is the key to mutually empowering and satisfying relationships?

This is a faulty question and if we were to take it seriously, it would take us on a proverbial wild goose chase. Let me explain.

Can you see anything wrong with the question, "What is the key to a locker?" This question is fundamentally flawed because, of course, the answer would depend on the lock. Typically, it would be a metal object and we could go on to describe keys in general, but I cannot see how knowing that would help us unlock anything, including the secrets to empowering and satisfying relationships.

To find a practical answer we need to ask a practical question. If I want to open a particular locker, my question should be, "*Where* is the key to *this* Locker?" or "*Which* is the key to *this* Locker?" In other words, the key to my heart is different to the key to your heart, but I believe that there is a key; of sorts.

Just like every lock and its key is supposed to be, every relationship is unique, requiring its own key. So, "How *does* one find the key to satisfying and empowering relationships?" The answer is, "Become a locksmith."

How does one become a locksmith? Reading books can help but you will never become a locksmith by reading books alone. It is a practical skill that you can learn in two ways; the hard way and the easy way. The hard way is to start from scratch and reinvent the wheel. The easy way is apprenticeship where you learn by watching others and trying out for yourself as you become more confident. Unfortunately, since the Industrial Revolution, the number of apprentices has dropped so much as to be almost extinct.

Every analogy breaks down at some point and the 'lock and key' analogy to relationships can become problematic if we take it even slightly too far. For example, locks and keys have complementary elements so that a trough in the key corresponds to a spike in the lock and vice versa. However, relationships work on the basis of both complementary and common elements. We explore this in more detail in § 47 (Common and Complementary Elements), but for now, let me get you started here.

An example of a complementary element is where one person has money, the other person has skills and they join forces to create a partnership. An example of common elements is when two people are enthused by the idea of conservation and work together on a common project to rally for saving the environment. The lock and key analogy works for the complementary type of relationship, but not the common elements type (§ 46 *Adjunctum communalis*).

The lock and key analogy breaks down in another very important way when we try to apply it to relationships. Locks and keys are static; they don't change over time. Relationships are dynamic which means that the key and the lock are adapting to their environment continuously. We explore this further in § 26.2 (Characteristics of Living Systems).

There is yet another type of relationship that cannot fit into this model. I have used a 'dative' type of chemical bond as an analogy to help explain that (§ 25 Relationships as Chemical Bonds).

Chapter 3

Writing Style

I can classify the books in my library into three broad categories; theoretical, practical and entertaining. Textbooks tend to fall into the first category, self-help books into the second and fiction falls into the third. I like to be able to understand the theoretical framework behind the practical advice that I am given. My favourite types of books are those that blend the first two categories and spice it with some of the third. *'The Power of Habit'* by Charles Duhigg is one such book that I would recommend to everyone. With a journalistic background, Mr. Duhigg's style is somewhat different from my style which has its roots in academia.

The most consistent guidance given to writers is to write as you would speak, adopting a conversational tone. My 'conversational tone' may seem a little odd to you, but that's what my friends have to contend with too. Yes, I do tend to talk in the hybrid fashion that I alluded to above. This is also reflected in my writing style (what you are reading right now). In other words, that's what actually goes on in my head when I'm thinking in English. I suspect that this is because I began to learn conversational English when I started secondary school in the UK [after I had completed my primary schooling in Iran]. As such, I missed out on the baby talk and the nursery rhymes and the language of the primary school in English. Another reason may be that, at that time, my grandfather told me that if I could learn 20 English words a day, I could know the whole of the dictionary by the time I finished secondary school. So, I did; I started to read the dictionary. I also began to use the words that I had learnt from the dictionary in my conversations. This, sometimes, raised eyebrows, but that's a story for another time and place. Nowadays, I do not recommend vocabulary-based approaches to learning or teaching a new language. My motto is this, "The unit of language is *the sentence* not *the word*."

Also, you may notice variations in 'tone' or style of writing as you progress through this book. For example, in some places, there are more exercises. In other places, it is more or less academic. And in other places, the level of explanation varies. I have been writing this book in my 'spare time' over a period of about six years. One of the central themes in this book is that 'who we are' depends on the situation. Since I have been writing this book under various physical and psychological situations, you may see the variations in my mood (serious, jovial, focused, curious, etc.) reflected in the writing style. The Scientist in me says that 'consistency' is very important. The Philosopher in me says, "Variety is the spice of life". The author in me agrees with the Scientist and the Teacher in me is more inclined to agree with the Philosopher. In the end, the Teacher won the debate.

3.1

Don't Complicate It

When my son was two-and-half years old, he saw a hammock made of interlaced twining and referred to it as 'spidery swing' [taabe-e-ankabooti in Persian]. *I began to think out aloud and said, "Wow! It's amazing what he has done. He has taken a concept from an entirely unrelated context, spider's webs in the garden, extracted the concept of a 'web' and associated it with the interlaced fabric of a hammock. He has then extracted the idea of a swing and associated it with the hammock. He has then taken a concept associated with a web, 'spider' and added the -y to the end of that word to denote that it is an adjective and put it all together to label the hammock as a 'spidery swing'. My wife said, "Don't complicate it."*

I believe that if we fail to see life's complexities, we lose the opportunity to appreciate so much that can be appreciated. Let me give you another example.

The first word processing software that I used was called 'Runoff' [and if we had had modern word processors then, I would have :-)] by Digital Corporation on VT52 terminals attached to VAX/VMS mainframe computers. There was no mouse and no graphics. All we had were characters on a green screen. I typed my entire PhD thesis with it. When I wanted to change the typeface, such as bold, underline, superscript etc., I had to use inline code, similar to HTML. But these inline codes were different for each printer that you wanted to print to. That meant that I needed to know which printer I was going to print on in advance so that I could insert the right inline codes for that printer. If I had to print to another printer, I had to go through the text again and change all the inline codes manually.

Fifteen years later, I was helping a friend with typing his research papers. We were using Microsoft Word 2003. Even though I had been using Word for years and was thoroughly familiar with its features, every time I used a shortcut or the mouse and saw the changes that occurred, as if by magic, I whispered, "I am so grateful (to everyone who has made this possible)." My friend said to me, "I think you appreciate this more than the likes of me because you know what has had to happen in the background to make this possible." And I realised that he was right. I was not only thinking about the ease with which I was able to make changes to the documents; I was also remembering the many hours that I spent writing code in FORTRAN (which I had done to map the way the dose of a drug affects the response of a tissue) and how a misplaced comma or semicolon could frustrate my efforts to get the program to do what I wanted for hours.

In response to my wife saying, "Don't complicate it" I said, "I am not complicating it, I am noticing the complexities that are already there."

I hope that you will bear this distinction in mind as we go on this journey together.

3.2
A Solution to the Footnote Problem

I am a great fan of footnotes. I appreciate their value in adding context and in providing the occasional brief detour and breather along the way.

When I am reading text that contains footnotes, especially for the first time, I feel compelled to read the footnote before continuing. This means that, if the footnote were in line with the text, my eyes would not need to flitter up and down the page. Therefore, for me the idea of footnotes only becomes advantageous on subsequent readings because when one is already familiar with the extra context that the footnotes provide, they can be ignored.

In the age of electronic books, implementing footnotes is slightly more problematic. Unlike with conventional books, the reader would have to take manual steps in order to access the footnotes (click somewhere and click back or hover a pointer). I find this to be more distracting than a traditional footnote. In this book, I have decided to integrate the footnotes into the main text. Bear with me as I tell you a story in support of my reasoning.

When I was conducting research in chemistry at Cardiff University back in the 1980s, we were told to use the referencing convention that is similar to what Wikipedia uses today; sequential numbers in square brackets, like this [123]. However, when I used this convention in my PhD thesis at the School of Pharmacy at the same university, my supervisor told me to change all the references to comply with the APA style which means putting the names of the authors being referenced and the year of publication inside normal brackets, like this: (John Doe, 1987). Then, in the reference section, works of these authors are listed in alphabetical order of first author and date. This means that, in order to maintain contextual continuity, the reader needs to both visually and mentally skip over the text within the reference brackets (the names of the authors and the relevant dates). As with everything else in life, repeated exposure leads to adaptation and I am able to skip over the content of those brackets when I read articles referenced in APA style.

3.2.1
Introducing Midnotes

Taking my cue from the above experience with referencing conventions, I have decided to blend footnotes into the text; with a difference. To help you, the reader, to distinguish visually between the main text and the supplementary notes, I have reduced the font size and changed the typeface of the supplementary information and have placed the 'footnote' text in square brackets [This is an example of a midnote]. Since these are not footnotes or endnotes anymore, I propose the use of the word 'midnotes' to distinguish them. I would welcome your feedback on your experience of this.

3.3
Brackets and Fonts

Square Brackets: For midnotes (formerly footnotes), in addition to using a different font and font size, I emphasise that the inserted text is related to - but an interruption of - the main flow of the text by surrounding the midnote in square brackets. I use normal brackets as I might use a change of tone during conversation to indicate that what I am saying is a short qualifier for what I have just said without veering us off course. For cross references, I use a different font. All of these are intended to be visual guides to compensate for the lack of dynamic visual cues that we would benefit from in face-to-face conversation.

Curved Brackets: In many cases, I have used curved brackets (like this) where grammatical puritans would use bracketing commas. My justification for this is that it avoids confusion with other types of commas without introducing any new complications.

3.4
Advantages of Speed Bumps

In § 61.1 (Genes as Potential), I explain that I am a slow reader which has its roots in my having a squint in one eye. Although I often feel that this has been a handicap (because it slows down my reading speed) it has had its advantages too. For example, I have noticed that few people can comfortably read in a car. I attribute this to their need to coordinate their eyes (which is more demanding than using one eye) when the target is constantly moving. The other advantage of reading slowly is that it allows me to reflect on what I have just read (the material spends longer in my short-term memory and has a higher chance of being transferred to long-term memory).

Along with the advantages that I have already mentioned in the above two sections on midnotes and brackets, another advantage of these 'visual speed bumps' is that, by slowing us down slightly, they allow the concepts to linger in our short-term memory for longer, saving us from our eagerness to skip to the next part at the expense of the requisite reflection.

3.5
Good or Bad?

I encourage my clients to avoid words like 'good' and 'bad' and 'right' and 'wrong' in both their internal conversations (thoughts) and their interpersonal communication.

Striving to avoid the duality that is often the destroyer of souls, I endeavour to practice what I preach. As such, throughout this book, I actively avoid the words 'good' and 'bad' (although I am not always successful). My favourite substitutes are 'empowering' and 'disempowering'. When you encounter these substitutes within the text of this book, try replacing them in your mind with the words 'good' and 'bad' and you will find that they instil a different *feeling* in you. Conversely, when you encounter words such as 'good', 'bad', 'right' and 'wrong' here and elsewhere, try replacing them with 'empowering' and 'disempowering' and see how the feeling that it evokes in you changes. Then you will realise why I am so actively against 'good' and 'bad'. We explore this in more detail in § 39 (Social Ranking Criteria).

3.6
Capitalization

In this book, I have tended to adhere to the conventional norms for capitalization of words. In addition, I have capitalised those words that have specific meanings in the context of affinitology. For example, a friend is a friend, but a (capitalised) Friend is an (capitalised) Identity which itself is not quite the same as what we mean by 'identity' in the conventional sense of the word (§ 42 The Anatomy of Identity).

3.7
Identities and Nexuses

In contrast to an 'Employer-Employee' relationship (Nexus), two Colleague Identities can form a 'Colleague-Colleague' Nexus which can also be called a 'Mutual Colleague' Nexus. For brevity, I have pluralized the Identities and have called the Nexus, a 'Colleagues' Nexus.

3.8
Types and Poles

Throughout this work, we come across many concepts that are often thought of as binary, when, in reality, there is a grayscale. Sometimes, we try to make reality easier to understand by drawing arbitrary lines somewhere along a spectrum so that we can call one side 'dark' and the other side 'light' or one side 'good' and the other side 'bad'. One of the most insidious words is when we categorise phenomena (objects, people, behaviours, patterns, etc) into *types*. I consider this to be the most prevalent thought pattern that results in prejudice and creates a barrier to the creation of healthy relationships.

Notice the number of times that we hear or think in terms of this or that 'type of person'. I propose that we would gain a more objective, flexible, adaptive and, overall, more empowering view if we replace the word 'type' with the word 'pole'. For example, in § 20 (Language and Levels of Persuasion), instead of saying, "There are two types of interference", I have said, "There are two poles of interference". Think about these two sentences and ask yourself which one makes you feel more empowered overall.

Chapter 4

Demographic Considerations

Traditionally, people write books targeted for a particular audience (a specific demographic). The tenet behind this approach is that you cannot please everyone. It is easier to market a product if you have a particular segment of the population in mind. For example, I could make this a technical book and target it at professionals or make it a non-technical book and target it at 'the general population'. Books aimed at 'the general population' tend to adopt a journalistic style [Although, personally, I would welcome reading the dissemination of basic research in a story format, it's just that, as scientists, we are neither trained nor encouraged to do that].

I feel somewhat uncomfortable with this idea of 'demographic' where education is concerned. You see, if I dumb down a subject to make it so-called more 'accessible' to the 'general public', I will have done a disservice to all. I think it is patronizing when I decide for 'the public' what they can or cannot understand. Secondly, I will be depriving people of the opportunity for a deeper understanding of the subject and the pleasures that come from that deeper understanding.

4.1
What Can People Understand?

When my son was still crawling, one of the first things that he said was "izieh" which sounded like, *"in chieh?"* which in Persian means "what's this?" and I responded to it as if that was what he meant. I began to point at the objects he appeared to be looking at and said their name. At one point, after he said "izieh", I pointed at a clock on the western wall of the hall and said, 'clock' [actually, I said 'saa-at' which is Persian for clock] and he turned his head, pointed at a clock on the northern wall and said "izieh". And I said, "Well done, that's a clock too." After that, for a while, he began to show a particular interest in clocks.

At one point, he pointed to the circular face of an analogue weighing scale and said, 'clock' ['saa-at']. I said, "Well done, that looks like a clock, but it isn't. That is a weighing scale." I then began to show him the different parts of a clock and to explain the 'hour hand', 'minute hand' and 'second hand'. Someone said to me, "You don't expect him to understand that stuff, do you?" I told him that I do not know how much he understands, but I prefer to assume that he understands more rather than to assume that he understands less. Also, what I am doing is not entirely about clocks. I am also teaching him,

a) The difference in tone and sentence structure when we are explaining things compared with other types of communication.

b) The different aspects of the environment that we can pay attention to (shape, movement, writing, colour, sound).

c) The differences between speech when describing a clock as compared with talking about the clock itself. [Also, hearing me talk about hours minutes and seconds in relation to the clock will allow him to combine these into a gestalt (§ 15.2 The Importance of Gestalts)]

But perhaps most importantly,

d) I am showing him that his curiosity is appreciated and rewarded with time, attention and a respectful response.

You might say, "But Bijan, what would a crawling baby know about respect?" And I would say, "Much more than we might realise".

My point is that, young children often surprise us with the words that they pick up and their level of understanding of those words. If we only utter words that we believe are within their ability to grasp, then in most cases, I fear that we will underestimate their potential and deprive them of opportunities.

The point I want to make here is that this does not simply apply to children. There was a time when it was thought that it is beyond the capabilities of most people to read and write. What this means is that, on the whole, I have tried not to hold back on using words on account of what I believe my readers may or may not understand.

This reminds me of an anecdote I heard about the James Bond movie, 'License to Kill.' Originally, it was to be called, 'License Revoked'. This was changed because the marketing people did some research and decided that Americans would not be able to connect with the word 'revoked' as much as with the words 'to kill'. I heard this story when I was a teenager and I remember thinking to myself, "What a wasted opportunity." If people don't know enough about a word, its connection to the well-known James Bond would motivate them to learn a new word. My basic views on this have not changed. Therefore, I am not going to go out of my way to deprive people who can learn new words and concepts from doing so because the course would be more popular if I did. Instead, I have tried to do what, in § 5.4.3 (Dealing with Diversity) I have admitted I was not able to do within a classroom setting, which is to differentiate the material for different groups of learners.

4.2

We Can Understand What We Are Motivated to Understand

[Actually, it works the other way round too, we are motivated to understand what we perceive we are capable of understanding. This, I believe is what teaching is at its core; motivating students to want to understand by impressing upon them that, a) they can understand (the understanding is not beyond their capability) and b) what is being presented is valuable enough to warrant expenditure of time and mental resources.]

One of my interests is in public engagement with science. I believe that the vast majority of people, even those who consider themselves technophobes, can engage with, and possibly even thoroughly enjoy, technical stuff. All that is needed is for the person to be motivated enough.

[If you are interested in this then, for starters, I encourage you to watch a TED talk by Benjamin Zander entitled, The Transformative Power of Classical Music (then apply the principles to technology instead of classical music)]

One of the things that doctors are taught at medical school is that patients with chronic diseases are likely to know more about their particular ailment than the doctor because a doctor has to know a little bit about every ailment whereas the patient focuses on her particular issue. This is an example of 'the public' knowing more than 'the expert' and highlights the importance of being 'motivated enough'.

Being able to identify with a subject, what in education circles we refer to as 'relevance', is the first step in motivation. For example, if I were to say to you that knowledge of the principles of spectroscopy could significantly improve your sex life, you might well find yourself inexplicably drawn to searching the internet for the term 'spectroscopy'.

Whenever my pupils tell me that they don't like a particular subject, let's say mathematics, I first ask them what their favourite subject is. Let's say it is geography. I then say, "Imagine there is a corridor with classrooms on either side and the name of a subject is on each door. Now, imagine that, as you walk down the corridor, you peek through the window of each of the classrooms. On your right, you see a door marked History. You look inside and you see students sitting at their desks listening to the teacher. To your left, you see a door marked 'English' and you see students busily writing quietly whilst the teacher is at her desk at the end of the classroom. Next, on the right, there is a door marked Geography and there you see students listening to the teacher talking. You keep looking through the windows and you see a similar scene until you get to a door marked 'Mathematics'. When you look through that window, you see students jumping up and down with excitement and

looking very happy. Which classroom would you rather be in?"
Invariably, the answer is "the Mathematics classroom". I then point out
that they have just chosen one of their least favourite subjects over their
most favourite subject. I then say, "Notice how this shows that your
choice is not about the subject itself, but about the feeling you get when
you are learning about the subject."

Nearly 30 years ago, when I was studying to become a chemistry teacher at
Bath University, we were told that in reality no one can teach anyone anything;
all we can do is facilitate learning. I was reminded of this recently when, on a
mug belonging to a teacher friend of mine, there was a slogan saying, "I can
explain it to you but I cannot understand it for you".

Whilst on the surface this sounds very logical, it makes several assumptions
that I am not very comfortable with. Firstly, it assumes that my explanation is
adequate. More troublingly, it assumes that everyone understands in the same
way. In other words, if my explanation is adequate for some people, it must be
adequate for everyone. Yes, it is true that I cannot understand things for you,
but if I claim to be a teacher, then the burden of responsibility lies on me to
explain things in such a way that will facilitate (make easy) your learning
(especially, understanding and not memorising *per se*).

How can I do that when some people understand what I say and some people
don't? It is easy to assume that those people who do not understand either
cannot understand or do not want to understand. But to me, this view is too
simplistic. What if you are explaining something very clearly in one language
(an auditory learner with a preference for abstract concepts, for example) to
someone who speaks a different language (a kinaesthetic learner with a
preference for concrete visualisation)?

[I appreciate that the ecological validity of such 'learning styles' has been contested and the whole concept is
controversial, but the examples serve to demonstrate the point.]

As a facilitator, my job is to have an arsenal (repertoire) of explaining tools so
that, if my explanation doesn't resonate with my audience, I can try different
approaches until it does.

In private teaching or in a consultancy/counselling situation, I can ascertain my
student or client's learning preferences and technical knowledge so as to pitch
(present) the material in a way that he is most likely to benefit from, but how
can I do that in a book or in an online course? If I make it too technical, I would
alienate the non-specialist and if I make it too general, I would not be able to
delve deeply enough into the subject-matter to facilitate changes that are

practically empowering; not merely intellectually stimulating or a passing curiosity.

The only way that I can think of that could resolve this dilemma is to explain each idea in different ways.

I did some research and found that audiences don't mind repetition as long as they feel that it is not redundant [Beethoven's fifth Symphony and Ravel's Bolero come to mind].

Another risk that might be involved in adopting this approach is that some of you who are more familiar with the subject-matter may feel patronised. I assure you that *that is not my intention.*

[This reminds me of a scene from Star-Trek Beyond. The team are trying to locate missing crew members on an uncharted planet:

Spock: Mr. Chekov, can you reconfigure the search parameters in order to compensate for this formula?

Chekov: Aye, Commander. But what is this formula?

Spock: It is Vokaya, Mr. Chekov. A mineral unique to Vulcan which emits low level radiation.

Chekov: I'll have to filter out all other energy emissions.

McCoy: Spock, what the hell would a Vulcan mineral be doing way out here?

Kirk: Where are you going with this?

Spock: Lieutenant Uhura wears a Vokaya amulet which I presented to her as a token of my affection and respect.

McCoy: You gave your girlfriend radioactive jewellery?

Spock: The emissions are harmless, Doctor. But its unique signature makes it very easy to identify.

McCoy: You gave your girlfriend a tracking device?

Spock: That was not my intention.]

We discuss intention in more detail, especially in the context of trust, in § 53.

In consideration of the above preamble, you may find the writing style in this book to be somewhat different in that it is a hybrid of academic and non-academic styles. You may notice that I explain a particular concept in one way and then clarify it in another way. This is deliberate. If you don't feel comfortable with scientific writing and find it a bit 'heavy', the idea is that, through this approach, by the end of this course, you will be more comfortable with scientific terminology and style and will be able to relate to it more easily.

4.3
Risk-Benefit Analysis

From the point of view of reaching the people who are most likely to benefit most from this work, perhaps the biggest risk I am taking by adopting this 'non-demographic' approach is getting mixed reviews. Personally, mixed reviews tend to intrigue me more than consistently favourable ones. In addition, Since I am presenting this work primarily for its social, rather than economic value, 'market penetration' is not as important to me as 'social penetration'. In other words, at this stage, breadth is more important to me than depth (§ 49.3 Depth and Breadth (Quantity and Quality)). My reasoning is that, rather than planting lots of seeds in one field, I am planting a few seeds in lots of fields. [This is also nature's (the evolutionary) way of dealing with seeds.]

Chapter 5

Give a Man a Fish

Laozi (Lao Tzu), the esteemed Chinese philosopher is quoted as having said,

> **"Give a man a fish and you will feed him for a day;**
> **teach him to fish and you will feed him for life."**

"But Bijan; what does teaching fishing mean when we are talking about relationships?" I hear some of you asking. I think I can explain this better through a couple of illustrative cases.

Case 1: A client asked me to help her to make a decision about two possible relationships because she was trying to make a 'logical' choice. However, logic is only as effective as its basic premises and assumptions. As we explored together, it transpired that the underlying problem was not the options themselves, but the direction in which she was trying to take herself. In this case, she was trying to use logic to avoid emotional involvement. She needed to resolve this issue because otherwise all the logic in the world would not have helped her to enter into a Mutually Satisfying and Empowering Relationship (§ 2.1 What is a SMER?). For her, a course in good decision-making principles would, perhaps, have helped her make a decision more easily, but it would not have helped her move in the right (more empowering) direction in that it would not have helped her to recognise the underlying issue; her need to learn to trust her instincts rather than to lock them up in a vault encapsulated in 'logic'.

Case 2: Once, a client came to me and said that he was financially comfortable and that he gave his girlfriend lots of money, but she would take his money but would go and fool around with other men. What should he do? It became clear to me that the underlying problem was his self-confidence and after we worked on this, he went away and came back three weeks later with a new girlfriend. Clearly, any advice on what he should *do* would not have helped him to figure out what he needed to *be* (or to *become*) first. He needed to learn how to move on. I have made some interesting observations about why we often find it difficult to move on. I discuss these in § 6-11 (The Journey). We will return to this case in § 40 (Self-Esteem and Self-Confidence).

The main point that I want you to glean from these cases is that what we *say* our problem is; our presenting symptoms, is often different to what the actual problem is; the underlying cause. That is, we are looking for a fish (or a magic pill) when what we need is to learn how to fish; the ability to consider the relationship from a number of different perspectives.

Talking of magic pills, before I decided to pursue psychology professionally, I was a research pharmacologist. There is not a single medicinal pill on the market that does not come with warnings about possible side effects. There are three main reasons for this. Firstly, when we ingest a pill, what ends up in our system is a mixture of the original drug and its metabolites. The effects of these metabolites are different from the original drug. Secondly, like our finger prints, even though we can classify them into general patterns, each of our livers are unique and we process (metabolise) different drugs differently. This means that we end up with different levels of metabolites in our bodies. Thirdly, our body is able to send signals to specific tissues, parts of tissues and cells so as to coordinate the actions of all of our tissues, organs and organ systems. When we ingest a pill, we send a drug into our bloodstream and it ends up everywhere. Think of our body as a gardener who can uproot a weed, whereas a pill is like an herbicide sprayed all over the garden. We can try to make our herbicides more and more specific for a particular species of weed, but whether or not we consider a plant as a weed has nothing to do with the plant and everything to do with *where* it is growing. Our problem with trying to develop magic pills, is that pills are 'systemic'. That means that they rely on the bloodstream to carry them to their targets and they cannot distinguish between a plant growing in the 'right' place and a weed. But the gardener (our body) knows. Yes, gardeners can make mistakes too, but I don't think it is a good idea to override their authority every time they make a mistake. I would prefer to point out the problem and to ask them to solve it themselves. [Now we are entering into the realm of another one of my pet interests; self-healing and the placebo effect. Let's leave that for another time and place.]

5.1
Give Fish or Teach Fishing

I have been thinking about developing distance-learning/online courses to help people find peace of mind, happiness, joy, love and confidence for some time. But, every time I started, I reached a point where I got stuck. And it was at the same juncture every time. The problem wasn't with the content; I was happy with that part. And it wasn't with the structure; I already have a lot of experience with that. My mental block was a conflict arising from my sense of obligation to provide value. Let me explain.

The pattern in the above two anecdotal cases points to the nature of the problem. On the one hand, if the course is too simplistic, my students would not be able to apply it effectively in real life to get real value from it. On The other hand, if it is too complicated then they wouldn't be motivated to follow it through to completion. [This is less of a problem in one-to-one sessions, as will become clearer shortly (§ 5.3).]

To make a course appealing enough to people who need it most, I would need to make it short. To do that, I would need to cut up the big picture into smaller pieces. Seeing part of a picture can arouse our curiosity for us to want to know more. However, to me, mere 'curiosity appeal' is not enough; it needs to be useful too. Therefore, I would need to try to make each piece of the jigsaw puzzle, not just meaningful, but practically applicable. Imagine that the whole picture is a car. It is easier to engage the listener/reader in the idea of the wheel and all the things that can be done with it than it is to ignite enthusiasm about the starter fuse [which is just as important as the wheel, by the way, because if we can't get the car started, then it is no longer a car in a practical sense, even though we may consider it *objet d'art*, so to speak. I just thought I'd take the opportunity to point out the interconnectedness of all the things big and small that can make or break relationships]. You see, I consider myself to be in the education business and not the entertainment business. Don't get me wrong, I have no reservations about being entertaining, but only as a means to an educational end. However, I also believe that,

---

knowledge that is not empowering is necessarily disempowering.

[you can quote me on that :-)]

You may see my problem now. For you and I to be ultimately satisfied with the outcome of an online course, or any course for that matter, I would need to teach fishing, whereas most people, especially those who look for answers to their problems online (or in a book) are looking to buy a fish; a quick fix. In fact, some of my clients have actually said to me, "Doctor, I hear what you're saying, but right now, I'm not interested in fishing, I just want a fish."

When it comes to relationships, quick fixes don't tend to last. This is because a quick fix would involve breaking up the big picture into smaller pieces. And what can you do with one or two pieces of a largish jigsaw puzzle?

5.2
Symptomatic Versus Root Treatment

Most people go to a doctor with symptoms and they expect the doctor to diagnose the underlying problem that is causing those symptoms. But with an online course in personal development, we don't tend to approach it in the same way. We look for keywords that relate to the *symptoms* and look for courses that address those symptoms. This may be a reason why many of us are dissatisfied with personal development books whilst our bookshelves are filled with them.

For example, you may be feeling anxious and so you look for a course on how to relieve anxiety and you expect to be given some information and some exercises to help you to overcome your anxiety. You don't expect - or want - to be told that "Your anxiety and all those other problems that you undoubtedly also have [because they tend to co-exist with anxiety problems] such as, your self-confidence issues, your relationship issues, your perfectionism, your health issues, your disempowering sleep patterns, your headaches and your problems with reminiscing past failures and unresolved relationships are interlinked and that you cannot address one without addressing the others." But that's the way it is; a genuine solution would be one that resolves all of these issues homogeneously (together without conflict) and does not treat them as isolated problems.

5.3

The Jigsaw Puzzle

In a consultancy session, as my client talks about her problems, I make notes about what I'm going to do about trying to resolve the issues, based on the person's beliefs, values and priorities. I then tell my client that what I'm going to present them with is a collection of stories, anecdotes, concepts, ideas and exercises and that each of these is a piece of a jigsaw puzzle. The more consistently a client attends sessions, the more of these items get ticked off on my list. When all the pieces are put together, the whole picture will take on a new meaning (the whole is more than the sum of its parts) and it will all make much more sense. I also explain that this approach will also help her become more independent since it will make it possible for the principles to be applied to different situations and not just the problem at hand.

In short, the purpose of the consultation is to eliminate, or reduce substantially, the client's dependence on me as the therapist by building up a toolset to help deal with different situations. After all, the idea that therapy can take longer than it takes for a person to train as a therapist seems somewhat absurd to me. Clearly in that time, I should be able to train the person to be her own therapist. Not that this means that the person will never need a therapist again; even therapists [some might say, especially therapists] need therapists from time to time.

One very important aspect of my approach is that the order in which the different pieces of the puzzle are presented to the client matters. This is based on some research I did some years ago which showed that the order of presentation of concepts can have a significant impact on students' retention and **understanding** [If you're interested in that research, get in touch (e.g., through introducingaffinitology.com].

To summarise my problem with creating online/distance courses; "Do I give people a short course to relieve immediate symptoms but leave the underlying issue untreated or do I risk drastically reducing the number of people that I can help, but give those people a fundamental psychological makeover?" Bear with me as I explain how I resolved this dilemma.

5.4
Catering for a Wide Range of Needs

Factors that affect the quality of our relationships include self-esteem and self-confidence. We explore these in more detail in § 40 (Self-Esteem and Self-Confidence). Bear this in mind as you read through the following sections.

5.4.1
Ability, Performance and Attainment

When you were at school, you may have heard people talking about your 'ability' in a particular subject or, as a parent, you may hear schools talk about your child's 'ability'. Unfortunately, this is completely the wrong word to use [i.e., this is a disempowering use of words] because 'ability' is not something that we can measure. What schools actually measure is something else.

Sometimes you hear educational establishments talk about *performance*. However, the word performance is also loaded with judgements about the child because Society tends to assume that people's performance is directly related to their own ability and effort.

The word 'attainment' is more accurate and is less value-laden (so far) and is somewhat more removed from the 'ability' label. Think of it this way; 'ability' is labelling a person's potential (an abstract, but emotive idea) whereas attainment is about outcome and many factors can affect outcome. Let me show you what I mean.

Education researchers know that only a small proportion of students' overall school results can be attributed to factors that the student has any direct control over. Here is a partial list of factors that have been shown to affect student *attainment*.

- **Relative age within the class:** The older students within a year group tend to perform better, both academically and in sports (and not just in the short term).

- **Socioeconomic status (SES):** This is a measure that takes into account a combination of parental income, education and social influence.
- **School related factors:** These include school type (public or private for example), teacher turnover, structure, and policies.
- **Teacher related factors:** Such as, teacher behaviour, experience, education level and teaching style.
- **Girl to boy ratio within the classroom.** "Really?" Yes really. And what might surprise you even more is that its effects depend on the student's gender and the subject. For example, increasing girl to boy ratio in a class tends to affect boys' Mathematics attainment positively and their attainment in English negatively.

Some of the other factors include,

- Methods of assessment (and reporting)
- Class size
- Hearing
- Eyesight
- Hand-eye coordination
- Other genetic factors
- Examination anxiety [This is a much bigger problem than tends to be acknowledged (causing segregation and distorting the playing field)]

As I am sure you know from your own experience, there are many other factors that can (and do) affect our attainment. These include:

- Hormone related factors [e.g., time of the month]
- Seasonal factors [diurnal cycles, pollen, light, precipitation, clothing]
- Social factors [peer group dynamics]
- Immunological factors [e.g., allergies]
- Mood [affected by all of the above and more]

Many other potential influences are more difficult to measure (need more time, money and patience). For example, some students grasp concepts better when the subject is taught through a concrete and practical approach, whilst others conceptualise the same ideas more readily when they are presented in abstract form [This is related to introversion and extraversion that I intend to discuss elsewhere]. Let's see what happens when we try to compare these two methods within a research setting and why I am saying that these are more difficult to measure.

5.4.2
Difficult to Measure

Let's imagine that we take a group of students and we teach them a particular mathematical concept through a theoretical approach and we find that 30% of students attain above a certain benchmark. We then take a similar group of students and teach them the same mathematical concept through a practical or more concrete approach; using real life examples etc. and this time our results show that 63% of students have attained above the benchmark that we happen to have set. I would be surprised if the researchers conducting such a study do not conclude that a concrete approach is 'better' (more effective) than the theoretical approach. Hardly anyone then stops to ask, better for whom?

You see, looking at the above results, the almost universal assumption is that there has been a 33% improvement (or 110% *increase*) in students' attainment [from 30% to 63%]. In reality, what is more likely to have happened is that the concrete approach appeals to a different subset of students who form a greater proportion of the student population. In other words, some of the substantial (around* 30%) minority who can relate better to the theoretical approach have been alienated in favour of the majority (63%) who prefer the concrete approach. [* Note that some of the students whose attainment was above the benchmark in the abstract approach may have been almost equally comfortable with the 'concrete' approach]

"But what about the other 7%?" I hear some of you asking. Well, some of the students may not have been able to relate to either approach. We need to look for different approaches that work for them; such as a hands-on approach or a game-based pedagogy.

The research design outlined above would not allow us to distinguish between these groups. **That's what I mean by difficult to measure.**

In summary, students' attainment is related to many factors most of which have little to do with their so-called 'ability'. **I propose that the quality of our relationships can be viewed similarly.**

5.4.3
Dealing with Diversity

OK, having got that out of my system, the question is, "What do you do with a class full of students whose attainment varies considerably?" Or in our case, with a group of students eager to learn more about how to improve their relationships when their needs vary considerably.

[Bear with me whilst I talk a little more about learning within the context of the education system and then I will put it all into perspective so that you will see what all this has to do with the main subject of this coursebook on relationships. Meanwhile, I suggest that you stop focusing on the outcome (i.e., trust me) and enjoy the journey.]

When I was at school, variation in attainment levels was called 'the ability gap' and was resolved by 'setting' or 'streaming'. In the first case, children are grouped into 'sets' according to their attainment in each subject. So, if your attainment in mathematics tests was high, you would be put in the 'top' set for that subject. In streaming, children are grouped at the whole year-group level depending on their overall 'ability' [This is related to the 'nature of intelligence' controversy (multiple intelligences versus 'g')]. In my first year of secondary school in England, we were streamed. For the rest of my Secondary education, I was at a school where children were put in different sets for different subjects.

When I began my teacher training in the early 1990s, the idea of 'differentiation' came into vogue. In this system, children of all 'abilities' attend the same class. It then becomes the responsibility of the teacher to make sure that each child gets material that is appropriate for his level.

I am not particularly skilled at multitasking and I used to find it difficult to do this. For example, I remember thinking to myself; I know what Simon's sticking point is and I know what Sarah's issue is and I know what Joe's problem is and so on and if I could sit with each of them individually, I could push each of them over their own particular hurdles, but since the issues were all different, I was unable to give each of my students the one-to-one attention they needed without losing control of the class. And so, I gave up classroom teaching and began to teach privately instead. This, not only allowed me to pick up on each student's stumbling block, it also gave me much more insight into the various factors that contribute to the occurrence of those stumbling blocks.

[Over thirty years ago, my Physics teacher solved this problem in a different and somewhat altruistic way. His approach was neither setting, streaming nor differentiation in the conventional sense. There were twenty of us in our Physics class. For ten of us, he was teaching at a comfortable pace. Five of us were finding it difficult to keep up and five of us were finding it too easy and were getting bored. Mr. Mitchell used to hold an extra class a week for the five who needed help to catch up and another extra class a week for the group who needed more stimulation. He was able to do this because we were in a boarding school and we spent our spare time not too far away from our teachers' homes or our classrooms. To me, Mr. Mitchell's solution was inspirational, becoming more so with time.]

I encourage my clients to look for win-win scenarios. So, coming back to the problem that I began this section with, it dawned on me that I could take my own advice; I decided not to entertain the idea that it has to be either a short and less effective course or a long and less appealing one. So, I started to ask a different kind of question, "How can I do both?" (§ 15.1 The Power of Questions). In our case, this would mean not cutting corners, yet keeping you, the reader/student engaged, in spite of the more detailed content.

5.4.4
A few Inspirational Ideas

In this section, I want to give you some pointers on how you may approach finding solutions to your relationship problems by taking advantage of what you learn in this book. Here are a few reasons why people come to me for help.

I want more satisfying relationships

Since this is a very general statement, we need to try to narrow it down. It could mean that you are not dissatisfied with any particular relationship, but you would like to improve the quality of all your relationships across the board, whether it be social, professional, family or romantic. If you identify with this interpretation of the question, I suggest you begin by going through the Table of Contents. Some of the sections may resonate with you more than others. Start with those. The book has been written in such a way that all the parts are related to each other somehow. That's only to be expected in the same way that every organ and every process in our bodies are related to all other organs and processes. If any part of the system fails the whole system begins to fail. Since your question is a general one, I suggest that you start with the parts that are most interesting to you. You will find that as you progress along your journey, you will be piecing together the different parts of the jigsaw puzzle until you have the whole picture.

Another possible interpretation of this question is that you have yet to find a relationship experience that you would call satisfying. In this case, if you look in the table of contents, you will find a section called, "What is the key to empowering and satisfying relationships?"

I'm having issues with...

… my boyfriend, girlfriend, mother, boss, colleague, etc.

This is another broad question that usually boils down to problems in one of four areas; trust, communication, confidence/fear, lack of direction.

You will be able to find sections about Trust, Communication and Self-Confidence easily. The sections related to 'lack of direction' may be less obvious. This is why I suggest that you skim through the whole book first, because then your mind will be primed to relate lack of direction to words like Goals, Values and Decision-Making, all of which have their own dedicated sections.

Having skimmed through the book first, you will also become aware that all of the issues mentioned above are related to our Psychological Defence Mechanisms - There is a big section in this book dedicated to that (§ 79).

Section 42.1 (The Mirror) is also relevant here.

I'm afraid of commitment

Skimming through this book, you will probably recognise that this question is relevant to the sections that deal with Decision-Making (e.g., § 62, § 64.9, § 72). However, it is also related to what goes on in our head when we hear any word [in our thoughts or uttered by other people]. Words often change our focus. In § 33 (Atasinex Cluster), I explain that how we feel in, and consequently react to, any situation depends on two factors; what we are focusing on and how we interpret whatever it is that we are focusing on. The point about words is that, not only do they change our focus, *words also come with a presupposed interpretation.* We need to consciously take a metaphorical step back from the word and re-evaluate its meaning and the impact of subscribing to that meaning on our psyche (mindset).

In this case, I would suggest that you start with § 33 (Atasinex Cluster). I also suggest that you look through the section on Relationship Frameworks (§ 92), especially, the section on Marriage.

I worry about what other people think of me

This one is related to our relationship with society and I have discussed this at length in § 39 (Social Ranking Criteria)". I suggest that you start there.

I am unhappy with my sex life

There are several possible questions here. It could be a question of quality, quantity or meaningfulness. For issues related to the first two, I would refer you to § 50.5 (The Sexual Dimension) and for the last one, I suggest that you start with § 50.3 (The Spiritual Dimension).

Other issues

Before starting to write this book, I created a long list of reasons that people have come to see me for. If I were to go through them one by one, the book would become several volumes and would detract from what this book has become; a theoretical outline for a new discipline. I have, therefore, decided to deal with individual issues elsewhere [keep an eye on introducingaffinitology.com].

SUMMARY OF UNIT 1

Whether we are looking to create more empowering relationships or to improve our existing ones, there is no magic pill. But being aware of some basic principles helps to direct our efforts in more empowering directions so that our trial and errors lead to progressively fewer errors. I suggest that you familiarise yourself with a map of the territory before you set off on this journey. To do that, I suggest that you browse through the entire book first. This will give you an overview (some kind of bearing) as to what is involved in a relationship and what we need to understand so that we don't leave the quality of our relationships to random chance.

After you have browsed through the book, choose a particular section that interests you most and start there. The course is structured in such a way that each section has something like a guide; a pointer, a reference that looks like this (§ X) that act as signposts that guide you through the relevant sections of the course until you complete the tour.

Unit 2

The Journey

> **The sea will be the sea, whatever the drop's philosophy.**
>
> Farid al-Din Attar

[The inspiration for using the image of migrating birds came from a work by the Persian mystic, Farid al-Din Attar (Attar of Nishapur). If you look up the words 'simorgh' and 'The Conference of the Birds' on Wikipedia, your experience of much of what I talk about in this chapter and the next is likely to be enriched.]

Fire, Aim, Fire

As a practical method for setting and achieving goals, the established sequence is Ready, Aim, Fire. Some argue that this is impractical because you will not be able to calibrate your aim unless you fire first. T. Harv Eker suggests dropping the 'Ready' phase and adopting a "Fire, Aim, Fire" approach.

Eliminating the 'ready' stage is acknowledging that, since nothing is absolute [which, dramatics aside, I accept, is an oxymoron] we will never be absolutely ready. We, therefore, need to make a 'judgement call' about the right time to 'fire' and then be ready to adjust if necessary. This approach is practiced by Google [So, I have heard] which considers itself to be in Perpetual Beta. It is also in line with Tim O'Reilly's point of view that,

> **"Users must be treated as co-developers"**

[source: https://en.wikipedia.org/wiki/Perpetual_beta]

Embracing this sentiment, I invite you, dear readers, to be co-cultivators of the ideas that I am seeding here. That is to say, I welcome feedback, ideas criticism and suggestions for thinking scientifically about relationships.

Chapter 6

Know Thyself

6.1
Self-Discovery

In the preamble section, I invited you to think of this course as a journey; a journey into the pendulous but enchanting, sometimes dangerous, often confusing, but always exciting land of relationships. So, let me take you by the metaphorical hand and let us wander together, through the wonders of the mind, on an adventure into allurement, in search of an itinerary for intimacy through a safari of self-discovery.

"Self-discovery?" I hear some of you asking, "But Bijan, you said that you were going to tell me about *The Art and Science of Being with People?*"

Yes, self-discovery. Because we might think we know what we want but without self-knowledge, our reasons for wanting it are likely to be precarious (shaky, unstable, temporary, unfounded). And unless we are clear about who we are (§ 37.7 The Emergence of Identity), what we want and why we want it, we are unlikely to end up in relationships that are both satisfying and empowering.

6.2
Knowing What We Want

The vast majority of us don't know exactly what we want from life. Our team at the Institute of Education (now a part of UCL) spent several years researching the ways in which young people make decisions about their future and even the ones at university weren't sure what they wanted to do afterwards. And I see no prospect of them finding out what they want from life in the near future because the system doesn't provide a mechanism for individuals to discover their individuality. We are on our own in that department (§ 39 Social Ranking Criteria).

Often, it is circumstances outside of school that can provide us with those knowledge and insights that help us to break free from the psychological constraints placed upon us by the education system.

"Think not what your country can do for you, think what you can do for your country" is great rhetoric, but that can only happen productively and spontaneously when my country doesn't *actively* interfere with my life in the first place. I do not see the wood for the trees, not because I cannot, but because I am not *allowed* to think beyond the confines of the wood. How can *I* do anything for my country when *I* do not exist in the eyes of my country; that is, when I am not allowed to be an individual. I am only 'counted' and compared against a 'normalised' sample. If you look at the trend in the Education systems' policies, it is a trend towards increasing interference with a view to narrowing the distribution curve [easier to control]. The natural (organic) way would be to let it *become* whatever it would evolve into if it were left alone (§ 91 Relationships as Self-Organizing Systems). The paradoxical message seems to be that we will celebrate 'diversity' as long as you conform to the narrow way in which we define it. You will get a glimpse of how this is done in § 39 (Social Ranking Criteria).

Chapter 7

Good Enough

7.1
You Make Me Want to Be a Better Man

These 'clips' from popular movies epitomise the spirit of this course.

The following is an exchange (from Star Trek Insurrection) between a 12-year-old boy, Artim, and an android, Data.

> Artim: "Do you like being a machine?"
> Data: "I aspire to be more than I am."

A deep message doesn't need to be any more complicated than that. We have an innate need to 'become better' (grow, develop, evolve). Without aspiring to be more than we are, we would feel lost (no direction) or empty (no motivation) or both. Interpersonal relationships are essential in this quest. Our relationships (*any* interaction with other people) facilitate, define and punctuate our development trajectory.

Whether or not I can identify with being a machine depends on the extent to which I have a mechanistic view of life. Nevertheless, the above exchange sums up "The Human Condition"; wherever I may be physically, emotionally, financially, intellectually, culturally, socially, or whatever (Unit 11 Dimensions of Human Experience), it is not enough because I am compelled by an unknown drive to want to be somewhere else; somewhere 'better'.

The following exchange from the movie, "As Good As It Gets", illustrates how becoming aware of this need, *and making it explicit*, can transform a relationship.

> Melvin: "You make me want to be a better man."
> Carol: "That's maybe the best compliment of my life."

You may have picked up on a potential conflict here. A conflict between 'being' and 'wanting'; "How can I enjoy *being* who I am when part of me is aspiring to be someone *better*?"

Let's resolve this conflict right now. The problem occurs when we think that wanting to be better means that we feel that we are not good enough as we are now. How we have come to think like this is a discussion for another time and place. Meanwhile, we only need to change our angle of view slightly to see that these two positions are not actually in conflict. When we can say (and believe) the following sentence, then many of our lives will be transformed.

> **"I am good enough and I aspire to be better"**

Again, it doesn't have to get any more complicated than that. Once we achieve (*regain* is probably a better word) this level of understanding, we can stop judging ourselves for aspiring.

You may be asking yourself, "Why would I want to aspire to be better when I am good enough?" One way of understanding this is through the lens of Herzberg's two factor theory of motivation [also mentioned in § 2.1.2 (What is Satisfying?)].

There are certain criteria through which we consider ourselves as being good enough. These are factors that we *choose*. If we don't choose them for ourselves, then other people and 'society' will choose them for us (§ 39 Social Ranking Criteria). If we allow other people to choose these for us, then we will, eventually develop a victim mentality (§ 44 Locus of Control) and will tend to lose our self-esteem (§ 40 Self-Esteem and Self-Confidence).

The criteria that we have for feeling 'good enough' will be different for each of the different aspects of our lives (Unit 11 Dimensions of Human Experience). For example, in the spiritual dimension, I suggest that knowing that I respect myself and others is me being 'good enough'.

Once we decide what makes us feel good enough in each Dimension, then we will have identified what Herzberg calls the 'hygiene' factors for that Dimension. After that, our motivators will arise from a comparison of *where I am* with *what I think is possible*. For example, within the spiritual dimension, I could say, "I am good enough because I respect myself and others, but I can aspire to be better by passing on that relative sense of 'at-one-ment' to whoever is looking for it." [special thanks to Eric Fromm for that insightful rendition of the word atonement]

Once I have reached a point where I can accept being whatever I am, no matter what other people think, then the rest of my journey will be about being willing to let that journey change me into something 'better' (more empowered). When we achieve this level of confidence, that is, when we 'self-actualize' [to use Abraham Maslow's terminology], then the destination becomes less important than the journey itself. Some of you may find this perspective counterintuitive. I hope that, after completing this course, any such conflict will resolve itself.

A lady came to see me because she had a vague idea that something wasn't right and she didn't know what. After I had explained the reasoning behind making the journey more of a priority than the outcome, she told me that she felt as if a weight had been lifted off her shoulders because she now realised that the source of her constant anxiety had been that she had always focused on the outcome rather than the journey.

I explain how we do this later in this course (§ 44 Locus of Control).

It is when we focus on the journey and not the destination that we can see stones in our path as stepping stones and not as stumbling blocks. Consider the following exchange between Artim and Data a moment later:

Artim: "I can't imagine what it's like to be a machine."
Data: "Perhaps it would surprise you to know that I have often tried to imagine what it is like to be a child."
- Really?
- Really.
- For one thing, your legs are shorter than everyone else's.
- But they are in a constant state of growth. Do you find it difficult to adapt?
- Adapt?
- A child's specifications are never the same from one moment to the next. It is a wonder you do not trip over your own feet.
- Sometimes I do.

This dialogue highlights another truism; tripping over our own feet is a sign that we are growing, which is another way of saying,

---

Those who have not 'failed', have not tried.

7.2

How Pain Can Lead to the Emergence of Something Sensational

The inventor of the thesaurus was Peter Mark Roget. He was born in 1779. His father died when he was very young. He struggled with depression for most of his life. As a child, he used to make lists. This was a coping mechanism that he used to bring order into the chaos around him.

Think for a moment about what this means. It means that we would not have had a thesaurus if Mr Roget had not been struggling with depression and using making lists as a coping mechanism.

This is one of the numerous examples I have come across of something sensational emerging from something painful. In short, when we are in pain, emotionally, we are just falling over our feet. That's what happens sometimes when we are growing, that is, when we are aspiring to 'become a better Man' [note the capital M].

I once gave a talk with the title, "Are depressed psychologists hypocrites?" What I explained was that it depends on how long they remain depressed for. I used the analogy of gravity and said that gravity is a force that acts on all of us. It is always possible for us to fall over, psychologist or not. The difference is that psychologists, like seasoned warriors, should be less likely to fall over and, if they do, they should be able to rebound from it more quickly. And this brings me to a personal example of how pain can be a conduit for becoming a better Man.

At around the time when I decided to become a psychologist, I went through a bout of depression. Someone said to me, "How can you help other people with their problems if you are depressed yourself?" I did not say anything to her but, when I was talking to another friend of mine, I said, "I had never experienced depression before this; how can I help a client with depression if I can't empathise with him?"

Nowadays, when someone comes to me with symptoms of depression, I explain to them in great detail what it *feels* like to be in a conflict where,

> *"On the one hand, you know (cognitively) that you are blessed and that you have a myriad of strengths through which you can contribute to society and you know that somewhere inside you there is a capacity for feeling joy and elation to the point of sensing a oneness with some kind of divine being, yet how you feel contradicts what you know. Your body refuses to respond to such positive thoughts and when you are not acting like an automaton to appease society, you feel like curling up (or actually being curled up) in the foetal position, with a lump in your throat and tears in your eyes hoping that a miracle would put you out of your misery, one way or the other."*

After I explain this to my depressed clients and then proceed to speak with an upbeat tone, often standing up and moving around animatedly, smiling, clicking my fingers, moving my shoulders and eyebrows to the rhythm of some music that I am hearing in my head, my clients begin to see that the end of their misery is not simply possible, but probable and secondly that such ending does not have to be 'one way or the other', but in the direction that celebrates life.

7.3
A Word of Caution

We don't become more than we are by trying to be better than other people; we will never win that game. That kind of mentality stems from a win-lose mindset (§ 39, § 31.2.1 and 66.2.2).

> **From a holistic perspective,**
> **when one person loses everybody loses.**

Most people aren't able (or are unwilling) to expand their consciousness to a level where they are able to appreciate that. Some people spend a lifetime trying to understand it. Most of those who do understand it, don't talk about it, they simply live it.

To want to be a better person is great, but consider some of the consequences of wanting to do it by becoming better than someone else:

a) Our sense of purpose will be linked to factors that are outside of us (other people). In § 44 we will explore the concept of locus of control (LoC), the detrimental effects of having an *external* LoC and some of the things we can do to break free from its chains.

b) Our comparisons will be flawed because we will not be comparing like with like and, therefore, any conclusions we reach will not be valid/useful (§ 39 Social Ranking Criteria).

There is opportunity for gaining more insight into this from the story of the doctor who thought that he wasn't successful (Unit 11: Dimensions of Human Experience) and from the story of the stonecutter (§ 39.3 SRC are Disconnected).

The point is that it is natural and empowering to want to be better than we are at the moment (in whatever way we choose to define that), but we can't do that by disempowering other people because that's like trying to knock a leg out from under a table and then trying to take its place. A lot of people do that and they think they're in a stronger position. What these deluded souls fail to realise is that they have just caused everything on the surface of the table to topple over. Why would we want to be a table leg when we don't care about what's on the table or the purpose of the table?

> **"For all sad words of tongue and pen, the saddest are these,**
> **'It might have been'."**
>
> - John Greenleaf Whittier

7.4
The Destructive Power of Competition

Once I was playing a simple game like Snap with a group of 5- to 7-year-olds. They became competitive and some of them began to cry when they 'lost'. I shouted, "Okay from now on the loser is the winner". Immediately a couple of them shouted triumphantly, "I'm the loser". It took them a moment to pick up on the contradiction and it gave them pause for thought; enough for them to learn a valuable lesson; our feelings about winning or losing depends on our interpretation and not on what actually happens. To quote from the ABBA song, Waterloo, "How could I ever refuse, I feel like I win when I lose." [Ok, the context was different, but the sentiment is what I am focusing on here].

Competing with others within Society is disempowering enough but even worse is the destructive effect of competing with someone with whom we are in a (more direct) relationship, especially if we want it to be a mutually satisfying and empowering relationship; a SMER (§ 2.1).

We need to be careful not to confuse competition with aspiration. In competition, as long as I feel 'higher' than someone else, that's enough; I have 'won'. It doesn't matter whether I reach this relative position by moving myself 'up' or by pulling my competitor 'down'.

The aspiring person has role models, not competitors.

7.5
Comparison without Competition

Comparing ourselves with others is so frequently disempowering that it is safer to avoid it. If, however, we are mature enough to compare ourselves with others in a way that *does not affect our judgement of our personal worth or value* (or others' personal worth and value), then we can reap the benefits of comparisons without falling into Social Ranking Criteria (SRC) traps (§ 39). This can happen when our comparisons with other people become completely objective, that is to say, when the comparison does not affect our sense of who we are (§ 37.7 The Emergence of Identity). To be able to do this, we must be able to look at other people without thinking, "Oh, I am inferior or superior to him/her" or anything like that. Instead, we look and think, "Hey, that's a place that I could aspire to reach." This is when we can look at others and see possibilities not competitors. For example, imagine looking at a seagull and feeling inferior to it because you cannot fly. Compare that with the feeling you get when you look at a seagull and say something inspirational to yourself like, "I want to be able to fly and that seagull is proof that it is possible", whereupon we proceed to try; as the Wright Brothers, amongst many others, did.

Chapter 8

What If

I frequently encounter a certain mental block in my clients. Having set a goal, they spend a disproportionate amount of mental energy thinking about what might happen if they don't reach it. Specifically, you may be having relationship problems at the moment and may be thinking, "What if I complete this course and still don't resolve my relationship issues?" The obvious answer is, "You won't know until you've tried it." And that's the reality of life. But that doesn't seem very reassuring, does it? So let me see if I can be somewhat more helpful here.

I have found that, far too readily, people brandish advice, especially through imperatives. For example, it is very tempting to follow the above answer with, "That's just the way life is so, get over it!" which is more self-serving than helpful because, if I knew how to get over it, it is unlikely that I would have asked the question in the first place. What I need is guidance that will show me *how* to get over it. So, let's do that.

In a moment, I am going to give you some exercises. Before that, here are a few tips that will help you to get more out of them. Fear of not reaching our goal or destination is almost universal. It's often referred to as 'fear of failure' because we have been programmed by society (§ 39 Social Ranking Criteria) to think of 'failure' as something to be afraid of.

To say, "Don't be afraid", is like saying, "Don't think of a pink elephant." Stop reading for a moment and try to focus on not thinking of a pink elephant. What happens? Exactly.

If I don't want you to think of a pink elephant, I need to say something like, "Think of pistachio flavoured ice cream." No elephants there. [Unless this inspires Disney/Pixar to make a popular animation featuring a pink elephant eating some pistachio flavoured ice cream, in which case, I'll need to think of another example.]

Say to yourself, "I'm not doing this to get the pot of gold at the end of the rainbow; the opportunity to ride the rainbow is far more valuable than that." The idea is to detach yourself from the outcome;

> As long as I am on a journey,
> I am not stagnant and that is success.

I used to jump out of aeroplanes. No, I was not suicidal; I was a member of a parachute club. I have not forgotten what our instructor said to us on our first day; "I have been doing this for twenty years and still, when I am looking down from the open door of a plane several thousand feet above the ground, I am scared. The day you stop being scared is the day you should stop doing this sport."

Fear keeps us alive. Fear's message is not "Don't do it"; it is "Be careful" which means, "Do your due diligence". Now let's get down to that exercise that I promised you earlier; an exercise to help you 'get over it'.

Exercise 1 How to handle "What if?"

Sit down somewhere quiet and think about the following couple of sentences for as long as it takes for you to stop thinking about what might or might not be at the end of the rainbow.

"I don't learn from the outcome. I learn from the journey. Whenever I'm focusing on the outcome, I am missing out on the journey."

Then you will be so engrossed in the beauty of the rainbow, and the excitement of following it, that you won't know when you reach the end. And when you do find that 'pot of gold' at the end of the rainbow, you will wish that you hadn't because the journey is over [until you decide to pick another destination].

Here's a personal story to demonstrate this.

One Sunday morning, when my children were 8 and 10 years old, I was taking them to a Persian language school. The journey was going to take us around 45 minutes. Within about 3 minutes of setting off, my daughter asked, "Are we there yet?" and my response was to immediately say to her, "Look, Ariana, I suggest that you imagine that we will not be there for another 24 hours. That will free your mind to start enjoying the journey. You have many opportunities here. You can play or talk with your brother, talk to me, listen to some music or look outside and see what's around you. Look at the buildings, look at the people. These are all opportunities that you will miss if you focus on are we there yet." Ariana then decided to roll down the window, stick her head out and start shouting, "Hello" and "How're you doing" at the passers-by and her younger brother started to follow suit (from the other window). Then it became a competition to see who could get the most reaction from people. It wasn't exactly what I had in mind, but I decided that no real harm will come of it and so I let them pass the time that way. In 'no time at all', we were at our destination.

[That reminds me of an exchange in a scene in Star Trek (TNG, Season 6, Episode 25):

Riker: "What are you doing?"

Data: "Recent events have compelled me to study how humans perceive the passage of time. For example, I have often heard people comment that time seems to pass more slowly in one instance or more quickly in another. In reality, the actual passage of time remains fixed."

- "I suppose it depends on how people perceive time. Every situation is different. It depends on how you feel."

- "I have been testing the aphorism, a watched pot never boils. I have boiled the same amount of water in this kettle 62 times. In some cases, I have ignored the kettle. In others, I have watched it intently. In every instance, the water reaches its boiling point in precisely 51.7 seconds. It appears that I am not capable of perceiving time any differently than my internal chronometer."

- "Why don't you turn it off?"

- "Sir?"

- "Data, people do not have internal chronometers. Why don't you see what happens if you turn yours off?"

- "Thank you, sir. I will try that."

- "Just don't be late for your shift."]

This idea of first setting an outcome then focusing on enjoying the journey, turns up in many guises in different disciplines. In educational circles, it is referred to as "Mastery Orientation" and contrasted with "Performance Orientation". Carol Dweck has popularised these as "Growth Mindset" and "Fixed Mindset". In motivational psychology, they are referred to as "Intrinsic motivation" and "Extrinsic motivation". In personality psychology, they are what is measured by the "Openness to Experience" dimension of the Big Five personality model. These are all significantly correlated with "locus of control" which we discuss in more detail in § 44.

Even though we tend to consider personality traits as stable, I would argue that the extent to which we are 'Open to Experience', for example, depends on many other factors including, on our mood (Unit 22: Thermodynamics of relationships), on which of our Identities (or selves) is dominant at the time

(§ 29.4 The Omniself and § 64 Values) and on which dimension of our human experience we are focusing on (Unit 11: Dimensions of Human Experience). *All of these are mediated by the environment.*

Unlike the black and white implication (§ 25.3 Polar Bond: Partial Sharing) of Growth/Fixed, Mastery/Performance and Intrinsic/Extrinsic approaches, treating these tendencies as a grayscale (whether it be categorised as a personality dimension or anything else) is more empowering on several levels. Firstly, it has the advantage of acknowledging that people (we) function within a movable point along a continuum between two extremes. Secondly, it allows us to move away from a victim (and victimization) mentality and the idea that I am (or he is) either this or that. I can be Mastery oriented, say, 70% of the time and Performance oriented 30% of the time (and more or less in one situation compared with another).

When we encourage ourselves (and our children) to stop thinking in binary terms (§ 39 Social Ranking Criteria), we say to ourselves, "Just because I do or say idiotic things at times, it doesn't make me an idiot." [Substitute idiotic and idiot for any adjective and its complementary noun that you like, including 'ingenious' and 'genius']

We veer into, or out of, binary-oriented thinking by what we focus on. For example, exams and grades are fixed, but learning is an ongoing and multidimensional journey. Destinations and goals are fixed, but journeys are the means through which we become experienced, develop mastery; grow.

"But, Bijan, I am here for the outcome." I hear you say; "I want to improve my relationships; I don't want to waste my time doing something that might not work."

"OK, OK!" I would respond, whilst thinking to myself, "Oh dear, it seems that one hasn't learnt to enjoy the flow of life yet."

"Let me tell you some more stories," I would continue, because everyone likes stories, especially inspirational ones.

The next story is about Steve Jobs. I was going to tell the story in my own words, but then I found it explained fluently by Simon Garfield on the CNN website, so, gratefully, I will quote him here:

> "[Steve] Jobs was the first to give us a real choice of fonts, and thus the ability to express ourselves digitally with emotion, clarity and variety... Jobs realized their value... and suddenly we were no longer dependent on professional printers, graphic designers and those long dark nights of the soul with rub-down letters.
> And who did Jobs himself thank for this advance?
> He credited the people who made the cost of his academic life so expensive at Reed College in Portland, Oregon. He said he dropped out to save his parents spending

their entire life savings. And if he hadn't dropped out, he may not have discovered calligraphy.

"Throughout the campus," he remembered at an address to students at Stanford in 2005, "every poster, every label on every drawer, was beautifully hand calligraphied." So, having dropped out and finding himself a free agent, he decided to take a class in this art. "I learned about serif and sans serif typefaces, about varying the amount of space between different letter combinations, about what makes great typography great. It was beautiful, historical, artistically subtle in a way that science can't capture, and I found it fascinating."

At the time, the student dropout believed that little he had learned would find a practical application in his life. But things changed. Ten years after college, Jobs designed his first Mac, and it came with something unprecedented -- a wide choice of fonts."

[Source: https://edition.cnn.com/2011/10/05/opinion/garfield-steve-jobs-fonts/index.html]

We never know how, what we learn on different journeys, will impact our life or the lives of others.

"But, Bijan, life is too short to spend it all on experimenting." I hear you say. And my response would be, "Life is too short *not* to be experimenting because, from my perspective, when we are not experimenting, we are not learning and when we are not learning, we're not growing."

"But, Bijan, if you spend all your time growing, when will there be time for *achieving*?" You might retort. And I would say, "Growing is not only a *means* of achieving, it is an achievement *in itself*."

Contrary to what we might have been led to believe, the process of growing is not endothermic, to use chemists' parlance. It does not only take in energy (resources); it is also a source. At some point, learning (growing) reaches a threshold; a point at which it wants to burst out and we feel an urge to do something with it. That is when we set off on a different kind of journey.

Learning is not a mere means to a foreseen end. It is inspirational and creative. Many 'achievements' have come about from watching children play. In fact, children don't 'play' in the way that adults perceive the word.

> **Where children are concerned, what we call playing is better described as experimenting.**

Another advantage of looking at children's play as experimentation, as opposed to entertainment, is that we would take the idea of children's play more seriously. We would also evaluate games differently and provide people with games that offer the greatest opportunity for experimentation. Anyway, I digress.

To go on a journey, that is, to grow, we need to set goals or destinations and will, from time to time, reach those goals. What I am saying is that, as unintuitive as it may sound to some of us, by focusing on the journey, we are more likely to achieve more satisfactory outcomes than if our focus were entirely on the outcome. Here's another story to demonstrate this.

> *Once, a couple came to me for counselling. One of them said, "I want to marry this person" and the other said, "Well, I do want to marry this person, but what's holding me back is that I don't know whether or not there is a future in it." I said, "When you're looking at your partner and you're thinking about the future, you are not completely present; in the present. In other words, part of you is not with your partner, it's wandering in I-wonder-what-the-future-holds-in-store fantasy land. Next time you're alone together, I want you to spend 5 minutes focusing only on the relationship as it is at the moment and how you can make the most of that moment. If you do that, what is the likelihood that your relationship will extend from 5 minutes to 10 minutes, from 10 minutes to an hour, from an hour to a day, from a day to a month and from a month to a lifetime? Now, compare this to a relationship where you are constantly second-guessing what might happen so that you hold yourself back from real intimacy?"*

Two years later they called me and they were still together.

Viewed from a different perspective, psychologists, J Nakamura and Mihaly Csikszentmihalyi explain what I have described above in this way, **"Viewed through the experiential lens of flow, a good life is one that is characterized by complete absorption in what one does."** The lesson here is that,

---
A good relationship is also one in which we are completely absorbed in the relationship, *in the moment*.

So, if I am out with my friends, I am completely absorbed in the experience of 'being with my friends' and if I am in a business meeting, I am completely absorbed in 'being with the people in the meeting'.

On many occasions, my clients have told me that they feel neglected when their romantic partner does not respond to their messages straight away. The dynamics of any relationship in which such feelings arise is the subject of another book/course. It involves dependence (§ 23.2 The Road to Interdependence), self-esteem (§ 40.3) and trust (§ 53) and it can have severe consequences for the relationship.

For now, if you empathise with the above sentiment, then I suggest that you begin by contemplating the idea that your partner is in 'the flow state', that is, focused on the journey that he is undertaking at the moment. The advantage of being like this is that your partner will be like that with you too. That is, when he is with you, you will have his complete undivided attention as he enjoys the journey of the moment with you.

Chapter 9

Inspirations, Conceptions and

Misconceptions

In my late teens, I discovered the Roget's Thesaurus. Actually, a friend introduced me to it (thank you Anne). I remember how excited I was. It was in the days before the internet; when the Roget's Thesaurus was a book that you could hold in your hands and flick through. Here's what Joshua Kendall has to say about it.

> "We tend to think of a thesaurus as a collection of synonyms and antonyms. But Roget's is essentially a reverse dictionary. With a dictionary, the user looks up a word to find its meaning. With Roget's, the user starts with an idea and then keeps flipping through the book until he finds the word that best expresses it."
>
> [Source: https://www.merriam-webster.com/words-at-play/rogets-thesaurus]

I have one of these antiques at hand. It is over 700 pages long and consists of two sections. The main section lists words by classification, listing words on the basis of their meaning. And then there is the index which is almost as long as the 'main' section. When I want to find a synonym, I look up the word in the index and it gives me a list of keywords for the word I am looking up along with relevant section numbers for each of the various meanings that the word could have.

The first page of the index of my version of the Roget's Thesaurus looks like this.

A1

A

A1
best 644 adj.
abacus
counting instrument
86 n.
abandon
relinquish 621 vb.
resign 753 vb.
not retain 779 vb.
excitable state 822
n.
abandoned
unpossessed 774
adj.
vicious 934 adj.
abasement
humiliation 872 n.
abash
humiliate 872 vb.
abate
decrease 37 vb.
discount 810 vb.
abatement
relief 831 n.
abattoir
slaughter-house
362 n.
abbey
monastery 986 n.
church 990 n.
abbot
ecclesiarch 986 n.
abbotship
church office 985 n.
abbreviate
shorten 204 vb.
abstract 592 vb.
abbreviation
smallness 33 n.
A.B.C.
beginning 68 n.
letter 558 n.
abdicate
relinquish 621 vb.
resign 753 vb.
abdication
loss of right 916 n.

ABJ

abdomen
maw 194 n.
insides 224 n.
abduct
take away 786 vb.
steal 788 vb.
abeam
sideways 239 adv.
aberrant
non-uniform 17 adj.
aberration
abnormality 84 n.
deviation 282 n.
inattention 456 n.
abet
aid 703 vb.
abetment
cooperation
706 n.
abettor
colleague 707 n.
abeyance
lull 145 n.
inaction 677 n.
abhor
hate 888 vb.
disapprove 924 vb.
abide
stay 144 vb.
go on 146 vb.
dwell 192 vb.
abide by
acquiesce 488 vb.
observe 768 vb.
abiding place
abode 192 n.
ability
ability 160 n.
skill 694 n.
abirritant
antidote 658 n.
abject
servile 879 adj.
contemptible
922 adj.
rascally 930 adj.
abjure
negate 533 vb.
recant 603 vb.

ABO

able
powerful 160 adj.
possible 469 adj.
intelligent 498 adj.
skilful 694 adj.
able-bodied
stalwart 162 adj.
able seaman
mariner 270 n.
ablution
ablution 648 n.
abnormal
disagreeing 25 adj.
abnormal 84 adj.
insane 503 adj.
wrong 914 adj.
abode
abode 192 n.
abolish
destroy 165 vb.
abrogate 752 vb.
abolitionist
revolutionist 149 n.
destroyer 168 n.
abominable
hateful 888 adj.
heinous 934 adj.
abomination
badness 645 n.
hateful object
888 n.
aboriginal
primal 127 adj.
native 191 n., adj.
abort
be unproductive
172 vb.
miscarry 728 vb.
abortion
abnormality 84 n.
undevelopment
670 n.
eyesore 842 n.
abortive
immature 670 adj.
unsuccessful
728 adj.
abound
superabound 637 vb.

ABS

about
concerning 9 adv.
nearly 200 adv.
around 230 adv.
about face
turn back 286 vb.
about to be
impending 155 adj.
about turn
reversion 148 n.
above
aloft 209 adv.
above-mentioned
preceding 64 adj.
above par
excellent 644 adj.
abracadabra
spell 983 n.
abrade
rub 333 vb.
abrasion
wound 655 n.
abrasive
rubbing 333 adj.
obliteration 550 n.
abridge
shorten 204 vb.
be concise 569 vb.
abstract 592 vb.
abroad
abroad 59 adv.
abrogate
liberate 746 vb.
abrogate 752 vb.
not retain 779 vb.
abrupt
instantaneous
116 adj.
vertical 215 adj.
hasty 680 adj.
abscess
ulcer 651 n.
abscond
run away 620 vb.
elude 667 vb.
absence
non-existence 2 n.
deficit 55 n.
absence 190 n.

401

[Source: Roget's Thesaurus, Penguin Books, 1979, ISBN: 0140510079]

One of the interesting things that one gleans from the index section of the Roget's Thesaurus is that most words have at least two meanings (are listed in more than one classification). For example, take a look at the word 'able' in the picture. we have four meanings to choose from; powerful, possible, intelligent and skilful. We then need to use the number reference in front of each word to go to the main section where that word and its synonyms are listed. I have found counselling to be a similar process. Let me illustrate.

We tend to have different interpretations of what a particular relationship means, in much the same way that we hold different interpretations of the word 'able'. It is not that we do not know that there can be other meanings, it's just that we are not consciously considering the other meanings at the time. This is what much of humour is about. Here's an example,

"A man walked into a bar and said, 'Ouch!'... It was an iron bar."

Similarly, two people can be in a relationship (any kind of relationship) and conflict can arise because each of them thinks that they are in a different kind of relationship (different meanings of the word 'bar' in the above joke).

In this course, we are going to encounter many assumptions about (and interpretations of) relationships that can cause conflicts. Awareness of these tripwires can, in themselves, be therapeutic.

In deciding on the structure for this course [when it was a 'course' and before it became a 'textbook'], I drew some inspiration from the paper version of the Roger Thesaurus. At one point, I included a 'lookup' section that contained a list of issues and related concepts along with relevant section numbers related to those particular issues. However, in the interest of time, I have decided to postpone that project.

9.1
Science as an Art

There is a popular misconception that science is about facts and laws and exact protocols and procedures that must be followed. In our research about the factors that affect young people's subject choices after the age of 16, we found that some young people choose a career in science because they believe it to be solid, robust and, ultimately, free of uncertainty. However, the greatest discoveries in science were not made by following procedure; they were made by creatively exploring a hunch. In short,

---

There can be no science without creativity.

There is a difference between a scientist and a technician. There is a TED talk by Clifford Stoll called '18 minutes with an agile mind'. Watch it and you will see what I mean. Here's a section from the transcript of that talk.

"The first time you do something, it's science. The second time, it's engineering. The third time, it's just being a technician. I'm a scientist. Once I do something, I do something else..." [Source: https://www.ted.com/talks/clifford_stoll_on_everything]

Note that we can be a 'scientist' even when we are labelled a 'technician'. In other words, being a scientist is not about what our job description says, it is about how we approach the job.

> *When I used to teach in classrooms, whenever I gave my students a test, I would look to see how many of them had answered the question correctly. If this number was fewer than two, I would tell the children that, clearly, I had not explained properly and I would, therefore, exclude the question from their test results. I also looked at the distribution of the marks to see whether it was normal or not. Sometimes, I found outliers (in both directions) which I reported to our educational psychologist so that she could keep an eye on those children.*

When I was studying chemistry at UWIST (now Cardiff University), one of our lecturers told us that when we are reading a paper, let's say about the synthesis (making) of some compound, the instructions may say that after mixing two substances in a solution, you should let it boil for eight hours. This is neither a magic number, nor a carefully calculated time. It usually simply means that the chemist went to have dinner and then went to bed, leaving the mixture to boil overnight and came back in the morning to see what had happened. Of course, this kind of thing happens at the creative stage. If something significant transpires that is of potential value to industry, then the next stage is to throw a lot of money and resources at it to see what the optimal conditions are for the reaction (best temperature, pressure, concentrations and duration).

The main point I want to make here is that when I talk about the art and science of relationships, I am not talking about 'art' and 'science' as two isolated and distinct facets of relationships; there is a significant 'art' (creativity) component in the 'science' (methodological framework) part too.

Through a scientific exploration of relationships, we can gain insights into techniques that can improve relationships. Without creativity, we will not be able to adapt those techniques to take full advantage of them in the ever-changing realm of interpersonal relationships.

In addition, scientific terminology may appear reassuring, but that doesn't mean that they are free of controversy within the scientific community itself. In scientific papers, you will find that the authors tend to define the main terms that they use so as to avoid any ambiguity. If the words were not open to multiple interpretations, this would not be necessary. For example, you may see a word like *dimension* and assume that this is a well-understood concept (§ 49.2 Excuse me sir, what is a dimension). I hope that by the end of this course, you will appreciate that this, and most other concepts in science, are fluid and renegotiable.

9.2

Everything That Is Easy Was Once Difficult

What is easy appears hard at first. Hard simply means that we still don't have the information, or experience, that makes it easy. I say this because I don't want you to think about whether making the changes proposed in this book are going to be hard or easy, just soak up the knowledge and enjoy the ride. All we have to do is feel the excitement when we see what could happen if we were to change and say, "Yes! I really really want that." Then, the change will happen all by itself, spontaneously, without effort.

My approach to both the acquisition and dissemination (imparting) of knowledge is grounded in the principle that the whole is more than the sum of its parts. More specifically, in the context of learning, this means that,

---

our understanding of *everything* changes when we learn *anything* new

---

In other words, changes in our understanding of **anything** can affect our responses to (behaviour towards) **everything**.

Relationships are no exception. Knowledge changes us and the knowledge outlined here will affect the way we approach our relationships and that will change the quality of our relationships. I am confident of that; not because it sounds good, but because I have seen the effects that this knowledge has had on hundreds of my clients.

Every part of this book will add a piece to an intricate jigsaw puzzle that changes, not only our perspective on relationships, but, more importantly, our *repertoire of perspectives* on relationships (§ 35.12 The Mind-Body Evolution). This gives us greater flexibility and manoeuvrability to use our own creativity to develop and build a wider range of empowering relationships.

This course, being an overview, is all about awareness. It is designed to give you an insight into the factors that shape relationships, especially SMERs (satisfying and mutually empowering relationships). Awareness is the basis on which self-directed (independent) growth (becoming more than we are) is founded.

9.3

Loyalty

A few years ago I designed a course; a series of seminars and workshops, which I called Psychology and Healthy Relationships. It consists of 15 weekly three-hour sessions which I split into three levels Beginner, Intermediate, and Advanced five sessions each. In the first session, I began by asking participants to complete a questionnaire. When I analysed the responses and followed up the results, my findings gave me some insights into those topics that the participants could benefit most from. I then modified the content and the structure of the courses accordingly. Let me tell you a little bit about some of those findings.

One of the questions tested how willing the participants were to end (or distance themselves from) a disempowering (dysfunctional) relationship. This was one of the lowest scoring items. In other words, at the beginning of the course, participants were very resistant to the idea of 'moving on'.

In every endeavour of life, we believe that experience is empowering, however, it appears that, when it comes to relationships, many of us tend to self-limit our range of experiences. We tend to believe that, once we enter into a relationship, we have an obligation to do our best to maintain that relationship. The reasons for this vary, but the justifications usually allude to 'loyalty', whether or not that is the actual underlying reason.

[There is, of course, a great deal of evolutionary value in the notion of loyalty. It can be one of the instruments through which each of us, as cells (§ 90 Fractals), are drawn to creating tissues, organs and organisms beyond ourselves (§ 50.3 The Spiritual Dimension and § 32 Extended Relationships). However, as with all of our other evolutionarily empowering capabilities, it can become disempowering if it manifests in inappropriate contexts.]

For some people, it is a fear that they may not be able to enter into a more empowering relationship later. This lack of self-confidence is, of course, linked to lack of experience [I am sure you can see how this can lead to a closed loop].

Another reason for not ending disempowering relationships is the value judgements that we attach to loyalty. We believe it is disloyal to end a relationship even if it is disempowering for both parties. Some people form emotional attachments easily and then find it painful to withdraw from such a relationship even if it is more disempowering to stay.

Another reason for people limiting their experience is the idea that ending a relationship is tantamount to failure. They interpret it to mean 'giving up' and they have associated giving up with being a 'loser'. Such perceptions tend to carry with them a sense of guilt; a feeling that we have not been strong enough, a feeling that, had we persevered, perhaps we would have 'won' the 'battle'.

I should clarify that when I talk about disempowering, I do not mean 'bad'; I mean that the 'partnership' is not in the best interest of both parties *in the given circumstances* [not a good 'fit' in the Darwinian (adaptive) sense].

I hear some of you saying, "Well that's 'bad' enough, isn't it?" Later in this course, we will be talking about Transactional Analysis (§ 73) and, after you know more about that, what I'm about to say will make more sense. The words 'good' and 'bad' tend to have a judgemental edge to them that trigger an emotional response (the Parent ego state affects the Child ego state) and can, to varying degrees, impair our judgement.

The words 'good' and 'bad' touch our emotions because, as we were growing up, the significant others in our lives (parents, teachers, carers and other authority figures) used them to describe us so we have associated them with our own sense of identity and anything that is linked to our sense of identity is not emotionally neutral (§ 37.7 The Emergence of Identity).

Anyway, let's get back to the interesting finding from those questionnaires. When I gave the same questionnaire again at the end of the courses and compared the results, the greatest difference was in this idea that if the relationship is not sufficiently empowering, it is acceptable to move on.

[Actually, it is not surprising for those in the know (research analysts) that the greatest improvement was with regards to the lowest scoring question. Change is not linear; it is easier to make improvements when we are at the lower end of a scale than at the higher end of it. The better we get at something, the more effort is required to make an incremental improvement. This is because the effort-result relationship is asymptotic. I explain what that means in § 64.10 (Values and Perfectionism)]

Chapter 10

The First Step

10.1
Orientation

Imagine that you're lost and you want to decide which way to go. What's the first thing that you do?

[When my son, Parsa, was very young we used to play a game called, 'guess what's in the box'. When it was my turn to guess, he would say, "Let me give you a clue; it's a sock (or whatever it was that was in the box)." In the same vein, I'm going to give you a clue.]

In embarking on any journey, the first step is orientation (we need to get our bearings). Where exactly am I? What is my starting position? That is, we try to establish where we are before deciding which way to go; we look for landmarks or other points of reference [which don't have to be on 'land', so we could call some of them, such as stars, 'skymarks'].

[Of course, we don't need to be lost to do that. The reason I asked you to imagine that you are lost is because if I had asked you to imagine that you are starting on any journey, you would most probably have imagined setting off from home. This wouldn't have demonstrated my point as clearly because, even though we do need to get our bearings before setting off on any journey, we don't consciously think about that when we set off from home.]

To get our bearings, we start by asking questions (§ 15.1 The Power of Questions) such as, "What are some of the reference points that I can use to allow me to establish where I am?"

10.2
How do you track progress?

By measuring, of course! What we measure and how we measure depend on what we are trying to track. So, if I want to lose weight, I track my progress using weighing scales. But it is not as simple as that. If I don't use the scales correctly, I will make decisions based on incorrect information. And I'm not talking about the accuracy of the instrument. Let me explain.

Does measuring my weight affect how much weight I lose? The intuitive answer is to say, "No." But let's not jump to that conclusion yet.

[You may be wondering why I am talking about weight loss in a book about relationships. The answer will become clear a little later when I talk about metaphors (§ 14.2) but, for now, let's just say that I want to get the basic concepts across as simply as possible before we apply them to relationships which, being more abstract, are more complicated.]

Throughout the day, depending on when we ingest, how much we ingest, how often we go to relieve ourselves and how much exercise we do, our weight fluctuates [as surprising as it may seem, this can be as much as 2 kg a day]. This is the noise in the system. I may be following an effective weight loss regime which enables me to lose weight at an average rate of 50g per day, that's about 1 kilogram every three weeks. So, what happens when I measure my weight too often? I will get a distorted view of what is happening because the noise will sometimes make it appear as if my weight has gone up in spite of my efforts or I may get the impression that the diet is working too well. Both of these will affect how I continue with my efforts.

So, the answer to the question is, yes, measuring *can* affect the outcome. In this case, measuring our weight can affect how much weight we lose or gain. One of the factors it depends on is how often we measure. Measuring too frequently can give us a distorted view of our progress. So, what is the solution?

The solution is to look at *trends* instead. The chart in figure 2 shows how weight can fluctuate from day to day. Compare this to the straight trend line. Notice how, if the person had taken just two measurements, one at the beginning of March and one on the 24th of March, he would not have noticed the effectiveness of his efforts and may well have given up.

Figure 3 Change of a Dieter's Weight Over Time

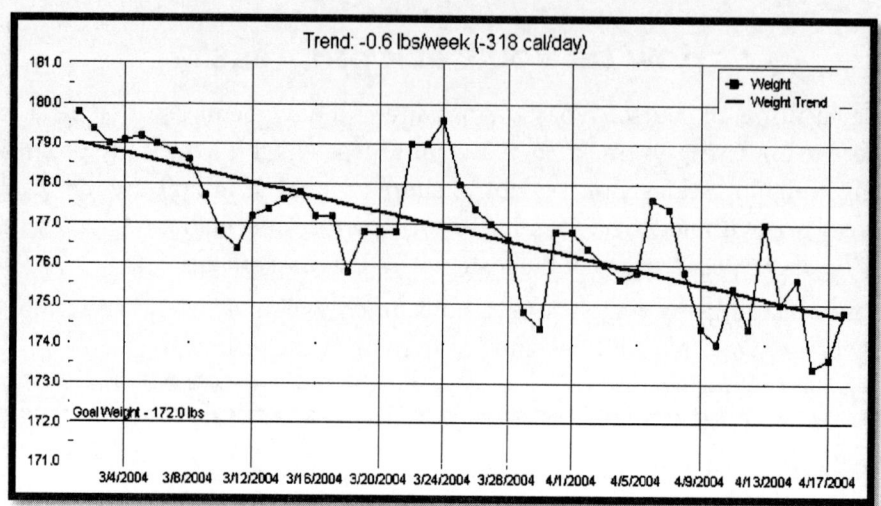

[Source: http://www.weightware.com/weighttrend.htm]

So what does all this have to do with *The Art and Science of Relationships*? Thank you for asking. I am trying to encourage you, somewhat *emphatically*, to take a baseline measurement before you go any further along in this book, that is, I urge you to answer the questions in the following link first:

www.introducingaffinitology.com/baseline_questionnaire/

There are two reasons for this. The questions help you to increase your self-awareness, which itself is therapeutic (§ 11 the Therapeutic Effects of Awareness). Secondly, your responses will become a baseline against which you can judge the effectiveness of this course for you. In other words, it is a standard against which you can judge the extent to which this course helps you to feel more empowered. If you do not do this, it would be like embarking on a weight loss program without knowing your starting weight.

Chapter 11

The Therapeutic Effects of Awareness

**Awareness can reduce our resistance to change
(expand our comfort zone)**

When I was in primary school, I read a book that explained how our likes and dislikes for foods can be affected by experiences which, rightly or wrongly, we have associated with those foods. For example, if I eat, let's say, *Spaghetti al dente* [my choice was inspired by the song, L'Italiano by Toto Cutugno that made the British Charts in the 1980s. It is a socio-political commentary on the Italy of its time] and later experience a stomach ache, in my subconscious mind, I may associate my stomach ache with that food. If I do, from then on, I will tend to avoid *Spaghetti al dente* even if the actual reason for my stomach ache had nothing to do with it. When I became aware of this, I began to eat some of the foods that I had refused to eat before and found that I didn't react to them as negatively as I had done before and I gradually began to enjoy eating them. This change in attitude happened over several days not years. This is an example of the therapeutic effect of awareness.

[The ease with which I managed to do this may have had something to do with me having been eight years old when habits are not so engrained and there is less resistance to change. Nevertheless, it demonstrates the point.]

When I say that, at an earlier age, there is less resistance to change, I don't mean that kids don't put up resistance. Actually, they make a point of doing so. However, the underlying reason for this resistance is different; it is not engrained habits. When my kids were sitting around at home, I used to encounter resistance when I suggested that we should go out somewhere. They would whine, stall and argue. I would eventually manage to get them out of the house. If after an hour or so of being let's say, in the park, I suggested that it was time to return home, I encountered resistance again, "Oh Daaad, can't we stay a little longer?"

That scenario is probably familiar to most parents. The difference between what kids do and what adults do when they resist change is that kids make a point of actively testing their carers' resolve. I intend to discuss this in more detail in a separate course about parenting. [Keep an eye on introducingaffinitology.com]

Adults resist change for different reasons. One hypothesis is that our limbic system is only interested in one thing; survival. This is how it thinks,

> "I have survived so far by doing what I have been doing and I don't see why I should change because anything new has not proven itself to have survival value, whereas what I have done so far has. So, let's not rock the boat, OK?!"

This is why many people remain in relationships that, to an observer, appears to be very disempowering (dysfunctional).

As the saying goes, "If you always do what you've always done, you'll always get what you've always got".

Therapy, any kind of therapy, requires that we change.
To get different results, we need to change what we do.
To do that, we need to change how we think *first*.

"But Bijan, if this is a book about relationships, why are you talking about therapy?" I hear you ask. Well, because that's what I consider any kind of practically empowering learning to be; therapy. By empowering, I mean the acquisition of a greater range of adaptive skills that can help us to deal with obstacles that may get in the way of us feeling fulfilled.

What we do; any decision that we make and any action that we take, however small or large, stems from a combination of two factors; our values (§ 34.1.2 Values) and how easy or difficult we think it is to put into action (§ 93 Energy). New evidence, that is, a new conclusion that we derive for ourselves or one that we accept from others, can affect our perceptions of how important and/or easy something is to accomplish. It is this new awareness that motivates us to change (or not). I consider **any kind of awareness that motivates us to change (grow or adapt) as being therapeutic**.

Although, on the surface, what I have just pointed out might seem quite obvious, the part that may not be so obvious is that,

---

Through awareness, change happens spontaneously.

That is, we don't have to 'work hard at it' for change to happen. Most of the changes that we need to make to create extraordinary lives and relationships for ourselves are not intrinsically difficult. What makes them appear difficult is our subconscious *resistance* to change (§ 94.2 The Frontal Lobe and Emotional Control). After an empowering change of perspective, however, our *resistance* to the actions that we need to take diminishes and that's how awareness facilitates change.

The therapeutic effect of newly acquired awareness is often fleeting (temporary) unless it is reinforced persistently. Think of the difference between going on a 'diet' and a lifestyle change. This is why one of the things that I tell my clients is that **nobody leaves my office without homework**.

11.1

Why Can Seriously Damage Our Health

(And the Health of Our Relationships)

The word 'why' can be an adverb, a noun, a conjunction or an interjection and can refer to cause, reason or purpose. That's a lot of versatility.

The word why, not only tends to attract our attention, we are prone to becoming oversensitive (§ 81 Emotional Allergens and Hypersensitivity) when we hear someone say 'why' to us. "Why is that?" I hear you wonder. It is because we become oversensitive to things that can potentially threaten our sense of identity. Our beliefs are the building blocks of our Identities (§ 42 The Anatomy of Identity) and the word why can potentially threaten our beliefs. Our intentions (§ 53 Trust) are also inextricably bound with our sense of identity and, in some contexts, the word 'why' can be perceived as casting doubt on our intentions.

'Why' is more likely to be damaging to our relationships when it is accompanied by the word 'you' in the same sentence, such as, "Why did you do that?" Similarly, it can be damaging to our relationship with ourselves (§ 29.4 The Omniself), when we use the word 'I' in the same sentence, "Why did I do that?"

Many of us have a propensity to overuse the word 'why' in our internal and external conversations. Here is an exercise to help us kick this habit.

Exercise 2 Exploring the Disempowering Effects of 'Why'

Before the exercise, I say, "I put it to you that questions beginning with 'why' cause more problems than they solve." I then explain the reasons behind this assertion. Then I say, "Until next session, your homework is to firstly become aware of the number of times you encounter (think, hear, say or read) a question that begins with 'Why'. Why did you do that? Why did he say that? Why do I feel this way? And so on. In other words, you need to become sensitive to this word. Then, I want you to eliminate all questions beginning with 'why' from your mental and verbal vocabulary."

Of course, this is like asking someone not to think of a pink elephant (§ 8 What If). To avoid the 'pink elephant' problem, we need to substitute the why with an alternative expression. I tell my clients that an empowering way of doing this is to restructure any question that begins with 'why' so that it begins with 'How can I'?

>>> **Change WHY to HOW CAN I** <<<

In the next session I ask, "Did you notice any changes in the way you think and react (emotionally, intellectually or behaviourally) towards others when you adopt this new question structure? What did you notice about the way others react to you? What insights did you gain from doing this exercise?

In short, this one simple change in the way that we think and interact with other people can transform our emotions, our relationships, our outlook; our entire life.

SUMMARY OF UNIT 2

In this Unit, I have explained that to get the most from this course, begin to read this book as if you are reading a novel. The first time you read through it, don't think about what it can do for you, because that way you will be focused on the outcome too much and, paradoxically, the outcome will elude you because those who appreciate the journey appreciate the outcome much more than those who are so focused on the outcome that they miss the journey. And if we are not to appreciate the outcome, what is the point of seeking it?

You see, if we are not transformed by the outcome that we seek, there is no real outcome; any semblance of an outcome is illusory. What I am saying is that, if the result of what we do does not change the way we percieve the world in some way, even if it looks like a result, it is not a result worth thinking about.

You might have sought this course because you are looking for answers to your relationship problems. What I am suggesting is that your relationship problems are likely to resolve themselves if you let this course transform you rather than looking for specific answers to specific questions.

In the next section, we are going to explore the language of relationships, that is, how we can talk (and think) about relationships in ways that empower us.

Unit 3

The Power of Language

[Image by Oberholster from Pixabay.
Source; https://pixabay.com/vectors/moses-religion-christianity-1564373/]

Chapter 12

Communication

At every moment, in every day, we take a great deal for granted; things that are crucial to our existence which we don't notice. Obvious examples include the beating of our hearts and the blinking of our eyelids. Of course, we notice them as soon as we *become aware* of them.

This isn't limited to abilities that we are born with; it also happens with acquired skills. For example, as babies, we try really hard to learn to walk but, later, we take it for granted; we don't even notice what we are doing. Similarly, a skilled driver is not conscious of the efforts that he had to put into learning how to drive are all the myriad of details that he needs to take into account whilst he is driving; it has all become automatic that is to say, unconscious.

With that in mind I would like to draw your attention to words. The words that we use every day and the words that you are reading on this page and even the words that we use for thinking. Without words our thinking would be severely limited.

Let me dwell on this just a little bit more because it's very important for the next part of our discussion and, of course, for understanding relationships.

Without words we couldn't answer the question, "Who am I". In fact, the whole concept would be meaningless. 'Who' is about identity and identity comes about through words; without words we would only be concerned with *what* not *who*. In other words, the question (which I wouldn't be able to frame as a question) would be, "What is that?" and not "Who am I?". Therefore, language gives as a means through which we can, not only explain, but actually know who or what we are. Not only that but we wouldn't even be who we are.

> **Words are not simply the means through which we explain or describe our identity; they are the building blocks with which we build our identities.**

I should clarify that it is not words but sentences because the *structure* of language also constrains us in terms of what we can think and how we can think.

Once, on a linguistics course, I heard that there is a language which forces you, through your sentence structure, to say whether or not you are sure of what you are saying. This made me wonder whether there is anything within the English language that I am forced to do and I realise that yes there is. English [and, I believe, Indo-European languages in general] forces me to conjugate a verb which means that I have to state the tense. That is to say I must say whether what I'm talking about is about now about the future or about the past. I cannot avoid inferring something about time in my sentences in English. In Chinese, on the other hand, this is optional. If I begin a sentence in Chinese with "I eat" what the listener perceives is that I am going to talk about something to do with me and eating. Unlike an English interlocutor, they do not assume that I'm talking about now or about something that I do habitually (whether I am talking about the past, the present or future is optional and needs to be qualified with a time-related adverbial clause; yesterday, later, now, etc.).

Another example is that if there is only one person involved and you're talking about them in the third person, English forces you to specify the gender of that person (he or she). In Persian there is only one pronoun for the third person singular; when you say 'oo' in Persian you could be talking about a he, a she or an it. If you want to be more specific, you will have to say 'that man', 'that woman' or 'that chair'.

I was speaking to an Assyrian friend of mine, a few decades ago, and she said that, in Assyrian, even the first-person singular pronoun is bound to gender. That means that when I say I, I must specify whether I am saying 'I man' or 'I woman'. That is not as redundant as you might think. Imagine you're reading a story and it begins with, "I was alone in a room with him." The gender of the 'I' could make quite a difference to our perception of the situation; I should say, our assumptions about the situation (§ 33 Atasinex Cluster).

There is even more to this than meets the eye, literally. There are an infinite number of possible colours in the rainbow and because of the way in which our eyes work we can only distinguish several million of them, but we reduce all of those into seven colours including green and blue. However, some languages, such as Vietnamese, use the same word for green and blue. In the same way that Persian uses the same word for camel and dromedary. The point being that research has shown that when you don't have a different word for green and blue you don't perceive the difference. This is the way they did the research. Let's say you have five Shades of Grey and the green blob on the screen and you ask the person to pick the odd one out. The results will be the same for both Vietnamese and English speakers. However, if you have five shades of green and a shade of blue in the mix, the Vietnamese will not indicate that there is an odd one to be picked out. The point is that consciousness depends on perception and perception is the interpretation of physiological signals and language affects that perception.

Language focuses our attention on some of the things that are perceivable and causes us to ignore (blinds us) to other aspects of what we can perceive.

A crucial implication here is that, since the perception of 'difference' is the root of prejudice,

> **The language we use and how we use it can affect the extent to which we become prejudiced.**

If the various so-called 'races' of humanity were different shades of blue and green, English speakers would be more susceptible to prejudice than those who speak Vietnamese.

All I want to do here, is to plant the seeds of awareness. I want us to become more acutely aware of the effect that the language that we have inherited from our ancestors has on our psyche; on the way we think and, consequently, on the way in which we *actually perceive* our world, including all the assumptions that go with it. This is particularly important to our current discussion because words and language are the building blocks of the Identities through which we connect with people and maintain relationships.

We tend to talk about communication as if it is a means of simply imparting information but that's not entirely true. The interaction between my psyche and the information that it receives create new information, new syntax, new meanings and, consequently, new attitudes and new behaviours.

> **Every time we use language, we are either changing or reinforcing our reality; what we see and how we see it.**

And I don't mean just subjective reality we actually change objective reality through the words that come out of our minds.

Searching through the internet for ideas that can only be expressed through metaphors, I came across an interpretation of metaphors as, "Alternative linguistic mechanisms for expressing ideas." However, I suggest that this is only a very small part of what metaphors are about because often metaphors are *the only way* to express ideas, abstract ideas in particular. In fact, I would go as far as to say that there isn't a single word in the dictionary that is not an abstraction. Words and even perceptions are simply derivatives of reality.

As I mentioned earlier, relationships are abstract. You cannot point to two people and say oh look there's a relationship, just as we can't say oh look there's love walking down the street or flying through the air. We can say that two people 'look like' they're in love because of what they're doing, the way they're looking at each other, holding hands and their facial expressions, etc., but in the end, *it's all assumption* (§ 33 Atasinex Cluster).

The word 'abstract' has its roots in the notion of withdrawal. It was originally used to convey the idea of distancing yourself from worldly interests, as in what monks do in monasteries. But now, it means anything that does not have material form. We need to give material form to the abstract ideas that we talk about, including the idea of relationships. We know it's there. We 'know' it's real. But we can't point to it, we can't show it. And, therefore, we have to present it in a way that is concrete. A metaphor does that.

When attempting to convey ideas, I believe that it is the teacher's responsibility to help the student to understand. In my private teaching, when my student doesn't understand what I'm trying to explain, I consider it to be my responsibility to find another angle or point of view that the student can identify with more than the previous explanations.

With regards to this course in relationships, if I were sitting with you one-to-one, I would first explore your experiences and your interests and then try to use metaphors that are closer to your experiences in order to explain the abstract concepts that we need to appreciate when creating and developing exciting, empowering and satisfying relationships. However, since I cannot do that here, I will try to do the next best thing which is to provide you with various angles from which you can look at the ideas I'm trying to explain and, hopefully, one will resonate with you more than the others.

Chapter 13

Language as a tool

Without communication there can be no interpersonal relationships and language is the primary mode of communication.

"But I thought that experts say that more than 90% of our interpersonal communication is nonverbal" I hear some of you saying. If you are not a perfectionist, that is to say, if a 90% success rate is good enough for you, then try this exercise: Try instigating and maintaining your interpersonal relationships without words for a week. If the theory is correct, its impact on your relationship should be less than 10% (and you can always compensate for that to some extent by improving your non-verbal communication skills). I can hear what some of you are thinking and, no, you can't use sign language because that's still verbal communication; only the symbolism is different. After all it's called sign language and not sign communication.

> **"It seems redundant to make a lot of noise about something when in fact there it is"**
>
> - S. Rushdie

I have come to conclude that the biggest threat to our mental health is language. Language is the medium through which we pass on knowledge and someone once said, there is no higher purpose than that. However, unfortunately, language is also the medium through which we corrupt knowledge (lie, deceive and impart falsehoods in general) and most of the time we do that, whether consciously or subconsciously, as part of our psychological defence mechanisms. This kind of 'false knowledge' can be and often is, much more destructive than ignorance because we can't pass on ignorance, but we can pass on false knowledge. Perhaps I shouldn't be elevating 'falsehoods' by calling them 'knowledge' because this associates them with that highest of all purposes, passing on real knowledge. I can't call 'false knowledge' a lie, because that implies deliberate deception and often, we pass on false knowledge without realising that this is what we are doing. OK, then let's stick with 'falsehoods' for now and carry on.

Language is the primary vehicle for bringing people together, especially since we seem to have lost our sensitivity to pheromones and other less overt cues. But then again, any common focus could bring people together. One such example is guns, which bring people together in the form of armies. However, the conflicts that this creates are much more destructive than the apparent 'unity' that holds an army together. So, am I saying that language is like a gun? Well, it can be, but I suggest that it is more like a knife. The sole purpose of a gun is to kill. You could argue that it is a deterrent and my response would be that, when it deters, it does so through threat of death, which fuels animosity by affirming hostile intention, rather than ameliorate the relationship by reducing barriers to communication. A knife, on the other hand can be, and often is, designed with the intention of enabling the user to improve his quality of life directly. In the wrong hands, however, that same knife can be used in destructive ways. The same applies to language and relationships.

Chapter 14

What's in a Word?

> **"In the beginning, there was the word ..."**
>
> - John, Chapter 1

14.1
Words are Meaningless

Words are meaningless *out of context.* One of our misconceptions about language is that we think of the 'word' as the basic unit of language. I contend that this is not the case. We do not learn languages through vocabulary, any more than we can learn to drive by knowing the Highway Code. Whenever I am asked to teach English, I begin by saying that,

> **a unit of communication is the 'sentence', not the 'word'.**

The shortest sentences tend to be imperatives ('do this' or 'don't do that') and the shortest imperative in the English language is, "Go!". This is a one-word sentence.

Depending on when, where and how we use words, what we communicate (the meaning), and its consequent effect on our relationships, can change dramatically (§ 11.1 Why Can Seriously Damage Our Health).

14.2
Metaphors

In the physical sciences, words are a means of describing or explaining the 'nuts and bolts'. In relationships, they *are* the nuts and bolts. Words create, maintain and empower or disempower relationships (Unit 16: Physiology of Relationships). However, this section is about how we use words in the first way; to talk *about* relationships.

Relationships are abstract. Therefore, in order to talk *about* relationships, we need to find ways of conceptualising them in concrete terms. As such, I make extensive use of metaphors in this course. This is primarily because, as George

Lakoff and Mark Johnson pointed out in their influential work, "Metaphors we live by":

> "The concepts that govern our thought are not just matters of the intellect. They also govern our everyday functioning, down to the most mundane details. Our concepts structure what we perceive, how we get around in the world, and how we relate to other people. Our conceptual system thus plays a central role in defining our everyday realities. If we are right in suggesting that our conceptual system is largely metaphorical, then the way we think, what we experience, and what we do every day is very much a matter of metaphor."
>
> [Source: Silver, M. (1982). *Metaphors We Live by* by George Lakoff, Mark Johnson. Leonardo, 15(4), 323]

Another reason for my extensive use of metaphors may have something to do with my first language being Persian in which the use of metaphor is even more pervasive than in English.

14.3

Situation vs Circumstance

Throughout our discussion of interpersonal relationships, I have emphasized the crucial role that the situation plays in determining our behaviour through the identity that either emerges or is evoked by that situation.

In § 33.2 (Perception), I define the situation as our perception of circumstances. Nowadays the words situation and circumstances are used interchangeably. However, for the purposes of this discourse, I wish to highlight some critical differences between them. The word situation is derived from a Latin word meaning position. In any given circumstance, I can change my position (point of view) and I can perceive that circumstance differently and for me, that change in point of view, changes the situation, as I perceive it.

In general, the word situation is used much more often in conjunction with emotive words such as, "The situation is hopeless" or "The situation is gratifying." The word circumstance(s), on the other hand, is used in more objective terms alongside words like mitigating or extenuating. The distinction I have made here between the situation and circumstances ties in with our discussion of locus of control (§ 44). We cannot change the circumstances but the extent to which we can influence the situation depends on our locus of control.

Chapter 15

The Power of Specialised Language

Here is a personal anecdote that demonstrates how timely use of specialised language can defuse a potentially volatile situation.

> *One morning, in Iran, my mother was in her study and I popped in to see her. I cannot remember what she said to me, but I responded somewhat curtly and stormed out* [I am not much of a 'stormer' and so, to someone who doesn't know me, it may not have looked out of the ordinary]. *A few moments later, she walked into my study and said something like* [it was in Persian], *"Hey Bijan, can you tell me what happened back there in my office earlier?" With a smile on my face, I replied* [in Persian], *"Oh, nothing; your Parent ego state spoke and my Child ego state responded." And that was the end of it; nothing more needed to be said.*

Later in this course, we explore the Transactional Analysis (TA) model of human relationships and how it can help us in our quest for SMERs. If you are not familiar with TA, I suggest that you return to this story once you have familiarised yourself with it (§ 73 Transactional Analysis).

15.1
The Power of Questions

Earlier (§ 73), I posed this question, "How do you track progress?"

As simple as this question may seem, thinking about it can have a profound impact on our lives. Here's why. Firstly, being a question, it compels us to begin to think about it. It also forces us, as questions do, to come up with some kind of answer; even if that answer is "I don't know" or "I don't care". Thinking about anything new veers our focus away from what we were thinking about before. This is an effective method that is often used in psychotherapy to change people's state.

Specifically, the question, "How do you track progress?" is asking you to think about a goal, and not just any goal; a goal that involves gradual or incremental change. And that is just for starters.

Having assumed that you have a goal and that the goal is related to a gradual change, the question then invites you to think about how you are going to measure that change. This is a very important aspect of goal-setting. As you probably already know, goals are more effective when they are SMART (Specific, Measurable, Achievable, Relevant and Time-bound). In addition, the word 'track' in the question suggests that we need to measure at least at two different times and then compare the results. Another subtle effect of this question is that it appeals to our positive value judgements. By directing our attention towards *progress*, it implies (unconsciously, of course) that something 'good' is about to come our way and makes us feel more positive inside.

Yes! All that in 5 words. Isn't that amazing?

Since I make use of questions extensively throughout my teaching and in my consultancy sessions and, of course, in these courses, I think it is important that you appreciate their power.

Questions are often used to instil beliefs in us which, by being posed as questions, appear to be innocent. The idea of changing minds through questions is well researched and I don't want us to be distracted too much by it here. At this point, I simply wanted to plant the seeds of interest in you.

15.2
The Importance of Gestalts

If, in a group of people, I ask everyone to imagine an Island, every person will create a unique picture in their mind. However, all of the images will have certain features in common; there will be a piece of land surrounded by a body of water [unless you are a lollipop lady (crossing guard) in which case, you might be one of the exceptions].

Now, if I ask the same group to then think of a lake, again, the details may be different but they will have no difficulty in imagining what will be a body of water surrounded by land.

Both 'island' and 'lake' describe a relationship between three concepts, the concept of 'land', the concept of 'water' and the concept of 'surround'. But each of the words 'island' and 'lake' are coded in our minds in such a way, that they evoke different images, feelings and memories. We will not be saying to ourselves,

"Oh, an island, yeah, I know, I know, it has something to do with land, water and surround, but there's that other thing that has the same three concepts in it, what was it again, oh yes, the lake, so which way round is it with island, is that the one where the water surrounds the land or is it the other way around?"

That does not happen because each of these two concepts has become a gestalt.

Now, imagine that you are in school and you are learning about atoms and molecules. You are told that "negative ions are called anions and positive ions are called cations". You are also told that in electrolysis, "the negative electrode is called the cathode and the positive electrode is called the anode." Then comes the dreaded exam and here is the question, "What is the charge on an anion?" and you think to yourself, "Anion, cation, anode, cathode, negative, positive, positive, negative! Oh, I hate chemistry, it's so confusing." Clearly, the concepts have not become gestalts yet.

In the first example, your gestalt regarding an 'Island' may evoke images of a small piece of land with a single palm tree or images of sitting on your father's lap as he reads Robinson Crusoe to you. In the second example, the word 'anion' will evoke feelings of frustration and images of sitting in a classroom with your head spinning and wondering whether you are the foolish one or chemical nomenclature. Now, sit back as I tell you a story about Alkemian* mythology.

*[Alkemia is a fictional place created by the author.]

Anions and Cations

In the days before the earth was created, the Gods were sitting around a large table and were thinking about the design of creatures to put on earth. They had already agreed that they would create two versions of Man, a male and a female. In one of the earlier designs, they gave man and woman one breast each. The Gods didn't call them breasts; they called them 'electa' (singular; electum). But then, Greedius, the God of Inequality, said that it would serve the purposes of evolution better if one of them had both electa because that would lead to greater diversity and so they gave woman two 'electa' and man got none.

They called the first man Andrew and that's why the prefix 'Andr-' means 'male' (the prefix 'an-' means 'without' as in, without electa). They called the first woman Catherine; remember, she's the one who got more than her fair share of 'electa'. As time went by, more Andrews came along and they wanted to balance the books by trying to take back an electum that they felt was rightfully theirs. An Andrew who hadn't found a Catherine who is willing to share an electum with him was called a Cation (a Catherine seeker 'ei' means go and 'eion', abbreviated to the suffix '-ion' means 'one who moves toward').

But the other Gods who did not agree with Greedius, imbued Catherine with a sense of obligation to share her electa with Andrew. In future generations, a Catherine who had not yet found an Andrew to share her electa with was called an Anion (a seeker of Andrews). Then the Gods built a convent (like a Cathedral) where all the eligible Catherines would wait for eligible cations to come along. They called this building a cathodral (abbreviated to cathode) and decorated it with representations of electa to attract cations.

The Gods also built a similar building (like a monastery) where all the eligible Andrews would wait for their anions to come along. They called this building the anodral (abbreviated to anode) and decorated it with representations that would attract anions. Since then, cations (Catherine Seekers) strive to reach the cathode and anions (Andrew Seekers) strive to reach the anode.

Once, an Alkemian social psychologist asked a group of anions, "How do you feel about having too many electa?" And the majority said, "Negative." When asked why, they said because they felt that it was unfair. This feeling was shared with the Catherines in the Cathodes. The social psychologists also asked the cations how they felt about not having any electa and they said, "positive." When asked why, they said that it was because it gave them a sense of purpose. The Andrews in the anodes shared this sentiment.

Now, if we tell that story to our teenage kids and then ask them to answer the earlier exam question, I am fairly confident that they are much less likely to confuse anion, cation, anode and cathode because, instead of being isolated concepts, they become integrated into a unified whole; a gestalt. The point is that,

> **facts are burdens until they become gestalts.**

And after they become gestalts,

> **facts are useless, unless they can be incorporated into *skills*.**

We can think of gestalts as mental resources that can be accessed through a variety of triggers. These triggers can be anything that is connected with the gestalt. For example, since you have just read the above Alkemian mythology, the word Cathedral is now a trigger for connecting to gestalts called anions and cations. The names Catherine and Andrew will also remind you of anions and cations (in addition to everything else that you previously associated with 'Andrew' and 'Catherine'). This is the power of gestalts.

Facts, on the other hand, strain our mental resources. If you are familiar with Microsoft Windows' search facility, you will probably know that indexed searches are quick whilst non-indexed locations are slow to search. It may be helpful for you to think of it this way; a gestalt is like an indexed item within your memory retrieval system whereas mere facts are unindexed and are not useful when we need to access and use them at short notice, especially on the fly. Gestalts have their downsides too. For example, searching an indexed location can return more results than the user can cope with and then she will need to narrow the search.

Some years ago, I used to offer my services as a court interpreter. One day at court, I was interpreting for a gentleman who had been accused of dangerous driving. When my client was called to the stand, the public prosecutor began his examination with these words, "I want to talk to you about undertaking". My mind froze, very briefly, as my head began to buzz. The courtroom went silent as everyone waited for me to translate. I quickly recovered myself and said, "Sorry, three meanings of the word 'undertake' came to mind".

In short, one of the disadvantages of gestalts is that they sometimes cause our minds to give us more information than we need for the particular situation.

Interpersonal relationships are gestalts too. As such, they also offer us the advantages and disadvantages of gestalts. If I were to ask you to think of someone you know, you won't just remember a name or a face; you will remember a myriad of details about this person and the images will include their shape and size, something that he is wearing along with one or more feelings and a context for each of those feelings.

If you meet someone for the first time and he is introduced to you as Henry and he happens to have red hair and a kilt, then your mind will immediately access all the gestalts related to 'Henry' and all the gestalts related to 'man with red hair' and all the gestalts related to 'man with kilt'. Your overall reaction to this opportunity for a connection will depend on the sum of the emotions aroused by the combination of the name, the characteristics of the person and the circumstances under which you meet.

To sum up, the lesson I would like you to take away is that, in spite of its drawbacks, if we try to convey ideas in gestalts as much as possible, we will save much confusion, conflict and heartache. The ancients understood this and that is why most of the cultural heritage that we have left from history is embedded in mythological and sociological *stories*. On the downside, this is, perhaps, also the reason for our predilection for gossip.

Chapter 16

To have or to be

> "Because the society we live in is devoted to acquiring property and making a profit, we rarely see any evidence of the being mode of existence and most people see the having mode as the most natural mode of existence, even the only acceptable way of life. All of which makes it especially difficult for people to comprehend the nature of the being mode, and even to understand that having is only one possible orientation."
>
> - Erich Fromm, *To Have or To Be*

16.1
Having, Being and Becoming

When it comes to relationships, we seem to either be *in* one, as if it is some kind of a container, or *have* one, as if it is something we can possess. Neither terminology seems satisfactory to me.

To my mind, 'having' a relationship is worse than being 'in' one because the idea of 'having' brings with it the risk and fear of 'losing'. On The other hand, when we are *in* a relationship, we have a choice of extending the metaphor to feel like being *in* a garden or *in* a relaxing hot tub or, conversely, *in* a prison or *in* a deep well.

I suggest that we attempt to escape from these restrictive perceptions about relationships that language is imposing upon our psyche. Replacing the word 'relationship' with 'connect' offers greater possibilities since 'connect' can be a verb as well as a noun; apparently, I cannot feel 'relationshipped' whereas I can feel 'connected'. And this brings us closer to what a relationship actually is. I put it to you that,

> **relationships are characterized through *feelings***

See also § 51.2 (Affect, Feelings and Emotions).

Let me explain. If something or someone does not evoke a feeling in me, meaning that I am emotionally disconnected from that object or subject, I cannot say that I have a relationship with it [note that the 'I' here refers to my Identity and not my physical entity (§ 29.4 The Omniself) and (§ 37.7 The Emergence of Identity)].

Throughout this course, we explore ways to improve our connections through reconnecting with our feelings. Mindfulness and conscious gratitude are two ways in which we can get in touch with our feelings.

16.2

Mindfulness and Conscious Gratitude

Mindfulness helps us to connect with things and people with whom we have lost our emotional connection (primarily through habituation). Habituation keeps us from being distracted by what we *have already*, allowing us to concentrate on other aspects of our lives. However, there is a major drawback to this.

What/who we *are* is defined/determined by what we are *connected to*, i.e., what we have *feelings* for (§ 16.1 Having, Being and Becoming). When we lose our emotional connection to something that is a part of us, or we are a part of (§ 41 Sculpturism), a part of us becomes atrophied.

Conscious gratitude can be thought of as mindfulness from a different perspective. One way of achieving the state of conscious gratitude is by becoming mindful of what our world would be like if something that is currently in our lives (a person or some other phenomenon that we feel connected to) were to no longer be there. This can help us to connect or reconnect with people, our environment or different aspects of our being.

Chapter 17

Chemical Nomenclature

The title of this section might intrigue you to ask, "What does naming compounds have to do with understanding relationships?" But, more fundamentally, this section is about a much broader issue, that being,

> **"What does naming anything have to do with understanding anything?"**

To put it another way, this section is about PERSPECTIVE. How we understand anything, including our relationships, affects EVERYTHING in our lives, especially our decisions which affect our behaviour, our emotions, our relationships, our finances, our trajectory and ultimately, our destiny.

There is always more than one way to understand anything. Actually, that is an understatement. There is a myriad of ways to understand anything, including any particular interpersonal relationship. It is a wonder that we understand each other at all. [Rebecca Saxe says that this has to do with a certain part of our brain called the RTPJ. Since you are interested enough in interpersonal relationships to pick up this book, I encourage you to watch her TED Talk entitled, *how we read each other's minds.*]

The way we use words, including how we label things both indicates and affects the way we perceive what is going on around us. Just as in society, such as in criminal law, we can talk about the accused, the suspect or the defendant, scientists can also look at natural phenomena from different perspectives and be affected by those perspectives.

In this section, I am going to demonstrate this in relation to the naming of chemicals for two reasons; it is one of my fields of expertise and chemistry is thought of as a 'hard' (as in 'robust') science and I just want to point out that even when the objective reality is the same, our minds can perceive them in different ways, even when we are looking at it as 'objective' scientists. The reason for that has little to do with *who we are* and much more to do with *how we observe*. With the help of chemistry, in this section, my aim is to demonstrate how our perspective changes our understanding and how this can get quite complicated and why we sometimes take shortcuts that do not always work to our advantage (§ 72.5 Cognitive Load and Heuristics). But, let's take it one step at a time, starting with how we name compounds.

Take a look at the compound on the left. It is known by many names. Some of these names are like Chinese characters; you simply have to be told what they are, you cannot work them out. Let's call this the you-just-have-to-memorize-it method. Other names are like German words, you can work out how they are pronounced as long as you know how Germans pronounce their alphabet. Let's call this one, the rule-based method. Some of the names of this compound are like English where you can take a good guess as to how a word should be pronounced, but you can't be sure. Let's call this the hybrid method [If you are not sure what I mean, take a look at a poem called *The Chaos* by Gerard Nolst Trenité]. We are going to look at this compound using the rule-based approach. But even that is not straight forward, not because there are any ambiguities in the standardized ways that we use to name compounds, but because of the different perspectives from which we can look at a compound. Let me explain.

This part of the molecule is made up of six carbon atoms joined together in a hexagon formation with one hydrogen atom attached to each of those carbon atoms. It is called benzene. Like Chinese characters, you just have to know that. Alternatively, you can be a purist and call it cyclohexa-1,3,5-triene. That would be like German, the naming follows rules that lets you work out the structure.

This part of the first molecule is called a hydroxyl (or a hydroxy-) group.

To name the compound on the left, we can put the two groups together and we get hydroxybenzene. Determining its structure from its name is like trying to pronounce an English word. The hydroxy part is in the rules and the benzene part you need to know. But it doesn't end there. This structure turns up often in chemistry and trying to say hydroxybenzene all the time is using five syllables when two will do. That is why we call it phenol. Let's carry on and see what happens.

I promise this is all going to be relevant to our discussion of our interpersonal relationships, so bear with me.

CH₃   Like the hydroxyl group, this group consisting of a carbon atom and three hydrogen atoms is everywhere in biology. It is called a methyl group.

CH₃   When a methyl group attaches to a benzene ring, we can be relatively principled about naming it and call it methylbenzene, which sounds logical enough. But people knew about this compound and were using a different name for it before the standard naming system was developed and so the old name stuck and we call it toluene [As in trinitrotoluene, better known as the explosive, TNT, the compound responsible for the establishment of the Nobel Prize].

CH₃   When a hydroxyl group is attached to toluene, we can call it OH hydroxytoluene. But that would be ambiguous because we wouldn't know how far away from the methyl group the hydroxyl group is. It can be in position 2, next (ortho) to the methyl group, in which case we can call it orthohydroxytoluene or 2-hydroxytoluene. And, like German, anyone familiar with the naming conventions would be able to draw the structure of this molecule.

OH   We can also look at 2-hydroxytoluene from a different CH₃ PERSPECTIVE. It can just as easily be seen as a methyl group attached to phenol. Therefore, it would be just as proper to call it orthomethylphenol or 2-methylphenol. This and the previous molecule are identical:

2-methylphenol   =   2-hydroxytoluene

If you rotate the molecule on the left anticlockwise by 60° and then rotate it along its vertical axis by 180°, you will see it from the same perspective [For the sake of completeness, note that not all molecules remain identical when rotated; they become mirror images of each other; they are called chiral molecules].

17.1
Relevance of Chemical Nomenclature to Affinitology

One of the reasons that 'identical' twins are *not* identical is because, each of them, when looking at the other, is seeing their twin in a different context and, therefore, experiences the other differently.

Imagine a scenario where a chemist sends someone to buy some 2-methylphenol. The stockist gives the messenger a jar labelled, 2-hydroxytoluene [actually, just to confuse matters, it's more likely to be labelled o-cresol]. The messenger may then complain that this is not what he asked for. The stockist can explain that the two are the same but, if the messenger knows a little bit of chemistry, he may say, "Hey, I know the difference between a methyl and a hydroxy. I asked for a methyl and you are giving me a hydroxy." This is where a little knowledge is more disempowering than no knowledge at all.

[It is my humble opinion that all of us spend most of our time operating on 'little knowledge' where we would be better off operating on the basis of no knowledge at all. I may have just opened a can of worms here, so I'm going to do what some naughty children do; knock on a door and run away.]

In the same way that those unfamiliar with chemical naming conventions may think of 2-hydroxytoluene and 2-methylphenol as being two different compounds, the different labels that we use to describe our relationships can also be misunderstood. This is when knowledge of affinitology can help.

Imagine a scenario where I work in an organisation with someone, let's call her Maggie. I could call Maggie my 'co-worker' or my 'colleague'. Let's also assume that it makes no difference to me which one of these labels I use, that is, I consider these two labels to have the same meaning. If, on the other hand, Maggie makes a distinction between these two labels, there is already a potential for misunderstanding. For example, she may understand a colleague to be someone who has similar goals whereas she may think of a co-worker as someone who does similar things but not necessarily for the same reasons.

[As we progress through this coursebook, the implications of perception of similar goals will become clearer (§ 23.4 Do I have what it takes to be part of a win-win relationship?)]

Consider what would happen if, at a gathering, Maggie overhears me refer to her as my 'co-worker'. Somewhere in her mind, a little alarm goes off; a conflict that needs to be resolved. [We call it cognitive dissonance. It happens to us all the time. It is part of a mechanism through which we adjust our perspective to be more congruent with reality.] With sufficient understanding of affinitology, she would not be like the messenger sent to buy 2-methylphenol. She would ask, "Could he have a different understanding of the words co-worker and colleague?"

Notice that I have not only created four levels of relationship here, I have also implied that they are hierarchical:

Stranger: No commonalities perceived we don't know (or are not interested in knowing) what we have (or may have) in common.

Co-worker: No common goals perceived we work in the same environment, but for different reasons.

Colleague: Common, but independent goals we both want to achieve similar objectives, but we are going about it in our own separate ways.

Collaborator: Common and interdependent goals we both want to achieve similar objectives and the actions we take towards those goals directly affect the action that The Other takes towards those goals.

We can continue with this line of reasoning and create a fifth level; a 'friend' (§ 92.8 Friendship).

Collaboration involves greater levels of interaction and mutual understanding than the other three types of relationship [you may argue that a 'stranger' is no relationship at all, but I would beg to differ § 62.1 (Beliefs) and § 18 (Art or Science)]. This provides greater opportunities for extending that understanding to beyond the professional domain.

In a parallel universe, I may be aware of the distinction between co-worker and colleague and know that Maggie is aware of it too (because we attended the same conference on Affinitology). I may have deliberately referred to her as a co-worker to signal my reluctance to being approached to take on new collaborative projects (where colleagues become collaborators). My reasons for this may include being overwhelmed with existing projects or it may be my lack of confidence in being able to control the progression of a relationship to one which may not be in the interest of both parties in the long run.

Chapter 18

Art or Science

[Originally, I called this chapter "The Dance of Relationships" and put it towards the end of the book because it did not seem to fit into any of the earlier categories. But I did feel that the content would be more beneficial if it appeared earlier in the book. And then I had a spark of inspiration; by putting a semantic twist on the title, I could justify putting it into the section on Language. So, here it is.]

No art is completely devoid of science and no science is completely devoid of art (§ 25.3 Polar bond). In this course, we use scientific terminology to create a range of new concepts by changing their context to interpersonal relationships. We then take these understandings to improve the way we think and talk about relationships with a view to improving the quality of our relationships.

Art is about being creative. In the context of interpersonal relationships, this means being creative about when, where and why we 'express' various beliefs and values [think of gene expression § 62.4 (Beliefs as Affinitological Genes)] . In this section, we are going to look at some examples.

18.1
A Stranger is a Friend
You Haven't Got to Know Yet

In § 62.4 (Beliefs as Affinitological Genes) I explain that when I used to take my children to various events on the London underground, they did not want to sit next to a stranger and that my response was to tell them that 'a stranger is a friend you haven't got to know yet.' A belief such as this, gives the believer of it a theoretical framework [and science is all about developing working theoretical frameworks]. That framework now becomes a tool; something that helps us achieve what we want to achieve more easily.

The 'tool' metaphor is helpful here because it allows me to relate it to the adage, "The right tool for the right job". It highlights the importance of treating theories as simply potential. Otherwise, 'theories' can obstruct our ability to move forward creatively by invoking a cognitive bias known as 'functional fixedness' [Look up the 'Candle Problem' on the internet].

To help us avoid functional fixedness, we need to be able to take as step back to consider the advantages and disadvantages of each of our beliefs or belief sets (theoretical frameworks).

Let's take the idea (or belief) that "a stranger is a friend you haven't met yet." I know that I was taking a risk here because, in practice, it depends on the stranger. However, the art is in balancing preventing my children from becoming antisocial, on the one hand, with the risk of them possibly trusting a dangerous individual, on the other. This meant taking into account what I knew about my kids.

18.2

Can You Bake a Cake?

Once we know how to bake a cake, we can experiment with different ingredients, timings and temperatures to see what works and what doesn't. With more experience, we can create an endless variety of highly desirable cakes. However, the first thing that we need to know is that we cannot make a cake without flour, water and heat as a minimum.

[Some of you may say, but what about baking powder, eggs and sugar? Well, that depends on your definition of cake. I looked up 'cake' on dictionary.com and the first definition says that a cake is 'sweet', but the second definition says that it is just bread with a flat shape. So, if you think that a cake must be sweet, then add the words 'and sweetener' just before 'as a minimum' in the last paragraph.]

There are two important points here. The first is that we need to have at least a minimal [I know that's tautology, but it's deliberate!] knowledge of the ingredients (or components or anatomy depending on your point of view) that need to go into a relationship for us to be able to call it a 'relationship'. We also need to have a minimal knowledge of how those components interact with each other (work together - physiology) and what is needed for that 'mixture' to become a 'cake'.

The second important point is this: When I mentioned the word, 'cake', I am fairly confident that what you imagined was sweet and swollen (leavened). However, as we can see from the second definition of the word, it is not guaranteed that the cake envisaged by the person we are talking to will be sweet (or leavened).

The same applies to relationships. We do have a limited number of words to help us convey our intentions, for example we can say, "Will you be my date?" or "Will you be my friend?" or "Will you be my business partner?" Whilst these concepts go a long way in resolving potential ambiguities, insofar as they are better than saying, "Would you like a cup of tea?", each of these relationship frameworks (§ 92) are still conceived differently by different people.

It is actually surprising how often people *do* understand each other's intentions. For example, most people would understand the intention behind a statement such as, "Would you like a cup of tea?" *in context*, which highlights the importance of context, including non-verbal communication (tone and gestures) in relationships. Whilst the ambiguities involved in "Would you like a cup of tea?" may, on the one hand, bring excitement, on the other hand, they can cause misunderstandings, lost opportunities and/or heartaches. Therefore, the 'art' of relationships also involves balancing the excitement of the unknown [Can she guess what I mean when I say, "Would you like to see my ballpoint pen collection?"] with the robustness of clear and concise communication. This reminds me of a TED talk by Rebecca Saxe in which she said:

> "Today I'm going to talk to you about the problem of other minds… a problem that is maybe… familiar to us as parents and teachers and spouses and novelists, which is, "Why is it so hard to know what somebody else wants or believes?" Or perhaps, more relevantly, "Why is it so hard to change what somebody else wants or believes?"
> I think novelists put this best. Like Philip Roth, who said, "And yet, what are we to do about this terribly significant business of other people? So ill-equipped are we all, to envision one another's interior workings and invisible aims." So as a teacher and as a spouse, this is, of course, a problem I confront every day. But as a scientist, I'm interested in a different problem of other minds, and that is the one I'm going to introduce to you today. And that problem is, "How is it so easy to know other minds?"
> …the crux of the problem is the machine that we use for thinking about other minds, our brain, is made up of pieces, brain cells, that we share with all other animals; with monkeys and mice and even sea slugs. And yet, you put them together in a particular network, and what you get is the capacity to write Romeo and Juliet. Or to say, as Alan Greenspan did, "I know you think you understand what you thought I said, but I'm not sure you realize that what you heard is not what I meant."

If you want to delve into this aspect of relationships in more detail, I would recommend Eric Berne's book, 'What do you say after you say hello.'

This course is about ingredients (Identities, beliefs, values and context) and possibilities; the different ways in which we can create, maintain and define our relationships. Once we know these, we can choose to specialise or diversify. In either case, we need to get creative.

18.3

How to Avoid Stagnation or Paralysis

Every noun in the dictionary represents a relationship. Take 'Plinth' for example (a noun I just picked at random). It is defined as a "slab at the base of columns." So, a 'plinth' describes the relationship between a 'slab' and a 'column'. A 'slab' also represents a relationship and so does 'column' and if we follow the trail, we will end up either going through the entire dictionary via meandering paths or, more probably, fall into an endless loop of circular definitions. The point to take away from this brief example is that what appears to be a very simple idea; 'plinth', can get very complicated and messy (confusing, overwhelming, futile, etc.) if we start to analyse and dissect it too much.

The idea of 'relationship' is abstract and complicated to begin with. Just imagine where it could lead us if we begin to analyse it too much. On The other hand, if we don't analyse enough, we won't know what we are doing and we will not recognize the pitfalls. Oh, what a predicament! How is an ordinary soul, such as you and I, supposed to strike the optimal balance? As I was writing this, I remembered this conversation from Star Trek - The Undiscovered Country:

> Spock: History is replete with turning points, lieutenant. You must have faith.
> Valeris: Faith?
> - That the universe will unfold as it should.
> - But is that logical? Surely, we must …
> - Logic, logic and logic. Logic is the beginning of wisdom, Valeris, not the end.

That's where the 'art' of relationships comes in.

Art is what brings eloquence to science and engineering. It is what separates the conscious from the machine (transcends logic to find faith and meaning and to create aesthetic beauty in the process).

"But Bijan," I hear some you saying, "Machines produce art too." Yes, machines can produce intricate shapes. However, it only becomes 'art' when it is interpreted by consciousness. Art is a product of our creative faculties. It is what separates the crowd or the collective (dogmatic and uncompromising) from the individual (flexible and adaptive). We explore this idea further in § 29.4 (The Omniself).

Sometimes, we fall into the trap of mistaking flexibility and adaptability for obedience, conformity and submissiveness. Flexibility and adaptability can be instruments of great personal power. The way I explain this in my sessions is to take a pencil and a piece of rubber of similar shape and size and indicate that if a force is exerted on a pencil and it 'resists' it will eventually reach breaking point, whereas if it bends to 'let the force pass', then it can return to its original form.

18.4
Flexibility, Adaptability and Creativity

From a psychological perspective, our 'flexibility' is the extent to which we are able to shift our viewpoint. It is what determines how successful we are at creating, building, maintaining and enjoying relationships. This kind of flexibility is also required for us to be able to manage our emotions. Flexibility requires creativity. The less creative we are, the more rigid, brittle, fragile and vulnerable we will become.

18.5
The Art and Science of Managing Relationships

Emotion Management (§ 51 The Emotional Dimension) is not something that we are born with. However, like walking, we are all born with the ability to do it. It is a skill; it can be learnt. Most importantly for the purposes of our discussion here,

---

Emotion management is the primary determinant of the stability of any interpersonal relationship.

The good news is that we are born with the creative faculties we need to develop our emotion management skills.

Circumstances change and relationships either adapt to those changes or whither. The more sensitive we are to changes, the better informed and equipped we will be to adapt appropriately (§ 34 Cells, Receptors and Sensitivity). Therefore, any exercise that can enhance our sensory acuity is a step towards empowering us to manage our relationships better. Painting or drawing, drama, dancing, socializing, writing, conducting research, journalism, making things, and so on can all help us to develop our sensory acuity. However, those activities that sensitize us to other people's needs and strengths are the most valuable when it comes to relationships.

We need to be sensitive to all three elements in the relationship; The Self, The Other and The Bond (Nexus). The three most important possible changes that we need to be sensitive to are beliefs, values and goals. A subtle change in any one of these three could derail a relationship. The reason that even a subtle change can have major repercussions is because, once a relationship begins to diverge then, as time goes by, the gap between the two parties grows to a point where it becomes unbridgeable. There is a theory of divorce that says when you ask divorced couples why they divorced, it is rare for them to point to a single behaviour or event as the primary cause. What they tend to say is that they gradually grew apart.

Creativity is an essential tool for adaptation. This is where the art comes in. Once we recognize that The Third Entity, 'The Bond', isn't as strong as it used to be (or could be), asking, "What can I do to improve the bond?" would not be as productive as asking, "How many different ways can I think of for improving the relationship." (§ 15.1 The Power of Questions)

Our psyche tends to look for the most concise answers to the questions that we ask of it. If I ask for one solution, it will tend to give me one solution. By asking for a list of alternative solutions, we can get creative. We could compare alternatives and choose one that might be better than the first answer that would have popped into our minds. We could combine different approaches, we could mix and match, we could tailor one method by taking inspiration from another. In short, we are much more likely to save the relationship.

In summary, the science of relationships is about **sensitivity** to factors that could threaten the bond and art of relationships is about **creativity** in finding and applying solutions that strengthen the bond.

Chapter 19

Quantity vs Quality

> **"There are a lot of similarities between dancing and wrestling. The costumes are the same, the spandex and all that, you have to be light on your feet to do both, and you have to remember choreography."**
>
> - Chris Jericho

Interpersonal relationships are about quality, "All intelligent people will agree on that." [I have taken that quote from the movie, Amadeus.]

Now, before we go any further, let me warn you that I am about to confuse you before clearing that confusion. That is because there is a difference between being ignorant and attaining ignorance through knowledge. [No, that gem is not mine, I am paraphrasing Socrates.] Here is the confusing statement;

> **quantity is a quality**

We tend to think of quality as being the opposite of quantity. Or, at least, that quality is one thing and quantity is something else. We also talk about things like qualitative vs quantitative research and make similar distinctions between art and science (§ 9.1 Science as an Art).

From a reductionist perspective, we can say that the quality of something is the sum of its characteristics or properties. From a holistic perspective, those properties only become relevant in the context of how they fit together and interact with each other and their environment [The whole is more than the sum of its parts].

I can talk about a human being in terms of character or personality or my overall feelings about that person [which we tend to express in 'objective' terms, for example, by saying he is 'handsome' or 'endearing'] and, in such cases, it would be said that I am talking about that person's 'qualities'. Alternatively, I can talk about the person's age, weight or height, which we tend to perceive as being quantitative measures. But it's not a simple as that.

If someone asks me, "How handsome is that man?" The Researcher Identity within me might think something like this, "I would say that about 80% of the heterosexual, female, Caucasian population living in the western hemisphere would probably fixate [place the image in direct view of her fovea] on that man for more than five seconds if he were to appear in her peripheral vision." [In other words, all other things being equal (itself, a tall order), the longer she fixates on him, the more handsome one could say he appears to the perceiver]. By simply changing the question from "What" to "How much" or "To what extent", we can change a qualitative view into a quantitative one. What I'm trying to show here is that quantity is an inherent part of quality and not separate from it.

There are times, however, when quantifying becomes an abstraction that detracts us from quality. For example, as soon as we begin to talk about equitable relationships, we start to count things. "Look at all the things I have done for you and what have I got in return?". We can discover where the problem lies in this kind of approach by rephrasing the question as, "Look at all the things that I have done in my attempts to strengthen this relationship and let's see to what extent each of these attempts have been effective in doing so." (§ 2.1 What is a SMER?)

Chapter 20

Language and Levels of Persuasion

A popular method of categorising communication is by intention; to persuade, to inform or to entertain [referred to by the acronym, PIE]. Here, we are only concerned with the first two. I am also going to suggest that for our purposes here, we can take 'intention' out of the equation. In other words, it does not matter whether the interference is incidental, accidental or intentional. If it persuades, it is invasive and if it informs, it is non-invasive. This raises the question, "What is the point of informing, if it does not have any effect on action, that is, if it does not persuade? Isn't that just wasting people's time?" And I would say, "Yes, I agree with you. I believe that the ultimate intention of any information given purposefully is to persuade. However, the difference is in the level (or more accurately, degree) of persuasion.

20.1
Persuasion Level 1:
Inform the Other of 'my Perspective'
of the Situation

Let's say that I am at a friend's house and I say, "I am feeling cold". **This is when I acknowledge that what I am saying is my opinion.** In this situation, my host can decide whether to bring me a blanket, make me a hot drink, close the window, turn up the heater, do nothing or say, "That's strange, I'm not feeling cold at all." Of course, I would not bother to 'inform' my host of the way I feel about the temperature if my intention were not to get some kind of help in reducing my discomfort. However, when I inform, I am not 'asking' for help, 'telling' or 'directing' my host to take action.

If someone comes to visit my house and tells me that she is feeling cold, I can feel,

a) Greater *intimacy* because she has been honest with me (without trying to put me under any obligations)
b) *Obligated* to do something about it

c) *Informed* that some of my guests may feel less comfortable with temperatures at which I feel comfortable

d) *Pleased* that I can help him to feel more comfortable

e) *Annoyed* that someone has the audacity to come to *my* house and to criticise it

f) *Embarrassed* because I attribute my guest's discomfort to my incompetence

g) *Curious* about why I am not feeling cold when she is

h) ...

I hope you can see where I am going with this. At this 'level of persuasion', my interlocutor has the most control over his or her response.

20.2

Persuasion Level 2:
Inform the Other of 'the Situation'

There is another way to 'inform' that steps up the level of persuasion. **This is when I express my opinion as 'fact'.** For example, I can say to my host, "It is cold in here." The difference is that when I say, "I am feeling cold", I am suggesting that it is a problem that I need to deal with *from within;* that is, the fact that I am feeling cold has something to do with me; it is subjective. When I say, "It is cold" I am suggesting that it is a problem that affects everyone; it is objective (and that if you don't feel cold too, it is you who has the problem and not me). The overt response of the host might not be different, but the psychological effect is likely to be. For example, when "My guest is cold" I can feel like I am helping her and that can be a slightly more pleasurable feeling than when "It is cold" because even if I do something to raise the temperature of the room, I have not done my guest any favours, I have simply adjusted the environmental conditions to what it 'should' be.

20.3

Persuasion Level 3:
Solicit the Other's Confirmation
of my Perspective

The next level of persuasion is to ask a question like, "Don't you think it is cold in here?" **This is when I invite The Other to agree with my opinion.** From the host's perspective, this comment is no longer about The Other in the Pactum (my guest) or about the environment, it is about 'The Self'; it is about how *I*, the host, feel. I might wonder whether if I disagree, it might put some tension on The Nexus and might then feel more obligated (persuaded) to agree. On the other hand, I may feel that this is an opportunity to strengthen the Nexus by helping my guest to understand some of our differences, in which case, I might say, "Well, actually, I have lived in colder climates most of my life, so I am used to it, but I can appreciate that many people can feel uncomfortable at this temperature, so let me bring you a nice hot cup of tea."

20.4

Persuasion Level 4: Create Expectation

(By Referring to Some Identity-Related Aspect of The Other)

The next level of persuasion is to ask something like, "Do you have any kind of temperature control system in here, because I am feeling cold?" **This is when I indirectly suggest something that can affect The Other's sense of identity** (note the word 'you' in the question), in this case, what the host *has*. The extent to which different people are influenced by such inferences varies depending on their worldview (§ 50.3 The Spiritual Dimension). Here, my host's focus will be directed towards his guest's expectation; "I should have something". The question is about *me* (the host) and, therefore, my answer would reflect on how I am (my identity is) perceived. Therefore, a question phrased in this way can elicit a response that is more influenced by emotion. The qualifier, "Because I am feeling cold" can attenuate that emotional response by changing the focus back onto the guest. We can attune (in this case, slightly intensify) the emotional response to "Do you *have*" by changing the "because *I am* cold" to "because *it is* cold" (it's not just my problem; it is yours too).

You might say, "But Bijan, my host may be genuinely more concerned about how I feel than the objective temperature." I suggest that, since I would not say, "It is cold in here" unless I were feeling cold, to a host who is genuinely concerned about how I feel, both statements would raise concern about my level of comfort. However, the second statement has the additional effect of making the problem 'external' (I *am* cold because *it is* cold and not because the temperature is beyond *my* tolerance threshold). In other words, "It is cold" is more 'projective' (projecting *my problem* onto the environment and my host). It is also indicative of a lower locus of control (§ 44).

20.5
Persuasion Level 5:
Attempt to Create Self-Doubt
(By Questioning the Judgement of The Other)

The next level of persuasion is to question the validity of the situation and to associate it with The Other. For example, "How can you live in a place as cold as this?" The response here will be more dependent on the host's (The Other's) self-esteem. For example, the host may feel

a) *Compassionate* and to think to himself, my guest is cold and respond by saying, "Oh, I am sorry about that, let me turn up the heating"
b) *Grateful* and say, "Thank you for bringing that to my attention."
c) *Curious* and ask himself, "Am I doing something out of the ordinary here?" and respond by saying, "I hadn't thought about that."
d) *Informed* and say, "I hadn't noticed"
e) *Threatened* and take a defensive stance and say, "Some of us like it this way."

You might be wondering why, in the last example, saying "Some of us like it this way" is being 'threatened'. Threatened is a feeling and 'defensive' is an emotional response to that feeling (§ 51.2 Affect, Feelings and Emotions). There are several tell-tale signs of defensiveness in that response. One is that it is not an answer that is based on a desire to resolve the guest's discomfort. It is a response rooted in trying to *defend* a position (why the temperature is the way it is and that it is fine the way it is, thank you very much). Secondly, the word 'us' tries to convey two things; it detracts from 'me' as the subject of the criticism and it implies that my opinion is based on a consensus (it is not just me who thinks this).

20.6
Persuasion Level 6:
Indirect Prompt for Specific Action

The next level of persuasion is to prompt for action with a statement such as, "I think we should turn up the heating in here." This statement acts at several levels (sways in several directions). The phrase "I think" implies that it is a personal point of view, but the word 'should' implies a moral imperative (if we don't do this, we have not done the right thing). The word 'we' says, "I am assuming that you are with me on this" and the phrase "turn up the heating" is offering a solution, that is, it is giving a direction for action. It assumes that there is a heating system and that the host has control over it. It is not leaving the host with an alternative option, for example, of offering a blanket or moving to another room. Of course, this does not prevent the host from suggesting alternatives, but doing so would mean contradicting the guest's 'suggestion' and the extent to which the host feels comfortable with doing this depends on her self-esteem, self-confidence (§ 40) and assertiveness.

20.7

Persuasion Level 7:
Direct Prompt for Specific Action

Changing the word "we" to the word "you" in the previous example; "I think you should turn up the heating in here", adds another layer of persuasiveness. You may have already noticed that,

---

as our language patterns become progressively more 'persuasive', they increasingly limit our choice/freedom[1] and, in doing so, interfere[2] with our decision-making[3] process.

---

[1] See § 50.3 (The Spiritual Dimension)
[2] See § 60.2 (Interference)
[3] See § 72 (Decision-Making)

20.8

Masked Imperatives

We can think of persuasion as the use of compelling language without resorting to direct imperatives (orders). If I say to someone, "Turn up the heating (please)", I am not persuading, I am demanding. The next level down from demanding is expecting; "Could you turn up the heating, please?" Structuring of the expectation as a question and the adding of 'please' are both pacifiers intended to reduce the chance of non-compliance (resistance) and the extent of possible subsequent resentment.

I propose the phrase "masked imperative" to denote this this kind of sentence structure; where an obligation is implied but not explicitly stated.

Part 2
Understanding
Relationships

Unit 4

Affinitology

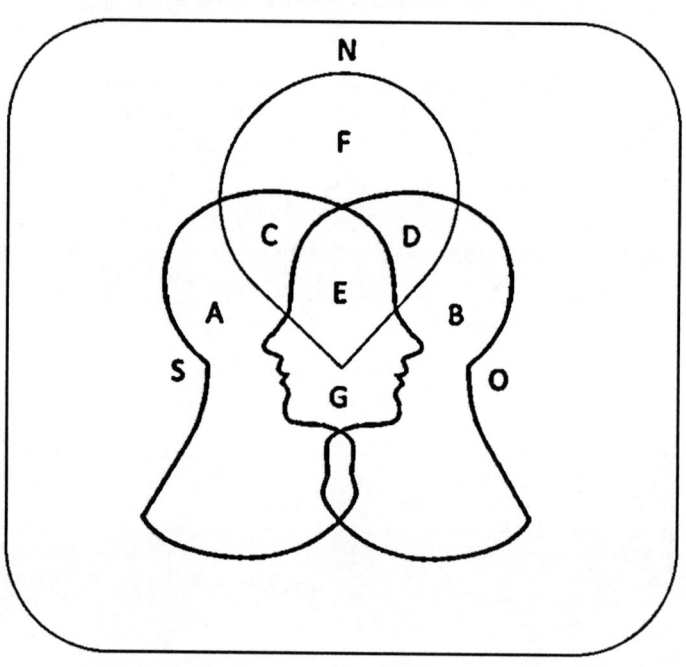

Chapter 21

What is Affinitology?

The word affinity stems from the idea of a border or boundary. This reminds me of what in Biology and medical science, we call a 'membrane'. If you relate better to the visual arts, think of 'contrast'. If you are into sports, think of the markings on a playing field. Without boundaries, there can be no interaction because we will simply not be able to define any elements and without separate elements, the idea of interaction would become meaningless.

Nowadays the word affinity is used synonymously with 'attraction' even though this is only one type of interaction at a boundary. Other types of interaction include physical exchange and information exchange.

affinity (n.)

c. 1300, "relation by marriage" (as opposed to *consanguinity*), from Old French *afinite* "relationship, kinship; neighborhood, vicinity" (12c., Modern French *affinité*), from Latin *affinitatem* (nominative *affinitas*) "relationship by marriage; neighborhood," noun of state from *affinis* "adjoining, adjacent," also "kin by marriage," literally "bordering on," from *ad* "to" (see **ad-**) + *finis* "a border, a boundary" (see **finish** (v.)). Spelling was re-Latinized in early Modern English. Used figuratively in English since c. 1600 of structural relationships in chemistry, philology, geometry, etc. Meaning "natural liking or attraction, a relationship as close as family between persons not related by blood" is from 1610s.

[Source: https://www.etymonline.com/word/affinity]

Affinitology is what I am proposing as a word to mean the study of *interpersonal* relationships. That is, interaction across human psychological boundaries. These boundaries separate our 'personal space' from whatever lies beyond it. Unlike physical space, our personal space is a fluid concept and exists along different dimensions (Unit 11: Dimensions of Human Experience).

For instance, we are more tolerant of incursions into our personal *physical* space when we are on a crowded train or in an elevator than we are when we are sitting on a secluded beach.

Our Identities play a very strong role in our perception of what we consider to be our personal space. If I identify with a car because it is 'mine', then I may consider it an invasion of my personal space if someone leans on it (or maybe even stares at it). In other words, my relationship with the car changes depending on how I perceive it and, more importantly, how I *identify* with it. If you aren't that attached to your car, perhaps replacing the image of the car with your 'significant other' may help you to relate to this idea more personally. We explore Identities in more detail in § 37.7 (The Emergence of Identity).

It is my hope that, by elevating the status of interpersonal relationships from being an adjunct to individual psychology or social psychology to being a separate science, we will create greater opportunities for exploring our various Identities and how they are shaped by our relationships. Perhaps through this science, humanity will be able to deliberate on the travesty of identifying more with our possessions than with the people whose pain makes possessions possible.

In summary, affinitology is about the boundaries across which Identities interact. This is akin to the medical science of physiology, which, in the final analysis is about how cells interact across their interstitial space. We explore this concept in more detail in § 55 (Taxis).

21.1
What is a Relationship?

The meaning of the word 'relationship' extends well beyond interpersonal relationships. Every noun in the dictionary is a representation of one or more relationships. Also, every research question* can be framed in terms of "what is the relationship between x and y?"

* [That encompasses all of knowledge: Science, Philosophy and Mathematics :-o)]

Relationships can be looked at from a functional or descriptive perspective. To keep it simple for now, I am going to use a table as a metaphor for relationships.

Imagine you are from the planet Mars and you ask someone to tell you what a table is. From a functional perspective, you might be told that a table is, "A piece of furniture specifically used for serving food to those seated at it." [Dictionary.com] Descriptively, it is, "An article of furniture consisting of a flat, slab-like top supported on one or more legs or other supports." [also, Dictionary.com]

In the second definition, there is a very important word that we are very likely to simply pass over. The word 'support' is not a conjunction, but our mind almost treats it as one. When we look at a table, we *see* a flat 'slab' and, typically, four legs. When we look at relationships, we typically *see* two or more people in certain relative (concrete or abstract) positions to each other. But *how* do a table's legs support its top? There are two aspects to this; *where* the legs are placed in relation to the slab and *how* the legs are attached to the slab. Together, these two considerations create the 'relationship', what I have called **The Third Entity** or **The Nexus** (§ 30.1); this Third Entity is what we need to be conscious of when looking at our interpersonal relationships.

I put it to you that the reason we do not think consciously about designing unique and beautiful interpersonal relationships in the same way that we do for a table is not so much because relationships are more abstract as it is about us not having developed sufficient specialist vocabulary; vocabulary that can extend the way we think about the elements that go into making a relationship and how they fit together (§ 15 The Power of Specialised Language).

This course is about looking at relationships in the same way a competent, proficient and efficient table maker/designer needs to look at a table. We explore this idea in more detail in § 30.1 (The Nexus) where we also extend the table metaphor a little further.

21.2
Identity and Vocabulary

When I taught in schools, I was intrigued by how different teachers used different words in their everyday conversations. For example, a Geography teacher would say that a student was 'eroding' her patience and a Chemistry teacher would talk about a student having a 'volatile' personality.

These words are not mere passive conveyers of thought, they affect our perspectives in subtle (and, sometimes, not so subtle) ways. For example, erosion is a long-term natural process which we have little control over. As a short-term solution, the geography teacher may erect a dam (ignore the student) or redirect the flow of water (send the student to someone responsible for discipline [presumably, being trained, this person's emotional 'banks' (as in 'river banks') are reinforced and less susceptible to erosion]). Volatility, on the other hand, is an inherent characteristic of a material, but it can be mitigated by cooling. If I think of a student as being volatile, my approach might be to try to 'cool' him down.

Meanwhile, a statistically oriented person may refer to the same pattern of behaviour as being 'random' or 'unpredictable' in which case he would focus on having contingency plans such as extra worksheets or may hedge her bets (put the child in different situations every lesson with different people or in different locations) rather than trying to change the behaviour directly.

What this demonstrates is that our internal dialogue is affected by the words that we are exposed to and this in turn affects what we focus on, and more importantly, *how* we focus on (and deal with) it. This is another way of saying that,

> **our perspectives depend on the words that we use.**

Perspectives can be broken down into two components; perception, that is, how we interpret the signals that reach us through our five senses (§ 33 Atasinex Cluster) and approach, i.e., what we do about it (§ 40.2 Behaviourism versus Humanism). Of course, it is our approach to interpersonal relationships that determines the outcome, such as 'happily ever after' or 'never again'.

What all this means is that, the answer to the question, "What is a relationship?" boils down to,

> **"It depends on who you ask."**

An economist would describe a relationship as some form of *exchange*. Indeed, we do have a 'social exchange theory' of interpersonal relationships which has its roots in economics and treats relationships in terms of cost-benefit analyses.

Meanwhile, from a legal perspective, a relationship is a social *contract*. My chemist Identity likes to describe an interpersonal relationship as a *bond* between two people (§ 25 Relationships as Chemical Bonds). As a therapist, I may decide to think of an interpersonal relationship using Eric Berne's model, in which case, I would think of it as a series of complementary *transactions* (§ 73 Transactional Analysis). Which of these positions we subscribe to at any one time depends on which of our multitude of Identities is dominant *at the time* (§ 29.4 The Omniself).

From an affinitological perspective, I propose that we consider relationships one 'bond' at a time whereby every relationship is seen as consisting of three elements; The Self, The Other and The Third Entity [AKA The Nexus, The Connection, The Bond]. Taking this as our starting point, I offer the following as our working definition of a relationship:

> **A relationship is The Third Entity (or Nexus) that emerges from the interaction between two Identities; The Self and The Other.**

We explore this idea step-by-step and in greater depth later in this course, beginning with § 35.1 (Embryology of Relationships).

Earlier, I said that the answer to the question, "What is a relationship?" depends on who you ask. **It also depends on *why* you ask.**

We can define concepts in one of two ways, descriptively or functionally [See also § 62.1 Beliefs]. From a descriptive perspective, we need to be able to say what a relationship looks like. However, since relationships are abstract, we can't do that. But leaving it there will deny us any opportunity to study relationships scientifically and to talk about them in any objectively meaningful way. After all, we need to be able to observe *something* measurable about a relationship, otherwise, everything we ever say about relationships will be mere conjecture. This is where functional definitions come to our rescue.

From a scientific perspective, we want to be able to recognise a relationship when we see one. Here is a functional definition that works for all relationships; not just interpersonal ones:

When a change in one system causes a change in another, then the two systems are related.

We can refine the above definition by applying it to different dimensions of human experience (Unit 11). For example, we can say, if a change in the physical state of one person causes a change in the emotional state of another, then there is a physical-emotional component to the relationship (§ 96 Directionality of Relationships).

21.2.1
Predictive and Non-Predictive Relationships

You might well say, "But Bijan, not all relationships are cause-and-effect relationships." And I would agree with you. Some relationships are indirect. For example, there is a relationship between the crop yield of maize and wheat in Lamjung District of Nepal but that doesn't mean that we can improve the crop yield of maize by increasing the crop yield of wheat. We do, however, say that there is a relationship between the yield of maize and the yield of wheat in that one can *predict* the other. In such cases, the relationship is mediated through external factors. In other words, we cannot do something to the maize to change the yield of the wheat; the wheat and the maize are not affecting each other, they are both being affected by something else [In this case, I would postulate the weather (sunshine and rainfall)]. Nevertheless, I suggest that in our definition of relationships, we confine ourselves to the cause-and-effect type because this kind of relationship is the only one that we can have control over. The importance of this becomes clearer through our discussions in § 44 (Locus of Control), § 40.2 (Behaviourism versus Humanism) and § 35.11 (Consciousness).

I feel that some clarification would not go amiss here. So, let me elaborate. In statistics, assumption of a cause-and-effect relationship is the defining difference between what we call correlation (no cause-and-effect implied) and regression (cause-and-effect implied). I believe that basing our definition of relationships on correlations rather than regressions is likely to be counterproductive. Confining our definition of relationships in the way that I have proposed helps us focus on what *causes* changes rather than what may or may not *inform* changes. After all, not all correlations are informative; sometimes, there isn't any relationship at all, even though the data strongly suggests that there is. **This can happen when we only look at the data and not at what the data represent.** For example, between the years 1999 and 2009 there was a 99.79% correlation between 'US spending on Science, Space and Technology' and 'suicides by hanging, strangulation and suffocation. This is where a **theoretical framework** is essential before we make (jump to) any conclusions.

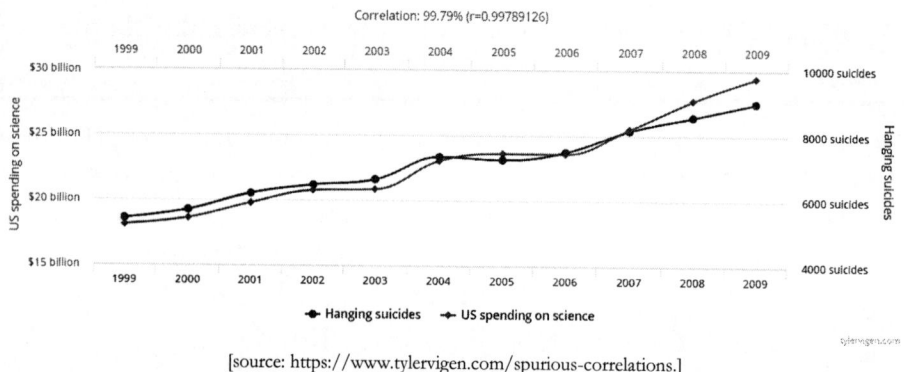

[source: https://www.tylervigen.com/spurious-correlations.]

21.3
Exchange versus Flow

The social exchange theory of relationships is based on the premise that all interactions are deliberate (premeditated) with the intention of getting something (material, intellectual or emotional) and that whatever we give in exchange for what we get is the 'price' that we have to pay for getting what we need or want. I propose that this point of view is applicable to some, but not all, interpersonal relationships.

Reaction to an action is not exchange. When we push one side of a see-saw down, the other side does not reward, punish or otherwise 'compensate' *us* by moving up; it just does. You might argue that the reaction 'compensates' for the action. And whilst this may be the case from a Newtonian physics perspective, it does not apply to interpersonal relationships because in Newtonian physics, choice is not a mediator in the reaction (§ 62 Beliefs and Decision-Making).

When two people feel connected [I prefer to think of them as *being* in a state of connectedness], that is, when two people feel that they are part of the same system, there is no 'me' and 'you', there is a dynamic *connection* and *flow* of energy, it is not an exchange; any reaction is not 'payment' for the action.

In order to make the distinction between 'exchange' and 'flow' in the previous paragraph, I sneaked in a word to act as a qualifier. I said, "When two people *feel* connected". I propose that **when we intellectualise a relationship (take the feeling out of it), we are no longer 'connected' in the affinitological sense.**

When we think of (intellectualise) a relationship as an exchange, "You scratch my back and I'll scratch yours", we perceive the 'you' and 'I' as separate entities.

> **In a connection, where you and I become part of the same system, the hand that scratches a another's back is scratching another part of itself.**

In other words, if I do something for you, I am doing it for myself, you owe me nothing for that.

If my arm were to be cut off and shown to me, I might say, "Hey look, that is *my* arm." However, when my arm is attached to me, I do not think of is as *my* arm, it is simply there, it is a *part* of me. If anything happens to *my* arm, it happens to *me*. I do not *give* nutrients to my arm *in exchange* for it picking up a glass of water for me and my arm doesn't pick up a glass of water for me *in exchange* for receiving nutrients from me.

In an *exchange*, I would be calculating how much nutrients I am giving my arm and how much value I am getting out of it in exchange, "Hey left hand, you are not pulling your weight as much as the right hand, so I am going to reduce the blood supply to you and give it to my right hand instead." [Actually, this does happen; the muscles that are working harder draw more nutrients from the blood, but the point is that it is the muscles that are taking what they need, it is not a negotiation between my body and my arm.] Although there are times when it can turn into a negotiation; at times of scarcity (starvation) or injury or overwhelm. However, in such cases, the negotiation is not about who can get the most, it is about who needs the least or stands to lose the most. Again, the point is that it is not about *exchange* it is about *flow*.

This also applies at the cellular level. The way that the cells in our bodies interact with their environment (the rest of the body) is also based on flow, not on exchange. Our cells interact with their environment in one of four ways:

1. Cell senses its environment (receptor activation)
2. Takes what it needs (active transport)
3. Uses from what is available (osmosis) and
4. Gives what is required of it (secretion).

[It sounds kind of Marxist, doesn't it? "From each according to his ability, to each according to his needs"]

If there is a disruption in any of these processes, the relationship between the cell and the rest of the body becomes problematic and beyond a certain point, the cell either kills itself or is ordered to self-destruct (apoptosis), is destroyed by immune cells or becomes cancerous, ultimately killing itself along with the organism that it was, once, a part of.

In interpersonal relationships, we exchange with those who we do not feel at one with (a part of). At all other times, **what is happening is not exchange, it is flow.** I propose that, even in a purely financial relationship, if it is based purely on exchange rather than on flow, that relationship cannot be a SMER.

21.4
What is a 'Healthy' Relationship?

It is tempting to define 'health' by contrasting it with 'disease'. That is to say, we can define being healthy as not having any pain or disease or any other impediments. But this is not very helpful because it can easily become a circular definition; I can just as easily define disease as being the absence of health.

There was a time when we would have had the same problem with 'light' and 'darkness'. A time when we didn't think of light as electromagnetic waves travelling through space. Imagine being there for a moment. In terms of our actual experience, we could either define darkness as the absence of light or define light as the absence of darkness. This means that any definition of light that refers to darkness, and vice versa, would be meaningless to anyone who doesn't already know both of them. And if she does, then the definition would be redundant (serve no purpose).

[Incidentally, lexicologists have a similar problem with the word 'the' because it is not easy to define 'the' without using it in the definition itself; "The is the definite article"]

Now we can see how appreciating light as being 'something' allows us to distinguish darkness as being the absence of that 'thing'. With this kind of understanding it would be skewed thinking to say that light is the absence of darkness; that would be like trying to imagine matter as being the absence of a vacuum.

[We could have some fun with that thought. Try looking at the moon one night and telling the person standing next to you, "Oh look, I can see a white hole in the vacuum of space." They will probably look at you as if you are suffering from some strange form of synaesthesia.]

So how can we avoid this problem of circularity when trying to define healthy relationships? How can we think about health in a way that does not refer to (or infer) disease? Learning from the light/darkness analogy, we need to think of disease as 'something' and health as the absence of that something or vice versa. I was tempted to think of that something as being conflict, so as to define a healthy relationship as the absence of conflict. But that doesn't work. Let me show you why.

[we explore the nature of conflict and its effects on relationships in the following sections: § 33.7.3, § 48, § 59.2, § 59.3, § 63.2, § 64.10, § 87.2 and § 87.3]

Life is a dynamic process of conscious change. In terms of personal growth and interpersonal relationships, conscious change can be viewed as being either a response to resolve a conflict or the cause of a conflict to which we need to respond. In any case, conflict is part and parcel of change, which is necessary for growth and adaptation (avoiding stagnancy). We can, therefore, conclude that a healthy relationship is one in which interpersonal conflicts are resolved without there being any detrimental effects on the Nexus.

Conflict resolution is the mechanism through which interpersonal relationships *grow*. We can therefore, also define a healthy relationship in terms of growth. But what is growth? Relationships being abstract, we cannot take out a tape measure to assess their growth. The concept of empowerment is more amenable to tangible evaluation, that is to say; it is easier to establish criteria for relationship empowerment than it is for relationship growth. In conclusion, a healthy relationship is an empowering relationship and therefore,

> **if a relationship can do something that neither of the individuals forming the relationship could have achieved by themselves, *without disempowering side effects*, that's an empowering relationship.**

The "without disempowering side effects" part in the above definition emphasises that, when instigating (and maintaining) any relationship, a risk-benefit judgement is involved. This is related to The First Law of Decision-Making that I discuss in § 72 (Decision-Making).

Related to the above is the point that, with power should come responsibility. If I am empowered by a relationship, I need to do my due diligence to assure myself that that power is not misused or abused. For example, a two-year-old with a knife is more empowered, that is to say, it is now capable of doing more than he could have done without the knife. However, that power, without the requisite responsibility can be very costly (disempowering) for all concerned, including the two-year-old. We can substitute 'any person who has power without the requisite responsibility that it entails' for 'two-year-old' and 'any form of empowerment'; be it social position or access to resources in other ways, for 'knife'.

The acronym, SMER, emphasizes the importance of all three of the concepts that comprise a healthy relationship; satisfaction, empowerment and mutuality. It enables us to ask questions such as, "Is this teacher-student relationship a SMER?" without having to spell it out.

Chapter 22

Components of a Relationship

This chapter is a preamble to Unit 6 (Relationship Anatomy), where we shall develop these concepts further. For now, I simply want to sow some seeds.

22.1
The Self and The Other

We tend to think of a relationship as something that ensues with two people (persons, individuals) interact. However, in essence, when we interact with someone, primarily, it is not our bodies that are interacting, it is our minds. More specifically, it is our Identities; one 'who I am' is interacting with another 'who I am'. Therefore, a relationship is, in effect, something that ensues when two *Identities* begin to interact with each other, not two people.

"But Bijan, isn't that just semantics?" I hear some of you asking. And my answer is a resounding 'NO'.

One of the pivotal concepts in affinitology is the Omniself (§ 29.4). The word Omniself is based on the idea that each of us are made up of several, sometimes many, selves (each 'self' being a separate Identity) and that, at any moment, one of these Identities is interacting with another Identity, either within the same or another Omniself (person/individual/physical body).

A relationship ensues when one of these Identities, The Self (§ 29.2), interacts with another Identity, The Other (§ 29.5). And, in case you are wondering, yes, that does mean that I can have a relationship with myself; it is called thinking (§ 73.1 What is Thinking). An example is where my Father Identity interacts with my Spouse Identity. I trust that all this will become much clearer as we explore the relationships terrain together throughout this course.

The Self is the Identity through whose 'eyes' we are exploring a relationship. The Other is another 'self' (Identity), who interacts with The Self. In other words, whether an entity is The Self or The Other is simply a matter of our point of reference [linguistically, 'first person or 'second person' In the field of Neurolinguistic Programming, these are called 'first position' and 'second position'].

22.2
The Third Entity (The Nexus)

To build any structure, we need the right materials and a blueprint for how the pieces fit together. In this section we are going to explore the materials or elements that make up the structure of a relationship. The word 'structure' is important. To put it into context, here is what Eric Berne said about structure in his book, *Games People Play*:

> "In everyday terms, what can people do after they have exchanged greetings, whether the greeting consists of a collegiate "Hi!" or an Oriental ritual lasting several hours? After stimulus-hunger and recognition-hunger comes structure-hunger. The perennial problem of adolescents is: "What do you say to her (him) then?" And to many people besides adolescents, nothing is more uncomfortable than a social hiatus, a period of silent, unstructured time when no one present can think of anything more interesting to say than; "Don't you think the walls are perpendicular tonight?" The eternal problem of the human being is how to structure his waking hours. In this existential sense, the function of all social living is to lend mutual assistance for this project."

When two people meet and begin to interact, something new is created from that interaction. Something appears that wasn't there before. This is called an emergent property. I am not talking about changes that happen inside the individuals who are interacting. It's more than that. You cannot see it, so you cannot point to it. Think of it like a distortion in space. It is perhaps similar to what Rupert Sheldrake calls a "morphic field". It is a conduit through which I behave differently when I perceive a relationship to exist compared with when I do not perceive there to be a relationship. For the purposes of this course, I am calling this emergent property The Third Entity or The Nexus.

It is curious that the dictionary definition of 'relationship' revolves around the idea of 'connection' and yet when we think of relationships, we often focus on the elements (people) that are connected rather than the connection itself. Without this 'connection', we, as individuals, would be too isolated to be able to give any sense of meaning to our lives. To reiterate, I have called this bond or connection The Third Entity to highlight the need to separate it from the two individuals (Identities) involved. The word Nexus is an alternative name that I am proposing for The Third Entity because it is more concise (two syllables instead of five). To get a feel for what I mean by 'The Third Entity', try this exercise.

Exercise 3

The Difference between The Other and The Nexus

Think about someone you're in a relationship with; any kind of relationship, not necessarily a romantic one.

Part 1

1. Ask yourself, "What can I do for this person?"
2. Contemplate that for a while and notice what comes to mind (intellectual dimension).
3. Notice how you feel about what comes to mind (emotional dimension).
4. Store your mind and body's responses to that question somewhere (give it a name, such as the "what-can-I-do" response).

Part 2

1. Clear the image from part 1.
2. Ask yourself, "What could improve the relationship that I have with this person?"
3. Contemplate that for a while and notice what comes to mind (intellectual dimension).
4. Notice how you feel about what comes to mind (emotional dimension).
5. Store your mind and body's responses to that question somewhere (give it a name, such as the "improve-relationship" response)

Part 3

1. Compare your mind and body's responses to the questions in Parts 1 and 2 above.
2. What differences do you notice at the intellectual level?
3. What differences do you notice at the emotional level?
4. What insights did you gain from this exercise?

By comparing the difference between focusing on the parties involved in the relationship and focusing on the relationship itself, we begin to realise the importance of considering The Relationship as a separate component that needs to be distinguished from the individuals that form that relationship.

The Third Entity, being an emergent property, comes about spontaneously and uniquely through the meeting of two people. Its uniqueness in every situation makes it unpredictable and that is what makes relationships exciting and confusing and frustrating and intriguing and fun and joyful and painful, sometimes all at the same time (or at least that's how our amazingly integrative mind remembers them). Which of these emotions we experience at any one moment depends on our viewpoint or perspective.

In summary, the three necessary components to every relationship are The Self, The Other and The Third Entity (The Connection or The Nexus).

22.3
The Pactum

We also need a word that will incorporate all three elements; two 'Identities' and the emergent Nexus. If we refer to it as a couple, in addition to the confusion of inferring a sexual relationship, we are, at the very least, side-lining the Third Entity. A duo or dyad leaves us with the same problem. A triad or trio would suggest three individuals rather than three entities.

After some deliberation, I settled for **Pactum** (plural, Pacta). This word is derived from the word pact and is related to packet, both of which suggest several elements coming together to form a single unit. We can say that the Pactum is **The Fourth Entity** that emerges from the interaction of two Identities. We explore Pacta elsewhere including § 30.2, § 32.3 and § 56.1.

22.4
The Bondle

Our physical bodies house the various Identities within us. We call this Identity package a 'person' or an 'individual'. In affinitology, we call it an Omniself (§ 29.4). Whenever two identities from two individuals form a Nexus, a connection is also created between the two individuals that house each of those Identities.

Imagine each individual being like a motorhome and each Identity being someone who lives in each of those motorhomes. When two Identities connect with each other, we can think of this as being like two people sticking their heads out of the windows of each motorhome to talk to each other. In this case, you would need to be an alien to see such a scene and perceive this as being the two motorhomes talking to each other [oh we are so alien to ourselves]. Now, imagine what would happen if one person from one motorhome wants to go on a trip with one from the other motorhome. Since each Identity is inseparable from its Omniself, everyone in both of the motorhomes would need to tag along. I have named this concept, a Bondle, being a cross between a 'bond' and a 'bundle' [you see, it wasn't a spelling mistake and it makes it more memorable because it rhymes with fondle ☺]. We explore this concept in more detail in Unit 13 (Paediatrics of Relationships).

Chapter 23

Two Types of Relationship

Whether we are talking about a person or a sausage, we can classify the way we feel about things or people into four basic categories:

1. I **need** (a relationship with) it
2. I **want** (a relationship with) it
3. I want to **avoid** (a relationship with) it
4. I **don't care** about (having a relationship with) it

In practice, the third and fourth categories do not lead to SMERs. That leaves only two types of relationship for us to consider here.

If the relationship is based on a 'mutual want', then we call that an Interdependent relationship and if the relationship is based on a 'need' (whether one-way or reciprocal), then we call that a Dependent relationship.

If the only thing standing between me and my demise is a sausage, then I *need* that (food↔feeder) relationship; I am dependent upon it. This is an example of **dependence**.

Similarly, if, instead of a sausage, that feeling of need is directed towards another person (The Other), that will lead to a '**dependent**' interpersonal relationship. In this case, I feel that my wellbeing, whether it be physical, emotional, psychological, social, financial etc. (Unit 11: Dimensions of human experience) **depends** on my relationship with a particular person.

If The Self and The Other both *want*, but don't *need*, the relationship, then that relationship is an **Interdependent** one. In this section we explore these two types of relationship in more detail.

23.1

Dependent Relationships

Earlier, I said that if I feel that my wellbeing depends on a particular person, then I will feel dependent on that person. Notice that I am focusing on *feeling* and not on reality. It may be true that my wellbeing depends on a particular person, but this only happens under extreme circumstances. In the vast majority of cases, dependent relationships stem from habituation. One type of habituation is learned helplessness.

Unlike attachment (§ 42.3 and § 51.8.10), whose primary indicators are sadness (in the absence of the attachment figure), comfort and gratitude, the main indicator of dependence is anxiety which is rooted in the fear of not being able to cope without some person, object, belief or value.

A dependent relationship may or may not be a SMER depending on the perception of the parties involved. As we shall see later, our feelings of dependency have much less to do with our real need than with our perceived need. Two of the factors that affect such perception are our self-esteem and our self-confidence. We explore these in more detail in § 40.3 (Self-Esteem) and § 40.4 (Self-Confidence).

23.2
The Road to Interdependence

23.2.1
Independence

Interdependence is the most common kind of relationship that leads to an SMER. To get there, we need to go through an intermediate step; independence. That's when The Self does not *need* the relationship which means that The Self is not looking for the relationship as its *only* means of survival, but sees it as a potential means of mutual growth.

You might say, "But Bijan, we are social animals and we all *need* each other for survival. We cannot become completely independent." And I would agree with you. I would also point out that that's why I have italicised the word 'only' in the previous paragraph. It is true that the less we need, the more independent we become.

[I have to come the conclusion that, lamentably, the greater prosperity that has led us to become less dependent on each other has also led us to be less caring towards each other. On the other hand, perhaps, at a holistic level, the benefits outweigh the costs (see 'opportunity cost' in § 62 Decision-Making). I will endeavour to explore this further at some other time and place. Keep an eye out on introducingaffinitology.com]

There *is* a way of becoming more independent *in spite* of our need and that's through *choice*. Think of it like this, "What is the difference between a monopoly and healthy competition?" If there is only one supplier of water, I am *dependent* on that person for survival. If there are two or more suppliers of water, I have choice. I am not dependent on any single supplier, but I am, nevertheless, dependent on what they have to offer.

"Bijan, are you saying that to be independent, we need to be fickle?" No. I would describe fickleness as mismanagement of choice. It is indicative of indecisiveness; of being lost, of not knowing what exactly it is that we want or not being able to make up our minds about what our priorities are. I would concede, however, that one cannot be fickle if one does not have choice.

Often, people associate being independent with being in control when, actually, independence is more about *self*-control (§ 44 Locus of Control).

"A river only reaches the sea because it is hemmed in by its banks."

[I have heard or read that somewhere, but I can't remember where, so apologies if due credit has been omitted.]

23.2.2
Types of Independence

There are two types of independence. Voluntary and obligatory. You might ask, "But how can anyone be independent and obligated?" And that would be a pertinent question. So, let's deal with it.

The movement of an asteroid through space is independent. There are no forces acting upon it, yet it keeps on moving. In fact, according to Newton's first law, it will continue to move unless it is acted upon by an external force. Although the asteroid is independent of anything outside of it for its movement (velocity), it *is* dependent on outside forces for *change*. That is, it moves, but that movement is obligatory. We can extend that analogy to people too.

There is a primitive part of our brain that reasons like this, "Doing what I have done so far, I have survived. Therefore, my current ways have proven themselves to be effective; as the saying goes, if it ain't broke, why try to fix it?" And then there is another part of our mind that says, "Hey, wake up. We are not here to merely survive. Survival is a means not an end. We are here to learn (to grow) and to pass on what we learn to future generations." And then, there is a third part of our mind that completes what the second one says by shouting, "AND ENJOY THE PROCESS."

What happens, therefore, is that, people (we) also continue to do what they were doing (physical behaviour) unless acted upon by an external force; specifically, a thought. That thought may emanate from The Self or from some other source. Whether or not we choose (§ 40.2 Behaviourism versus Humanism) to be influenced by that external thought is the 'voluntary' aspect of independence.

23.2.3
Control

Sometimes, overprotective parents come to me and complain that their children aren't well behaved. They present the problem as something like, "How can I control my child?" This tends to turn out to be the wrong question because, in most cases, the specific behaviours that these parents want to have control over, whilst inconvenient, often don't present a physical risk to the child.

Trying to exercise control over children often results in the very behavioural issues that their parents are trying to control. In such cases, the problem needs to be reframed as, "How can I feel less anxious whilst relinquishing *some* control?" This reframe clarifies the issue as being related to self-confidence. Here, parents' anxiety stems from a belief that they need to be able to control their child's behaviour. When that happens, our sanity becomes *dependent* on being able to control. And the problem is that

> **the need for control creates dependence.**

In case you are saying to yourself, "Yes, Bijan, the *need* to control creates dependence because it implies that control isn't there yet, but having achieved control, one becomes more empowered." My answer would be, "Yes and no" because to 'control' and to 'restrict' are intimately connected. And

> **when we restrict someone to whom we are connected, we restrict ourselves.**

Our need to control often stems from our need to feel safe and that comes at a cost. To feel safe, I need to create an environment where change is minimised and, of course, *so is growth*. The result is often stifling for myself and for others, even if I don't recognise it. The question then becomes, **"When is 'control' empowering?"** The answer is simple; **when it empowers all concerned**. Control can be potentially empowering when it is relinquished voluntarily (through choice) by The Other in the relationship, that is when The Other *is willing* to be controlled. Having said that, people tend to relinquish control to others (allow others to tell them what to do) for two reasons; fear or guidance. One is empowering and the other is not.

In summary, our level of independence is a function of choice. Unless we can *choose* to connect or disconnect with a person (through want, not need), we cannot instigate and develop an interdependent relationship which is a prerequisite for a SMER. Let me clarify. I am not saying that, to be independent, we must not *need* relationships. What I am saying is that we become more independent (do not feel that we are stuck in a relationship) when we have a choice of relationships. If there is only one lender, and I desperately need to borrow money, then the potential for an SMER is reduced; I become vulnerable to exploitation. But if there is more than one lender and there is healthy competition, i.e., no oligopolies or cartels are involved, then that creates fertile ground for a healthy lender-borrower relationship. You might say, "But Bijan, does that not create possible conflict with the notion of 'loyalty'?" And I would thank you for your question and refer you to § 9.3 (Loyalty).

23.3

Interdependence

Interdependence is a required but insufficient condition for a SMER. Here's a story that demonstrates this.

> CK was a top manager at a large firm. One day, he was with some friends and lost track of time and realised that he was late for the office. Only a few days earlier, he had told his workforce that he would not tolerate anyone being late to work, because he was never late himself.
>
> He jumped into his flashy car and sped down the road only to be stopped by a police officer who took his time asking questions and checking his credentials. As the clock ticked away, CK became more and more angry and frustrated.
>
> When he got to the office, the first person he saw was his sales manager.
>
> "Good morning, CK" said the sales manager in a friendly tone.
>
> "What's good about it?" shouted CK, "I want to see you in my office, NOW!"
>
> With some trepidation, the sales manager followed him into the office.
>
> CK yelled at the sales manager, "What happened to that big client that you were supposed to bring in?"
>
> "It looks like it's not going to happen, but we are working on a new equally good potential client." The sales manager said.
>
> "If you don't do better, I'm going to have to look for another sales manager." CK said.
>
> The sales manager went out of the office muttering to himself, "Doesn't he realise what an asset I am. Without me, the company would have gone down years go." As he was brooding, he saw his secretary.
>
> "Did you send out those letters that I asked you to?" He shouted.
>
> "You told me that the letter to AB & Sons was a priority, I'm still working on that." Said the secretary.
>
> "I am sick of hearing excuses." said the sales manager, "If you can't do the job right, perhaps I should be looking for someone who can."
>
> The secretary picked up the letters and stomped off, mumbling to herself, "If it weren't for me, this guy would have been sacked years ago and this is the treatment I get for my hard work and loyalty."

Further along the corridor, she saw the telephone operator and said to her, "You seem to be sitting idle, not doing anything all day. The least you can do is post these letters." and thumped them on her desk.

The telephone operator was furious. How dare she talk to her like that? She was much busier than anyone else at the firm. When the telephone operator got home, she saw her young son sitting on the carpet with muddy shorts, watching television.

"You don't seem to appreciate how hard I have to work to put food on the table here. Is this how you repay me, spreading dirt all over the house and lazing in front of the TV?" She said, "Go to your room, right now."

As the little boy was on his way to his room, the family cat walked in front of him. That was a mistake. He kicked the cat saying, "Get out of here. You've probably been up to no good yourself."

[I am grateful to Zig Ziglar, the inspirational speaker who told this story. Zig goes on to explain that if someone behaves rudely or abruptly towards you, it's nothing personal. Someone has kicked his cat. Actually, he called the manager Mr B. I changed the name to CK (short for Cat Kicker ☺)]

This story has other merits. For example, it also demonstrates that:

- Each of us is a 'node' in a web of connections
- Emotions are contagious
- Lack of emotional control can have far reaching consequences
- Any one of those involved in the chain could have chosen not to propagate the wave of discontent.

Do I have what it takes to be part of a win-win relationship?

Life is a lot *less* like football than you might have been led to believe. The more we think of life as being like a game of football, the more we make it like a game of football for ourselves. This reaffirms our original false belief (§ 33.8 Confirmation Bias) and, when we do that, we begin to miss out on far more than we could imagine. In games like football, there are always losers (at least in terms of score). In life that need not be the case. If you find that difficult to believe, then I suggest that you stop playing games, especially competitive games (§ 39 Social Ranking Criteria). I mean that in more ways than one.

Let me recommend a book to you. It is called, "Games People Play" by Eric Berne. From a relationship point of view, you will discover much about the destructive effects of treating life as if it is a series of games. It is lamentable that nowadays, we need to be extra-alert and highly self-aware [not to be confused with self-conscious] to avoid falling into the social games trap. On the other hand, those who do manage to discover the sense of liberation that comes from integrity and sincerity are careful not to fall into the soul-sucking snare of games. This is in spite of the fact that not playing games can (at least initially) lead to a heightened sense of vulnerability.

You see, when we believe that there always has to be a winner and a loser, we will tend to find (put) ourselves in situations where there *are* winners and losers. That belief becomes self-fulfilling because of certain flaws in our thinking processes, in this case, confirmation bias (§ 33.8). Confirmation bias is when we see evidence in support of our beliefs, but fail to notice evidence that contradicts our beliefs. It will then become inevitable that sometimes we end up feeling like a loser. This fans the fires of a 'dependency' mindset.

> **"Most people have been deeply scripted in the win/lose mentality since birth."**
>
> - Stephen Covey, The 7 habits of highly effective people

In a dependency mindset, you are out to get things. If you get, you are a winner and if you don't get (or sometimes even if you give), you are a loser. Such a mindset sabotages the possibility of developing and nurturing SMERs. How can we feel content in a relationship where we need to constantly battle to get the upper hand, lest we feel inferior?

In relationships, the antithesis to dependency is what Steven Covey calls *interdependence*. This is where the parties in a relationship no longer feel the need to prove themselves; they already believe in themselves and their potential. Without the need to focus on who you are or what you are, you can pay attention to nurturing The Third Entity (The Nexus); the bond that makes the difference between being 'disparate parts' and being a 'coherent whole'. So, when we are focusing on The Nexus, what exactly are we focusing on? I am going to try to explain that through another chemical analogy.

By itself, sodium is a highly reactive, soft silvery grey metal. Chlorine is a poisonous gas with a pungent smell. When sodium and chlorine react (bond with each other) the outcome is nothing like either element. They both lose each other in the relationship and what results is something stable, crystalline, beautiful, nutritious and tasty [assuming there aren't too many cooks].

Here's another analogy to help clarify the difference between focusing on the individual within a relationship as compared with the relationship itself. Imagine you're a farmer. When you're ploughing the field, planting the seeds, fertilising the soil, watering the soil and protecting the crops, if you do not focus exclusively on what the wheat needs to thrive your crop is less likely to be as good as if you do. In other words, your own needs are better satisfied by focusing on the needs of the land as it pertains to the development of the wheat. The soil is The Nexus, the bond that joins the farmer to the crop. In interpersonal relationships each person's needs are better served by focusing on the common goals [if common goals are the basis of the relationship (§ 92 Relationship Frameworks)].

Here's a thought for you to dwell on. I put it to you that:

---
the greatest freedom is the freedom of having nothing to lose

---

Now with that thought fresh in your mind, imagine this scenario. It is holiday time and you want to go camping. Your partner, on the other hand, wants to go skiing. What are the possible outcomes? Get creative. Notice how you feel about each of the possible alternatives.

- Do you see yourself winning in one case and losing in another?
- Do you see some options as a compromise?
- Can you imagine a scenario where there is no bartering, no winners, no losers and no compromise? If you can, you are ready for an interdependent relationship, a SMER at that.

Unit 5

Classification of

Relationships

[Image by OpenClipart-Vectors from Pixabay.
Source: https://pixabay.com/vectors/file-cabinet-office-equipment-file-146157/]

Prelude to Unit 5

Relationships are abstract (§ 21.1 What is a Relationship?) and can only be understood through metaphors. As such, the way we classify relationships depends on the metaphors through which we understand them. All metaphors break down at some point [otherwise, they wouldn't be metaphors, they would be descriptions]. When we use several metaphors for the same concept, we can compensate for the shortcomings of one metaphor by switching to another.

In this Unit, we explore four different metaphors that can help us to understand and to classify relationships. These are,

- Relationships as chemical bonds
- Relationships as living (biological) systems
- Relationships as part of a hierarchical organisation
- Relationships from a material science perspective

There are many other ways in which we can look at relationships. We encounter some of these later in this course, including,

- Relationships as a part of an ecological system
- Relationships as mechanical systems

Each of these metaphors gives us a different perspective on the nature of relationships. In this way, we can try to touch different parts of Rumi's elephant before jumping to conclusions about what an elephant actually is (§ 64.9 The Origin of Values) [To be accurate, Rumi did not come up with the story, he simply popularised it through his eloquent rendition in Persian].

Chapter 24

Affinitology as a Material Science

24.1
What do Tables and Relationships Have in Common?

In § 14 (What's in a Word) and § 30.1 (The Nexus), I use a table as a metaphor for relationships. This metaphor allows us to focus more on the different ways in which a connection can be made.

A table leg and a table top can be joined together in various ways, including glue, nails, screws and hinges. Each of these have their own unique set of properties (strength, flexibility, resistance to pressure, temperature, solvents, corrosion, etc.). A connection between two people can also be made in various ways depending on the 'properties' of the 'materials' that we want to join and the nature of the joint that we want to create.

In affinitology, the 'properties' of the materials that we have to work with can be thought of as being the beliefs, values, knowledge, skills, experiences, strengths, weaknesses and expectations of the Identities (The Self and The Other) that form the Nexus.

If someone were to ask me, "What is the best way of connecting two objects?" I would say, "Well, it depends on what you are trying to connect with what and what you want to do with the final product." What if we were to think along the same lines when we think about connecting with other people (or connections between people)?

If you were to ask me, "How many different ways can you think of for joining two objects together?" My mind would race through a plethora of alternatives including paperclips, starch, wax, mortar, chewing gum, various types of sticky tape, including electrical tape, knots, rivets, screws, nails, dovetailed joints, magnets, hinges, rope, staples, stitches, cement, hairspray, glue, glue guns and other types of fusion, such as through welding. And if you were to ask me how many different materials can I think of that can be joined together through these methods, again my mind would race and come up with things like, paper, card, bricks, stones, various types of wood and plastic, various types of metals, wax and human skin. If you were then to ask how many different structures can be made by joining two or more materials together, the possibilities are, of course, only bounded by our imagination.

The means by which we join these materials together depend not only on the materials, but also on what we intend to do with the final product. I can join two pieces of wood together with glue, but this would not be very useful if one of those pieces of wood is part of a door frame and the other is intended to be its door. Similarly, a connection between two people (Identities) can be made in various ways and depends on the 'materials' we have and the means that we use to join them. We discuss what constitutes (the equivalent of) 'materials' in § 47 (Common and Complementary Elements) and 'the means of joining them' in Unit 16 (Physiology of Relationships).

A material science metaphor helps us to switch our perspective on interpersonal relationships from the two Identities involved to the nature of the connection. It can also open communication channels by giving us words that allow us to focus more specifically on factors that connect people to each other rather than the individuals themselves. These factors can be emotional, intellectual, environmental, social etc. (Unit 11: Dimensions of Human Experience).

Chapter 25

Relationships as Chemical Bonds

25.1
Atomic and Molecular Orbitals

At school, we are generally taught that there are two types of chemical bond; ionic and covalent. However, neither chemical bonds nor relationships are as black-and-white as that. We can think of ionic and covalent bonds as two extremes of a spectrum (grayscale).

Chemical reactions (bond making and bond breaking) only involve the outer electrons of atoms. We could think of it as the atom's 'skin' or 'interface' or 'surface' or 'membrane'. Actually, this idea of 'surface' (more specifically, surface area) is a pivotal and crucial aspect of all of biology and, as we shall discover, of affinitology.

At school, we are also taught that every atom consists of a core; a nucleus, with 'particles' called electrons rotating around this nucleus similar to the way in which planets revolve around stars. Later we are taught that actually, electrons are less like solid balls with predictable orbits and more like clouds of negative charge whereby we cannot determine for certain where the electron is going to be, but we can use statistical methods to work out the probability of finding the electron in any particular location. When represented graphically, each of these probability density maps looks like a 'cloud' and we even call it an electron cloud, or more 'scientifically', an orbital. There are two types of orbitals, atomic orbitals and molecular orbitals. This means that when two atoms interact, the probability density maps of their electrons change shape.

If the above concepts of orbitals are already familiar to you, you may see similarities between these and my graphic representations of The Omniself (§ 29.4) and the Pactum (§ 30.2). Later in this course, we shall append these to other concepts, such as Core Values or Principles (§ 29.4.1), Identities (§ 37) and the Nexus (§ 22.2 and § 30.1).

If we think of an atom's nucleus as a metaphor for each individual's Principles and his various Identities as being akin to an atom's electrons, then what I am calling the emergent Third Entity or Nexus is like a molecular orbital.

The reason for my use of multiple analogies for relationships in this way (placing relationships in the context of atoms and molecules, cells and organs, organisms and ecosystems) should become clearer when we discuss fractal structures (§ 90).

25.2

Ionic and Covalent Bonds

At school we are also taught that when an atom that doesn't want one of its outer electrons gives it to an atom that does want one, then the donor becomes a cation (positively charged) and its receiving counterpart (anion) becomes negatively charged and then, since opposite charges attract, a force of attraction; an ionic bond, is formed. In this type of bond, there is no sharing involved, just a straight forward, one-off (static) exchange (one gives and one takes). The distinction between static and dynamic is an important one, especially with regards to interpersonal relationships. This will become apparent as we continue through this course.

We are also taught that there is another type of relationship that atoms can have with each other whereby two atoms who each feel that there is something missing in their lives, namely, an electron, share one of their outer electrons with each other to form a covalent bond.

Strictly speaking, in a covalent bond, electrons do not share in the way that two people 'share' an experience. It is more like, I'll scratch your back with my electron, if you scratch my back with yours. It is a dynamic exchange; a continuous give and take. The atoms take one of their outer electrons and pass it backwards and forwards to each other rather like a two-person juggling act.

[Actually, although that is what we teach kids in schools, electrons aren't like balls at all and covalent bonds aren't like what I have just described, but it is a useful place to start so, let's go with that model for now and see what happens when we apply it to interpersonal relationships.]

Let's say that someone has surplus money that they want to lend and I am keen to borrow some. Here, an exchange takes place and, to use our chemical bonding analogy, an ionic bond is created because now the lender is attracted to me since she wants to get her money back and I have a commitment to her by virtue of an obligation to give that money back. In theory, and on the surface, that could be all that there is to the relationship. That is to say; the relationship is unidimensional, based purely on the financial dimension (Unit 11: Dimensions of Human Experience).

But it would seem that life is never quite that simple because the lender would have to trust me to some extent first before he will lend me money and I would have to trust the lender to some extent as well. For example, that he will not demand 'a pound of flesh' before I proceed to borrow money [for those of you who are unfamiliar with this idiom, it is a reference to Shakespeare's Merchant of Venice].

Trust (§ 30.1.2, § 51.8.3, § 53, § 54.1 and § 83.1.2) requires us to evoke both our cognitive acumen (intellectual dimension) and our emotional faculties (emotional dimension).

25.3
Polar Bond (Partial Sharing)

In the good old days (like when I was a student), when I needed to borrow money, I would walk into my branch and speak to my bank manager who would look at me and talk to me and he would base his decision, in part, on his impression of me. Whenever impressions are formed, an emotional component is introduced into the relationship. Let's say that, in my meeting with my bank manager, we find that we have common interests such as playing chess. Then, I could tell him that I am a member of the chess club nearby and he might say, "Oh, I would like to come to that."

[It is lamentable (at least for me) that so many opportunities like this are being lost to automation. Personally, I tend to avoid automatic tellers at supermarkets and inside banks and when ushers try to persuade me to go out of the queue and start using one of these devices, I usually explain that I prefer to wait and have a human interaction because if I don't, I will be doing my part in helping humanity to become cyborgs (cybernetic organisms; part human and part machine where the human part is unable to operate without its machine part and vice versa). My daughter would argue that this is the 'boomer' in me talking and that every older generation laments 'the good old days'. But I would argue that I do not lament what we have gained, I lament what we have lost (and are losing). Anyway, I digress.]

I hope it is becoming clear that, unless we are dealing with machines or cyborgs, a relationship instigated through one dimension has the potential to expand to include relationships in other dimensions (Unit 11: Dimensions of Human Experience).

This is also true for ionic and covalent bonds between atoms. Purely covalent bonds only happen between identical atoms of the non-metals family. There is no such thing as two identical people, even if they have identical genetic structures, so we can't do that; we can't share anything exactly 50-50. All other chemical bonds exist on a grayscale from almost purely ionic to almost purely covalent.

So when a hydrogen atom and an oxygen atom form a bond, the hydrogen says to the oxygen, "I can see that you need this electron more than I do (you become more unstable without it), so you can have a greater share of it, but I still feel better knowing that you're around than me being on my own (I am more stable too)." On reflection, it would seem that we can learn a lot about relationships from hydrogen.

[By the way, hydrogen is the most versatile element. Have you ever wondered why it is often placed on its own in the middle top portion of the periodic table, as if it does not belong to any of the groups? Far from being a loner, it is very gregarious. It belongs to both group 1 elements (for example when it forms hydrogen fluoride) and group 7 elements (e.g., sodium hydride). It has the ability to give when the stability of the relationship requires it and to take, again when the stability of the relationship requires it. And without hydrogen and its versatility, there would be no water and without water there can be no life or at least 'not as we know it' (as Spock of Star Trek might say).]

We now have an arrangement whereby the negatively charged electrons spend more time around the oxygen atom than they do around the hydrogen atom. That makes the oxygen relatively negative and the hydrogen relatively positive. Note that this is not an ionic bond in the classic sense and it is not a covalent bond in its classic sense. We call it a polarised bond or a dipole. I found this depiction of the continuum I am talking about on the University of West Indies (Jamaica) website.

Figure 4 Grayscale is the norm

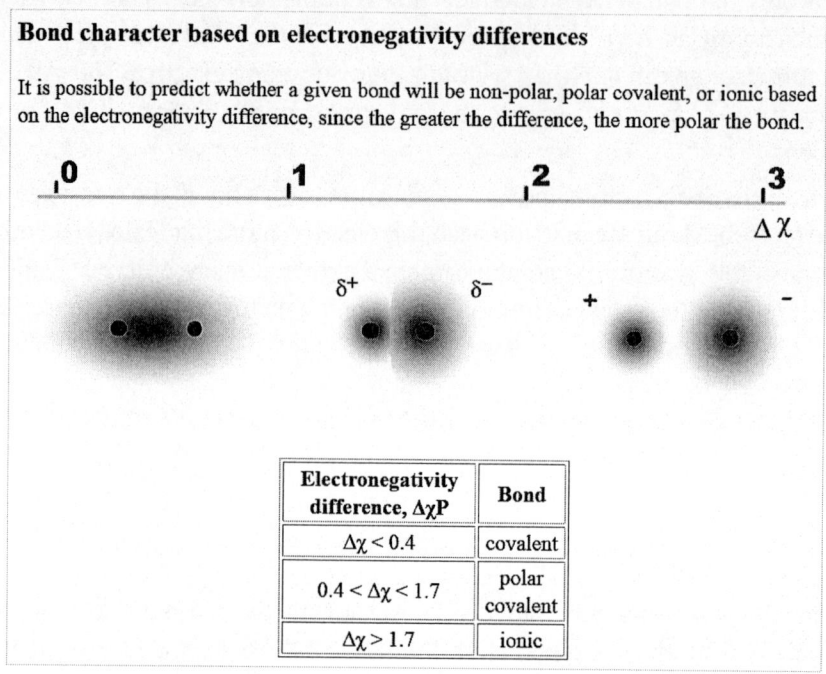

Bond character based on electronegativity differences

It is possible to predict whether a given bond will be non-polar, polar covalent, or ionic based on the electronegativity difference, since the greater the difference, the more polar the bond.

Electronegativity difference, $\Delta\chi P$	Bond
$\Delta\chi < 0.4$	covalent
$0.4 < \Delta\chi < 1.7$	polar covalent
$\Delta\chi > 1.7$	ionic

[Source: http://www.weightware.com/weighttrend.htm]

Notice that we are so keen to be able to establish black and white parameters that we draw arbitrary lines somewhere along the spectrum so that we can impose 'blackness' (covalent-ness: <0.4) and 'whiteness' (ionic-ness: >1.7) onto the *continuum*.

This kind of mental partitioning seems to be characteristic of all of us. We seem to consider grayscales as being too messy and we try to impose 'structure' on them. A notable case is the colours of the rainbow. Our eyes can distinguish about ten million colours and we would become conscious of that fact if we had a name, or an algorithm for deriving a name, for each one. However, we have arbitrarily split the rainbow into seven colours; seven being the average number of items that we can hold in our short-term memory.

In his book, Marital Myths Revisited, Dr Arnold Lazarus, cites one of the myths as, "Marriage should be a 50-50 partnership". With regards to this, it might be enlightening to reflect on this point: The fact that the relationship between oxygen and hydrogen is not a 50-50 partnership is what makes water such an amazing substance [if we care to ponder its amazingness for a moment].

Earlier, I touched on the idea that interpersonal relationships are based on *complementary* and *common* elements. We explore this idea in more detail in § 47. Here, I suggest that the 'complementary elements' on which our relationships are based are like the ionic component in a dipole and the 'common elements' are like its covalent component. Notice that, by implication, I have just reinforced the idea that relationships are not 50-50 (and they don't need to be in order to be a SMER).

25.4

Dative Bond (Give and Share)

There is a third type of chemical bond that we hear much less about. In a dative [AKA coordinate] bond, an atom gives two of its electrons to another atom without acquiring a charge. This means that what holds the two atoms together is neither the forces of attraction arising from opposite charges nor the 'exchange' of electrons (in the usual 'give one' and 'take one' sense). Juggling is still involved; it is just that both of the electrons being 'juggled' between the two atoms come from one of the atoms.

So how can we apply this understanding to relationships? To expand on my earlier example, in an ionic type of bond along the financial dimension, you borrow money from me and use it to go to the movies. Our relationship is based on you owing me money.

In a covalent type of relationship, we each pay for our own movie tickets but come together and share the experience.

In a dative type of relationship, one of us pays for both tickets and we go together to share the experience and neither owes the other one anything. Note that, although money is involved, there is no financial relationship; this money is being exchanged outside of the relationship, it is in Zone X (§ 35.1 Embryology of Relationships) [In its chemical counterpart, one atom is donating both electrons for the sake of the relationship. I know that's somewhat anthropomorphic, but it helps in making the point]. This kind of relationship is illustrated well by the following quote from Antoine de Saint-Exupéry [the author of 'The Little Prince'].

> **"Love does not consist of gazing at each other, but in looking outward together in the same direction."**

Actually, this definition of love includes both the dative and the covalent type of relationship, as I have described them here. In other words, as long as we are going to the movies together, love is there and it doesn't matter who pays for the experience.

[It might be enlightening to contemplate the fact that without dative bonds, we would not have haemoglobin (the molecule that make oxygen safe for transport through our blood and which is responsible for the red colour of blood) without which we would not be alive. Similarly, it is dative bonding that allows for the formation of the chlorophyll molecule without which there would be no plant or animal life on earth. We might include in our contemplation how this understanding could affect our approach to the concept of love.]

25.5
Metallic Bonds

In metals, individual electrons are not bound to specific nuclei. They roam freely between them. In § 32 (Extended Relationships), I explain that there are situations [Note: § 14.3 Situation vs Circumstance] under which people lose their sense of individual identity and merge into what I have called a Collective Identity. If the electrons in a metal were to have a slogan, it would be, "All electrons are created equal and are free to roam as they please", although that perceived freedom to roam is constrained by the size of the metal fragment and the absence of electrical fields. You could use your imagination to come up with equivalent slogans for these two determinants of 'freedom within a collective' for social systems.

25.6
Chemical Equilibria

A chemical reaction is said to occur when two atoms or molecules, which we call *reactants*, 'bump' into each other (interact) in such a way that bonds are broken and/or made resulting in new chemical species. These new chemical species are referred to as the *products* of the reaction. In some reactions, called addition reactions, nothing has to come off a molecule for another species to be added onto it [Strictly speaking, there is temporary disruption; a bond breaks and re-forms - usually not with the same atom, but with an identical one (but for the purposes of our discussion here, let's ignore this complication)].

Similarly, people can 'bump' into each other (interact) and create new Pacta (§ 30.2) which may or may not be at the expense of existing Pacta.

Some, I suggest most, chemical reactions are reversible. This means that the reactants can become products and the products can become reactants. The most prevalent and most important case in point is water which exists in dynamic equilibrium with hydronium ions and hydroxide ions.

Reactants		Products
$H_2O + H_2O$	$\rightarrow$	$H_3O^+ + OH^-$
$H_3O^+ + OH^-$	$\rightarrow$	$H_2O + H_2O$

[Note that this is the basis for the vital concept of pH and of sourness (something to think about next time you put some sweet and sour sauce on your chips)]

Similarly, within society, we have eligible single people and couples in dynamic equilibrium with a continuous stream of single people getting hitched whilst others become available. The same applies to buyers and sellers, colleagues and friends.

From a chemical perspective, the relative proportions of the reactants and products in a dynamic equilibrium depend on factors such as temperature, pressure, concentration and presence of other chemicals, as well as the presence of electromagnetic and nuclear radiation. Similarly, factors such as economic policies and conditions, media manipulation and cultural norms affect the equilibrium positions for various types of Pactum.

At a more personal level, **the equilibrium theory of social interaction** [look up "Argyle and Dean 1965"] proposes that there is also a dynamic equilibrium between the various interactions between two people. According to this theory, in order to maintain a certain level of intimacy [nowadays we would say rapport], if one supporting aspect of a relationship (such as level of eye contact) wanes, another (such as physical proximity or amount of smiling or a more 'intimate' subject of conversation) would need to take over.

Chapter 26

Relationships as Living Systems

26.1
Advantages of considering relationships as being alive

The analogy of relationships as organisms has many advantages. Let's consider some of these. By tapping into the vast existing research-based knowledge about organisms, we can take advantage of existing structure and terminology of biomedical sciences. Additionally, if you are unfamiliar with medical science and its vocabulary, this approach could encourage you to become more familiar with it in the context of an alluring topic [That was the teacher Identity in me having his say (§ 29.4 The Omniself)]. If, on the other hand, you are well versed in basic biology and/or medical science and you are also interested in relationships, then this course marries the two [hopefully, they will live happily ever after].

Since relationships are abstract ideas, the 'relationships as organisms' approach allows us to use medical terminology as metaphors for describing relationships in more concrete terms. Here are some medical terms that I use in this book along with a brief description showing how I have applied them to interpersonal relationships.

Physiology: The dynamics between the constituent parts of a relationship; how they work together, especially communication in all its forms.

Behaviour: How a relationship (the Nexus) reacts to its environment (or chooses to act in a given environment). Note that this is related to, but separate from, how the individuals that make up the relationship (The Self and The Other) react to their environment.

Ecology: The dynamic interplay between the environment that a relationship needs to thrive and the environment to which a relationship needs to adapt.

Taxonomy: How can relationships be classified? In particular, how can relationships be classified in ways that allow us to keep track of their progress over time (evolution). This is related to our discussion in § 92 (Relationship Frameworks) and Unit 21 (Diversification and Speciation of Relationships).

Anatomy: The parts that make up a relationship (The Self, The Other and The Nexus) and how they fit together.

26.2

Characteristics of Living Systems

We have not found a way of defining life yet. Personally, I would prefer to characterise life in terms of consciousness, which I would define as "the ability to exercise choice" (§ 35.11 Consciousness). For the time being, however, let's limit ourselves to what we are taught in high school biology where we learnt that, although we cannot define life, we have come up with seven signs that, when they occur *together*, indicate life (Movement, Reproduction, Sensitivity, Growth, Respiration, Excretion, Nutrition - you may remember the mnemonic, MRS GREN or MRS NERG). In other words, **we can attempt to *describe* life, but we cannot *define* it**; at least not yet. Similarly, we could try to use the same seven signs, or criteria (MRS GREN), to describe relationships. Let's look at each of them in turn.

[As my biology teacher once pointed out (thanks Andy), an important item missing from this list is death. That reminds me of a movie that I once saw about a man who fell in love with an artificial life form (I can't remember its name and, no, it wasn't Blade Runner. Perhaps if anyone out there knows the film I'm talking about you will let me know). He asked his friend how one can tell the difference between something that's alive and a machine and the friend said that a machine is not afraid of dying.]

26.2.1

Movement

Relationships are dynamic. Every aspect of every one of our relationships is subject to change; in quality, intensity and direction. Just like living systems, the constant movement (manoeuvring) in relationships is also proactive. That is to say, choice is involved (§ 35.11 Consciousness); if we choose to exercise that choice (we often don't because we are not aware that we have a choice).

If I am moving rapidly downward (like a brick) because I am one thousand meters above the ground, that movement has nothing to do with me being alive. However, movement that I instigate (in a way that a brick can't), like jumping out of an aeroplane, is an indicator of life, but only if it is in association with the other six signs; a robot jumping out of a plane doesn't count. Although relationships can also be reactive; that is, be subject to outside forces that compel them to change in quality, intensity and direction, as living organisms, relationships would also be expected to be instigators of movement, including compensating for that which compelled them to change (§ 35.5 Homeostasis).

26.2.2
Reproduction

Organisms can replicate. In the context of relationships, we can think of it as their ability to be modelled. The relationship that we call 'marriage' is a case in point. Marriage is a conventional phenomenon which means that someone made it up and others thought it was a good idea and started doing it too.

> **As soon as we label a Relationship Framework, we create a mechanism through which it can replicate.**

We explore various Relationship Frameworks in § 92.

When replicating a relationship, we are in fact, replicating a set of beliefs. We explore this in more detail in Unit 14 (Genetics of Relationships).

26.2.3
Sensitivity

Relationships are sensitive in the same way that living organisms are; they react to changes in their environment. For example, the quality and the intensity of a Marriage relationship is sensitive to many external factors, such as changes in financial circumstances and the social environment, such as the proximity of other people.

In § 64.4 (Values as Receptors), I propose that the sensitivity of each of our Identities is determined by that Identity's values. There, I also propose that each of our Identities' values are like a receptor on the surface of a cell membrane. These receptors (values and value systems) are important in terms of the common and complementary elements that lead to the formation (and determine the dynamics) of the Nexus.

In addition to the pre-existing sensitivities of The Self and The Other, the emergence of the Nexus (Unit 12: Embryology of Relationships) brings with it a new set of sensitivities (including expectations) that would not be present in the absence of the Nexus.

26.2.4
Excretion

In terms of relationships, we can think of excretion as the unwanted emotional by-products of a relationship that need to be cleared out of the system; jealousy, anger, guilt, regret, envy, spite and distrust [not to be confused with caution] come to mind.

26.2.5
Growth

Relationships can grow in their breadth and intensity. A relationship can be instigated or 'fertilised' (Unit 12: Embryology of Relationships) in an art gallery by two people who share a common liking for a particular piece of art and can grow from there to encompass many other aspects of each of those individuals' lives as well as the lives of others. We explore this to some extent in § 35.2 (Paediatrics of Relationships).

26.2.6
Respiration

Relationships don't breakdown simple sugars to produce energy [although the individuals that comprise the relationship do]. I propose that the equivalent to respiration for relationships is the *conversion of one type of motivational energy into another type of motivational energy*. We discuss this in more detail in Unit 22 (Thermodynamics of Relationships).

26.2.7
Nutrition

The question here is, "What is food for relationships?" Well, it would have to be something that can be broken down into the equivalent of simple sugars; something that can be converted into motivational energy through an equivalent to respiration. That should give us a clue.

If we define the relationship equivalent of respiration as the 'conversion of *attention* into motivational energy', relationships can be nourished through anything that provides the kind of attention that can be converted into motivation. How about saying "hello", a smile, a wink, a touch, a handshake, an email, a postcard, a single red rose, time spent together, a joint project or a random act of kindness?

Anything that attracts any kind of attention, can kindle and nourish relationships.

Unit 6
Relationship Anatomy

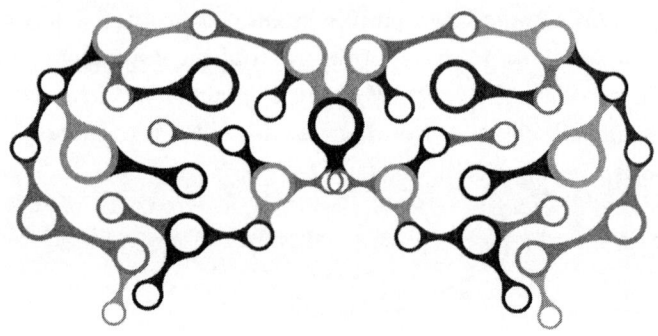

[Image by OpenClipart-Vectors from Pixabay.
Source: https://pixabay.com/vectors/brain-cognition-design-art-2029391/]

Chapter 27

The Meeting of Minds

We explore minds, Identities and creativity in greater depth later on in this course. Here, I am simply going to lay some foundations. When two people meet, the ensuing relationship is not based on the meeting of two bodies; it is based on the meeting of two minds. More specifically, the meeting of two Identities. Even when the relationship appears to be based on the meeting of bodies, it is each person's interpretation of that touch that defines the relationship at that specific moment. And it is each person's *mind* that is doing the interpreting (§ 33: The Atasinex Cluster).

Notice I said 'at that specific moment'. That's because relationships are dynamic. They change from *moment to moment*. However, this 'resonance' of relationship bonds (Nexuses) is more like music than Simple Harmonic Motion.

Figure 5 Music and Simple Harmonic Motion

Sample music wave form

A sinusoidal wave (simple harmonic motion)

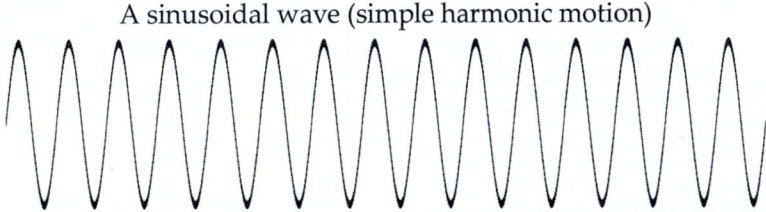

Just like music, relationships tell a story over time. And, as with music, people have different tastes when it comes to relationship dynamics. The arrangement and harmonics in one piece of music will resonate more with some people than others. We will encounter this concept later when we discuss the role of 'Values' in relationships (§ 64).

> *One morning, on a Christmas Day, many years ago, I was walking along the quiet streets of Bournemouth with my girlfriend when, through the windscreen of a van, I saw a couple struggling. Then I heard the lady shout out, "Help!" I grabbed the door handle and pulled. The man, whilst trying to hold the door shut, fell out of the van, turned to me and said, "It's none of your business." I simply told him that I was responding to a cry for help and that he would expect someone to help him if he ever shouted for help. He backed off. I asked the lady whether she wanted to leave and told her that she could be our guest. She said that the man had locked her belongings in the back of the van. I asked him to open it and he did. When we were ready to go, the lady who had called for help changed her mind and said that she would stay with him.*

I was quite surprised at the time. I have had more than twenty-five years of experience since then. In that time, I have seen a wide range of relationship styles and, although I still get an uncomfortable feeling inside when I see submissive behaviour of that kind, I am far less judgemental about it. There are many reasons why we may choose to remain in disempowering or 'poisonous' relationships and lamentably, one of them is a misunderstanding of the concept of loyalty (§ 9.3).

In some situations, people appear to behave like a square wave (on-off) type of relationship whilst others prefer more smooth and stable types of resonance.

This reminds me of a scene in the 1989 comedy, *Parenthood*:

Karen: Life is messy.

Gil: I hate messy. It's so messy!

Grandma: You know, when I was 19, Grandpa took me on a roller coaster. Up, down, up, down. Oh, what a ride.

Gil: What a great story.

Grandma: I always wanted to go again. It was just interesting to me that a ride could make me so frightened... so scared, so sick, so excited... and so thrilled all together. Some didn't like it. They went on the merry-go-round. That just goes around. Nothing. I like the roller coaster. You get more out of it...

Karen: She's a very smart lady...

Gil: A minute ago I was confused about life. Then Grandma came in with her wonderful and effecting roller coaster story. Now everything is great again.

Karen: I happen to like the roller coaster, okay? As far as I'm concerned, your grandmother is brilliant.

27.1
'Who' is a Fluid Concept (Situational)

Through the influence of society (§ 39 Social Ranking Criteria), we create different Identities (Unit 9 Identities, Roles and Personas) for ourselves for different situations (§ 29.4 Omniself). Here's is an exercise to demonstrate this.

Exercise 4 Who are you?

Step 1

Imagine you're walking down a secluded street and a policeman walks up to you and asks, "Who are you?" Let's call this scenario 1.

Step 2

Imagine that you are at a business conference and someone asks, "Who are you?" Let's call this scenario 2.

Step 3

Imagine that you are at a dating club and a potential date asks, "Who are you? Let's call this scenario 3.

Step 4

You've gone to a parent-teacher convention at your child's school and an usher ask, "Who are you?" Let's call this scenario 4.

Step 5

In each of the above situations, assuming that you volunteer more than just your name, how would your response be different? That's what I mean by different Identities. I explain this idea in more detail in the section on the Omniself (§ 29.4) but, for now, it gives you an idea of how complicated human relationships can get.

Each of our Identities has a different personality and a different set of goals congruent with that personality in that situation. This can be a blessing and a curse. It's a blessing because, in similar situations, we will meet similar Identities. For example, in a business conference, if you ask someone, "Who are you?" there are unlikely to say, "I'm James and I live down the Road at number 53, why do you ask?" It only becomes a curse when we meet the same person in different situations; since Identities are situation-dependent, we will see changes in that individual's personality.

27.2

Identities meet impressions

Throughout this discourse, we have talked about a relationship being the formation of a Bond (Third Entity) between two Identities, The Self and The Other. However, in reality, four different perceptions, or impressions, are involved here.

A. The Self's image of itself

B. The Self's impression of The Other

C. The Other's image of itself

D. The Other's impression of The Self

In The Self's mind, A meets B

In The Other's mind C meets D

In reality A meets C.

In order to study relationships with a view to creating SMERs, we need to ask three questions (§ 15.1 The Power of Questions)

a) What affects how we see ourselves [Through the lens of the interacting Identity, The Self, in a specific situation]?

b) What affects how we see The Other?

c) What affects how The Other sees us?

Exploring these ideas in too much detail here would make the subject more complicated than I believe to be warranted for this introductory course. Suffice it to say, these are related to what I have briefly delved into in § 33 (The Atasinex Cluster).

Chapter 28

First Law of Satisfactory Relationships

One of the 'principles' that I stress to my clients is what I call **The First Law of Satisfactory Relationships**. It states that,

---

Others have the right to express their opinions and I have the right to accept or reject them. Conversely, I have the right to express my opinions and others have the right to accept or reject them and
I ACCEPT THE CONSEQUENCES.

This idea that others don't have to accept my point of view, no matter what it is and I don't have to accept their point of view either and in both cases, I accept the consequences, can be very liberating; intellectually, emotionally and socially.

We don't usually take offence if a good friend calls us an idiot, because we believe that his intention is not to offend. If a total stranger walks up to us and calls us an idiot, again, we don't usually take offence because he doesn't know us enough for us to feel that his comments can be any threat to our Identity.

[Both of these scenarios assume that we are of 'sound mind and body' which means that our intellectual faculties are not compromised. Unfortunately, this assumption is warranted much less often than I would like to think. We touch upon this in Unit 22 (Thermodynamics of Relationships)]

Under normal, 'sound mind and body', situations, we only take offence at what other people say when we feel that our Identity; who we think we are, or want to be seen as being (§ 38 Personas), is being threatened. For example, if I am amongst a group of people and how some of those people perceive me is important to me, then I may take offence at a total stranger calling me an idiot. In situations like these, we may feel an urge not to adhere to the 'First Law of Satisfactory Relationships'.

Here is another example. If some stranger pulls their car in front of ours when we are driving and then proceeds to call us an idiot, if we are not practiced enough at exercising "The First Law of Satisfactory Relationships" our emotions may take over our intellect and we may begin to engage in, at best, a futile exchange. This is when another belief, if we take the time to internalise it, can come to our rescue;

> **"I am not who I am because of what happens to me, I am who I am because of the way I respond/react to what happens to me."**

Did I hear you say, "How do we internalise it?" Thank you for asking. We look into that in § 68.5 (Habits).

Chapter 29

The Self, The Omniself and The Other

29.1

Know Thyself

Know thyself. That sounds like simple enough advice, doesn't it? After all, it is advice that goes back to at least 3000 years ago. But if it were that simple, you would think that after 3000 years, there would be no argument over how we should go about doing it. But, alas, I fear that we are more conflicted about who we are than those thinkers, scholars, sages and mystics of antiquity.

So why have we not been able to solve the mind-body problem and why have we eagerly embraced this question as 'The Hard Problem'? I propose that the hardness of the problem stems from two inherent assumptions in the phrase itself; "Know thyself" implies that,

a) I have 'a' Self and

b) It is knowable.

It is not possible to know anything from within. For me to be able to know any kind of self, I need to be able to step outside of that self and look at 'it' (me) from outside (as an observer). But, if I step out of a room and look inside, surely, I will no longer be in the room to be observed by the me who is outside.

The great Persian Mystics such as Attar, Rumi and Hafiz approach the question of the Self from a different perspective. Their stance is that the Self is an illusion and a burden and they talk about the seventh and final stage of enlightenment being 'annihilation'. This is the point at which the Self [the ego, the Identity, the persona, the I, the me, the who I am; call it what you will] is extinguished. These mystics do not suggest that we step out and look in to see the Self. Instead, they say that the Self is a veil or cloud that obfuscates our perception and prevents us from being able to see The Truth. In other words, trying to discover the nature of the Self, is like focusing on what is muddying the water rather than focusing on the clarity that would result if there were no suspended particles in the water.

Frankly, that is a very difficult concept to grasp. If I get rid of the *me*, then what would be the nature of the consciousness that would remain to be anything?

And these mystics would say, that this is like saying, "But how can I know the elephant if I cannot touch it?" (See The Parable of the Elephant in Darkness in § 64.9) and the mystics would say, with your inner eyes; the observer that lies beyond the self.

[Through his observations of people under deep hypnosis, Ernest Hilgard proposed that there is a 'Hidden Observer' within each of us that overseas, but does not interfere with what is going on in our mind, but which simply observes. If you want to explore this topic further, look up 'Neodissociationist Theory']

Here, we are not going to try to take such giant leaps, not least because disciples spent many years in direct contact with their spiritual guides and the vast majority were still not able to unshackle themselves from the chains of, what I am going to call, 'self-referential perception'; the idea that my 'sense of self' has to be present for my consciousness to be able to conceive reality.

Instead, I am going to base our discussion on the old riddle, "How do you eat a horse?" One bite at a time. I propose that trying to perceive who I am through a 'sense of self' implies that there is one (coherent) self and that it is this assumption that *creates* 'the hard problem (of consciousness)'. In other words, what we call 'The Self' is, in fact, a conglomerate of lots of little selves and that these various selves, or what I am calling Identities, are in a state of flux, with each Identity manoeuvring in or out of our consciousness depending on internal (thought) and external (environmental) triggers (stimuli).

In short, the mind-body (hard) problem becomes easier when we stop looking *for* 'the mind' and start looking *at* the mind<u>s</u>. This is because, a single observer can experience, but it cannot 'know' that it is experiencing, unless it is able to look at itself from the outside. This is the literal meaning of the word ecstasy. Multiple identities, can, however, observe/experience each other.

[This has been amply demonstrated in 'split-brain' experiments where the corpus callosum is severed. Interestingly, Pinto et. al (2017) have concluded that "severing the cortical connections between hemispheres splits visual perception, but does not create two independent conscious perceivers within one brain."]

If you are looking for a materialistic view (a theoretical framework based on physiology) that could, perhaps, allow us to look for the 'mind' in 'the body', then I suggest that we need to start by activating each of our separate Identities and look for the neural circuits that pertain to that particular Identity. Then we can look to see whether we can find circuits that integrate these separate experiences. Whilst our individual Identities are also adaptive and idiosyncratic [idiosyncrasy being the nemesis of scientific enquiry into anything, including the mind], our 'consciousness' is what unifies those multiple perspectives and interpretations (§ 33 Atasinex Cluster) into a unified experience that imparts to us, a sense of being one entity, a whole, a 'me'.

If this section seemed somewhat deep or heavy, let me assure you that this section will become easier to understand once you have read through the book (when you see how the other pieces of the jigsaw puzzle fit together).

29.2

The Self

In § 21.1 (What is a Relationship?), I explained that in affinitology, when we talk about The Self and The Other, we are not talking about the physical side of our being. When I interact with someone, as I am doing with you right now, it is not my body that is interacting with your body, it is our minds. More specifically, it is our Identities; my *who I am* is interacting with your *who I am*.

It is clear that my Identity is embodied within a physical structure which I call my body. And yes, I need my body as a means through which the content of my mind can materialise (manifest). However, *I* am not my body, in the same way that *I* am not my leg. I can lose my leg and *I* can still be here and *I* (myself, the person, the Identity) will still be intact. Therefore, even when we touch each other, it is not our bodies that are interacting, it is our minds *through our senses*.

[This reminds me of a 2006 TED talk by Sir Ken Robinson where he says that university professors "are disembodied, you know, in a kind of literal way. They look upon their body as a form of transport for their heads." And whilst the academic in me pleads guilty to that accusation, In defence of my Omniself (§ 29.4), not all my Identities think like that.]

There are exceptions, of course. If I strongly associate who I consider to be with a part of my body, then losing that part could have an impact on my sense of Identity. For example, if my sense of Identity is intertwined with me being a dancer, then I will feel that I have lost a significant part of my *Self* if I am no longer able to dance.

It is all a matter of expression. For any given situation, I create an Identity for myself (or accept an Identity that society imbues me with (§ 39 Social Ranking Criteria) and then use my body as a means to *express* or *manifest* that Identity.

The extent to which my body affects my sense of Identity (at any given moment) is something that, to a large extent, I can choose. An anorexic person's sense of Identity and her body are inseparable [to be more specific, an 'anorexic Identity' within an anorexic person's mind is inseparable from her body (§ 29.4 The Omniself)]. Steven Hawkins, on the other hand, was able to create a sense of identity for himself that was largely independent of his body; as long as he was able to express his ideas, his identity was intact.

[Of course, I am only guessing here. If Steven Hawkins were here, he may disagree with my interpretation insofar as the separation of his body from his Identity was not a personal choice and that it is possible that he may have created a new identity for himself in which his inability to use his body became an aspect of his new Identity, but let's not read too much into what I am trying to say here. All I am saying is that, under the circumstances, he was able to separate his body from his identity such that he could function in a way that an anorexic cannot.]

The most important point that I want you to take away from all this is that,

> **in our interpersonal relationships,**
> **it is our Identities that interact with each other.**

These Identities may be tied to our physical bodies to a lesser or greater extent depending on how much we have chosen to associate our bodies with our sense of Identity [in any particular situation]. Becoming aware of this distinction between 'who I am' and 'what I am' can be very liberating. It also allows us to appreciate that, when we are talking about The Self and The Other as two components of a *Pactum* (what we used to call 'two people in a relationship'), our focus is on the meeting of Identities.

As we mature, we tend to increasingly disassociate our Identities from our physical structure. That is to say, 'who I am' becomes more important than 'what I am'.

In addition, although I have been talking about each person's Identity, we shall soon discover that each of us has multiple Identities (§ 29.4 The Omniself). In other words, depending on when and where I ask the question, "Who am I?", the feeling that I get from the answer that my mind gives me will be different. Awareness of this can be very empowering in our interpersonal relationships.

29.3
Integrity

I often tell parents that, **it is better to be respected than to be liked.**

It is easier to be liked than to be respected because respect requires integrity. Integrity means being rooted in one's Core Values (Principles) and goes hand-in-hand with robustness and self-discipline. We may disagree with other people's Principles (§ 29.4.1 Identities, Core Values and Principles and § 64.5.2 Expediencies versus Principles), but we tend to respect those who stick to them. Here is a story to demonstrate this.

> *Many years ago, one of my uncles received a large inheritance. He told his family that he felt it to be his moral duty to give away 20% of it to charity. My cousin, who was in his 20s at the time, staunchly believed that this was a mistake. After a couple of weeks of tension and arguments in the household, one day my uncle walked into the house and said, "There is no point in arguing about it anymore because it has been done; I have paid my dues." Later, my cousin said, "I disagreed with what he did, but if he had given in to our demands, he wouldn't have been my father."*

This demonstrates how we respect people who remain true to who they are, *with the proviso that they do not harm themselves or others.*

Conflict can compromise integrity. This is vitally important to understand because without integrity,

- we begin to dislike ourselves and our self-esteem suffers.
- we are not able to trust in ourselves and our self-confidence suffers.
- we find it hard to make decisions and our self-efficacy suffers.
- our behaviour becomes inconsistent and our relationships suffer.

What does integrity look like?

From the outside, integrity looks like consistency. It makes people around us feel that they know where they stand with us. We are predictable in areas that really matter and this stems from being true to our Core Values (§ 29.4.1). It logically follows from here that, in order to have integrity we must have beliefs that we consider to be 'core' or fundamental; that is, unshakable.

The previous sentence may sound like stubbornness, so let me elaborate. Integrity is not about refusing to budge (change our position or perspective), it is about needing a very strong reason to change. And when we do, we do it, not for convenience, but as a matter of principle.

Parental integrity is also an important factor that has a direct impact on the development of children's self-confidence. I intend to write more about this elsewhere [keep an eye on introducingaffinitology.com].

29.4

The Omniself

One body, many selves (Identities)

Have you ever thought to yourself, "Part of me thinks this, but another part of me thinks that?" If so, have you ever stopped to wonder what the nature these 'parts' might be? Here, I am proposing that we consider each of these 'parts' as a separate identity.

So far, our discussion has assumed that, when we talk about a 'self', we are talking about something that each person only has one of. One self, one Identity, one ego, one set of (coherent) values, expectations, etc. Fortunately, life isn't as simple as that [or perhaps unfortunately, for some of us who have yet to learn the art of enjoying its intricacies]. Let me explain.

Many years ago, I had an idea in my head about a book that I wanted to write. I haven't written it yet, but the idea keeps coming back to me. The story begins with a scene in which a young man asks a gentleman for his daughter's hand in marriage. The rest of the story revolves around what goes on inside the father's mind where there are many people, all sitting around a large oval table [The scene reminds me of Alfred Hitchcock's 'Twelve Angry Men']. *There is a philosopher, a father, a scientist, a husband, a young man, an old man, a leader, a manager, a linguist, an accountant, an artist, a warrior and others. Each of the people around the table presents his case or his opinion about what has just happened. For example, the 'father' says, "I am not going to let anyone take my little girl away. She is too young and still needs my protection". The 'philosopher' says, "It is inevitable that children will leave the nest; it is the way of the world". Meanwhile, the 'Scientist' says, "We'd better do some genetic testing to make sure that there will be no potential problems for their children". The 'husband' says, "I need to speak to my wife about this" and the 'accountant' says, "How much is this going to cost?" The conversation turns into a heated debate culminating in the father's response to the young man, only a few seconds later.*

Afterwards, I thought of an extended version of the story where each of the characters has three ego states; Parent, Adult and Child (§ 73 Transactional

Analysis). This gives us a glimpse of how amazingly complicated the inner workings of our mind can be (become).

29.4.1
Identities, Core Values and Principles

The notion of the Omniself (multiple Identities) is central to our discourse here and is a fundamental part of affinitology. It explains much about ourselves and, consequently, of the nature of our interpersonal relationships. As such, it is a concept that we shall come across frequently in our exploration of the subject here. Later, we shall look at what an Identity is and where it comes from (§ 37.7 The Emergence of Identity).

Figure 6 A graphic representation of a (unified) Omniself

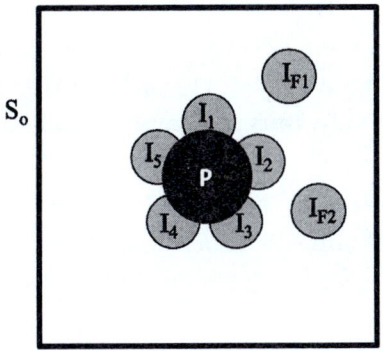

Figure 6 depicts a generalised Omniself (S_0), a container (a physical body, an individual) consisting of a single set of Core Values (the black circle, P) along with any number of situation-dependent Identities (grey circles, I_1-I_5) that share the same Core Values (Principles), but have their own sub-values (expediencies). Two 'False Identities' (Personas) are also shown (I_{F1} and I_{F2}). Personas (§ 38 Personas) do not share the same core values as 'True Identities'. They are temporary defences against potential threats to our Core Values. However, they can, sometimes, interfere with and disrupt our Core Values.

Similar to the way The Self and The Other interact with each other in interpersonal relationships, the way in which each of our various Identities interact with each other, within the same individual (Omniself), depends on the extent to which they have common perceptions in each of the situations in which they are dominant.

Some Possible Implications

I sometimes wonder how our judicial system may be transformed if we were to consider the 'criminal' to be one Identity amongst many non-criminal Identities within an individual. Or to quote Sister Helen Prejean, "People are more than the worst thing that they have done."

From this perspective, incarcerating people is like punishing an entire community for the misdemeanours and felonies of one of its members. This is similar to what we do when we pigeonhole people into demographic groups based on race, colour, creed, nationality, faith, gender, sexuality, neighbourhood and tribe. These labels and their consequent prejudices result from our perception that without such heuristics we will not be able to function adequately. I propose that it is precisely such heuristics that prevent societies from functioning adequately, thus providing the judicial system with its *raison d'être.*

I am inclined to believe that immoral Identities within an Omniself are primarily the product of unhealthy societies (§ 39 Social Ranking Criteria). I would go even further and suggest that every one of us harbours potentially criminal Identities ["Let the sinless man among you be the first to throw a stone at her." John 8:7]. I further propose that what prevents those 'antisocial' Identities within us from becoming activated/manifest is the presence of a sufficient number of other Identities (above a 'critical mass') with the prerequisite strength of character (e.g., self-esteem and self-confidence) to subdue the potentially offending Identity. The practical implication of this belief is a proposal that, rather than punishing every Identity within an Omniself for the crimes of one of its Identities, we can empower the constructive Identities within that individual to a level that makes the Omniself as a whole more personally and socially empowered.

"That all sounds great in theory Bijan, but how do you propose to do that?" I hear you ask. And I think to myself, "You see, Affinitology is already causing people to ask empowering questions." I would then say, "I would begin by referring you to the quote from Rumi's Poem ["Through compassion, the bitter becomes sweet"] that I referred to in § 38.3 (Alternatives to Personas) and its associated anecdote.

29.4.2
The Omniself versus Multiple Personality

Personalities vs Roles

We almost exclusively hear the phrase 'multiple personality' followed by the word 'disorder'. Here, I propose that multiple personality is a 'condition' and not necessarily a 'disorder'. It only becomes a disorder when the condition disrupts a person's (an Omniself's) ability to create SMERs or leads to the disruption of other SMERs. Before we explore this line of thought further, let us consider what Multiple Personality is from an affinitological perspective and how it differs from an Omniself.

Another name for Multiple Personality (disorder) is Dissociative Identity (disorder). If we consider these two terms to be interchangeable then, this implies that Personality and Identity are different words for the same concept.

From this perspective, each of us are only *supposed to have* one identity/personality and, if we have more than one, as I have postulated here, then we are all suffering from some kind of mental disorder. On the other hand, it is deemed healthy for us to play several 'roles'.

The model presented here postulates that this distinction between 'roles' and 'personalities' creates a false dichotomy, where the adoption of different 'roles' is accepted as adaptive behaviour and the adoption of different 'personalities' is considered to be maladaptive behaviour stemming from some kind of underlying 'disorder'.

To help you to further appreciate what I am trying to say here, contemplate this for a moment: If we could tell the difference between a role that someone is playing and that actor's personality, the entire film/movie industry would be jeopardised.

What is a Personality

In its most fundamental sense, personality is what personality tests measure [Actually, I have adapted that from a similar definition that I have seen regarding the definition of intelligence; "intelligence is what intelligence tests measure"]. There are, however, many problems with the way we measure personality.

Personality measures are not objective. They are based on 'self' assessment. Measuring personality relies on asking people to answer questions about how they feel about various ideas about themselves and how they think they would generally behave in some abstract situation. This means that in order to answer each question, I need to mentally create a situation and then imagine my feelings or behaviour in the context of that imagined (self-created) situation.

Depending on the conditions of the test, my mood and my experiences, I am likely to imagine different contexts for the question that I am about to answer. It may be argued that this is accounted for through the construct of test-retest validity, but I am yet to be convinced of this.

I remember, when I was studying chemistry, when we wanted to take a boiling point or a melting point, we needed to take at least three measurements and take an average. If people were as rigid as melting points and boiling points, then I would say that the whole process of evolution will have been in vain. And yet, we are quick to label people on the basis of a single test. Even if we took three tests at three different points in time, we would have reduced our belief in the variability of people's behaviours to the status of a melting point.

The validity of personality tests (inventories/assessments) is measured, not by whether or not they work in practice (ecological validity), but by whether or not they are *internally consistent*. For example, if I ask you five different questions about your feelings (or ethical stance) on theft and get similar answers each time, then I assume that those five questions really do measure your ethical stance on theft. However, as we all know, when push comes to shove, we sometimes surprise ourselves in terms of how we behave in different situations. So much for self-assessment.

You might say, "But Bijan, we cannot expect these tests to predict unusual situations (where we surprise ourselves), they are there to give us a general probability for how we are likely to behave." And I would say that that's exactly my point. Statistical probabilities are 'colligative' properties (§ 39.6 SRC are Unstable at the Individual Level). They carry the flaws of comparative judgements (§ 39 Social Ranking Criteria). In addition, we are often prone to self-deception. How can a self-assessed personality measurement determine whether or not I am deceiving myself?

Even if it is in the form of an interview, the subject is asked to tell the interviewer about themselves. Those tests that are called 'objective' refer to the objectivity of the person scoring the test and not the person (subject) doing the test. I wonder if you can see the problem with that? Let me explain.

There is a paradox that I am going to call the, 'I am a liar paradox'. If I said to you, "I am a liar" what can you deduce from that? If I am a liar, then what I have just said must be a lie, therefore, I have just lied about myself being a liar. This means that I am not a liar. If I am not a liar, then why did I just lie?

Let's see how this relates to our notion of personality in the context of personality testing. Let's assume that I have a personality disorder. If that does not affect the way that I answer the questions, then how can I be said to have a disorder? And if it does affect the way that I answer the questions, then the test itself becomes invalid because the answers are tainted by my 'disorder' and, therefore, cannot be considered to be valid answers.

- Ah Bijan, but we will know that there is something abnormal about the answers, so we will know that there is something abnormal about the person providing those answers.
- But the answers are also invalid because there is something abnormal about the person providing them.
- OK, so at least we know that there's something not right with the person, even if we cannot rely on the answers to tell us *what* is wrong.
- But, you also cannot rely on this person to tell you whether your questions are right (for him/her).
- Oh, we know that there's nothing wrong with our questions because we have calculated a mean and standard deviation and so we have a 'standardized framework'.
- What if the person who you think is abnormal is the only seeing person in a room full of blind people? Then your questions will be similarly biased towards assessing the blind as 'normal' and the seeing as abnormal.
- OK, then. We will create two sets of tests; one for the vision impaired and one for the less optically challenged.
- What if you are one of the optically challenged? How can you devise a test for those who are able to see what you cannot see?

This hypothetical dialogue points to flaws in our understanding of the concept of 'normal' (§ 71 What is Normal?).

There is plenty of evidence that even our perceptions are situation dependent [For a primer on this topic, I suggest that you begin by reading 'The Person and the Situation' by Lee Ross and Richard E. Nisbett]. Note that taking a personality test is, itself, a situation. It affects how we feel, how we perceive and, of course, by extension, how we imagine the questions and consequently respond to them.

Based on what I have proposed in this discourse, that our 'personality', or what I have preferred to refer to as Identity, changes (adapts) depending on the situation, then, under the conditions that personality tests are administered, at best, an introspective personality is active and, at worst, our 'questionnaire filling' Identity is at work. This will make more sense as we near the completion of this course, that is, when we begin to see the different parts of the jigsaw from the perspective of a unified whole.

In essence, if we use such tests to assess mental health, we are using what a person says about themselves as a means of determining whether or not she is mentally 'stable'. A further problem is that,

> **We do** [should] **not want people to be 'mentally stable',
> we want people to be mentally 'adaptive'.**

My proposal for circumventing this is to suggest that a 'healthy' individual has a single set of Core Values (Principles), along with a set of associated 'true' Identities [as in being 'true' to the Omniself's Core Values]. However, sometimes, we find ourselves in situations where sticking to our 'usual' Principles would be maladaptive (disempowering/dangerous). In this case, we need to create a separate set of Principles for those situations. It is the existence of more than one set of Core Values within a single Omniself that can become unhealthy (a disorder). Even then, what makes this unhealthy is that it can be socially disruptive and it is the repercussions of that social disruption that has unhealthy consequences for the Individual and not the 'split' set of Core Values *per se*.

You may be wondering, "But Bijan, why not simply expand our current set of 'Core Principles'?" And I would thank you for that observation and say, "Because, sometimes, the situation creates a fundamental (uncompromisable) conflict between two sets of our essential values [it becomes essential that I believe one thing in one situation and something else in another situation]." We resolve the conflict by creating two sets of Principles and it is this that causes an individual to 'split' into two or more separate 'people' [Dr Jekyll and Mr Hyde, etc.]. Clearly, such conflict would need to be intense [and perhaps even unbearable for the individual concerned].

> **"The occurrence of dissociative symptoms in the wake of a traumatic experience has been a topic in the scientific literature for more than a century."**
>
> - Armour et. al. (2014)

[Source: Armour, C., Karstoft, K. I., & Richardson, J. D. (2014). The co-occurrence of PTSD and dissociation: Differentiating severe PTSD from dissociative-PTSD. Social Psychiatry and Psychiatric Epidemiology, 49(8), 1297-1306.]

Borrowing some jargon from the field of Management in general, and Strategic Planning in particular, may help us appreciate these concepts more easily. I propose that our 'Core Values' or 'Principles' guide and inform our lives' *missions* and *strategies* [and ultimately, our lives' trajectories and our 'destinies']. Our Identities are responsible for developing *policies* and *procedures* that allow us to navigate through (adapt to the constraints of) the real world. In doing so, these *executives* recognise that different situations call for different approaches (presumptions) and behaviours (including improvisations).

Character vs Personality

In his highly influential book, The Seven Habits of Highly Effective People, Stephen Covey makes a distinction between what he calls the 'character ethic' and the 'personality ethic'. Adapting this distinction to our model here, we can say that our Principles underpin our character and determine our mission and strategies whilst our Personality is made up of our policies and procedures.

Here, I define an Identity as 'the sum total of everything that we identify with in *a particular situation*' (§ 37.3 Is Identity Definable?). Now, if in a particular situation, I identify with what I am supposed to *do*, then that Identity's actions will be driven by Covey's Personality Ethic. If, on the other hand, in that particular situation, I identify with who I am supposed to *be* (what is congruent with my Principles and my mission), then my Identity, at that moment, will be driven by Stephen Covey's character ethic. Notice the similarity between this and what Erich Fromm calls the *being mode* and *having mode* of existence (§ 16 To Have or to Be). In one case, my decisions and actions are driven by 'who I am' and in the other case, by 'what I should be doing' in that particular situation. From this perspective, multiple Identities (or personalities) become **normal and adaptive responses**, there being no need to label them as disorders. The problem arises (disorders arise) when our Core splits so that we begin to house two or more Characters with separate missions and strategies within the same psyche or Omniself.

Figure 7 is an extension of Figure 6 depicting an Omniself with three conflicting Characters (sets of principles; P1, P2 and P3) each with its own set of associated Identities. It shows how, for the Core Values to split, and for multiple personalities to emerge within an individual, different sets of Identities would need to cluster around different sets of Principles. Just like the Parent, Adult, Child scenario in Transactional Analysis (§ 73), I would not be surprised if we found overlaps and interactions across all the boundaries shown.

Figure 7 A graphic representation of a split Omniself

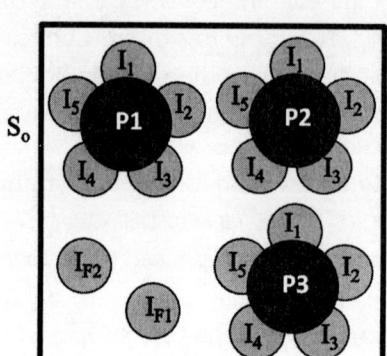

Introducing the term Personette

I propose the term Personette to describe a set of Principles along with its associated Identities. Adopting this terminology, Dr Jekyll and Mr Hyde, each become a different Personette. Figure 7 shows an individual who has split into three personettes, along with two false Identities (§ 38 Personas).

I propose [and shall discuss in greater detail in my future writings] that our psyche only concerns itself with reality insofar as it pertains to survival. At all other times, its primary focus is on the avoidance of inner conflict. In other words,

---

Everything that we do beyond survival, we do to avoid inner conflict.

[In § 72, decision-Making, I describe decision-making as a process of conflict resolution. This links the idea of personality, character, Identity, values and conflicts to decision-making. And these are just some of the parts. The whole is much more than the sum of its parts.]

Ideally, we can resolve our inner conflicts within the boundaries of a single set of Core Values or Principles. However, if our core values become conflicted with each other, we split our psyche into two or more separate Personettes; each Personette being triggered by some aspect of the environment.

Imagine a scenario where an Individual has two sets of Core Values, one based on the belief that theft is immoral and another on the belief that life is transient and has no meaning and, therefore, hedonism is the best way to make the most of life. For as long as these two Core Values are not in conflict with each other, one Character (set of Principles and associated beliefs, values and expectations) will suffice. However, if at some point, I discover that I derive a highly pleasurable thrill from stealing [or as Eric Berne may put it, playing the game of "Catch me if you can"], then I will experience an inner conflict between two of my Principles, not stealing and hedonism. Such splitting of a unified Omniself into two Personettes may be *triggered* by, for example, the Omniself (Individual) walking into a shop. At this point, a conflict arises between one set of Core Values (the Honest Person) and another set of Principles (the Hedonist). In such a situation, instead of *suppressing* the ethical (stealing is wrong) Core Value, the individual *steps out* of (dissociates from) that Personette and *into* the Hedonist Personette, thereby *avoiding* the need to resolve any conflict [avoidance is a psychological Defence mechanism (§ 79)].

From this perspective, the difference between Dr Jekyll and Mr Hyde is not that they have different personalities/Identities (policies and procedures), it is that they have different Personettes (principles, missions and strategies), divided by their conflicting Core Values and creating two distinct 'character ethics' within a single Individual (Omniself).

29.5
The Other

Earlier, I said that a relationship consists of three components, The Self, The Other and The Nexus. In the last section, we focused on The Self.

> **Everything that we have already discussed in the section on The Self also applies to The Other.**

Relationships are only made possible where there is mutual allure. There is no point in one party trying unless the other party is also willing (or at least has the potential to be willing). We can do everything in our power to facilitate a relationship. However, as Hafiz, the 14th century Persian mystic says,

> **"What does trying avail if there is no allurement from that [other] side."**
>
> From 'The Collected Lyrics of Hafiz of Shiraz', translated by Peter Avery

Just like The Self, The Other also has a host of potentially conflicting factors within him/her. At a minimum, we need to be aware of the potential existence of these conflicts; not to expose or exploit them (lest the same be done unto us, so to speak), but to buffer the relationship against any strains (Unit 97: Pressure, Stress and Strain) that The Other's Identities and their associated conflicts may put on The Nexus.

29.6
Aspects of The Self

There are many words that refer to different aspects of what we might call the Self. These include personality, character, ego, self-esteem, self-confidence, self-efficacy, self-concept, temperament and identity. When we are focused on any of these aspects of the self, we are not looking at the building, or even the wall that is it a part of, but at bricks in a wall [there is nothing inherently disempowering in that. In fact, in some situations, it is necessary. Just like a knife (§ 13 Language as a Tool), it is not the concept that is the issue, it is where, when and how it is applied]. This reminds me of the adage, "can't see the wood for the trees". I suggest that, when we are being reductionist in our approach; looking for the self by focusing on different aspects of the Individual, we are looking at the trees and not the wood.

Although, in this course, we encounter some of these different aspects of the self, our primary concern will be with Identity. I propose that each of our Identities [evoked by different situations] has its own personality, ego, self-esteem, self-confidence, self-efficacy, self-concept and so on - although we expect to see less variation in these constructs within each Individual because the Identities originate from the same Core Values.

In § 17.1 (Relevance of Chemical Nomenclature to Affinitology), I mentioned that even identical twins are not identical because, each of them, when looking at the other, is seeing their twin in a different context (e.g., background) and, therefore, experiences the other differently. Similarly, each of our Identities does not have exactly the same experiences as the other Identities residing within that individual because, in different situations, different Identities, having different values, are sensitive to, and therefore pay attention to, different aspects of the environment.

When my children were young, I made up a story to demonstrate the differences in the effects of optimism and pessimism on our attitudes (§ 65 Attitudes). Although the story is more about what we pay attention to and how we interpret what we focus on (§ 33 Atasinex Cluster), I will tell you part of it here because it helps us to see how different Identities (whether inside the same individual or in different individuals) can be in the same situation, but experiences that situation differently (§ 14.3 Situation vs Circumstance).

> Eric and Florence were two brothers, but they were very different. Eric was grumpy most of the time whilst Florence was mostly cheerful. One day, Eric said to Florence,
> "Why are you so cheerful? Can't you see it's raining?" and Florence said,
> "Yes, that is why I'm happy. It's because the plants are getting the water they need to grow."
> "But, it's too wet to go out." Said Eric.
> "Isn't it wonderful?" Said Florence. "I can try out my new raincoat."
> The next day the sun was shining but again Eric was grumpy.
> "Why are you so unhappy?" Asked Florence.
> "You shouldn't be so happy either." said Eric. "Can't you see that your precious plants aren't getting any water to grow? And you are not getting a chance to wear your new raincoat."
> "Isn't it wonderful?" Said Florence. "Yesterday, the plants got the water they needed and today they're getting the sunshine that they need to grow. And, I get to try on my new sun hat."

The point here is that, in any given situation, each of our Identities devotes attention to different aspects of the environment and will, therefore, experience it differently.

Chapter 30
The Other, The Nexus, the Pactum and The Bondle

30.1
The Nexus

Earlier (§ 14 What's in a Word), I talked about the importance of words and used a 'table' as a metaphor for interpersonal relationships. I said that relationships can be looked at from a functional or descriptive perspective. Probably no one appreciates a table more than a professional and competent table designer. The designer needs to be able to look at a table from many different perspectives. For example, she needs to

- Know ergonomics (even though she may not think of it as such) because the table must not be too high, too low, too sharp, etc.

- Know something about material science, that is, what a table can be made of, what the relative merits of each material are, taking into account aesthetics, durability, cost, ease of manipulation, etc.

- Know economics, accounting and marketing to be able to ascertain the cost of production in relation to who will buy at what price.

- Know management (or, at least, have some organisational skills).

- Have technical knowledge so as to know when and where a bevel, a screw, a nail, glue, a rivet, a dove-tailed joint, etc. can and should be used.

- Have analytical skills to be able to ascertain what worked and what didn't and why, as well as what sells well and what doesn't and why.

- Have some understanding of physics and forces otherwise the table might crack easily or topple over.

- Have some understanding of sociology and of interior design so as to be able to answer the question, "Which demographic group am I making this table for and what is the ambiance of the overall space that this table is going to occupy?"

All that for a 'simple' table that we take so much for granted. Now, compare that with the relative complexity of our interpersonal relationships. What factors do we take into consideration when it comes to what is, undoubtedly [I, at least, don't doubt it :-)], the most important aspect of our lives? Just as crucially, what important aspects of the relationship do we fail to notice and pass over?

Despite the multiplicity and complexity of the factors that need to be considered in the design of a functional and reliable table, this is miniscule when compared with the much wider set of factors, within a broader range of dimensions that we need to consider if we are to create simply functional, let alone extraordinary, relationships. These include emotional, spiritual, social, financial, physical, sexual and ecological dimensions (Unit 11: Dimensions of Human Experience).

Without a connection, there is no relationship. Just as, without a means of joining a slab to its legs, there can be no table. The quality of any relationship is the quality of the connection. I call this The Third Entity or The Nexus to draw our attention away from the individual parties involved. That is because *the relationship is the connection* not the individuals, just as a table is the *relationship* between the slab and four stumps and not a slab and a pile of stumps.

30.1.1

Sustained Attention

The most important factor that determines whether or not a relationship becomes more stable or less stable is the extent to which the involved parties *consciously* focus on, and pay *sustained attention* to, The Nexus (the thing that makes them more than the sum of their individual parts). To do that, we need to understand ourselves. In doing so, we need to become independent of, let's call it, *the social noise*, that can interfere with being a part of the process of SMER creation (Unit 12: Embryology of Relationships). We also need to know what relationships can do *to* us (not just *for* us) and what we can do *with* relationships as well as *for* relationships. Later (Unit 22: Thermodynamics of Relationships), I propose that, in interpersonal relationships, attention is the equivalent to the direction component of a force field in physical systems.

Relationships exist in a state of dynamic equilibrium (§ 58.2 Good Vibrations). To maintain the stability of this equilibrium, active attention is required. This is comparable with active transport and passive transport across cell membranes. Passive transport (diffusion or osmosis) is where simply being in the right place at the right time is enough for something to happen [This reminds me of the 1979 movie, 'Being There', starring Peter Sellers and Shirley MacLaine]. Active transport, on the other hand, involves choice (§ 35.11 Consciousness). That is, the cell 'chooses' to (actively draws into itself) a substance that it 'wants'.

30.1.2
Trust and Reliance

The word trust is defined in terms of reliance. This means that if we don't need to rely on someone, trust becomes irrelevant. The logical conclusion here would be that,

---

The more self-reliant (independent) we become, the less we need to concern ourselves with the issue of trust.

Some of you may be thinking that this would be great because becoming independent of other people would mean needing fewer interpersonal relationships and, by extension, fewer visits to therapists and spending less on books and courses about relationships. "Not so fast" I would say because it would also move us into the realm of psychosis. Excessive detachment from other people (whether by choice or through a combination of social and genetic factors) is the hallmark of psychosis. On the other hand, if we become too dependent on others, we move in the opposite direction; neurosis. In other words, neurosis and psychosis lie at two extremes of the same (dependence-independence) continuum.

[Notice that the above paragraph implies that there is an overlap between attachment and dependence. I have made this point explicitly in § 42.3 (Identity, Attachment and Dependence)]

We are social (interdependent) animals and interpersonal relationships are as important to us as the air that we breathe. And, as I have just indicated, trust is an integral part of this aspect of 'the human condition'. We discuss trust in more detail in § 53.

30.2
The Pactum

Figure 8 shows two circles, each representing an Identity. Although strictly speaking, these two Identities can be from within a single Individual (Omniself), such as my Father Identity and my Husband Identity, for the purposes of our discussion here, I shall be assuming that these are two Identities from two separate individuals.

Figure 8 A diagramatic representation of The Pactum

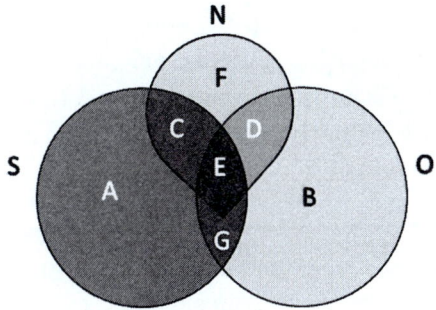

When two Identities interact, a Third Entity, a Nexus (the piriform region in the diagram) is created. The superimposition of that Third Entity on the two Identities, S and O, creates seven potential new regions [You could argue that, strictly, only five 'new' regions are created since regions A and B are those aspects of each of the original Identities that are unaffected by the Nexus. However, I would argue that the original identities are no longer the same because a part of them has been 'chewed off' (influenced/commandeered by) by the Nexus]. We shall return to the Pactum in § 56.1 (Fertilisation) where we shall explore Figure 8 in more detail.

30.2.1
A few words about sacrifice

If at any point within this course, you get the impression that The Self needs to be sacrificed for the sake of the relationship, then some clarification is probably in order. Forming a relationship, or becoming part of a team, is not about sacrificing our selves or our egos. It is about reframing our Identity to be part of something more; in the sense that 'the whole is *more* than the sum of its parts'. Coming back to our table metaphor, a rectangular or circular prism doesn't lose its Identity when it becomes a table leg, it gains an *additional* Identity as part of something bigger, a table. This means that if you think that you are making sacrifices because of a relationship, you need to reframe your Identity (when it is operating within the parameters of a given 'relationship') as being different from the Identity that is independent of that relationship. Alternatively, you can consider your new Identity (as part of the Pactum) as being enhanced (more valuable) than your Identity as an individual. In this context let us ponder the words of the 13th Century Persian mystic, Rumi, who said,

> **"A drop is the ocean for as long as it is with the ocean,
> otherwise, the drop is a drop and the ocean is an ocean."**

[Actually, it sounds much more eloquent in the original Persian; it loses something in translation (c'est la vie). Also this quotation may appear to be in conflict with some of what we discussed in (§ 39 Social Ranking Criteria). However, the main point of that section was to highlight the flaws in Social Ranking Criteria. SMERs (healthy Pacta), on the other hand, do not suffer from those inherent flaws.]

Returning to the table metaphor, just as we need some kind of design (so that we don't put the legs in a dysfunctional place), we also need to have a design plan for each of our relationships before we can decide whether to acquire the affinitological equivalent of glue, bevels, tacks, dove-tailed joints, nails, screws, hinges or some other creative means of attaching the legs to the top. In human relationships, *creative* is the operative word. This is the *art of relationships*. We explore the art of relationships in more detail in § 18 (Art or Science).

30.3
The Bondle

I introduced the concept of the Bondle in § 22.4. A Bondle is a connection between two Omniselves through one or more Pacta. Figure 9 demonstrates this concept. It shows a relationship between two people (Omniselves). The depicted relationship (Pactum) consists of The Self's I_2 (e.g., Father) Identity and The Other's I'_2 (e.g., Child) Identity from which the Nexus R [for relationship] emerges. Like the respective inhabitants of two mobile homes, all the other Identities within each of the Omniselves become physically bound to each other through this relationship. Therefore, if R happens to be a Father-Child Nexus and I_5 is a Recluse Identity that tries to avoid getting 'caught up' in a Pactum, then I_5 cannot retreat to a monastery when this Nexus is activated.

Figure 9 The Bondle

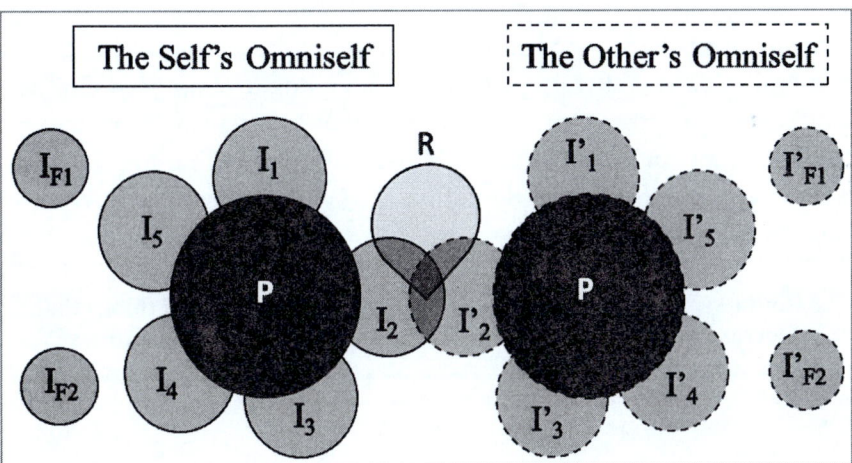

Chapter 31

Symbiosis

[After I wrote this section, I debated with myself whether or not to include it in this book. The problem is that, through this discourse, I want to highlight the importance of the relationship itself; the Nexus. When you read this section, you might notice that the 'symbiosis' perspective reduces the Nexus to a mere tool, rather than a 'living' and adaptive entity **(see also § 36.9 Holons)**. I decided to leave it in with a view to it being a seed for future development of ideas. You see, since we are looking at the Nexus as a separate entity from The Self and The Other, we can extend our exploration to include the idea that there is a relationship between, for example, The Self and The Nexus, as a separate entity from The Other and that The Self can have a separate relationship with the Nexus, independently from The Other (see Zone C in Figure 30 - § 56.3 Differentiation and Gestation). For example, I can think of 'my marriage' and what 'my marriage' means to me and what I can do to improve 'my marriage' and how much 'my marriage' is costing/benefiting me and so on.]

31.1
The Concept of Symbiosis

Symbiosis literally means 'living together'. In biology, the term is used for when one or both of two organisms (from different species) do things that increase the chances of survival of one or both of them. Since I think this is a very useful concept and worth usurping, I am going to adapt its definition for affinitological purposes and replace the word 'organism' for the word 'Identity' and the concept of 'living together' with 'interacting with each other'. This leads to the following definition of symbiosis where interpersonal relationships are concerned.

Affinito-symbiosis is when one or both of two Identities do things that increase the chances of survival of one or both of those Identities*

[* Notice that here, we have gone backwards a little in that, we are back to saying, "It's about you and me baby", which, as I mentioned in § 1.4, creates a blind spot].

And since, every interaction has a consequence that ultimately affects the survival of each of its constituent Identities in some way, every Pactum can be considered to be a form of symbiotic relationship.

From a symbiosis perspective, the Nexus is a means of exchange or a portal. This point of view detracts our focus from the emergent property of the relationship and onto 'who gets what'. I am going to invent another new word here and say that, where interpersonal relationships are concerned, the symbiotic perspective is 'counter-holistic'.

> **In contrast to reductionism, which takes what is already whole and breaks it into smaller pieces, the counter-holistic approach prevents the perception of the whole by creating or highlighting (overemphasizing) boundaries.**

Symbiosis is also related to Game Theory. If one becomes too engrossed in these theories, one runs the risk of seeing all interpersonal relationships as no more than 'survival strategies'. That is, a means to an end, rather than an end in themselves [For an insight into my own perspective on this, see § 6-11 The Journey]. It is also reminiscent of the 'social exchange theory' of interpersonal relationships (§ 21.2 Identity and Vocabulary).

31.2
Types of Symbiosis

Symbiosis can be categorised into six types as shown in Table 1.

Table 1 The six types of symbiosis

		The Self		
		Benefits	**No effect**	**Is harmed**
	Benefits	Mutualism	Commensalism	Parasitism
The Other	**No effect**	Commensalism	Neutralism	Amensalism
	Is harmed	Parasitism	Amensalism	Competition

Note that, [as I have often pointed out in this course, and contrary to the way in which they are labelled and presented,] these relationships are not binary. They lie on a spectrum. In other words, whilst the overall impact of the relationship on one party may be harm or neutral, it does not mean that no benefit was imparted by the relationship. In addition, since relationships are abstract, the relative harm and benefit is often not easy to judge; what appears to be a benefit may lead to harm in the long run and vice versa.

31.2.1
Mutualistic (Win-Win) and Parasitic (Win-Lose) Relationships

In a mutualistic relationship, both parties (identities) 'benefit' from the relationship. These benefits may be along different dimensions of human experience (Unit 11). For example, the benefit may be sexual satisfaction for one and financial security for the other.

In a parasitic relationship, one party benefits whilst the other party is harmed. Hopefully, in interpersonal relationships, The Self and The Other each have a higher level of consciousness (§ 35.11) than viruses and leeches. See also § 40.2 (Behaviourism versus Humanism). Therefore, I anticipate that a truly parasitic relationship will only ensue when the parasite uses either force or deception. We explore these concepts further in the context of goals in § 66.2 (Dimensions of goals).

31.2.2
Competitive Relationships (Lose-Lose)

In biology, competition is *an interaction between organisms or species in which, on the whole, both of the organisms are harmed*. This is contrary to much of what we are led to believe by society (§ 39 Social Ranking Criteria).

Many years ago, in a brief conversation in a corridor at the Institute of Education (UCL), a colleague said, "I do not subscribe to the philanthropic model of social justice." Even though the interaction was very brief, it planted a seed that has had a profound effect on my perception of social structures. Writing this section reminded me of that.

Recently, a friend referred to me as a 'socialist'. In context, he meant that I am not adept at [perhaps it would be more accurate to say, inclined to] adapting to a capitalist society. There was a time when I used to think of capitalism as a viable social framework if it were based on 'perfect competition' and that the problems we face within capitalist societies is a reflection of the abuse of the system through the creation of non-competitive advantages, such as through monopolies and cartels. Gradually, I veered away from this point of view because I realised that even in 'perfect competition', the focus is on *division* of resources rather than on their mutual utilisation. The consequence is massive waste leading to social atrophy. At one point, I remembered the mathematical concept of Limit Theory and when I applied it to the notion of capitalism, I astonished even myself. Let me show you why.

Within a capitalist framework, the success of any organisation is measured by the extent to which it can maximise income (what it takes) and minimise expenditure (what it gives).

In absolute terms, we can express this as, **Income = Revenue - Expenditure**

And in relative terms as, **Efficiency = (Revenue-Expenditure)/Expenditure**

From a capitalist perspective, therefore, the most successful organisation is one that can take without giving. Taking this to its ultimate conclusion, the best possible scenario for a pure capitalist (the most successful organisation within a capitalist framework) would be one that can **take everything and give nothing**. And since this capitalist 'best case scenario' does not make me feel optimistic about the future of humanity, I am inclined towards seeking a more promising framework.

31.2.3
Other Types of Symbiotic Relationship

Commensalistic Relationships (Win-neutral)

Since emotions play a central role in relationships (§ 51.3.2 Feelings Trump Logic), it is difficult to contemplate a situation where the consequence of an interaction for one of the parties is neutral. For example, even when someone pays money to a beggar, he or she does it because there is some level of emotional satisfaction in doing so. [Therefore, for us to be able to contemplate commensalistic relationships, I suggest that we change our understanding of the word 'neutral' by thinking of it as meaning 'negligible'.]

Neutralistic Relationships (Draw)

Can we really call it an interaction if neither party is affected by it? The alternative is to consider there to have been no 'net' effect. This would presumably be a situation where the advantages of the relationship outweigh the disadvantages to an equal extent. I contend that there is a fundamental flaw in this kind of argument. I explain this in § 19 (Quantity vs Quality).

Amensalistic Relationships (Neutral-Lose)

As conscious beings, we tend to ignore those things we do not perceive as having any effect on us and avoid things (including relationships) that can potentially harm us. Therefore, the only time that I can conceive that we would intentionally enter into an amensalistic relationship is when we expected a payoff that did not transpire. In other words, this kind of relationship is *post hoc*.

We return to symbiosis in Unit 17 (Pharmacology of Relationships) and Unit 18 (Immunology of Relationships).

31.3

Beyond Symbiosis

A misleading implication in the six categories of symbiosis described above is that neither party is fundamentally changed by the relationship.

Let us assume that two organisms are living independently of each other. At some point, one organism begins to leech (beg or steal) from the other. It is apparent that, the more the parasitic organism adapts to this way of life, the more dependent it will become on its host. After a while, it will not be able to live independently from the host.

The organism has not merely taken from the host,
it has been transformed by it.

The organism is now, qualitatively, a different kind of organism because, not only is it no longer independent, it is limited in how it can evolve.

We can apply a similar line of reasoning to mutualistic relationships. In what I have called a SMER (§ 2.1), the emergent entity (§ 22.2 The Nexus) leads to the creation of a new organism, the Pactum (§ 22.3) whereby, the creation of two independent, but cooperating organisms leads to greater potential for adaptation and evolution. What I am saying is that healthy relationships lead to the emergence of, not only the Nexus, but also of a *superorganism*. We have seen this happen when prokaryotic cells became eukaryotic cells. This provided them with the potential to create animals and plants. Similarly, in the absence of competition, individuals form groups and groups form communities and communities form societies (§ 36 Levels of organisation), each an organism in itself; just as a mitochondrion is an organism within a cell; an organism within an organism (§ 36.9 Holons).

Chapter 32

Extended Relationships, Communities and Beyond (The Superself)

32.1
Overview

The pivotal notion throughout this discourse is the idea that three components are needed for any kind of relationship to exist: The Self, The Other and The Nexus. A question that may arise is, "How does this paradigm work for teams and communities?" Since we are looking at relationships from the point of view of individual connections, our relationship with groups can take one of two forms; we can ask,

a) "What is (or can be) my unique connection with each and every member (Identity) within the team?"

   or

b) "What is (or can be) my unique connection with the Identity of this collective?"

In this section, we explore how we can treat a community as a single organism, what I have called a Superself, having its own unique Identity (The Collective Identity). Using our chemical bond analogy (§ 25 Relationships as Chemical Bonds), each member of the team is like an atom in a molecule. A potential new member is like a 'substrate'. From this perspective, each team is held together by individual bonds between individual Identities and each molecule will then exhibit qualities that are unique to that combination of atoms. It also means that the addition of each new member can, initially, partially disrupt the overall functionality of the team before a new Collective Identity, incorporating the new member, is formed. This is because some bonds will need to 'loosen' to make room for the new member. In chemistry, even when the reaction is exothermic, this first step in the reaction is endothermic; it requires the input of energy (resources) to break existing bonds and leads to initial instability in the molecule. This is akin to the storming stage of the four stages that we discuss in § 59.1 (Stages of Relationship Development).

Like group 1 and group 7 elements, some Identities can only form one bond; the Husband Identity in a monogamous society, for example, whilst others such as the Business Partner Identity, are more like the transition metals which have multiple valences.

Notice that, from this perspective, just like a molecule, the 'team' or 'society' is built through one-to-one bonds that extend to become one-to-many and many-to-one relationships (§ 58.2 Good Vibrations).

32.2

Communities

When more than two Omniselves (§ 29.4 The Omniself) connect through a set of common beliefs (reinforced through rituals), they form a new social entity, a community, such as families, teams, organisations, support groups, action groups, nations and crowds. Such communities are united by (created through) common sets of beliefs and Core Values.

[If you are interested in the last category and want to know how, under certain circumstances, individual Identities give way to crowd mentality, becoming 'zombified' in the process, I suggest that you begin with a book called 'The Crowd - A Study of the Popular Mind' by Gustave Le Bon (1896). According to Wikipedia, Hitler, Mussolini, Lenin and Freud were amongst the people who were influenced by this book.]

> **A community that emerges (through a culture) becomes an entity
> that has different characteristics, and dynamics,
> from the individuals that comprise it.**

A few years ago, I was at a gathering of minds, where one of the academics at the University of London was talking about her research. She was looking into why soldiers stationed in foreign countries were more likely to commit sex crimes, especially against the indigenous population. She and her team were trying to understand and explain these observations through the lens of Individual Psychology, but the results did not seem to make sense. I suggested that she was looking in the wrong direction. I mentioned Gustave Le Bon's 'The Crowd' and suggested that the reason the data cannot be explained with reference to the theories that govern Individual Psychology is that institutional behaviour (of the type that she was investigating) is governed by different rules.

Here, I propose that, when a part of us (one of our Identities) becomes attached to a set of Core Values or Principles that The Omniself perceives to be bigger, stronger or otherwise, more valuable than The Omniself, it surrenders its 'will' to the perceived 'higher purpose', *in a particular situation.* I cannot overemphasise the importance of the situation because,

---

Meaning is created through context

One of the practical consequences of looking at a community in this way is that a community can be regarded as a new Superself. Like an Omniself, a Superself is made up of its own set of Core Values along with a set of associated 'Collective' Identities to which special 'Allied' (community-induced) Identities within Omniselves are attached. This is depicted in figure 10.

[Originally, I called the Superself, the MegaSelf on the basis that a community is 'bigger' than the individual. On reflection, however, I decided that the word Super, meaning 'above' fits better because, although becoming part of a community is becoming a part of something bigger, the most salient aspect of this is the idea that we lose our 'selves' within that community; we rise 'above' our individuality. Or to put it another way, "The needs of the many outweigh the needs of the few... or the one." (Thank you, Mr. Spock :-)]

This tendency in us to seek to become a part of something bigger is facilitated by our seemingly innate, instinctive or primeval need to be tribal. This is borne out by research that has led to what has come to be known as the 'minimal group paradigm' (I encourage you to look it up).

So far, our discussion has centred around two identities that can form a potential relationship (lead to the emergence of a Nexus), The Self and The Other. The Superself is like a fractal (§ 90) derivative of the Omniself. Like an Omniself, a community (Superself) has its own set of Core Values along with a potential for a multiplicity of Identities (§ 64.6 Principles and Expediencies). Each of these Identities also have the potential to create a Pactum.

Figure 10 The Superself as a Fractal Derivative of the Omniself

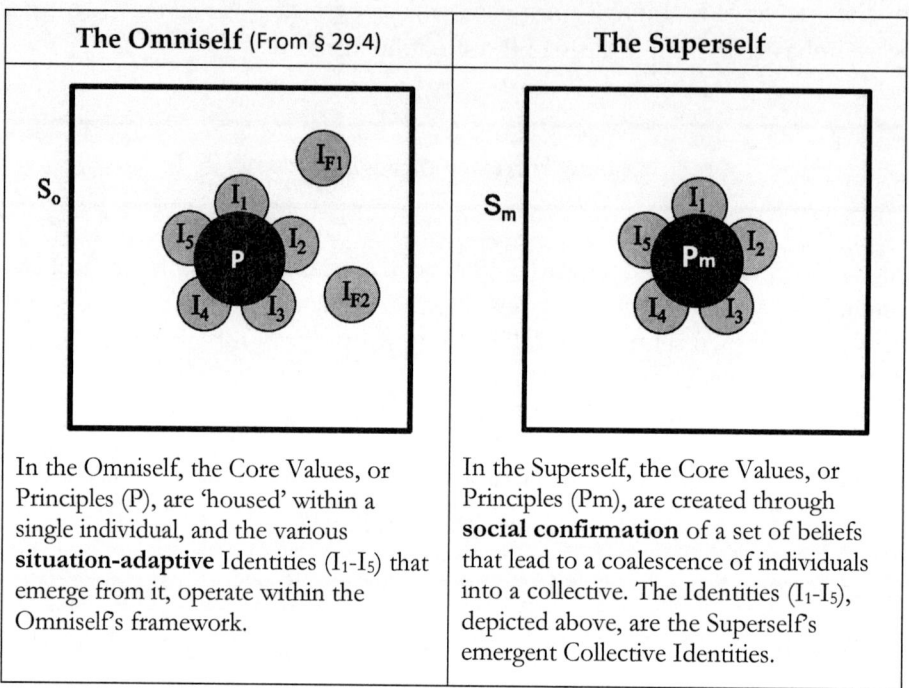

The Omniself (From § 29.4)	The Superself
In the Omniself, the Core Values, or Principles (P), are 'housed' within a single individual, and the various **situation-adaptive** Identities (I_1-I_5) that emerge from it, operate within the Omniself's framework.	In the Superself, the Core Values, or Principles (Pm), are created through **social confirmation** of a set of beliefs that lead to a coalescence of individuals into a collective. The Identities (I_1-I_5), depicted above, are the Superself's emergent Collective Identities.

When an Allied Identity within an Omniself is activated and forms a relationship with a Collective Identity within the Superself, that Allied Identity adopts the Core Values of the collective in addition to its own. That creates a 'Superbondle' (§ 22.4 The Bondle) as depicted in Figure 11.

[* Each Identity is specific to a particular collective (and situation). For example, my Chess-Club-Member Identity would be different from my Neighbourhood-Association-Member Identity.]

In Figure 10, I_2 represents an Allied Identity attached to the Omniself's Core Values in a relationship with a Collective Identity (I'_2) attached to the Superself's Core Values.

Figure 11 The Superbondle

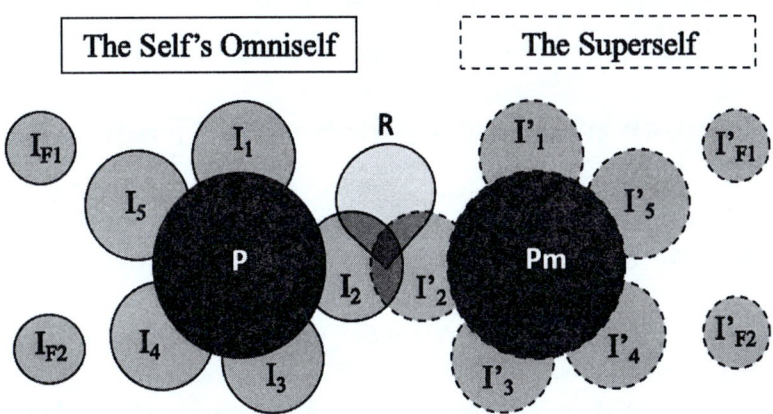

P = Omniself's Principles (Core Values) | Pm = Superself's Principles (Core Values)

Notice that, like an Omniself, a community; a Superself, has a set of Core Values with which multiple Identities are associated. For example, I remember that the character of my school, being a boarding school, was generally quite introverted. Most of the time, we were not really too concerned about what was going on outside the walls of the school. However, the character of the school became decidedly exhibitionist on Open Day, when parents and potential parents were going to visit, and we all wanted to make a good impression. In other words, 'the school' had a Routine Identity (introvert) and an Open Day Identity (extravert).

We can now say that, an Individual can either relate to [enter into a relationship with] another Identity within an Omniself, or (through an Allied Identity) to a Collective Identity that is bound to the Core Values of a Superself. The presence of a Superself creates four different categories of Identity:

1. Unallied Self (Su)
2. Allied Self (Sa)
3. Unallied Other (Ou)
4. Allied Other (Oa)

Here, the word allied means 'emotionally attached to the Core Values of the community' (§ 51.3.2 Feelings Trump Logic) meaning that an Identity within an Omniself has chosen to bond with (become a part of) the collective. This leads to a potential for the creation of four basic types of community-related Pactum, as described below [I say 'basic' because it can, of course, get more complicated, such as when we make distinctions between the individual within a community as an individual, as a member of the community, as a representative of the community, etc., but let's keep it simple for now].

32.3
Types of Community-Related Pactum

In Figure 12, I have depicted and described four different types of community-related Pactum.

Type 1 (Su-Ou) represents the standard Self-Other relationship. It is where the Identities in the relationship are not affected by the presence of the Community Identity (the Superself). "My relationship with you is independent of our relationships with the community that one of our Omniself's other Identities is associated with."

In Type 2 (Su-Oa), The Self's relationship with The Other is contingent upon The Other's relationship with the community (through The Other's Omniself). Here, the Self's interest in The Other is because of his association with the Collective, "I am connected to you because of your membership of this community." In this case, The Self ceases to Identify with The Other if he breaks his Bond with the Community. [The two Individuals/Omniselves can, however, create other Relationship Frameworks (§ 92) through their other Identities (§ 58.3 Multi-Nexus Relationships)]. Alternatively, changing the direction of the association [which cannot be shown through a Venn diagram) The Self may be connected to the Superself because The Other is attached to it, even though The Self is not. We can think of this as community membership by proxy. In practice, this means that The Self ceases to identify with the community in situations that do not involve The Other.

Type 3 (Sa-Ou) is the counterpart to Type 2, where The Self is attached to the Superself and The Other is not.

In Type 4 (Sa-Oa), the relationship between The Self and The Other is contingent upon both of them being a member of the community. If one Identity ceases to Identify with that community, this particular Nexus between the two Omniselves disbands.

Figure 12 Types of community-related Pactum

Type 1 (Su-Ou)	Type 2 (Su-Oa)
The Self's relationship with The Other is not contingent upon any other relationship that the Other has: *"my association with this community is only because of my connection to you."*	The Self's relationship with The Other is contingent upon The Other being a member of the community: *"I am connected to you only because of what the community means to me."*
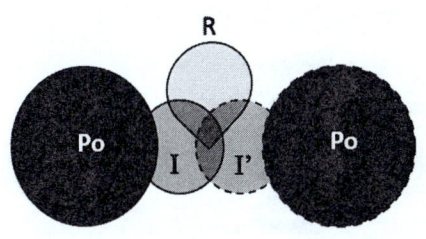	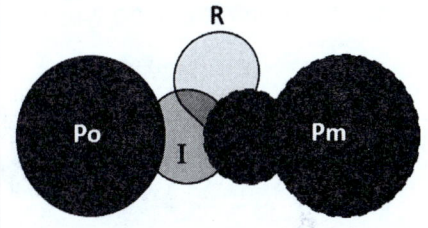
Type 3 (Sa-Ou)	Type 4 (Sa-Oa)
The Other's relationship with The Self is contingent upon The Self being a part of the community.	The Self's relationship with The Other is contingent upon both being a part of the community.
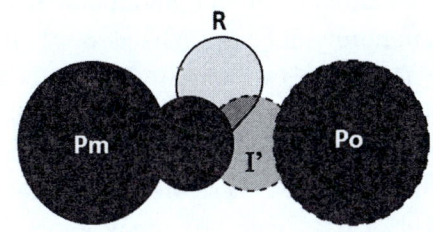	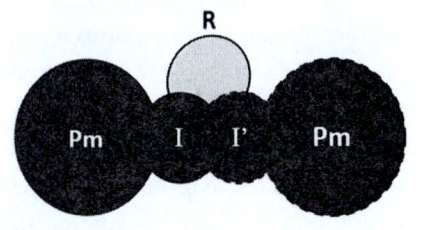

32.4

Collective Identity

In the above cases, a Nexus is created between two Individuals (Omniselves) through relevant Identities attached to each Omniself's Core Values. In other words, a member of one community connects with someone who may or may not be a member of that community. There are situations, however, when the collective becomes an abstract concept; a Collective Identity in which the Individuals lose their individuality as they merge with the collective. For example, if I identify with a particular nationality and consider myself to be loyal to what that concept stands for, then I can connect with that concept without being in contact with anyone who shares my sentiment. In other words, when connecting with an Identity within an Omniself, The Self and The

Other retain their individuality, whereas, when connecting through a Collective Identity, the Individual becomes irrelevant. We can think of this as a separate type of community-related Pactum. My proposed name for this is 'Immersed Pactum' as depicted in Figure 13.

Figure 13 A Representation of an Immersed Pactum

Immersed Pactum

"I don't care who you are, as long as you are *one of us*."

Pm

In an Immersed Pactum, the Nexus effectively disappears. From a chemical perspective, this is like a metallic bond (§ 25.5).

In practice, the above possibilities create two options for an Individual seeking to interact (create a relationship with) a community. If I ask, "What is, or can be, my connection with each and every member of this community?", my focus would be on the Identities of the Individuals that comprise the community. Alternatively, asking, "How can I fit into this community?" would direct my focus towards the community's Core Values. Clearly, these are not mutually exclusive, they simply create different Pacta with different practical consequences. In the first case, the practical consequence is that the Collective (team, group, community, etc) becomes an emergent property of the interactions of the individual team members with each other. Like molecules, such a Collective would comprise individual bonds between members of the group where people don't bond to group concepts; they bond to individual members of those groups through their Common or Complementary Elements (§ 47) (e.g., "I am a part of this research team").

In a Collective, Individuals do not connect with individual members of a team or community, but with a particular ideology; irrespective of the Individual members that comprise it (e.g., "I am a scientist.").

Unit 7

The Atasinex Cluster

This is a short unit consisting of one chapter. It is short because the topic is vast and, at this stage, all I want to do is to plant a seed. It is a separate Unit because I want to highlight its central importance.

[I propose that, in some form or other, the concepts presented in this unit are applicable to all living organisms. For example, a cell needs to pay attention to its internal and external environment in order to function for its actions to be goal-directed (**§ 66 Goals**)].

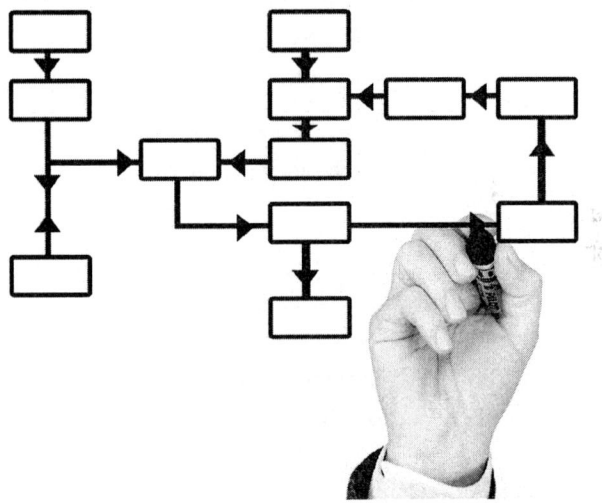

Image by Gerd Altmann from Pixabay

Chapter 33

Attention, Assumptions, Interpretation, Evaluation and Expectations

Attention, assumptions, interpretation, evaluation and expectations are part of the same system. I am introducing it here as the Atasinex [At-As-In-Ex] Cluster. This cluster constitutes all the interrelated internal processes that link the input that we receive from our senses to their physiological repercussions. This includes our affect, our feelings and our emotions (§ 51.2), as well as our behaviour (reactions) – See also § 40.2 (Behaviourism versus Humanism).

The Atasinex Cluster is the *second step* in the process of perception (§ 33.2). The first step is sensation (§ 26.2 Characteristics of Living Systems).

33.1
Sensation

Throughout this book, I have consistently emphasized the importance of the situation. The *situation determines* the Identity that is evoked in any set of circumstances, that is, *who we become*. Perception is the process that leads to our understanding of the circumstances in which we find ourselves. In other words, our perception determines how we interpret our circumstances and it is the result of that interpretation that I am calling the 'situation' (§ 14.3 Situation vs Circumstance).

Circumstances are external and the situation is about how we relate to (place ourselves mentally) within the boundaries of those circumstances. Another way of saying this is that the situation is the outcome of our interpretation of the circumstances. From a psychophysiological perspective,

> **circumstances provide the sensory input that
> our mind uses to determine the situation.**

We could also say that the situation is our subjective interpretation of objective circumstances.

33.2
Perception

Who we are is characterised by what we do. We can take a systems' approach (§ 67 Feedback Loops) and summarise everything that we do as consisting of four components; input, process, output and feedback.

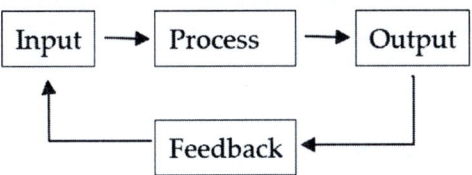

Perception is about the entire process (everything that happens) from the moment we sense something (input) to *just before* we react in some way to that sensation (output). We can, therefore, think of perception as the combination of sensory input, the Atasinex Cluster, affect and feeling, but *excluding* emotion and behaviour. In this unit, we are going to take a closer look at the process indicated as 'Process 1' in Figure 14.

Figure 14 The Relationship between Perception, Atasinex Cluster, Reaction, Emotion and Behaviour

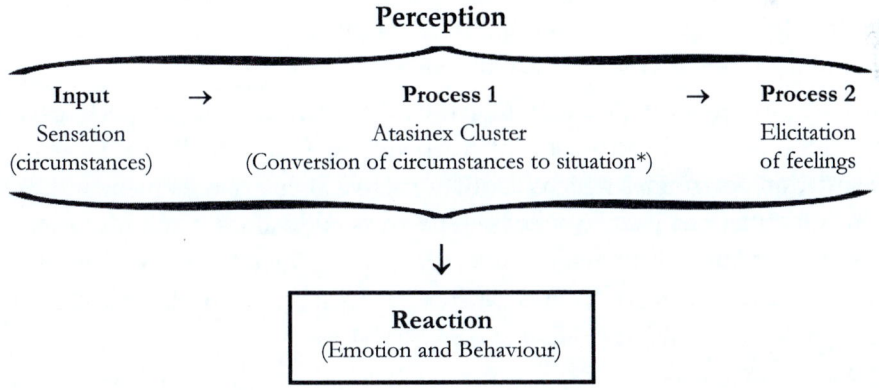

* See § 14.3 (Situation vs Circumstance)

33.3
Attention

In Unit 22 (Thermodynamics of Relationships), I explain that Energy is transferred whenever there is a change in the relationship between mass, distance, time and direction. I then propose a new type of energy that we can apply to interpersonal relationships and call it 'motivational energy'. From this, thermodynamic perspective, attention would be the 'direction' component of motivational energy.

At any one moment, we become connected to (a part of) whatever our attention is directed towards; the observed influences the observer and [perhaps less intuitively] the observer influences the observed. In fact,

---

the observer becomes a part of the observed.

I am not simply talking about the, often misunderstood, quantum observer effect. I am talking about a conscious experience that each of us can verify subjectively for ourselves. Our feelings change depending on what we are looking at and how mindfully (deliberately) we are looking at it. In other words, depending on what we observe and how we observe, the strength of the connection between I, the observer, and whatever it is that I am paying attention to changes. From an affinitological perspective, the observer is The Self and the observed can be The Other or The Nexus.

What we pay attention to is determined by the situation, our perspectives and our values. These are, of course, not independent of each other. That is because the situation determines which Identity is active at any one moment and each of our Identities has its own set of perspectives and values (§ 29.4 The Omniself). These assorted perspectives and values are held together by a set of core values, rather like the way in which the branches of a tree are supported by its trunk. We explore values in more detail in § 34.1.2 (Values).

The quality of our observation is mediated by our feelings. This means that we interpret what we see differently depending on our physiological state. This is related to the 'warm cup of coffee' experiment I describe in § 42.4 (Identity Homeostasis).

I have been interested in attention and attentional mechanisms for over twenty years; you may notice that attention is an integral part of the main thread that runs through this course. It deserves a separate course/book. Here, I simply want to draw your attention towards the central part that it plays in our interpersonal relationships, especially attraction. In short,

> **Life is not about where we are, it is about where and how we look.**

33.4
Assumptions

We cannot interpret anything without making assumptions. At the very least, we must assume that the information that our senses are giving us is congruent with the reality that is outside of us. In other words, we must assume that what we are experiencing is not entirely based on our imagination. Assumption is, therefore, an integral part of interpretation.

If I could go through life simply seeing things and hearing things and I could say to myself, "Well, it is what it is" and put myself into such a *state* of being, then I could exist; purely exist without identifying with, without evaluating, without judging, without the notion of having and without wanting. Take a moment to imagine that. Does that feel like heaven or hell to you?

Isn't that annoying? There you were blissfully going about your business of imagining not having a care in the world and I went and spoilt it all with a question. And there is a reason for that. You see, questions invite us, compel us even, to interpret, evaluate, judge and conclude. "It is what it is" does not require any interpretation. Therefore, interpretation (giving meaning) necessitates that we go beyond direct experience and we do it because we are compelled by some inner drive to fill in the gaps [look up 'the law of closure'] between what we experience and our perception of who we are (§ 37.7 The Emergence of Identity). This is where assumptions come in. At any given moment, we make so many assumptions that we can safely assume that,

> **we assume much more about reality than we sense directly.**

Yes, you got it. What I am saying is that **we are all living in our own fantasy land**. The line between fantasy and imagination is so blurred that we have no idea about the extent to which we are in The Matrix or 'down the Rabbit Hole' or chained in a cave looking at shadows on a wall.

[The last is a reference to the 'allegory of the cave' told by Plato about 26 centuries ago. Actually, Plato was more optimistic than me because he suggested that education can break the chains of illusion. My point is that this blurred line between reality and illusion is not a new idea.]

So, how can this understanding help us in our quest in creating more SMERs? Simple. If we want to instigate a SMER or to move an existing relationship towards a SMER, then we can begin by asking questions (§ 15.1 The Power of Questions). Exercise 5 is an example.

Exercise 5 Creating a SMER by Questioning our Assumptions

Think of a person with whom you want to have a more empowered relationship (§ 2.1.1 What is Empowering). Ask yourself,

1. Which of my assumptions about this person or this situation is preventing me from doing what I need to do to get the result (SMER) that I want to get?

2. What can I do about it?

If the answer that comes to mind is beyond your comfort zone, then try dissociating your associated 'Identity' from the situation (§ 51.2 Affect, Feelings and Emotions).

Since our assumptions are linked to our beliefs, challenging our assumptions is an indirect way (back door) to changing our beliefs whilst encountering less resistance. We can do this by asking questions (of The Self or The Other). There are plenty of examples here in this book. In the end, it boils down to 'reframing' (§ 63.1 Changing Beliefs).

33.5
Interpretation (Creating Meaning)

Interpretation is the process through which we *create* **meaning.** Nothing has any intrinsic meaning. It is us, as individuals and as a collective (society), that give meaning to (make sense of) what passes through our senses. *What* we interpret depends on what (which aspect of the situation) we are paying attention to at any one time. *How* we interpret (the meaning that we give to things) determines how we react and interact with everything. I am going to risk my reputation on this and assert that,

> **attention and interpretation are the *only* determinants of our quality of life.**

Everything else that we discuss and explore here, including our beliefs, values, wants, needs, personality, character and so on, ultimately revolve around what we pay attention to and the meaning that we give to it.

Direct experience does not require interpretation; it is what it is. The only time [and that turns out to be all the time] that we need to interpret something is when we want to make sense of it and the only way that we can make sense of something is to *relate it to ourselves*. This means that, ultimately, interpretation is **not** about, "What does this mean?", it is about "What does this mean *to me?*" The more broadly we perceive the *me*, the more integrated we will feel, that is, the more we will feel that we belong. And it is that sense of belonging that, I would venture to say, is the primary (most important) determinant of our self-esteem (§ 40.3).

Our sense of belonging is reduced by the extent to which we disassociate ourselves from various aspects of our environment. Note that, whether or not we feel associated or disassociated with something is a *choice* that we make.

[See the example of the arm that is about to receive an injection in § 51.3 (Feelings, Emotions and Impulse).]

33.6

Evaluation

After interpreting the situation, we need to *decide* what to do about it. That decision is based on our evaluation of the situation. Evaluation means assigning value to each of the options that the situation presents us with. *How* we evaluate depends on our beliefs (§ 34.1.2 Values) and our goals (§ 66 Goals).

33.7

Expectation

Everything that we do and feel is based on our expectations and not on physical reality. *Everything*. You could argue that these expectations are, ultimately, based on physical reality and I would say that,

---

> **When we decide to cook something, it is neither the ingredients nor the recipe that attracts us; it is the image of the food when it is ready to be eaten**

"But Bijan, you can't mean everything that we do and feel." Yes, I do mean everything. Even the feeling of tiredness that appears to come from our muscles; our stamina, does not mean that there is any stress on the muscles; it means that our brain is telling us that the **change** in the amount of work that we are asking our muscles to do is more than the **pattern** that it is used to experiencing and, therefore, it is not in line with expectations and therefore, 'bad'. In other words,

our physiology is managed on the same basis as our feelings and behaviour. But, in the light of our discussion about feelings and emotions, this is not surprising (§ 51.2 Affect, Feelings and Emotions).

"But Bijan, what about direct injury?" There are many reports of people not feeling pain, including not noticing that they are bleeding or even that their limb had been severed because they were highly focused on something else; in the heat of battle is a common example. These are times when our attentional resources (§ 93-95 Thermodynamics of Relationships) are too stretched for us to use them to interpret the signals that are coming in from the injured area. No interpretation, no expectation, no expectation, no pain (or pleasure).

Expectation is the primary consequence of interpretation. We can think of it this way; there is no point in deciding on the meaning of something if it does not result in some sort of prediction. For example, if we interpret what we see about someone as meaning that he is 'educated', with that interpretation comes certain expectations. These may include a certain level of knowledge, broadmindedness, tolerance, intelligence, understanding or experience (social, cultural, academic). There is an example of this in § 53.7 (Experience).

33.7.1
Expectation and Belief

In § 62.1 (Beliefs), I define a belief as cause-and-effect associations or a set of 'if-then' statements that we live by. That makes expectations (the 'effect' side of a cause-and-effect association) and an integral part of beliefs. In other words, where there are no beliefs, there can be no expectations and conversely, where there are no expectations, there are no beliefs. To put it another way, I cannot believe in something without it creating an expectation (in situations where that belief becomes relevant) and I cannot have expectations, unless it is prompted by an underlying belief.

33.7.2
Expectation and Values

In § 64.4 (Values as Receptors), I assert that, for something to have value, we must believe in it first and that this makes values a subset of beliefs; values are beliefs about beliefs. This means that, everything that we say about beliefs also applies to values [but not everything that we say about values can be applied to beliefs]. Since expectations are prompted by beliefs and values are hierarchical beliefs, our beliefs and values create a hierarchy of expectations.

33.7.3

Expectation and Conflict
(Divergent Expectations)

Conflict can occur through what I am calling 'divergent expectations' (§ 59 Affinito-Adolescence). These include conflicting expectations, unfulfilled expectations and misunderstandings. The extent to which a divergent expectation can disrupt a Nexus depends on the hierarchical rank of the Value that creates the expectation (§ 64.7 Hierarchy of Values). This is affected by two interrelated factors,

   a) How related the expectation-causing Value is to the Omniself's Principles and,

   b) How relevant the Value is to the integrity of the Nexus.

Conflicting Expectations

Conflicting expectations can be qualitative (inappropriate, unexpected or untenable) or quantitative (too much or too little). They occur when The Self expects The Other to behave in a certain way [do or say certain things in a specific situation, such as, for example, in defence of The Self or The Nexus] and The Other does not fulfil that expectation. The effect that this has on the Nexus depends on The Self's Values (which will determine The Self's reaction) and The Other's Values. The Self's expectation of The Other's reaction creates a feedback loop that can ameliorate or exacerbate the tension (Unit 23: Mechanics of Relationships) created in the Nexus.

If, for example, both Identities decide that the conflict is the result of a misunderstanding or incompetence (§ 53 Trust) rather than an indication of blatant disregard for the integrity of the Nexus, then the conflict will resolve itself.

Unfulfilled Expectations

Expectations emerge from our beliefs and their impact on the Nexus depends on where that belief ranks in our hierarchy of values (§ 64.7). There are two types of unfulfilled expectations;

   a) Unexpressed assumptions (or values on which those assumptions are based) and,

   b) Broken promises.

The first type of unfulfilled expectation can be summarised in the sentence, "But everyone knows that." There are many examples of a cognitive distortion known as 'mind-reading'. This is one of them. The problem is that in most cases, our assumption pays off; people do as we expect without us needing to tell them. This makes it more difficult for us to accept that, sometimes, what is obvious to us is not so obvious to others. The second type of unfulfilled expectation (broken promises) does not need explanation.

The extent to which unfulfilled expectations can cause conflict and disrupt the Nexus depends on, the extent to which we believe that the unfulfilled expectation was intentional (§ 53 Trust).

Misunderstandings

Divergent expectations can arise through misunderstandings. Although, these are related to both conflicting and unfulfilled expectations, I have decided to treat them separately because, unlike the other two, in misunderstandings, communication attempts have been made, but have been ineffective. In other words, the problem here is not so much about the *quantity* of communication, it is about the *quality* of communication (Unit 3: The Power of Language). Misunderstandings can arise through ambiguity (vagueness/lack of clarity) or because The Self assumes that The Other has received the message, such as when The Other is preoccupied and not paying attention (§ 33.3 Attention).

33.7.4
Expectation and Consciousness

One of the recurring themes in this course is the relationship between consciousness and choice (§ 35.11.1 Defining Consciousness). We cannot make a conscious choice without some degree of expectation. Actually, the word conscious is redundant here because choice implies that the decision is not random. And if a choice is not random [potential tautology notwithstanding (if it is a choice, can we call it random? And if it is random, can we call it a choice?)], I suggest that it is safe to assume that some kind of consciousness is mediating that choice. Therefore, expectation and consciousness go hand in hand; there can be no expectation without consciousness and there can be no consciousness without expectation. If you are inclined to argue with me over the last point, I suggest that our argument can be resolved without even starting it. Let me explain.

When we think about expectation, we tend to mean those expectations that occupy our awareness (we are consciously aware of), such as 'anticipation' or what we consider to be 'right' or 'wrong'. However, expectations can reside at different levels of consciousness. Even if I put myself into a meditative state where I feel totally at one with everything so that even the notion of 'I' ceases to exist [I can tell you from personal experience that this is possible, but staying in such a state is like trying to squeeze a bar of wet soap without it slipping out of your hand. Nevertheless, it is a great feeling while it lasts], the least that I am assuming, unconsciously (§ 35.11.2 Subconscious and Unconscious) is that the experience is real or that the experience is an illusion. Either of these assumptions carries with it a set of expectations, irrespective of whether or not I am aware of them.

The relevance of this section in our pursuit of SMERs is that whenever we are dealing with a conscious being, we are dealing with expectations. The level and quality of our consciousness, affects our expectations and conversely, our expectations affect the level and quality of our consciousness. Both of these affect the level and quality of our relationships.

In the previous paragraph, you may have noticed an implied feedback loop [the input is a function of the output]. This is a necessary quality for Self-Organizing Systems (§ 91) and for the creation of fractals (§ 90).

33.8

Confirmation Bias

Although our expectations are the result of how we interpret what we perceive, it can work the other way around too; we can begin with an expectation and actively select evidence that match (confirm) that expectation and ignore evidence to the contrary. This is the basis of one of our most prevalent biases, confirmation bias.

Confirmation bias is one of a myriad of cognitive biases that distort our experience, making the 'reality' that we perceive incongruent with what is actually happening in the real world. In fact, a brief contemplation of the range, depth and breadth of our cognitive biases [look up 'List of Cognitive Biases' on Wikipedia], will leave us in awe of how we manage to maintain even a semblance of sanity and harmony. This is another reason why we cannot live without relationships.

> **We instinctively know that our cognitive processes are prone to errors and misinterpretation and we need others to confirm our perceptions.**

[And when they do, we call it objective reality, even though our reference individuals are prone to the same biases.]

Once, when my son was about three and half years old, a family who had a four-year-old boy came to visit. Someone in our household observed that the little guest was physically abusing my son and was clearly exhibiting 'antisocial behaviour'. We had seen him push my son and strike out at him on several occasions for 'no reason'. I decided to take a closer look.

I had made a little safehouse for them to play inside using square seat cushions and a blanket. It was a rectangular structure with enough room for both of them. At one point, I noticed that the little guest had occupied one side of the bunker and my son was trying to get inside from the same end, but he was not getting physical. He was simply getting very close to his guest and saying, "I want to come in." The other side of the bunker was completely open and there was plenty of room for him at that end. It was then that the little guest struck out with his palm, trying to tell him not to 'invade his space'.

I realised that, although our little guest had a tendency to be more physical, it was my son who was being provocative by being over-possessive of what he perceived to be his space or perhaps he was simply experimenting (probing the consequences of his actions).

So, what does this have to do with confirmation bias? Well, if I had looked for evidence of hitting, the behaviour of the little guest may have 'confirmed' the notion that the boy was 'exhibiting antisocial behaviour'. Instead, I looked for the 'triggers' of that behaviour and found the 'real' culprit. Figure 15 shows how I perceive what I am proposing as the Confirmation Bias Cycle.

Figure 15 Confirmation Bias Cycle

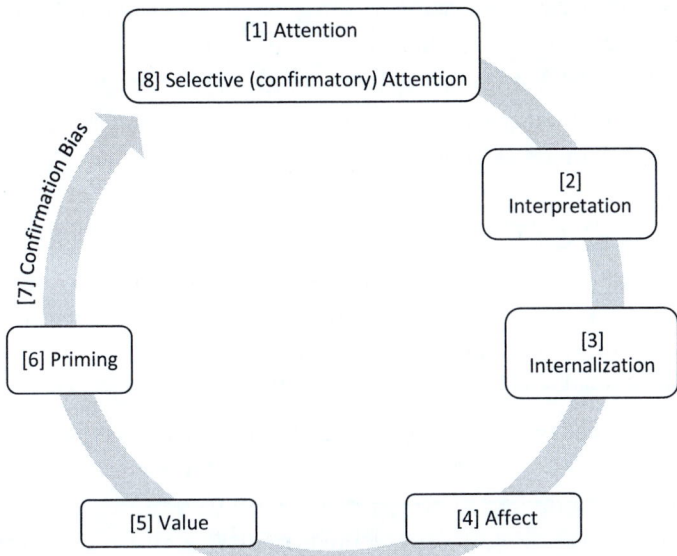

Stage 1: Attention

Attention means what we focus on. It is the process through which, at any one instant [when the little guest is hitting out], we choose a subset of data for mental processing [only the behaviour of the little guest (ignoring the possible [hidden] causes/preamble)]. This 'selection' can be data that we select from the vast amount of potential information streaming in from our senses (neurological transducers) or it can be data selected from the content of our memories. In Figure 15, I have shown attention as the beginning of a cycle that ends in confirmation bias leading to selective (confirmatory) attention. From this perspective selection bias becomes a mediator of confirmation bias. In other words, we can reduce the risk of falling victim to confirmation bias by changing our focus from what we expect to other cues in the environment. This one change alone can have a magically empowering effect on our interpersonal relationships.

Stage 2: Interpretation

Interpretation can be summarised as being our answer to the question, "How is this data relevant to me?" To generate an answer, we begin by looking for patterns. We then try to match those patterns to existing patterns in our memory. The misunderstandings that arise in interpersonal relationships are due to differences in those existing patterns. That is, insufficient common experiences for the situation (§ 47 Common and Complementary Elements). However, common experiences do not necessarily result in similar interpretations. This is because people pay attention to different aspects of the situation. Nevertheless, the common experiences allow us to appreciate each other's perspectives when that different way of looking at (experiencing) the situation is pointed out (made explicit).

For heuristic purposes (§ 72.5 Cognitive Load and Heuristics) we classify patterns into groups. The model I have in my mind for understanding how we classify patterns is inspired by the way our colour vision works. We only have three types of colour receptor in our eyes. These allow us to distinguish between millions of different colours. Similarly, I propose that,

> **we only have three different categories that we use to classify patterns; safe, dangerous and useful.**

These lead to three categories of feelings; neutral, avoid and approach. We label these feelings as indifferent, like and dislike. I propose that the whole range of feelings that we experience arise from the interaction between these three interpretations.

[Notice that what I am implying here is that we tend to ignore what we deem to be merely safe. This is also part of the mechanism that leads to desensitization, including not appreciating what we have (AKA taking things - in our case, each other - for granted).]

Stage 3: Internalisation or Identification

Internalisation means different things in different disciplines. In sociology, the emphasis is on how we make other people's perspectives our own. The way I use the word here is closer to the psychoanalytic interpretation. When we internalize a belief or a value, we integrate it into one of our true Identities (§ 29.4 The Omniself) and make it our own. It does not matter whether these beliefs and values are based on our own experiences or others'.

[You might say, "But Bijan, if the beliefs and values are created by ourselves, aren't they 'internal' already? And I would thank you for paying attention and thinking about it and would continue by asking, "Have you ever created something that you were not particularly attached to? What did you do with it? Usually we throw it out." So, what I mean by internalised, is not, where it was created, but whether we are inclined to keep it inside (identify with it).]

We can also think of the opposite of internalisation as dissociation. When I dissociate myself from something, what I am saying to myself is, "This is not a part of me" or "I do not wish to be associated with this" or "this is not congruent with who I am (perceive myself to be)" and so on.

At this point, I need to make a distinction between active and passive rejection. In active rejection, the act of rejecting something becomes an aspect of me, something that I identify with. If I call myself an anticolonialist, then that becomes a part of who I am because I am defining a part of who I am through something I oppose (§ 40.3 Self-Esteem). This has repercussions for the next stage in this cycle.

Stage 4: Affect

If I do not identify with a pattern that I perceive, then it will not affect me and, as such, it will not trigger an affect; the thing that leads to feelings and emotions (§ 51.2 Affect, Feelings and Emotions). Once I am affected by a pattern, then how that pattern affects me becomes its valence and how much it affects me becomes arousal. The combination of valence and arousal determine the nature and quality of our feelings.

Stage 5: Values

Our values are determined by the level of arousal that is induced in us by a particular pattern. We tend to place greater value on those patterns that result in higher valence within the 'approach' (like) domain. Our values as lie along the spectrum of has-vital-value to has-no-value. To put it another way, we tend to think of things as worth getting/keeping or not worth getting/keeping. The former are things that we identify with and the latter are things that we don't identify with.

What we actively dislike also becomes part of our Identity. Therefore, it becomes a value, albeit a negative one. The significance of making this distinction is that, whether something has positive or negative value, it will attract our attention more than something which has neutral (zero) value.

Stage 6: Priming

Once we determine that a pattern has value, whether positive or negative, our minds become primed to be on the lookout for such patterns and to deliver them to our conscious or subconscious awareness (§ 35.11 Consciousness).

Stage 7: Confirmation Bias

Since priming brings patterns that we identify with to the front of the queue, it obscures our awareness of potentially contradictory patterns. And this strengthens our belief, i.e., it leads to the reinforcement of previously similarly activated neural pathways.

Part 3
Medical Affinitology

Unit 8

Introduction to

Medical Affinitology

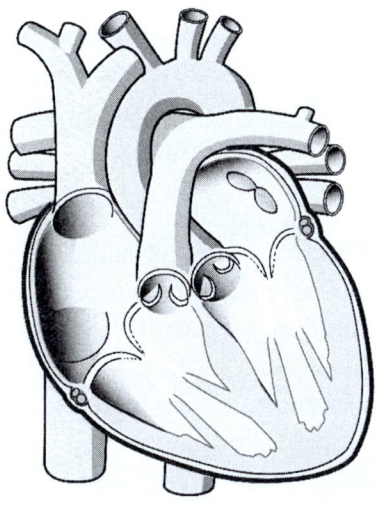

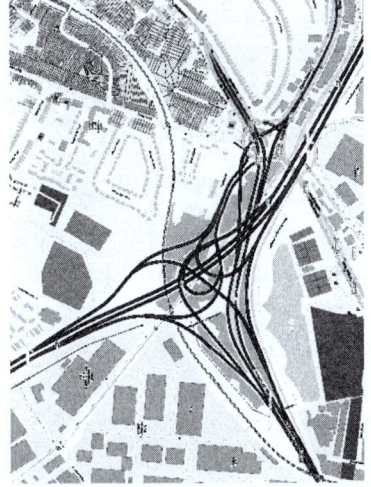

[source:
https://upload.wikimedia.org/wikipedia/commons/c/cc/Diagram_of_the_human_heart_%28no_labels%29.svg]

[source:
https://upload.wikimedia.org/wikipedia/commons/f/fc/Gravelly_Hill_Interchange_OpenStreetMap.png]

Chapter 34

Cells, Receptors and Sensitivity

I never used to pay much attention to gold until, many years ago, a friend of mine told me that she likes multi-coloured gold jewellery Ever since then, my attention is drawn automatically towards multi-coloured gold whenever I look at jewellery displays.

Our senses are designed to perceive a limited range of stimuli from the environment, such as the limited range of colours that lie between the infrared and ultraviolet region of the electromagnetic spectrum or the limited range of sounds that, for example, are less high pitch than the frequencies that dogs can hear. On top of that, we do not notice everything that we have the potential to notice. This is why we fall for conjuring tricks. They are exercises in misdirection.

By increasing or decreasing the number of receptors on their surface, cells can adjust their sensitivity to environmental stimuli. You and I can also change our psychophysiological sensitivity to what happens around us. When we do this to *reduce* our sensitivity, we call it 'acclimatisation' or 'desensitization' which means that we don't consciously notice it any more. In other words, we get used to things; we ignore things that become familiar. Sadly, this also leads us to take such things for granted so as not to appreciate what we have when we have them. Acclimatisation and desensitisation usually happen so gradually that we are not consciously aware of the process; the incremental changes are too small for us to discern.

We can also change our sensitivity to stimuli in the opposite direction in that we can become (make ourselves) *more* sensitive. Cells do this by either increasing the number of receptors on their surface or by switching those receptors on and off.

The various Identities within each Individual (§ 29.4 The Omniself) are formed by our values (§ 64) which are derived from our beliefs (§ 62). These determine the extent to which we become sensitive to different factors in our environment. For example, my 'scientist' Identity is interested in (sensitive to) patterns and processes and my 'father' Identity is interested in growth and adaptation and the extent to which these can relate to my children's current and future sense of fulfilment. The point is that we shape our Identities and, by extension, the type and quality of our interpersonal relationships, by changing our sensitivity to various factors in our environment. In short, from an affinitological perspective,

---

sensitization is a process through which we begin to *identify* with something (a phenomenon).

And the context in which that sensitization expresses itself determines The Self, or the Identity that manifests at the time (§ 29.4 The Omniself).

34.1
The Three Sensitivity Concerns

How can we apply the understandings that we gain from our discussion of cells, receptors and sensitivity to our interpersonal relationships? We can begin by asking three questions (§ 15.1 The Power of Questions). Let's call them the three *sensitivity concerns*; factors, values and adaptations [The acronym FAV can help us remember these].

34.1.1
Factors

Factors are things that *potentially* influence what we are sensitive to. We can identify these by asking, "What are the things (factors) that, if we notice them, can affect the quality of our interpersonal relationships?" In other words, "What factors attract, repel, maintain and disrupt relationships?"

The answer to this question lies in the three types of components that make-or-break relationships; Complementary Components, Shared Components and Conflicting Components. We explore these in more detail in § 46 (Adjunctum Communalis).

34.1.2
Values

Having identified the factors, we can focus on the second sensitivity question, "How do we decide which factors are more important?" That is to say, "Which factors do we need to become more or less sensitive to?" Another way of putting this is, "How do we prioritise so as to maximise the quality and efficiency of the relationship at hand?" From yet another perspective, what we are asking is, "What factors do we need to pay more attention to (prioritize) in order to improve the quality of any given relationship?"

We can only answer these questions by determining (choosing) and identifying our values. To do this, we need to become sensitive to The Self and The Other's values (§ 34.1.2 Values).

34.1.3
Adaptation

Adaptation is about asking, "How can we go about changing the extent to which we are sensitive to each of these factors?" This is sensitivity question three and is primarily about habits (§ 35.5 Homeostasis).

Chapter 35

Terminology

Here, I want to introduce you to some of the medical concepts that help us take a 'living systems' approach to exploring interpersonal relationships. In later sections, we shall delve into these in more detail.

35.1
Embryology of Relationships

Embryology of relationships is about how relationships are instigated (fertilisation) and the subsequent stages that they go through in order to become stable, independent and resilient in the face of environmental factors.

There comes a point at which at least part of the relationship becomes independent of the two people who instigated it. If you find it difficult to get your head around this one, consider this: Once a relationship between two people becomes public, for example by announcing the marriage of A and B, then the marriage itself becomes a separate entity; we begin to talk about a happy 'marriage', a productive 'marriage', a 'marriage' being on the rocks and so on. We explore the embryology of relationships in Unit 12.

35.2
Paediatrics of Relationships

This is about how relationships mature. Continuing with the example of marriage, unlike in fairy tales where the story ends with marriage, marriage is the birth of a new relationship which needs to be nurtured to maturity. Not the maturity of the individuals, but the maturity of the marriage relationship (Pactum), so that the relationship (Nexus) becomes less vulnerable to outside influences. This principle applies to all kinds of interpersonal relationships; not just to marriage (§ 92 Relationship Frameworks).

35.3
Developmental Affinitology

This is about how relationships change as they mature.

Earlier (§ 25 Relationships as Chemical Bonds), I mentioned that we seem to have the need to impose arbitrary points of demarcation (division) along what is, in essence, a continuum or spectrum. We talk about (and label) stages of development; stages of cognitive development, moral development, physical development, emotional development and so on, in the same way that we split the rainbow arbitrarily into seven distinct colours. From now on, whenever you see words such as 'stages of', remember that the rainbow consists of ten million colours and not seven; even that ten million is a limitation placed on us by our physiology.

Developmental Affinitology is concerned with such questions as, "What factors affect the trajectory of a relationship?" and "Are there any predictable milestones that can inform such trajectories?"

35.4
Affinitoimmunology

Affinitoimmunology (the immunology of relationships) is about how relationships protect themselves from threats to their inner processes. It is about answering the question, "What happens to relationships when they become subject to interference from outside forces?" These outside influences could be from other Identities, individuals, relationships or environmental factors. How (and how much) these affect the relationship depends on how equipped the relationship is to defend itself against such interference.

Relationships can become resilient to outside influences in one of three ways, toughness, flexibility or active protection (immune response). Toughness is when a relationship is impermeable to outside influences. Flexibility is when the relationship changes temporarily to accommodate the environment and then returns to its original state. These are relatively passive processes.

An immune response is an active process. It seeks out potential threats and eliminates them. Such active protection also makes relationships susceptible to autoimmune disorders. We explore the Immunology of Relationships in Unit 18.

35.5
Homeostasis

How do/can relationships keep their inner environments to within optimal parameters? For example, what can we do to ensure that any one of our relationships doesn't get too hot, too cold, too tight, too loose, too deep, too shallow, too isolated, too open, etc.? [For 'too' read 'disempoweringly'].

Homeostasis is based on having a point of reference for each of the characteristics of a relationship, along with their associated tolerance levels. Our affinitological tolerance levels (how much variation we can accept within different aspects of a relationship) are determined by our flexibility. In this context, another word for flexibility is 'open-mindedness'.

[I appreciate that open-mindedness is a value-laden concept. It can make some of us uncomfortable to think that, if my relationship is not a SMER (§ 2.1), it may be because I am closing my mind to certain possibilities; that simply (or not so simply) expanding my comfort zone can redefine the 'normal' parameters under which the relationship can be considered to be a SMER. I suggest that we try to remove our value-judgements from the meaning of the word open-minded and simply see it as how far back we are willing to pull pack the curtains to let in the sunshine. It is not 'good' or 'bad' it is a matter of preference, which can, of course change depending on circumstances.]

Tolerance is also the antithesis to conflict. In other words, conflict is synonymous with intolerance. Actually, not exactly synonymous because intolerance is the mechanism and conflict is the outcome, but you can see what I mean; the less I need to tolerate something, the less conflicted I am about it.

We explore this idea further in Unit 15 (§ 67-69 Relationship Maintenance).

35.6
Pathology

What can go wrong with the inner workings of interpersonal relationships and how?

Pathology and homeostasis are closely related because, essentially, **pathology is about disruption of homeostasis**. Pathology is about how and why those factors that make a relationship functional are pushed to outside normal or nominal levels. The distinction between normal and nominal is an important one. Normal is a statistical construct, it is about what is generally *observed* and nominal is a criterion that is *chosen* deliberately. It is likely that the nominal standard is based on a statistical norm, but it need not be (§ 71 What is Normal?).

The most prevalent factors that result in conflict in interpersonal relationships are assumptions and expectations (§ 33 Atasinex Cluster).

We explore what can go wrong in relationships, including intolerance and conflict in Unit 19 (Pathology of Relationships).

35.7
Thermodynamics

The Encyclopædia Britannica describes thermodynamics as the

> "Science of the relationship between heat, work, temperature, and energy. In broad terms, thermodynamics deals with the transfer of energy from one place to another and from one form to another."

Let's compare that with the description of *economics* offered by Wikipedia;

> "Economics is the social science that studies the production, distribution, and consumption of goods and services."

Notice that both thermodynamics and economics revolve around two central concepts; **flow and exchange**. In the first case, the focus is on energy and, in the second case, on goods and services.

We explore the 'flows and exchanges' that can characterise the dynamics of relationships in Unit 22 (Thermodynamics of Relationships).

[I am in two minds as to whether or not to introduce a new word such as 'affinitodynamics or affinitonomics' or to stick to 'thermodynamics of relationships'. The jury is still out on that one. Perhaps we can reach a consensus through discussion and debate (Keep an eye on introducingaffinitology.com)]

35.8
Prevention

How can we prevent damage to relationships?

Prevention is about anticipating and mitigating any potential shift from homeostasis to pathology. It is about identifying possible factors that could disrupt homeostasis and taking measures to reduce or eliminate the potential effects of such factors. For example, it goes without saying that a dearth in the quality and quantity of our communication can have severe detrimental effects on relationships. Therefore, in affinitology, one very important aspect of prevention is healthy communication (Unit 16: Physiology of Relationships). Another possible preventable factor that could otherwise be detrimental to our relationships is not having clear goals for the relationship (§ 66 Goals). We can also prevent damage to a relationship by developing its ability to recognise and to deal with interference (§ 60.3 Relationship Interference).

35.9
Pharmacology

From an affinitological perspective, pharmacology is the science that seeks answers to questions such as, "How are relationships affected by outside influences?" and "How do relationships affect those factors that influence them?" We discuss these in more detail in Unit 17 (Pharmacology of Relationships).

35.10
Toxicology

Poisons (Toxic* substances or toxins) can make us ill. They can also kill us. Similarly, affinitotoxins can turn SMERs into unhealthy relationships and even lead to the ending of a relationship (breaking of the Nexus).

[* This reminds me of when my daughter was very young. After hearing the song, Toxic, performed by Britney Spears, I explained to her what toxic meant and she said, "Oh. I thought she was saying talk sick." And, from an affinitological perspective, that would also work; when we 'talk sick' we communicate in a manner that is toxic to the relationship :-)]

We explore the toxicology of relationships in § 75.

35.11
Consciousness

35.11.1
Defining Consciousness

The idea of consciousness is implicit in almost everything that we talk about. Here, I am going to try to bring 'consciousness' out of the shadows and into a more demonstrable realm so that, perhaps one of the oldest bastions of philosophy, can be made to succumb to science (become amenable to scientific investigation).

I have a mental allergy (§ 81 Emotional Allergens and Hypersensitivity) to sweeping statements. My mind recoils on hearing words such as 'always' and 'never'. However, there are times when absolute conclusions are inescapable. Here is one of them (even after assuming that our questions are rational and relate to something that is falsifiable [courtesy of Karl Popper] in the first place),

---

Science will never be able to answer all of our questions

[The reason I am so confident about this is that for anything to be open to scientific investigation, two conditions are absolutely necessary. Whatever it is that is being investigated must be **measurable** AND it must be **reproducible** (consistent). The purpose of science is to **make predictable.** And what is not measurable *and* reproducible is not predictable. To predict accurately, we rely on mathematics, yet some of the most fundamental units in science and mathematics are irrational (unpredictable). The one that we are most familiar with (there are lots of others) is the ratio of a circle's circumference to its diameter. Pi is an irrational number. It is not possible to predict the sequence of numbers in Pi because it can be calculated to an infinite number of decimal places without it ever becoming a repeating pattern. For as long as there are irrational numbers, there is unpredictability in the universe. Why? Because of something called sensitive dependence on initial conditions. We explore this concept in Unit 21 (Diversification and Speciation of Relationships).]

To make consciousness available to scientific enquiry, we need to define it in a way that allows us to measure something about it. For example, no one has ever seen an electron, but we believe it exists because that assumption has successfully allowed us to *predict*, and manipulate, the world around us. How can we do that when no one has ever seen an electron? We use a fundamental assumption of all science:

If anything (a change) happens, something has caused it to happen

---

With electrons, we saw effects and assumed (theorised as to) a cause. The theory is still working, so we can go on assuming that electrons exist until there is evidence to the contrary.

Perhaps you can see where I am going with this; I propose that consciousness is the cause of behaviour, i.e., *consciousness is that which causes behaviour*. But this definition is missing something very important, so let me clarify:

Consciousness is the cause of goal-directed behaviour.

If behaviour is not *goal-directed*, it is random. Although organisms can, and apparently do (sometimes), behave randomly, it is their *potential* for goal-directed behaviour that makes them conscious. And that brings me to the main point of my argument; it is the potential to exercise choice that characterises consciousness. In other words,

---

Where there is the potential to exercise choice, there is consciousness

---

The importance of this discussion and its conclusion to our quest for 'empowering and mutually satisfying relationships' will become more apparent as we develop the arguments in this book.

35.11.2
Subconscious and Unconscious

Often, the words subconscious and unconscious [not to be confused with non-conscious] are used interchangeably. Here, I have made a distinction between the two. [The reason for this will become clear in our discussion about the role of attention in thinking and how this relates to interpersonal relationships.] Both of these words mean 'unaware'. However, we can be unaware of things for different reasons.

The prefix sub- means below. When I am looking up or straight ahead, I may not be aware of things that are 'below' at my feet. However, I *can* become conscious of what is at my feet by directing my attention downwards. Similarly, there are things that are happening inside my mind and body that I am not aware of as long as my attention is elsewhere, but I can become aware of them if I choose to redirect my attention. For example, are you conscious of how often you blink? No. *Can* you become conscious of it? Yes. Therefore, you blink <u>sub</u>consciously.

On the other hand, there are things happening around us that are not accessible to our conscious attention because they may be obscured (e.g., behind a rock) or be beyond our perceptual range, such as radio waves or ultrasound (accessible to a greater extent to bats and dogs). Similarly, there are processes that are going on inside my mind and body that I *cannot* become aware of by simply redirecting my attention because they are either obscured or I do not have the necessary faculties to perceive them. These are what I would refer to as <u>un</u>conscious content and processes.

With the environmental examples above (radio, ultrasound and rocks) we can construct devices that can make the directly inaccessible, indirectly accessible (perceivable and measurable) to us. Although biofeedback and neurofeedback are procedures through which we can gain access to some of our unconscious processes, I am curious as to how far these can go and, to me, the prospect is exciting.

35.11.3
Consciousness and Thought

Can there be thought without consciousness? That was the easy question. Here comes the hard one.

Can there be consciousness without thought? I would postulate that, since such a hypothesis is not falsifiable, it is not open to scientific enquiry and dwelling upon it is a mere distraction. On the other hand, having an opinion about the answer could simplify our exploratory journey into the realm of interpersonal relationships. I am, therefore, going to rely on my instinct and say that there can be no consciousness without thought. How does this simplify our journey? Well, let's see. If there can be no thought without consciousness and there can be no consciousness without thought, then we could, through a leap of presumption, conclude that thought is consciousness and consciousness is thought.

[This is reminiscent of Descartes' *cogito ergo sum* and, whilst I am tempted to discuss this further, like Odysseus and the Sirens, I am going to tie myself to the mast so that I am not able to give way to the temptation to veer into that philosophical quagmire].

Since we are much more familiar with the concept of thought (cognition) than we are with consciousness, we can reduce our cognitive load [strain on the brain] (§ 72.5 Cognitive Load and Heuristics) by making a mental note that, whenever we talk about consciousness, we mean thought and whenever we talk about thought, we mean consciousness. Just before we move on; from a philosophical perspective, one could argue that *thought is what happens in the brain* and *consciousness is what happens in the mind*, but for all practical purposes, we can consider them to be the same thing [for now ;-)].

35.11.4

Extended Consciousness

The interaction of two conscious entities (entities that have the potential to exercise choice) leads to extended (higher) consciousness, increasing the number of options (potential for making choices) than there would be in the absence of such interaction.

Endosymbiosis is a process by which one organism lives inside another to their mutual benefit. I propose that this is an example of extended consciousness. But the idea that an organism is simply living inside another is too simplistic because it is too dissociative/reductionist.

Atoms can exist as individual entities, but when they combine (bond) to form molecules, both their individual characteristics and colligative properties (§ 39.6 SRC are Unstable at the Individual Level) change drastically. Yes, it is still possible to separate the parts from the whole, but doing so will destroy the thing that is the whole. Similarly, two microbes (prokaryotic cells) that do not have a nucleus can 'merge' together. If this 'merging' is of the form where one goes inside the other, it is called endosymbiosis. There is a potential problem (conflict) here (§ 59.1 Stages of Relationship Development). Both of the original prokaryotic cells contain genetic code (DNA and/or RNA) inside their cell membranes. If they get mixed up neither 'component' would be able to function properly.

If I have a room to myself. I can spread my belongings in any way that I please (see fit). However, if I decide to have a roommate, then I will need to clear up my belongings. This is where cupboards and wardrobes and compartments come in handy. Eukaryotic cells; the cells that make up the bodies of 'higher' organisms, including humans, evolved from an endosymbiotic relationship between two prokaryotic cells; a larger cell decided to have a roommate. To do this, it had to clear up the 'room' and put the important stuff (genetic material) somewhere where it could not potentially cause conflict. In eukaryotic cells the nucleus is the 'wardrobe' for the host's DNA and the smaller cell became the mitochondrion. The combined consciousness of the two prokaryotic cells, leads to the emergence of an entity with a higher consciousness.

To wit, when two conscious beings interact, a higher consciousness emerges that could not exist otherwise.

35.11.5
Consciousness and Levels of Organisation

We discuss levels of organisation in § 36. At this stage, I simply want to point out that,

> **every level of organisation has its own communication systems, goals and values and makes decisions at its own level.**

This means that consciousness works differently at different levels of organisation (from viruses to ecosystems and from information to humankind). In other words, we can extend the argument in the previous section fractally* and say that at every level of affinitological organisation, each of the emergent entities (including Pacta, Bondles, Communities, Societies, Cultures and Humankind) have their own separate consciousness, including the 'will' to adapt (survive) and to grow.

* [I searched the internet and was relieved to find that others are already using the word fractally, so I didn't need to make up another new word :-)]

35.12
The Mind-Body Evolution
(Beyond Medical Analogies)

35.12.1
Adaptation

In 1975, I had recently moved to Yorkshire, England. It was one of the coldest winters on record, with ice forming on my hair in the couple of minutes that it took me to go to the corner shop at the top of the road. I remember that I could not make snow balls because the ice crystals were too cold to stick together. It wasn't long before I was sliding on the ice in the street wearing just a tee-shirt.

In September 1982, I arrived at Cardiff Railway station to start university there. It was raining. I don't know how long it had been raining for before that, but there was no respite for the next seven weeks. Basically, it rains a lot in Cardiff (or at least it used to). Within three weeks, I had adjusted to it.

A couple of years later, I went to Iran for my summer holidays and the weather was very sunny (hurt my eyes), very hot (and sweaty) and very dry (clothes dried faster than putting them in a tumble dryer). Within three weeks I was used to it. Now, I am equally comfortable in heavy rain and the strong sunlight.

In 1996, having lived in the UK for over twenty years, I went for a regular visit to Iran to see my family. When the officer at border control looked at my passport, he said that since I was an Iranian citizen and had not done my National Service, I was not allowed to leave the country until I did. That winter, the temperature in London reached -6 °C. For my 'combat training', I was sent to a region in the desert where the temperatures fluctuated from -10 °C at night to +47 °C during the day. It took me about three weeks to adapt.

Nowadays, I am much more comfortable with variations in temperature, humidity and precipitation than I would have been had I not had these experiences. My adaptation to temperature is both at the physical and at the psychological level; I sweat less and when I do, it is not as distracting. The important point here is that I have not merely *adapted* to cope with a different environment, I have added to my arsenal of adaptive strategies. This is also what evolution does.

I know! You are waiting to see what all this has to do with relationships. Well, so far, we have piggy-backed our affinitological concepts on the back of medical terminology. However, interpersonal relationships are a step passed the body in terms of evolution. What I mean is that relationships have features that go beyond the physical body and into the abstract. Therefore, we need to extend our terminology so as to be able to discuss and explore these.

Even though our bodies and our minds are part of the same system, our minds appear to have developed to a level of sophistication that surpasses the complexity of our bodies. This means that, having adopted scientific terminology to explicate affinitological concepts, we need to extend those scientific concepts to include those aspects of relationships that do not fit into the existing medical-scientific lexicon. I have begun this by exploring areas of human concern that go beyond physiology.

At first, I struggled to conceive of medical equivalents for some of the aspects of relationships that we are exploring in this unit. In § 48-50 (Unit 11: Dimensions of Human Experience), I have discussed certain aspects of our lives that do not seem to fit neatly into categories of processes that can be considered to be analogous to anything within the biological domain. Eventually, I realised that this is beyond the realm of medical science and we need to stop piggy-backing and start to toddle on our own.

There is, of course, a very strong relationship between our minds and our bodies. This has been known for centuries. Back in the 13th Century, the Persian sage, Rumi, in his work, *Masnavi*, wrote about how a psychologist was called by a king to help a young lady who was suffering from depression. Historically, the word for psychologist in Persian [hakim-e-khaarchin] translates literally as "thorn plucking expert" which I think is a beautiful allusion in that, when we are feeling psychologically unwell, we need to have the thorns removed from our minds [Incidentally, according to Etymology Online (etymonline.com) the word 'psychology' didn't appear in Europe until the seventeenth century]. Anyway, Rumi describes how the psychologist, having asked everyone to clear the building (note confidentiality) began to casually chat to the girl about her life and her travels (built rapport). Significantly, the psychologist did something that the psychology profession has only relatively recently begun to pay any attention to; the mind-body connection. He monitored the lady's pulse throughout the conversation. When the lady began to talk about a certain aspect of her life, her pulse changed. The psychologist used that as a sign that he needed to explore that aspect of the woman's life in more detail. If you want to find out what happened, you're going to need to go and read it for yourself (my version is in the original Persian, I'm afraid) [I can tell you that the psychologist's findings led to a conspiracy that is reminiscent of Machiavelli (The Prince) and Sun Tzu (The Art of War)].

To return to our subject, the point I'm trying to make is that our body and our mind are intricately connected. Continuing with my argument, our mind is an evolutionary *extension* of our body and not an appendage or an annex of it. It has even been said (and I am inclined to agree) that the mind and body are one and the same system, in the same way that our hearts and lungs and brain and liver and blood etc. are working together as one system - a change in one part affects all other parts in some way and 'the whole is more than the sum of its parts'.

Before leaving the concept of Medical Affinitology, I need to lay down some foundations and so, bear with me as we begin to enter a new realm.

35.12.2
Repertoire

The amoeba is one of our earliest eukaryotic (non-microbial) ancestors. It is sensitive to blue light. It doesn't move towards the light and it doesn't avoid it; it simply stops moving in the presence of the light. To detect light, the amoeba needs photoreceptors (light sensors), but that's just stating the obvious. What may not be so obvious is that the cell's ability to sense light continues to exist in various forms in 'higher' animals, including humans. Studies have found that, even the functionally blind (those who have lost all rods and cones due to genetic disorders) still have light-responsive daily rhythms amongst other 'seeing' abilities. Our skin can detect light. In fact, since every cell in our bodies carries our entire genome, including the genes for creating specialist light detecting cells, such as the rods and cones, in theory, every cell in our body carries the potential to become light-sensitive. What I am trying to demonstrate here is that,

Evolution is not about mere adaptation;
it is about *extending our repertoire of adaptive strategies*.

This means that we can survive in a wider range of environmental conditions than we could before. As organisms and, by extension, societies, evolve, they extend their repertoire of adaptive strategies. This means that we are not *completely different* from an amoeba; we are an amoeba *and more*; a conglomerate of supercharged amoebae.

As I have argued elsewhere in this discourse, relationships can be considered to be living systems too. As such, as they evolve, they do not merely adapt, they extend their repertoire of adaptive strategies. This includes creating new phenomena that form facets and aspects of our relationships that do not fit into our current medical lexicon [Note that these new phenomena emerge from new relationships created between existing phenomena].

Chapter 36

Levels of Organisation

This section is about how our interpersonal relationships fit into the grand scheme of things.

When we use words like simple or complicated, we are talking about different *levels of organisation*. The fewer the number of interacting units, the fewer levels of organisation can be created, meaning that there is less potential for complexity. [From a statistical perspective, think 'degrees of freedom' and from a mathematical perspective, think combinations and permutations.]

36.1

Viruses

The jury is still out on whether viruses can be classified as being alive. You might say, well, just see if the MRS GREN criteria (§ 26.2 Characteristics of Living Systems) apply to viruses? And trying to do that leads to the conclusion, "Weeell, kinda." And you might think, "What do you mean 'kinda'? It either fits or it doesn't."

The thing is that, viruses are more like molecules than cells. Molecules are not alive, but virus molecules become 'alive' (become an integral part of a living system) once they enter a host cell. It is like a person eating some simple inanimate object like sand and turning into a zombie. The zombie is alive, but it has surrendered its will to the sand. But how can something that is not alive, like sand, know what it wants a zombie to do? Well, that's the bit that makes viruses difficult to classify. It's like asking, "Is a car without fuel a car?" Strictly speaking, no, because it can't do what a car is supposed to do. However, it is close enough to a car, not to be classified as a mere doorstop or bunker.

Molecules are tiny compared to cells. We can think of viruses as being more like a navigation system for the car in our analogy. Virus molecules are different to your regular molecules in that they contain genetic information. This means that they can reprogram the host cell to do what they want it to do [I am not sure if 'want' is the right word, because that implies free will; you can see why it gets complicated].

Some people hypothesise that from an evolutionary perspective, viruses are precursors to cells. But I am not convinced. How can something that needs a cell to replicate gather the genetic information necessary to control a cell? I think it would make more sense to think of viruses as genetic material that is left over after the cell that contained it was destroyed, perhaps because of faulty programming. This could explain why viruses, if left unchecked, eventually destroy their hosts.

Luckily, we have immune systems that recognise zombified cells and 'take care' of them. From an affinitological perspective, we can say that:

> **An affinitological virus is faulty information that is fed into a relationship to serve someone else's agenda to the detriment of the relationship. ***

[* Actually, perhaps that's a bit unfair to viruses because we now have evidence that, like bacteria, most viruses do not harm their hosts and are often in symbiotic (§ 31 Symbiosis) relationships, doing something beneficial for their host. In order to squeeze this aspect of viruses into our affinitological concept, we would need to change the definition of an affinitological virus to "information that enters the relationship from the outside that can either help or hinder the relationship." But, based on how the majority of us perceive viruses at the moment, this is less intuitive (and less dramatic) than the first definition. In addition, the first definition has more utilitarian value in that by calling some piece of information a 'virus', we are being explicit in focusing on the detrimental effects of the information, rather than then needing to go on to explain that this is a 'good' or 'bad' virus. Perhaps in the somewhat distant, future, when we start to warm to viruses more, in the same way that we look at bacteria (there are good ones and bad ones), we will need to find another word that will convey this 'detrimental' idea but, for now, let's stick to affinitological viruses as being 'bad'.]

An example might be someone who gives false information about a colleague to their boss in order to win favours with the boss. Note that it is the *information* that is the virus and not the individual 'Identity' (§ 29.4 The Omniself) who conveys that information.

In March 2018, *Science* published an article by Soroush Vosoughi, Deb Roy and Sinan Aral showing that "Lies spread faster than the truth". The researchers compared how true and false news stories spread on Twitter from 2006 to 2017. They looked at around 126,000 stories tweeted by around 3 million people and found that,

> **falsehoods spread "significantly farther, faster, deeper, and more broadly than the truth in all categories of information"**

Amongst many other interesting details, the authors found that false news spreads more than the truth because humans, not robots, are more likely to spread it. These conclusions suggest that we are just as apt at being vectors for 'information viruses' as our cells are for molecular viruses. And both are contagious. It is also, perhaps, not a coincidence that we talk about content going 'viral' on the internet.

[The authors of the above study also found the spreading of false information to be "more pronounced for false political news than for false news about terrorism, natural disasters, science, urban legends, or financial information (but that was before the COVID-19 pandemic)."]

Notice how applying biomedical terminology to interpersonal relationships can be empowering. In this case, it helps us to appreciate the similarities between the effects of misinformation and the devastating effects of viral epidemics.

> **Each of us can be a vector for misinformation. At that moment, we are weakening the collective and contributing to our own demise.**

36.2
Cells and Receptors
(Identities and Values)

Every cell has all of the features that we use to describe life (MRS GREN). As we continue to develop more advanced tools for studying cells, our discoveries of the incredible sophistication of cells continuously amaze us. [I would go as far as to say that cells are conscious, but that is a discussion for another time and place.] Cells are very versatile. They can differentiate into different types of cells. This is why we can get a whole organism (such as a human being) from a single cell (a fertilised egg). Notice that, from an affinitological perspective, Identities can also replicate and differentiate into different 'types' of Identities from a single set of Principles or Core Values (§ 29.4 The Omniself).

Cell differentiation is triggered by the extracellular environment of the cell. For example, if an undifferentiated (stem) cell is placed inside a heart, it differentiates (specialises) and becomes a heart cell. I am not aware of any evidence to suggest that once a cell has differentiated, it can go back to becoming a stem cell [the adage, 'you can't teach an old dog new tricks' comes to mind] although, I would not be surprised if that were possible.

Like stem cells, we adapt to our environment, or situation, by creating different (specialised) Identities (§ 29.4 The Omniself). Being much more evolved, [I presume (§ 33.4 Assumptions)], Identities are more versatile than cells .

Cells connect to (communicate with) other cells through receptors on their surface. They only notice those things about their environment that their receptors equip them to notice; just as we can only notice those things in our environment that our senses equip us to notice. Cells can also actively 'decide' to become more or less sensitive to what goes on in their environment. One of the ways in which they do this is by increasing or decreasing the number of sensitive receptors on their surface. This is one of the mechanisms of drug tolerance (how drugs lose their effect with extended use) as well as desensitization and acclimatisation (how we become less sensitive to certain stimuli in our environment).

Affinitologically, we can think of each Individual's multitude of Identities as individual cells. We develop this line of thought further in § 35.1 (Embryology of Relationships), § 37.7 (The Emergence of Identity), § 29.4 (The Omniself) and Unit 14 (Genetics of Relationships).

If Identities are cells, what are the affinitological equivalents of receptors on the surface of those cells? I propose that these are each Identity's values (§ 64.4 Values as Receptors). These values change depending on the Identity that is 'active' at the time (§ 29.4 The Omniself). We discuss these in more detail in § 42.2 (Beliefs, Values and Attitudes).

36.3

Tissues (Individuals)

When similar cells connect to each other, they form a tissue. When similar Identities coexist within a person, they form an individual (an Omniself). Notice that I am proposing a fundamental shift in perspective from a materialistic orientation where the 'body' is the individual to a more spiritual one. Here, the individual is a collection of Identities (Selves) that emerge within an individual to help it adapt to different social situations.

> **'The human condition'** then becomes the challenge to coordinate these various Identities so as to minimize conflicts between them.

One of the characteristics of physiological tissues is that the cells within each tissue share a common embryonic origin. Similarly, Identities within an individual emerge from that individual's developmental origin (experiences).

36.4

Organs (Pacta)

At this point, it would be helpful to take a look at how various sources define an (anatomical) organ.

1. "An organ is a self-contained group of tissues that performs a specific function in the body."
2. "Organ, in biology, a group of tissues in a living organism that have been adapted to perform a specific function."
3. "A differentiated structure (such as a heart, kidney, leaf, or stem) consisting of cells and tissues and performing some specific function in an organism"

The common theme in these definitions is that

a) Organs consist of more than one tissue and
b) Organs are concerned with specific functions.

In spite of the apparent consensus in defining organs as structures with 'specific functions', organs often perform several functions. For example, the lung is considered to be a single organ, yet it is multifunctional; in addition to its role as a regulator of oxygen delivery to the body, it acts as a conduit for the elimination of dead cells and microorganisms from the body [Phagocytic cells use the lung's mucociliary apparatus as a sanitation system (these cells also use other outlets such as the tear glands and the sweat glands to perform the same function)]. Our lungs also have an important role in regulating blood pH levels [much more so than our kidneys, actually].

Defining organs as units that perform specific functions [or, as I have indicated, several 'specific' functions] does have an important implication. The ability to perform specific functions is not conducive to adaptation; the more functions an organism can perform, the more adaptive [able to survive changes in the environment] it becomes. This means that organs cannot survive in isolation. By extension, cells (Identities) and tissues (Individuals) cannot survive in isolation either.

You might say, "But what about single-celled organisms such as an amoeba?" and I would say, "The answer is in your question". An amoeba is an 'organism' it is not merely a cell. Yes, cells can be organisms in themselves [just as the word 'go' can be both a word and a sentence (§ 14.1 Words are Meaningless)]. Cells have 'little organs' called organelles that perform 'specific functions' within the cell. So, what is the difference between a cell that forms a part of an organism and a cell that is, itself, a complete organism? Its ability to survive *independently* [be alive think MRS GREN (§ 26.2 Characteristics of Living Systems)]. What is important to note, however, is that an amoeba cannot form interdependent relationships (§ 23 Two Types of Relationship); it cannot create a 'society'; a multicellular (much more adaptive) living organism.

As we shall see later, our maturing understandings of the nature of interconnectedness in general, and our own interconnectedness in particular, can help us create more empowering and more satisfying SMERs (§ 36.9 Holons and § 90 Fractals). For example, since organs do not perform their functions at random, we can describe each 'specific function' that an organ performs as a goal (§ 66 Goals). Let's explore this in the context of the way in which we have defined relationships here.

A Pactum consists of a *pair* of individuals that connect to each other through common or complementary elements (§ 46 *Adjunctum Communalis*). We can think of each of these elements, or ingredients, as resources that form the basis for setting goals within relationships (§ 66 Goals).

[We explore the idea of Pacta in more detail in § 35.1 (Embryology of Relationships) and their extended interactions in sections § 32 (Extended Relationships, Communities and Beyond) and Unit 13 (§ 58-60 Paediatrics of Relationships and Adolescence).]

In physiology, several tissues make up an organ. In affinitology, a pair of individuals make up a Pactum. I am suggesting that the Pactum is the affinitological equivalent to a physiological organ. The usefulness of this analogy will become clearer in Unit 21 (Diversification and Speciation of Relationships). The implication here is that relationships (Pacta) do not operate in isolation. They influence and join with other Pacta as part of a larger collective.

36.5
Organ Systems
(Communities/Organisations)

When several organs join together to perform a series of interrelated functions, we call them Organ Systems. For example, the gastrointestinal (digestive) system consists of organs that include the mouth, teeth, oesophagus, stomach, duodenum, ileum and rectum. Being the next level up from an organ, I propose that we think of a community as the affinitological equivalent to an organ system.

When Pacta come together, social groups (clusters) are formed. These can include families, business or government organisations, NGOs and other sub-cultures or communities. The common goals of each of these clusters are usually confined to a limited number of dimensions of human experience (§ 48-50).

36.6
Organisms (Societies)

A community that can thrive, if it were detached from the society that it is a part of, can be thought of as a small (self-sufficient) organism. By our definition, that would make it more like a small society than a community. If this smaller society interacts with another community or society for their mutual benefit, this would create a symbiotic relationship (§ 31 Symbiosis), and not an organ system within a single organism. As independent units, these organisms (Societies), whether large or small, can then create and be part of a larger collective; an ecosystem.

What I am proposing here, therefore, is that a society is the larger collective that is formed through the interaction of social groups (communities) that are, themselves, dependent on the society that they are a part of.

Note that, like most concepts, these distinctions become blurred at their boundaries.

36.7
Culture (Species)

In § 32.4, I implied that culture is the fractal equivalent of Identity for communities. In terms of Levels of Organisation, they are analogous to species.

Cultures are categorised according to their distinctive characteristics, including common beliefs and values. They are a set of rules, guidelines, rituals and common frames of reference (such as artistic forms and mythoi) that reflect the combined historical knowledge of previous generations of a particular society. These rules, guidelines and rituals are 'social adhesives' that strengthen the connections between individuals within a society and lead to the creation of a common Identity. Without an attachment to such a Collective Identity (§ 32.4) or cultural affiliation, the Omniself remains culturally undifferentiated and can 'morph' to fit into any culture without becoming attached to that culture. Although such Omniselves are able to adapt, they do not carry cultural beliefs from one culture to another. This means that they do not diminish, enrich or disrupt their new host culture. Although I have met individuals who are (almost) like that, I believe them to be exceptionally rare.

Immigration often involves disconnecting from one culture and reconnecting with another culture. This requires 'turning off' certain Identities and their respective beliefs (genes) and turning on and acquiring new beliefs. This process also involves dealing with feelings of loss and various conflicts of Identity. We discuss this in § 63 (Epigenetics of Relationships).

The main criterion that determines whether two organisms belong to the same species is their ability to mate (or pollinate) to produce fertile offspring. When two societies share Common Elements within their respective cultures, then individuals from each of those societies can interact and the Pactum that emerges can incorporate aspects of both cultures.

36.8
Ecosystems and Humankind

When I was in primary school in Iran, the following poem by the early thirteen century Persian sage, Saadi Shirazi, was required reading for all school children there. Here is a literal (less poetic) translation:

> The children of Adam are members of the same body,
> Who in creation are from the same jewel,
> Should circumstance inflict pain upon one member,
> Other members cannot remain calm,
> You who are not upset by other people's suffering,
> Do not deserve to be called a human being.

When organisms rely on other organisms for their survival, an interconnected network of organisms emerges; an ecosystem. Similarly, when societies begin to interact in such a way that they begin to depend on each other for their survival, members of those societies become members of the same collective whole; an inter-societal ecosystem [some 'members', like Saadi, reach this understanding sooner than others ;-)]. This inter-societal ecosystem is what we sometimes refer to as 'the human race'. This is a misnomer, of course, because a race is a subspecies and the so-called 'human race' consists of many races within the same species. Actually, I would argue that there is no such thing as race. What we call race is simply (flawed) mental clustering based on the most rudimentary and primitive distinctions, such as the colour of skin, simply to create an in-group and an outgroup to compensate for our own weaknesses/laziness (§ 72.5 Cognitive Load and Heuristics).

[This is related to the Minimal Group Paradigm that we also encounter in section § 32.2 (Communities) and section § 78 (Active Protection)]

Thinking about what we could call our affinitological ecosystem, the word humanity came to mind. One meaning of this word fits the bill well. However, thinking it through, the word can be ambiguous because it has several other meanings too. Here, I propose the word Humankind to describe our network of interdependent cultures or 'Collective Identities' (§ 32.4).

[In our search for a more suitable term, we could borrow some concepts from computing. The word, Internet, is a contraction of the phrase, 'interconnected networks'. Networks are groups of computers working together. A Pactum is a single interactive unit. It is a network of two Identities. Perhaps, a vast network of interconnected Pacta (an ecosystem of Identities) could be called an Interpact. These were just thoughts that came to mind and I decided to share them with you because it may spark insights that could advance this topic.]

An important feature of ecosystems is that a disruption in one part of the ecosystem affects the whole ecosystem. It is the same with Humankind. When societies, especially cultures and subcultures, are disrupted in any part of the world, be it through war, oppression, colonisation, immigration, terrorism or in some other way [e.g. media infiltration through satellite broadcasts or social media], its effects resonate throughout Humankind and, in one way or another, affect everyone (§ 90 Fractals). The most lamentable of these effects is the loss of some part of our common human cultural heritage; that is, *our roots*.

One consequence of this is that disciplines like archaeology and anthropology emerge to try to salvage bits and pieces of the vast knowledge and experience that has been lost. Such loss of our common cultural heritage is equivalent to loss of experience (amnesia) at the individual level which leads us to continue to make the same mistakes. These mistakes are then manifested in history 'repeating itself'. Note that, by 'lost' I mean lost to our collective awareness or consciousness (no longer a part of our culture).

36.9

Holons

We have yet to identify the most basic level of organisation. A hot contender for this position at the moment is one-dimensional 'strings', but many of the details remain to be worked out. Whatever that most-basic-level-of-organisation may be, it will be indivisible and, as such, a 'whole' something. But that whole something is itself part of another whole something, a subatomic particle, for example. And that 'whole' subatomic particle, is part of another whole thing, an atom, all the way up to the universe, which may still turn out to be a part of something bigger [but that would defeat the purpose of the word 'universe' ;-)]. A holon [a term coined, so I am led to believe, by Arthur Koestler in his 1967 book, *The Ghost in the Machine*] is a whole something that is, itself, a part of a whole something.

What I am trying to say is that, even though we have defined an organism as a collection of organ systems and each organ system as a collection of organs and each organ as a collection of tissues and each tissue as a collection of cells and each cell as a collection of organelles, by invoking the concept of holons, we can look from a perspective that sees each of these as organisms that are a part of bigger organisms. Notice the similarity between this and our discussion of endosymbiosis in § 35.11.4 (Extended Consciousness). We can extend the argument to conclude that Humankind is an organism and that each organism that we call an individual human being is a part of it. And this would take us to the Saadi quotation above (§ 36.8 Ecosystems and Humankind).

36.10
In Summary

There are different levels of organisation in biological systems, beginning with cells (or simpler even) and growing hierarchically into ecosystems and, ultimately, into an ecosphere/biosphere. We can conceive of similar levels of organisation and hierarchical structures for networks created through interpersonal relationships which, of course, ultimately link into the ecosphere (joins with the biosphere). Rumi puts this eloquently.

> **"A drop is the ocean for as long as it is with the ocean, otherwise, the drop is a drop and the ocean is an ocean."**

[We return to this quotation in other sections of this course as it is relevant to other aspects of our current discussion about afffinitology.]

Since we have been talking about a relationship (Nexus) as being different from the two Identities (The Self and The Other) through which that relationship emerges, we need a different word to describe the structure that is formed when these three elements form a single unit. I have called this collective consisting of The Self, The Other and The Nexus, a *Pactum* (plural *Pacta*) which we explore in more detail in § 35.1 (Embryology of Relationships).

Pacta organise themselves into communities and communities organise themselves into societies. Societies interact to become interdependent, leading to the formation of ecosystems. I have proposed the word Humankind for this ecosystem.

In § 35.11 (Consciousness), I have related levels of organisation to the concept of consciousness and to Self-Organizing Systems (§ 91).

Unit 9
Identities, Roles and Personas

[Source: https://upload.wikimedia.org/wikipedia/commons/8/85/MooneyFaces.jpg]

Chapter 37

What *is* an Identity?

37.1

The Concept of Identity

The concept of Identity forms the basis for all our discussions here regarding the nature of relationships. It is, therefore, very important for us to have a clear understanding of what we mean by Identity in this context.

The word Identity has its etymological roots in the idea of sameness. Therefore, in principle, Identity is comprised of those aspects of the psyche that do not change over time. However, as a wise man once said, "Change is the only constant."

It is now widely believed (generally accepted) that life is a process of adaptation. And, clearly, there can be no adaptation without change. The idea of Identity, therefore, becomes a paradox because we are looking for sameness in a system that is designed to be dynamic. And if we look hard enough, we *are* able to find constant elements in our psyche, but, as I frequently point out, meaning is created by context. In other words, I am arguing that the meaning of Identity is situation dependent, even if some of the elements that comprise it are not.

Think of it like this. If water had a psyche similar to ours, and we subjected it to our tests to determine its sense of Identity, we would conclude that it is suffering from a severe case of "Disturbed Identity" [Yes, that is a real proposed diagnosis]. This is how the assessment may proceed:

Clinician: "Do you know who you are?"

Water: "Well, that depends on the situation. Sometimes I am a river and at other times I am a lake. Sometimes, I am the content of a cup and at other times I am freefalling from the edge of a ridge."

Clinician: "Do you imitate other people, instead of being yourself?"

Water: "Well, I don't quite know what you mean by 'yourself', but I do take the shape of whatever container I am put inside, except when it is very cold, then I keep the shape of the last container I was in."

Clinician: "I think you may have a severe case of 'disturbed Identity'. I recommend a course of psychoanalysis."

If nature, including its derivatives, such as the human psyche, is predicated on the principle of change [call it 'adaptation' if it makes you feel more at home], then why are we so adamant to impose sameness on it as an indicator of (mental) 'health'? The answer lies in, a) our need to connect and b) what we need to connect. The latter is the focus of our discussion in § 35.1 (Embryology of Relationships). For the components of any system (including a Pactum) to work together, they need to interact and, in order to do so, there needs to be some level of predictability (sameness). I am, therefore, not denying the concept of identity. What I am saying is that looking at it out of context will distort our understanding of it [thus, adding to our growing list of cognitive biases (§ 33.8 Confirmation Bias)]. To put it another way, if we *do* look for an individual's identity out of context, we shall continue to chase shadows.

37.2
Who are you?

Figure 16 Trend in the use of the word Identity in English

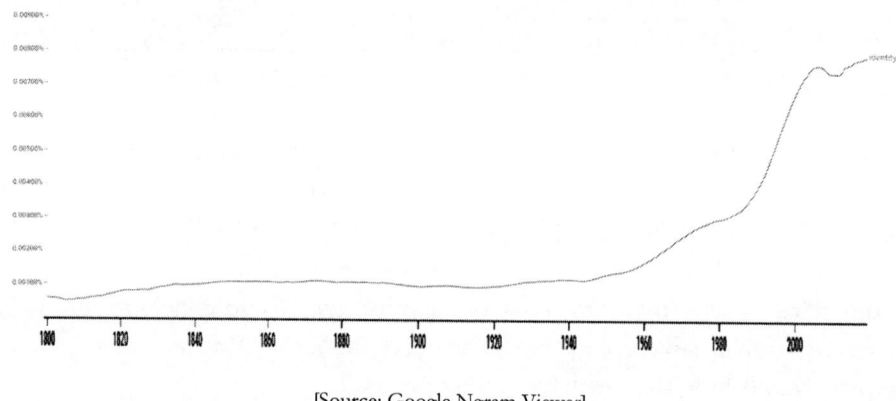

[Source: Google Ngram Viewer]

Some words become so deep rooted in society that they become, in the words of Carl Jung, archetypes. I propose that,

---

the idea of *who* is the archetype of archetypes.

The need to invoke the concept of identity arises from our need to connect and predictability is a prerequisite for that connection.

Now let's imagine the following alternative dialogue between a 'patient' (I've called him the interviewee) and a clinician:

Clinician: Who are you?
Interviewee: I am the entity talking to you
- Well, that's obvious.
- You asked a question that has an obvious answer.
- Ok, but how do you think of yourself?
- *How?* Through a cognitive process that I do not fully understand.
- Ok, but *what* do you think of yourself?
- I don't.
- So, what do you usually think about?
- I think about whatever the situation induces me to think about.
- So, you have an external locus of control?
- I would have to be inanimate not to react to the environment. Actually, come to think of it, inanimate objects react to their environment too, otherwise there would be no Newton's laws and no science of Chemistry.
- So, what does this situation induce you to think about?
- The answers to your questions.
- But what do you normally think about?
- I need to know more about what you think 'normal' is before I can answer that question.
- Ok, let's try this from a different angle; what do you do?
- I talk, I walk, I think, I drink...
- Yes, yes, but what gives meaning to your life?
- What is meaning?
- What is the purpose of your life?
- My purpose is to survive, to connect and to grow.
- I think I understand you now.
- I am glad.
- You have an identity problem.
- What is a problem?
- A problem is an inability to adapt.
- I adapt, otherwise I would not have survived so far.
- That's true.
- So, what is the problem?
- The problem is that you don't know who you are.
- I *do* know who I am.
- Then who are you?
- I am the entity talking to you.

Such a conversation would probably be so alien to a clinician that she is likely to be compelled to attach some kind of label to their interlocutor, turning him into a 'patient'. However, there is no internal incongruity in the answers that the interviewee was giving. He simply refused to be drawn into a conversation involving abstract archetypes.

37.3
Is Identity Definable?

Exploration of the literature on the subject has led me to conclude that, like the notion of life itself (§ 26.2 Characteristics of Living Systems), we can talk extensively about identity but it is not something that we have managed to define conclusively. Furthermore, the way the term is used (even by authorities on the subject) makes the concept indistinguishable from personality, character, self-concept and motivation. Here are a few examples.

A search for the term 'identity' in the fifth (2013) edition of the Diagnostic and Statistical Manual of Mental Disorders returned 194 results. Throughout the manual, the term 'identity' is not defined, but a meaning is sometimes alluded to. For example, for 'dissociative identity disorder', the diagnostic criteria are,

> "Disruption of identity characterized by two or more distinct personality states... The disruption in identity involves marked discontinuity in sense of self and sense of agency..."

If 'disruption of identity' is characterized by multiple 'personality' states, then a consistency in 'personality' is characterized by coherence of, or lack of disruption in, 'identity'. This implies that identity and personality can be regarded as being synonymous (at least in *this context*).

Focusing on the assertion that 'disruption of identity' involves a disruption (discontinuity) in the 'sense of self/agency', another way of talking about 'sense of agency' is through the concept of 'locus of control' (§ 44), which the APA dictionary defines as,

> "A construct that is used to categorize people's basic motivational orientations and perceptions of how much control they have over the conditions of their lives."
>
> [source: https://dictionary.apa.org/locus-of-control]

This relates the concept of identity to motivation. It indicates that we can gain insights into our sense of self, by looking at factors that motivate us.

In his influential 1968 book, *Identity, Youth and Crisis*, Erik H. Erikson, referring to a quote from William James, states,

> "James uses the word "character," but I am taking the liberty of claiming that he describes a sense of identity."

In other words, the word 'character' can be a substitute for 'identity' too.

In the same book, Erikson [optimistically] states,

> "But one may note with satisfaction that the conceptualization of identity has led to a series of valid investigations which, if they do not make clearer what identity is, nevertheless have proved useful in social psychology."

From a clinical perspective, attempts have been made to establish 'norms' for identity so that 'normal identity development' can be measured. The types of questions used in such questionnaires [social scientists call them 'inventories'] are context-neutral. Indeed, in some inventories, agreeing with the statement, "I change a lot depending on the situation" would be indicative of a 'Disturbed Identity'.

Let me break down the process through which I arrived at the definition of Identity [note the change in capitalisation] that I am going to use in this discourse. Originally, I phrased the definition like this, **"An Identity is the sum total of everything a person identifies with in *a particular situation."*** But decided to be more specific because it sounded somewhat like a circular definition. I, therefore, changed it to, **"An Identity is the sum total of everything that affects a person's value judgements in a particular situation."** But this raises the question, "What is a 'person' and how is that different from an identity?" A more robust concept than 'person' is the notion of 'Self'. We explore the concept of Self in detail in § 22.1 (The self and The Other), where I have proposed that what we perceive as a 'self' is a dynamic community of Identities held together by common or Core Values. To distinguish this from our common understanding of the self as a single entity (and to act as a reminder of the inherent multiplicity of our psyche), I have called a 'person' an Omniself (§ 29.4). Integrating this idea into the previous definition, for the purpose of our discussions here,

> **An Identity is the sum total of everything that affects a self's value judgements in *a particular situation.***

Our (sense of) Identity, therefore, is determined by what we Identify with in a particular situation which affects our sense of self, or *who*, we *become* in that situation. The critical point here is that, our Identities are situation-dependent (§ 29.4 The Omniself). We identify with those aspects of the environment that we associate with our values and principles. These determine what we *notice* and, therefore, what we are sensitive to (§ 34 Cells, Receptors and Sensitivity) in a particular situation and this, in turn, guides or triggers (§ 40.2 Behaviourism versus Humanism) our behaviour. Whether something about an environment guides or triggers a behaviour depends on the extent to which that behaviour has been repressed or habituated/conditioned (§ 68.5 Habits). In either case,

> In *any particular situation*, my Identity is made up of everything that I identify with *at that moment*.

37.4
Identity and Sensitivity

To identify with something, I must first notice (become aware of) it. Depending on the situation, we become sensitive to different aspects of the environment (§ 64.4 Values as Receptors). For example, the mother of a toddler would be sensitive to those aspects of the environment that could cause a potential threat to the child (sharp objects, corners of furniture that could be at the toddler's eye level, slippery floors, etc.). In other words, in a situation where a toddler is present, the Mother Identity becomes active/prominent. Now, compare that with the Father Identity of a teenager who is more likely to be sensitive to (notice) how his daughter is dressed and the time of day or night that she leaves or enters the house, but may not notice a sharp object on the floor.

How can we recognise something that we identify with? I identify with things that I feel I am part of, or things that I feel are a part of me. Herein lies a clue as to how we can recognise something that we identify with; what we identify with evokes a feeling in us. In other words,

> where there is a feeling, there is a connection to an Identity.

You might say, "But Bijan, I sometimes see a complete stranger who evokes a feeling in me. How can I identify with a complete stranger?" And my response would be that you are not identifying with the complete stranger, you are identifying with those aspects of the stranger that evoke a *feeling* in you (§ 47 Common and Complementary Elements).

37.5
Identities, Memories, Feelings and Values

A critical question that arises here is, "What connects an Identity to a feeling?" Memories. If a noticed pattern in the environment matches a pattern in our memory archives, it evokes a feeling. Often, the memories are not consciously accessible.

Our Identities determine our values (what we are sensitive to) and our values are triggered by patterns in the environment that we are primed to notice by the 'active' Identity. Patterns in the environment trigger our memories. Our memories evoke feelings and our feelings direct our emotions. See also § 51.2 (Affect, Feelings and Emotions) and § 65 (Attitudes).

You might be wondering, "But Bijan, what about those feelings that we get from something (call them patterns if you like) that we have not encountered before or have any memories of?" To say that we have no memories of something is misleading. We may not have any memories of an event if we never experienced it. However, if we did experience it [or something similar enough to lead to a pattern match], then 'I have no memories of it' means 'I cannot *recall* that experience'.

Memories and remembering are two different phenomena. Memories are what is stored in our psyche (content) and remembering is what we are able to *recall* from that archive (process). How well we recall something depends on the way in which we organise and index our memories [I propose that this is something that we can (and 'should') teach our children from a young age, but that discussion best be left for another time and place].

I propose that we have two main mechanisms for organising and indexing our memories; cognitive association and emotional association. Think of them as being like serial and parallel processing. [As with most apparent dichotomies in life, the true picture is a grayscale (§ 25.3 Polar Bond: Partial Sharing)]. The distinction can help us understand why some memories are easier to retrieve than others. Some memories have a greater cognitive component and some have greater emotional component.

Cognitive association helps us to memorise *processes*. Processes are about how various phenomena fit together through space and time. They are serial in nature. For example, earlier, I was listening to a piece of music from my student days; decades ago. It has a musical introduction before the lyrics. The moment I heard the first bar of the intro, I began to remember and anticipate the next bar, but it wasn't until the music had reached the stage just before the lyrics that I began to remember the lyrics, even though I was straining my mind to remember the lyrics as soon as the music started. Memorising the anatomy of a flower is also primarily cognitive in nature; unless it becomes a gestalt (§ 15.2 The Importance of Gestalts). It requires us to build a mental picture of how the different parts of a flower fit together in space and time. If we were to learn the anatomy of a flower dispassionately (with minimal emotional component), then the only way to trigger the recall of this knowledge would be through exposure to one of the components in the process. For example, if I say the word 'flower' to you, that is more likely to trigger memories with a strong emotional component (see below). However, if I say the words 'anther and stigma', then, those of you who have been exposed to these words are likely to recall the image of a diagram of a cross-section of a flower from a textbook. Dispassionate information seems to be stored in deeper archives within our psyche making them less readily accessible.

Emotional association helps us to memorise *events*, including gestalts (§ 15.2). Rather than being in deep archives, it is as if such memories are on display in the library of our minds and categorised by emotional arousal and valence.

Here is an example to demonstrate the difference between cognitive association versus emotional association-based memories. In most people, the phrase 'school biology' is likely to evoke images of a classroom and specific images of times when we were particularly emotional (excited or upset). However, for me, it evokes images of me skipping in the heathlands of Southwest England and shouting "Go wild in the country" [which was the title of a song by a group called 'Bow Wow Wow']. That's because, at around the time that the song was in the British charts, my Biology teacher took me under his wing and I spent a couple of weeks of Easter holidays at his house [thanks, Andy]. I have just scanned my memory for anything else associated with 'school biology' and most of them have emotional content of relatively high intensity. I then scanned my memories with the key phrase, "content of biology syllabus" and this time, the first thing that my probe recovered was an image of the green cover of my school biology textbook. I began to mentally flick through the pages and I remembered words and diagrams associated with 'photosynthesis', 'Krebs cycle', 'evolution' and so on. In these cases, the memories take more time and effort to retrieve.

37.6
Being and Playing
(Identities, Roles and Personas)

In this section, I expound on the idea that there is a difference between *being* a father and *playing* the role of a father (pretending to be a father). [Note that, as we are about to explore, my (real) role as a father is different from me playing the role of a father. See also § 56 (To Play or Not Play).]

In psychology, the word Identity is rarely seen in isolation; we talk about national identity, racial identity, gender identity, ego identity, etc. I can, therefore, have a national identity which is different from my racial identity which is independent of my gender identity and so on. In addition to emphasising the critical influence of context on the notion of identity, it highlights the similarities between our affinitological (context-dependent) perception of Identity and what is understood by the term 'role' within a psychological context. The APA Dictionary of Psychology defines 'role' as

"A coherent set of behaviors expected of an individual in a specific position within a group or social setting."

The difference between this definition of the term 'role' and our definition of the term 'Identity' lies in the word 'expected'. Now, the APA definition of 'role' does not indicate expected by whom. If I expect myself to behave within certain parameters in a certain situation, and I do so, then I have fulfilled a specific 'role' in that situation. And fulfilling that role is tantamount to 'who' I am in that situation; hence, my role becomes my Identity.

Taking a closer look at the above definition, if we assume, as is generally the case, that the word 'expected' is a reference to what society expects rather than what the individual expects of himself, then we notice that a 'role' is being defined as a form of *dissociative state* where the individual is not being true to herself, but is, instead, behaving in accordance with society's expectations in a given social situation. That is to say; the individual is 'acting' as she is expected to act rather than as she would act naturally. This is akin to Jung's concept of Persona (§ 38), which the same dictionary defines as,

"The public face an individual presents to the outside world, in contrast to more deeply rooted and authentic personality characteristics... The term is taken from the mask worn by actors in Roman antiquity."

Earlier, I defined the term Identity as, "The sum total of everything that a person identifies with in *a particular situation.*" By deliberately defining the concept of Identity in terms of the situation, I have implied that, even though one may behave differently, or more pertinently, *inconsistently*, in different situations, this need not be incompatible with the individual's core sense of self; what I have called 'Core Values' (§ 29.4 The Omniself). This approach makes the concept of 'roles' redundant in that, if my behaviour in any particular situation is not consistent with my core sense of self, then the term 'persona' (mask) would be a more accurate depiction of what is happening.

In § 29.4 (The Omniself), I use the example of playing the role of a father and being a father to explain that the former is a persona whereas the latter is something that the person identifies with (in the situation) and is, therefore, not a mask, but an adaptation.

**When a chameleon changes its colours to camouflage (adapt) itself,
it remains true to what it is** (its integrity remains intact);
it does not become something else.

37.7

The Emergence of Identity

The emergence of Identity is synonymous with the emergence of a Self within the Omniself. From this perspective, we are the result of the amalgamation of all the Identities that we have created for ourselves or have been created for us.

[This reminds me of the following dialogue from the opening scene of the movie, Parenthood:

Young Gil: Look, you have to understand. My father, in his own childhood, was without a positive male influence.

Usher: Huh?

- His own father kicked him out when he was 15, so my dad was taught to see child-raising as a job, a burden, a prison, rather than a playground. Do you understand what I'm saying?

- You don't talk like a kid.

- Yeah, well, I'm not really a kid.

- You're not a duck.

- This is a memory of when I was a kid. I'm 35 now. I have kids of my own. You don't really even exist. You're an amalgam.

- A what?

- A combination of several ushers my dad left me with over the years. I've combined them into one memory.

- Why?

- This was a great symbolic moment of my life, my father dumping me with you. It's why I swore things would be different with my kids. That's my dream; strong, happy, confident kids.

- That's great. That's great, you know, you got a lovely family, and I'm a goddamn amalgam.]

37.7.1

Identities are Created and Maintained by Attentional Biases

At any one moment, our experience of the world around us is not determined by the reality of the situation, but by those aspects of the situation that we choose to focus on (§ 33 Atasinex Cluster).

We are inherently pattern-seeking animals. Without patterns, our mind would be filled with nothing more than randomness. And randomness is not exactly conducive to consciousness (§ 35.11). Therefore, in any situation that we find ourselves, we either see patterns that are already there or we impose patterns that are not there (and then proceed to see them). An obvious example of the latter is our perception of 'constellations'. There are no such things. They are mental projections of our collective psyche onto the night sky. Nevertheless, they have given rise to many human endeavours and pursuits including astronomy and significant cultural development through mythology, beliefs in the predictability of the future through clairvoyance [and the sense of security that it bestows] and very lucrative enterprises through astrology.

Once our mind decides that a pattern exists in a particular situation, it proceeds to focus on that pattern, almost to the exclusion of all other patterns that may be discernible [or imposable] upon that particular situation. This is the basis for our attentional biases. Let me demonstrate.

Imagine that, one day, you look up into the sky and see the scene shown in figure 17. What do you see? You might say, "I see a bunch of clouds." And I would say, "I appreciate that, but I want you to use your imagination to see what *patterns* you might be able to see within those clouds." [Yes, it *is* a bit like the Rorschach test].

Figure 17 A typical image of clouds

The first thing that I saw was something that looks like a grizzly bear [inside a rectangle whose diagonal line extends from (11,1) to (17½,8)] and a 'fire-breathing wolf' [rectangle (12,10½) to 17½,8½)]. I then closed my eyes and pretended that I am at a BERA [British Educational Research Association] conference, where I have been immersed in discussions about science education. When I opened my eyes, I saw what looks like a fish [its eye is at grid reference (16,10.5)] and the ocean theme prompted me to see a Manta ray (just above and to the left of the fish) and a turtle with its head at (5½,6). I also saw a swan [(11,9) to (17½,2]. I then repeated the exercise, but this time, I imagined that I am browsing the pictures on the walls of an art gallery. When I opened my eyes, I saw the profile of a witch [her eye is at (11½,4½)]. Then, when I imagined a domestic scene, I saw a pet cat pouncing playfully on a baby [the eye of the cat is at grid reference (9.8,4.3)]. After that, my mind went into playful (pattern-seeking [as opposed to meaning or coherence seeking]) mode and began to see lots of other patterns [including a poodle wearing black goggles (13,10) to (15,11) :-)]. What this shows is that,

---

our mental state determines what patterns we see and the patterns we see determines our mental state.

[I know that this leaves many questions unanswered, including, "What exactly is a mental state?" but for the sake of brevity and to keep our focus on the problem at hand, let's leave that discussion for another time and place.]

It is easier [reduces our cognitive load (§ 72.5)] to take a pattern 'off the shelf' than to create a new one. Words anchor patterns (package them and put them on our psychological shelf). A concept is a ready-made pattern that we can fit reality (the situation) into. When we become familiar with a word, we become familiar with the concept that the word packages for us.

This is why our mind tends to seek patterns that it is familiar with (§ 33.8 Confirmation Bias). When we find a pattern, especially one that matches a word in our vocabulary, that pattern then becomes one of the defining features of the situation for us. We then decide which of our existing Identities is best suited to that situation [or word] (combination of perceived patterns). We do this by asking two questions,

    a) "Which of my values is this situation best suited for?" and

    b) "Which of my Identities is best suited to take maximum advantage of* this situation?"

    * [as in, derive maximum (holistic) benefit from, not as in abuse]

37.7.2
Attitudes and Identity

What are attitudes? Attitudes are beliefs that are linked to emotions (§ 65 Attitudes). This is why attitudes are difficult to change; the change would somehow threaten the integrity of my current Identity. The implication here is that, for us to be able to change an attitude, we first need to disentangle its intellectual components (the beliefs) from its affective components (§ 51.2 Affect, Feelings and Emotions). We discuss attitudes in more detail in § 42.2 (Beliefs, Values and Attitudes).

37.8

Self-Concept and Multiple Identities

APA defines self-concept as

> "One's description and evaluation of oneself, including psychological and physical characteristics, qualities, skills, roles and so forth. Self-concepts contribute to the individual's sense of identity over time."
>
> [source: https://dictionary.apa.org/self-concept].

In other words,

Our sense of identity is created through our self-concepts.

The main difference between the definition of self-concept, above, and the notion of self-esteem (§ 40.3) is that self-concept is about how we *perceive* ourselves whilst self-esteem is about how we *evaluate* (determine the *value* of) the identity that we derive for ourselves on the basis of our self-concept. These definitions and their distinctions may seem straightforward enough except that they are not. Let me explain.

As far back as the 1970s, it was recognised that we do not have a single self-concept. Semantically, the idea of self-concept is like the idea of 'colour'. We can talk about colour and we know what we are talking about, but the notion of colour is abstract until we decide to be practical. At that point, we need to specify the colour that we are talking about. It is the same with the self-concept. Let us begin the rest of our discussion with an excerpt from a paper published in 2000.

> "Until the late 1970s it was commonly accepted that self-concept was a unidimensional construct. Little support for subscales among self-concept scales was found in factor analyses, and consequently global self-concept tended to be the major unit of study in research. Shavelson, Hubner, and Stanton (1976) leveled charges against the field more than 20 years ago when they lamented that "(self-concept research) has addressed itself to substantive problems before problems of definition, measurement, and interpretation have been resolved" (p. 10); Wylie, in her seminal reviews of self-concept, expressed similar concerns (1974, 1979). Although the question of whether self-concept is a unidimensional or multidimensional construct has been settled during the past 20 years in favor of a multidimensional theoretical structure, there has been little empirical effort expended to determine the primary domains that underpin the construct."
>
> [Source: Bracken, B. A., Bunch, S., Keith, T. Z., & Keith, P. B. (2000). Child and adolescent multidimensional self-concept: A five-instrument factor analysis. *Psychology in the Schools, 37*(6), 483-493.]

The authors then go on to propose a multidimensional self-concept, being hierarchical and consisting of six higher order dimensions, as shown in figure 18 [Source: *ibid*].

Figure 18
Representation of the Dimensions of self-concept by Bracken et. al.

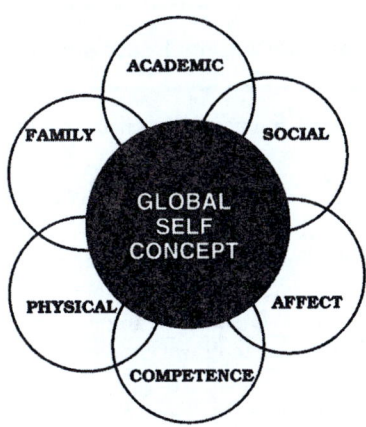

In this discourse, I have repeatedly implied that such 'dimensions' only become relevant *in context*. In other words, I contend that it is *the situation* that determines our self-concept. What I am proposing here is that,

---

Self-related constructs are *dynamic* and change depending on the situation.

In § 25.3 (Polar Bond), I explained how we have a tendency to impose blackness and whiteness by drawing arbitrary lines somewhere along what is essentially a grayscale. In § 89 (Evolution through Relationships), I use the example of a tree to explain how we also have the tendency to look for, and mentally extract, common features from what are, essentially, distinct phenomena and group those phenomena into abstract generalisations. We can also see this in figure 18; the idea that there is a 'global' self-concept. I contend that there is no such thing as a global self-concept (just as there is no such thing as the 'average' person); whether or not I think well of myself (my self-concept) depends on when are where I am. If I had a 'global' sense of who I am (or my worth), the situation would not make a difference, but even the most severely depressed person is cured, not by changing who he believes himself to be, but by changing his (perception of) the situation.

At the beginning of this section, I pointed out that APA's definition of identity is based on the premise that 'our identity is based on our self-concept'. This means that,

> **If our self-concept is situational, so is our 'sense of identity'.**

Let's take a look at an excerpt from an illuminating study published in 2002:

"The most important finding of the present investigation was the existence of a clearly defined, multidimensional structure of self-concept based on the self-report responses of 4- and 5-year-olds. This finding implies that very young children are able to distinguish between multiple dimensions of self-concept at an even younger age than has been demonstrated in studies based on other self-concept instruments and provides strong support for those like us who argue for the importance of self-report as a research tool in developmental and early childhood research."

[Source: Marsh, H. W., Ellis, L. A., & Craven, R. G. (2002). How do preschool children feel about themselves? Unraveling measurement and multidimensional self-concept structure. Developmental psychology, 38(3), 376.]

In § 29.4 (The Omniself), I proposed that we can think of each individual as a container [for want of a better word] in which several 'people' reside at the same time. You could think of our bodies as time-share properties occupied by different Identities at different times, except that, since affinitology is a fledgling discipline, there is no research as yet to help explain how these time-share contracts are negotiated between the various Identities. Nevertheless, it is clear that context (including social expectations) plays a critical role.

To see what this notion of multiple Identities looks like in practice, imagine that you meet someone at a gathering, let's say, a research conference, and you start a conversation. You would naturally assume that you are talking to one person. It would be very unlikely for you to be saying to yourself, "I wonder which one of her multitude of Identities is communicating with me right now." However, you would see a 'different side' to this person if you meet again at a wedding. We explore this idea in more detail in § 27 (The Meeting of Minds).

37.9

Are Identities Alive?

In § 26.2 (Characteristics of Living Systems), I mentioned that I would prefer to define life in terms of consciousness, that is,

> **If it is alive, it is conscious and if it is conscious, it is alive.**

I hear some of you protesting that there are many people lying 'unconscious' in hospital and yet, they are alive. This is a semantic problem, not a functional one. As I have discussed in § 35.11 (Consciousness), there is a difference between unconscious and non-conscious.

From this perspective, the question of whether or not each individual Identity (that comprise the Omniself) is alive becomes, "Are each of our Identities capable of exercising individual choice?" And I would say, "Yes, each of the Identities within an Omniself can and does exercise independent choice." For example, *at any particular moment* when I am alone with my wife, my Father Identity can choose to either be present or absent. If present, it can relate to my wife as a father figure (supportive and nurturing) or as a father (having mutual interest in our children).

[We could classify these as sub-Identities of the Father Identity or as two separate Identities. More research needs to be carried out to work out the details].

This Father Identity can also decide which of its ego states to manifest, The Child (I want this for my children), The Adult (what is the best course of action?) or The Parent (why doesn't she do what I tell her to do?). Therefore, not only can an Identity exercise choice, it can have a conversation with itself (§ 73 Transactional Analysis).

37.9.1

The Decision Ratifier

A question that remains unanswered is this, "Does each Identity decide for itself whether to 'take the podium' or is there an entity at the top of the hierarchy that decides which Identity should be active/dominant at any moment?" Experience from observation of human and animal organisations suggests that every 'purposeful group' chooses an ultimate decision-maker of some kind. Actually, it may be more conducive to the establishment of SMERs (which is what all this is about) if we think of, and call, such a person or entity a **decision** *ratifier*. This reduces the chances of the ratifying entity losing sight of their role and becoming side-tracked by notions of being 'in charge' or 'in control' or 'the leader'. It also implies that, even in the presence of a ratifying or coordinating entity, each Identity is not simply a passive participant in the process.

[In § 38.2 (Persona versus Self-Deception), I talk a little more about this and touch upon Ernest Hilgard's concept of The Hidden Observer. This is a possible candidate for that coordinating entity or decision ratifier.]

Earlier (§ 1.2 The Seed), I quoted Professor Norman from the movie, Lucy:

> **"The sole purpose of life has been to pass on what was learned."**

This points to another distinguishing characteristic of life; purpose. More specifically, to "pass on what has been learned". From this perspective, we can ask, "Does it appear that each of our Identities has a purpose?" and "Does that purpose relate to the collection and dissemination of what has been learned?"

[I am sticking to 'learned'; steering away from words like knowledge and information, because knowledge and information are very different, but I don't want to get side-tracked into a discussion about that, especially since we would have to bring wisdom into the equation. Not that the idea of 'learning' is not controversial, it's just that it is more generic (includes both memorisation and understanding at all its levels). I encourage you to search for 'Bloom's Taxonomy' to find out more).]

In conclusion, Identities, having a purpose and the ability to exercise choice are alive (and conscious).

37.10
Summary

To summarize, rephrase and reiterate, I put it to you that, Identity is only definable in the context of change. However, since the whole concept of Identity is a quest to create a sense of continuity (consistency/sameness), defining Identity with explicit reference to change may appear to create an internal inconsistency. This apparent contradiction stems from the original intention which led to the creation of the concept of Identity which was (and has been) to allow us to feel secure in the knowledge that people are predictable and, therefore, 'safe' to interact with. By defining Identity (sameness) in the context of change (the situation), I hope to help us feel safe in interacting with people without needing to constrain, label or pigeonhole them in the way that we are generally inclined to do at the moment. This means changing our language patterns by reducing the number of adjectives that we use to describe ourselves and others (*cf.* § 40.3 Self-Esteem) by changing phrases such as, "He is" and "I am" to "He does" and "I do" or even more empowering, "He tends to" and "I tend to" *"in these kinds of situations"*.

Chapter 38

Personas

Don't worry, I am not going to turn this section into a discourse on Jungian Psychology, but the concept of persona allows us to make a distinction (appreciate the difference) between what I have called True and False Identity.

The words person, persona and personality all come from the same Greek root meaning 'mask' which, in Latin became the word to describe a character in a play. The allusion being that characters in a play are not true characters, they are imitations. Its later use in French (Persone and Personne) to denote a human being makes me wonder whether those who adopted this word implicitly bought into the idea that, who we see someone as being, is different from who they actually are. From one perspective, such an assumption would be very reasonable because, in a sense, all of our knowledge is superficial let alone our knowledge about 'who' other people are.

There is another sense in which we can interpret the adoption of the word 'mask' to mean a 'person' that can be more disturbing. It would imply that a 'person' is someone who *deliberately* hides his true self and presents to the world what he is not. Or, to put it more bluntly, it means that you can only be classed as a 'person' if it is in your character to lie about who you really are.

There is extensive research and literary exploration of lies and deception that delve into these concepts from every conceivable angle [It's probably safer to say, 'from every angle that has been conceived so far']. Given our current concern, namely SMERs, it is not necessary to consider every conceivable angle. Let me clarify.

Every relationship consists of only three primary elements, The Self, The Other and The Nexus. The Self and The Other are the same concept viewed from two separate points of reference. The Nexus emerges through interactions between The Self and The Other. In short, everything in affinitology revolves around the concept of The Self. Therefore, it is crucial for every student of affinitology to be able to determine whether The Self (and The Other) in any particular relationship is rooted in openness or misrepresentation.

In affinitology, the underlying assumption or premise is that each Identity is true to itself. This means that when we see our colleague with his offspring behaving as a father does, he is not pretending to be a father and he is not assuming the role of a father. At that moment, his Father Identity is in control and he *is* a father. In being a father, he is in no way masking or denying his Colleague Identity. To put it a different way, when he is being a father, he is not pretending not to be a colleague. He is being true to himself (his Identity) as a father and that is not in conflict with him being true to himself as a colleague (or husband or lover or friend or whatever).

The idea of persona or mask only becomes relevant when we create an Identity that pretends to be what it is not. For example, if I do not enjoy the company of children and I pretend that I do, creating a false Father Identity within myself, then my interaction is not through my true Identity, but through a Father Persona. So, what is a False Identity or a Persona?

A Persona is an Identity that does not believe in the values that it purports.

38.1
Personas are Rooted in Doubt

For affinitological purposes, the question, "How can we distinguish a true Identity from a Persona?" is an important one. Of course, this is easier to do in relation to The Self than The Other. However, being able to do that for ourselves solves half of the problems that can thwart our efforts to create and maintain SMERs. The trick is in being able to recognise a niggling feeling of 'what if' in the back of our minds. "What if she doesn't like me?", "What if I don't get the job?", "What if I lose my reputation", "What if I don't get what I want?". In a word; **doubt**. See also § 51 (The Emotional Dimension).

Doubt is the opposite of faith. In Persian, the word for 'faith' is *îmān* (a loanword from Arabic). The root of this word is *amn* which means secure. In other words, faith is the means (or *a* means) through which one attains a sense of security, that is to say,

---

one who has faith is one who feels secure.

Viewed from the opposite direction, this means that **fear is a sign of lack of faith**. Faith means trust and another word for trust is confidence. Hence, we can extend our previous understanding and say that **fear is a sign of lack of confidence**. Putting it all together, it follows that, where there is doubt there is fear and, where there is fear, there is a sense of vulnerability and the practical point of these deliberations is that,

> **where there is a sense of vulnerability, there is often an overwhelming temptation to evoke psychological defense mechanisms.**

So, what does all this have to do with Persona? I am glad you asked. Invoking a persona (a mask) is one of numerous psychological defence mechanisms (PDMs). Lamentably, PDMs are prevalent and generally have a detrimental role in our relationships. We explore PDMs in § 79.

38.2
Persona versus Self-Deception

A persona is a false image that we present to the world, *knowing* (being consciously aware) that what we are portraying is in conflict with 'who' we really are; our Core Values (§ 29.4.1 Identities, Core Values and Principles). The downside to invoking a Persona is that if the Persona occupies a seat on, let's call it 'the council of Identities', for too long, it becomes an honorary member. We explore this idea in more detail in § 29.4 (The Omniself).

As we have noted, the main difference between a Persona and a True Identity is that a Persona is at odds with some of our Core Values; the principles that harmonise our real Identities. This means that the Persona becomes a disruptive influence because, with a permanent seat on 'the council', it can influence our behaviour in ways that we cannot justify on the basis of our principles. This leads to inner conflict. And nothing drains our psychological resources like 'chronic' inner conflict [This is related to the soundbite; "Any decision is better than indecision" (§ 51.8.7 Indecision)]. The draining of our resources can disrupt our decision-making processes and can have disastrous consequences for our physical health, mental health and, naturally, our interpersonal relationships (§ 93-95 Thermodynamics of Relationships).

What happens when we begin to believe our own personas? Imagine what would happen if an actor playing the role of Hamlet in a play, did not let go of that persona after the play is over and began to believe that he *is* Hamlet [or Hercules, or Captain America, or Homer, or even, just an 'extra']. I propose that,

> **Self-deception is when we are fooled by ourselves because we are not able to distinguish a Persona from an authentic Identity.**

This is the risk that we take when we evoke personas. I can hear what some of you are thinking, "Who is the 'we' who is not able to distinguish?" This could be Hilgard's Hidden Observer [also mentioned in § 29.1, § 37.9 and § 78], but I would suggest that it is the other Identities on the council (united by having the same Core Values). For example, if I create a false Father Persona within myself, one who pretends to prioritise children's welfare over and above his own [because, for whatever reason, I am incapable of creating a true Father Identity within me and society expects me to have one] then, in that particular situation, I begin to *act* like a father without the requisite Values (value systems) to *be* a father. As long as I am aware that this is an act, I am not deceiving myself, I am deceiving society [This also requires that I dissociate myself from that (society) which I am a part of (§ 36.9 Holons)]. If my other Identities begin to accept this imposter as a genuine article, then they become prone to confirmation bias (§ 33.8) and will overlook evidence that indicates that the father character is a Persona and not a true Identity.

An important point here is that we will only evoke a Persona when we perceive ourselves to be separate from society. That is to say, when I take a 'me and them' approach to interpersonal relationships. Otherwise, I will not be able to conceive of a way of deceiving society without simultaneously deceiving myself. This takes us back to the following quotation by Rumi [which we also discuss in § 36 (Levels of organisation) and § 30.1 (The Nexus)]:

> **"A drop is the ocean for as long as it is with the ocean,
> otherwise, the drop is a drop and the ocean is an ocean."**

So, one might well wonder, "What would be our motivation for deceiving society if we are a part of it?" And one might find some insights into this in § 39 (Social Ranking Criteria).

38.3

Alternatives to Personas

(And other Psychological Defence Mechanisms)

Some people argue that personas are both normal and necessary. I do not reject that premise outright. However, I would argue that, in this context, 'normal' (§ 71 What is Normal?) is a statistical construct and it does not mean 'healthy' and 'necessary' is a situational concept and is meaningless in the absence of a context. Personas may be normal and necessary in contemporary society, but that does not mean they are healthy. To put this into a more tangible context, a fever may be a 'normal' and 'necessary' response to a viral infection, but in a healthy (uninfected) individual, a fever is neither normal nor necessary.

Similarly, playing interpersonal games, putting on an act, adopting a persona, etc. may or may not be 'normal' and 'necessary' responses to a society depending on the extent to which that society is healthy. This brings us to the Krishnamurti quotation that I have cited in § 86 (What is Mental Illness?),

> **"It is not a sign of good mental health to be well adjusted to a profoundly sick society."**

This suggests that creating a false (unhealthy) Identity, a Persona, in the face of possible rejection by society may be an unhealthy response. Note that there is a contradiction between this point of view and my viral infection analogy because it suggests that, even if my environment is corrupt, to respond to it by creating an unhealthy inner environment (in the case of the virus analogy, a fever, and in the case of an unhealthy society, a Persona) is not a sign of a healthy individual.

You might say, "But Bijan, are you suggesting that the immune system (the fever producing process) should not kick in when our body is infected with a virus?" And my answer is, maybe. I cannot speak too much for the body. I am not sure whether a fever is a 'normal' and 'necessary' response to a particular viral infection. Personally, especially with regards to the common cold, my own body rarely responds with a fever. I sometimes feel the slightest of sore throats, but I usually know when my body is fighting an infection from a feeling of lethargy along with a loss of appetite that tell me to slow down because energy is needed elsewhere (§ 93-95 Thermodynamics of Relationships). That having been said, the root of the contradiction that I referred to in the previous paragraph is in that there is an important difference between an immune reaction in response to a viral infection and a defensive psychological reaction in response to a threatening social situation. This contradiction arises from my analogy's assumption that, like the relationship between viruses and human cells, individuals in society are separate from society itself. Clearly, this is not the case. A more accurate analogy would be to imagine a scenario where conflict ensues between two or more of the body's own cells. In this case, a defensive reaction against any group of the body's own cells by another group of the body's own cells is an attack on the body itself. Similarly, if I, as a member of society, interrupt healthy communication with other members of society, either through putting up psychological defences or through intolerance or prejudice, then my reaction would be akin to an autoimmune response, damaging the fabric of the structure (society) that makes my existence possible.

"But Bijan, what am I supposed to do when someone behaves badly towards me?" If I were to say, 'Turn the other cheek', I am sure that your response would be, "Get real." So, I am not going to say that, especially since, I believe that the concept needs to be tweaked a little. Instead, I will demonstrate through an anecdote.

> *Once, a newly appointed colleague of mine told me how, before starting to work there, she had plenty of spare time and used to spend much more time with a certain friend. But now, she had less time because she wanted to put in some extra effort so that she would make the most of the opportunity that she had been given so as to achieve certain ambitions. Her friend would call her from time to time and tell her that she was not a true friend and that her new position at a prestigious institution had gone to her head and it had made her forget her old friends.*

I told my colleague that the answer lies in what one of my favourite Persian mystics, Rumi has said,

---

"Through compassion, the bitter becomes sweet."

[The full poem is fourteen stanzas long and contains twenty instances of the phrase "Through compassion …". According to Rumi, the bitter becoming sweet is just one of the effects of love. I shall endeavour to translate it in full soon. Keep an eye out for it on introducingaffinitology.com]

I then suggested that she listen to what her friend had to say and then to simply say, "I have heard everything that you have told me, my friend, and all I can say is, I still love you." Sometime later, my colleague told me that her friend was calling to speak to her so often that it was disrupting her work and could I now suggest a way of keeping her as a friend without her feeling rejected if she asked her to call less frequently.

That's the power of love.

The moral of this story is that whenever, in the face of injustice, we feel like responding in kind, we can think about responding in kindness instead. To help us do that, I suggest that we become sensitive to the early indications of the feeling of being incensed so that, whenever we notice that feeling coming on, we can evoke the memory of the song, 'The Power of Love' by Huey Lewis & The News [fans of the movie, Back to the Future, will be able to relate to that song easily] and use it as a prompt for reminding ourselves of the Rumi quote above so that we can be guided by it so as to respond accordingly.

38.4

In Summary

A Persona is a false Identity that we create so as to pretend to be what we are not (have values that we do not). This is a psychological defence mechanism (§ 79) to protect us against being (mis)judged by society. The danger for us is that through repetition, we sometimes forget that we are pretending and begin to accept our Persona as a real part of ourselves. However, since the Persona's values contradict our core values, this creates conflicts within us. These inner conflicts can be debilitating and very detrimental to our quest for becoming a part of SMERs. When we are feeling vulnerable in the face of society, love and compassion are [in the vast majority of cases] healthier and more effective alternatives to resorting to personas.

In § 58.1 (Core Values Probing), we discuss why it is that, sometimes, we talk to other people about aspects of their lives that have little or nothing to do with the nature of their current relationship. There, I suggest that part of the reason is that we are trying to assess the authenticity of the Identity with whom we are in a relationship at that moment.

Chapter 39

Social Ranking Criteria (SRC)

Once, a client said to me, "I can't have a girlfriend because I don't have a flashy car" ...

We live in a society that propagates values on the basis of irrelevant comparisons. Such comparisons create false Identities [leading to an ultimately disempowering Omniself] which we subsequently struggle to defend. They also detract us from our true selves and lead to false pride. These derail our efforts, and sometimes even our quest, to create and maintain SMERs. When almost every one of our interactions serves to reinforce disempowering values, what can we do to escape the increasingly unwinnable rat race? Or, in the words of Wayne Dyer, "Leave the tribe".

Here's the secret. The criteria (academic, physical, financial, intellectual, social, professional, and so on) that people use to compare us (and put values on us) have certain flawed features in common. We can exploit these flaws to break out of the rat race or social prison. In fact, the system is so flawed that the thing that is holding it together is not its quality, but its quantity; it relies on repetition. If you are bombarded by falsehoods often enough you begin to believe them as being the absolute truth, *especially if you are also led to believe that your livelihood depends on believing it.*

Consider a scenario where, if I believe in a falsehood then I will live and if I don't, I will die. This death need not necessarily be physical; it can be emotional, social, spiritual or intellectual. Obviously, I don't want to die and the prospect of living in conflict, which is what the first option is offering, is too painful to contemplate. Caught in what seems to be a catch-22 situation, I choose to change my beliefs to relieve me from the conflict. I begin to believe in the falsehood that society is feeding me, even though somewhere in the back of my mind, I know that something isn't quite right, but I supress that intuitive voice and push it into the depths of my unconscious [put is somewhere where my attention is not drawn to it (§ 33 Atasinex Cluster)]. This helps me to avoid the pain that I would feel if I were conscious of it. It is not uncommon for us to transmute so much that we become hostile towards those who challenge the falsehoods that the status quo has led us to believe. In fact,

> **one of the signs that we might be conflicted inside is becoming hostile towards someone whose beliefs or opinions do not physically harm others.**

As I mentioned earlier, the secret to breaking away from conventional forces (chains) is to become aware of the defects in the system. Here is a list of some of those defects. Social Ranking Criteria (SRC) are

a) unidimensional,
b) binary,
c) embody elitism and competition,
d) superficial and
e) unstable at the individual level.

Let's see how each of these defects in SRC can provide us with opportunities for escaping the rat race.

... I told the young man who thought that he needed a flashy car that he was trying to hide his lack of self-confidence behind a status symbol and that a woman who is more likely to be attracted to him if he has a flashy car is more interested in the 'owner of a flashy car' than 'a beautiful soul'. He brightened up.

39.1

SRC are binary

> **"I will not be pushed, filed, stamped, indexed, briefed, debriefed, or numbered! My life is my own!"**
>
> - The Prisoner (1967), Season 1, Episode 1 *Arrival*

In every 'normal' population (and being normal is 'good') half of the people will always be *below* average (that's 'bad') and half will always be *above* average (that's 'good'). This is true for any 'normal' population. In a 'normal' population of geniuses, half of them will be above average (more worthy) geniuses (that's 'good') and half of them will be below average (less worthy) geniuses (that's 'bad'). Similarly, in a population of morons, half of them will be above average ('better') morons (that's 'good') and half of them will be below average ('worse') morons (that's 'bad'). This is what 'groupthink' [look it up] does to us. The very nature of this kind of groupthink is that it first reduces us to a number; we become first, second, third, above average (1), below average (0), last, n^{th} or otherwise a mere 'centile' (IQ score, SAT score, height, weight, BMI, etc.). The soul-destroying characteristic of SRC is that, after reducing us to a number, those numbers are used to reduce us again into value-judgement-laden binary categories; good or bad, guilty or not guilty, pass or fail, in or out (one of *us* or one of *them*), winner or loser… that ultimately reduce to **worthy or unworthy**.

[Incidentally, that's also the mainstay of modern consumerism. Without such false value judgements, much of what capitalism is offering us becomes unnecessary (worthless). Yes, I am aware that I just implied that consumerism and capitalism go hand in hand.]

How does this defect in SRC help the enlightened to escape the rat race? An important distinction that we need to make here is that we are not talking about real comparisons. Groupthink tricks us into believing that social and statistical comparisons are as real as comparisons like, "That's an Alsatian and that's a Poodle." The most important difference between real comparisons and SRC comparisons is that one is empowering and the other is disempowering. Awareness of this comparison trap is the beginning of freedom. I will explore freedom and practical ways of achieving it in more detail in a separate course.

[keep an eye on introducingaffinitology.com]

39.2
SRC are Unidimensional

Once, after talking to me at length, what a 56-year-old client was saying can be summarized as, "I am lonely and I am broke. What can you do for me?" I asked her what skills she had and she said, "None."

It was clear that her biggest issue was with self-confidence. She felt that she was not good enough at anything to stand out and be successful. That is an example of unidimensional thinking. It is the perspective or the assumption that, you are a 'loser' unless you are 'the best' in a single field of endeavour. It is no wonder that we have a growing epidemic of anxiety disorders and depression when, in any one field, there is one, so called, 'best' and a limited number of 'aspiring' runner ups and everyone else is a 'failure'.

I asked my client to tell me a little more about herself. In our casual conversation she told me that she was able to do sewing and tailoring at professional level, that she had a firm grasp of statistics and that she had worked in public relations for a while. This client was in Iran, so I asked her, "Can you speak Persian?" She said, "Well, yes of course, but everyone can do that." So, I said, "Actually, no. Only about 1.5% of the world population can speak Persian." (that's about one in every 67 people in the world).

Then I asked her, "Of the 1.5% Persian-speaking population of the world, what proportion have sewing and tailoring skills that are at your level or above?" We concluded that this would be less than one percent. At this point, I reminded her that with those two skills alone, Persian and Tailoring, she was already about one in seven thousand. I then asked her, "Of those one-in-seven-thousand Persian speaking professional tailors, what proportion would you say are as competent at statistics as you are?" She said, "Probably none." I said, "Congratulations! With just three of your myriads of skills and experiences, you have just become unique."

The next thing I said to her was, "Without water, all life would disappear, but gold doesn't have many practical uses. So, why is gold much more expensive (valuable) than water?" For the remainder of my session with her, we extended this line of thought until she could see herself as a highly desirable gem with much to offer society.

The biggest lesson here is that we do not need to be the best at any single skill to be unique. In fact, being at the top of any specialised field requires such single-minded focus that it comes with a very high risk; it can make us blinkered and can deprive us from experiencing the beauty and satisfaction that a holistic perspective can bestow.

Simply becoming aware of our uniqueness in this way is therapeutic in itself in that it helps us to see a way out of the tyranny of social comparisons (§ 11 the Therapeutic Effects of Awareness).

39.3

SRC are Disconnected

Let us begin with the story of the stonecutter which I think demonstrates this flaw in SRC quite well.

The Stonecutter

There was once a stonecutter who was dissatisfied with himself and with his position in life.

One day he passed a wealthy merchant's house. Through the open gateway, he saw many fine possessions and important visitors. "How powerful that merchant must be!" thought the stonecutter. "I wish I could be like the merchant."

To his great surprise, he suddenly became the merchant, enjoying more luxuries than he had ever imagined. Soon a high official passed by, carried in a sedan chair, accompanied by attendants and escorted by soldiers beating gongs. Everyone, no matter how wealthy, had to bow low before the procession. "How powerful that official is!" he thought. "I wish that I could be a high official!"

Then he became the high official, carried everywhere in his embroidered chair. It was a hot summer day, so the official felt very uncomfortable in the sticky chair. He looked up at the sun. It shone proudly in the sky, unaffected by his presence. "How powerful the sun is!" he thought. "I wish that I could be the sun!"

Then he became the sun, shining brightly down on everyone. But a huge black cloud moved between him and the earth, so that his light could no longer shine on everything below. "How powerful that storm cloud is!" he thought. "I wish that I could be a storm cloud!"

Then he became the cloud. But soon he found that he was being pushed away by some great force, and realized that it was the wind. "How powerful it is!" he thought. "I wish that I could be the wind!"

Then he became the wind. But after a while, he ran up against something that would not move, no matter how forcefully he blew against it a huge, towering rock. "How powerful that rock is!" he thought. "I wish that I could be a rock!"

Then he became the rock, more powerful than anything else on earth. But as he stood there, he heard the sound of a hammer pounding a chisel into the hard surface, and felt himself being changed. "What could be more powerful than I, the rock?" he thought.

He looked down and saw, far below him, the figure of a stonecutter.

You see, we are all much more interconnected than we realise and it is SRC that impede that realization. This is much less of a problem for small societies living closer to nature.

[Before he passed away, my friend, Dr. Parviz Farvardin, an Iranian psychiatrist, gave me a copy of his book, "Statistical Sociology" in which he demonstrated how social aberrations increase exponentially with rising population, with the threshold being communities having a population of around 10,000 people and rising most rapidly when it reaches about 250,000 people.]

39.4

SRC Embody Elitism and Competition (E&C)

I say 'embody' because they literally need bodies to carry around, manifest and propagate their common ideologies and to create groupthink. Elitism and competition are incompatible with healthy relationships. Let me explain.

SRC create people who walk around with elitist and competitive tendencies. You want yourself or your children to be the best. However, as we saw with the example of my Persian-tailor-statistician client earlier (§ 39.2 SRC are Unidimensional), each of us is unique. **This isn't mere rhetoric; it is a fact.** And uniqueness is in direct conflict with competition. Two unique items are not compatible unless we strip both of them of some of the qualities that make them unique. This is the basis for labelling and stereotyping. To me,

stripping someone of their uniqueness is tantamount to destroying their soul

[The challenge, and the art of being a citizen, then changes from "How can I mould myself to fit society?" to "How can we incorporate the uniqueness of each individual into the tapestry of society?"]

The exploitable flaw here is that, again, this effect relies on the idea of 'normal' (§ 71 What is Normal?). As every statistician can tell you, 'normal' populations always have two extremes (tails), the lowest ('bottom') x% and the highest ('top') x%, which Groupthink interprets as, the worst and the best and then there is everybody else. Those at the 'top' don't tend to stay at the top for very long because there's a lot of competition for that spot. The 'bottom' tends to have different dynamics which is mainly passive (a bit like diffusion), making the bottom more stable because those who *see and believe themselves to be* at the illusory 'bottom' are more prone to learned helplessness. The x, that is, the arbitrary line that is drawn between the 'bottom', 'top' and 'the rest', depends on what is deemed to be convenient at the time. If it is a political election, a majority of 1 in several thousand is an acceptable majority but, in social science research, a probability of 'getting it wrong' of less than 5% is required for the results to be considered to be 'statistically significant'.

Let's see how this flaw can be exploited to escape the rat race. I am going to explain this through a surfing metaphor. Like a surfer, instead of either fearing the wave (resisting E&C) or getting caught up in the wave (submitting to E&C) or becoming a wave (identifying with E&C), we can first take a moment to become an objective observer of it; looking at the situation from the outside to get a bird's-eye view (rising over and above E&C). Then we can choose the right moment to ride on the wave and enjoy the process immensely. The following three exercises can help us understand how we can do this.

Exercise 6 How to Bypass Elitism and Competition
Part 1

1. Think about something that you aspire to achieve. Got it? Good. How does that make you feel? Take a snapshot of that feeling and give it a name. A name that I came up with was the "Not-There-Yet" feeling.

2. Now imagine how you would feel about this thing that you aspire to achieve if, after you achieve it, it doesn't make the slightest difference to the way that others see you (society judges you). How does it feel now? Let's call this the "no-one-else-cares" feeling.

3. In what ways is this feeling different from the "not-there-yet" feeling?

4. Would you still aspire just as much to achieve it?

5. What insights did you get from doing this exercise?

6. Could these insights affect what you want to be and where you want to get to?

7. Without the need to seek approval from Society, in what ways do the qualities and directions of your aspirations change?

8. Why?

9. Think again about what can make you happy. Has anything changed?

Exercise 7 How to Bypass Elitism and Competition
Part 2

1. Think about something that you are proud of; an achievement, a position, a relationship. Focus on it until you really get a sense of the feeling that's associated with that thought. Got it? Give this feeling a name such as the "I-am-proud-of-myself feeling".

2. Now imagine how you would feel about this thing that you are proud of if it didn't make the slightest difference to the way that others see you. How does that feel now? Let's call this feeling, "no-praise".

3. In what ways is this feeling different from the I-am-proud-of-myself feeling?

4. What insights did you get from doing this exercise?

5. Could these insights affect what you want to be and where you want to get to?

6. Without the need to seek recognition from Society, in what ways would the qualities and directions of your aspirations change?

7. Think again about what can make you happy. Has anything changed?

Exercise 8 How to Bypass Elitism and Competition
Part 3

1. Imagine that the world that you are living in is a holographic stage. Everything is a simulation. Imagine that you have chosen to be here because you want to take an objective look at what it is like to be in this situation. You are here because you are curious. You are trying to get a real sense for what it is like to be in your shoes. Immerse yourself in your role as an objective and curious observer. Give this character a name, such as 'the ethnographer' or 'the alien visitor'. As you may have already gathered, I'm a Star Trek fan, so I call this character "Mr. Spock".

2. From the point of view of this observer, what does it feel like to see a society where some people use flawed criteria to judge themselves as unworthy and end up in the "not-there-yet" state or, worse, in the "not-good-enough" state?

3. How does that make you feel about the person who is internalising these false comparison criteria and is judging himself by them?

4. How does that make you, the objective observer, feel about that society? Give this feeling a name. The name that came to my mind was, "The Wall" because it reminds me of the song of the same name by Pink Floyd.

5. What did you learn from these exercises?

6. What new insights did you glean?

7. Can you notice any differences in the way you think about yourself now?

If there is even the slightest bit of difference in how you feel about yourself, then I have just planted a seed. You now need to attend to, and to nourish, that seed with love and devotion. Before long, you will notice an inner transformation.

The inner transformation that I refer to in the above exercise may happen so gradually that you may not notice it happening in the short term, rather like the accumulation of tiny changes that occur in a small child that are less apparent to the parents than to those who visit every few weeks.

39.5
SRC are superficial

The mother of a preschool child once said to me, "My son is blind in one eye and I am worried that this will affect his chances with women later in his life." I told her that, in this respect, this was a blessing...

Social ranking criteria only rely on those factors that are externally observable; on the surface; they lack depth or substance.

Society does not care about how we feel. People do, but 'Society' (The conglomerate, the crowd, the herd, the system, the collective, the hive, etc.) does not (§ 32 Extended Relationships, Communities and Beyond). If it appears that it does, it is only to the extent that it affects our behaviour (what we do, not how we feel). This creates conflicts within us;

"I want to be part of Society but how can I justify having a relationship with something that does not care about my feelings?"

And we do, indeed, 'justify' such a relationship to ourselves. Justification is one of those self-preservation tactics that Anna Freud called Psychological Defence Mechanisms (§ 79).

Justification usually means justifying *the methods* employed in pursuit of a goal; an outcome. However, outcomes are never certain. Relying on outcomes to make us happy is always a gamble. We would be gambling our time (our life) and all the possibilities of enjoyment that now (the present moment) offers on a hope that this sacrifice will *one* day pay off and, *one day*, we will be happy (Unit 2: § 6-11 The Journey).

Let's see how that relates to entering into a relationship with a Society that does not care about how I feel, but only about what I do. This kind of relationship is contractual. In such relationships the only things that matter are the terms of the contract. As long as I deliver, the other party in the contract, Society in this case, does not care whether I am happy, sad, satisfied, dissatisfied, alive or dead.

Just to remind you, *individuals* within society do care, but the collective (the Order, the masses, etc.) don't care. For example, do you care how the head of state is feeling at the moment? No. You care about his policies and how it affects you. You care about what he *does*. If caring about his feelings affects what he does, then you begin to care about that; as a means to an end. This is what social welfare and healthcare policies are about. Such policies may appear to care about me, the individual, but they need me to think that when, in fact, what they actually care about (if we can call it that) is my 'contribution'. I am not saying that we do not need to contribute, what I am saying is that such contribution should not be because we are drawn into a game through which we are distracted from our real (unadulterated) Self.

Outcome-based relationships, being contractual, are gambles that may or may not pay off. In the meantime, however, our moment-to-moment possibilities for experiencing joy, happiness and satisfaction are held to ransom by the hopefully-one-day image of the outcome. We try to escape the feeling of being trapped in this way by convincing ourselves that it is only 'right and proper' that we do what Society expects of us. As such, we continue to aspire to receive its prizes, awards, accolades, standing ovations and other metaphorical pats on the back. Meanwhile we fail to notice that this conditioned compulsion to conform and perform is gradually draining our soul, leaving it empty. We do not notice (or notice too late) that this contractual and disempowering relationship with Society has not left us with enough time (life) to nurture satisfying, empowering and meaningful relationships.

Sometimes we consciously decide to do something for Society because the intrinsic value that we have assigned to it makes it a worthwhile activity in itself. This is very different from believing that the beneficiaries appreciate us or care about the feelings that we get from doing it.

The important point for those of us who want to experience a sense of freedom is to become aware of whether or not what we are doing is for its intrinsic or extrinsic value; see § 8 (What If) and § 44 (Locus of Control). In educational circles, these two perspectives are called mastery orientation and performance orientation (§ 8 What if). Those trapped by SRC become performance oriented.

> ... *I told the mother of that preschool child that his blindness in one eye was a blessing because most men have to work hard to determine whether the interest a girl is showing in him is superficial or not. In her son's case, he would attract girls who are more likely to be genuinely interested in him as an individual rather than as someone that she wants to show off to her friends. There was a clearly visible sense of relief in the mother's face.*

SRC are Unstable at the Individual Level

SRC are dynamic; they change. They are not stable on a micro scale (the scale of the individual), even though they may appear to be stable at the macro scale of contrived categories, such as class, caste, rank, income or demographic. A useful analogy would be to consider the question, "What state is a molecule of water in? Is it a solid, a liquid or a gas?" As soon as Society begins to compare these three states of water from an SRC perspective, it will start to impose its value judgements on it. It starts to say to the molecule, "Oh, you are an ice molecule, are you? So, you're one of the *restricted* ones. You want to be a gas like me. I'm free to go wherever I want." Note that there is no such thing as an ice molecule. It is a water molecule (H_2O) like any other. It is its *relationship* with all the other molecules in its vicinity that determines its physical state.

Physical states (solid, liquid or gas) are known as colligative properties; they are properties that arise (emerge), when a very large number of particles get together. They are properties that cannot be assigned to individual atoms or molecules. Let's continue with our analogy and see what happens when we try to impose colligative properties on individual particles.

The aforementioned pompous water molecule, that thinks of itself as a gas, has no idea what 'free' means. He has just heard it somewhere and 'knows' that it is 'good' and good means that it is something that I can use as ammunition to declare myself superior. Of course, this deluded water molecule doesn't realise that, it too, is 'trapped' in the water cycle like all the other water molecules, whether frozen in an iceberg, flowing with the prevailing current (of water) or feeling free whilst at the mercy of the wind.

Note that the need to declare one's self as superior is closely related to the need to prove one's self as 'worthy'. It stems from an underlying sense of unworthiness [itself, a social construct]. Our feeling of unworthiness stems from a sense of separation from the whole and the sense of isolation that it entails. [This is related to our discussions in § 79 (Psychological Defence Mechanisms) and to the Rumi quote in § 30.2.1, 36.10 and 38.2].

How can becoming aware of this flaw in SRC help us free ourselves from its chains? If you can think of someone that you can identify as *one of us*, then you've just recognised one of the shackles that your mind is chained to. This is like saying, "Hey you're an ice molecule like me." Remember, *there is no such thing as an ice molecule* insofar as it is not possible to distinguish an ice molecule from a steam molecule at the individual molecular level. Of course, a water molecule could say,

"You are a water molecule trapped in a block of ice like me" or, "You are a water molecule blowing in the wind like me", but the difference is that it is no longer labelling the other water molecule, it is focusing on the common circumstances that they find themselves in (§ 14.3 Situation vs Circumstance). And that is a very different perspective which leads to very different outcomes (quality of Nexus).

Here is another analogy. Imagine a nail judging its intrinsic value or worth by whether it is holding up a painting on a wall or connecting the panels in a baby's cot. Now imagine this conversation between the two identical nails (except for where they have happened to have ended up).

- "I'm better than you because I am holding up an expensive painting and you aren't."
- "Don't be stupid," says the other nail, "Babies are much more important than paintings."

So, what would a nail that is not trapped by SRC say?

- "It feels so good to be me. I hope others feel just as good about who they are."
- "Oi!" comes a voice from the other side of the room, "But you're inferior."
- "If this is what inferiority is, I seem to be fine with it" thinks the self-actualized nail to himself.

A teenager hears the conversation (as one does). Recently, he has been reading about holism and he thinks to himself,

"Yes, I'm sure that to a reductionist, I can be seen as being inferior in an infinite number of ways to an infinite number of things, but holistically, I am unique which means that I cannot be inferior or superior to anything. Being unique means that I can do things that no one else can do. What makes me unique is the combination of my experiences, my genes (potential), my age, the kind of people that I know (and can, therefore, connect to each other), where I am and when I happen to be there and many many other factors that make me a 'One and Only'."

And at that point, he remembers a Gloria Gaynor song that his father used to listen to called *"I am what I am"*.

39.7
Social Ranking Criteria Summary

In summary, the *only* factor that influences our self-esteem is social comparison. Self-esteem is about our perception of our self-worth and without a frame of reference, there can be no value judgement; think supply and demand. Something is expensive in comparison to something that is not, something is good in comparison to something that is not. Our frame of reference for judging our self-worth is other people. Therefore, without SRC, self-esteem would be a meaningless concept. You may be able to envisage yourself being the only person on earth and thinking, "I am great and I like who I am" but you can only do that because you have your *current* frame of reference. If you were the only person on earth, 'self' would not have any meaning because there would be no 'other' to provide the necessary frame of reference. In other words, if I were the only person in the world, it is most unlikely that I would even think about whether or not I like myself because I would not be aware of any sense of self.

We have seen that social comparisons are inherently flawed at several levels and that we are using a defective and unreliable system through which to judge our own self-worth. I'm calling this *Original Spin*.

We noted that one of the flaws of SRC is that they are unidimensional and that we can use this to break out of the rat race. We saw this with the example of my Persian-Tailor-Statistician client, who realised that she did not need to be the best at anything to be unique and therefore, extremely valuable. The only person who needs to realise this is 'me' because I know that those who do not appreciate my uniqueness and judge me by society's ranking criteria are using slime as a yardstick.

Eight centuries ago, Rumi realized this. He opens one of his momentous works, the Masnavi, with a poem in which he compares himself to a flute. It contains the following couplet.

> **Each interprets my notes in harmony with his own feelings,**
> **But not one fathoms the secrets of my heart.**

[Source: Masnavi i Ma'navi Teachings of Rumi, The Spiritual Couplets of Maulana Jalalu-'d-din Muhammad i Rumi, Translated and abridged by E.H. Whinfield, M.A., Published by Omphaloskepsis (2001)]

Another flaw inherent in SRC that can provide an escape route out of the rat race, is that its criteria lie on a grayscale or continuum. However, society sells it to us as black or white or nothing; you are either at the top or the bottom or mediocre. In the movie, Amadeus, the composer Salieri, being jealous of Mozart proclaims to have killed Mozart and calls himself "The patron saint of mediocrities everywhere". This is what SRC can do to us. If we buy into this mentality, then we are either struggling to get to the top or have resigned to our status as a failure. This can have detrimental effects on any relationship. The following simple reframe allows us to evade this.

> **I, being unique, am at the top and the bottom of a scale that only has one point on it, me. I am part of a statistical population that can only have one member (n=1); me. Therefore, any attempt to 'generalize' me is an attempt to defy my uniqueness and the only reason for that would be to devalue me in preparation for exploitation. I am not going to buy into that paradigm.**

You might say, "But Bijan, what about those who are praised for what they do?" And I would suggest that unless one is at no risk of becoming attached to such praise, then one becomes vulnerable to entrapment. Such potential Achilles Heels include the need to keep one's reputation (fear of loss of acquired status). Here's another thought-provoking question for you to think about:

> **Without SRC, what would happen to each of the 'seven deadly sins' (pride, greed, lust, envy, gluttony, wrath and sloth)?**

Chapter 40

Self-Esteem and Self-Confidence

There are many other self-related constructs. I mention some of them, in passing, later in this chapter (§ 40.7). However, self-esteem and self-confidence are the ones that I work with most with my clients. In addition to our interpersonal relationships, our self-esteem and self-confidence affect many aspects of our lives (Unit 11: Dimensions of Human Experience), including our aspirations and our views of personal choice. We begin this chapter by looking at the last two first.

40.1
What do you want to be when you grow up?

In 2008, I began to work with a team at the Institute of Education (now merged with University College, London) looking into the factors that affect young people's decision-making. It was funded by the British government because it wanted to know how to increase the number of students who decide to study Mathematics and Physics at university. Although we were interested in Mathematics and Physics in particular, what we really needed to know was why students choose to study anything. It was like trying to answer the question, "What do you want to be when you grow up (and why)?" but because we were asking teenagers and not primary school kids, and since this was a high-profile University study involving a team of experienced researchers, we called it "Understanding Participation rates in post-16 Mathematics and Physics" (UPMAP).

To me, one of the most striking revelations was that most people who are at school don't know what they want. We interviewed students in their first year of university and most of them didn't know what they wanted either. What also surprised me was that I should have been surprised at all considering that I was no different when I started university.

Here are some of the reasons that students gave for wanting to study whatever it was that they wanted to study.

- Because I'm good at it
- Because I like it
- Because my family wants me to do it
- Because my friend wants to do it
- Because a friend I trust said that it was a good subject to study
- Because it leads to a secure future
- Because my career advisor recommended it for me
- Because my older brother is studying the same subject
- Because a computer program suggested it

What I would like you to notice about these responses is that they are unidimensional, that is to say that they focus only on a single facet of the issue. Notice also that the responses are framed in binary terms. In other words, I am either good at it *or not*, like it *or not*, my family wants me to do it *or not*, there is a secure future in it *or not* and so on. I am sure that there was a myriad of factors that affected students' decisions and, as I have explained elsewhere in this course (§ 72 Decision-Making), our decisions are mediated by our emotions.

> **Whenever we are called upon to explain (intellectualize) our decisions (emotions and their consequences), we resort to justification.**

As I mentioned earlier (§ 39.5 SRC are Superficial), justifications are psychological defence mechanisms (§ 79).

We followed up these children every year over a period of three years to see if there were any changes in their perspectives and, if so, what could have caused those changes, but I'm not going to go into that here. Instead, let's look at the case of a client who came to me because he had a similar problem.

40.1.1
A Case Study of a Career Decision

A 26-year-old man was referred to me by his sister because he was frustrated and didn't know what he wanted to do with his life. In the course of our conversation, he told me that he likes travelling and seeing new places. The first exercise that I suggested was for him to remember a time when he was really happy. I then asked him to think about another time when he was really happy, and another time, until we had about five different situations in which, in the past, he had felt happy. We then looked for common elements that ran through all the examples that he gave of times when he was happy. We were looking for a pattern. Two of the commonalities in the times when he had been happiest were that they involved him being with his friends and him being outdoors.

In the second part of the exercise, I asked him to remember a time when he was really proud of his achievement; any achievement. Again, I was looking for a pattern. We wanted to know what sort of things made him feel good about himself. He told me with a great deal of pride and excitement that once he had been asked to supervise the parking arrangements for a large conference in an area where the parking facilities were not well-designed. He spoke with enthusiasm as he described how he supervised the arrangements so that it all flowed smoothly without congestion.

I told him that he seemed to have spatial skills, management skills, people skills and an interest in groups and outdoors. We then started to explore the kind of activities that one could make a living from that involved both the things he was good at and the things he liked. He had been to a lot of places and had seen many historical and natural sites in Iran, so I said, "How about starting a tour business." He found the idea exciting but he was hesitant because he didn't know where to start. I told him that he could start by taking three or four people in his car to a place that he knew well and that he liked and he could charge them for it. He would need some business cards and some leaflets. He could gradually get to a point where he could hire a minibus. He could also negotiate a discount with (or offer incentives to) hotels and restaurants.

Now you might be thinking, "Yes Bijan, this is all very interesting but what has it got to do with relationships?" Quite a lot actually. Just as we need to consider different aspects of ourselves when we are deciding on a career (skills, interests, family, society, friends and so on), we also need to look at the different dimensions that affect our interpersonal relationships. We explore this in more detail in § 48-50 (Dimensions of Human Experience).

40.2
Behaviourism versus Humanism

This sound bite from B.F. Skinner (depicted in figure 19) summarises the behaviourist school of thought: *"Behaviour is shaped and maintained by its consequences"*.

Figure 19 The Behaviourist Perspective

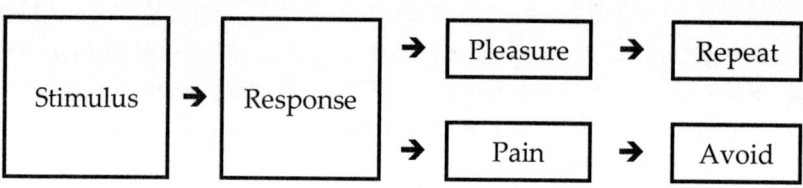

Context (the situation) leads to a stimulus which leads to a reaction which leads to a result which leads to a feeling which leads to a reaction and, eventually, an attitude (§ 65 Attitudes).

From a behaviourist point of view, it doesn't matter whether the thing that is reacting is an earthworm or a saint, what matters is pleasure or pain. In this model, we don't determine our destiny because we simply react to our environment through a compulsion to repeat what has already given us pleasure (which initially happened by chance) and to avoid what has already given us pain (which also initially happened by chance). If you buy into this paradigm then you can throw up your arms and say, "It's not my fault; I am not responsible. I am a victim of my conditioning." This is what psychologists call having an external locus of control, that is to say I am controlled by factors that are outside of me (§ 44 Locus of Control).

Although behaviourism became very popular in its heyday, I am sure you can see how the idea that people are not responsible for what they do can be a very discomforting thought. Then came the Humanistic school of psychology. Humanists did not reject the basic tenets of behaviourism because there's a lot of strong research evidence behind it, they just made one small change to the model and it is this: *Between stimulus and response people have a choice.*

Figure 20 Humanist Adaptation of the Behaviourist perspective

This seemingly small change makes a huge difference. Now, in order to believe that we are in control of our destiny (i.e., not victims of our circumstances), we simply need to consciously *decide* how to respond to a stimulus. We can extend this idea of choice to beyond the consequences.

Figure 21 More choice

That is, we can also decide whether or not to repeat what is pleasant and to avoid what is painful. This is the principle behind various techniques for desensitising people to pain or expanding our comfort zones (feeling the pain and doing it anyway). It also explains the idea behind delayed gratification; giving up something that is pleasurable in the short term for the sake of greater empowerment in the long-term.

40.3
Self-Esteem

Self-esteem is a belief. This is how I explain it to my clients:

> **Self-esteem is a belief that my presence in this world makes the world a more beautiful place than it would be without me**

It is about intrinsic value. It is also about implicit value; we don't need to prove it to anyone. My mere presence in this world is enough for me to feel worthy of receiving that which it bestows or offers. Self-esteem is independent of the situation and as such, it can be classed as a 'Core Value' (§ 29.4 The Omniself). Viewed from a different perspective, we can see self-esteem as being the extent to which an individual needs other people's approval to feel worthy.

- "Worthy of what, Bijan?"
- "Worthy of that which we have the potential to receive."
- "What do we have the potential to receive?"
- "Love, money, food, respect, a job, clothes, presents, appreciation, clean air to breathe, a roof over my head, a healthy body, peace of mind and so on."
- "You say, 'potential to receive', but what is potential?"
- "Potential is that which would be available to us if we chose to avail ourselves of it."

The more I need other people's approval to consider myself worthy of receiving, the less self-esteem I have. Taken to its limit, the highest level of self-esteem is achieved when we don't need anyone's approval to feel worthy of receiving. This can create a paradox because, since I have just defined the concept of self-esteem in terms of other people's approval (albeit an inverse relationship), when other people's opinions cease to matter, self-esteem becomes meaningless.

But to what extent can we actually ignore other people's opinions when Society is built on individual interactions and each interaction is mediated through opinions? Let me rephrase that. The question I am asking is this, "Can I care about other people's opinions without it affecting my self-esteem?" I would argue that this is possible through a simple reframe:

> **People's opinions matter only insofar as the practical consequences of those opinions matter.**

This changes our focus from the opinion to its 'practical' consequences. I no longer care what people think *in vacuo* (out of context), but I do care about the effect of those thoughts on the individual thinking them and on the wider society and environment. Let's see how thinking like this pans out in practice.

Let's say I want to help a beggar and a friend of mine thinks that that's a stupid thing to do. If I have low self-esteem, I would doubt my judgement (or I would wish to avoid my friend having a low opinion of me) and refrain from helping the beggar. On the other hand, I can examine my friend's opinion from a pragmatic perspective and say to myself, "I think that what I'm about to do will have a positive impact on the world at large, but my friend seems to think the opposite. Here is an opportunity for me to learn something from my friend."

[You might say, "But Bijan" if I start to analyse every little interaction, I have with someone in such detail, then my life will become staccato rather than being smooth flowing." And I would argue that we see this pattern in the learning of every practical skill; disjointed or discontinuous at first, becoming smoother with practice. I put it to you that, in those things that you are skilled at (such as walking or driving), you will surprise yourself if you stop and think of the depth of analysis that you perform in a split second.]

Notice that, in thinking this way, I have not attached value to the word 'stupid'. To a person with high self-esteem, the word stupid doesn't register as, 'I think less of you for it', it simply means, 'I am looking at the situation from a different perspective'. In other words, people with high self-esteem don't take other people's opinions personally, even if those opinions are about them. The easiest way to do this is to start distinguishing between who *I am* and what *I do*, that is, between my intention and the consequences of my actions. This is also a distinction that I encourage parents to make when interacting with their children. The earlier we start removing labelling of people, the sooner we will eradicate this scourge from our society.

> ### Labels (adjectives) create false readings on our self-esteem scale

---

Here is an anecdote that shows how getting rid of labels can feel liberating.

> *Once, I met a friend of mine at a reunion and asked him how things were going for him. He told me that all was well and that he was happy with his life and his job except for one thing; whenever he told people what he did, he felt that people judged him negatively. I asked him what he did and he said, "I am a lorry driver." I told him that the problem was not with his job, it was in the way in which he was associating himself with it. He said, "How's that?" And I told him about one of my favourite quotes from Rumi;*

> **Clean out of your mind all the adjectives you use to describe yourself, so you may behold your pure and clear essence.**
>
> Masnavi Ma'navi* of Rumi (1207-1273)
> Translation by the author

* A Masnavi is a 'book of verse' consisting of rhyming couplets. Ma'navi means 'pertaining to meaning' (i.e., Spiritual). The work consists of around 27000 couplets (stanzas) in six volumes ('Books'). The above quotation is a translation of couplet number 3460 from Book 1 of The Masnavi.

I then told this friend of mine that, in his case, what this means is that, by using the verb 'to be' (saying I am a lorry driver), he is labelling himself and identifying with the label. This creates blinkers that make people focus on his 'lorry driver' Identity rather than the wholesome person behind it. He said, "What am I supposed to call myself then?" [or something to that effect]. I told him that he could simply say that he drives lorries. In other words, he is not a lorry driver, but someone (a person) who drives lorries. He immediately had a flash of inspiration and said, "Actually, I could say that I deliver goods to people, because that's the part of the job that I enjoy." And I said, "That's brilliant, because you are now focusing on the service and the benefit that you give people and that is a more accurate indication of who you are."

When, in the light of this realisation, we put self-esteem aside, that is, when the idea of whether or not we are worthy becomes *implicit*, our focus will turn to what we *want* rather than what we *don't want*. This opens the path to pursuing those things that give genuine meaning to our lives; with the proviso, of course, that we do not infringe on other people's rights to the same.

[This is related to what, in psychology, is called approach (towards) and avoidance (away from) motivation.]

True self-esteem is stable. False self-esteem is as fragile as the diversity of opinions (and the ever-fluctuating values) of those around us. In fact, no matter how much 'better' than others we perform, as long as our sense of self-worth is determined by comparing ourselves with others, we have self-esteem issues. In § 39 (Social Ranking Criteria) I explained society's role in propagating the self-esteem trap and what we can do to free ourselves from its shackles. In § 5 (Give a Man a Fish) I mentioned the case of the young man who came to me because he wanted to improve his relationship with his girlfriend.

He said that in spite of spending a lot of money on her, she would take his money and fool around with other men. In his case, the issue wasn't with how to improve his relationship (as he had originally thought), it was with how to have enough self-esteem to end a disempowering one. He was uncomfortable approaching women because he thought that a rejection would be a threat to his sense of self-worth. I suggested to him that the only reason for someone to say no would be that her circumstances, external (environmental) or internal (psychological) are not conducive to her saying yes. That is to say, she either can't engage with you because of her circumstances or she won't engage with you because she doesn't recognise your value. Reframing the problem in this way cleared his way by removing the 'fear of rejection' barrier. We went through some exercises and his homework was to continue to do those exercises twice a day (our first session was three hours long).

When he came back to see me with his new girlfriend three weeks later, she told me that she did not believe in the effectiveness of psychology and I thought to myself, "If only you knew!" I asked her why and she told me that she had read many books on psychology and they had not been helpful. I explained to her that,

> **knowledge is not a solution. It is a burden.**

Knowledge only *becomes* a solution when it can be put into action. That happens when we use the knowledge as an indicator of the direction in which we need to target our efforts. These efforts will eventually lead to skill and, hopefully, wisdom. At that point she picked up one of my business cards. Fortunately, she did not ask me what wisdom is, but if she had, I would have begun by saying this,

> **Understanding comes from appreciating knowledge and wisdom comes from appreciating understanding.**

[now you can see why I said 'fortunately']

40.4
Self-Confidence

Confidence means trust. We explore trust in more detail in § 53.

> **Self-confidence is another way of saying,**
> **"To what extent can I trust myself to do something adequately."**

Sometimes, our self-confidence suffers at the hand of our self-esteem. That is, we do not trust our own ability because we relate it to our self-worth, "I cannot do it because I am not worthy of the payoff of the action." This can happen when we substitute the word 'adequately' with 'perfectly' (§ 64.10 Values and Perfectionism). This is also related to our ability to trust our own judgements, which links in with our discussion about locus of control (§ 44).

Like self-esteem, self-confidence, is about beliefs. More accurately, it is about a collection of beliefs which, in combination, condense (summarise, generalise, decontextualise) how we feel about our ability/competence to meet challenges or to cope with adversity. It is about how independent we believe we are or can be (§ 23.2 The Road to Interdependence). This is a reflection of the extent to which we feel that we can cope with *the consequences* of our own actions. Therefore, from another perspective, we can say that,

> **Self-confidence is about the extent to which we**
> **fear the consequences of our actions.**

Context affects our self-confidence more than our self-esteem. Both of these constructs are closely associated with the concept of locus of control (§ 44).

40.5
The Relationship between
Self-Esteem and Self-Confidence

Self-esteem and self-confidence are the two biggest determinants of independence; in thought and action respectively, affecting our interpersonal relationships, especially our ability to create SMERs (§ 2.1). We explore Dependence, Independence and Interdependence in § 23.2 (The Road to Interdependence). Self-esteem and self-confidence go together because laying down the tracks, or smoothing the way (self-esteem), is not in itself enough to get us from A to B; we also need the locomotive (self-confidence) to push us along the tracks. Another way of looking at this is through this question,

> **"I'm not afraid of being rejected, but how do I go about increasing my chances of being accepted?"**

This perspective is related to Herzberg's two-factor theory of motivation that we look at in § 2.12 (What is Satisfying). This is when the art and science (§ 18 Art or Science) of communication (Unit 3: The Power of Language) come to the fore. It is also where our understanding of The Nexus comes into prominence, e.g., Exercise 4 in § 22.2 (The Third Entity). To wit,

"I know what to do and say because my focus is on building the connection and not on The Self or The Other. I am confident because I understand that I need to practice to improve and that every attempt is a practice attempt until it is successful, at which point it becomes a successful outcome."

40.6
Self-Esteem, Self-Confidence and Optimism

Self-confidence nurtures optimism and vice versa. Let me show you how. Often, my clients say to me, "It can't be done" or "It can't happen" or "I can't do it". At this point, all they need is a simple shift in perspective (reframe). So, I tell them to write this statement on a piece of paper and stick it on a wall somewhere where they can see it every day:

> **It can't be done means**
> **I don't know how it can be done, YET.**

This simple reframe can have a profound effect on our psyche because it changes our focus from our current beliefs and assumptions (§ 33 Atasinex Cluster), specifically our 'ability' (§ 5.4.1 Ability, Performance and Attainment), which we tend to think of as being fixed, to our 'knowledge' which we can extend through learning. This change in belief also changes our attitude (§ 65) from lack of confidence to optimism. It means that I can at least grow by trying to find a way and if I don't find a solution, at least I will have found some ways it cannot be done which would at least veer other people (and myself) away from those unsuccessful directions.

This was Thomas Edison's response to a reporter who questioned his lack of results, a few months before he invented the light bulb; **"Results! Why, man, I have gotten a lot of results. I know several thousand things that won't work."**

Once we break free from the shackles of our limiting beliefs, we can revitalize our curiosity and creativity in pursuit of new evidence and knowledge to support the new *possibilities*. The easiest place to start is to see whether others have been able to do what we are trying to do. If so, then the possibility is already established and the next question becomes, how can *I* do it too. This leads to another reframe for us to stick on our wall,

> **If other people can do it,**
> **it is possible that I will be able to do it too.**

It is more common for people to say, "If other people can do it, so can you." But experience with my clients has shown me that I am less likely to encounter resistance when I talk about the possibility of being able to do what others have done as compared with a certainty that they can do what others can do. There are two reasons for this. At some psychological level, the first assertion can be perceived to be a threat to a person's individuality, "But I'm not like everyone or anyone else." And at some level, that's quite true. Another reason for resistance is that the idea of being told that we can definitely do something can be a potential threat to our self-esteem; "If I am supposed to be able to do it and I can't, then there is something wrong with me."

As with anything else, including starting maintaining and ending relationships, the reason and the mechanism (the end and the means) are not independent of each other. Knowing *why* we want to do something affects *how* we go about doing it. And knowing *how* something can be done affects whether or not we want to do it. At this point the question becomes, "Does the end justify the means?" If we believe that something can be done, but requires more effort (or sacrifice) than the value that we feel that we will gain from it, then we are less likely to *want* to do it. Often, people don't change their relationships for the better, not because they don't believe it can be done, but because they think it is too hard to do. What 'too hard' really means is that the outcome doesn't justify the effort that is required; "It just isn't worth it".

Our self-esteem is one of the factors that determines whether or not we believe a relationship (Nexus) is worth making or breaking.

One day a client came to me with a relationship problem and she couldn't decide what to do. She had also mentioned that she had a younger sister. I asked her, "If your sister had the same problem, what would you advise her?" She was quick to offer a solution. I asked her, "Why is it that you can make a decision so quickly if your sister had the same problem but you can't do that for yourself?" She started to say things like, "Well, that's different... she is my little sister and I want the best for her ..." I pointed out that this shows that she is conflicted inside; harbouring double standards, in this case, one for herself and one for her sister. I also pointed out that this was a clear sign of low self-esteem because she felt that she was less worthy than her younger sister and that she needed to think about her own value (self-worth). She said, "But, wouldn't that make me a selfish person?" I explained that she would only be selfish if she believed herself to be more worthy than other people whereas self-esteem is about not considering ourselves to be any less worthy than other people.

40.7
The Role of Self-Confidence in Relationships

How we see ourselves (self-image) affects how we think about ourselves (self-concept) and what we think we are capable of doing well (self-confidence) and how well we believe we are performing in relation to a perceived potential (self-efficacy). When any of these are based on social comparisons, they affect how much we value ourselves (self-esteem). Obviously, all of these have an impact on the quality of our relationships. However, considering all of them together can get quite complicated. In this section, I am going to focus on Self-confidence, because this is one of the most practically-oriented 'self' constructs. Along with self-esteem, it is also one of the issues that I most frequently need to address in my counselling sessions.

> **Self-confidence only becomes an issue when there is a perceived gap, or a conflict, between what we can actually do and what we think we can do.**

This gap arises from fear and is often self-fulfilling. Let me explain.

You may have heard it said, "If you think you can and if you think you can't you are right." The implication here is that thinking that I can do something makes me capable of doing it and thinking that I can't makes me incapable of doing it. **This may or may not be true.** If I think that I can tie my shoelaces and I think that I cannot grow a second head, I am right in both cases; there is no conflict there and I don't think anyone is going to accept the notion that if I believe in it enough, I will be able to grow a second head.

There are times, however, when not believing in what you are actually capable of doing can be a handicap. This is where self-confidence becomes an issue. In such cases, the problem is not about whether or not I can go through the motions; it is about whether or not I can cope with the consequences (that's the fear part). Let's look at an example.

> *I was eleven years old and had only been in the UK for a few months. In an English class, at a Grammar School in Barnsley, the teacher asked me to read a passage from a book in front of the class. When I got to the word 'Greenwich' (pronounced by the British like gren-itch), I read it as "green witch". My classmates exploded with laughter.*

That experience could have made a big dent in my self-confidence, but it didn't. This was partly because it was blatantly obvious to me that there was no way that I could have known how to pronounce that word and therefore I knew that the laughter was more directed at the unexpected pronunciation than it was at me as a person. However, any doubt that I may have had about this last point was cleared up by the teacher who turned immediately to the kids and said something like, "When you can read, write and speak a second language like Persian, to the extent that Bijan can do in English, then you may have the right to judge."

A year later, I was told that I had to give a public speech. I had recently moved to a boarding school. Every Wednesday morning, all the pupils were split into four groups, called Houses, and for each group, one of the students was expected to make a speech. With trepidation, I stood in front of the gathered and started to read from a passage in an unfamiliar book. Feeling acutely self-conscious, I stammered throughout. No-one laughed. In fact, as I was reading and blushing, without even daring to look up, I could feel the vibes of sympathy in the room.

Of course, I might have been imagining these vibes, but that is how I remember the experience. Was I confident? No. Did I fear the consequences? Yes. Did I go through with it? Yes. Why? Because long before, I had learnt to think like this;

> **There are some people who will judge me fairly and there are some people who won't. The latter are not a group that I want to have within my circle of friends anyway and their judgement will simply allow me to recognize them, leaving only those who judge me fairly and I have nothing to fear from them.**

You might be wondering why, with that kind of reasoning, I should have been self-conscious, blushing and keeping my eyes down? The answer is that, the feeling that my logic was sound allowed me to go through with it. However, I knew that I was not competent. Exposing our weaknesses and being emotionally comfortable with the feeling of vulnerability that it entails takes a lot of practice. Four years later, I was the fall-back guy when someone pulled out of one of these speeches at the last minute.

Self-confidence in our interpersonal relationships also has the same two elements. We need to have a theoretical position that allows us to take risks and the practical understanding to trust that competence grows with experience. I intend to delve more deeply into some practical techniques that we can use to make self-confidence work to our advantage and in the direction of building even more empowering relationships in a separate course on self-confidence and decision-making [keep an eye out for it on introducingaffinitology.com]. For now, try this exercise.

Exercise 9
An exercise in building self-confidence

1. Think of something that you would like to do and that you know that you can do it insofar as, if you do it, the result won't be a disaster, but which you are reluctant to do.

2. Now, ask yourself (in each case notice how the statement changes your attitude),

    a) I will never get better if I don't try.

    b) I can't lose what I don't have.

    c) I can't learn from what I haven't done.

3. What insights did you gain from this exercise?

[When I focused on the answer to this question for myself, the words 'carpe diem' came to mind and it reminded me of one of my favourite movies; "Dead Poets Society".]

Chapter 41

Sculpturism

I debated with myself [my Philosopher Identity debated with my Teacher Identity] as to whether or not to take a slight detour into an existential journey before returning to our quest to find SMERs and I decided that it is not really a detour, but extra spice in our SMER-creating recipe. You see, the quality of our relationships is strongly linked to our existential view of life. That is, I would behave differently towards others and others would respond differently to me depending on whether I believe that I am an individual acting with my own volition (§ 44 Locus of Control), or a cog in the machinery of society (§ 39 Social Ranking Criteria), or a member of a self-organizing system (§ 91) or a creative element in an emerging social structure; a living sculpture?

Personally, I veer towards the viewpoint of societies being like living sculptures. I have not come across a word to describe such a point of view, so I am going to propose, Sculpturism. Feel free to suggest an improvement on this term.

[I thought that autosculpturism (§ 91 Relationships as Self-Organizing Systems) may be more accurate, but then, Sculpturism is unique enough not to cause confusion and being shorter, slips off the tongue more easily.]

From a sculpturist perspective, I am not merely a part of society, society is also a part of me. You may find this point difficult to digest, thinking, "How can something that is bigger be part of something that is smaller?" So, let me elaborate.

Every cell in my body [with a few exceptions, such as the gametes and erythrocytes] contains all the necessary genetic information required to build another complete individual who, physiologically, is almost identical to me. What, presumably, my cells do not contain is the sociocultural information that would allow a group of such individuals to replicate our society as it is today. If a disaster were to strike and I were to be left alone on this earth with one other (female) individual, our combined knowledge of our respective societies would allow us to build a society that is imbued with the knowledge, values and norms that our respective societies has imbued us with. What will emerge will be very different from a society built by individuals without such a cultural base.

[This can be a basis for an argument for focusing more on 'culture' within our school systems, but I will leave that discussion for another time and place. If you are interested in that, I suggest that you keep an eye on introducingaffinitology.com]

"So what, Bijan? What does all this have to do with SMERs?" I hear some of you asking, impatiently. The point is that it is much easier to create healthy relationships in healthy societies and healthy societies are created through healthy relationships. Therefore,

---

I have the power to move a society, overall, towards it being a more healthy or more unhealthy society through the quality of the individual relationships (Pacta) that I (help to) **create.**

Once we are able to acknowledge this power, then, in order for us to build healthier relationships, we need to think about, and focus our attention on, how each of our relationships can, directly or indirectly, influence the health of society at large.

In § 90 (Fractals), we explore the concept of fractals and how they can enhance our perspectives on interpersonal relationships. One of the essential features of a fractal equation is that the term in the subject of the equation also appears on the other side of the equation $[x=f(x)]$. This means that in every iteration (~repetition), the old result affects the new result. You may have noticed that this is similar to what I have just pointed out about the relationship between Pacta and society at large; healthy one-to-one relationships lead to incremental improvements in the health of society which, in turn, lead to incremental improvements in the health of our one-to-one relationships [and vice versa ;-)].

Chapter 42

The Anatomy of Identity

42.1

The Mirror

Continuing with our medical analogy, I suggest that what we are doing in this section is akin to histology where we slice an organ and look at its tissues (Omniselves) and cells (Identities) under a microscope. In our case, instead of using a microscope (psychoanalysis, for example) we can begin by simply looking into a metaphorical mirror.

> *A few years ago, a lady came to me for help. She was complaining about her daughter and how her daughter's behaviour was putting a strain on their relationship. I explained to this mother that she was the one who needed to change and gave her some strategies that she could use. The following day, her daughter came to see me. After the daughter had told me about the problems she was having with her mother, I explained to her that she was the one who needed to change and gave her some strategies that she could use.*

In order to have satisfying relationships, we need to turn our attention inwards *first*. How often do we say to ourselves, "I must take a serious look at the effect I am having on my relationship and what is it about my own sense of self that is responsible for these effects?" Not often enough, I venture to propose. One of the most exciting turning points that takes us from a feeling of being reliant on others to a feeling of empowerment and maturity is the realisation that *the buck stops here*. If anything in my life isn't the way I want it to be; if I perceive anything to be 'wrong' with my life, *I am the one who has to deal with it*. That includes my relationships. (§ 44 Locus of Control)

In this chapter, we take a look at some of those important aspects of ourselves which, if we simply pay closer attention to, can transform our relationships (as we perceive them) in many gratifying and rewarding ways that we could not have imagined before.

Each of us can only change ourselves. Whether others change (in the way that we want) as a result of our change is beyond our 'circle of influence' (§ 44.4 Circle of Influence and Circle of Concern).

42.2
Beliefs, Values and Attitudes

> **"The only important changes from whence the renewal of civilisations results, affect ideas, conceptions and beliefs."**
>
> - Gustave Le Bon (1896) in 'The Crowd A Study of the Popular Mind'

How can we become conscious of the Identities that we have created for ourselves (or we have allowed others to create within (impose upon) us) when they are so deep-rooted that we don't notice them? Simple. Just, start a sentence with 'I am' and complete it. Here's a revelation:

> **The basic unit of Identity is belief**

This means that each of our Identities (§ 29.4 The Omniself) is derived from (composed of) a combination and configuration of beliefs [LEGO™ bricks would be a useful metaphor to imagine here]. A belief is simply a cause-and-effect association; whenever I think that something causes something to happen (or does not cause something to happen), that thought is a belief (§ 62.1.1 What is a Belief).

"But Bijan," I hear you say, "What if I simply believe in the existence of ghosts or that Persian cats are prettier than Siamese cats?" And I would say that, at some level, you are right. But when we dig deeply into both of these beliefs, we find that, at their core (in the final analysis), they boil down to cause-and-effect associations. For example, if I say that I believe in the existence of ghosts or multiple universes or love or a supreme intelligence or aliens or clairvoyance and so on, what I am really saying is, "Some of the experiences that I have had, and the way I have interpreted (§ 33 Atasinex Cluster) those experiences, lead (causes) me to conclude (effect) that these things exist."

In the objective, observable, measurable, repeatable and verifiable realm of science, it is much easier to pinpoint the actual cause-and-effect bases for our beliefs (what we call hypotheses or theories or laws) than it is in the invisible and subjective realm of the psyche. Nevertheless, I put it to you that,

> **there can be no beliefs without cause-and-effect associations.**

The more important practical implication of this is that any change in belief ultimately involves changing the cause-and-effect associations that we make. If we can identify the associations, the belief change will be easier, i.e. more cognitive and less emotional. (§ 63.1 Changing Beliefs)

> **A belief becomes a part of my Identity when that belief affects the way I think about myself (who I am).**

Our beliefs have a profound effect on the quality of our relationships.

Where do beliefs come from? I don't know but the following sentence just sprang to mind: *Allow me one miracle and I will explain everything else.*

This implies that if we delve too deeply into the sources of our beliefs, we risk finding ourselves in a situation where our whole world falls apart around us. If that were to happen, it would not, in itself, be either good or bad; it is the way that we react to it that would make it so. You might be thinking, "But Bijan, how can the whole world falling apart around us not be bad?" So, let me elaborate. But first, I should clarify that I am talking about a mentally created world and not the physical world. Nevertheless, I am going to use physical metaphors to shine light on this notion.

If we see a building falling down unexpectedly, our first reaction is to think, "Oh, that is bad." However, we would not have that reaction if we knew in advance that the building is being knocked down because it is derelict and dangerous and that it is being demolished to make way for a better one. This is an example of what in psychology is called priming; knowing something in advance of an experience (§ 33.8 Confirmation Bias). We would also change our mind about it being bad if we were given that information after the event. This is an example of a meaning reframe (§ 63.1 Changing Beliefs).

A belief such as "the earth is flat" is one that I can choose to accept or reject. Whether I accept it or not, as long as I don't identify with it, it has no relevance to me and, therefore, has little value (§ 64 Values); it's not important to me and it does not elicit any emotions in me. But if adopting or rejecting this belief has an impact on something that I *do* value (especially other's opinion of me), then it will affect my sense of Identity. In that case, I can choose to either identify with the belief or to distance myself from it. The belief in the earth being flat is now important to me and I *react* to thinking about it (or someone expressing it); it will not be something that I am (can be) impartial to.

> **The stronger my reaction, whether it is to affirm or reject an idea (a belief), the more I identify with it.**

Notice that we can form an Identity around rejecting an idea (or belief) too.

To reiterate, a belief is any cause-and-effect association. However, beliefs in themselves do not have any intrinsic value, they are a means to an end. They inform our judgements and our values. This is a two-way (reciprocal) process.

> **Our beliefs become our values by the extent to which we perceive them to affect an Identity that we have sculpted for ourselves.**

In other words, whether I believe in evolution or intelligent design is not important until I begin to judge myself and others through that belief. This means that,

> **our values are the standards by which we judge ourselves and others.**

That is what makes this topic particularly relevant to affinitology because **it is our judgement of other people that determines the people that we establish relationships with, and the quality of those relationships.** And those judgements are mediated by our values which are mediated through our beliefs.

Beliefs are not isolated concepts, they are building blocks. We use our powers of imagination to put these blocks together creatively to produce what we then perceive to be reality. In other words, we sculpt our Identity using our imagination and creativity which, primarily, involves filling in the gaps in our knowledge. What makes life interesting is that we are all unique (§ 39 Social Ranking Criteria) because we all fill in the gaps in our knowledge in our own unique ways. And it is these differences that make interpersonal relationships possible (§ 47.2 Complementary Elements).

We encounter some of these concepts again in § 62 (Beliefs and Decision-Making) when we explore beliefs in the context of decision-making.

42.3
Identity, Attachment and Dependence

Attachment and dependence are often confused. Dependence is a practical concern. It is about how much help we need to be able to look after ourselves physically. It is related to self-confidence (§ 40.4) and locus of control (§ 44). Attachment is an emotional concern. It is about the extent to which my emotions are aroused by something which, in turn, depends on the extent to which I identify with that thing. In other words, Identity and attachment are two sides of the same coin. We become emotionally attached (to a lesser or greater extent) to what we identify with.

It has been suggested that one of the characteristics of attachment is that the attachment figure is seen as a 'secure base'. I would argue that this is more a characteristic of dependence (§ 23.1) than attachment. If I am going bungee jumping, although I am physically *attached* to the rope, I am not emotionally attached to it; I am *dependent* upon it.

42.4
Identity Homeostasis

In § 35.5 (Homeostasis) we explore how relationships (Pacta) respond to change so as to maintain their integrity. Individuals also have characteristics that remain relatively stable in similar situations. This is the mainstay of the field of 'individual psychology' and the concept of personality. We have seen elsewhere in this course (§ 29.4 The Omniself) that individuals assume different Identities in different situations. Since the stability (predictability) of each Individual's responses depends on the situation, it is not Individuals, but their Identities, that have characteristics that remain relatively stable.

42.5
What is a Situation?

In a hard science such as chemistry [hard as in 'robust', not as in difficult], the situation (conditions of the experiment) is relatively easy to define; there are relatively few variables (the main ones are temperature, pressure, concentration and duration).

[That is, of course, an oversimplification, but let's stick to that simple view for now. If you really want to delve deeper into the more slippery variables that can confound even the 'hard' sciences, you could get started by looking at this paper: https://www.ncbi.nlm.nih.gov/pmc/articles/PMC4776714.]

Defining 'situation' in a social science context is much more problematic. For example, research has shown that a subtle change in the environment, such as holding a warm or cold cup of coffee in our hand before we meet someone, can affect how receptive we are to that person; that is to say, whether we perceive the person as being a 'warm' or a 'cold' individual. The point is that our different Identities emerge from our psyche and what emerges can vary depending on even slight changes in the environment (circumstances) and the situation (§ 14.3 Situation vs Circumstance).

Chapter 43

Attribution Theory

Throughout this course, our aim is to become aware of how the way we think (including our beliefs, perspectives, interpretations, decision-making processes, self-confidence and locus of control) affect the quality of our interpersonal relationships. These constructs [ideas, labels, words, concepts, ways of trying to make sense of things, ...] are highly interconnected and often overlapping. If you were to ask me for some sort of thread that can bring and hold these ideas together, I would propose Attribution Theory as a strong candidate. The work of the Gestalt Psychologist, Fritz Heider [Especially the 1958 publication of his book, The Psychology of Interpersonal Relations], has been influential in bringing about some of the major developments in psychology since the second half of the twentieth century. These include theories of motivation, cognition and emotion as well as trait theories of personality [big names in psychology, such as Ajzen, Bandura and Lazarus].

Elsewhere in this book (§ 33 Atasinex Cluster), I have explained that our beliefs form the foundations of our emotions and our actions. I described beliefs as "cause-and-effect associations" and explained that each belief can be expressed in the form of an if-then statement. Attribution Theory takes these understandings to a deeper level by delving into why we believe what we believe. For example, if I say something like, "If I let go of this apple, it will fall" and someone asks, "Why do you believe that?" I am being questioned about the way I have reasoned (§ 33 Atasinex Cluster) in order to arrive at that belief. In other words, the question can be restated as, "What do you attribute as the reason for your belief that the apple will fall if you let go of it?"

[and my answer might be something like, "I attribute it to an invisible field called gravity whose strength is directly related to the mass of the earth, the sun, the moon and the apple and their distances and relative positions to each other." And if the questioner is my daughter when she was eight, she might follow that answer with, "Why?" and my answer would then have to be, "Because I believe my physics teacher." And from then on, we would be venturing into the realm of another fascinating subject; metacognition and then, this midnote will stop here. However, the why's from an inquisitive child would probably not.]

Similar to our concern here, Fritz Heider's primary concern was with people's attributions regarding other people's behaviour; he wanted to know why people believe what they believe about why people do what they do. In other words, instead of the example of the apple, he would probably have preferred a more interpersonal example. Maybe one like this: One friend says to another,

"If I ask this person out, I will embarrass myself." And if the other person then asks, "Why [do you believe that]?", she is asking about the friend's 'attributions'.

In this course we shall frequently encounter the concept of reframing (§ 63.1). Another way of looking at reframing is to think of it as changing attributions. An example is the anecdote about the girl who had lost interest in studying because she was no longer at the top of her class. I talk about this case in § 83.2.1 (Damaged Self-Confidence) in Unit 19 (Pathology and Therapeutics of Relationships).

Chapter 44

Locus of Control

44.1
What is Locus of Control?

"Que Sera Sera", "You can't escape fate", "Where there's a will there's a way", "Believe in yourself", "Expand your comfort zone", "It's just my luck", "Date with destiny". All these phrases refer to mental attitudes that psychologists call locus of control (LoC) or 'internality' or the 'Internal-External locus of control Scale'.

LoC is a measure of the extent to which we believe that we are able to control our destiny. These perspectives lie along a scale ranging from, "My efforts don't make the slightest difference" to "My efforts make all the difference." Those who lean towards the former belief are called 'externals' and those who fall into the latter camp are called 'internals'.

From a behavioural point of view, it is about whether or not we are reactive or proactive and what makes us so. It is also the main difference between the Behaviourist and the Humanist schools of psychology (§ 40.2 Behaviourism versus Humanism), the former advocating external LoC (it's all about the environment) and the latter, internal LoC (it's all about the choices that we make).

In this section, we look at where LoC comes from, how it affects us (and our relationships, of course) and what we can do about it.

Locus of control is highly correlated with such constructs as Mastery/Performance *Orientation* which is related to Carol Dweck's Growth/Fixed *Mindset* and to Intrinsic/Extrinsic *motivation*. These constructs are all also related to (correlate significantly with) what is measured by the Openness to Experience dimension of the Big Five *personality* 'traits'. The relevance of these constructs to this part of our discussion is that they point to deep-rooted beliefs and have a significant influence over our sense of Identity and its trajectory. I say trajectory because, depending on our Orientation [Mindset, Motivation Direction, Openness to Experience, etc.], we will have a greater or lesser chance of changing what we believe. And what we believe determines who we are and who we become; our sense of identity and, ultimately, our interpersonal relationships, including our chances of (or ability to) create SMERs.

Our beliefs can also empower or disempower us with regards to the range of Identities (§ 29.4 The Omniself) that we can create within ourselves and, therefore, the depth of breadth of relationships that such flexibility can bestow. Note that, like self-confidence, from an affinitological perspective,

> **our locus of control depends on both the situation and the Identity that is active in that situation.**

44.1.1
Locus of Control and Self-Confidence

Self-confidence is about our belief in our abilities. Locus of control is about our belief in the extent to which those abilities can make a difference to the situation, to our life's trajectory or to our destiny (depending on our projected timeframe).

Self-confidence is a necessary, but insufficient, condition for having high Internality. In terms of Levels of Belief (§ 62.5 The Three Levels of Belief), Self-confidence is in Belief Level 2 (I can do something about it). LoC, on the other hand, is closer to Belief Level 3, which I have defined as our answer to the question, "Is it worth it?".

We can feel 'in control' or 'out of control' in two different ways. That is, there are two facets to locus of control; 'chance' and 'powerful others'. Let's take a look at each of these.

44.2
Chance

Once, a friend of mine, who lived in London, said that she wanted to find translating and interpreting jobs. We spent several hours putting together an elegant looking CV (Résumé) and then I went home. I saw her again a couple of months later and asked her how her job hunting was going. She said, "Bijan, you need luck to get anywhere in life. I just don't have the luck." I asked her how many of those CVs she had sent out and she said, "four". I asked her whether her 'luck' would have been the same had she sent out 400 CVs. This did not change her attitude or behaviour. I assume that believing in luck, the way she did, had certain psychological payoffs.

This story illustrates one of the facets of LoC; the extent to which we subscribe to the underlying belief that our life is governed by randomness; sometimes we get lucky and sometimes we don't.

44.3
Powerful Others

The second facet of LoC is the extent to which we believe that we are actively controlled by powerful others. Of course, the world is littered with people who believe that the way to achieve fulfilment and happiness is through controlling others in whatever way it takes. However, just because there are people out there who are on the lookout for people to control, it doesn't mean that I must subscribe to the notion that I am helpless to do anything about it. In the words of Viktor Frankl,

> **"The one thing you can't take away from me is the way I choose to respond to what you do to me. The last of one's freedoms is to choose one's attitude in any given circumstance."**
>
> - Viktor E. Frankl: Man's Search for Meaning

The following couplet by a Persian poet demonstrates how those who are obsessed with control operate (even though the motivator here appears to be love, not power).

> **Through guile or guise, wailing or whip*,**
> **I shall, eventually, dig a route into your heart of stone.**
>
> - Rezagholikhan Hedaayat (1800-1871)

* I have taken poetic licence here. In the original, he uses a word that literally means 'force' (not whip)

[You could argue that I am corrupting a beautifully romantic love poem by associating it with power-seeking. Actually, there was a battle between my romantic Identity and my teacher Identity and the latter gained the advantage by invoking the Machiavellian argument; the end justifies the means. And then the Teacher Identity in me intervened and asked whether Machiavellian philosophy is congruent with the spirit of teaching, and the jury is still out on that one...]

Notice that when I was describing each of the two aspects of locus of control, I used the phrase, "the extent to which". This is because, LoC is a scale; it is not that we either have an internal LoC or an external one. Our LoC also varies depending on the situation. Secondly, as I have already pointed out, LoC is *belief-based*, which means that it is *acquired*; we are not born with a particular LoC disposition, it is something that we learn, usually, quite early in life.

Since both determinants of LoC lie on a scale, at different times we can feel more or less in control of our destiny. If our LoC becomes too external, then we become prone to learned helplessness and depression.

Conversely, when our success has more to do with outside influences than we think, we can develop false self-confidence. [This is related to a pervasive and much researched cognitive bias known as Attribution Error. I encourage you to look it up.] This often happens when we lack experience. The more experience we have, the more we appreciate the relative influence of internal and external factors.

LoC can be generalised (applied to specific or broad areas of our lives) to a greater or lesser degree. For example, my perception of my employer may lead me to believe that I am helpless in changing my current work conditions; that is, I believe that, where my work conditions are concerned, my employer is in control. The extent to which I generalise my LoC, that is, how much of my life I believe I have control over, depends on whether I *believe* that my inability to influence my employer is related to who I am (Internal attribution) or to who he is (external attribution) (§ 43 Attribution Theory). Secondly, my LoC would be more external if I focus on where I am rather than where I could be. In other words, I can believe that I have some control over who I work for which means that I have control over whether or not to continue to work for that particular employer. [This reminds me of a book called, "Who Moved My Cheese" by Spenser Johnson]

In conclusion, becoming aware of the concept of locus of control and our own position along its spectrum in any given situation can, itself, alter our perception and the trajectory of our relationships (§ 11 The Therapeutic Effects of Awareness).

44.4
Circle of Influence and Circle of Concern

Through his influential book, *The Seven Habits of Highly Effective People*, Steven Covey introduced us to the notions of circle of control and circle of concern. In my coaching sessions, I use these concepts as a means of explaining the roots of our anxieties.

I begin by writing down a list under the heading, "What is important to me". I then draw a circle and say let's imagine that we can put 'everything that is important to me' into this circle. I then draw a smaller circle and say that this circle represents 'those things in life that are important to me AND which I can do something about'. Then I draw lines from each of the items in the list of 'what is important to me' to either the outer circle and the inner circle (figure 22).

Our circle of influence is where we can make decisions that we can act on.

Figure 22 Circle of Concern and Circle of Influence

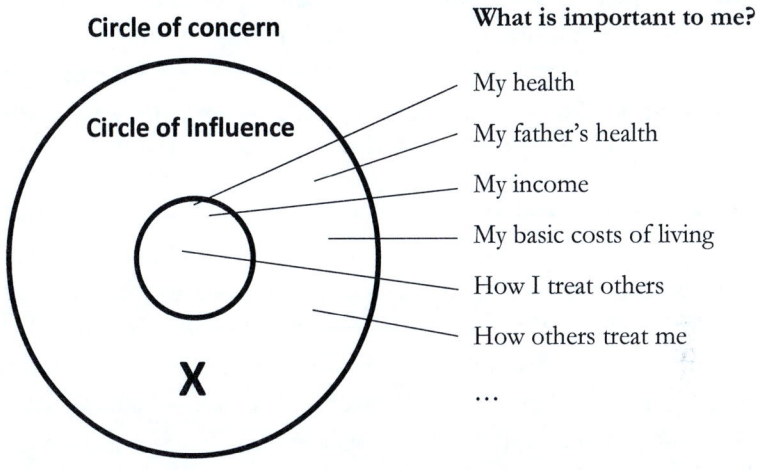

Circle of concern   **What is important to me?**

Circle of Influence

My health

My father's health

My income

My basic costs of living

How I treat others

How others treat me

X

...

44.5
Zone of Anxiety

In figure 22, region X represents those things in life that are important to me, but where there is little that I can do to affect them. For example, where my own health is concerned, I decide what I eat or drink or smoke, whether or not I practice good personal hygiene and the extent to which I exercise, and so on. In contrast, however much my father's health may be important to me, it is he who ultimately decides whether or not he engages in behaviours that promote good health. Similarly, by focusing on my income, I can come up with ideas that *I can act upon* to improve my earnings whereas, focusing on rising house prices is more likely to leave me feeling frustrated and helpless. The difference between the two is the extent to which I am able to **take action** (do something) that would affect whatever it is that I am focusing on. I then explain to my clients that

> **Anxiety is a feeling that stems from focusing on things that** (we believe) **we are unable to predict or influence.**

When we cannot predict an outcome, we have no criteria for making decisions. Anxiety stems from this unpredictability. You could say, "But Bijan, most things in life are unpredictable and many of those are important to all of us, so if what you are saying is true, we should all be anxious wrecks." And I would say, "That's a great point, thank you for paying attention." And speaking of attention, that's the difference between the anxious and the active.

> **Anxious people ask *why*, focusing on what they cannot change and active people ask *how*, focusing on what they can do.**
>
> cf. § 11.1 (Why Can Seriously Damage Our Health)

Whenever we are feeling anxious, it is because we are focusing on something that is important to us but which we believe we have no control over. Once we recognize this as being the root of our anxiety, we need to identify the direction and focus of our attention (Unit 22 Thermodynamics of Relationships) that is making us feel anxious. We then have a choice; we can either change our focus or change our interpretation (§ 33.5 Interpretation: Creating Meaning), such as, I *can* do something about it. To wit, we can consciously change our locus of control (and the consequent level of anxiety that it can induce) by changing our beliefs (§ 63.1 Changing Beliefs).

Both fear and anxiety are about not feeling safe (§ 38.1 Personas are Rooted in Doubt). The difference between fear and anxiety is that fear is about an immediate threat in the here and now, whereas anxiety is an *expectation* (§ 33 Atasinex Cluster). It is about something that may or may not happen at some time in the future. It is a very useful feeling because if you are not sure whether you left the gas on before leaving the house, then anxiety nags you until you *do something about it*. This *doing something* can be a change in focus or a change in interpretation - involving a change in belief level (§ 62.5 The Three Levels of Belief). In short,

> **Action is the antidote to anxiety.**

"But Bijan, I am running around all the time and I am still feeling anxious" Here, we need to make a distinction between 'action' and 'movement'. Just because I am moving it does not mean that I am taking action. I may simply be running around like a headless chicken. [I know it is not a pretty allusion, but the more emotive it is the more memorable it will be and the more impact it will have]. We cannot relieve ourselves from anxiety by taking random action. The doubt in the back of my mind that I may have left the gas on will continue unless I,

a) Become absorbed in something else,

b) Decide that I have not left the gas on or, if I have, it is not important, or

c) Go back and check

For option (a) to be effective, my 'complete' attention needs to be diverted elsewhere (until I get back home). For example, I could be focused on the more immediate problem of making sure that a loved one gets to the hospital in time.

Option (b) is an example of a change in interpretation. Ways in which we can do this includes changing our perspective (I am sure I did not leave the gas on) or our belief level, in the example above; deciding that it is not important (§ 62.5 The Three Levels of Belief).

Option (c) is about changing our locus of control by moving the item (thought) from our Zone of Anxiety into our Circle of Influence.

I hear some of you saying, "But Bijan, sometimes I am anxious and I don't know what is making me anxious; I am not thinking about anything specific at the time." And I would say, "I understand that but, just because I don't know what is making me anxious, it doesn't mean that I am an irrational being; it simply means that the reason is not immediately accessible to my consciousness. It may have been forgotten or temporarily lost, but *there is a specific reason that is making me anxious at any one time.*" What I am saying is that, in my humble opinion, Generalised Anxiety Disorder (as the DSM calls it) doesn't mean that the reason for the anxiety is 'general', it means that the anxiety is with the person in 'general' *situations*. When we find the 'specific' reason and deal with it, the 'general' anxiety will go away.

To see how this relates to our interpersonal relationships, go back and change the example of 'I wonder whether I left the gas on' to something like, 'I wonder whether I upset him/her' and take it from there.

This is clearly a big topic and I have gotten somewhat carried away, so let me leave the rest of this discussion for another time and place. Suffice it to say that anxiety has disempowering effects on our relationships and to deal with it, we need to find what it is that is both important to us *and* we currently believe to be outside of our circle of influence that is occupying our mind.

44.6
Catch 22

We encounter the importance of expectations throughout this discourse (§ 33 Atasinex Cluster). Here, I want to take a brief look at the potential effect of other people's expectations in the context of locus of control. Fear of rejection (§ 40.3 Self-Esteem) can compel us to act in ways that are contrary to our Core Values (§ 29.4 The Omniself and § 39 Social Ranking Criteria). Sometimes we may find ourselves in a conversation that boils down to this:

- Why do you always treat me like a child?
- I treat you the way you expect me to treat you (I get the most this-Nexus-enhancing responses from you).

The problem is that, when we act according to other people's expectations because we want to cling to the relationship and not because those expectations are congruent with our Core Values, resentment is likely to be the consequence. And,

---

Chronic resentment is a slow poison that can gradually corrode our soul.

Using the above dialogue as reference, here is the catch; if I don't want to be treated like a child, I may need to cease to act in a way that my interlocutor expects. If I cease to behave in a way that he or she expects, I might lose the relationship (§ 92 Relationship Frameworks). This only becomes a problem if I am dependent on that person (or that particular Relationship Framework) in at least one domain of human experience (Unit 11: § 48-50). Here are some possible questions that can help us resolve such conflicts (dilemmas):

1. Can I change the Relationship Framework (§ 92) without losing that which I am dependent upon? For example, I may want to maintain a comfortable relationship with my mother because it fulfils my need for a sense of belonging and/or continuity. In this case, I may decide to assert myself and demand that I be treated as an adult. Here, I would be asking for a change in our Relationship Framework from a Mother-Child Nexus to a Friends Nexus [Henceforth, her Mother Identity would need to resist the temptation of 'butting in' even when my actions remind her of my childhood and trigger her 'mother-of-Bijan' Identity].

2. Can I replace the Relationship with one that fulfils those needs without compromising my Core Values? For example, by creating a new Pactum with another Individual for situations when I need a mother figure.

3. Can I continue in my current relationship without compromising my Core Values? For example, I can create a False Identity (§ 38 Personas), such as a Child Identity, which is not inclined to resent acting like a child or being treated like a child and which only emerges in relation to this particular Pactum (§ 56 Fertilisation, Differentiation and Gestation). Note that in a different situation, I may be in a different Pactum with the same Individual, but through a different Identity (§ 58.3 Multi-Nexus Relationships).

44.7

The Two Ways of Feeling in Control

We can feel (believe/perceive ourselves to be) in control of a situation in one of two ways; by believing that

a) I can adapt myself to this situation, or

b) I can change the environment to suit me.

From an affinitological perspective, 'suit me' means a situation in which I do not feel the need to be on the defensive (§ 79 Psychological Defence Mechanisms).

Chapter 45

To Play or Not to Play

Nowadays, we live in a culture that encourages us to play games in our pursuit of any kind of relationship. Paradoxically, this is particularly true in our quest for intimacy, which is, in essence, the antithesis to playing games. If you doubt that you ever play games yourself, especially where your most intimate relationships are concerned, ask yourself whether you ever think twice about what you might have initially wanted to say to someone. If so, you were playing a game. The game is, "How should I best twist (spin) what comes to mind so that I get a response that I want or to avoid a response that I don't want?" The reward you are looking for may be anything from a smile to acknowledgement to cooperation to money to sex.

You may say, "But Bijan, what you have just described is 'foresight' not playing games." And you may be right. But foresight has its drawbacks too; it prevents us from being spontaneous. "And what is wrong with that?" You might well ask. Perhaps, at this point, it might be better for me to pass the baton to the illustrious Eric Berne, the founder of Transactional Analysis (§ 73). Here are his closing comments in his book, *Games People Play*.

> "After Games, What?
> … For certain fortunate people there is something which transcends all classifications of behavior, and that is awareness; something which rises above the programming of the past, and that is spontaneity; and something that is more rewarding than games, and that is intimacy. But all three of these may be frightening and even perilous to the unprepared. Perhaps they are better off as they are, seeking their solutions in popular techniques of social action, such as "togetherness." This may mean that there is no hope for the human race, but there is hope for individual members of it."

Looking at it from Eric Berne's view, 'foresight' (lack of spontaneity) is tantamount to behaving in accordance with prior programming (being trapped inside a program) and when we rise above that programming, we will be able to achieve something that is more rewarding than games; intimacy.

I define intimacy as a situation where there is no fear of being judged. In other words,

> **Intimacy is where positive intention is taken for granted.**

This is actually the basis behind a school of therapy (Rogerian Counselling) instigated by Carl Rogers whose main tenet is "unconditional positive regard".

We have come to think that being entirely honest is likely to leave us desolate and unloved. Ironically, we expect others to play by the same rules and employ similar subterfuge. If they don't play the game, we consider them to be unworthy as potential companions or business partners (too naïve, too gullible, too open, too predictable, too trusting, too blunt, too forward, etc.). We can even become hostile to those who are blatantly honest with us. This is yet another example of being "well-adjusted to a profoundly sick society" (§ 86 What is Mental Illness?).

Awareness of such perspectives and inner conflicts in ourselves, along with an appreciation that The Other in the relationship is prone to the same conflicts, can go a long way to facilitating more empowering and satisfying relationships. Here is an exercise for you to try.

Exercise 10

Steps Towards Greater Intimacy

1. Ask someone the following questions (one at a time)

   a) What is your greatest weakness?

   b) How do you deal with it?

2. As you hear their answer, pay close attention to how you *feel* about the answer. What does your intuition tell you? Is this a guarded or an open response?

3. Taking that answer at face value, how do you think you could use it to *improve* the quality of your relationship with that person? Here are a few suggestions:

   a) Empathise with that weakness if you can; if you also feel that vulnerability, share (express) it.

   b) Share one of your own vulnerabilities.

   c) If you have had this vulnerability in the past, explain how you got over it.

4. Compare the dynamics of your relationship before and after this exercise.

"But Bijan, *what if* I make myself more vulnerable and get exploited?" You may well ask. And I would refer you to § 8 (What If) and I would add that we need to take that risk and feel confident (§ 40.4 Self-Confidence) that we can deal with the consequences. This is also the spirit of entrepreneurialism (§ 53.6 Trust and Vulnerability). We discuss this trade-off between vulnerability and intimacy in more detail in § 79 (Psychological Defence Mechanisms).

Unit 10

The Composition of

Relationships

The quality of a Nexus and the trajectory of any Pactum depend on each and every transaction or interaction between The Self and The Other. In this section we explore some of the factors that mediate our interactions and transactions.

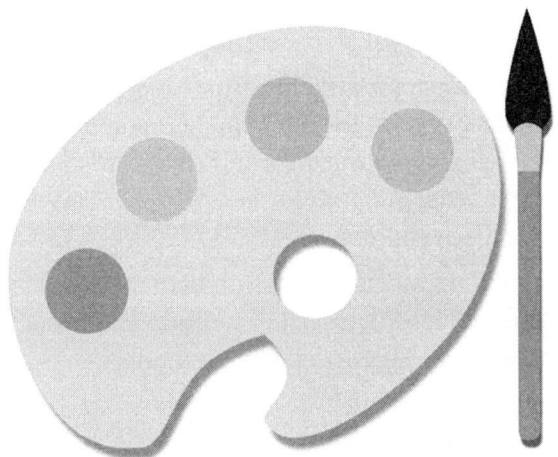

Chapter 46

The Adjunctum Communalis

(The Backbone of Relationships)

What we call the backbone is not a bone; it is a fantastic structure blending the rigidity of many bones with the flexibility of the cartilages that hold them together to give us the best of both worlds. The backbone of a relationship; the structures that hold a relationship together yet allow it to remain flexible, are what I have called Common and Complementary *elements*.

The Self and The Other have characteristics (akin to biological 'structures') that have the *potential* to create a connection. Affinito-Receptors exist on both The Self (A.R.S.) [Affinito-Receptors of the Self] and The Other (A.R.O.) [Affinito-Receptors of the Other] which are designed to recognise the potentially bond-forming characteristics in others. These Affinito-Receptors make each respective Identity in the relationship more sensitive (more receptive) to the Common and Complementary elements (§ 47) in The Other's dominant Identity (§ 37.9.1) *in any given situation*. We explore the nature and characteristics of these Receptors in other sections of this course - (§ 34 Cells, Receptors and Sensitivity) and § 64.4 (Values as Receptors) and § 33 (Atasinex Cluster).

In biology, the interstitial space is the environment through which cells interact with each other. Affinitologically, it is the environment through which The Self and The Other can interact. This is depicted in figure 23.

Figure 23 The Potential for a Relationship

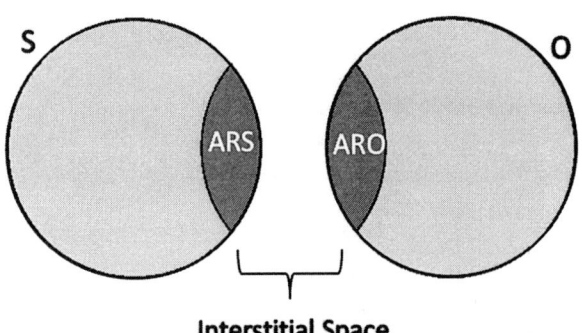

Interstitial Space

A.R.S. and A.R.O are regions consisting of Common or Complementary Elements; factors which can, potentially, lead to a connection. Molecular biologists call such potential for connection 'binding sites'. Cellular biologists and pharmacologists call them receptors. Molecular biologists call the counterparts to binding sites (i.e., that which binds to the binding site), ligands and pharmacologists call them agonists. Note that in chemistry, the word ligand has a different meaning; it is a moiety that binds to a metal atom via a coordinate bond (§ 25.4 Dative Bond). The interesting point is that the ligand also needs a binding site for there to be a connection. So, which is the ligand and which is the binding site? The answer is, it depends on your perspective; whichever side you call the binding site, the other side is the ligand. That is not as outlandish as it sounds. Think of the word spouse. Whichever side you are on, the other is your spouse. Here, the ligand is the spouse.

Similarly, we can think of A.R.S. as the interpersonal binding sites for an Identity that we use as a reference point and A.R.O. as the other party's ligands. This section is about the nature of those binding sites.

[In physiology, the ligand and the binding site are distinguished by their location. If the binding site is on the surface of a cell, it is a receptor. If it is in the interstitial space, it is an agonist and if it is in a synapse, it is referred to as a neurotransmitter even though, at the molecular level, they all simply refer to two molecules interacting with (causing changes in) each other].

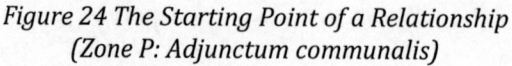

*Figure 24 The Starting Point of a Relationship
(Zone P: Adjunctum communalis)*

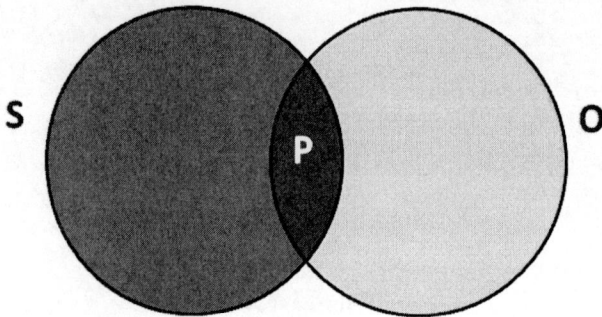

Clearly, by virtue of being human [alive, even], we have innumerable things in common with everyone that we meet. Some of these characteristics allow us to bond with some people more than others along certain dimensions of human experience (Unit 11: § 48-50). My humanity allows me to connect at an emotional level [somewhere along the emotional dimension] with almost* everyone to some extent [hopefully more than we are often led to believe] whereas, the extent to which I can connect with people along the sexual dimension depends, in part, on my gender. Similarly, the extent to which I can connect with people at an intellectual level depends, in part, on the language that The Self and The Other can speak and/or understand. [*I was hesitant as to whether to say 'almost', but the side of me that resists absolute statements prevailed, saying, "There are always exceptions. This reminds me the 'I am a liar paradox' (§ 29.4.2).]

Zone P [for potential] represents the bases [plural of basis, not base] on which a relationship *can* be founded and maintained. That is, those factors (affinito-receptors) such as, common or complementary beliefs, values, interests, needs and capabilities within each of the two Identities that could potentially lead to the creation of a specific Pactum. Note that at this point, there is no interaction yet, simply pure potential. Prior to some kind of interaction, these potentials remain unnoticed. As the number of interactions increase, more of these potentials become manifest, making them available for strengthening the bond. In some cases, the manifested potential can weaken the bond [if you are familiar with pharmacology, think 'antagonist']. We delve into these concepts more deeply in § 56.1 (Fertilisation: Pactum Formation).

"But Bijan, I am reading this book because I am looking for practical advice on how to improve my relationships. How does knowing these things about your, so-called, *adjunctum communalis* help me to do that?"

Thank you for asking. In § 62.4 (Beliefs as Affinitological Genes), I tell a story about how I tried to encourage my children not to avoid sitting next to strangers by suggesting to them that 'a stranger is a friend that you haven't got to know yet.' Appreciation of the *adjunctum communalis* directs our attention (§ 33 Atasinex Cluster and Unit 23: Mechanics of Relationships) towards those aspects of ourselves and others that can facilitate the transition of people from strangers into friends (§ 92 Relationship Frameworks).

Viewed from a different perspective, we (as healthy individuals) are only likely to make a move towards establishing a connection with someone if we consider there to be a *potential* for a beneficial (mutually empowering) relationship. Knowledge of the *adjunctum communalis* makes us aware that there are *always* potentials for establishing at least some kind of relationship with others, if we understood what the Common or Complementary elements are.

Chapter 47

Common and Complementary Elements

47.1
Common Elements

As the name implies, common elements are those aspects that The Self and The Other have in common. This is a necessary but insufficient condition for creating SMERs. Why it is insufficient will become apparent when we begin to discuss Complementary Elements in a forthcoming section (§ 47.2). Let's begin by taking a look at a few examples of Common Elements.

47.1.1
Common Language

Without a common language (verbal or non-verbal), there can be no interpersonal connection. I can anticipate what some of you are thinking, so let me clarify. In this context, a common language is not one that is spoken by both parties, it is one that is *understood* by both parties. For example, a person can interact with a dog, not because he can wag his tail, but because he can understand what it means and conversely, a dog cannot say, "Sit!" but it can understand what it means. This principle also holds true for two people. I know some people who find it very difficult to utter the words, "I love you", but find it relatively easy to present someone with a bunch of flowers. For someone else, the reverse may be true. It is possible for these two people to create a SMER if they both understand and appreciate the gestures without expecting the other to speak their 'language'. This is related to Gary Chapman's '*Five Love Languages*' (cf. § 93.2 Manifestations of Motivational Energy) which reminds me of Rumi's *parable of the four travellers*.

The Parable of the Four Travelers

"Four persons, a Persian, an Arab, a Turk, and a Greek, were traveling together, and received a present of a dirhem. The Persian said he would buy "angur" with it, the Arab said he would buy "inab," while the Turk and the Greek were for buying "uzum" and "astaphil" (staphyle), respectively. Now all these words mean one and the same thing, viz. "grapes;" but, owing to their ignorance of each other's languages, they fancied they each wanted to buy something different, and accordingly a violent quarrel arose between them. At last a wise man who knew all their languages came up and explained to them that they were all wishing for one and the same thing."

[Source: The Masnavi, by Rumi, tr. by E.H. Whinfield, (1898)]
[Available from: https://www.sacred-texts.com/isl/masnavi/msn02.htm]

47.1.2
Common External Environment

Being in the same place at the same time or having had experience of being in the same place at different times can provide a basis for a connection.

47.1.3
Common Beliefs, Values and Interests

Common beliefs are essential in establishing a connection between The Self and The Other, but that is not enough. For example, The Self may believe that cigarettes cause cancer, yet this may not deter him from seeking the pleasures of smoking [whatever they may be; I wouldn't know]. In other words, In this case, The Self values immediate pleasure more than long-term health. Here, the belief in cigarettes causing cancer may facilitate a connection at an intellectual level. However, if The Other values long-term health more than short-term pleasure, there will be potential conflict at the values level. Without common beliefs, there cannot be common values, after all, how can one value what one does not believe in? Nevertheless, if the common beliefs affect our value systems differently, it is the value systems that will determine the quality of our relationships and not the beliefs *per se*. Our values determine our interests (pastimes). As such, our pastimes are better indicators of our values than our words.

47.1.4
Common Perspectives

Our perspectives determine how we perceive and interpret what goes on around us. These can either provide a potential for connection or deny us the opportunity. Throughout this course, we encounter many examples of different perspectives such as,

- Whether we focus on the outcome or the journey (§ 6-11)
- Which part of the elephant in darkness we touch (§ 64.9 The Origin of Values)
- Whether what others say makes a difference; The Frog Race Story (§ 62.5.1 Belief Level 1)
- Now or future (§ 5.1 Give Fish or Teach Fishing)
- Trust or doubt (§ 53 Trust)
- Black and white or grayscale (§ 25.3 Polar Bond: Partial Sharing)
- Give or take (§ 25 Relationships as Chemical Bonds)

Clearly, the perspective that we choose for observing our reality will affect both our perception and our interpretation of the world around us (§ 33 Atasinex Cluster). In particular, how we interpret The Other, whether in an existing or a potential relationship will, obviously, affect the quality of our relationships.

You might say, "Bijan, if it is obvious, why are you wasting my time telling me about it?" And the answer is that, new meaning emerges from established meanings (the obvious). In a logical argument, we call these 'obvious' declarations, premises.

[If these premises appear obvious, but are, in fact, false, then we exit the domain of logic and enter the realm of sophistry. But, alas, pursuing this fascinating line of thought will detract us from our current concern.]

The conclusion that I want to reach is this: The fundamental question that we need to ask in each encounter with another person is,

---

Which of the myriads of perspectives at my disposal is likely to have the most empowering impact on this relationship?

Notice that whatever perspective (point of view) we choose to observe a situation from, our interpretation of the situation is still dependent on our beliefs and values. In other words, we can choose to view a situation from a perspective that is more conducive to a more empowering relationship as long as there is no conflict where our values are concerned.

In the early days of management science, two perspectives on management were identified and labelled Theory X and Theory Y. Theory X managers consider the typical worker to have little ambition, be motivated by self-interest and responsibility avoidant. Theory Y managers assume employees are internally motivated, enjoy their job, and work to better themselves. Such perspectives are not limited to management. They affect the way in which all of us perceive people. And what a difference this makes to our relationships.

[I once told my mother that I am a Theory Y type of manager and she told me that I should not tie myself into a single perspective and that my management style should be informed by my observations of my employees' behaviour. In other words, some people perform better through a Theory X approach and others through a Theory Y approach. Here, I am arguing that, at least sometimes, the employer's approach results in complementary behaviours/attitudes from the employee. There is one concept that can consolidate these potentially discordant perspectives; *calibration*.]

For another example of perspective, we can point to the Teacher-Student relationship. One student may see the teacher's role as a resource and another as a gatekeeper. Clearly, depending on whether or not the teacher shares the student's perspective, the potential for connection and the quality of the connection will differ.

Our perspectives are shaped by our sociocultural background and our own personal experiences to a greater or lesser degree depending on various factors (§ 39 Social Ranking Criteria).

47.1.5
Common Experiences

Common experiences provide us with common frames of reference, that is, something to talk about that the other party can relate to. Without common experiences, we may be able to sympathise (imagine) with others, but we would not be able to empathise (relive) with them.

Consider the following exchange from Star Trek, *The Voyage Home*. Spock has been brought back from the dead and McCoy is trying to have a conversation with him about the experience:

McCoy: Perhaps we could cover a little philosophical ground, life, death, life, things of that nature.

Spock: I did not have time, on Vulcan, to review the philosophical disciplines.

- Come on, Spock. It's me, McCoy. You really have gone where no man's gone before. Can't you tell me what it felt like?
- It would be impossible to discuss this subject without a common frame of reference.
- You're joking.
- A joke is a story with a humorous climax.
- You mean I have to die to discuss your insights on death?

47.2
Complementary Elements

Without Common Elements, we would not have common frames of reference to form the basis of our communications (means of connecting). But that is not enough; common elements are also necessary, but insufficient, for creating a SMER.

A door frame and a door need to have at least one common 'element', the common purpose (function) of opening and shutting access to a particular space. However, for the door frame and the door to perform their joint function (fulfil their joint purpose) they need to be a **good fit**, in their case, their size and shape (and, if aesthetics is important, in terms of their texture and colour too). This is related to the lock and key analogy of relationships that we discussed in § 2.2 (What is the key to mutually empowering and satisfying relationships?). There, we noted that the **grooves in the lock must complement the troughs in the key** and vice versa for the two to function. Such Complementary Elements are essential for the formation of Interdependent relationships (§ 23.2 The Road to Interdependence) without which, I would argue, SMERs are not possible.

In § 21.4 (What is a 'Healthy' Relationship?), I defined a healthy relationship by saying, "If a relationship can do something that neither of the individuals forming the relationship could have achieved by themselves, *without disempowering side effects,* that's an empowering relationship." This highlights the value of complementary elements.

Complementary elements are those factors that, when they come together in a Pactum, enable it to achieve what neither of the Identities that comprise the Pactum can achieve independently.

Here are a few examples of various elements that can bring people together. These can be common or complementary depending on the interacting Identities. For example, depending on the sexuality of The Self and The Other, gender can be a common or complementary element.

- Behaviour
- Character
- Feelings
- Goals (Intentions)
- Habits
- Internal State
- Personality
- Physiology
- Gender
- Values
- Physical features

Note that,

a) These are not mutually exclusive and

b) Are not binary; they lie on a grayscale (§ 25.3 Polar Bond: Partial Sharing)

47.2.1
Exchangeable Elements

Exchangeable elements are things that one can 'give' and another can 'take' (be the recipient of). These can be as tangible as a potted plant or as intangible as 'a piece of my mind'. As soon as we can think of something as being giveable and, by implication, takeable, we have created a means (a tool) for creating a connection with another person [or to put it affinitologically; for creating a nexus with another Identity (The Other)].

There are an infinite number of 'things' that we may want to give, take or share but, in the final analysis, they can all be summarised in one word, **feelings** (§ 51 Emotional Dimension).

We do not give, take or share for any other reason than to create feelings.

Focusing on this (feelings) aspect of relationships alone can transform the quality of our relationships.

47.2.2
Opposites Attract

The word 'opposite' is quite versatile and potentially ambiguous. It can be a noun [The opposite of 'relationship' is 'no relationship', i.e., disconnectedness], an adjective [An opposite point of view] or a preposition [He sat opposite me]. To further complicate matters, we sometimes use the word 'opposite' when, strictly, we are not talking about opposites. For example, if I were to ask you, "What is the opposite of black?" I expect you would say "White." [unless you don't take the question at face value]. However, black and white are not opposite to each other, they are *in contrast* to each other and in being so, they can complement each other too. In other words,

---

**when we talk about opposites attracting each other,
we can be talking about contrasts complementing each other.**

Not all contrasts are complementary however; sometimes, they can be quite garish.

The word 'opposite' comes from the same root as the word 'position'. Therefore, strictly, you need to be in a relative 'position' to something to be 'opposite' it. However, since interpersonal relationships are abstract, there is no relative position and therefore, there can be no tangible opposites where relationships are concerned. We can, on the other hand, be in opposition to someone because 'opposition' is about what we do [even though it is a noun], whereas 'opposite' is about where we are [physically or metaphorically]. By putting the word opposite before a noun (use it as an adjective) we can turn it into something that we can have. Hence,

> we can *have* opposite points of view, yet not *be* in opposition to each other.

You might ask, "Bijan, how can that be? Are you talking about compromise?" And I would think to myself, "I hope not" because the idea of compromise does not sit well with me, perhaps because it means that each party is willing to 'settle for less'. The implication being that both parties have come to get something and any giving is a means for taking. The nature of 'compromise' then becomes, "I will take less if you are also willing to take less." I wonder if you can see the fundamental problem with this approach? Both parties are being asked to lower their standards. I would argue that this leads to the creation of weaker relationships than the alternative that I am about to propose.

To wit, two phenomena can be opposite, but not in opposition to, each other. This distinction is critical in creating and maintaining SMERs because it highlights contrast without implying conflict and,

> contrast can be complementary but conflict cannot.

This is because conflict emerges from apparent incongruence of values, whereas contrast is a call for distinctions to be made; distinctions that can lead to the emergence of Complementary Elements.

Notice how the words that we use (or think) can make relationships possible or, indeed, impossible (Unit 3: The power of Language). When we can take a concept like 'opposite' and perceive it as something that we can *have*, such as, "I have an opposite point of view" and make a distinction between that *having* and something that we can *do* (oppose) (§ 16 To Have or To Be), then, for any particular situation, we will have increased our options by one degree of freedom (§ 49.4 Degrees of Freedom). This is because I now have a *choice*. I can choose to take what I *have*, an opposing point of view, and either use it to 'oppose' someone (create conflict) or use it to mean 'contrast' as a way of creating a more empowering perspective; potential for connection through Complementary Elements (§ 47.2).

Contrary to what we would like to believe, our lives are not about *what is*; they are about how we *perceive* what is and what we do in response to that *perception* (§ 33 Atasinex Cluster). Let's look at an example. Consider the following transaction (§ 73 Transactional Analysis):

> Sam: "Gold is more valuable than water."
> Alex: "No, water is more valuable than gold."

Here, we have two opposite points of view, but they are not in opposition (conflict) with each other. If I look 'up' and someone else looks 'down', we see different things and perceive things differently. We are looking in opposite directions, but the things that we see are not in opposition to (conflict with) each other. The sky and the ground are two different *perspectives*. A conflict would only arise if we were to consider them to be two perceptions of the same phenomenon. There is an opportunity here to create Complementary Elements (§ 47), that is, a basis for a connection which can be realized by simply asking each person to look in the opposite direction. Now, we have a mutual understanding that both the sky and the ground are different aspects of the same moment – that we have the good fortune of sharing.

In the case of above dialogue, the differences in point of view arise from different belief systems and values. These are triggered by different imagined *situations*. For example, Alex may be imagining a life and death situation in a desert whist Sam is thinking about investment opportunities in New York. This reminds me of the following stanza from Hafez:

The dark night, the dread of the waves and the horror of the maelstrom,
What would the carefree ones on the beaches know of our plight?

From Ode 1, Divan of Hafez of Shiraz (1315-1390 CE)
Translation by the author

If Alex were to say to Sam, "Imagine that you are stuck in a desert with no water and a truckload of gold and someone offered you enough water to save your life, then what?" Sam may say, "Get real." But she would not say, "I still think you are wrong."

Compare that with a 'compromise' position which would be for both parties to agree that "Gold is as valuable as water." Can you see anything amiss with that conclusion?

The following are four perspectives which can potentially either be in conflict (relationship-disempowering) or complementary (relationship-empowering).

Perspective 1: "Ultimately, everyone does everything for selfish reasons." (Initial premise).

Perspective 2: "Only a selfish person would think like that because they are using themselves as their frame of reference." (Opposing, but not in direct conflict: You are not necessarily wrong from your own point of view, but your perspective is, perhaps, too narrow).

Perspective 3: "I disagree." (in opposition to the initial premise) [I may choose to voice the reasons for my disagreement or keep it to myself].

Perspective 4: "From *my* perspective, our selfish reasons are tools with which we can achieve unselfish (altruistic) goals." (Opposes the conclusion but not the premise, paving the way for a more empowering connection)

[I know, it was only supposed to be an example of different perspectives and perceptions, but it ended up becoming a basis for a potentially 'deep and meaningful' discussion, or debate, about ethics. My Philosopher and Teacher Identities appear to have conspired together to intervene here and I decided to let them have their way.]

I mentioned earlier that having Common Elements is a necessary, but insufficient condition for creating SMERs. This is true for *any* kind of relationship, not just SMERs. To appreciate why, let's go back one step and look at what a (generic) relationship is (§ 21.2):

> **When a change in one system (or phenomenon) causes changes in another, then the two are related.**

Two identical systems (or two people who only have Common Elements) cannot cause a change in each other [assuming that two people *can* only have Common Elements, but this is practically impossible because they would have to occupy the same space at the same time, but let's not get distracted by semantics here]. Let's put it this way, would you really want a friend who is exactly like you in every way? If you said yes, you need to think a bit more about the consequences (or lack thereof) of such a relationship. Two hypothetical people who lie on exactly the same position along every dimension of human experience (Unit 11: § 48-50) cannot be complementary to each other and, therefore, cannot create anything new, including a new Relationship (Pactum).

In summary, opposites may or may not attract. They will attract if they complement each other, albeit through contrast, but they will repel if they, or more specifically, their values, oppose each other.

If we visualise interpersonal relationships through the lens of the lock and key analogy (§ 2.1 What is a SMER?), then Complementary Elements in the relationship would need to be opposites. That is, a 'spike' in one person would need to correspond to a 'trough' in another. This would work for what I have called 'Exchangeable Elements' (§ 47.2.1). However, these 'elements' would not need to be opposite to be complementary. In the following sections, we will explore these concepts in a little more detail.

Chapter 48

Conflicting Elements

Conflicts do not arise from contrast; they arise from opposition (§ 47.2.2 Opposites Attract). In other words, conflicts are caused by actions, not by situations or circumstances (§ 14.3 Situation vs Circumstance). These actions, including reactions, can stem from thoughts (cognition), feelings or conditioned responses, including habits. Even though those actions and reactions can *potentially* cause conflicts, any ensuing conflict stems from, not only, how The Other processes/interprets the response (§ 33 Atasinex Cluster) but also on how he *acts* upon them (§ 40.2 Behaviourism versus Humanism).

Our minds *act* on (process) the sensory inputs being received and *change* them, through interpretation, into perceptions (§ 33 Atasinex Cluster). These perceptions then *act* on (activate) our autonomic nervous system to create physiological changes that we call feelings. These feelings then manifest as emotions (§ 51.2 Affect, Feelings and Emotions).

Although our behaviour is based on our perceptions, between perception and behaviour, we have choice (§ 40.2 Behaviourism versus Humanism). We can reduce conflict in our relationships greatly by adding the following belief to our belief set:

> **"In spite of how it may appear, my actions and reactions to anything or anyone stem from choice; not from obligation."**

Even if our interpretation creates a *potential* for conflict, whether or not that potential is realised, that is to say, whether or not an actual conflict situation arises, depends on how we react to The Other's position.

Now, you may well say, "So Bijan, what you are saying is that I can either deal with it there and then or sweep it under the carpet, i.e., suppress it in some way." And I would say, firstly, that depends on what you mean by 'deal with it' and secondly, it seems to me that you are overlooking a third and a fourth option.

The third option would be to present or re-present (§ 63.1 Changing Beliefs) the situation that shows it to be either an opportunity for growth or as being insignificant in the grand scheme of things (the main purpose of the relationship). The fourth option would be to defer the resolution of the conflict to more favourable circumstances.

> *One day, I told some of my colleagues that, without asking me first, my wife had thrown out a pair of shoes that I had been wearing for over 15 years. One of them said, if my partner did that with me, I would 'up and leave'.*

Clearly such a scenario presents many opportunities for conflict. Let's call this the "I-threw-your-shoes-away" scenario. Three of the possible 'elements' that could be in conflict here are values, expectations and perceptions. Let's explore each of these in turn.

48.1
Conflicting Values

Looking at the I-threw-your-shoes-away scenario from my perspective, affinitologically speaking, my Spouse Identity would become The Self and my wife's Spouse Identity would be The Other.

In Table 2, I have listed some of the values that would veer me in favour of keeping old shoes and a positive counterpart to that value that would encourage me to throw them away. I have assigned the latter to my wife as a possible 'justification' for her action. My reaction to my wife throwing away my shoes (and the trajectory of our relationship) will depend on the scenario (value pair) that I create in my mind. Note that these values (and perceived values) are not intrinsically in conflict with each other but the context can place them in conflict with each other.

Table 2 Value pairs based on the 'I-threw-out-your-shoes' situation

The Self's Values	The Self's Perception of The Other's Values
Comfort	Appearance
Memories	Living in the present
Preventing waste	Creating employment
Possessions are sacrosanct	Intentions are paramount

Internal dialogues between The Self (S) and The Other (O):

Note that these are not real conversations, they are different possible imagined conversations that I could have with myself to try to determine what my wife's intentions were. Of course, the simplest thing to do is ask and then take the answer at face value and decide what to do based on my interpretation of that answer. But we tend not to do that. However, even assuming that each of these conversations are based on actual transactions then notice that, ultimately, it is my *interpretation* that determines my final reaction; emotional response (§ 51.3.2 Feelings Trump Logic). These could be appreciation (strengthen Nexus), tolerance (may create tension in the Nexus) or 'up and leave'. In the following scenarios, in every 'up and leave' scenario, a conflict in 'Core Values' or Principles is implied (§ 58.4 Multi-Nexus Breakdown)

Scenario 1 (appreciation)

Other: Bijan, why do you want to keep old shoes anyway?

Self: Because they are comfortable.

O: But it does nothing for your reputation to be seen in those shoes.

S: Oh! I can see how she had my best interest at heart and how this is congruent with the way 'women' think because I see them wearing stiletto heels even though there's plenty of evidence that this can damage their spine. I do not agree with her, but I am going to decide to focus on her positive intention and thank her for caring about my reputation.

Scenario 2 ('up and leave')

O: Bijan, why do you want to keep old shoes anyway?

S: Because they are comfortable.

O: I don't care about how comfortable you are, how do you think it makes me look going out with someone whose shoes look like they've been fished out of a landfill site.

S: I'm not going to stay in a relationship where we are supposed to feel at one with each other, but my partner is more concerned with her own image than my comfort, so I am going to 'up and leave'.

Scenario 3 (appreciation)

O: Bijan, why do you want to keep old shoes anyway?

S: I have a lot of good memories with these shoes.

O: But if you are living with your memories, you are missing out on all the new experiences that you could have. A new pair of shoes can help you focus on the present and the future which is more conducive to your personal growth.

S: Well, that makes sense. I really appreciate how she understands what my priorities should be.

Scenario 4 ('up and leave')

O: Bijan, why do you want to keep old shoes anyway?

S: I have a lot of good memories with these shoes.

O: Your memories are not as important as what I want right now.

S: I'm not going to stay in a relationship where what gives me my sense of Identity (my past) is being berated for the sake of instant gratification. Therefore, I am going to 'up and leave'.

Scenario 5 (appreciation)

O: Bijan, why do you want to keep old shoes anyway?

S: It would be a waste to throw away shoes that can still be used.

O: But Bijan, if we hold on to shoes just because they are well-made and endure we will discourage shoe manufacturers from making high quality (durable) shoes and we will not be supporting innovation in shoe manufacturing and besides, it creates employment.

S: Although I don't agree with creating false employment, I hadn't thought of it from the perspective of quality and innovation. I really appreciate the way she helps me see things from a different perspective.

Scenario 6 (tolerance)

O: Bijan, why do you want to keep old shoes anyway?

S: They are my shoes and I will do with them as I please. You had no right to throw them away.

O: I know you liked them, but I really felt that if I didn't take the initiative, you would not make the kind of good first impression that you need to make in your job.

S: I do not agree with what she did, but I can appreciate her intention was focused on what would benefit our relationship.

Scenario 7 ('up and leave')

O: Bijan, why do you want to keep old shoes anyway?

S: They are my shoes and I will do with them as I please. You had no right to throw them away.

O: I know you liked them, but I really felt that if I didn't take the initiative, you would not make the kind of good first impression that you need to make in your job.

S: I don't care what you thought, not respecting my possessions is the same as not respecting me. Therefore, I am going to 'up and leave'.

Note that my ultimate response to the situation will depend on which values, or value pairs, I take into consideration and the relative impact of each of these interpretations on my overall feelings (§ 72 Decision-Making).

48.2

Conflicting Expectations

In the following table, I have indicated some of the expectations that The Self and The Other may have and how they can create conflict. Again, the consequence of each scenario may be appreciation, tolerance (§ 68) or 'up and leave'.

Table 3
Expectation pairs based on the 'I-threw-out-your-shoes' situation

The Self's Expectations	The Other's Expectations
Communication	Appreciation
Respect for possessions	Attention
Respect for wishes	

Internal dialogues between The Self (S) and The Other (O):

Scenario 1 ('up and leave')
S: I expect her to let me know that she intends to throw my shoes away.
O: I expect him to appreciate the fact that I am relieving him of the internal conflict that he faces between holding on to his memories (and appearing miserly) and wearing something new (and feeling like a new man).
S: There is a lack of healthy communication in this relationship so I am going to 'up and leave'.

Scenario 2 ('up and leave')
S: I expect her to respect my ownership of my possessions.
O: I expect him to pay attention to what is worth keeping and what is not.
S: She is making decisions for me and does not appreciate that my possessions are part of my personal space and not respecting that is like invading my private space which is tantamount to rape. Therefore, I am going to 'up and leave'.

Scenario 3 (tolerance)
S: I expect her to respect my wishes.
O: I expect him to respect my wishes. I don't like to see him wearing those ugly things.
S: I can see how I did not respect her wishes and made her tolerate seeing something that she thought was ugly for so long.

48.3

Conflicting Perceptions

Table 4 shows some of the conflicting perceptions that may arise in the 'I-threw-out-your-shoes' situation.

Table 4
Possible Perception pairs based on the 'I-threw-out-your-shoes' situation

The Self's Perceptions	The Other's Perceptions
Comfort	Beauty
Possession	Utility
Separateness	Togetherness

Internal dialogues between The Self (S) and The Other (O):

Scenario 1 (tolerance)

S: My old shoes are comfortable (my perception of comfort is based on what I feel).

O: I wouldn't feel comfortable in shoes that look that old (my perception of comfort is based on what I see).

S: I can't understand that point of view but I can respect it. Presumably, she would also be uncomfortable with seeing me wearing those shoes and I wouldn't want to cause discomfort and I perceive myself as someone who can adapt to wearing new shoes.

Scenario 2 (tolerance)

S: I perceive my shoes as being mine and I have the right to collect junk if I want to.

O: I think that possessions should fulfil a useful (utilitarian) purpose. If they don't, then I don't see them as possessions, I see them as burdens. You can have shoes that serve you better and I can help you make that decision by throwing away your old shoes.

S: I can appreciate her perspective, but what if I see utility in something that she does not? I need to let her know that my perspective may be just as valid as hers.

Scenario 3 ('up and leave')

S: I perceive my shoes as being mine and other people should not take it upon themselves to decide what to do with them.

O: I consider us to be one unit and anything that does not serve to maintain the harmony of the relationship should be removed.

S: On the one hand, I appreciate her feeling of being at one with me, but on the other hand, I am not ready to lose my sense of self in this relationship. If she needs that level of commitment, perhaps I should not stand in her way of trying to find one. Therefore, I will 'up and leave'.

48.4
Summary of Conflicting Elements

The examples given here are, of course, simplistic and imply that the relationship is held together by a single fragile thread. Whilst, in theory, this can happen in the early stages of a relationship (§ 35.1 Embryology of Relationships), in practice, this is rare and many similar scenarios are required for a Nexus to break and each new scenario provides opportunities for Norming after the Storming (§ 59.2 The Conflict Cycle).

What the examples here do indicate, however, is that, the extent to which we can appreciate or tolerate conflicting values, expectations or perceptions depends on the extent to which these are linked to our Core Values or Principles (§ 29.4 The Omniself).

Unit 11

Dimensions of Human Experience (DHM)

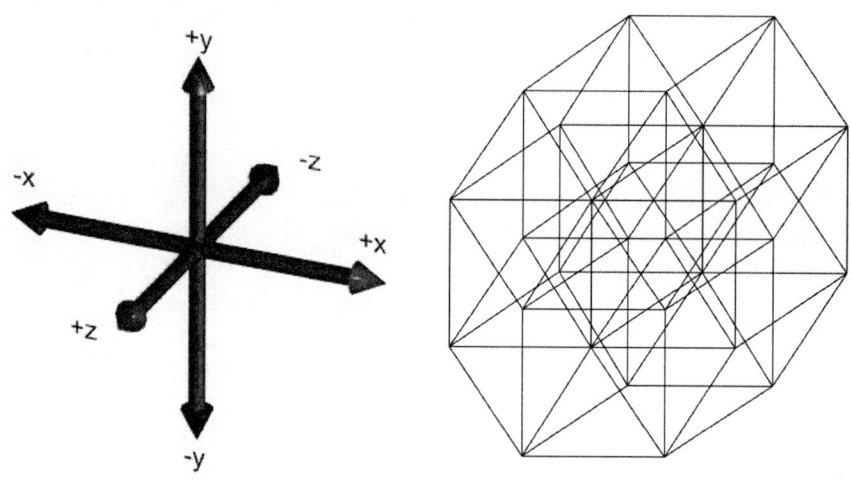

[Source: https://commons.wikimedia.org/wiki/File:Eixos.jpg]
[https://en.wikipedia.org/wiki/5-cube#/media/File:2d_of_5d_3.svg]

Chapter 49

Introduction to Dimensions of Human Experience

49.1
Chapter Overview

This chapter is intended to serve three purposes. The first is for us to become more attuned (alert/aware/sensitive) to the various aspects of our lives that affect the quality of our relationships. Secondly, I hope that it will help us appreciate that the quality of a relationship (with ourselves (§ The Omniself) and with others), is not only a question of *what* we perceive; it depends considerably on *how* we perceive. Note that, in this context, how we perceive is predominantly acquired (learned). It is about what we choose to focus on and how we choose to interpret what we focus on (§ 33 Atasinex Cluster). Therefore, the third aim of this chapter is to help us develop a more 'graded' (less binary) perspective.

We can categorise our experiences into various domains and we can think of each of these domains as a potential ingredient in our relationship-making recipe. The chemist Identity in me called them Common and Complementary *elements* (§ 47). From an academic research perspective (theoretical model building), we can think of them as *factors*. And from a mathematical perspective, we can think of them as *variables* (in our interpersonal relationship equations). I could also have called them domains, building blocks or constituents. In the end, I settled for dimension. The reason for this will become clear shortly.

One of the factors that determines how we relate to people is the extent to which we appreciate that relationships are not absolute or binary (black and white); we can move closer or further way from other people (Identities) *incrementally*, that is, we can drift apart and 'drift closer'. This moving (deliberate) or drifting (unplanned) can be along various 'dimensions' [scales/ranges/spectra].

Looking at these relationship building blocks from a dimensional and graded perspective paves the way to introducing the notion of calibration; a precursor to homeostasis (§ 35.5), into our relationships. Looking at the situation in this way can also help us to realise that relationships are not brittle; they can stretch and do, indeed, oscillate without breaking (§ 58.2 Good Vibrations).

It is important for us to be aware of where our beliefs and perceptions lie along *each of these dimensions* because they [or, more accurately, their combination and interactions] determine the nature of the Relationship Framework (§ 92), that is, whether (and to what extent) each factor becomes a Common or Complementary Elements (§ 47) in the construction of the Nexus.

49.2

Excuse me sir, what is a dimension?

This section might be a bit of an indulgence; think of it as a footnote; you can skip it if you wish [not that you couldn't skip the whole book if you were so inclined, but you know what I mean].

> *In my early days as a private tutor (over three decades ago), a student once asked me what 'dimension' means. I started to move my hands and fingers around in perpendicular and horizontal motions and to um, ah and stutter as I struggled to come up with a way to describe it and, in the end, I said, "Well, it's a kind of direction", but I knew that this was inadequate. I still feel a change in state, not dissimilar to embarrassment, when I think about it all these years later.*

The various dictionary definitions also fail to describe it as clearly as the idea is in my head. And since I'm going to be talking extensively about dimensions, I feel the need to explain what I mean when I am using the word. As an introduction, let me tell you a little story.

A mathematician invited his engineer friend to a mathematics conference. There, they were talking about eleven-dimensional space. The engineer came out of the session saying to his friend, "I struggle to even conceive of four dimensions. How can you get your head around eleven dimensions?" The mathematician replied, "It's easy. I just set dimensions, D, equal to n and then set n equal to 11."

Let's see if I can be a little more helpful than that.

All the things that we can measure can be divided into two categories. Statisticians call them 'discrete' and 'continuous' variables. If you are into electronics, think digital and analogue signals. If you are into languages, think countable and non-countable nouns. If you are into music, think note and timbre.

Most of us consider dimensions as simply being about length, width and height. And that is right insofar as everything that is not abstract has these three dimensions and these three dimensions *only*. So, what is it that makes length, width and height dimensions? Firstly, they are all continuous variables. In other words, they are not countable. The secondly, when you measure one, there is no interference from the other; our measurement of an object's height is not affected by its width. Notice I'm not saying that an object's height is not related to its width because, otherwise, you would get very disproportionate elephants, for example. What I am saying is that the *measurement* of an elephant's height is not affected by the elephant's width. To use a psychological example, I can measure someone's feeling (The Emotional Dimension) without needing to know (or it affecting) his 'rules of conduct' (Moral Dimension). In other words, I can measure someone's emotional state [this usually means just asking, "How do you feel?"] and then measure their rules of conduct *separately* ["Do you think that a certain behaviour is justifiable in a particular situation?"] and look to see whether there is a 'relationship' (correlation) between these two without needing to take into consideration that how I measure the emotional state [*the act of asking* a person about how they feel] will in some way affect her rules of conduct or vice versa.

[Based on the above explanation, you can judge for yourself whether the aspects of human experience that I discuss in this section fall into the category of dimension or not. Alternatively, you could decide to just go with the flow and not to analyse the theory too much and to simply concentrate on the practical benefits you could get out of the discussion.]

In isolation, a single dimension is meaningless because everything requires a context for us to be able to give it any kind of meaning. (cf. § 32.2 & 37.1) Epistemologically [from the point of view of what we can know and how] we can only create knowledge (meaning) by comparing. In the case of dimensions,

> **we can create knowledge by looking at the boundaries between dimensions.**

As such, we need to consider each of the dimensions that we are going to explore [perhaps it would be more accurate to say 'touch upon'] in this section from the point of view of how it can (or does) interact with other dimensions when they come together to create a Relationship Framework (§ 92).

49.3
Depth and Breadth (Quantity and Quality)

Usually, when we think about dimensions, the image of a straight line (or three mutually perpendicular straight lines) comes to mind. Although this is very convenient from a mathematical perspective, I consider it to be too reductionist for our purposes.

Each of the concepts that I have presented here as a dimension of human experience, can be thought of as having at least two aspects; depth and breadth or, in our case, a quantitative aspect and a qualitative aspect. This means that when two dimensions of human experience meet, it is not a meeting of two lines, it is a meeting of two planes (figure 25).

Figure 25
Dimensions as planes

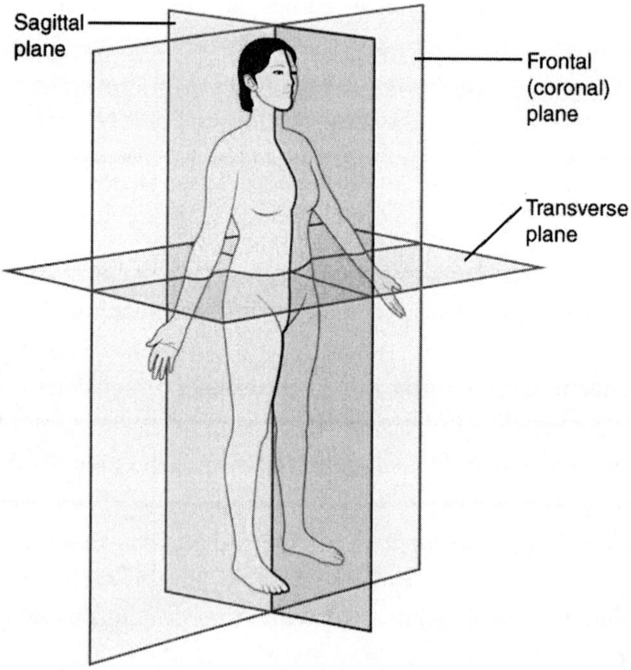

Source: https://commons.wikimedia.org/wiki/File:Planes_of_Body.jpg

49.4
Degrees of Freedom

Degrees of freedom is about the number of ways in which a system can change. For example, in how many different directions can a car (legally) move down a one-way road? One. Forward. When we are looking at direction of movement, this car has *no option* but to move forward. Having no options means it has *zero degrees of freedom*. If we consider putting the car into reverse gear as an option (albeit illegally), then the car can now move in two directions, forward and back. Therefore, in comparison to having no options (can only move forward), the car now has one more option than it had before, therefore, the car now has *one* degree of freedom.

[Some of you might be thinking, "But what about the option of stopping?" Since the question is asking about the number of ways in which a car can 'move', the question is not considering stopping as a possible option.]

Often my pupils have difficulty in grasping this concept. A car can move forward and back so it has two options, but only one degree of freedom. The problem is a semantic one. It is created by what we understand by the word 'option'. An option implies an ability to choose. If I cannot choose, I have no options, but that does not mean that I cannot move, it means that I can only move in one direction; along a single line or road (albeit a meandering one).

So, here is a question for you, "If I have one option, do I have an option?" No. 'One option' is not an option because there can be no 'choice'; it is an oxymoron. If I have two options, I have one *alternative*. Each *alternative* is a degree of freedom.

[Incidentally (and as something for the discussion amongst your mathematics pupils if you have them), I think the word 'option' is a little quirky in that it is about an arithmetic series, starting with zero and having a common difference of one, but which skips the number 1. I decided to share that little nugget with you because you don't come across examples like that very often.]

In statistics we often see the term n-1. What this is doing is that it is taking the 'number of options' and converting it to the 'number of alternatives' because without alternatives, even though we can still be doing something, it is not a choice.

Now that we are (hopefully) clear about what degrees of freedom are, I can say what I want to say in the way that I want to say it: This part of the course (Unit 11) is about the *degrees of freedom* that have been afforded to us that, on the whole, go beyond what medical science has equivalents for. It is about those aspects of life that make us human. It is about what the mind can do that the body cannot.

49.5
Selected Dimensions

The following table, in addition to being an overview of some of the factors that we can consider from a dimensional perspective, provides the basis for upcoming exercises that can help us improve the quality of our interpersonal relationships.

Table 5
Overview of the Dimensions of Human Experience
(Under Consideration in this Unit)

Dimension	**"To what extent does * affect the quality of the Nexus?"** [replace the * with the following phrases]
Values	What I consider to be important
Social	How I am affected by the other people in my life
Emotional	The range, quality and intensity of my emotions
Language	How and what I communicate
Intellectual	The range of factors that I consider (am capable of considering) in any situation
Spiritual	The criteria I use to create meaning
Financial	My understanding of the role of money
Sexual	My approach to the notion of sex
Cultural	The degree to which I am bound by cultural norms and expectations
Occupational	My approach to my job and career in relation to The Other
Family	My perception of 'who' is family and the obligations that this perception evokes in me
Dependence-Independence	My perception of my ability to cope in the absence of The Other
Psychological	How I perceive, interpret, internalise and respond to situations
Physical and Environmental	My reaction to who and what is present and what is happening around me
Aesthetic/Sensual	What I consider to be pleasing to the senses (beautiful, delicious, fragrant, engaging)
Ethical/Moral	My self-imposed limits on my behaviour
legal	That which is mandated by law
Temporal	The passage of time

Each of these factors can potentially become Common or Complementary Elements (§ 47) in a Nexus. The extent to which each dimension affects the relationship depends on the Relationship Framework (§ 92). I have selected these particular 'dimensions' because I consider them to have the most critical or influential impact on the quality of most relationships.

49.6

Related Exercise

Here is an exercise that will help us to appreciate how, looking at the concepts in Table 5 from a dimensional perspective can help improve the quality of our interpersonal relationships. Spending some time to actually do the exercise can be both diagnostic and therapeutic.

Exercise 11 Thinking dimensionally about the factors that affect our interpersonal relationships.

Think of a relationship that you want to explore in greater depth [you can, obviously, repeat this for as many relationships as you wish]. For each of the 'Dimensions' listed in Table 5, rate your answers to the following questions *as a percentage*.

1. To what extent have I consciously taken this aspect of the relationship (Nexus) into consideration in my interactions with The Other?
2. What is my own (The Self's) position along the continuum?
3. What is The Other's position along the continuum?
4. Is our relative positions putting any kind of strain on the Nexus?
5. How flexible can I be, without compromising my integrity (Core Values) so as to remove the strain from the Nexus. That is, "Can I be more elastic or is rigidity a defining feature of this particular Nexus?" [i.e., Is it a matter of my comfort zone or is my stance more fundamental than that?]
6. What are the pros and cons of expanding my comfort zone in this aspect of the Nexus?

Note that our relative position along each of these dimensions determines, not only the quality of the Nexus, but also the nature of the Relationship Framework (§ 92) itself. In other words, our relationship with an Omniself [what we used to call a person] may be strained because we are in a less empowering relationship with that person than we *could* be. That is to say, whilst we appreciate the PRESENCE of this person in our lives, we have not chosen the most appropriate Identity to create a Nexus with. A common example is where, after a certain age, trying to hold on to a 'parent-child' Nexus can create a strain on the relationship and a change in the relationship to a Friends Framework may be more suitable. And, as I have consistently pointed out in the course, every interaction is situational. This means that there may be times when it is mutually empowering and satisfying for the Parent-Child Nexus to emerge, even when the 'child' is a grandparent. And this is where the science of relationships gives way to the art of relationships (§ 18 Art or Science). Here, I am going to take the Values dimension as an example, but I encourage you to do this with each and every concept in Table 5.

49.7

Application of Exercise 11 to the Values Dimensions

Based on what I have explained about table 5, the question we are deliberating here is, "To what extent do my values [what I consider to be important] affect the quality of my relationship (Nexus) with someone?"

We explore the concept of values in detail in § 34.1.2 (Values). Here, I simply want to discuss this idea from a dimensional perspective. Note that the title of this section is 'Values Dimensions' and not 'Values Dimension'. This is because, as I explained earlier, each of the concepts in table 5 lies on a plane (has two dimensions), a depth and breadth. In the case of values, this translates as,

   a) Depth: How important (emotive) is it?
   b) Breadth: What does this particular Value encompass?

Although, in Table 5, I have cited 'Ethical/Moral' as a separate Dimension, often, the nature of our ethical *dilemmas* is rooted in (derives from) the depth and breadth of our values. For example, consider the statement, "I value my children's wellbeing." On the face of it, this is a noble and time-honoured sentiment. In terms of depth, it runs deep and, in terms of breadth, it spans the relationship between the parent and his or her children.

> *Sometimes, I see clients who tell me that they are in an abusive relationship, but do not want to leave because of the effect that it may have on their children. Clearly, there are many issues to consider here, including all those factors associated with the parent's physical, social and spiritual wellbeing. Nevertheless, in the minds of these parents, all other considerations become secondary to the wellbeing of their children.*

You might say, "But Bijan, you said that the breadth of this value only spans to the wellbeing of the children, but it is clearly affecting many aspects of the parent's life." And I would say, "Thank you for being alert and noticing this." This means that, in spite of the fact that this value has a specific 'domain', its effects can go beyond that domain, but this does not invalidate our notion of confinement. For example, an individual, such as myself, is confined to a physical body. I can, nevertheless, have influences that go far beyond the limits of my body. When all my (often overestimated) 'needs' are satisfied, those influences become primarily nurturing. If, however, I feel that my needs are not satisfied, my priorities become the acquisition of those needs.

[This reminds me of a local hero who was challenged to slay a dragon (or some such menace). Being clear to him that he would not succeed, he declined the challenge. Someone told him that he would lose his 'hero' status, to which he replied, "Being a hero is only valuable when one is alive to enjoy it." (Adapted from a Persian proverb)].

For parents facing such a dilemma, I reframe the problem by telling them that research has shown that a dysfunctional family environment is more detrimental to children's wellbeing than a relatively stress-free single-parent family.

To appreciate how being aware of our values can have empowering effects on our relationships, I encourage you to do the following exercise:

Exercise 12

Focusing on the Values Dimension within a relationship

1. Think of someone that you have some kind of relationship with.
2. Focus on the nature of your relationship (The Nexus [not The Other]) with that person.
3. Ask yourself, "What do I believe about this relationship that makes it important to me?"

   [This is another way of saying, "What do I value about this relationship?"]

4. Depth: *How* important (emotive) is this to me?

   [This is another way of asking, "What am I willing to sacrifice to maintain this particular aspect of the relationship (the thing that is important to me about this relationship)?" (See also § 72 Decision-Making).]

5. Breadth: How many different aspects of my life (including the Nexus) does this aspect of this particular relationship have an impact on?

   [Sometimes, as in the case of the wellbeing of our children, the full potential impact does not become apparent until it falls into conflict with other values. This points to the hierarchical nature of our values (§ 64.7 Hierarchy of Values)]

49.8

Other Factors

Now that we have seen the benefits of looking at the various factors (ingredients that we use in our relationship-making recipe) that influence each of our interpersonal relationships from a dimensional perspective, in the following chapter (Relationship Ingredients), we are going to delve deeper into some of the prevalent factors that go into the creation of the Nexus, i.e., can become Common and Complementary Elements (§ 47).

After reading each of the relevant sections, I encourage you to return to Exercise 11 and use our treatment of the Values Dimensions (§ 49.7 Application of Exercise 11 to the Values Dimensions) as a template and to apply it to any relationship that you wish to improve and to develop your relationship building (and empowering) skills.

Chapter 50

Dimensions of Interpersonal Relationships

50.1
Alternatives to the Word Dimension

After some debate with various parts of myself, I decided to call them 'dimensions' (for the reasons that I explained in the previous section). However, there were plenty of candidates for the job. This variety is afforded to us through the fact that the concept of relationships and its parts are abstract which means that our minds can shape them in any way that we please. The following are a few alternatives to the word dimension and arguments for their appropriateness for various purposes. See also § 15 (The Power of Specialised Language).

Ingredients

The Teacher Identity in me likes this word. It is easy to understand and it alludes to cooking which is very familiar to us. It also implies that we can devise an infinite number of recipes to suit every palate and that we are in control of what stays out and what goes in and how much.

Factors

This word appeals to my Scientist Identity. From a mathematical or statistical perspective, a 'factor' is a variable; a component of an equation. Here, the optimistic implication that we may have the potential to, one day, describe interpersonal relationships mathematically appealed to my Researcher Identity.

Components/Constituents/Parts

These words are more likely to evoke three-dimensional imagery of a mechanical device or a conveyor belt reminiscent of Taylorism. It has the advantage of allowing us to think of each aspect of the relationship as a building block.

Realms

This word appeals to the Adventurer within me. Realms can be vast expanses of territory that can be explored and conquered. They can include a variety of peoples and cultures that we can learn from, as well as demons, ogres and other exciting challenges for the Dungeons and Dragons enthusiast and, of course, the ardent relationship explorer.

Influences

I also contemplated calling them 'Influences' but decided against that because the word is often associated with 'external influences' such as interference which we explore elsewhere in this course (§ 60.3 Relationship Interference).

Elements

Not surprisingly, this word appeals to my Chemist Identity. It suggests that the 'things' that make up a relationship consist of very small and finite particles and that the properties of the relationship depend on how these 'atoms' join and or interact with each other.

Building blocks

This combines the notion of Components with the idea of Elements and appeals to the side of me that likes playing with LEGO bricks. It also gives us a sense of control and flexibility within certain structural constraints.

All of the above words can be seen as viable alternatives to the concepts presented in this section, depending on which aspect or property of the Nexus we want to highlight or focus on (§ 33.3 Attention).

50.2

The Intellectual Dimension

Intelligence is an emotive and contentious subject. It is intriguing that we speak so confidently about our measures of intelligence and yet we are not able to define intelligence satisfactorily. One of the least controversial definitions is that 'intelligence is what intelligence tests measure'. There is little to argue about in this circular argument, except to say that it is circular, and that it tells us nothing about what intelligence actually is. However, since I'm going to be talking about intelligence, I really should explain what it is that I'm going to talk about. So, here is my definition of intelligence.

Intelligence is the extent to which we are able to relate.

This raises the question, "Relate what to what?" My answer? Phenomena. That is anything that we can think about, including objects, concepts, notions, thoughts, ideas, beliefs, values and perceptions. So, the more we are able to relate different concepts to each other, the more intelligent and, as the following quote from the movie, Good Will Hunting, demonstrates, the more farsighted we become:

> "Why shouldn´t I work for the N.S.A.? That´s a tough one, but I´ll take a shot. Say I´m workin´ at the N.S.A. and somebody puts a code on my desk. Something no one else can break. Maybe I take a shot at it and maybe I break it. I´m real happy with myself because I did my job well. But maybe that code was the location of some rebel army in North Africa or Middle East. Once they have that location, they bomb the village where the rebels are hidin´. Fifteen hundred people that I never met, never had no problem with, get killed. Now the politicians are saying, "Send in the Marines to secure the area," ´cause they don´t give a shit. It won´t be their kid over there gettin´ shot, just like it wasn´t them when their number got called ´cause they were in the National Guard. It´ll be some kid from Southie over there takin´ shrapnel in the ass. He comes back to find the plant he used to work at got exported to the country he got back from, and the guy who put the shrapnel in his ass got his old job ´cause he´ll work for 15 cents a day and no bathroom breaks. Meanwhile, he realizes the only reason he was over there in the first place was so we could install a government that would sell us oil at a good price. Of course, the oil companies used a skirmish over there to scare up domestic oil prices. A cute little ancillary benefit for them, but it ain´t helpin´ my buddy at 2.50 a gallon. They´re takin´ their sweet time bringin´ the oil, of course. Maybe they even took the liberty to hire an alcoholic skipper, who likes to drink martinis and play slalom with the icebergs. It ain´t too long till he hits one, spills the oil and kills all the sea life in the North Atlantic. So now my buddy´s out of work, he can´t afford to drive, so he´s walkin´ to the job interviews which sucks because the shrapnel in his ass is givin´ him chronic haemorrhoids. Meanwhile, he´s starvin´, ´cause every time he tries to get a bite to eat, the only blue plate special they´re servin´ is North Atlantic scrod with Quaker State. So, what did I think? I´m holdin´ out for somethin´ better. I figure, while I´m at it, why not just shoot my buddy, take his job, give it to his sworn enemy, hike up gas prices, bomb a village, club a baby seal, hit the hash pipe and join the National Guard? I can be elected president."
>
> [See https://www.youtube.com/watch?v=mJHvSp9AKYg]

In terms of relationships, this means that the more intelligent we are, the more we are able to relate what we do or what The Other in the relationship does to its effects on the Nexus.

In this section, I hope to demonstrate that intelligence can have a significant impact on the quality of our relationships and, whilst it is partially genetic, *it is not fixed* (cf. § 61.1 Genes as Potential).

50.2.1
Intelligence and Vocabulary

There is a correlation between the number of words that people know and their intelligence. I think this is because, as I've mentioned elsewhere (§ 18.3 How to Avoid Stagnation or Paralysis), every noun and verb in the dictionary is about a relationship (as in association). So, the more words we know the greater our repertoire of association-making skills becomes.

The good news is that, just as the research on vocabulary shows, intelligence is more of a skill than a talent. We can become more intelligent through greater awareness and experience, including extending our vocabulary.

50.2.2
Intelligence and Appreciation

My earlier definition of intelligence implies that appreciation is also linked to intelligence. The more intelligent we are (or become), the more we are able to appreciate what we have. This is because, appreciation emerges from our 'ability to relate' events, concepts, objects and potentials to all the myriad of things that need to have happened for us to be 'blessed' with them.

It follows that, the more intelligent we are, the more we can appreciate our relationships. The quality and dynamics of any relationship is to no small measure determined by the extent to which The Self and The Other appreciate each other, including the extent to which this is expressed.

50.2.3
Intelligence and Emotion

Emotions are primarily processed through our brains' limbic system, whilst our thoughts (cognition) are primarily processed through the frontal lobe. Thinking (using our frontal lobe) is quite energy intensive and so, when other systems need that energy, the energy budget of the frontal lobe is cut and its responsibilities are passed on to the less energy-consuming limbic system (Unit 22 Thermodynamics of Relationships).

In practice, this means that the extent to which we have access to the intellectual centres of the brain (our intellect) varies depending on the level of stress, physiological or psychological, we are experiencing at the time. This means that, in fact, intelligence is much more fluid and variable than we tend to imply when we are talking about it. We can all verify the truth of this assertion by looking at the number of times that, on reflection, we have made stupid [poorly considered] decisions because we have been emotionally compromised (worried, nervous, overwhelmed, hungry, fighting an infection, digesting too many fats and carbohydrates, etc (Unit 22: Thermodynamics of Relationships).

50.2.4
Intelligence and Thinking

Thinking is processing information to reach a conclusion. If we accept our own conclusion, it becomes a belief. If we doubt our own conclusion, it becomes a hypothesis (an unverified belief i.e., in the absence of evidence to the contrary, we will act (behave) as if it is true, that is, I will use it as a rule of thumb).

We can reach conclusions through two types of reasoning: inductive and deductive. Depending on the time and place this could also be called generalising and analysing, synthesis and analysis, or constructive and reductive reasoning. Having said all that, to coin a phrase, "Houston, we have a problem". And it is this. In science, questions become hypotheses, hypotheses become theories, theories become laws and, in the final analysis, laws are susceptible to Heisenberg's uncertainty principle and the kind of unpredictability demonstrated by Chaos Theory and depicted by the Butterfly Effect (§ 90 Fractals), so that laws become, well, stop-gap measures until something better comes along. This is because we can never have enough information to reach an absolute conclusion; everything is too chaotic and interconnected for that. In the next section, we explore some of the ways in which we cope with uncertainty.

50.2.5
Intelligence, Optimism and Compassion

So, what do we do with this situation of perpetual uncertainty that we find ourselves in? The answer reminds me of a conversation between Dr McCoy and Spock from Star Trek, The Voyage home:

McCoy: You present the appearance of a man with a problem.

Spock: Your perception is correct, Doctor. In order to return us to the exact moment we left the 23rd century, I have used our journey back through time as a referent, calculating the coefficient of elapsed time in relation to the acceleration curve.

- Naturally. So, what's your problem?
- Acceleration is no longer a constant.
- Well, then you're just gonna have to take your best shot.
- Best shot?
- Guess, Spock. Your best guess.
- Guessing is not in my nature, Doctor.
- Well, nobody's perfect.

So, yes, in the face of perpetual uncertainty, that's what we do; we guess. And we are making our best guess all the time [For many of us, being conscious of this makes us feel uncomfortable and we look to others to reveal the 'truth' to us].

When we have no choice but to face the uncertainties of life, we can deal with it in one of two ways; with optimism or pessimism. Some people think that they can resolve this dichotomy by invoking the concept of 'realism'. However, in practice, a so-called realist is being optimistic about the extent to which he can make a prediction with accuracy and/or precision. Some of the things that people say about optimism lead me to conclude that they are not distinguishing between wishful thinking and optimism. My interpretation of an optimist is someone who gives (a situation) the benefit of the doubt. When that optimism is with regards to people's *intentions*, then I would consider that to be an expression of compassion. It is also an indication of a certain type of trust (§ 53 Trust). In contrast, a person who buys a lottery ticket is not an optimist; he's either misinformed, a wishful thinker or desperate.

Let's look at the possible consequences of optimism as I have interpreted it here. If someone is innocent and we give them the benefit of the doubt, that's clearly an empowering (Nexus-enhancing) approach in that we will have avoided a potential strain on the relationship.

One of the possible effects of not giving an innocent person the benefit of the doubt (such as in the case of an excessively suspicious partner in a relationship) is that the person may lose faith in The Other's judgements and conclude that since I do not have a reputation to keep, I am released from any obligation arising from such reputation. I'm not suggesting that this is a mature line of reasoning, but it is not an uncommon reaction. Let's look at what could happen if we give a guilty person the benefit of the doubt (treat her with compassion). She could,

a) Believe that she can get away with their deception and become more confident in their ignoble behaviour.
b) Become cautious because she has just had a 'close shave', so to speak.
c) Acquire a hitherto absent reputation that she may wish to keep.

It seems to me that, overall, the empowering consequences of giving people the benefit of the doubt outweigh its disempowering effects. There's more to this than I have outlined here, but to discuss it further, I would need to go into statistics, 'Type I' and 'Type II' errors and p-values and so on, which is a discussion for another time and place, but let's take a quick peek at where this could take us.

The purely rational approach as to whether or not we give someone the benefit of the doubt (assuming that we are not emotionally compromised) should be governed by Probability Theory, taking into account the potential consequences. This can be reduced to a simple mathematical formula:

$$risk = proportional\ gain \times probability\ of\ loss$$

Let me demonstrate this through an example. If I buy a lottery ticket for $1 and the jackpot is $5,000,000 and the probability of my winning is 1 in 30 million then putting the figures into the formula this is what we get:

$$risk = 5,000,000 \times 1/30,000,000 = 1/6$$

This means that only one sixth of the money goes back to the people who put that money into the system. This is like saying let's throw a die and if you throw a six, I will give you $2, otherwise you give me $1. Would you accept such a bet?

"But Bijan, we are talking about relationships here, not about betting money." Ok, I hear you. So, let's see how this applies to relationships. The argument could be that things like relationships are about quality (as are aesthetic values such as beauty), whereas money is about quantity. You can apply mathematical principles to quantity but not to quality. If that's the case, how does one decide what to pay for a piece of art? Or how much to spend on a night out with a beautiful woman or man? Like it or not, to decide anything our mind has to turn quality into quantity. How much effort? How much time? How much money? In return for how much satisfaction? Or how much pleasure?

Let's assume that I suspect that my partner is having an affair [I prefer to think of it as, "Keeping from me information that could be potentially detrimental to the quality of our relationship"]. Logically, I need to balance the risk to my relationship if I'm right, against the risk to my relationship if I'm wrong. Now how I assess that risk depends on my self-esteem and my self-confidence my assessment of what I can and cannot forgive/tolerate and the consequences in terms of all the other dimensions of human experience that we are talking about in this course. It can seem overwhelming when we lay it out like that, so let me tell you a story.

When I used to teach mathematics, some of my pupils believed that they were not good at it. So, I would throw a ball at them and tell them to catch it. I would then explain to them that the greatest mathematician in the world couldn't describe mathematically the process through which the eyes, the brain, the muscles of the hands, legs, neck and the rest of the body and all their nerves and other cells coordinate and interact for that seemingly simple act of catching a ball that we take so much for granted. I would then explain that it is not that we are not good at mathematics, it is more about learning how to deal with the way in which our innate mathematical abilities have been formalized through mathematical language.

So, let's put this understanding into the context of relationships. In much the same way that lots of subconscious mathematical computations are involved in catching a ball, our intellect is also involved in how we assess the quality of our relationships and how we quantify those qualities subconsciously. The more intelligent we are, the more factors we take into consideration when forming and maintaining satisfying and empowering relationships. The 'art' of relationships is in what factors we focus on and what factors we ignore.

50.3
The Spiritual Dimension

Take a look at the graph in Figure 26. From about the 1970s there was a surge in the use of the word spirituality. My guess is that before the 1970s the concept of spirituality was subsumed within the domain of religion. I postulate that the gap between disillusionment with religion and the perceived futility of nihilism was filled by the concept of 'spirituality'.

As a definition of spirituality, "The quality of being concerned with the human spirit or soul" sounds about right. Unfortunately, when described in such abstract terms as 'spirit' and 'soul', it becomes very difficult to explore objectively. We need to find a way to make the idea of 'spirituality' more amenable to objective discourse. In other words, we need to make it easier to talk about spirituality with minimal chance of there being any misunderstandings. How can we do that? A look at the second part of dictionary.com's definition gives us a clue: "... as opposed to material or physical things." (Figure 26)

Figure 26
Use of the word spirituality over time

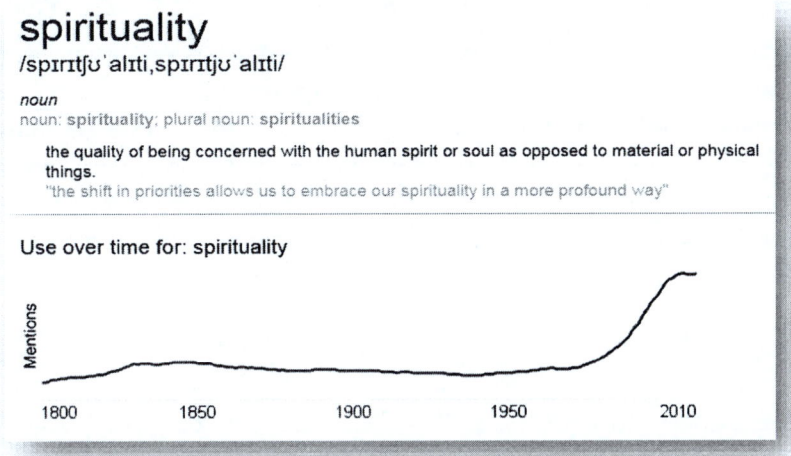

What if we said that the spiritual side of us, our spirit (or our soul), is the part of us that is concerned with concepts and ideas that do not have material existence? i.e., Those things that we cannot express without resorting to symbolism, including metaphors. This is why Carl Jung was so interested in symbols, because they provide a means of penetrating and interacting with our spirits (souls).

We could look at spirituality from another angle and say that it is about those things that we believe to exist without having any direct evidence (through our 'five' senses) for their existence. This definition implies that, **if it is not material and I believe in it, it is a spiritual concept**. This can open a big can of intellectual worms, so I am not going to elaborate on that point here. I just wanted to stimulate some grey cells.

[The reason I have put 'five' in quotation marks is because I think the argument is convincing that 'pain' should be considered as one of our senses since it is one of the ways in which our body tells us about our external world and it does not neatly fit into the other five categories.]

In our relationships, we use symbols extensively to interact with each other at the spiritual level. So, what kind of things are we talking about? Love, Freedom, Purpose, Joy, Pride, Forgiveness, Trust, Sacrifice, Belonging, Loyalty, Beauty, Gratitude and Happiness. These concepts represent some of our highest values and how we perceive and interpret each of them can have a profound effect on our relationships. The problem is that, in spite of their importance, they are intangible which means that they are open to a wide range of interpretations. Therefore, in addition to symbols, we need to clarify to each other what we mean by those symbols. We can do this by trying to help each other understand what our beliefs are about each of these ideas. We explore beliefs about each of these concepts in greater detail in § 35.5 (Homeostasis).

I said that Love, Freedom, Purpose, Joy, Pride, Forgiveness, Trust, Sacrifice, Belonging, Loyalty, Beauty, Gratitude and Happiness represent some of our highest values. But what are values? Values, in addition to determining the hierarchy of our priorities (§ 64.7 Hierarchy of Values) are those things (concepts) that give meaning to our lives. There is a whole school of psychology instigated by Viktor Frankl called Logotherapy that focuses on how we give meaning to our lives. This is another way of looking at spirituality.

What makes me happy and how can I get it?

When we are happy, we are less likely to be sensitive to things that might have otherwise upset us. We also influence those around us in more empowering ways so that they too become less sensitive. Clearly, understanding what makes us happy or sad can greatly improve the quality of our relationships (§ 11 the Therapeutic Effects of Awareness).

I explore some of the ways in which we drive happiness away from ourselves without realising it, and how we can reframe our notion of happiness to something that we can have control over, in a separate course [keep an eye on introducingaffinitology.com]. Meanwhile, try this simple, but enlightening exercise.

Exercise 13 What Makes me Happy?

Part 1

Begin by asking yourself, "What makes me happy?"

Dwell on that for two to three minutes and write down what comes to mind. Don't read on until you have done this part of the exercise.

(What comes to mind is often either vague or wishful thinking)

Part 2

Ask yourself, "When have I felt happy in the past?"

Again, dwell on it for about two minutes and write down what comes to mind.

Part 3

What did you notice about the difference in responses that your mind presented to you?

Part 4

What insights did you gain from doing this exercise?

Understanding how our minds generate feelings of happiness can have an enormous impact on our own mental wellbeing and, consequently on our relationships spiralling up from there.

Freedom

How can I be in a relationship and still have a sense of freedom?

In § 15.1 (The Power of Questions), we saw that how we pose questions to our mind affects the answers that our mind gives us. Notice the way I phrased the above question. I did not ask, "Do relationships kill freedom?" or "Can I be in a relationship and still have a sense of freedom?" I asked a question beginning with *"How* can I …?" This is very important because it *forces* me to assume that it *can* be done (§ 62.5 The three Levels of Belief) and the only question is *how*. It veers my mind away from the possibility that it cannot be done. So, if, in the past, I equated being in a relationship as a loss of freedom, it now *allows* my mind to consider the possibility that the two may not be linked in that way.

Another important detail in the above question is that I did not say, "How can I be in a relationship and still have freedom?" I said, "… have a *sense* of freedom". This emphasises the idea that freedom is not about our circumstances (§ 14.3 Situation vs Circumstance), but about how we perceive and interpret (§ 33 Atasinex Cluster) those circumstances.

How often do we stop to think about how our freedom has been taken away by society's imposition that we must wear clothes in public? It is an imposition on our individual freedom, isn't it? But we don't perceive it in that way. Instead, we focus on the possibilities that this has opened up. As a result of this simple restriction, a whole world of fashion and other forms of non-verbal communication has emerged. We now have the opportunity to be more beautiful than peacocks. I delve into this in more detail in a separate course (What is Freedom and how to experience it?) [keep an eye on introducingaffinitology.com]. For now, it is important for us (our mental wellbeing) to realise that our feeling about whether or not relationships hamper our freedom depends on what we think freedom is, what we want to do (our goals and priorities) and how we structure the relationship. You may find it helpful to (re)read the bit about the 'pompous' water molecule in § 39.6 (SRC are Unstable at the Individual Level) and, if you feel trapped in a relationship (in any way), try this exercise.

Exercise 14 Am I really trapped in a relationship?

Ask yourself,

1. **What is preventing me from leaving this relationship?**
   Notice that it's the thing that is preventing you from leaving this relationship that is curbing your freedom and not the relationship itself. The simple realisation that the relationship itself (The Pactum) is separate from what holds the relationship together (The Nexus) can be very liberating.

2. **Can I change the way I perceive the relationship (§ 33 Atasinex Cluster) so that the thing that is preventing me from leaving the relationship becomes less daunting?**

3. **What would I have to sacrifice (give up) to leave this relationship?** [see also § 24.1 (What Do Tables and Relationships Have in Common?)]

4. **In what ways would I (or could I) be empowered if I were to leave this relationship?**

5. **How can I change my perception (§ 33 Atasinex Cluster) of the relative value of my answers to questions 3 and 4 to make me feel more empowered?**

To use the table analogy (§ 24.1 What Do Tables and Relationships Have in Common?), gluing a table leg to a tabletop can fix a relationship in such a way as to make each part less flexible. Using a screw can make the table easier to dismantle and reassemble when needed, such as for transport. If portability is important, another type of joint that is less restricting than glue and faster than a screw, is a hinge. With this analogy in mind try the last exercise again and see if you notice any difference in the way your mind approaches the question, "How can I be in a relationship and still have a sense of freedom?"

50.4
The Financial Dimension

> **"Money will buy you a bed, but not a good night's sleep, a house but not a home, a companion but not a friend."**
> Zig Ziglar

How does money affect interpersonal relationships? That depends on the Relationship Framework (§ 92). If I am in a 'Lender-Borrower' relationship, then money has (almost) everything to do with the relationship [Note that we are talking about the Nexus connecting two specific Identities here. The other (non-lender/borrower) identities may have a different relationship with The Other (§ 29.4 Omniself)]. For those who do not feel that they have enough money, money becomes a *goal*. For those who feel financially secure, money is a *means*.

In any relationship, the 'money factor' can be a strength, a weakness, an opportunity, a threat or irrelevant. Some of you may be asking, "But Bijan, can money ever be irrelevant?" Here, I need to remind you that we are talking about relationships between different Identities within an individual, an Omniself (§ 29.4) and that every relationship is situational. For example, when I am teaching, or helping someone with an emotional problem, I do not perceive the relationship to be a financial one. In other words, the relationship is not *about* money. Money is a *facilitator* [the chemist Identity in me thinks of it as a *catalyst*]. What I am saying is that we need to clarify the role of money in each of our Nexuses. I can be in a relationship,

a) Because of money
b) In spite of money
c) With the help of money

Consider a situation where, I am helping a client with a problem and she has had three sessions with me and I feel that she needs another two or three sessions to resolve her problem to our mutual satisfaction. From a financial perspective, I can perceive the relationship to be of the first, second or third kind. Now, imagine that after the third session, she tells me that she can no longer afford the sessions. The fate of the relationship will depend, in part, on how I perceive the role of money in this Nexus.

If I am offering my services because of money, I would apologise, saying something like, "I am sorry to hear that and I wish you luck."

If I am offering my services in spite of money, I might say something like, "Well, don't worry about that for now, we have come this far already and it would be a waste to stop when you are so close to resolving your issue."

If I am offering my services with the help of money, I might say something like, "I don't want you to stop when you are have come this far, but it would be difficult for me to continue without payment, so let's see if we can reach a compromise. How much can you afford and can you pay in instalments?" In this example, money is an indirect facilitator. It is an exchange that takes place outside of the therapeutic (or any other service) relationship. In other words, the financial relationship is a separate, but necessary stage, so that the non-financial aspect of the relationship can proceed.

A situation where who pays the restaurant bill is not important (does not affect the Nexus) is another example of a relationship that is independent of money (§ 25.4 Dative Bond: Give and Share).

Another situation where the financial dimension does not interfere with the Nexus is when the nature of the financial aspect of the relationship is so clear that it does not affect the main 'purpose' of the relationship. An example may be when two Identities agree to split the cost of the trip so that they can focus on their Travel Companions Nexus.

Sometimes, money can be a direct facilitator of the relationship. For example, research has shown that there is a relationship between how much we pay for something and how much we appreciate (value) it. This is particularly relevant in a therapeutic relationship. If I have to pay (what seems to be) a lot (to me) for a consultancy session, then I am more likely to try to extract as much value from the session as possible. In a therapeutic setting, this means that the therapy is more likely to be more successful because the client will be paying more attention and will be more mindful of the exercises that she has been assigned. In this case, money is not an adjunct, but an integral part of the relationship.

"You can get everything money will buy without a lick of character, but you can't get any of the things money won't buy happiness, joy, peace of mind, winning relationships, etc., without character."

- Zig Ziglar

50.5
The Sexual Dimension

When you hear or see the word sex, what is the image that comes to mind? No, you don't have to tell me. Just notice. Sex means different things to different people at different times. Not that long ago, 'making love' was synonymous with petting. In social science research, sex is approached from the perspective of the thing that you *are* (male/female) and not something that that you *do* [even though we call it 'having']. Nowadays, in non-academic circles, the word sex is synonymous with coitus and this is the sense that I mean when I am referring to sex here. Sex is a very emotive subject because it is associated with intimacy, security, friendship, fun, ecstasy (the spiritual experience), procreation, loyalty, survival, family, tribe and responsibility to name a few.

> *A few years ago, I was asked to give a talk to a group of newlyweds, the theme being, "The role of sex in marital satisfaction". My first reaction was to tell the organizers that such a talk would have been more useful before marriage. One of the things that I told the audience was that they should not base their values on a limited set of opinions on the subject. This is because perspectives on sex range from it being just a brief period of pleasure like having an ice cream or a cup of coffee to something that is sacrosanct and should be a means of reproduction only, whilst others believe it to be a barrier to a relationship with God, so they then go off into a monastery and devote themselves to a life of celibacy. For most of us, however, our perspectives lie somewhere between these extremes. And it doesn't matter what our perspective is, regarding sex. What matters is that our partner should have a similar perspective.*

In practice, this means that, if your partner has an 'affair', whether or not he is being unfaithful depends on what he thinks sex is about, especially the extent to which he associates sex with love.

What damages relationships is not the act itself but the secrecy and deception (lack of openness) that it entails.

As I explained earlier (§ 49 Introduction to Dimensions of Human Experience), each of the factors that we are discussing here as 'relationship ingredients', including sex, can be considered to lie along two dimensions signifying depth and breadth (see figure 24: Dimensions as planes). These translate as,

a) "How emotive is the subject?" and

b) "How pervasive is its influence on the relationship?"

These are determined, primarily, by the meaning that each if the Identities in the Pactum assigns to sex (§ 33 Atasinex Cluster) and may include sexual appetite (quantity) and the nature of the sexual encounter, that is, its context and quality [by which I mean those qualitative measures that The Self and The Other are sensitive to (§ 34.1 The Three Sensitivity Concerns)]. For any particular Nexus or Relationship Framework (§ 92), sex can mean one or more of several things. Some of these are outlined in Table 6.

Table 6 - The possible meanings of sex in a relationship

Meaning	Explanation The fact that I am having sex with you means that...
Appraisal	I am trying to gain some insights into your character
Appreciation	I appreciate being with you
Connection	I want to connect with you (get to know you better)
Exclusivity	You are mine
Fear	I don't want to lose you
Forbidden Fruit	A source of curiosity, excitement, anxiety and guilt
Growth	I am trying to gain experience
Inappropriate	A negative influence/infringement on an existing Nexus
Intimacy	I love you
Pleasure	I derive hedonic pleasure from the interaction
Power	I am an alpha
Procreation	I want to have children with you
Release	I can focus on other aspects of my life more effectively
Simplification	There are fewer complications in my life
Spiritual	You are a part of me (you and I are [at] one)
Utilitarian	It is a means for getting something that I want

Note that each of the above can be a constituent in a cocktail of perspectives that can make each encounter a unique experience depending on the 'recipe' and the situation.

In short [as with the other 'Relationship Ingredients'], we need to clarify for ourselves what a sexual encounter means to us in the context of any given Nexus and the value that we attach to that meaning. Then, to create and maintain a SMER (§ 2.1), we need to be able to communicate (Unit 3: The Power of Language) our perspectives and values effectively to The Other in our Nexus.

The Cultural Dimension

According to Hofstede's cultural dimensions theory, culture (or what I have called Collective Identity - § 32.4) can affect our values along six dimensions:

1. Individualism-collectivism
2. Uncertainty avoidance
3. Power distance (strength of social hierarchy)
4. Masculinity-femininity (task-orientation versus person-orientation).
5. Long-term orientation
6. Indulgence versus self-restraint.

These dimensions have been extracted from quantitative data using statistical methods, such as factor analysis. To be able to do this, the factors need to be amenable to measurement through Likert-style questionnaires. However, there are many aspects of culture and micro-culture that sensitise us arbitrarily in favour or against certain behaviours or groups which cannot be measured so conveniently but which, nevertheless strongly influence our choices. Ethnographic studies are one way of accessing some of these. Here is an exercise for you to try:

Exercise 15 Effect of culture on affinitological fertilisation

You are sitting by yourself in a restaurant and you notice a handsome (or beautiful) person sitting alone at a nearby table. You are contemplating whether or not to approach him/her. Just then, the waiter places a tray of food consisting of a plate of rice, elegantly decorated with saffron along with two skewers of shish kebab. As you gaze at the scene, you see your mark plunge into the rice with her hands and begin to tear the kebab with her teeth. Are you now more or less interested in connecting with this person? The direction of your answer will depend on factors that include,

1. How honest you are with yourself,
2. Your cultural background,
3. Your range of experiences with other cultures,
4. The extent to which you are curious about other cultures,
5. Your personality such as 'Openness to Experience' and
6. The extent to which you find the target attractive

We can become desensitised to cultural influences (biases) in two ways; cultural and individual. Cultural desensitisation can occur through intermixing of cultures which includes Immigration, gentrification, incursion, war and colonisation. The method affects the extent and direction of the cultural shifts. Individual desensitisation (mind opening) to cultural biases can occur through personal experience. Methods include, travel, immigration, reading and mingling with people of different cultures within one's own society.

50.7

The Occupational Dimension

Our vocation (what we do for a living) affects what we experience and how. This, in turn, affects our focus and interpretation of events, especially other people's behaviours (§ 33 The Atasinex Cluster). These experiences include,

- The demographic sections of the population that we meet and associate with [I was going to say, the 'kind' of people that we meet, but decided that this turn of phrase is reminiscent of stereotyping and its associated biases (I have Dr Yvonne Reynolds, at the Institute of Education to thank for that insight)].
- Our language patterns which affect our thought processes (Unit 3: The Power of Language), and
- Our physical environment (§ 50.10 Environmental Factors).

All of these affect our mindsets, outlooks and priorities. These, not only affect who we want to meet and why, they also affect why, when, where and how we interact with people. Becoming aware of this can help broaden our minds and may affect our thinking in ways similar to the following:

- Maybe the reason that I am having difficulty connecting with this person is because my job limits the experience that I have with people.

- Perhaps my choice of vocation should also reflect the characteristics of the people that I want to meet.

- To what extent does my job limit the depth and breadth of my social experiences and what can I do to minimise the possible negative impact of this on my life and relationships?

The Family Dimension

Dictionary.com lists 24 different definitions for the word 'family'. This itself is enough to cause possible communication problems in relationships where the concept of 'family' is a focal point. Here is an exercise to help us explore the possible effects of our notions of 'family' on our relationships:

Exercise 16 Your notion of family

Part 1

Take a moment to think about your answer to each of the following questions.

    a) What does family mean to you? [Genes, contracts, commitments, common goals, common beliefs, looking out for one another, or something else.?]

    b) What would have to happen for you to consider someone to be a part/member of 'the family'?

    c) Do you distinguish between immediate family and extended family? What are your criteria for that?

    d) Do you think that there might come a time (or maybe it already has) when you would put the welfare of a 'friend' before a 'family' member?

Part 2

Think of someone that you are in a relationship with (any kind of relationship). How does your answers to the above questions and your views impact the quality of your relationship with that person?

Part 3

1. Repeat part two with at least two more people.
2. What insights did you get from doing this exercise?
3. Are these views always empowering or can they sometimes be disempowering for some of your more cherished relationships?

In § 60.3.2 (Inter-Pactal Interference), I have included an anecdote about a client who had issues with her father. There, I talk about how I challenged her notions of what a 'father' is.

50.8
Temperament and Personality Dimensions

We discuss personalities in the context of the Omniself in § 29.4. Here, I simply want to say a few words about how this could affect the nature and quality of our relationships.

The consensus of opinion is that, under similar conditions, there are predictable patterns in a person's behaviour. In other words, we are likely to behave similarly in similar circumstances. This isn't a very complicated idea. It simply means that, if you know your friend well, then you will be able to predict quite accurately how he would react in a particular situation.

There are many different theories of Personality each with its own set of dimensions [Three factor models, four factor models, five factor models, etc.]. You'll be relieved to know that I'm not going to go into the details of these theories here. I am just going to introduce a popular personality model that I have worked with and I am quite comfortable with. The model is called the Big Five. It is a model that splits people's predictable characteristics into five dimensions. The acronym for remembering these five dimensions is OCEAN (Openness, Conscientiousness, Extraversion, Agreeableness, Neuroticism). Let's take a closer look at this friend of yours. Try the following exercise.

Exercise 17
Can you predict what your friend will be like?

Imagine you have gone to a party with a friend.
1. How likely is she to,
    a) be on time?
    b) either mingle or to pair off with one person?
    c) be loud or quiet?
    d) nervous or relaxed?

2. What kinds of conversations is he likely to be involved in? Are those conversations going to be centred around certain topics or varied and diverse?

These seemingly predictable characteristics fall within the realm of Personality Psychology. I say seemingly predictable, because, as I have also pointed out in § 29.4 (The Omniself), the predictability of these so-called 'traits' depends on the situation and for some people, these traits are more stable across different situations. To see what I mean, try Exercise 17 again, but this time imagine your friend being in a different situation, such as at work or in a small gathering amongst family. To what extent have your predictions about how she will behave changed?

What I am pointing out to you here is that the relative effect of each of the Big Five personality dimensions on any of our relationships will depend on the situation which includes the Relationship Framework (§ 92). In other words, [to the dismay of many] our 'personalities' are not as stable as our security-seeking limbic system would like it to be. What I am also saying here is, **don't be surprised if someone describes a person you think you know and the description doesn't match your mental image of that person**; it is due to what psychologists call "context effects". Incidentally, whether we call these 'predictable' behaviours, 'temperament' or 'personality' depends on whether we believe them to be innate or acquired (learnt).

50.9

Environmental Factors

To put you into the right mood for this section, try the following exercise.

Exercise 18

The effect of the environment

Part 1

1. Imagine that you are walking alone on a secluded beach. How does that make you feel?
2. Now imagine that there is someone else with you. Who is it?

Part 2

3. Now, imagine you are in a secluded warehouse. How does that make you feel?
4. Now imagine that there is someone with you. Who is it?

[Note that your answer may have been different if I had reversed the order of the parts in this exercise (because of a phenomenon called 'priming' see § 33.8 (Confirmation Bias).]

The difference in feeling, mood, ambiance, atmosphere, vibes, etc. that we feel is what I mean when I talk about the effect of the environment. This 'environment' can also be changed by the presence of other people.

I am sure you can see how being in a different environment can affect our relationships. The Nexus is more susceptible to environmental variables in its early stages (§ 35.1 Embryology of Relationships). For example, if you have just started a new job and your daughter walks in and starts to scream and shout, this will make a greater impression on your relationship with your boss and your colleagues than if this happens three years after you have been with your boss and colleagues.

50.10
The Aesthetic Dimension

Once I had a client who was concerned because she felt that she had no sense of style. I asked her how she had come to think like that, and she said that her friends were constantly telling her so. I asked her to mentally put herself into a situation where she was choosing something to buy. At first, she was saying things like, "Well, there is this dress that I like, but, if I buy it, my friends may make fun of me again." I said, "So, what you are saying is that you like it, but your friends don't?" and she agreed. I said, "Whilst you are doubting yourself and being influenced by your friends, you are dismissing the sense of style of the person who designed it, the manufacturer who made it and the retailer who stocks it. They all must have liked the design. Are you saying that you and none of them have a sense of style and your friends do?"

Sometimes having different tastes in art and music can be a facilitator of relationships by becoming complementary elements in the Adjunctum Communalis (§ 46). At other times, having similar preferences can become Common Elements that facilitate the establishment and maintenance of a Nexus. And there are other situations where the nature of the Nexus, the Relationship Framework (§ 92) is such that these things become too superficial or irrelevant.

50.11
The Ethical/Moral Dimension

The dictionary was not very clear about the distinction between 'ethical' and 'moral' so I looked into the etymology of these words and found that the former has its roots in Greek and pertains to the study of 'proper behaviour' and the word 'moral' has its roots in Latin and is about 'doing the right thing'. Therefore, we could say that "What is right and wrong?" is an ethical question, but asking whether what someone is doing is right or wrong (§ 3.5 'Good or Bad' and § 39.1 SRC are Binary) is a question of morality.

We can define ourselves (who we are) at two levels; at the level of our Identities and at the level of our Core Values or Principles (§ 29.4 The Omniself). At the Identity level, who we believe ourselves to be, depends on the situation (§ 14.3 Situation vs Circumstance); I am a teacher, a father, an astronaut, etc. Even the extent to which we identify with our gender is situational; we only think about it in situations where the distinction serves a purpose (§ 66 Goals).

There is, however, another sense in which we can talk about who we are that is much less situational such as when we say things like, "I am honest", "I am caring", "I am loyal" or "I am dependable". The more our Identity is bound to the situation we are in, the more sensitive we become to threats to its integrity. For example, if, at a party, someone were to say to me, "You are not a teacher now." I would not dwell on it and would probably simply agree [or concede depending on the context]. However, if someone were to say that to me whilst I am teaching in a classroom, I might be much more tempted to defend my Teacher Identity. However, there are aspects of who I perceive myself to be that I would be much more likely to be sensitive to, irrespective of the circumstances. For example, if someone were to say to me, "You are not being honest with me", I probably would feel the urge to invoke a psychological defence mechanism (PDM) or two (§ 79).

The ethical/moral dimension is concerned with where we draw our boundaries. That is, the level of incursion into our sense of self that we are willing to tolerate before mobilising our defences (PDMs). Our very essence is defined by our boundaries. Without boundaries, we would be boundless [That's not as obvious as it sounds]. Since, it is our boundaries that define us, being boundless makes us undefinable and that would make us everything or nothing, neither of which sounds very appealing by itself [cf. § 79 (Holons)].

From a behavioural perspective, our morals are where we draw the line between what we are willing to do and what we are not willing to do and the grey areas in between. From a social and affinitological perspective, this is about those things that we are willing to do or not do *that affect others*. The grey areas arise because, from a holistic perspective, everything that we do affects everyone [I encourage you to watch a movie called 'Sliding Doors' to get a deeper sense of what this means].

The extent to which we appreciate the repercussions of our smallest actions on others depends on

   a) our ability to relate (§ 50.2 The Intellectual Dimension) and

   b) our ability to empathise (§ 51.7.4 Empathy and Compassion).

Both of these are critical in terms of the extent to which we can create and be a part of a SMER (§ 2.1 What is a SMER?).

Finally, the moral factors that we tie to our Identities are situational, whereas our Principles are not.

50.12

The Legal Dimension

From a legal perspective, a relationship is a social contract. [An 'agreement' is morally binding. A 'contract' is legally binding.] Ostensibly, a contract is an agreement between two people and there is, in fact, a legal doctrine called "privity of contract" which says that "a contract cannot confer rights or impose obligations upon any person who is not a party to the contract." This means that, in theory, any agreement between two people is private and no one else has the right to interfere. When we begin to refer to an agreement as a contract, we are either automatically involving a third party or anticipating that a third party may need to become involved at some point, most commonly, in case of a dispute.

One of the most private of contracts in which we deliberately involve other people is marriage. We also invoke legal terminology when we feel that our personal space has been (or is being) invaded. A common example being 'harassment'. In essence we reserve the law as an insurance policy against any unexpected happenings in our relationships with other people. The relationship between the Individual, the Nexus and the Law is bidirectional. In other words, the law doesn't just stand by waiting to get involved in case of a dispute. The law imposes its own restrictions on individuals and relationships too. I will not delve too deeply into this here because the purpose of this section is to merely make you aware of this aspect of relationships and its possible effects on various Relationship Frameworks (§ 92).

50.13
The Temporal Dimension

Imagine we are playing a word association game and I say the word 'time', what is the first thing that comes into your mind? A clock, a time machine, a sense of urgency, being on time (promptness), the passage of time, aging, antiques, timelapse photography, history, short-term and long-term goals/contracts, or something else? Our views about each and any of these can affect the quality of our interpersonal relationships.

Sometimes, I get some strange telephone calls.

> *Once, a lady called me to tell me that her sister had three suitors and she had chosen to marry one who was fourteen years older than her and could I kindly dissuade her from doing so. I told her that it was not my job to dissuade people from getting married to someone if they wanted to, but I could help her sister to consider her criteria for marriage from different perspectives. When I met the sister, I found that she was very eager to learn and open to new ideas...*

When people tell me that they intend to escalate their relationship with someone who is somewhat older or younger and ask for my opinion or advice, my stance tends to be that if both parties are attracted to each other and have compatible beliefs and values, then age need not be a deal breaker, unless this creates practical constraints that could have a detrimental effect on the relationship. This was one of those cases.

> *...One of the many questions that I asked her was, "Do you want to have children?" and she said, "Not in the short-term, but later." I asked her if she had discussed this with her intended and she said no. I pointed out that someone who is fourteen years older is likely to want children sooner rather than later.*

[There are many more aspects of time, as they pertain to relationships that we could consider here, but this book/course is already larger than my comfort zone. I shall, therefore, endeavour to develop this further at some other juncture.]

50.14
The Social Dimension

Our circle of friends has a significant impact on our circle of friends. No, that is not tautology; who we associate with determines who *else* we associate with. It can also affect who we *can* associate with. Have you ever been in a situation where someone you care about does not approve of the company you keep? How did that affect the quality of your relationship with that person? How did it affect the quality of your relationship with the company that you keep/kept?

This is clearly a vast topic that we cannot cover adequately here. However, as I keep saying, awareness itself is therapeutic (§ 11 The Therapeutic Effects of Awareness). This awareness will hopefully plant seeds in your mind by getting you to ask yourself questions like, "Is my relationship with the people with whom I am associating with helping me to create and maintain SMERs?"

a) If so, am I aware enough of this to appreciate (§ 51.75 Gratitude) what I have and to express it?

b) If not, what might be preventing me from seeking a more empowering social circle? (§ 68 Tolerance and Comfort Zones)

Chapter 51

The Emotional Dimension

51.1
A Relationship is a Feeling

> Our emotions affect *why* we want a relationship, *who* we want to have a relationship with, *what* kind of relationship we want, *how* we want to go forward with that relationship and *when*.

In § 16 (To Have or To Be), I said that a relationship is a feeling. Here is an exercise to help you grasp the significance of this assertion:

Exercise 19 The role of feelings in relationships

1. Think about any interaction with someone that you can remember well. What was exchanged at the overt level? (Money, a smile, a hello, a handshake, a hug, …)
2. Now think about what was exchanged at the feelings or emotional level.
3. Now ask yourself:
   a) What was more important; the things that were exchanged or the feelings that the exchange produced?
   b) In terms of feelings, did I achieve what I intended to achieve?
   c) Was that the best way of achieving it?
   d) If I wanted to achieve a better thymic outcome (mood, feeling, emotion, state) what could I have done differently?

51.3
Affect, Feelings and Emotions

We do not tend to hear the word 'affect' (used as a noun) outside of academic circles. It was introduced in the 1960s to refer to those aspects of our psyche that [ostensibly] are not 'pure thought'. Try this exercise to see what I mean. Look at the following questions and compare your answers:

1. How are you feeling?
2. What are you feeling?
3. How do you feel?
4. How does it feel?
5. What does it feel like?
6. How does it make you feel?

Except for questions 4 and 5 where the word 'feel' can also be interpreted to mean 'feel to the touch', the others are variously asking you about your mood, emotional state and emotional reaction. These include whether you are feeling 'good' or 'bad', 'high' or 'low', motivated or bored, elated or depressed, and so on. In academic circles, when dealing with such matters, we sometimes use the word 'affect' as an umbrella term for emotions, feelings, states or moods. It helps us to separate out the idea of thought; the mental processes that we use to try to make sense of the world (whether we are conscious of them or not) from how thoughts 'affect' us.

Often, we use the words affect, feeling and emotion interchangeably (as if they have the same meaning). However, not making the distinction that they deserve can deprive us of some important understandings and insights.

Affect

We can think of 'affect' as being about physiological changes in our bodies; intrusive thoughts, or something about the environment, 'affects' us and changes our focus. These physiological changes are, in effect, *changes in muscle tone*. In each of our bodies, there are an estimated 50 billion tissues that can be classified as muscle. Of these, less than one thousand are skeletal muscle (more amenable to voluntary control) and the rest are smooth muscle (less amenable to voluntary control).

Feelings

If we envisage each of our muscles as being like a button on a giant control panel, then, different 'feelings' are evoked depending on the combination of these buttons that we press. However, each combination of muscle tones needs to be coded; genetically, epigenetically or through experience [including social construction], to render certain feelings. In other words, feelings are about the (programmed) *meaning* that we give to physiological changes that take place in our bodies; that is, how we *identify* with them. In other words, feelings are about how we relate physiological changes (combinations of muscle tones) to our sense of who we perceive ourselves to be.

Emotions

Emotions are about how we *react* to the meaning that we give to that which has affected us. In other words, emotions are behaviours that are coupled to feelings. For example, crying is an emotion that is coupled to sadness which is a feeling coupled to a perception of loss [which we would only feel if that which we lost formed part of our sense of Identity]. Understanding this difference between feelings and emotions can significantly improve the quality of our relationships because it helps us appreciate that the same level of *feeling* can result in different expressions of *emotions* in different people. In other words,

---

Just because someone does not become emotional, it does not mean that he or she is not experiencing deep feelings.

Emotions (reactions to feelings) are primarily social. They are there to *show* other people how we feel. Yes, we can become emotional when we are alone and that can happen for three reasons. Let me demonstrate.

51.3.1
Why we become emotional when we are alone

The grounds of our house is separated from the main building by a tall wall. This means that we rarely feel the need to lock the door to the main building. When we have young children in the house, I lock the door to the building. Sometimes, I do this when there are no children in the house. And in the second situation, sometimes I am consciously aware that I am doing that and sometimes I am not.

We can understand why I might lock the door when I am not consciously aware of it; it has become a habit, a shortcut that allows us to be *doing* one thing (that has been tried and tested and proven itself to be safe) and be *thinking* about something else at the same time. But what about the times when I am consciously aware that I am locking the door when there are no children in the house? In those cases, I sometimes pause briefly and wonder whether I should do it or not and then *decide* in favour of taking the action. I do this because I tell myself that I do not want to lose the habit of locking the door because that would mean that I might forget to lock the door when there are children in the house and that can be dangerous. In other words, I prefer to lock the door when it is not necessary (it doesn't do any harm for the door to be locked when there are no children in the house) than to omit to lock the door when there is a need, that is, when it could be dangerous for young children to have unsupervised access to the garden [I am not talking about a grass lawn]. This has to do with what researchers call Type I and Type II error. It is also why, in our criminal system, we err on the side of letting a criminal go free than punishing an innocent person.

So, what does the above explanation have to do with why we become emotional when we are alone. Well, one explanation is that it has become a habit. We have let it become a habit because we have decided to err on the side of openness when we are in public. In other words, we have decided that the benefits of expressing those feelings (becoming emotional) outweighs the disadvantages of not showing them. This is the equivalent to me locking the front door even though there are no children in the house; I am not consciously thinking about it, it is a habit.

Another reason for us becoming emotional when we are alone is that, mentally, we are almost never alone. Even when we are physically alone, we imagine ourselves not to be alone. We act as if we are being watched (sometimes by a 'higher' being). This appears to be an innate need; children begin to have imaginary friends at a very young age. As I am confident you already know, we react to what we imagine and not to physical reality. Start thinking about chocolate or strawberries and your body will respond by producing saliva (and that's only part of it).

So, what about the times when I am conscious of there being no children in the house and lock the door anyway? That can be like an actor practicing his act in front of the mirror in preparation for the real performance.

There is yet another reason for us expressing our feelings even when we are alone. This has an evolutionary origin. Some feelings, like anger or fear, prepare our bodies for *doing* something (fight or flight). This is when hormones such as adrenaline are released into our system which *compel* us to do something (they rev our engine and release our clutch). If that energy has nowhere to go (if the car's bumper is touching a wall or if the handbrake is on), this can lead to internal damage. So, when we know that there is no one around, but we start to think about something that makes us angry (compelled to move), if we do not release that energy, we put a lot of strain on ourselves. We look at the differences between strain and stress in Unit 23 (Mechanics of Relationships).

51.4
Feelings, Emotions and Impulse

Emotions are the primary determinants of the quality of our relationships. For a relationship to be instigated, maintained, changed or severed, emotions *must* be involved (§ 51.3.2 Feelings Trump Logic). Our feelings (precursors to emotions) affect who we want to have a relationship with, what kind of relationship we want, how we want to go forward with that relationship and when. *All the other dimensions of human experience* (Unit 11: § 48-50) *are only important insofar as they affect our emotions.*

Our ability to choose our emotional state is the single most important skill that we can aspire to acquire.

The more control we have over our emotions the more control we can have over our relationships and vice versa. Earlier (§ 51.2 Affect, Feelings and Emotions), I explained the difference between affect, feelings and emotions through an anecdote. Here, we will explore those concepts in a little more detail.

What is an emotion? An emotion is a *behavioural* reaction to a feeling. What is a feeling? A feeling is a *physiological* reaction to a stimulus. This distinction is made in many languages which suggests that it is important not to confuse the two. Let's explore this difference.

The more we identify with a stimulus, the stronger the feeling it evokes in us. Imagine that you are about to receive an injection in your arm. If you focus on the fact that this is 'your' arm and that 'you' or 'your body' is being violated, that injection is likely to *feel* much more painful. It is also likely to be accompanied by fear (expectation of pain). On the other hand, if we look at 'the' arm and perceive it to be just an arm *not* 'my' arm (§ 37 What is an Identity?), we are likely to *feel* less pain. Yes, literally. This is the difference between being in an associated state and a dissociated state [In some disciplines, such as Neurolinguistic Programming (NLP), the former is called 'the first perceptual position' and the second is called 'the third perceptual position'.]. This is how hypnotic anaesthesia works; it diverts conscious attention from the self to somewhere else. By dissociating from the self, the I, the me and the my, we leave more room in our psyche for associating positive feelings to the experience of having an injection or anything else (think relationships). For example, we can feel curiosity or gratitude.

The corresponding *emotions* arising from each of these situations will also be different. In the associated state, the *feeling* of fear may manifest itself in the *emotion* of fear [we don't seem to have a word that distinguishes between these two, perhaps because we rarely separate the feeling of fear from its emotional counterparts] This emotion can express itself in different ways in different people and may include sweating, blushing, tensing of the arm, breathing differently, changes in facial expression, etc.

To summarise, an emotion is a behavioural reaction induced by an associated feeling (a physiological response). The behavioural reaction may be as simple as a smile or a grimace. In the absence of an ensuing behavioural reaction, what we are experiencing is a feeling, not an emotion.

We can put this idea into a broader perspective by reminding ourselves of the difference between the behaviourist and the humanist schools of thought (§ 40.2). A stimulus causes a physiological response. That response is a feeling and that feeling becomes a stimulus (or precursor) for a behavioural response; an emotion. In the same section, we also saw that from a humanist perspective, what distinguishes us from our 'less developed' evolutionary ancestors is that, between stimulus and response, we have the potential to exercise choice. When we relate this to our understanding of the Atasinex Cluster (§ 33), we can control our emotions, that is to say, we can choose our feelings and/or how we react to those feelings.

You might well ask, "But Bijan, what about spontaneity? Isn't that what makes life interesting? If we consistently analyse how we are thinking and how we are going to respond to situations, doesn't that defeat the purpose of life which is for us to experience the excitement that comes from the unexpected?" And I would say, "Thank you for asking. That is a very relevant question." My answer is that, when travelling at several thousand feet above sea level with a view to skydiving, being spontaneous requires a parachute, otherwise, it is not spontaneity, it is stupidity, suicide or desperation.

This reminds me of a teenage pupil of mine who told me that she wanted to be a writer but she did not want to read because being influenced by existing ideas would curb her originality. I suggested that reinventing the wheel is not original and that what she needed to do was to find innovative applications for the wheel. To do that, she would have to be aware of the existence of a wheel first.

Similarly, being able to choose how we react to a stimulus, gives us greater scope for choosing the feelings that we experience. It does not preclude spontaneity. The greater our repertoire for reacting to feelings, the more options we have regarding the emotions that we can choose to experience. In short, knowing that there is such a thing as a parachute, and knowing how to use it, does not deprive us of the choice to jump out of an aeroplane without one, but it does afford us the opportunity to jump from high altitudes relatively safely. "What does all this have to do with relationships?", you may well ask. Well, if you replace the idea of 'parachute' with 'emotional control' and the idea of jumping out of an aeroplane with 'jumping into a relationship', the relevance will jump out at you.

51.4.1

Thermodynamics of Feelings

The first law of thermodynamics (§ 95 Entropy) states that energy cannot be created or lost it can only change from one form to another. This is a useful metaphor to use for feelings as well. We could say that feelings do not disappear; they just change from one form to another. In other words, it would be useless for me to try to *stop* feeling angry (make the feeling disappear). Trying to do so will eventually result in the feeling being 'transferred' to other feelings like guilt and frustration. When I'm working with my clients, I tend to find it easier to substitute [or 'transfer' to use engineering parlance] the feeling of anger with feelings of compassion or curiosity depending on what he can manage at the time. Similarly, I reframe the concept of guilt to arrogance which we tend to be more motivated to expel from our psyche.

51.4.2
Feelings Trump Logic

Research has shown that those who are neurologically impaired, in a way that makes them unable to experience feelings, are incapable of making the simplest of decisions. We may believe that we are thinking through a decision logically and making a logical choice, however, that logic has to appeal to us emotionally for us to be able to take action on it (cf. § 73 Transactional Analysis). We explore this topic in more detail in § 51.5.3 (Emotions are in the Driving Seat).

51.4.3
Impulse

In this discourse, I sometimes make a distinction between feelings and impulse. By 'impulse' I mean, 'a feeling that does not linger', that is, the urge recedes as soon as we 'act' upon it or as soon as we are removed from the situation that induced it; physically or psychologically; through a change of focus/attention (§ 93.1 Motivation and Motivational Energy).

51.5
Emotions and Intellect
(Affect and Cognition)

51.5.1
Feelings and States

Feelings veer our attention (§ 93.1 Motivation and Motivational Energy) from thinking to doing - from *contemplating* the way things are (or should be or could have been, etc.) to *doing* something (taking action).

You might say, "But Bijan, when I feel sad, I don't feel like doing anything." Like other emotions, sadness is, to quote Tony Robbins, a "call to action". We don't perceive it that way when we do not understand its message. Sadness is not saying, "Don't do anything." It is saying, "Do what needs to be done for you to be able to move on."

"Move on from what, Bijan?" Move on from the feeling of loss, that is, "I am feeling sad because I believe that my link with a part of my Identity has been severed." [understanding the process of grieving allows to cope with any kind of loss, not just the loss of a loved one.]

Fear is the temporal counterpart to sadness. Fear is the feeling that emerges from a belief of *impending loss* and sadness is the feeling that results from the belief that we *have lost* something that we identify with (we are attached to, i.e., is or was 'a part' of us).

There are two types of feeling; feelings that are directed inwards and feelings that are directed outwards. Feelings that are directed outwards tend to be focused on a specific object, concept or phenomenon. Feelings that are directed inwards tend to be focused on 'I' as a general concept.

> **Fear is an example of a feeling that is directed outwards. When we are afraid, we are afraid of something. Anxiety, on the other hand, is an example of an emotion that is directed inwards; it is not about what I am afraid of, it is about whether or not 'I' can cope with the uncertainties ahead.**

I propose that this is the difference between a 'feeling' and a 'state'. Feelings are physiological action signals directed at something *outside of us* [this is related to our discussion about locus of control (§ 44)] and states are physiological conditions related to something *inside of us*.

Here is another way of looking at this. Think of the difference between the words 'want' and 'dance'. Want is a transitive verb. "I want" is not a complete sentence (it is a phrase); it needs an object. That is, it leaves the listener waiting for more, "*What* do you want?". Dance, on the other hand, is an intransitive verb. "I dance" is a complete sentence. Feelings are like transitive verbs and states are like intransitive verbs. We sometimes use the same word, such as grateful (§ 16.2 Mindfulness and Conscious Gratitude) to refer to both states and feelings.

51.5.2
The 'Why' of Emotions

When it comes to emotions the 'why' isn't directly accessible. Try the following exercise to get a feel for what I mean.

Exercise 20
Can we Really Get to the Root of Why We Feel What We Feel?

Part 1

Imagine a time when you wanted something that you didn't need, an ice-cream for example. Just as you say, "Oooh, I really fancy an ice-cream right now", someone asks, "Why?" What do you say?

Notice that the 'wanting' part of us doesn't really know why. The 'why' of emotions is not directly accessible to our consciousness, I cannot say to myself, "Why am I feeling this way?" and get a straightforward answer from my consciousness. To answer the question, which we feel compelled to do, (§ 15.1 The Power of Questions) you need to invoke the intellect to come up with some kind of *justification* that is convincing to either your own intellect or the person you're trying to convince. But how accurate is that justification, really? To find out, let's try another exercise.

Part 2

Imagine that, this time, just at the time when you say, "Oooh, I really fancy an ice-cream right now" (or whatever it is that you fancy), someone asks, "What would happen if you don't have it right now?" What would your response be this time?

Part 3

Compare your answers to Parts 1 and 2 of this exercise.

If your answers *feel* different, your intellect is justifying your feelings. What insights do you gain from this exercise?

Although thoughts affect our emotions, the same thought can cause different feelings and emotional responses in different people. The thought of having a baby, for example, affects everyone emotionally in some way. However, in one person, the predominant feeling may be joy and, in another, it may be anxiety. The practical implication here is that, when we have issues with any of our relationships, we need to become aware of,

a) *How* our emotions are involved (because they invariably are),

b) *What* those emotions are doing to (how they are affecting) The Nexus,

c) *How* the emotions of The Other is affecting their perspective and

d) *How* those perspectives are affecting The Other's involvement in the relationship (The Nexus).

51.5.3
Emotions are in the Driving Seat

In § 51.4.2, I said that *feelings trump logic*. In this section, we are going to explore that notion in more detail.

Improving anything, including a relationship, requires a change in behaviour. In other words, we need to *do something differently* to get a different result. There is an old adage that says,

> **"If you always do what you've always done,**
> **you will always get what you've always got."**

[Actually, that is not entirely accurate, but the message it sends is close enough to what I want to convey.]

To change what we do; our behaviour, we need to change whatever it is that drives that behaviour. There are only two things that drive behaviour *habits* and *emotions*.

"What about intellect and consciousness?" I hear you shout. I am not saying that intellect doesn't have anything to do with it, but intellect is not in the driving seat. Think of intellect as the navigator sitting next to the driver. Intellect can influence emotions, but in the end, if emotions are not changed, behaviour will not be. Another way of saying this is that the effect of intellect on behaviour is mediated through emotions. If my thoughts don't activate or arouse my emotions, there will be no change in my behaviour which means that I will continue to do what I was doing before.

In physics, the law of inertia (Newton's first law of motion) states, "An object will continue to move in a straight line and at constant speed unless it is acted upon by a force." In humans, that object is our body (the part of us that manifests what we call behaviour) and that force is our emotions.

We can't use the same physics principle for the effect of intellect on emotions because emotions can change in the absence of the influence of our intellect. This can happen when there is a change in the external environment (such as when we panic or act on impulse). It is true that sometimes we fail to recognise the emotion that is driving our non-habitual behaviour, but that doesn't mean that emotion is not involved. To wit, everything about relationships revolves around emotions.

> **To change any aspect of a relationship, we need to change the nature of our**
> **emotional connection with that aspect of the relationship.**

51.5.4
Emotional Control and The Will

There is a big difference between having no feelings and showing no emotions (§ 51.2 Affect, Feelings and Emotions). We can control our behavioural response to stimuli either at the feeling level or at the emotional level. For any emotion to manifest in me, there must be some kind of stimulus. A stimulus is the thing which could elicit a feeling that could lead to an emotional response from me; *if I allow it to* (§ 40.2 Behaviourism versus Humanism).

Emotional Control at The Feeling Level

Physiologically, a feeling is what happens at the 'neurotransmitter' level. This is when, neurotransmitters have been released [into synaptic clefts], but hormones have not [been released into the bloodstream]. Neurotransmitters are released when nerves begin to 'talk' to each other. This is the stage at which sensory messages have been received (usually from the Peripheral Nervous system) and a 'board meeting' has been convened to decide what to do about them. If the sensory messages are interpreted; perceived (§ 33 Atasinex Cluster) to be important enough not to be ignored, then this is followed by some kind of state change. Although a state change often has observable features, such as piloerection (goose pimples), unlike emotions, such changes are not for other people's benefit. It's simply the body preparing itself for a possible change of plan.

We can change how we feel by changing what we think about (our focus) and how we think about it (our interpretation). The first is like changing the meeting agenda (to some other topic) and the second is like reaching a consensus that the matter needs no further action to be taken.

Control at The Emotional Level

If at the 'board meeting', it is decided that action needs to be taken, a memo is sent out. Physiologically, this means that a hormone is released into the bloodstream. At this level, the body (or to be more precise, the somatosensory system) becomes involved. The original 'signal' (or signals) has now induced 'an emotional response'. This is when we say that our emotions have been aroused (woken up).

The Will

The next stage is where we need to exercise that elusive phenomenon that we call The Will. We need The Will when,

a) Our feelings resist the behaviour that our intellect demands (I don't want to do this. Oh but, you should.) And

b) Our feelings demand behaviours that our intellect considers unwise (I want to do this. Oh, but you shouldn't).

Controlling feelings requires cognitive manipulation. Controlling emotions requires corporeal regulation. In other words, we need to *do* something; we need to *move* (hence the word e-*motion*).

[Actually, there is a feedback loop between our body and the central nervous system such that, if we do something that creates a physiological pattern that resembles the effects of a hormone, the relevant feeling is aroused (the hormone that regulates that pattern of response is released). It is as if the mind is saying, "Somebody has bypassed the protocols" but instead of supressing the body (and punishing it for not following protocol), it issues the necessary permissions and licenses.]

51.6
Feelings, Emotions and Identity

Our feelings are inextricably tied to our sense of identity, especially the dominant Identity in that situation. If we do not identify with a stimulus (if we think it has nothing to do with who we think we are), we would be indifferent to it.

[You could argue that indifference is a feeling, and that is, of course, your prerogative. I wouldn't argue with that because I can see how, sometimes, it is useful to talk about black as a colour. However, for the purposes of understanding the role of feelings in relationships, I think it would be simpler to consider indifference to be a lack of feeling, because it gives us a different kind of canvass to work with. What I'm saying is that I can accept indifference as a state of being but not as an actual feeling because it does not have the potential to manifest as a behaviour into something that could be called emotion. In § 51.2 (Affect, Feelings and Emotions), I have discussed the difference between feelings and emotions which may clarify what I have just pointed out a bit more. You may be wondering whether all this isn't somewhat pedantic. I suggest not, because subtle nuances in words can make the difference between a person being set free or sent to jail. In this context, it is often referred to as 'a technicality'.]

An emotion is an urge to move. The urge stems from a feeling that we experience in response to a stimulus which can be something that happens in our thoughts or in our external environment. That feeling becomes an emotion when it interrupts our normal flow. In other words, a feeling that either makes me stop doing what I was doing, start doing what I wasn't doing or makes me do what I was already doing differently in some way, is an emotion. To put it another way, feelings are physiological changes in our bodies and emotions are our behavioural responses to those changes.

Showing no emotion is where I feel an urge to do something, but I somehow resist the temptation to interrupt my normal flow. Sometimes we do this so often that it becomes a habit and we don't realise that we are doing it. Being poker-faced is an example, meaning that we cannot tell what a person is feeling. Tony Robbins calls being cheerful as the quality of 'telling your face about it' when you are happy. Clearly, being aware of the extent to which we express our feelings can have a profound impact on the quality of our relationships.

Emotions can be manipulated (intentionally aroused or suppressed) and cultivated (habituated). This is done by a process called reframing (§ 63.1). Let's look at an example. If I said to you, "I just found a piece of paper." You might well ignore me, saying to yourself (ever so briefly), "So what?" But now, imagine that I follow that up by saying, "It has a picture of your mother on it." Did you notice your state change? Now it becomes relevant (related/associated with something that you identify with); the meaning of the piece of paper has been *reframed* in your mind to arouse the feeling of *curiosity*. If you subsequently act on that impulse (even if it be just raising an eyebrow), that feeling of curiosity has found expression; it is now an emotion (emotional response).

Controlling or managing our emotions does not simply mean being able to choose whether or not to respond to a feeling. It goes further than that. It also allows us to *choose* the feelings and emotions that we want to experience. For example, what if we could choose to be indifferent or to feel sympathy towards someone who is rude to us or treats us unfairly? How would that affect our relationships? I'm not suggesting that this is appropriate for every occasion, but I am saying that it is a useful tool to have in our kitbag. Since this is an introductory course all I'm doing at this stage is planting seeds. I'm making you aware of what's involved. I'm helping you see what we need to look at. I am highlighting possible blind spots.

In summary, understanding our own emotions and knowing how to be more in control of them can have a fateful impact on our relationships and all that it entails. Emotions are invoked by the stimuli that we associate with our sense of identity.

51.7
Emotions and Relationships

When we have issues with our relationships, one of the first things we need to become aware of is how the emotions of each party to the relationship (The Self and The Other) are involved and what they are doing to The Relationship. Not to Me, not to The Other, but to The Third Entity, The Nexus. Here's an exercise to help you do this.

Exercise 21

The Effect of What we Observe about a Relationship on the Relationship

Think of a relationship that you are in. Again, this can be any kind of relationship, not just a romantic one.

1. When you look at yourself in that relationship, what is the predominant emotion that you feel?

2. When you look at The Other person in that relationship, what is the predominant emotion that you feel?

3. When you are thinking about the relationship itself, what is the predominant emotion that you feel?

Now ask yourself,

4. How does the way I feel about myself affect the relationship?

5. How does the way I feel about The Other affect the relationship?

6. How does the way I feel about The Relationship (The Third Entity) affect the relationship?

7. What insights did you gain from that exercise?
   [please share your insights on introducingaffinitology.com]

If there is one take-away message from this section, it is this: Emotions don't happen to us; we can control them. Perhaps not as much as we can control our fingers, but at least to the extent that we can control our breathing.

51.8
Examples of Nexus-Empowering Feelings and Emotions

In this section, we explore some emotions that, in general, are conducive to forming and maintaining SMERs. I say, 'in general', because the meaning and significance of anything depends on its context.

The positive or negative associations that some words have for us can sometimes blind us to the possibility of their having opposite interpretations and effects. For example, we generally associate trust with positive emotions. However, some people, especially those who have had negative experiences in relation to trust, may consider trust to be tantamount to naivety. When my clients feel that they have been a victim of being too trusting, the greatest casualty is their self-confidence, a topic that we explore in more detail in § 83.2.1 (Damaged Self-Confidence). For now, I simply want to make you aware that the following concepts need to be looked at from a grayscale rather than a black and white perspective (§ 25.3 Polar Bond: Partial Sharing).

51.8.1
Curiosity

Curiosity is one of my favourite emotions [I have often thought of the phrase "Driven by curiosity" as being a suitable epitaph for my gravestone."]. Curiosity follows a similar hierarchy to beliefs (§ 62.4 Beliefs as Affinitological Genes) and can be summarised as being any thought that can be rephrased as a question beginning with, "I wonder…" Here are some examples:

1. I wonder what it is.
2. I wonder what it does.
3. I wonder what that (effect) can mean to me.
4. I wonder what it can do.
5. I wonder what that (potential) can mean for me.
6. I wonder what I can do with it.
7. I wonder what effect that would have on the people around me.
8. I wonder what effect that would have on the universe.

51.8.2
Love

Love is probably the most pervasive word in any spoken language and tends to have the most profound effects on interpersonal relationships. In spite of its omnipresence, its usage is so diverse as to confuse any uninitiated alien.

The holy grail of physics is the discovery of a unified field theory. I propose that a 'unified theory of love' would be its affinitological equivalent. I have been pursuing this. However, although I have mentioned 'love' in various contexts throughout this book, the subject is so alluring and so potentially expansive, that I intend to dedicate a separate work to it [keep an eye on introducingaffinitology.com].

51.8.3
Trusting

We explore 'trust' in detail in § 53 (Trust), where I propose that there are two types of trust; trust in *intention* and trust in *ability* and that not being aware of this distinction can severely affect the quality of our relationships.

[In case you are curious, the title of this subsection is Trusting and not Trust because there is another section called Trust and it would have messed up the cross-referencing system :-)]

51.8.4
Empathy and Compassion

I propose that empathy is a feeling and compassion is its complementary emotion. When we can empathise with someone, we can feel their joy and pain [our mirror neurons are both active and sensitive]. Being compassionate means being moved to *do something* to either create more joy or to reduce suffering.

Empathy is a potential (an implement, a tool, an ability); something that we can have more or less of. However much of it we have the potential to manifest, we can either choose to lock it away in a closet (not act upon it), to take it out once in a while or to carry it around with us all the time. What we *choose* to do with this potential determines both our level of compassion and the quality of our interpersonal relationships. The following adage conveys the idea of compassion better than any other way that I can think of [at least at the moment]:

It is better to be kind than to be right.

51.8.5
Gratitude

Gratitude is synonymous with appreciation. We have touched upon gratitude in various sections of this book, including § 16.2 (Mindfulness and Conscious Gratitude). Like love (§ 51.7.2) and happiness (§ 2.1.2 What is Satisfying?), we can perceive gratitude in different ways. And like other Dimensions of Human Experience, it lies on a plane, having both depth and breadth (§ 49.3).

Gratitude as a State

The state of *being* grateful is when we are 'consumed' by the feeling. At that (often fleeting) moment, the feeling is not focused on any particular aspect of life, it is just there, like anxiety, it is generalised (§ 44.5 Zone of Anxiety). As a 'state', gratitude is intransitive (§ 51.5.1 Feelings and States). It does not have an (external) object. When we are in a grateful state, we are not grateful *to someone* or *for something*. It simply feels as if fortune is smiling upon us and we feel blessed to be (simply conscious).

Gratitude as a feeling

Although, in the above section, I have defined a state in terms of it being a feeling, in § 51.5.1 (Feelings and States) I proposed that the fundamental difference between a feeling and a state is that one is focused on some external phenomenon whilst the other is focused on what 'I' need, can or should do. As such, gratitude becomes a feeling when its intellectual component (the thought that leads to its emergence) is focused on something specific outside of us. For example, when we say something like, "I am grateful to…" or "I am grateful for…", we are describing a feeling. We can however, simply 'be' grateful, that is, in a state of gratefulness.

Gratitude as an expression

Another way of conceiving the concept of gratitude is to think of it as the things we do, rather than the feelings that we have. In other words, if the feeling does not lead to action, then, since no gratitude has been expressed, it is passive and, therefore, irrelevant. I am in two (several) minds as to whether or not I subscribe to this interpretation, but I am open to persuasion either way.

Gratitude as give and take

If we subscribe to the above idea that gratitude is not a passive process, then we will need to reassess some of our current notions about gratitude. For example, the expression of gratitude can then become a form of giving and a taking, akin to the 'stroke' that Eric Berne talks about in Transactional Analysis (§ 73). Even when we are simply focused on being alive and feel grateful for that, we are 'taking in', through our attentional mechanisms (§ 33 Atasinex Cluster), and experiencing feelings, that we would not experience otherwise and this will, subsequently affect what, and how, we 'give out'.

Grades of Gratitude

Some people believe that gratitude is only applicable where someone has done something for them that is beyond the call of duty. Others believe in saying 'thank you' for the smallest act [if there is such a thing (§ 90 Fractals)] of giving. These are two extremes of a grayscale (§ 25.3 Polar Bond).

51.9
Examples of Nexus-Disempowering Feelings and Emotions

In this section we discuss some feelings and emotions that are toxic to relationships. Before we continue, however, bear in mind that emotions can be like double edged swords to a greater or lesser degree. Depending on the relationship and the circumstances, a particular emotion can be empowering or disempowering for the Nexus, (e.g., § 59.1.2 Storming). However, some emotions are riskier (more likely to be disempowering) than others.

51.9.1
Superiority

It is curious that although we often lament those happy times of childhood, many adults' behaviours towards children suggests that their approach to children is from the perspective of superiority. Before puberty children don't learn to resent in the way that adults do. However, looking at it from an adult's perspective, if I were treated the way many children are treated by adults, I would be using my emotion management skills to combat the resentment that I would feel.

If you ever experience a feeling of superiority, consider this. A sense of superiority, or inferiority for that matter, is divisive. It creates a barrier between me and you and it limits the potential of the relationship. A feeling of superiority or inferiority has its roots in false comparisons. See § 39 (Social Ranking Criteria).

Also bear in mind that a sense of superiority is often a psychological defence mechanism (§ 79) to compensate for a (often subconscious) perception of inferiority.

51.9.2
Inferiority

A feeling of inferiority is a symptom of low self-esteem, that is, a feeling of not liking ourselves. There is a book by Stephen Carter called, "Men like women who like themselves". It's not just men who like women who like themselves, I believe that,

---

Everyone with high self-esteem likes to see everyone else have high self-esteem

---

A feeling of inferiority limits our contribution to the Nexus and is not conducive to empowering and satisfying relationships. If you experience the feeling of inferiority, look at § 39 (Social Ranking Criteria) to get some insights into the probable roots of this feeling.

51.9.3
Hate and Resentment

Although, in this course, our focus is on Satisfying and Mutually Empowering Relationships (§ 2.1 What is a SMER), negative feelings, such as hate, can also lead to the creation and strengthening of a Nexus, albeit a disempowering one. For The Hater, this is a dependent kind of relationship in that he feels unable to 'let go' of the resentment that he feels (§ 23.2 The Road to Interdependence).

Hate and resentment are both 'harboured' feelings; infestations that tend to be invasive, pervasive and persistent in our psyche.

In addition to being binding, hate is also blinding. This is related to this quote by Sister Helen Prejean that we touched upon in § 29.4 (The Omniself); "People are more than the worst thing that they have done."

Hate prevents us from disassociating the object of our hatred from the situation that led to the feeling.

51.9.4
Disgust

Unlike hate and resentment, which are binding, disgust is a form of repulsion. It prevents bonds from forming or leads to severance of bonds. I suggest that we categorise disgust, as an impulse (§ 51.3 Feelings, Emotions and Impulse), a feeling that fades away quickly when one is removed from the situation that evoked that feeling. Sometimes disgust is accompanied, or followed, by feelings of pity or compassion.

51.9.5
Anger

Anger can be a feeling or an impulse. It is usually the former when it pertains to something that relates to our own sense of Identity. However, it appears in the form of an impulse when, although one of our principles has been violated, it is not perceived as being personal. For example, I may feel angry when I hear that a country in the middle east has been invaded by a foreign power in violation of all international treaties. However, that is an impulsive feeling when I do not lose sleep over it or allow it to spill over into my relationship with my children. It becomes a 'feeling' when I make it personal.

51.9.6
Indifference

Indifference is the greatest impasse to relationships. Where there is indifference, there is no mechanism for connection. Indifference is more psychologically damaging, especially to children, than even physical violence.

> *I used to teach science and mathematics to a 15-year-old girl at her home. One day she said to me, "Bijan, my mother is always shouting at me." So, I said, "Does she shout at the girl next door?" and she said, "Of course not." I said, "Why do you think she shouts at you and not at the girl next door?" She said, "I'm her daughter." And I said, "Exactly! Your mother is spending her emotional energy on you and that is a sign of love. You may not like the way the message is delivered, but try to focus more on the message than on the way in which it is being delivered."*

Once, I heard a story about someone telling Adolf Hitler that people were saying bad things about him and his response was, "As long as they're talking about me, I don't care what they say."

51.9.7
Indecision

Strictly, indecision isn't a single emotion, it is a conflict of emotions. Nevertheless, it is an emotional problem and it can be very detrimental to relationships, whether it be forming or maintaining them. The first trick here is to try to prioritise based on probable consequences of each possible option. If that doesn't resolve the problem, then here's a second strategy. It would appear that, right now, you do not have enough information to be able to ascertain which option will have the more favourable consequences. At this point,

> **any decision is better than indecision because indecision leads to stagnancy and stagnancy is a soul killer.**

If you're too scared to flip a coin, you need to take action to resolve your self-confidence issues because the reason you can't flip a coin is because you feel that no matter which direction you go you may not be able to cope with the consequences. As my friend, Michael Reiss, is fond of saying, "Few things in life are disastrous". I think it's a very empowering philosophy to live by.

51.9.8
Doubt

Doubt is the antithesis to confidence. Self-doubt is lack of self-confidence. Doubting others is a lack of trust (§ 53 Trust). The irony is that people tend to respond to us in accordance with our expectations of them. Therefore,

> **the more we doubt people, the more untrustworthy they tend to become.**
> [where 'we' is concerned]

Doubt is a state of purgatory; it's not heaven (trust) and it's not hell (distrust). Being in limbo erodes the soul. If you doubt enough, break the relationship and if you trust enough carry on with it. Again, if you can't make up your mind flip a coin but get yourself out of that state.

51.9.9
Lust

I consider lust to be a natural evolution-friendly physiological reaction. It is as good a starting point in a relationship as any. In contrast to the impression I get from most commentators, I believe that lust is not necessarily an antithesis to love; it can be a precursor to it.

What makes lust empowering or disempowering is not the impulse, but the accompanying intention.

I can feel lust and say to myself, "I intend to be honest with this person." On the other hand, my psychological defence mechanisms (§ 79) may kick in and that is when we begin to sow the seeds of conflict within ourselves and in our relationships. As the saying goes, "Oh what a tangled web we weave when first the seeds of deception we conceive."

[This is a quote I remember from a long time ago, attributed to The Bard. However, it appears to be a variation of the following quote from an early nineteenth century Scottish author, Sir Walter Scott: "'Oh what a tangled web we weave, when first we practice to deceive', but I prefer the version I remember having first heard.]

51.9.10
Attachment

Attachment is an emotional state. Dependence is a practical concern. Attachment can lead to dependence and dependence can lead to attachment, but they are separate phenomena.

When people come to me for parenting advice, I notice that they often confuse 'attachment' and 'dependence'. For example, they say things like, "My son is very dependent on me." After I make the distinction, they will say, "Oh, well, no; my son is very independent, but he is very attached to me." At this point, I reassure them that this is a very positive thing because research has shown that the more (securely) attached children are in their early childhood the more easily there go through the rebellious phase in their adolescence.

However, attachment can be a double-edged sword because it can cause our feelings for the person with whom we are in a relationship to continue in their absence and this can interfere with other aspects of our lives. For example, if

I'm supposed to be working on a project at work and my emotions are not congruent with that task because I am wondering what the person I am attached to is doing, that is not conducive to my financial health or career health and this will, at some point, have an impact on my other relationships too. Notice that the main side-effects [or complications, depending on whether you are looking at it from a pharmaceutical or clinical perspective)] of attachment are attentional in nature. See also § 33 (Atasinex Cluster) and Unit 22 (Thermodynamics of Relationships).

The main emotional indicator of dependence is anxiety, whereas the main indicator of attachment is sadness.

51.9.11
Fear

I put it to you that fear only has one source;

Fear is the perception of impending loss

The 'perception of impending loss' is what is also known as a 'threat'. In other words, fear is rooted in the 'perception' of threat.

Whether we perceive the message of fear to be 'avoid it' or 'be careful' depends on the extent to which we value that which we stand to lose in comparison with that which we stand to gain.

The only thing that will make the feeling of fear go away is a DECISION.

Where fear is concerned, what paralyses us is indecision. Once we decide (§ 72 Decision-Making), then our attention moves from, "How do I handle this situation (minimise the loss)" to 'doing what needs to be done' (doing what our decision mandates). Here is another way of expressing this. When you feel afraid, ask yourself,

---

"Is whatever I am afraid of losing worth the consequences of the paralysis that remaining in this state induces in me?"

I consider this to be very important, so let us explore it a little more.

Sometimes we spend so much time (and mental and emotional resources) wallowing in a fear that we are unable to achieve anything. In most cases, making any decision, even a 'wrong' one, releases us from this paralysis because it changes our focus from how we feel to what needs to be done. If we do not get into the habit of making quick decisions, often, the 'paralysis period' extends to longer than it takes to simply try a number of possible plans (A, B, C, …) until a satisfactory (or at least a minimum viable) solution is found.

If our fear is related to our relationships, then here are some questions that may help us to decide more quickly:

a) What am I afraid of losing? (Unit 11: § 48-50 Dimensions of Human Experience)
b) What do I have to believe about The Other to feel this way?
c) How vulnerable is the Nexus to this situation?
d) What can I do to strengthen the Nexus against this vulnerability? Then focus on implementing (making happen) your answer to this question.

An empowering answer to question (d) above is,

> **"Work on strengthening mutual TRUST in the relationship."**

We explore trust in § 53.

Continuing with the topic of fear for a moment; fear can be a saviour (real fear), but it can also be a barrier to progress (false fear). So, how can we determine which of these types of fear we are dealing with?

The question, "What have you to lose?" is often overused and sounds like a cliche. But that is not a problem with the question, it is a problem with the way it has come to be (over)used. With the help of this question, we can distinguish between 'real fear' and 'false fear' by looking at our minds' answers to the question. That is, we can look to see whether the answer relates to physical or psychological consequences.

If, in response to, "What do you have to lose?" my mind says, "My reputation" or "My pride" or "My self-esteem", then we are talking about fear that needs to be overcome through expanding our comfort zone. If, on the other hand, the answers that come to mind relate to loss of health, relationships or property (shelter), then the fear is justified (we can consider it to be 'true' fear).

51.9.12

Jealousy and Envy

Once a lady came to me with her husband and said, "Doctor, whenever we go to a party, my husband flirts with pretty women, can you please make him not do that anymore?" I said to her, "Madam, if I had a magic wand that I could wave to remove all desire for women from his head, then you would no longer be desirable to him either. From the moment that the egg and sperm met, your husband's nervous system was destined to be wired in such a way that he would find the female form attractive and yours was destined to be wired in such a way as to find masculine forms attractive. It is like having a field of beautiful flowers. Imagine picking one flower from that field whereupon that flower expects all the other flowers to suddenly become ugly to you."

Although the words jealousy and envy are often used interchangeably, there is a significant difference between them [Persian also has two words that make a similar distinction, emphasising the importance of having both words]. According to etymonline.com (quoting Century Dictionary), "Jealousy is enmity prompted by fear; envy is enmity prompted by covetousness."

In the age of increasing gender, racial and cultural integration and tolerance, I propose that the word enmity in this context is somewhat archaic and that we can replace it with 'competition'. Since, all fear can be distilled to fear of loss [I intend to expound upon this concept elsewhere (keep an eye on introducingaffinitology.com], we can say that, **envy is about something that we want** (that someone else has) **and jealousy is about something that we fear losing.**

[The latter is primarily psychological and relates how we think we are perceived by others. In other words, "I am jealous because I think that this (apparent) inequality makes others think less of me."]

Bringing the idea of competition into the equation, we can now say that,

---

Jealousy is competing to keep and envy is competing to get.

"Keep what Bijan?" I hear you ask. Thank you for asking. When I am (one is) jealous, I do not want to get better. I want to stay where I am but keep my sense of self-worth. This is rooted in a comparison mindset whereby my self-worth is contingent on comparing myself [superficially] with others (§ 39 Social Ranking

Criteria). If someone has something that, in my mind (Unit 7: Atasinex Cluster), makes him appear more valuable then, if I am jealous, I want him not to have whatever it is that is making me feel less valuable.

When we are envious, our focus being on getting/becoming, we have a wider set of options regarding how we go about acquiring what we 'covet'. If I see someone who has something that I covet, I can aspire to acquire something similar or 'better'. It is more difficult to think in these terms when our focus is on something that we fear losing.

From yet another perspective, we can say that Jealousy is more personal (less dissociated) than envy because with jealousy, we are competing with an adversary who we see as a threat; someone who can take away what I consider to be mine [because we can only fear the loss of something that we believe we already possess], whereas with envy, we are primarily competing *for* that which is coveted, not *with* the person who has it.

Some people consider jealousy to be a sign of love and try to make their partner jealous as a test of that love. The problem here is that there is a fundamental conflict between love and jealousy. When I see someone I love enjoying themselves without me,

> **if I want to take that enjoyment away from them because it does not involve *me*, then clearly, it is not love that I feel for that person, it is possessiveness.**

And that does not lead to a SMER (§ 23.3 Interdependence). The question then becomes, "Do I want a healthy relationship or *any* relationship, even if it is unhealthy?" If the answer is the latter, then The Other becomes a prop for me to hang my insecurities on and not someone through whom I can realise higher potentials (§ 2.1 What is a SMER).

The Little Prince by Antoine Saint Exupery is on my recommended reading list for anyone interested in the human condition. One of the many enlightening parts is a section in which the author demonstrates the difference between *my* flower and all the other flowers in the world by drawing parallels between the taming of a fox and what makes *my* flower special.

Unit 12

Embryology of Relationships

[Image by BellaDonna from Pixabay.
Source: https://pixabay.com/vectors/easter-egg-chick-egg-red-1324892/]

Chapter 52

Introduction to Affinito-embryology

52.1
Definition of Embryology

I searched the internet for a definition of embryology that wasn't too restrictive so that it could be applied to relationships easily and I found this one on biologydictionary.net

---

Embryology is the branch of biology concerned with the development of new organisms.

"What does the development of new organisms have to do with relationships, Bijan?" I hear some of you ask. Well, you may have noticed already that society (which is a conglomerate of interpersonal relationships) bears an uncanny resemblance to living organisms. The purpose of this section is to cement that idea by highlighting some of the more salient aspects of that resemblance. You might also have noticed that my tone is veering away from biological sciences and living systems being a mere analogy, to it becoming a model for what society actually is, a living organism, with all the features of MRS GREN (§ 26.2 Characteristics of Living Organisms).

52.2
The Gametes

In biology, gametes are those cells that can fuse together to form the cell (zygote) that is capable of growing into a complete organism. In affinitology, gametes are the individual Identities who can potentially create a relationship by connecting with each other in some way. In biology, the gametes need to be a male (e.g., sperm) and a female (e.g., egg) cell. This means that in biology, the term gametes are only applicable to sexual reproduction. In affinitology, we use the term more broadly to describe the two Identities who instigate a relationship - any kind of relationship (§ 92 Relationship Frameworks). An individual may have an Identity that has reached the gamete stage for instigating a healthy mother-child relationship, but may not have developed a suitable Identity for creating a healthy Employer-Employee relationship (in a specific situation; i.e., with a specific employer or employee).

Based on our definition of relationships, anyone can potentially have an interpersonal relationship with anyone else on this planet. Therefore, the term 'gamete' is only useful *post factum* [they have formed a Pactum, therefore, they were gametes], otherwise everyone could be called a gamete and that would make the idea redundant and defeat the purpose.

From an affinitological perspective, gamete formation is the process through which each individual develops the qualities and skills required to form a SMER. Let me remind you that here, we are talking about Identities; The Self and The Other (§ 29.4 The Omniself) and not physical entities or attributes [Compare masculinity and femininity (identities) with maleness and femaleness (anatomies)].

52.3

Preconception

Before instigating a relationship, we form an impression of The Other. The criteria that we use for forming that impression is based on our preconceptions, that is, the way we think things *should be*, not the way they *actually are*. The more preconceptions we have, the less objectively we are able to observe other people. This means that we see much less of them than they actually are.

Our preconceptions determine the extent to which we trust others (before we get to know them).

52.4

What is required for a bond to form?

Serendipity and desire. Let's look at each of these in turn.

52.4.1

Serendipity

The notion of serendipity/luck/happenstance is related to our locus of control, which we explore further in § 44. Our locus of control is the extent to which we believe that we are in control of what happens to us. Do I 'fall in love' or do I 'choose to love'? The less I choose to choose, the more serendipitous my relationships will be. However, who I meet is never 100% under my control; nor is it 100% out of my control. As we observe repeatedly in this course, grayscale is the norm.

I may decide that I want to meet someone who is interested in the visual arts and, therefore, decide to frequent art galleries. In this case, I will have considerably reduced my chances of meeting someone who is not interested in art. However, I still don't know who I am going to meet there. And I will not know whether I want to instigate a relationship with that person until we meet.

A different scenario may be that I want to borrow some money. I, therefore, decide to approach a venture capital firm or an angel investment network. In this case, I will have reduced my chances of meeting someone who is not interested in investing money, but I still don't know who I am going to meet and whether we would be willing to enter into a business relationship with each other. The more I focus on what I want and move towards getting it, the more likely I will be to get something close to what I have in mind. Nevertheless, there is always an element of chance; I may get more or less than I expect in spite of the most meticulous of plans.

Another factor that determines whether I get what I want is how broadly I define what I want. For example, if I specify the age, gender, height, weight, eye colour, hair colour, accent, taste in music, and so on to minute tolerance levels, then I am setting myself up for disappointment. The more flexible I can be, the more likely I will be to meet someone who meets my criteria.

The more flexible we are, the more independent we can be. The more independent we are, the more freedom (choice) we have.

We discuss independence and dependence in more detail in § 23.2 (The Road to Interdependence). For now, here are a couple of examples.

The less dependent I am on other people for money, the less I need to look for someone who has money to support me. This means that I can be more flexible in terms of who I enter a relationship with; rich *and* kind is more difficult to find than just 'kind'. This gives me an extra degree of freedom. I explain degrees of freedom in § 49.4. The same principle applies to dependence or independence in other domains (Unit 11: Dimensions of Human Experience). For example, in the social domain, the less dependent I am on other people's approval (§ 39 Social Ranking Criteria), the more flexible I can be in terms of who I choose to form a relationship with.

52.4.2

Desire

In order to form a bond (instigate a relationship), we must *want* it, whether consciously, subconsciously or unconsciously (§ 35.11 Consciousness). Two factors affect desire; belief and value. The first is about the extent to which I consider something to be possible and the second about how much I think it is worth the effort (§ 62.5 The Three Levels of Belief). In other words,

---

for any kind of bond or connection to form between people, there must be a how (mechanism) and a why (reason).

[Initially, I was going to include "belief" in here. Then I realized that belief is already implied in the how; if I know how to do something, I already believe that it *can* happen].

You might say to me, "But Bijan, I know plenty of people, including myself, who desire things that they know (believe) they can't have; that is to say, I cannot conceive of a mechanism for achieving it." Even if your logical mind tells you that it can't be done, in your imagination, you still entertain the possibility that it can be done. Otherwise, it would be too conflicting for your mind to dwell on it, let alone desire it. Also, we need to make a distinction between real desire and entertainment. Entertaining the idea of being a butterfly is not the same as desiring to become a butterfly. Entertaining the idea of being a butterfly will not motivate one to work hard towards becoming one, unless, of course, the person truly believes that it is possible.

Motivation (A Reason)

Before 1904, the word motivation hadn't been invented and 'desire' was much more in vogue. In 1943, Abraham Maslow published his paper called "A Theory of Human Motivation" and 'motivation' came to the fore. There is a difference between desire and motivation. Desire is one-way, it is about attraction only and does not deal with repulsion; unless we negate it with a not. Motivation, on the other hand, deals with the whole spectrum from 'I desire it to the exclusion of everything else' (obsession) to 'I would rather die than go anywhere near it' (Avoidant Personality Disorder* if the 'it' is other people).

[* Actually, I am being somewhat facetious here. A little introspection told me why. It is because I feel that we throw these labels around too frivolously, but that's a discussion for another time and place. I will open the subject on the introducingaffinitology.com soon. Meanwhile, take a look at a TED talk by Jon Ronson called, *Strange answers to the psychopath test.*]

All the reasons that we could have for wanting anything, including relationships, can be summarised in one word; affect.

Affect is, a change in feeling, emotion, mood, or state (§ 51.2 Affect, Feelings and Emotions). We can achieve a change in affect by changing our focus, our environment, our interpretation or our physiology (how we use our body, including what we do or do not put into it). Note that changing any of these factors will influence the other factors, it's a question of which one we consciously change first.

A Mechanism (How)

The why and the how are not independent of each other. If I think something is too hard to achieve, my mind will tend to protect me from the expected pain of 'failing' (§ 8 What If) to achieve it. In other words, we do not tend to desire what we believe to be too far beyond our reach. This suggests that when we desire something (including a relationship) we probably have at least a vague idea of how we might go about getting it.

Our estimate of how much effort is required and how likely we are to succeed at anything (including relationships) depends on two things; our own personal experience and what other people tell us. The more self-confident we are (§ 40 Self-Esteem and Self-Confidence), the less we are affected by what other people tell us (§ 39 Social Ranking Criteria). This means that, the more experience (internal resources) we have, the less we need to rely on other people (external sources of information) and the more self-reliant we will be (become).

Experience and self-confidence are interconnected. However, it does not necessarily follow that more experience leads to greater self-confidence. If our initial experiences do not lead to desired or expected outcomes, it can take a toll on our self-confidence. This happens when we interpret our unsuccessful experiences in a disempowering way. Attribution Theory (§ 43) is a persuasive model for explaining how this happens.

Many factors, both internal (§ 33 Atasinex Cluster) and external (§ 14.3 Situation vs Circumstance), can affect the results that we get. If we attribute too much of the outcome to ourselves and too little to outside influences, we can lose our self-confidence. We frequently attribute our lack of success to ourselves when, in fact, outside factors have a greater influence on the outcome than we perceive - see the anecdote in § 83 (Structural Damage).

52.4.3
Focus and Situationality

Whether or not a bond forms (a connection is made), as well as the type of connection and the consequent Relationship Framework (§ 92) depends on what the Gametes (§ 52.2) focus on in the situation that provides the opportunity for a connection. Some relationships are more situation-dependent than others.

I propose that the most important factor that determines the nature of the bond (Nexus) and the Relationship Framework (§ 92) is the nature of the common memories that are evoked by the transaction and the extent to which The Other considers those memories to have been a factor that has shaped their current sense of identity (who she is today). Let's explore these through a couple of scenarios.

Scenario 1

Imagine that I bump into someone in the street one day and say, "Hey, do you remember me? I bought a chewing gum from your shop about twenty-five years ago." The response may well be, "I don't work there anymore." Which roughly translates as, "That particular relationship ended when you paid for the chewing gum." From an affinitological perspective, this means that the common and complementary elements (§ 47) that held that relationship together [very briefly] are no longer relevant. However, if I continue the conversation by asking, "What happened to that shop, by the way?" I am,

a) veering the conversation towards something that is (probably) a part of The Other's sense of Identity [I identify with the shop I owned (or worked at) more than with the chewing gum that you bought because my experience at the shop was a factor in shaping at least one of my identities (and consequently, my sense of who I am today)] and,

b) prompting to continue the conversation and indicating that I want to explore a possible new relationship because you made an impression on me or because we have a common interest in that locality.

Note that at the time that I bought the chewing gum, I was not aware that I was creating a Common Element with the shopkeeper (The Other), that common element being what the shop represents; a memory of some significant period in my life, such as the shop being next to the hotel where I met my business partner (which, in turn, changed the trajectory of my life), for example.

Scenario 2

Compare the above scenario with the opening [Transactional stimulus (§ 73 Transactional Analysis)], "Hey, do you remember me? I used to help you with your maths problems when we were in secondary school together. Do you remember that prank we played on Mr. Morgan?" This is more likely to evoke an immediate connection because, having occurred during the formative years of our lives, our experiences are much more likely to be associated with 'that which has made me who I am today.' There are exceptions, of course, such as when someone's memories of school are disturbing and he prefers not to be reminded of them.

Chapter 53

Trust

In § 30.1 (The Nexus), we looked at 'trust' as it is usually defined; in terms of reliance or dependence. Here, we explore trust as a tool for creating and maintaining relationships. From this perspective trust becomes highly intertwined with communication (verbal and non-verbal). The quality of our communication is critical in the development of trust. We explore communication in Unit 16 (§ 70-73: Physiology of Relationships). Let's focus on Trust for now. From an affinitological perspective, we can say that,

---

Trust is our answer to the question, "To what extent do I need to expend my mental and physical resources into ensuring that The Other will not, intentionally or through incompetence, do anything that will be to the detriment of the Relationship?"

Framing the idea in these terms allows us to look at trust from a more pragmatic perspective. It focuses our attention on resources, intention, competence and that which holds the Pactum together.

In § 68.4 (Examples of Homeostatic factors), I point to the work of Ickinger and Morris (2003) who found that our need for interpersonal space depends on how secure we feel. This highlights a critical factor in interpersonal relationships; the extent to which we tolerate invasion of our personal space (or, indeed, any other 'homeostatic' factor) depends on our defensiveness. This is determined, in part, by how confident we feel in our ability to control the situation (§ 44 Locus of Control) and, in part, by social and cultural norms. However, there is another very important factor that can affect the extent to which we put our guards up; trust.

53.1
Trust is perception

Perception is *an interpretation based on the input we receive from our senses.* Trust is our answer to this question, "How secure do I feel in this situation?"

[The 'how secure' is the interpretation part and 'this situation' is the senses part. You could argue that the situation is highly subjective too. But I have mentally moved the interpretation aspect of the situation into the feeling that it evokes (how secure do I feel). What is left, is hopefully, the more objective aspect of the situation. Nevertheless, I grant you that this can get complicated, so let's not complicate it for now.]

Trust is based on beliefs. In § 63.1 (Changing Beliefs: Reframing), we see how beliefs can be changed through reframing. This means that trust issues can also be resolved through reframing.

53.2
The Two types of trust

There are two types of trust; trust in *intention* and trust in *competence.* Not being aware of this distinction can severely affect the quality of our relationships.

In § 28 (First Law of Satisfactory Relationships), I explain that we only take offence if we feel that someone is threatening our sense of Identity. Often, we defend our Identity with more vigour than we defend our physical body. Our sense of Identity and our intentions are closely bound. If someone questions our intentions, we can react in the same way as we would when we feel that our Identity has been threatened. So, what does this have to do with trust? Everything or nothing depending on which kind of trust we are talking about.

53.2.1
Trust in Competence

When we call into question someone's competence, that person may or may not become defensive depending on the extent to which he identifies with that competency (considers it to be a part of his Identity). Even if he does become defensive, the opportunity is there to demonstrate competence and, therefore, a line of communication remains open with regards to that aspect of the relationship. In addition, our competence need not be too tightly bound to our sense of Identity. In other words, if someone else can do something that I cannot do, I don't necessarily think less of myself. That reminds me of this snippet from a TED talk in 2007 by Hans Rosling called, *New Insights into Poverty* [I encourage you to watch the entire presentation, especially the ending]:

"I have a neighbour who knows 200 types of wine. He knows everything. He knows the name of the grape, the temperature and everything. I only know two types of wine: red and white. But my neighbour only knows two types of countries; industrialized and developing. And I know 200."

53.2.2
Trust in Intention

In contrast, if we doubt someone's intentions, we touch the person's sense of Identity to the core; whether the person's intentions are, indeed, honourable is usually irrelevant to the accused.

[This is borne out by the opening story about 'Two Gun' Crowley in Dale Carnegie's iconic book, 'How to Win Friends and Influence People.' And no, I am not going to tell you the story; I consider the book to be a must for anyone interested in mutually empowering and satisfying relationships.]

In practice, this means that, in order to maintain the quality of our relationships, we need to choose our words carefully (Unit 3: The power of Language) so that we do not invoke Psychological Defence Mechanisms (§ 79).

53.3
Components of trust

In the final analysis, trust can be reduced to two factors: probability (risk) and value (importance). It is easier to trust someone with something that is not very important to us. For example, it is easy to ask a neighbour who has just moved in next door (high risk) to look after our son's goldfish (low value) whilst we are away on a week-long holiday [apologies to goldfish everywhere]. However, we are much less likely to trust the same neighbour with the key to our house, especially if there is a safe inside containing our life's savings (high value). The lesson here is that to move closer to a SMER, it behoves us to ask, "What is really at stake here?" comparing the potential of the SMER with the potential risk involved. So, how do we assess that? Let's take a look.

The extent to which I can trust others depends on how secure I feel and how secure I feel depends on my answers to these questions:

- How vulnerable do I feel?
- How self-confident do I feel?
- How much value do I place on this situation?

You might say, "Hey, Bijan. What about the guy that I am going to be dealing with? What if I don't have any insecurities, but I have sufficient reason to believe that the guy is not trustworthy?" And my answer would be that, in all three of the bullet points above, The Other is *implied*; they can be rewritten to make The Other explicit:

- How vulnerable do I feel (in relation to The Other)?
- How self-confident do I feel (in relation to The Other)?
- How much value do I place on the situation (what is the Benefit:Risk ratio when dealing with The Other)?

Nevertheless, the fewer insecurities I have in general (the less I feel that I have to lose), the more I can trust, which means that I can spread my net wider.

You might ask, "But, Bijan, why would I want to try to instigate a relationship with someone who is 'high risk' (unlikely to be trustworthy)?" Because since you are judging the person before you experience a relationship with them, you are only 'assuming' that this person may not be trustworthy. This assumption will either be based on the person's reputation (what others have said) or superficial factors such as their appearance.

I am, by no means, advocating that we should not do our due diligence. What I *am* saying is that the less vulnerable we feel, the more risk we can take and sometimes we will be disappointed, but at other times we could be pleasantly surprised. If we feel too vulnerable and try to minimise risk, we are unlikely to experience either the disappointment or the pleasant surprise. [see also the excerpt from the movie, Parenthood, mentioned in § 27 (The Meeting of Minds)].

53.4
Trust and Vulnerability

Our answers to the questions I posed in the previous section also indicate the extent to which we can be open or sincere. Although openness and sincerity are closely associated with vulnerability, they are also closely bound with Trust. We can think of vulnerability as being in dynamic equilibrium with sincerity which itself is in dynamic equilibrium with Trust. Therefore, [and in accordance with the 0th law of thermodynamics] trust and vulnerability are in dynamic equilibrium with each other.

$$\text{Vulnerability} \underset{\leftarrow}{\overset{\rightarrow}{\rightleftarrows}} \text{Sincerity} \underset{\leftarrow}{\overset{\rightarrow}{\rightleftarrows}} \text{Trust}$$

What this means in practice is that we cannot have it both ways; we cannot expect to be trusted if we do not make ourselves vulnerable to some extent. This is a lesson that I learnt from the father of a former private pupil of mine; a successful businessman.

> *Someone I knew asked me to ask him whether he would invest in a particular business venture. When he asked for details of the venture, my acquaintance said, "That part of it is confidential". Of course, the businessman's answer was a resounding 'no'. He told me that he could understand that some people may be worried that their idea may be stolen but, without taking that risk, there is no way that any partnership*

can move forward. And yes, from time to time the idea will be stolen and, therefore, we need to have enough ideas to keep trying.

All of this requires experience.

53.5

Experience

Once, someone said to me, "You have a PhD, how can you not know that (some fact or other)?" I replied, "What do you think a PhD means? In academia, you start with knowing almost nothing about almost everything, then, as you move up the academic ladder, you get to know more and more about less and less until, at the PhD level, you know almost everything about almost nothing."

[Actually, this is only true if you are differentiating the learning curve (looking at what you are learning moment by moment). However, learning is integrative. This means that we stack knowledge (and, hopefully, understanding) as we go along So, if you have a PhD, don't take my reply to heart.]

Experience has two dimensions: depth and breadth. With depth of experience comes specialization. As empowering as this may sound, there is a possible problem here in that, if we are not careful, specialization can lead to reductionist thinking; the idea that we can understand the whole by looking at its individual parts. In the case of relationships, this means that if we have a lot of experience with only a few relationships, we risk believing that other potential relationships, perhaps even, *all* other relationships are likely to have a similar quality to the ones that we have experienced, since we don't have a frame of reference to think otherwise.

The sequence of experiences also matters. If my first 'deep and meaningful' relationship leads to major disappointment, then I may well be 'primed' (§ 33.8 Confirmation Bias) to be more cautious/reluctant to make myself vulnerable than if this happens after one or more empowering experiences.

'Breadth' is about the variety of our experience. It is the kind of experience that allows for more creative approaches to problem-solving.

Once I heard someone on a recruitment panel say, "Some people talk about having 10 years' experience when what they really mean is that they have repeated 1 year of experience ten times." We could consider this to be a third kind of experience; whilst it doesn't increase the depth or breadth of our experience, it does have its advantages. Repetition leads to tasks becoming subconscious. In addition to increasing speed, it clears our conscious mind and facilitates multitasking.

53.6
In Summary

The quality of our relationships is affected by how much we are willing to trust and, by extension, to make ourselves vulnerable. This in turn depends on the kind and range of experiences that we pursue. In other words, it is about the extent to which, and the direction in which, we are willing to expand our comfort zones (§ 68 Tolerance and Comfort Zones).

Being consciously aware (§ 11 the Therapeutic Effects of Awareness) of the kind and range of relationship experience that we *want* will help us to develop both the depth and breadth of our understanding of relationships in general [If I want to know what works for me, I need to also be aware of what does not work for me]. In Unit 19 (Pathology and Therapeutics of Relationships), we look at some of the ways in which trust issues can disempower relationships.

Chapter 54

Secure and Insecure Relationships

54.1
Trust and Security

Trust and a sense of security go hand in hand. In § 44 (Locus of Control) we see that our locus of control is a function of (depends, in part, upon) our self-confidence (§ 40.4 Self-Confidence). In the context of relationships, security can be viewed from three different, but interrelated, perspectives.

1. How secure The Self or The Other feel *within* the relationship?
2. How secure The Self or The Other feel *about* the relationship?
3. How secure the Nexus is against external interference?

The first is about our answer to the question, "Does being in this relationship affect how secure or insecure I feel?"

The second is about our answer to the question, "How likely do I think it is for this relationship to continue to be mutually empowering?".

The Third is about our answer to the question, "How often do The Self or The Other feel that something has been able to rock the foundation of The Nexus?".

For the rest of this chapter, we look at some of the factors that can influence the relative security/vulnerability of the Nexus and the Pactum.

54.2
The Shell (Nexus Membrane)

Like a cell, a Nexus needs a shell (a membrane) to control the flow of Elements (Unit 10: The Composition of Relationships) in and out of the relationship. Ideally, this should be a semi-permeable membrane, facilitating the exchange of Elements that empower the Nexus, whilst being a barrier to disempowering Elements. From an affinitological perspective,

> **the membrane that keeps the relationship secure is Trust.**

The quality and efficiency of this protective shell, that is, the level of security of the Nexus to internal (§ 33 Atasinex Cluster) or external influence and interference (§ 60.2) depends on two key factors,

a) The level of dependence (§ 23.2 The Road to Interdependence) of either of The Self or The Other on the Nexus and

b) The Self and/or The Other's locus of control (§ 44).

Table 7 shows how LoC and Dependence affect the extent to which a Nexus is secure (not vulnerable). Note that, although, for the sake of simplicity, I have presented these in binary terms, it would be more useful to think of them as grayscales.

Table 7
The Relationship between Dependence,
Locus of Control and Nexus security

		Dependence	
		Dependent	Independent
Locus of Control	High	Q1: Secure	Q2: Secure
	Low	Q3: Insecure	Q4: Secure

Table 7 shows us that the Nexus only becomes vulnerable (think cracked shell) when an Identity within the Pactum (The Self or The Other) has an external locus of control AND that Identity perceives himself or herself to be dependent on the Nexus. Let's put this into context with the help of some examples and further explanations.

54.2.1
Quadrant 1 (Q1)

Consider an Employer-Employee Nexus. The Employee is financially and occupationally dependent upon The Employer. The Nexus is secure (robust) when both the Employee and the Employer Identities perceive themselves to have sufficient control over the relationship. In other words, both parties are confident in their understanding of what is required for this particular Relationship Framework (§ 92) to remain intact.

54.2.2
Quadrants 2 and 4

Only Independent Identities can form Interdependent relationships (§ 23.2 The Road to Interdependence). When I am in a relationship because I *want* to be and not because I *need* to be, I can feel in *ultimate* control.

There are levels of control. For example, I can feel (be in) control of the details of what happens within the relationship or I can feel that I can leave the relationship if it becomes incongruent with my Core Values (threatens my integrity). This; being able to leave the relationship without loss of integrity is what I mean by *ultimate* control. In other words, if I do not have control over much of what happens in the relationship, I can choose whether to accept that situation and remain within the relationship or leave. This is still a secure relationship; there are no cracks in the shell. External forces are less likely to disrupt the Nexus because the Nexus is held together by both Trust and Choice.

54.2.3
Quadrant 3

When choice is reduced, the security of the Nexus is compromised (cracks appear in the shell). This is when the integrity of the relationship becomes precarious and the Nexus becomes vulnerable to external influences. This happens when at least one of the Identities is dependent on the Nexus in at least one of the dimensions of human experience (§ 48-50) AND feels powerless to either control or adapt to or leave the relationship (§ 44.7 The Two Ways of Feeling in Control).

Note that the dependence or *need* can be self-imposed. For example, if I feel that I *should* be in a relationship because of a sense of responsibility that I am *bound by*, then I still *need* (no choice) to be in that relationship otherwise I will *lose* my sense of happiness/tranquillity/contentment or whatever I *need* to feel alive (vivacious).

SMERs do not have cracks in their shells; their Nexus membrane is intact. This renders them secure against internal and external interference (§ 60.3 Relationship Interference).

54.2.4
Affinitological Vulnerabilities

A relationship becomes vulnerable to interference (external or internal) when the Nexus makes The Self or The Other 'uncomfortable' in some way. such *feelings* include frustration, annoyance and disappointment. Note that external interference can only be disruptive to a Nexus if it leads to (or catalyses) internal disruption, for example, by inducing negative (Nexus disempowering) feelings in The Self or The Other.

Internal versus External Interference

External interference is one that is instigated, either by a change in the context or by what an Identity outside the Pactum does. Internal Interference consists of negative thoughts and feelings about the Nexus or The Pactum because of what happens within the Relationship Framework.

For relationships, the most destructive type of interference is one that causes doubt (§ 51.8.8).

Doubt (dearth of trust) is the greatest vulnerability in any relationship.

Chapter 55

Taxis (Attraction)

I have borrowed the term 'taxis' from physiology in order to,

a) help us explore the concept of interpersonal attraction through a biomedical metaphor and,

b) to highlight the similarities between the cells in our bodies and the units of society (Identities). This links into our discussions is § 36 (Levels of Organisation) and § 90 (Fractals).

In biomedical science, Taxis is defined as, "oriented movement of a motile organism in response to an external stimulus." In everyday language, this means attraction (pull towards) or repulsion (push away). However, as far as I am aware, our cells do not have a mechanism for repelling each other.

[Likewise, a muscle cannot push, it can only pull. When you are pushing something away with your hands, the muscles necessary to do that are pulling (contracting). How? By pulling on the other side of a lever, the fulcrum of which is a joint)].

[As I have argued elsewhere in this book, organisms are conscious and consciousness implies choice and choice implies options and options indicate that a decision needs to be made. In other words, choice and decisions are involved in taxis (the extent to which we are aware of that choice is a different matter). This connects this topic with decision-making (§ 72).]

Physiologically speaking, chemotaxis is when some cells in the body release chemicals that attract other cells. For example, there are cells that act as 'informant scouts' (mast cells) which roam around the body and if they spot trouble, such as damaged or misbehaving cells, they release chemicals (e.g., histamine) that signal (attract) immune cells to the trouble location. The result is inflammation. Chemotaxis occurs in many other situations too. Particularly relevant to our discussion is that chemical signals also attract sperm cells and guide them towards the egg.

For fertilisation to be initiated, the gametes must move close enough to each other to make contact. For affinitological gametes (§ 52.2) to meet, there needs to be **opportunity**, **attraction** and a **mechanism for connection**. Mechanism is any means of communication. Communication is a huge field that we touch upon elsewhere in this book (Unit 3: The Power of Language and Unit 16: Physiology of Relationships). In this section, our focus is on attraction.

55.1
Mechanisms of Attraction

In this section we build upon the ideas that we discussed in § 22 (Components of a Relationship) and Unit 10 (The Composition of Relationships). To act as a reminder, here are three figures from those sections.

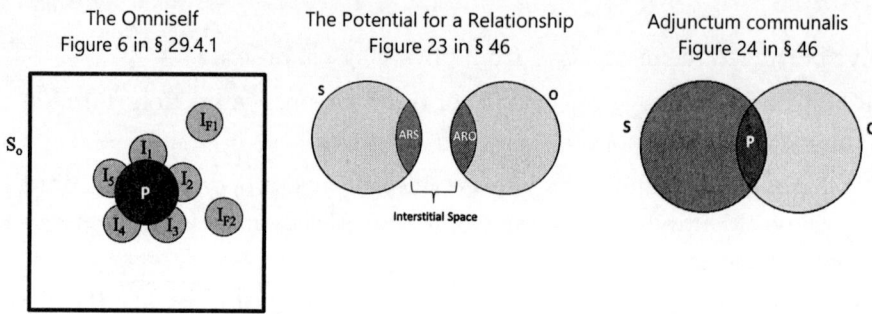

The Omniself	The Potential for a Relationship	Adjunctum communalis
Figure 6 in § 29.4.1	Figure 23 in § 46	Figure 24 in § 46

When we recognise at least one pair of common or complementary elements (§ 47) that can potentially lead to a meaningful connection, that becomes an opportunity for a transaction/interaction (§ 73 Transactional Analysis). This can only be realised through communication (Unit 16: §70-73 Physiology of Relationships). The question is, *"How* do we go about making the most of this opportunity?" Or in the words of Eric Berne, (§ 73 Transactional Analysis) "What do you say after you say hello?" [This is the title of one of his influential books]

55.2
Identity Differentiation

Figure 27 Stage 1
In the beginning there was The Self...

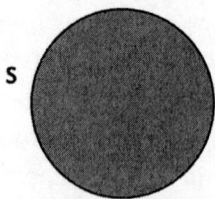

[Note that, here, we are only looking at The Self (a single Identity within an Omniself) with respect to a single impending relationship and we are ignoring all the myriad of other relationships that this Individual, consciously or unconsciously, is involved with.]

Figure 28 Stage 2

...And then, The Other appeared on the scene

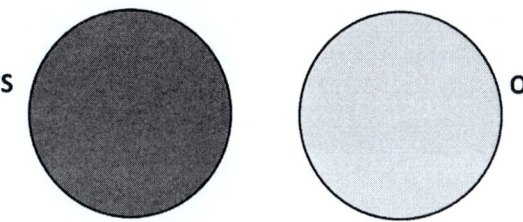

S   O

(But this is not the starting point)

[It is rare for chemical reactions to involve isolated atoms (free radicals). In the vast majority of cases, atoms are already 'involved' with other atoms; they are already a part of a molecule (or a lattice). Similarly, people connect with each other in the context of their existing relationships.]

From a chemical perspective, to understand the mechanism of formation of any bond between two atoms, we need to zoom in on each atom's outer electrons. From a biological point of view, it is like looking at cells and zooming down to the receptors on each cell's membrane. From an affinitological perspective, we are looking at two separate Identities and we need to zoom in on each Identity's sensitivities (§ 64.4 Values as Receptors).

At this stage, assuming that there are no presumptions or initial posturing [and, in today's overcomplicated world, this is a big assumption], each of these Identities are generic, undifferentiated; rather like stem cells. In its broadest sense, this is when the Omniself is open to any kind of relationship, that is, the creation of any kind of Identity and its consequent Relationship Framework (§ 92). In such a case, I am in a position to start a conversation with someone under circumstances where I can keep an open mind about the kind of relationship that may or may not ensue. For example, I may be sitting next to a stranger in an airport lounge and may strike up a conversation to pass the time. As the conversation develops, I may become interested in certain aspects of my interaction with her. I may begin to appreciate (value) her knowledge or demeanour or perspectives on life or I may find that we have common interests, experiences or values. By the end of our journey, my relationship with her may be as Friends, a Mentor, a Mentee, a Tennis Partner, a Pen-Pal, a Contact, a Business Partner, a Guide and so on [Capitalised because each of these become affinitological Identities with a Relationship Framework]. Each of these relationships require a different set of values. In other words, for me to be able to establish a relationship within each of these Relationship Frameworks (§ 92), I will need to be sensitive to different aspects of The Other (§ 64.4 Values as Receptors). Values determine what The Self pays attention to, and consequently notices, about The Other and vice versa. Each relationship, consisting of different Identities, is sensitive to different aspects of the environment, i.e., our values/receptors or sensitivities change to accommodate different relationships. This is how Identities proliferate within our psyche (§ 29.4 The Omniself).

55.3

Types of Attraction

Attraction may not be very easy to explain, but it is easy to recognise, especially in oneself. To recognise the kind of attraction we feel towards anyone, all we need to do is to start a sentence with, "I want" and finish the sentence with a phrase that includes The Other. For example, "I want to know more about him".

The type of interaction that we have with someone *at any given moment*, depends on the types of attraction (values) that are at work *at that particular moment*. The overall quality of a Nexus is determined by the combination (stacking) of these interactions.

The type of attraction is determined by *what* attracts, *why* it attracts and *how much* it attracts. Anything that lies along any of the dimensions of human experience (Unit 11) can attract; physical, financial, intellectual, etc.

There is a school of thought that says that everything we do is for one of two reasons, to gain pleasure or to avoid pain. The first sounds like attraction and the second sounds like repulsion, but it is not quite as simple as that. We could be attracted to power to avoid the pain of insecurity. And we might be attracted to someone who shows an interest in us to avoid the pain of loneliness. We can classify attraction into two groups; want and need.

> **Am I attracted to this potential relationship
> because of a *want* or a *need*?**

Where interpersonal relationships are concerned, need implies dependence and want implies interdependence (The Road to Interdependence). This is related to our discussion in § 23 (Two Types of Relationship).

55.3.1
Giving and Taking

Needing and wanting are not only about taking. Once our primal needs, along any of the dimensions of human experience (Unit 11), are satisfied, we begin to feel an innate drive to connect through contribution (giving). In other words, there comes a time in our life's journey when we begin to feel a *need* to give, not simply a *want* to give, or to give as a means of receiving. Indeed, one of the ways in which we can give is to receive graciously, that is, to acknowledge the pleasure that the giver derives from giving without feeling *obliged* to reciprocate.

Let me clarify why I think that, at some point, giving becomes a *need* and not something that we merely *want* to do or feel *obliged* to do. We have an innate need to reciprocate [give something back in return for something that someone gives us]. Such obligation is as compelling as it is pervasive. It is neither socially constructed nor is it limited to humans. In a 2021 paper in Nature, researchers Kettler, Schweinfurth and Taborsky report findings that show that rats also reciprocate. Here is some anecdotal evidence from my own personal experience.

> *A few years ago, I saw an African Grey parrot in a pet shop. Whilst all the other parrots there appeared to be relatively calm, this one was clinging to the edge of the cage and squawking and threatening anyone who got close. To me, it seemed to be brighter than the others. I bought it and brought it home* [I would have preferred to have released it into the wild, but I felt that it would be unsafe for it]. *I do not know what kind of traumatic experience it had been through, but it took weeks for it not to tremble at the sight of a human being and it took at least a couple of years for it to begin to trust us. Nevertheless, after it calmed down, I do not recall the parrot ever having failed to acknowledge us (or to express gratitude, in its own way) for something that we did for it, whether it be giving it food or water, cleaning its cage, taking it outside, giving it a bath or even simply giving it special attention.*

'Giving' thanks for something that someone has done is related to extrinsic motivation (§ 44 Locus of Control). And to the exchange theory of interpersonal relationships (§ 21.3 Exchange versus Flow). However, we also have altruistic needs, that is, **a *need* to give without expectation of return** (not even gratitude) such as the need to nurture, support (especially the vulnerable) and show appreciation for someone's mere being.

On a subconscious level, we are also aware that there is this thing called Society or Humanity "or something" that is giving us a lot of things. This is not about what individuals do for us (directly), it is about what everyone is doing for everyone; we also have a relationship (Nexus) with that 'everyone'. In much the same way that, in a relationship with one other person, we feel the need to reciprocate, we have a similar need to reciprocate in our relationship with 'society at large' [This is related to our discussion in § 32 (Extended Relationships: Communities and Crowds)]. This is what phrases such as, 'a sense of contribution' and 'wanting to give something back' are about. More importantly, if this need is not satisfied, we feel a sense of emptiness, a void, a sense that something missing in our lives. In the vast majority of our interactions, this giving and taking is not tangible; it is not a physical thing that is being given or taken. We could say that, in affinitology, giving is when Life Energy is transferred from The Self to The Other and taking is when this happens in the opposite direction.

[What I mean by Life Energy is not some obstruse or occult concept. It is something that I, originally, began to explain as part of this course, but decided to take it out and incorporate it into another book that deals with relationships from a Newtonian mechanics and thermodynamics perspective. If you are interested in that, keep an eye on introducingaffinitology.com]

Most interpersonal exchanges consist of a simultaneous give and take. The act of giving (when it is sincere) contains within it, the pleasure of giving. This pleasure is something that we 'receive' as part of the giving process. What we notice here is that, affinitologically speaking, 'give and take' is not like juggling. They are two sides of the same coin. Give and take is never exactly equal or completely one-sided; it lies somewhere along a dipole; a grayscale (§ 25.3 Polar Bond: Partial Sharing). Even in the case of slavery, the slave submits to the will of the master in exchange for a sense of security. Of course, since our focus in this course is on SMERs, this kind of relationship is beyond the scope of this book.

There are many types of giving. These include giving gifts, help, reassurance, acknowledgement, attention, support, time, and knowledge.

55.3.2
Intensity of Attraction

From a physics perspective, attraction is a force. Forces are vectors and vectors have both intensity (magnitude) and direction.

The intensity with which we [one of our Identities (§ 29.4 The Omniself)] feel inclined (desire) towards connecting [creating a Nexus] with another Identity depends on several factors including, the type of attraction (§ 55.3), the situation, our affective state (§ 51.2 Affect, Feelings and Emotions) and the availability of other options for satisfying our need or want. It involves the interplay between many factors including our motivation (§ 93.1), our belief level (§ 62.5 The Three Levels of Belief), our self-confidence (§ 40.4) and our perception of the possible consequences of acting on our sense of attraction [See also, § 40.3 (Self-Esteem) and § 72 (Decision-Making)].

Note that, since attraction is the stage *before* the instigation of a relationship, it is based on speculation and assumptions about what *could* happen (§ 33 The Atasinex Cluster). These imaginings are not about the other person, they are about what the *relationship* could mean to us. Also, this attraction may not necessarily be directed at a person. It could be an attraction towards connecting with a social group concept, such as a team, a club or other organisation (§ 32 Extended Relationships).

55.4
Domains of Attraction

Attraction can be along different domains such as financial, emotional, social, etc. (Unit 11: Dimensions of Human Experience). This means that the basis for our wanting to connect is different for different people. For example, I may want to connect with a person or a group for financial reasons (e.g., my bank manager), intellectual reasons (such as with an author), for security or for sexual reasons (§ 50.5 The Sexual Dimension).

[I am not going to single out emotional reasons because emotions have the first and last word in all our interpersonal relationships (§ 51.3.2 Feelings Trump Logic).]

55.4.1
Types and Domains of Attraction

We can determine the type of attraction that we have for a potential relationship by filling in the blank in the sentence, "I want to _____ him/her." Table 8 shows a few examples. Note that the examples given in the table are not mutually exclusive.

Table 8- Examples of different types of attraction

I want to … him/her	Domain	Primary Direction*
Be hugged by	Emotional	δ Take
Be in the presence of	Spiritual	δ Give/Take
Exchange ideas with	Intellectual	δ Give/Take
Exchange objects	Material	δ Give/Take
Give to	Material	δ Give
Help	Practical	δ Give
Hug	Emotional	δ Give/Take
Learn from	Intellectual	δ Take
Plan with	Intellectual	δ Give/Take
Sleep with	Sexual	δ Give/Take
Take from	Material	δ Take
Teach	Intellectual	δ Give
Touch/smell/hear/taste/ogle at	Sensual	δ Take

* δ Give (tends towards more giving than taking)

δ Take (tends towards more taking than giving)

δ Give/Take (the tendency can be either way)

Notice that the 'domains' correspond to the 'dimensions' that we explore in Unit 11 (§ 48-50 Dimensions of Human Experience). These are not mutually exclusive and one dimension may be a mediating factor for another. For example, the sexual attraction of one person to another may be mediated through the Physical and/or the Financial dimension (she is sexually attractive because of her physique or financial status).

We can finetune this classification by adding a qualifier to our question; "I want to _____ him/her, *because…*" And our answer would be a reflection of our active Identity's *values*.

55.4.2
Ways of Classifying Attraction

By Intention

We can think of the first column in Table 8 as an indication of 'intention'. This can be further narrowed down to the intention of The Self, The Other or The Nexus.

Let me clarify what I mean by the intention of The Nexus. In § 5.3 (The Jigsaw Puzzle), we explore the concept of the whole being more than the sum of its parts and in § 30.1 (The Nexus), I proposed that The Nexus is a separate entity that emerges through the interaction of two identities. This Third Entity is capable of doing things that neither of the Individuals that led to the emergence of the Nexus and The Pactum would have been able to do in the absence of the relationship. We can, therefore, also look at intention from the point of view of The Third Entity's intention. For example, if two people connect with the aim of creating a school, soon 'the school' begins to take on a life of its own and will have its own demands and agendas that go beyond what the individuals that led to its emergence even envisaged and, therefore, could not have intended.

By Values

The attraction between two people can be viewed from the perspective of their common values. Each Identity's values determine what we colloquially call 'who' that person is, that is, the characteristics of the Identities [situation-dependent values] or Individuals [Core Values or Principles] that intend to create a Nexus.

By the Situation

Two interconnected factors that can influence the depth and breadth of Taxis are **Time and place.** This *situation* (§ 14.3 Situation vs Circumstance) affects our focus; what we pay attention to, and therefore, what we see and how we perceive that which we see. It also affects how we interpret that which we perceive (§ 33 The Atasinex Cluster).

By Its Dynamics

Attraction can be planned or impulsive that is,

a) "Am I attracted to someone because of something that I was looking for [such as an employer, a business partner, a customer, a lender, a friend, a lover, etc.] or

b) I am attracted to something about The Other that I didn't know I was looking for?"

Chapter 56

Fertilisation, Differentiation and Gestation

56.1
Fertilisation (Pactum Formation)

Simply being present in the same environment and having Common and Complementary elements that can, in principle, form the basis of a relationship are not enough for fertilisation to be initiated. The 'gametes' (§ 52.2) must *interact* with each other, either physically, emotionally or intellectually.

[Actually, behaviour, emotion and cognition are part of the same system, we cannot affect one without affecting the other two, but I am not going to elaborate on that here].

Figure 29 Stage 3
The Self interacts with The Other

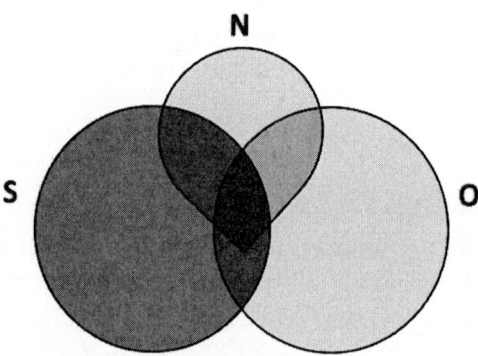

As soon as we *interact* with someone in any shape of form (a look, a smile, a message, a nod of the head, a piece of writing), The Third Entity, shown in figure 29 as N [for Nexus], emerges [Emergence is something out of nothing compare with entropy (§ 95)]. At this stage, at least one party has made some kind of impression on The Other.

When does a relationship begin?

There is a great deal of controversy over the question of when life begins; at conception or at birth or at some point in between. The same arguments can apply to affinitology. When does a relationship begin?

[I, personally, believe that life is already there, in the sperm and the egg. The question should be, "At which point do we care enough about what it is to give it special protection from deliberate interference in its natural progression through life?" Different cultures place different values on different animals. If we discover that an animal that we previously didn't pay much attention to is on the verge of extinction, then it suddenly becomes more valuable. At this point, it is not the individual life that we value, it is what it represents, otherwise we would have cared about it irrespective of how many of them there were. We can extend this argument to soldiers in a war. It is not the individual soldier that is important, it is what he represents, namely, King and Country. If in a particular culture, arranged marriages are on the point of extinction, should we take action to preserve such historical relics or, maybe, erect an icon in their memory? Anyway, I digress.]

In § 92.8 (Friendship), I recount the story of how Sir Peter Avery and I met. It began with me looking through a bookstore and finding his translation of the Rubaiyat of Omar Khayyam. Strictly, there is no 'interaction' yet because the word interaction implies reciprocity, that is, it is not an interaction unless it is two-way. I, for example, I say 'Hi' to someone and they do not hear me, have I interacted with that person? What if I say 'Hi' to someone and she ignores me? Have I interacted with her? I suspect that you, like me, would be less sure of your answer to the second question.

As you can see, this can get very complicated. Here, Eric Berne and his Transactional Analysis (TA) model (§ 73) can come to our rescue. Instead of interactions, we can talk about transactions. In TA, a transaction is one-way and is considered to have taken place when one person says or does something that the other person can potentially respond to. And this is how I am going to use the word 'transaction' in the context of Affinitology.

Now that we have cleared up that point, we can get back to the story of how I met Peter Avery. The initial transaction here, would be this: He wrote something that I could potentially respond to, if I were to receive the message. When I picked up his book and read it, I was moved, that is, I was not inclined to ignore it. I suggest that, from an affinitological point of view, this is the point at which a gamete is formed. Think of an egg and a sperm. In humans, having been formed, the egg is relatively passive. It sits there and waits for sperm to find it.

[Of course, you can argue that the system is not so passive (and that is why I said, 'relatively') because the egg releases chemotactic factors to attract the sperm. Hormones are also released to change the behaviour of the woman in ways that signal the readiness of the egg to be fertilised, but let's not go there.]

When someone writes something, that is a message sent. When someone reads it, the message is not necessarily received unless the recipient is changed by it in some way. The question is, "Is there a relationship if the sender of the message does not receive a response?"

For me to be moved by what Peter Avery had written, we had to have something in common; an interest in Omar Khayyam. At this point, I would argue, whilst the relationship is not yet fertilised (no two-way interaction), the gametes have been created; Common and Complementary Elements (§ 47) have been identified.

56.3
Differentiation and Gestation

After biological fertilisation, cells begin to proliferate and differentiate specialising into specific types of cells, such as skin cells, heart muscle cells or light sensitive cells in the eyes. After affinitological fertilisation, different Zones (sub-Identities) emerge. Figure 30 shows how, at this stage, seven new Zones are created.

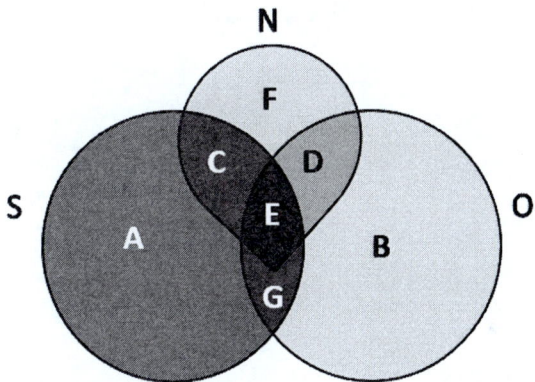

Figure 30 Stage 4
7 New 'Zones' are Created

Zones A to G are created out of a single interaction. If the relationship grows and develops, each of these zones will change both quantitatively (in their size or strength) and qualitatively (in what they can do or affect). Thinking about relationships in terms of these Zones helps us to clarify the purpose of each interaction within the relationship. Additionally, appreciating that it is possible to value people for who they are, without needing to know too much about them, allows us to avoid unnecessary complication.

By referring to these 'Zones' as 'sub-Identities', I am implying that, not only does The Nexus have a separate Identity (its own set of Values, characteristics and agendas), each Zone may also emerge to be, at least partially, independent, requiring us to treat it as a separate aspect of the relationship that has separate values, demands and agendas.

56.3.1
Gestation

In biology, gestation is the period during which an embryo develops within the safe confines of a mother's womb until it can survive without needing a live host. In affinitology, gestation is the period during which the relationship is not subject to influence by other relationships; internal or external. We discuss internal and external influences on relationships in § 58 (Post-Natal Development).

During affinitological gestation, each of the seven new Zones develops uniquely and at different rates, both qualitatively and quantitatively. The combination of these qualities and quantities defines the relationship and the extent to which it is a SMER (§ 2.1).

An important point here is that no two relationships are identical despite any Relationship Frameworks (§ 92) that we may define for them, assign to them or impose upon them.

The Independent Differentiated Self

Zone A represents those aspects of The Self that are independent of The Other or the Relationship (The Nexus). For example, if The Other is a work colleague Identity, Zone A represents those aspects of The Self that are *not* directly relevant to a 'work colleague' relationship, such as what I did for my holidays. I may choose to share that information for two reasons.

Figure 31 Zone A (The Independent Differentiated Self)

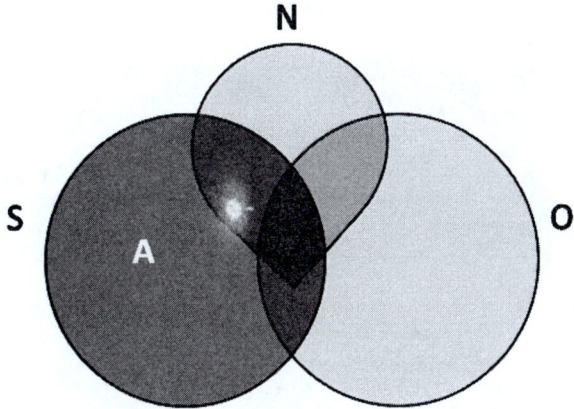

Often, people feel that they need to know more personal details about someone before they can be productive in a relationship (within a relationship framework) that does not depend on that extra information. Sometimes the information is given inadvertently (the person is not focused on the current nature of the relationship). At other times, it may be a deliberate invitation to a different kind of relationship. For example, I could be inviting one of the other Identities in The Other's Omniself to create a separate Nexus, such as a Friends Nexus (§ 92 Relationship Frameworks). It is also possible that I may be using this as a means of validating the authenticity of The Other; "Am I interacting with a True Identity or a Persona?" I call this 'Core Values Probing' (§ 58.1).

[A case could be made that the what-I-did-on-my-holidays situation will evoke a different Identity. Perhaps it would be more accurate to say that Zone A represents those aspects of the, in this case, Colleagues Identity that is independent of the relationship and the Other. Or perhaps we can do away with Zones A and B altogether arguing that, since each Identity is unique to the relationship, it is difficult to conceive of a situation where my Colleague-of-Jane Identity, emerging to serve the need of the relations, has any sense of Self that is independent of the relationship and the Other. Any such self would need to be independent of this particular Identity. You see, since this is a fledgeling field, there are many questions that still need to be answered.]

The Independent Differentiated Other

Zone B is Zone A's counterpart. It represents those aspects of The Other that are independent of The Self and the relationship (The Nexus).

Figure 32 Zone B (Independent Differentiated Other)

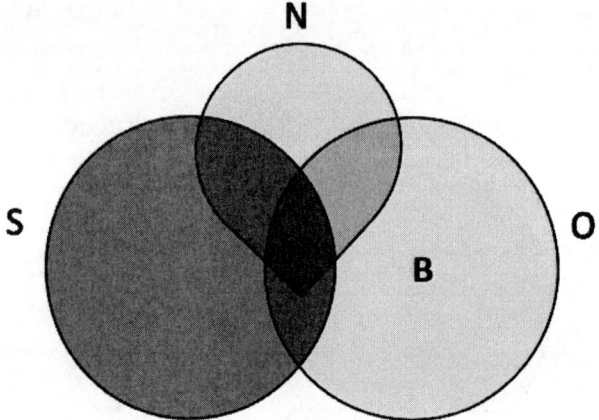

Peripersonal Zone

Zone C, Peripersonal Zone, represents those aspects of the relationship (The Nexus) that affect The Self but not The Other. For example, depending on my relationship with my wife, our Nexus *may* affect how I look at other women in ways that do not directly affect her (e.g., with restraint or relief).

Figure 33 Zone C (Peripersonal Zone)

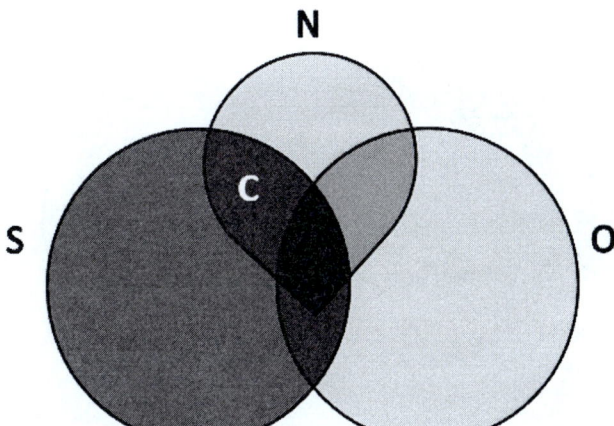

Here is another example. I cannot be in a Father-Child relationship with my son at *the same time* that he is at school (a time when I have agreed to delegate parental responsibility to the school), unless he decides to contact me directly from the school. My father Identity may be intact and may even be active (doing things that fathers do for their children), but this is me doing something *for him* and not me being in a relationship *with* him at that specific moment. When my Father Identity is active in his absence, then The Nexus is affecting me, but it is not affecting him *at that moment*.

Perialter Zone

Zone D, the Perialter Zone, represents those aspects of the Relationship that affect The Other but not The Self. It is the counterpart to Zone C.

Figure 34 Zone D (Perialter Zone)

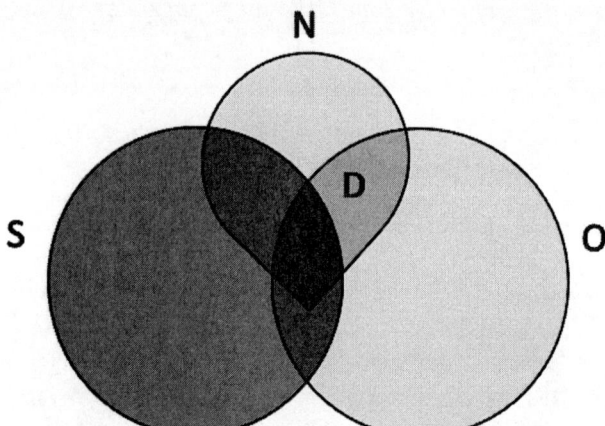

For example, a Spouses Nexus may affect how the Wife perceives other women in ways that do not affect the Husband directly, e.g., as a potential threat [In this example, the relationship is on shaky grounds (it is not a SMER yet) and suggests that there are multiple issues here; see Trust (§ 53), Self-Esteem and Self-Confidence (§ 40), locus of control (§ 44), Interdependence (§ 23.2)]. Note that reversing the words Wife and Husband in the above example would also be a valid example [Which reminds me of Mike Oldfield's 1982 hit, *Family Man*].

Interdependence Zone

Zone E, the Interdependence Zone, represents those Common Elements (§ 47) that affect, or are affected by, the relationship in some way (§ 56.4 Relationship Dissection: Cutting Across Zones). For example, my relationship with my wife affects both of us in terms of where we live and some of our activities and goals. The interdependence zone is also the region that contains the elements that bring the Identities together and maintain the relationship. That is, common goals, values, interests or complementary strengths and resources.

Figure 35 Zone E (Interdependence Zone)

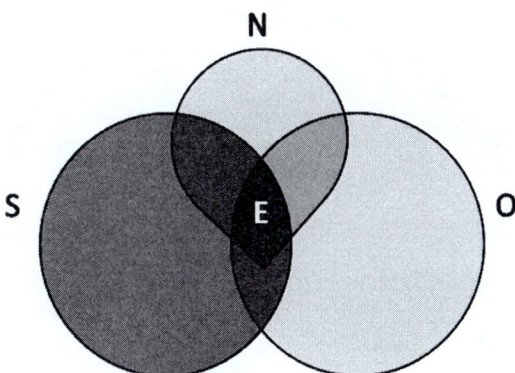

I have called region E the interdependent zone on the optimistic premise that relationships strive to become SMERs (§ 2.1). In non-SMER relationships, elements in region E can become means of exploitation. This can be one-way (dependent-independent) or two-way (dependent-dependent) see § 23.2 (The Road to Interdependence).

Parapersonal Zone

Zone F, Parapersonal Zone, represents those aspects of the relationship that do not directly influence the individuals who led to the emergence of the Nexus, but which, nevertheless, influence other individuals and other relationships.

Figure 36 Zone F (Parapersonal Zone)

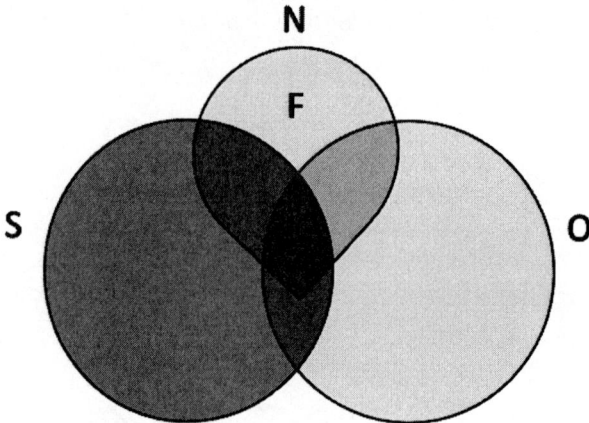

For example, sometimes my clients tell me how their lives have been disrupted by the thought that their ex-partner has married. For other examples, see section 58.8.1 (Three Types of Exo-Nexus).

Latent Shared Zone

Zone G, the 'Latent Shared Zone', represents that which The Self and The Other have in common (or that could be complementary to each other) but which do not affect the current Relationship. For example, a cardiologist and her patient may both be interested in entomology. I have called this region 'Latent' because it represents 'unrealised potential'.

Figure 37 Zone G (Latent Shared Zone)

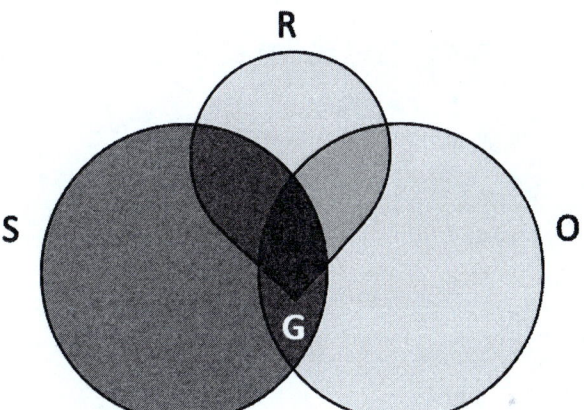

I cannot conceive of a situation where this mutual interest could be directly relevant to a Doctor-Patient Nexus. However, the same two individuals may instigate a different relationship [e.g., "Would you like to see my insect collection?"] based on this shared element *via separate Identities* (not 'doctor' or 'patient'). Note that this would be a different Pactum. To use the mobile home analogy (§ 22.4 The Bondle), this would be like two other members of the family living in the mobile homes connecting by sticking their heads out of the respective windows.

Independent Self

Zones can be combined to create new categories, as indicated below.

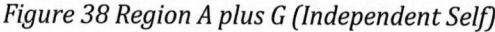

Figure 38 Region A plus G (Independent Self)

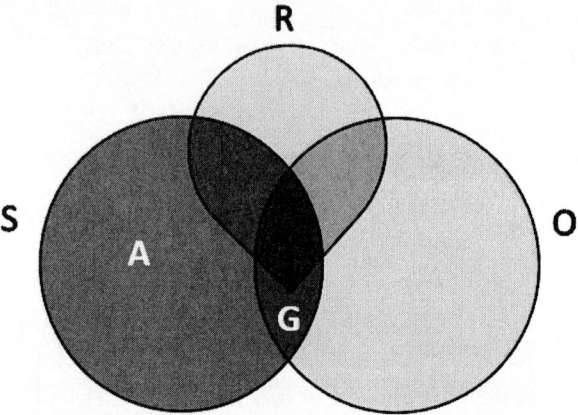

In Figure 38, Zones A and G [or A ∪ G if, like me, you like that sort of thing] have been categorised as the 'Independent Other', that is, those aspects of The Self that are not directly affected by his or her relationship with The Other.

Independent Other

This is depicted in Figure 39. It is the counterpart to the 'Independent Self'.

Figure 39 Region B plus G (Independent Other)

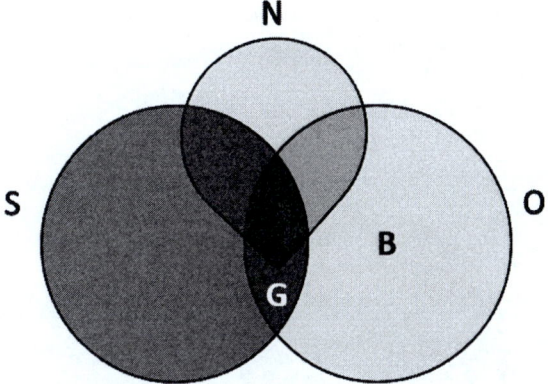

The Connected Self

Zones C and E together represent the 'Connected Self', that is, those aspects of The Self that either affect the Relationship or are affected by it. The practical significance of this is that any change in this region will have an impact (change the dynamics) of the relationship, either temporarily or long-term.

Figure 40 Region C plus E (The Connected Self)

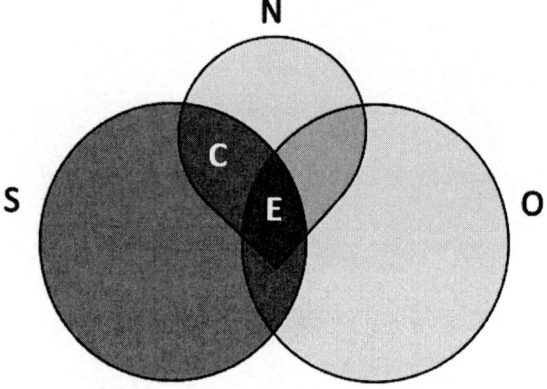

The Connected Other

Zones D plus E together make up The Connected Other. It is the counterpart to the Connected Self.

Figure 41 Region D plus E (The Connected Other)

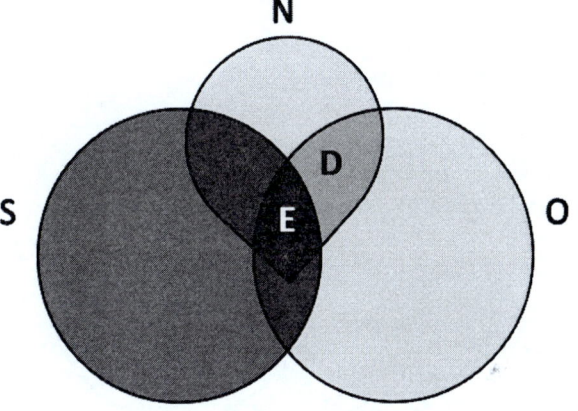

The Pericular Region

In combination, Zones A, B and G represent the "Pericular Region', that is, those aspects of The Self and The Other that are unaffected by, and do not affect, the Nexus.

[I know, I know, from a holistic perspective, everything affects everything else, but thinking that way here will not allow us to make practical use of these concepts; it is a question of degrees (§ 25.3 Polar Bond Figure 4). In statistics, we make a distinction between probability, significance and effect size. Here, I am talking about effect size. In other words, those changes in the Pericular Region that do not have any practical significance with regards to the relationship.]

Figure 42 Region A, B and G (The Pericular Region)

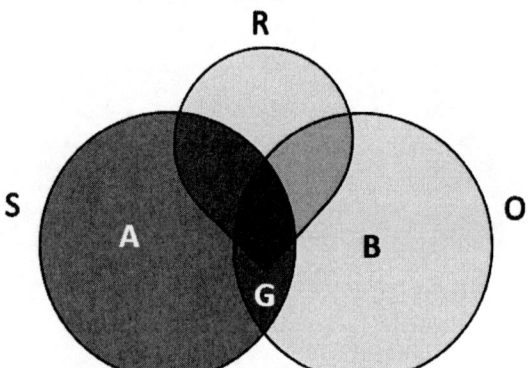

Imagine you are taking to your spouse about your relationship (and you are both students of affinitology) and she says something that you feel has nothing to do with your relationship and you want to bring her focus back onto the subject at hand. You could simply say, "That's pericular." She could,

a) agree with you and re-focus,

b) agree with you and say that her mind is preoccupied with other things and ask to have this conversation under different circumstances,

c) disagree with you and point out how what she is saying is related to your Spouses Nexus.

In all the above cases, the relationship will be empowered by the new quality of connection (communication) that is afforded by the specialist vocabulary. This is related to the anecdote in § 15 (The Power of Specialised Language).

The Interdependence Region

Zones C, D and E together represent the 'Interdependence Region', that is, those aspects of the relationship that affect, or are affected by, either or both Identities in some way.

Figure 43 Region C, D and E (The Interdependence Region)

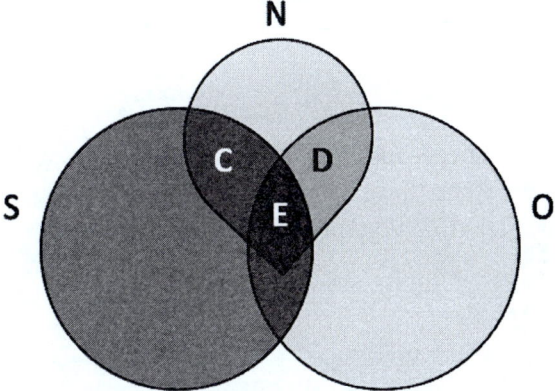

This is where The Nexus directly affects either The Self or The Other or both. The Interdependence Region is the counterpart to the Pericular Region. From a different perspective, it is also the union of Connected Other and the Connected Self regions.

56.4
Relationship Dissection (Cutting Across Zones)

---

dissect [dih-sekt, dahy-]

verb (used with object)

1   to cut apart (an animal body, plant, etc.) to examine the structure, relation of parts, or the like.

2   to examine minutely part by part; analyze:
    to dissect an idea.

[source: dictionary.com]

Although Venn diagrams are useful for giving us an overview of the relationship terrain, they have a significant drawback. As I am about to demonstrate, they lack directionality.

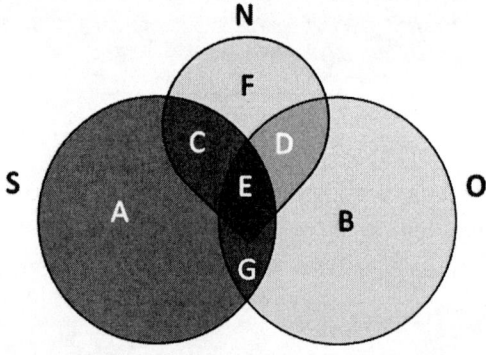

[This is copy of figure 30 which we discussed in § 56.3 (Differentiation and Gestation)]

Let's zoom in on Zone C for a moment. It represents those aspects of the relationship that affect The Self but not The Other. For example, my relationship with my son or daughter may motivate me to acquire more wealth than I might otherwise be inclined to do. That motivation is triggered by an interaction (or a memory of an interaction) between myself (my Omniself) and my son or daughter's Omniself. That interaction will have involved my Father Identity, represented in the diagram by the circle S.

Actually, a Father Identity was present in me before my children were born. It manifested itself as a protective feeling towards all children. However, after the emergence of the Nexus, N, between my Father Identity and my son's Son Identity (circle O), part of my Father Identity moved from Zone A (less motivated to acquire wealth) to Zone C (more motivated to acquire wealth). We can depict the direction of change as, $A \rightarrow C$. By definition, $C \rightarrow A$ is not possible because 'A' represents those aspects of The Self that is *not affected* by the nexus.

We can perform dissections along the borders between each of the Zones to help us better understand the processes that are operating across each of the boundaries and the effects of these processes on the relationship.

Let's take a closer look at the boundary between zones E and G. Both Zones are part of *adjunctum communalis* (§ 46). Zone G represents those aspects of The Self and The Other that can *potentially* form bonds based on common or complementary elements. Zone E represents those Common and Complementary Elements (§ 47) within each Identity that *actually* take part in creating and maintaining the Nexus. When each of the potentials in Zone G is *realised*, a common or complementary element becomes part of the relationship (strengthening that relationship in the process), that element moves from Zone G (potential) to Zone E (actual).

Imagine a situation where an employer mentions to her assistant that her family is expecting visitors from a landlocked area and they have expressed an interest in experiencing water sports. Her assistant tells her that one of the men who is contracted to oversee the IT systems is an avid water sports enthusiast. The employer approaches the IT man and explains the situation. He agrees to make the necessary arrangements for the guests to experience diving and water skiing. Following a successful experience, the employer may decide that such experiences can be arranged for employees for team-building and boosting morale.

In the above scenario, there was a hidden potential in the 'Employer-Contractor' Nexus in Zone G. Once the potential was discovered, and a connection made through that Complementary Element [I need someone who knows about water sports / I am someone who knows about water sports], then the connection (Employer-Contractor Nexus) between The Self and The Other was empowered because a potential from Zone G became actualized and moved into Zone E.

[Since this happened spontaneously, from a biological perspective, it is like diffusion. Or perhaps 'osmosis' would be more accurate since the transfer of the potentially bonding elements (in this case, I need-I have) was mediated through something that we can conceive of as being similar to a semi-permeable membrane; the assistant.]

Dissection would need to involve making a deliberate incision across Zones E and G to see what happens below the surface. The 'scalpel' that would allow us to do this would be a combination of attention, curiosity, research and sensory acuity, ultimately, leading to awareness (§ 35.11.2 Subconscious and Unconscious). If this backstory were to remain unknown, then the *process* through which the Employer-Contractor Nexus was empowered would not have been noticed.

Having applied our metaphorical scalpel to analysing the situation, we can similarly dissect across the other boundaries within a Pactum.

56.5
Premature Birth

Unfortunately, many (probably most) relationships (especially romantic ones) do not complete the required gestation period before being exposed to external influences (other relationships). Sometimes, this is because The Self or The Other actively seek the interference (advice, presence, evaluation, intervention) of others. At other times, the interference happens spontaneously or unintentionally and at other times, others interfere deliberately. In certain societies, the last type of interference is culturally rooted. [This reminds me of the movie, My Big Fat Greek Wedding].

When the seven new zones are not sufficiently developed, it is more vulnerable to outside interference. That is, when The Self and The Other have not had enough opportunity to appraise each other so as to move enough elements from Zone G into Zone E to create the trust (§ 53 Trust) and stability (§ 35.5 Homeostasis) required to create a SMER (§ 2.1), the Nexus remains fragile.

56.6
Chapter 56 Summary

With the simplest of interpersonal interactions, a complex web of potential is created. We can categorise the effects of the interaction and the consequent relationship into seven Zones. This categorisation helps us to focus on different aspects of the relationship in the same way that having names for different parts of the body [e.g., head, shoulders, knees and toes] empowers us to communicate in ways that would make it unduly difficult in the absence of such labels.

A Venn diagram highlights the significance of The Third Entity (The Nexus) in ways that simply talking about it does not. It gives us an image through which we can probe for answers to questions such as,

> **"How is my relationship with my partner affecting him in ways that it is not affecting me?"**

This image also helps us not to confuse one type of relationship with another, simply because the Individuals (§ 29.4 Omniself) that embody the interacting Identities are the same (§ 39.4 SRC Embody Elitism and Competition). We caught a glimpse of this in the doctor-patient-entomology example earlier (Figure 37). As we progress through this course, the significance of these distinctions will become more apparent.

Chapter 57

Organ Systems

In § 36 (Levels of Organisation) we looked at organisms from the point of view of their hierarchical structure with 'organ systems' being the level before complete 'organism'. In this chapter, we explore the extent to which we might be able to find parallels between human organ systems as they might pertain to relationships.

57.1

Digestion and Respiration

Digestion

What is the equivalent to the digestive system for relationships? The purpose of digestion is to process food (a substance that, in its unprocessed state, is unusable by our cells) into glucose, minerals, amino acids, fatty acids and other usable sources of energy and structural materials. It also has the equally important function of ensuring that unwanted or potentially dangerous substances do not enter the body.

To find an equivalent to digestion for interpersonal relationships, we need to ask, "What are the equivalents to that-which-can-be-converted-into energy and structural materials that are needed for a Nexus (§ 30.1), to be created and maintained?" and "What mechanisms are potentially available to prevent disempowering 'elements' from disrupting the Nexus?"

We explore the 'structural materials' needed to build a relationship; Common and Complementary Elements, in § 47. I propose that for interpersonal relationships, motivation (§ 93.1) is the equivalent to energy and any transaction (§ 73) that results in motivation to connect or maintain a relationship is the equivalent to glucose. The direction of motivation (Unit 23: Mechanics of Relationships) is determined by attention. There are two sources of attention: internal (memories) and external (communication).

If a motivating transaction is the equivalent to glucose and Common and Complementary Elements are the structural materials needed to build relationships then we can say that,

> **Affinitological digestion is the sum of all the processes through which Common and Complementary Elements are converted into motivation for the maintenance and further empowerment of the relationship.**

We can extend this analogy and say that 'motivating transactions' can be converted into memories and stored for use in the absence of direct transactions (just as glucose is converted into glycogen and fat).

It is noteworthy that normal digestion is not an entirely physiological process; it is psychophysiological. It does not begin with ingestion; it begins with the recognition of food. Try this exercise to see what I mean.

Exercise 22 Expectation is the Beginning of Digestion

Imagine you're in a restaurant and someone has just brought you a dish with your favourite food on it. You don't have to dwell on that image for long before your body responds by secreting saliva into your mouth.

Can you feel it? If not, *do* the exercise, don't just read about it.

The above exercise highlights an important aspect of the way our bodies (and, I believe, living systems in general) operate:

> **Inanimate objects *react* to changes in their environment whereas living systems *anticipate* changes.**

[Although the nature and extent of the anticipation varies from organism to organism.]

This is why cars with manual transmission tend to be more fuel efficient than their automatic counterparts. An automatic transmission car cannot anticipate what the driver is going to do, so it only changes gear when there's a strain on the engine whereas with manual cars the driver knows when he's about to accelerate or decelerate and will change gear before there is too much strain on the engine. This is also why our expectations, which are determined by our assumptions, have a huge impact on every aspect of our lives (§ 33 The Atasinex Cluster). This includes what we expect of others and what we expect them to expect of us; all of which, of course, strongly influence the quality of our relationships.

Exercise 22 also highlights what I said about the nature of journeys (§ 6-11 The Journey); the journey does not begin when we get into the car; the journey begins with the *decision* to go somewhere. The journey of creating and maintaining a relationship begins with the decision to do so (§ 62 and § 72).

The next step is to supply the right nutrients; attention (§ 33.3 Attention and § 93.1 Motivation and Motivational Energy) and communication (§ 70-73 Physiology of Relationships), to allow the Nexus (§ 35.1 Embryology of Relationships) to emerge (§ 95 Entropy) and to develop. Whatever the sources of these nutrients are, they need to be converted into a form that can be used by the Nexus and this, in turn, depends on the nature of the Identities (The Self and the Other) that instigate that particular Relationship Framework (§ 92) and that particular Pactum. Different Pacta, just like different organisms, have different nutritional needs, but they all need the equivalent to glucose [For the pedantic amongst us, I am ignoring anaerobic respiration].

Respiration

Respiration (not to be confused with breathing) is the process through which we combine glucose and oxygen to produce all the other types of energy (heat, movement, sound) that we need to sustain all of our physiological needs. I propose that we think of the equivalent of oxygen for relationships as being 'intention'. The combination (interplay) of attention and intention give us 'desire'. In other words,

---

**attention and intention
are the two sources of the energy that fuel relationships.**

Attention and Intention

In summary, the purpose of the digestive system is to absorb the material resources that we need to do whatever it is that we need energy to do. We can do all sorts of things with attention and intention. Make proteins, make conversation, make goods, make love, make sense; make it happen.

It is important to note, however, that for every type of relationship, there is an optimal range of attention and intention. Too much or too little of either of these can become pathological in the same way that too much or too little glucose (depending on where it is or what the body does with it) can lead to hyperglycaemia, hypoglycaemia, obesity or starvation. Similarly, too few or too much other nutrients (Common or Complementary Elements) can become disempowering to the Nexus (§ 35.5 Homeostasis).

The amount of nutrients that reach the body through the digestive system depends on many idiosyncratic mechanisms involved in intake, absorption, metabolism and excretion. Some people can eat a lot but, because they do not absorb or metabolise as much, remain thin whereas others have a more efficient system for absorbing glucose and storing fat and, as such, gain weight more easily. The same applies to the attention, intention and Complementary and Common Elements for relationships. In other words, for each Nexus, the processes that determine the final amount of nutrients that it uses are different, even if the same amount is available to begin with.

57.2
Endocrine and Nervous Systems

What are the equivalents to the human endocrine and nervous systems for relationships? The endocrine and the nervous systems are complementary to each other in that they are both communication systems. The difference is that the endocrine system is slower and more generalised whilst the nervous system is faster and more specific.

Imagine an organism being like a military base. Giving a direct command to a soldier to do something is the equivalent of what the nervous system does; it is direct, specific and fast. Issuing a red alert, on the other hand, is what the endocrine system does. When a hormone is released into the bloodstream, it travels to different parts of the body and each of the cells respond to that message in the specific ways in which they have been 'trained' or 'programmed' (designed or habituated) to respond [I know, we can design to create habits, but here, I mean hardwired. Again, there is a problem here because habits are also, kind of, hardwired, but not genetically. I think I will leave this discussion for another time and place]. For example, in response to adrenaline, blood vessels in our skin contract (our skin becomes colder and paler) whilst the blood vessels in our biceps dilate [we want to punch something].

Another way of looking at it is to say that hormones change our state or mood and nerves communicate specific actions that we need to take. Affinitologically, we can think of the kind of communication that changes the *quality* (mood) of a relationship as being akin to the hormonal type of communication and the kind of communication that changes the *dynamics* of a relationship (albeit temporarily or minutely) as being a neural type of communication.

Examples of hormonal types of communication may be statements such as, "I love you" (especially for the first time) or "I am not happy with this contract" or "I don't think this relationship is working". These change the 'state' of the relationship (§ 51.5.1 Feelings and States).

Examples of a neural type of communication may be statements that have an immediate effect on the dynamics of a relationship such as, "Please make yourself comfortable" or "Sit your ass down". These two examples also highlight the close relationship between the endocrine and the nervous systems. Although, superficially, both of these commands are asking for the same behaviour, depending on the kind of relationship and one's cultural background, they can, in addition to short-term dynamics, cause different changes in the longer-term quality of a relationship [perception of 'she wants me to sit down' versus 'she does not respect me'].

Since these seemingly small distinctions can make a huge difference to the quality of our relationships, let me give you an example using the analogy of our physiology to show you how the interrelationship between our hormonal and nervous systems can affect our wellbeing.

Asthma is not a disease. Asthma is a word that describes the symptoms of a range of possible diseases [we could have, more informatively, called it a 'breathing disorder']. There is a type of asthma called stress-induced asthma. As the term implies, when a person becomes stressed, they become short of breath. This is somewhat paradoxical.

When we think of stress, we think of the fight and flight response and adrenaline is the 'red alert' signal for that. To prepare us for fight or flight, adrenaline diverts energy into our muscles, away from our digestive system (we forget about hunger) and away from our frontal lobe (we start to act on instinct instead of thinking things through). During stress, our heart beats faster (to capture more of that oxygen and send it through to the tissues that need it). We need more energy and for that we need more oxygen and, to get more of that, the muscles in our airways dilate (our lung function improves). This is where it becomes paradoxical for stress-induced asthma. Our normal response to stress is for our lung function to improve. However, in Stress-induced asthma, the opposite happens.

Salbutamol is a drug that is given to people who are at risk of getting asthma attacks. It mimics adrenaline so that, when it is inhaled, cells in the airways react as if a 'red alert' has been issued; the airway muscles dilate and breathing becomes easier. However, our body is much more coordinated than we sometimes give it credit for. Imagine you're a soldier calmly wandering around the barracks and you suddenly see a group of soldiers running towards battle stations. You have not heard a red alert siren, nevertheless you won't ignore what your eyes see, so you take up your assigned position, just in case. Another soldier sees you running towards your battle station and does the same. Soon, everyone's at battle stations waiting for their orders. Similarly, when salbutamol causes airways to dilate, the heart responds by pumping faster and the whole body starts going into stress mode. Now, if your asthma happens to be stress-induced, guess what happens.

Let's see how this would translate if we were to apply it to relationships. What we communicate can either have a transient effect on the status of our relationship (similar to neuronal communication) or it can alter the state of the relationship (similar to a hormonal effect). And, just as we saw in the case of stress-induced asthma, sometimes what we communicate can have paradoxical effects on the relationship.

57.3
Reproductive System

What is the equivalent to the human reproductive system for relationships? Reproduction is, in effect, the passing on of genetic information. Clearly it is not reproduction itself that is one of the seven signs of life, it is the *potential* to reproduce [otherwise an organism would only be deemed alive whilst it is reproducing ☺]. It is important to make a distinction between reproduction and cloning because, just as each individual is unique (including homozygous twins), each relationship is unique also, even if it has been reproduced (see below).

In § 62.4 (Beliefs as Affinitological Genes), I have argued that, the genetic information pertaining to relationships are beliefs and belief systems. There, I proposed that we think of beliefs as being equivalent to genes. Perhaps we can think of belief systems as being equivalent to chromosomes; chromosomes pack genes and belief systems chunk (group) beliefs.

In § 26.2.2 (Reproduction), I said that we can think of reproduction in relationships as their ability to be modelled, 'marriage' being an example.

> **As soon as we label a Relationship Framework, we provide a mechanism through which it can replicate.**

We explore various Relationship Frameworks in § 92.

If replication is the modelling of a Relationship Framework, what is the equivalent to its reproductive system? The way in which we instigate and maintain relationships is, to a great extent, culturally determined. And culture itself is a set of beliefs and belief systems. In other words, culture can be seen as being the provider of the mechanisms through which relationships can diversify and replicate (create new Relationship Frameworks).

57.4
Immune System

Immunology is the study of how organisms protect themselves from threats to their integrity. Integrity is "The state of being whole, entire, or undiminished." Affinitologically and psychologically, this would include honesty, including being true to oneself. Affinito-immunology is about how relationships protect themselves from threats to their inner workings.

From a physiological perspective, what we lump together as 'the immune system' is an interconnected network of different specialised cells which, in addition to dealing with mechanical injury (cuts and bruises) and microbial infection, also deal with misbehaving cells (such as cancerous cells). It is a highly intricate and sophisticated system. It is the equivalent to the military, the police force, the fire service, the ambulance service and the security and intelligence services combined.

So, what is the equivalent to the human immune system for relationships? To explore this question, we need to ask, "What happens to a Pactum when it becomes subject to interference from external or internal forces?" and "What could be the nature of such forces?"

External forces could be other individuals, other relationships or other environmental factors and internal forces can be conflict through misunderstandings or changes in the perspectives of the Identities involved. The effect of such forces on relationships depends on how equipped the relationship is to defend itself against any possible detrimental effects.

Like its physiological counterpart, relationships are also susceptible to autoimmune disorders. We explore the Immunology of Relationships in more detail in § 35.4 (Affinitoimmunology).

Unit 13
Paediatrics of Relationships

Image by Irina_kukuts from Pixabay.
Source: https://pixabay.com/photos/baby-toy-newborn-girl-childhood-5842506/

Chapter 58

Post-Natal Development

Rarely does the Pactum remain isolated for long. There comes a point in the development of any Pactum where other Nexuses begin to have the potential to influence the relationship. A Pactum's gestation period depends on where and how The Self and The Other meet.

The 'environment' of a Pactum can include objects, images, a person, movie characters on a screen or a concept, such as an opinion or a doctrine. The effect of any aspect of the environment on the Nexus depends on The Self and The Other's *relationship* with that phenomenon. More specifically, on how The Self or The Other *react* to it [cf. § 40.2 (Behaviourism versus Humanism)]. In other words, for any aspect of the environment to influence a Pactum, that phenomenon must be in some kind of relationship with The Self or The Other. We can relate this to our earlier metaphor of chemical reactions (§ 25 Relationships as Chemical Bonds). For an atom or molecule to influence another atom or molecule, it must *interact* with it in some way. This involves an initial collision (meeting) followed by a change in the configuration of outer electrons. This change in configuration may or may not lead to a change in molecular structure.

Affinitologically, this is equivalent to a change in the individual's active Identity which may or may not lead to a change in the structure of the Pactum depending on the kind of change. If the Identity changes completely, that is, if The Self or The Other is replaced by another Identity, then for that moment, the Pactum disengages and is replaced by another Pactum. For example, if Jack is having a romantic evening out with Jill and his business partner, Mark, walks in and they begin to interact, then at that point, Jack's Romantic Partner Identity gives way to his Business Partner Identity and the Romantic Partner Pactum is temporarily disbanded. The extent to which Jack and Jill can resume their Romantic Partner Pactum (relatively unaffected) after Mark leaves depends on Jack and Jill's reactions to the interruption.

It is also possible for the environment to change without replacing either of the Identities in the Pactum. In this case, the Pactum remains, but its quality changes. For example, if instead of Jack's business partner, an old flame walks into the restaurant then Jack's Romantic Partner Identity may remember the mistakes he made in that relationship and may become more attentive to Jill. In this case, the encounter will empower the Pactum. Alternatively, Jack may become distracted and less attentive to Jill in which case, the Pactum will be disempowered. Environmental influences on a Pactum can be along any of the Dimensions of Human Experience (Unit 11).

Sometimes external influences or relationships can become a defining feature of a relationship. For example, a Father-in-law relationship is defined through a Spouse relationship. Similarly, a Mediator or Referee only has relevance in the context of an existing or an impending relationship. Theoretically, a Mediator or Referee relationship emerges in response to a need or a demand and vanishes once it has served its purpose. In practice, however, they often leave a trace; "It was Jack who introduced us to each other". In our mind, we being introduced to each other is no longer simply a historical event; we create an Identity for Jack with whom we continue to have, at least, a conceptual relationship. Jack is now our 'matchmaker'. The practical consequence of this is the Jack is not simply a cause of something that happened but has a continuing (mental) presence as a Matchmaker Identity in the relationship. This presence may be strong or very weak depending on many factors, including whether the Omniself has any other relationships with Jack through its other Identities. Let me demonstrate.

> *Once, in a dispute between a husband and a wife, let's call them John and Mary, a mutual friend, Harry, supported John's point of view. Mary complained indignantly, "But Harry was my friend first."*

In Mary's mind, introducing Harry to John was not merely a historical event, it is an ongoing aspect of her relationship with both Harry and John, whereas Harry has moved on from that event and now considers himself to be an independent friend of John and of Mary. Therefore, in assessing the merits of each of their arguments, Harry is not influenced by the Identity of the person who is putting the argument forward and considers the argument on its own merits. Mary's expectation of Harry is, of course, irrational. It is a cognitive bias. I suggest that we call this the *Loyalty Bias* - see also § 9.3 (Loyalty) - and add it to our impressive list of irrational tendencies [look up 'list of cognitive biases'].

Like a child, a Pactum is initially very vulnerable to outside influences and needs to be nurtured through its early stages of development. This is when slight influences by significant and, sometimes, not so significant, others in the lives of The Self and The Other can have nurturing or disruptive effects on the trajectory of a relationship.

> **The longer its gestation period, the less vulnerable a Pactum will be.**

Imagine that you have just met someone and you are exploring possibilities. Knowing very little about this person, at this stage, you are more likely to be influenced by other people's opinions. The more you are able to get to know this person for yourself, without outside interference, the more likely you will be to trust your own judgement and the more stable (resistant or resilient to outside interference) the relationship can become.

[I was tempted to explain how the distinction between resistance and resilience is an important one and then to go on to explain the significance of such a distinction, but then decided to leave that discussion for another time and place. NB. This midnote is not as redundant as it appears (Unit 3: The Power of Language).]

I say other *people's* opinions because this is how we have tended to think about relationships up to now. However, in Affinitology, we are primarily concerned with Identities. It is our Identities that are interacting to form and maintain a relationship and not our physical bodies that house a multiplicity of Identities (§ 29.4 The Omniself). This is similar to the way in which chemists are primarily concerned with what happens on the surface of atoms (outer electrons) and molecular biologists are mainly concerned with what happens on the surface of cells (receptors).

For example, my Neighbour Identity may be in a relationship with my neighbour's Neighbour Identity. This would be a Neighbours Pactum. My Neighbour Identity is about the way in which I perceive my neighbour differently *because* we happen to dwell in relative proximity to each other. For example, I may trust the person more than I would someone who does not live close to me or I may expect certain behaviours that I may not expect from a non-neighbour or I may pay more attention to that person or place greater value on that person merely on the basis of where that person lives. Of course, such predispositions can facilitate the development of other types of Pacta (based on other Identities) such as friend, business partner, lover, travel companion and so on.

58.1
Core Values Probing

Sometimes, when we are in a particular relationship, such as a Colleagues relationship, we ask questions about a person's life that are unrelated to our Nexus, but which probe the Individual's other Identities, what we could call his Exo-Identities (Identities that are external to the Nexus, but a part of The Other's Omniself). Such probing may be direct, by asking the Other, or indirect, by asking other people about The Other. These are the kinds of question that can prompt a response (or feeling) such as, "It is none of your business". In most cases, however, we do not tend to resent such 'probing' because we recognise that same tendency in ourselves too. But why? Why do we want to know about other aspects of a person's life when, apparently, it has no bearing on the existing relationship (Nexus)? Our affinitological model provides a framework for understanding this.

As we have seen, the difference between a False Identity (§ 38 Personas) and a True Identity is that the latter is rooted in a set of Core Values or principles. Viewed in isolation, it is not possible to determine whether the Identity that we are dealing (interacting) with is a False or True Identity. We try to assess this by probing into the Omniself's other Identities. The common values exhibited by different Identities within an Omniself point to that Individual's Core Values. In this context, the seemingly irrelevant questions/intrusions begin to make sense. The intention is not to interfere (§ 60.2 Interference), but to a) understand and b) feel safe in the existing Nexus. In addition, such probing provides opportunities for establishing Multi-Nexus relationships (§ 58.3).

58.2
Good Vibrations

Colloquially, we sometimes talk about getting 'good vibes' or 'bad vibes' from other people. Despite what you might have thought, this idea of vibes or vibrations is not a mere metaphor. There is a physiological basis behind it. Our feelings are actual vibrations. Yes! Literally. For us to feel anything our body must react physiologically in some way. Specifically, there has to be some change in muscle tone somewhere in our body. This 'tone' is indeed a vibration. Let me demonstrate.

In physics, we learn that work is not done (energy is not converted) if there is no change in motion. This means that if you put a cup on top of a plank extended from a table, the force pushing up the plank is equal and opposite to the force that is pushing the cup down onto the plank. After this equilibrium is reached, the plank doesn't need to do any extra work to hold the cup in position (to resist gravity).

[Bear with me for a moment. You will see where I'm going with this and what all this has to do with interpersonal relationships very soon. Meanwhile, if you are one of those people for whom the very word 'physics' sends shivers down your spine, this is an opportunity for you to associate it with something more alluring.]

Let's imagine that we are holding the cup on the palm of our hand with our arm extended out. We are not able to hold that position for very long and, quite soon, we will begin to feel tired. Notice that, if we resist this tiredness, our arm will begin to shake (vibrate). Try it.

But isn't that contrary to the laws of physics? Your hand isn't moving. The cup isn't moving. Therefore, theoretically, there is no expenditure of energy and so, we shouldn't get tired. What's going on here? Tiredness is a feeling and I began this section by explaining that our feelings are actual vibrations. I then mentioned muscle tone before plunging into the laws of physics. Now we're ready to appreciate the connection here.

Even though my hand and the cup on it may appear to be as stationary as the extended plank, a significant difference is that I am able to **choose** whether to keep my hand there or not whereas the plank does not have that luxury. This choice is afforded us by the fact that our muscles are not in a static state. They are not either relaxed or contracted. They are constantly oscillating (vibrating) between a state of contraction and relaxation. The more frequently our nerves send signals ['action potentials' if you're interested in reading more about it] to the muscles, the more contracted the muscles become (higher muscle tone) and vice versa. Since our muscles are always vibrating, to a greater or lesser degree, and vibration is a consistent change of movement, it requires energy. In short, my arm uses energy to hold up a cup whereas a plank does not. The former is in *dynamic equilibrium* and the latter is in *static equilibrium*.

So, what does all this have to do with relationships? Here is the crux. Our relationships are in *dynamic equilibrium*. That means that they require expenditure of energy just to keep them stable. But that's just the tip of the iceberg. Dynamic equilibria resonate far beyond their own system.

[Before continuing, let me just explain that I happen to be one of those people who likes to delve into things more deeply than might be practically necessary for the immediate task at hand, but, sometimes, this can give us a more satisfying picture of existence. You could think of it like this; I am not doing it for practical reasons, I am doing it for spiritual reasons. Again, it is not as black and white as that (§ 25.3 Polar Bond: Partial Sharing)]

For a dynamic equilibrium **not** to affect **everything else in the universe**, it would have to be in an adiabatic system (a system that is so closed that no energy can move in or out of it). In reality, there is no such thing; it is just a theoretical construct (like the notion of an ideal gas). In the same way, our relationships, being in dynamic equilibrium, both affect, and are affected by, everything that's going on around them; especially by other relationships. Since I have a chemistry background, I'll use molecules as an analogy.

[Using ideas from chemistry as metaphors for relationships can be slightly disconcerting to some of you who could not connect well with chemistry at school. The upside, however, is that looking at these concepts from a perspective that interests you (relationships) could help you to connect with chemistry more than you may have done in the past. If you are averse to science, forget everything you think you know about it and just go with the flow for now. Hopefully, it will 'resonate' with you and, if it does, then you will have extended your repertoire of thinking strategies.]

A molecule is two or more atoms held together by bonds (connections) between pairs of atoms. Meet ethane

Figure 44
Structural Formula of Ethane

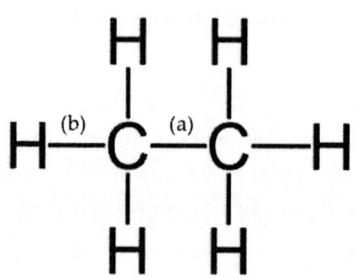

Ethane is a relatively harmless, albeit explosive, gas. It doesn't dissolve in water. If you breathe it in, you will just breathe it out again. It's a 'community' of eight atoms; two carbon atoms and six hydrogen atoms.

The relationship (the bond) between each pair of atoms affects all the other bonds in the molecule; just as your relationship with one of your friends will affect your relationship with all your other friends, to a lesser or greater extent. There's no escaping that. The stronger the bond, the greater the reverberating effect.

Since ethane is a simple, symmetrical, molecule, we will only see three main types of vibrations (or resonances). There is one type of vibration which has to do with the relationship between the two carbon atoms; C-C bond type marked (a). Another one has to do with the relationship between the hydrogen atoms and the carbon atoms; C-H bond type marked (b) six of them. Ethane's absorption spectrum (figure 45) shows that there is a third type of vibration too. The two types of vibrations that I just mentioned are where the atoms move backwords and forwards relative to each other, like the piston in a car's engine. But dangling atoms and groups of atoms can vibrate in a pendulum-like (bending) fashion too. That gives us the absorption that we see at around 1450 cm^{-1} range.

Figure 45 Infrared Spectrum of Ethane

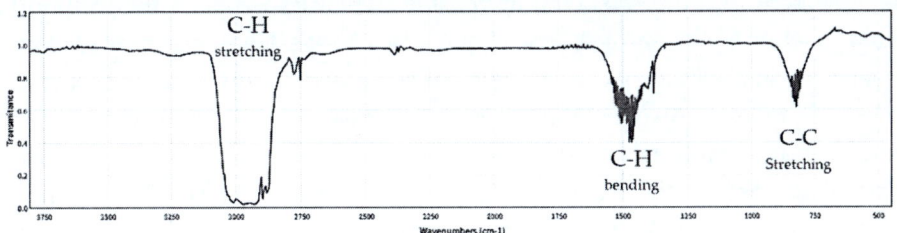

Source (without labels):
https://webbook.nist.gov/cgi/cbook.cgi?ID=C74840&Type=IR-SPEC&Index=1#IR-SPEC

Now, let's see what can happen to a relationship when we introduce another element; the mother-in-law, for example. Meet Ethanol

Figure 46
Structural Formula of Ethanol

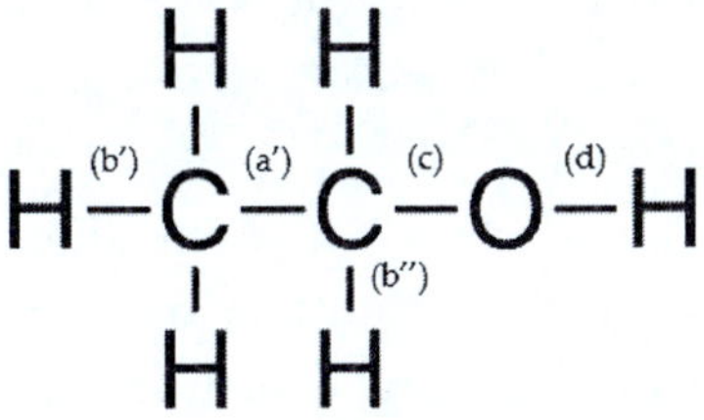

Ethanol is a liquid at room temperature and has rather well known, and often coveted, intoxicating effects on people. Unlike ethane, ethanol is very soluble in water. All we have done is introduced a single oxygen atom into our group. What a difference that made! Look how that atom affects the resonances between the other pairs of atoms (the ones not connected to the oxygen).

Figure 47 Infrared spectrum of Ethanol (Gas Phase)

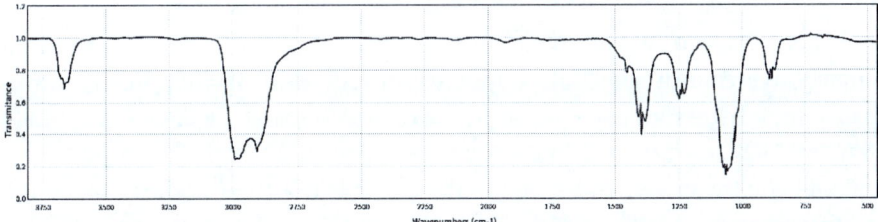

Although I find all this fascinating, you are not here for a chemistry lesson. All I want you to glean from this spectrum is that relationships are interdependent (they affect one another even at a distance). Notice how all the 'vibes' have changed with the introduction of just one extra element into the group. Similarly, the passing of one stranger through a community can have a profound impact on the whole community. What's more; molecules are infinitely simpler than people and 'no man is an island' as the saying goes, is a gross understatement. [This reminds me of the 1997 film, The Postman)]

Continuing with our chemical analogy, what we notice when we introduce a new element into the molecule is that the dynamics between the individual atoms, including the nature of each bond, also change. Comparing ethanol with ethane, by just looking at their chemical structures, one would expect to see two extra types of resonance frequency; one pertaining to the carbon-oxygen bond (c) and another for the oxygen-hydrogen bond (d). However, what actually happens is quite astounding. The nature (dynamics) of the C-C and C-H vibrations have changed; they are no longer (a) and (b), they are (a′), (b′) and (b″). Also, new types of vibrations have been introduced (an extra dip in the spectrum). I think the point has been made.

Beyond Analogy

I'm sure you've heard people say things like, "There's great 'chemistry' between those two people." But actually, whilst I have drawn some parallels between chemical bonds and human bonds, analogies have their limitations. Here, I want to point out a few of the fundamental differences between chemical bonds and human bonds [No, this is not a mere intellectual exercise. It helps us appreciate some of the important features of interpersonal relationships].

In chemistry, to form a bond, atoms or molecules must collide with each other. People don't usually form relationships by colliding with each other. However, meeting each other in some way is a prerequisite for instigating a relationship. Although it is possible for people to have a relationship with someone that they haven't met, such as an imaginary friend, in this course we will limit our discussion to relationships where people actually meet either physically, or through written or spoken communication.

A collision between two atoms or molecules is not enough for a bond to form. Similarly, we cannot say that people are in any kind of relationship simply because they have met [unless we start to go down the philosophical or holistic root and define the word relationship so broadly as to make it practically unusable. We won't go there.]

Unlike in chemistry, when two people meet, it is not their bodies that collide, it is their minds. More specifically, it's their Identities (§ 29.4 The Omniself). Chemical bonds don't negotiate their relationships. Once a chemical bond is formed, its quality [resonance frequency, dipole moment, and dissociation energy], does not spontaneously change over time. In human relationships, even in the absence of interference from others, the quality of our relationships changes from moment to moment and from situation to situation. This change can make Nexuses more or less stable or vulnerable in different circumstances (§ 14.3 Situation vs Circumstance).

Macromolecules

When we connect with someone, anyone, we are not simply connecting with just one person; we are in fact connecting with *a 'node' of a community*. In any one of our relationships, we are in a relationship with a person whose thoughts and behaviours are affected by all his other relationships. These relationships may not necessarily be with other people. They could be with his other Identities or places, objects, professions, other relationships and other self-related concepts that he identifies with. The more we appreciate this interconnectedness about ourselves and others, the more we will be able to develop satisfying and empowering relationships. One of the empowering and liberating aspects of such realisation is that we will be less inclined to judge ourselves or others. Many of the constructs, such as 'personality' and 'character' lose much of their (ecological) validity in the context of relationships.

Good Vibrations Summary

In summary, relationships:

- Are in dynamic equilibrium
- Do not take place within an isolated system
- Are multidimensional
- Can be very susceptible to changes in the environment [internal or external]

58.3
Multi-Nexus Relationships

My 'neighbour' [not friend, colleague or anything else *yet*] and I may meet at a gathering serendipitously (§ 52.4.1 Serendipity) and discover that we have a common interest in Amnesty International and may decide to become collaborators in such humanitarian campaigns (create a Collaborators Pactum) through our respective Collaborator Identities. In this case, my neighbour and I would now have two separate relationships with each other through two separate Nexuses, a Neighbours (N-N) Nexus and a Collaborators (C-C) Nexus. Theoretically, two *independent* Pacta can emerge from two pairs of Identities within two individuals. From this perspective, our Neighbours relationship need not have any impact at all on our Collaborators Pactum on an Amnesty International campaign. This is depicted in Figure 48. And, in theory, this is possible.

Figure 48 Two Individuals (Omniselves) forming two Pacta

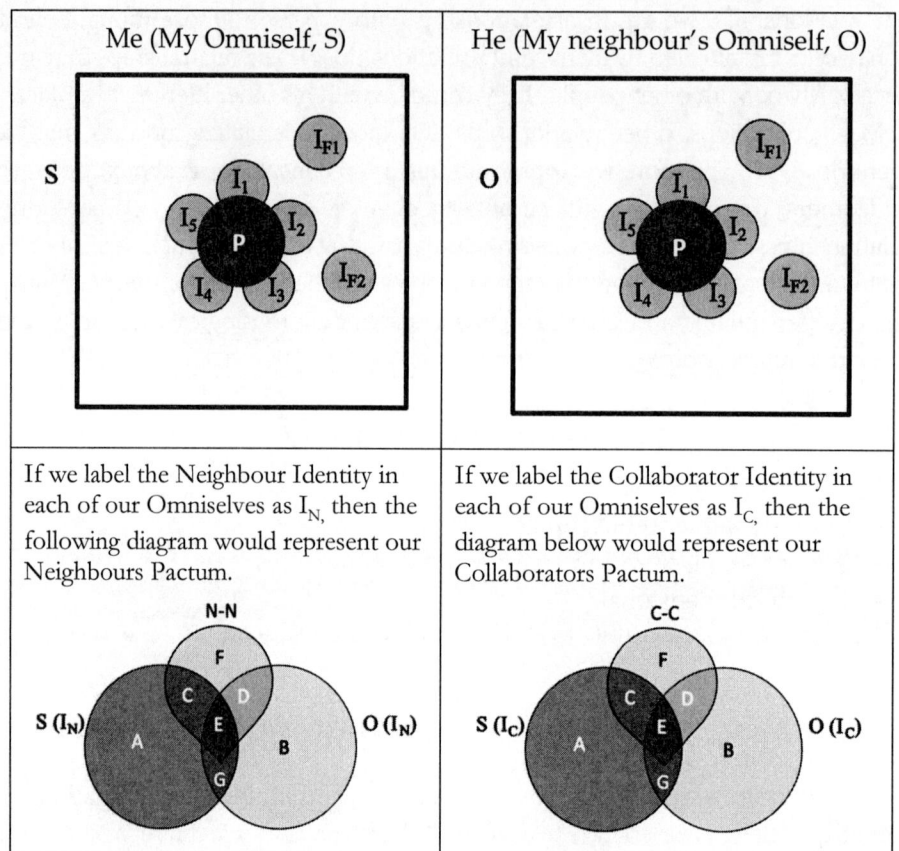

Note that when we are talking about the Neighbour Identity, we are not talking about the physical proximity of our respective dwellings. My neighbour 'situation' and my Neighbour 'Identity' are two separate things. When we talk about Identities, we are talking about values, attitudes, expectations and behaviours that emerge as a result of perceiving someone as a Neighbour. From a physical or geographical point of view, I cannot decide not to be a neighbour when I decide to become a collaborator, but I *can* put aside the notion that this person is *related* to me by virtue of my perception of him as *my* neighbour. Think of it as being similar to the difference between beer and being drunk. Beer (neighbour) is what it *is* and drunk (Neighbour Identity) is what it *does* to my perception (§ 33 Atasinex Cluster) and my behaviour.

58.3.1
Bilateral Influences

Earlier (§ 58 Post-Natal Development), I said that the more we are able to get to know someone (an Identity) for ourselves, without outside interference, the more likely we will be to trust our own judgement and the more stable (resistant or resilient to outside interference) the relationship can become. The above example of Neighbour and Collaborator Identities can help us to appreciate the point that the 'outside interference' is not necessarily from other Individuals. The interference can come from other Identities within the same Omniself. In the above example, my Neighbour Identity can interfere with the Collaborators Pactum through its preconceptions. Such interference can either be empowering or disempowering. We discuss interference in more detail in § 60.3 (Relationship Interference). For now, let's look at a graphic representation of this situation. Figure 49 shows two Individuals and their Core Values (Principles) forming two independent Pacta on the basis of each of their Neighbour and Collaborator Identities. C-C and N-N represent their respective Nexuses.

Figure 49 Two independent Pacta between two individuals (Omniselves)

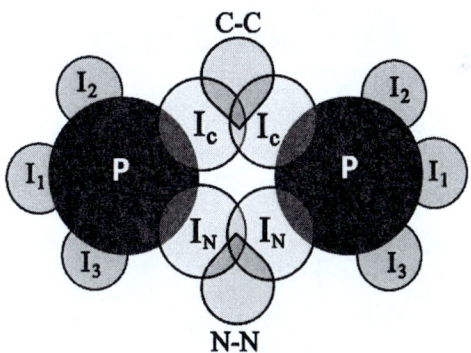

Let's assume that, ordinarily, I would complain to my neighbour about noise or rubbish being dumped in inappropriate places or my driveway being obstructed, but because I am now also in a C-C relationship with him, I decide not to complain [or complain when otherwise I might not]. In this case, our Collaborators Nexus is interfering with our Neighbours Nexus. This shows that, it is not only factors from outside of our Omniselves that can interfere with a relationship, other Nexuses resulting from different Identities within the same individuals can also influence or be influenced by a particular Nexus. In other words, interference occurs when a Nexus causes a change in our attitudes (§ 37.7.2) or behaviours towards another Nexus irrespective of whether the other relationship is with the same person (Omniself) or another person.

One possible depiction of intra-Individual interference is shown in Figure 50 where, P1 and P2 represent the Core Values (principles) of The Self (in the above example, me) and The Other (my neighbour) respectively.

Figure 50 Intra-individual (bilateral) Influences

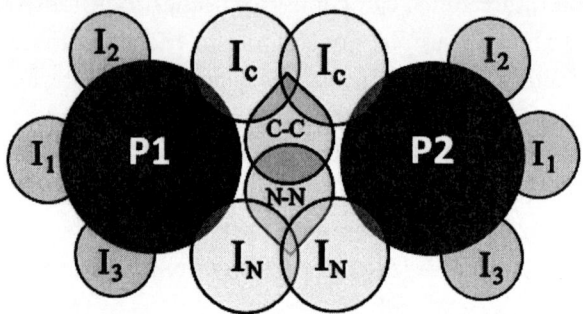

[Strictly speaking, the C-C- and N-N labels should be outside of the piriform shapes because they refer to the entire shape and not just the non-overlapping regions that the labels reside in.]

58.3.2
Trilateral Influences

Alternatively, the affected (or affecting) Nexus can be part of a Pactum involving another Individual. For example, my Father-Son relationship may affect my Neighbours Nexus. Depending on my son's age and my Father Identity's values, I may be more or less tolerant of my neighbour's behaviour. For instance, I may become more sensitive to my driveway being obstructed depending on the extent to which my son needs me to drive him to and from his extracurricular activities. This situation is depicted in Figure 51.

Figure 51 Inter-individual (Trilateral) Influences

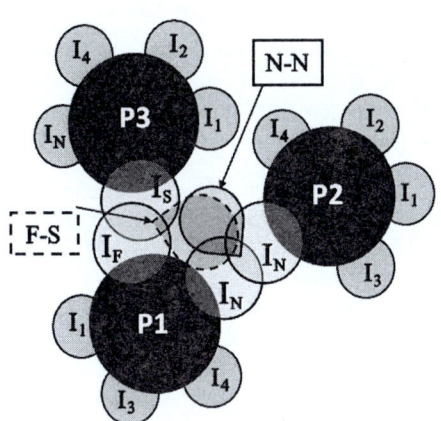

Key

P1: The Self's [my] Core Values (Principles)

P2: The Other's [my neighbour's] Principles

P1: The Third Party's [my son's] Principles

I_N: Neighbour Identity

I_F: Father Identity

I_S: Son Identity

N-N: Neighbours Nexus

F-S: Father-Son Nexus

58.4

Multi-Nexus Breakdown

My various relationships with my neighbour may include, for example, Collaborators, Fellow Commuters, Sports Partners or Local Activists Nexuses. Each of these separate Nexuses have their own place within the lives of the Omniselves and the nature of their interference with each other is not usually so much as to radically affect each Nexus. There is, however, a significant exception to this.

As we have seen, each of our 'real' Identities (not Personas) is rooted in our Core Values. If, in a Multi-Nexus relationship, one of 'The Self' Identities perceives there to be a conflict with her own Core Values (Principles), or in the Other's Core Values (§ 58.1 Core Values Probing), then this can affect every other Nexus between the Omniselves.

> *I know of two friends who started a business partnership together. Within the business context, one partner signed a contract with a client without informing The Other. That dissolved both their partnership AND their friendship because two core values of Trust and Openness had been violated.*

58.5
The Exo-Nexus

Now that we have seen what Identities and Nexuses can look like in context, in figure 52, I have cleared away the distracting parts of the diagrams to show you a clearer picture of the possible influences of another Nexus on a Pactum. I have called this other Nexus, an Exo-Nexus. We have seen that, in a Pactum, whether an Identity is The Self or The Other is simply a matter of choosing a point of reference. Similarly, whether a Nexus is a Nexus or an Exo-Nexus is also merely a matter of our point of reference. In the above examples, our point of reference has been the Neighbours (N-N) Nexus making the Collaborators (C-C) and the Father-Son (F-S) relationships Exo-Nexuses to N-N. In figure 52, the Exo-Nexus is indicated by the piriform area confined by the dashed line.

Figure 52 Post-Natal Environment and Influences

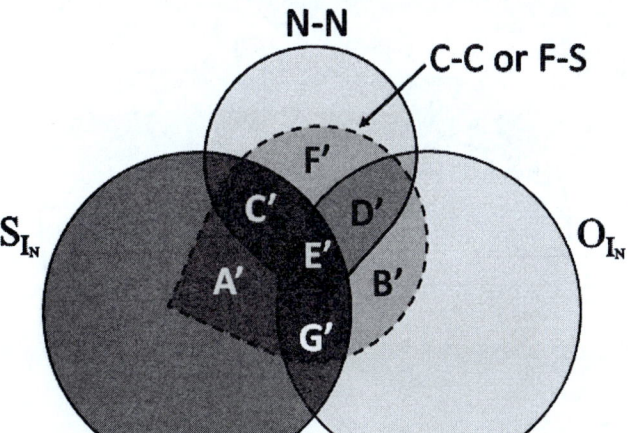

Figure 52 also shows that an Exo-Nexus can potentially impact any of Zones A-F in an existing Pactum (§ 56.3 Differentiation and Gestation).

58.5.1
Three Types of Exo-Nexus

Other relationships (Exo-Nexuses) can either affect or be affected by the Pactum. Figure 53 shows three types of Exo-Nexus. I have borrowed some terms used by chemists and have called them Ortho-Nexus (ON), Meta-Nexus (MN) and Para-Nexus (PN).

Figure 53 Post-Natal Environment and Influences

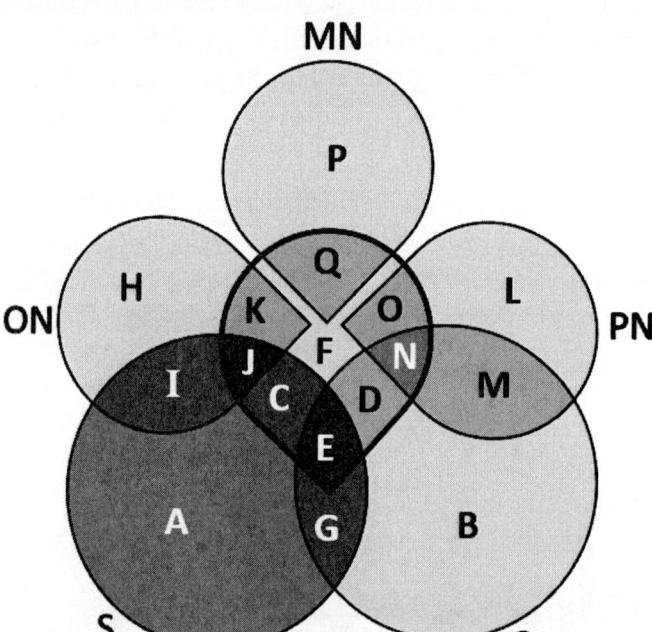

Here, we see that, whilst the original 7 Zones (A to G) are still there, ten potential new Zones (H to Q) can be created through the interaction of each of the three types of Exo-Nexus with the reference Nexus.

Let's say that Luke and Mary are husband and wife and circle S represents Mary's Spouse Identity [i.e., we are looking at the Pactum with Mary as our point of reference] and circle O represents Luke's Spouse Identity. At work, Mary has colleagues with whom she interacts. In figure 53, Mary's relationship [through her Colleagues Identity] with one of those colleagues, let's call her Stella, is shown as a separate Nexus, ON [the circle that would represent Stella's Colleague Identity is not shown].

Zone H represents those aspects of Mary and Stella's Colleagues relationship that have no bearing on Mary's Spouse Identity or Luke and Mary's Spouses Nexus and where Luke and Mary's Spouses Pactum has no influence on Stella's Colleague-of-Mary Identity, such as when Mary and Stella are talking to each other about the specifics of their work. If, however, Stella says to Mary, "I wish I had a husband like yours" and Mary responds by saying, "I guess I am a lucky girl" then, Mary is no longer responding to Stella through her Colleague(-of-Stella) Identity; she is responding to her through her Spouse Identity. At this point, Stella and Mary's Colleagues Nexus begins to impinge on Mary's Spouse Identity. If this interaction has no effect on Mary and Luke's Spouses Nexus, then the effect will be confined to Zone I, otherwise, its effects will also extend to Zone J. If we imagine similar scenarios with Luke and one of his colleagues, creating Nexus PN, then Zones L, M, N and O would be the counterparts to Zones H, I, J and K respectively.

Zones K, O and Q show areas where the relationship between S and O passively affect other relationships without either The Self or The Other being aware of them. An example may be if someone says to his girlfriend, "Why can't our relationship be more like Luke and Mary's?" Similarly, imagine that Teri and Judi are two friends who are acquainted with Mary and Luke. One day, Teri says to Judy, "I wish I had a man like Luke in my life." And Judy replies, "I didn't know you found that kind of man attractive. I have a cousin who reminds me of Luke, I will introduce you to him." Mary and Luke's relationship is not affected by this conversation, but Mary and Luke's relationship has had some effect on Teri and Judi's relationship (Nexus MN). This effect is represented by Zone Q.

Chapter 59

Affinito-adolescence

In this section, we discuss what is required for a connection to become stable. Interpersonal relationships are in a constant state of flux, preferably moving towards maturation. We can start a debate about the end point of maturation, but this is not the time and place for that.

> *This reminds me of a BBC Radio interview I heard back in the mid-nineties with an accomplished author who was a lady from native American descent* [Sadly, I don't remember the details]. *The interviewer said something like, "Your tribe must be very proud of your achievements" and the lady said, "They don't consider anyone under 50 to be mature enough to be taken seriously. They still treat me like a child" or something to that effect.*

In other words, we may have objective criteria for physical maturity, but other types of maturity are generally socially constructed. For example, I debated with myself whether to call this section Puberty or Adolescence. Puberty relates to measurable physiological changes. Adolescence is a sociocultural construct. Although adolescence is associated with puberty (insofar as the relationship between society and the child changes more rapidly and is more turbulent during that period), its focus is more on social behaviour and social responsibility, the outcome of which depends on the development of a robust sense of personal and social Identity and, of course, the successful integration of the 'self' (§ 6 Know Thyself). As you can see, in the end, I settled on 'Adolescence' because it reflects the messiness (slipperiness) of the real world of interpersonal relationships.

Stages of Relationship Development

After reviewing 55 articles dealing with small group development, in 1965, Bruce Tuckman proposed that groups go through four stages over time. These are,

1. Testing and dependence (Forming)
2. Intragroup conflict (Storming)
3. Development of group cohesion (Norming)
4. Functional role relatedness (Performing)

Forming

Fitting this model into what I have explicated here, Forming represents the fertilisation, gestation and the post-natal development stages. It can be summarised in the following exchange.

- "I think we can mean something to each other."
- "So do I."

Storming

Tuckman's 'Storming' stage is akin to what we have described here as 'adolescence' and is broadly summarised in the following exchange.

- "I don't like this."
- "And I don't like that."

This is a period of conflict. Sometimes, couples come to me and say that their relationship is on the rocks because of some conflict or other. I reassure them that, not only is this not unusual, it is a healthy part of the process of becoming closer. Or to put it another way, it is not an aberration, it is a *necessary* part of becoming a functioning team.

When growing up, we go through two main stages of 'Storming'. One is during the 'terrible twos' and the other is during adolescence. In the first instance, the toddler begins to develop a 'theory of mind' through which she realises that her perceptions and interpretations of reality are different from other people's. A conflict then arises between a child's need to be supported and her need to consolidate her own perspective of the world. Since her communication skills have not yet developed sufficiently for her to be able to articulate her feelings, wants and needs, these feelings manifest as a pattern of screaming, shouting, hitting and resisting followed by an intense need for emotional support.

The second stage happens during adolescence, when the conflict is not about asserting the right to independent action or interpretation. The adolescent child already knows that his actions are independent of the actions of the others (he can *choose* how to act) and that he can interpret events differently to others, what he wants is the opportunity to experiment with *consequences* within a 'sand-box' of a home environment. In other words, he is asserting his right to take risks and face the consequences knowing that he would be prevented from taking risks that are too dangerous. This is when we begin to experiment with, and create, multiple Identities within ourselves (§ 29.4 The Omniself). We take a closer look at conflict in relationships in § 47 (Conflicting Elements).

59.1.3
Norming

Once the conflicts (and potential conflicts) become apparent, the parties to the relationship, The Self and The Other, acknowledge the threats and challenges that their conflicts pose to their relationship *whilst at the same time acknowledging the opportunities that resolving such conflicts will bring*. This is summarised in the following exchange.

- "Let's set some ground rules."
- "I agree."

59.1.4
Performing

- "Hey, it looks like we can make it work."

The Conflict Cycle

We can think of these four stages of relationship development, not as a line to a destination, but more like a cycle, so that, once an organisation, in our case, a Pactum, reaches a 'performing' stage, the relationship takes on a new form and can start the cycle all over again. I have depicted the first cycle in Figure 54. I call it The Conflict Cycle.

Figure 54 The Conflict Cycle

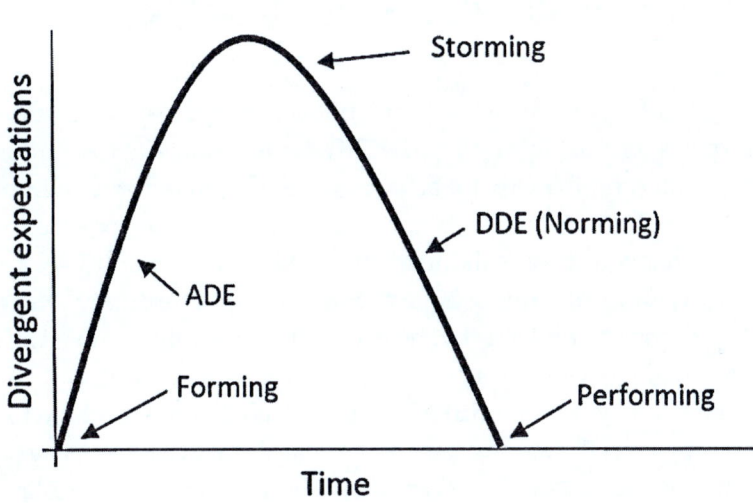

ADE: Ascending divergent expectations (increasing sources of conflict)
DDE: Descending divergent expectations (decreasing conflict and increasing conflict resolution)

What I have called 'divergent expectations' include conflicting expectations, unfulfilled expectations, and misunderstandings. The last stem from vague, unclear, ambiguous or unexpressed (assumed) expectations (§ 33 Atasinex Cluster).

'Performing' sounds like the final stage of building a Nexus or team, it is reminiscent of fairy tales where the boy and girl eventually marry and 'live happily ever after'. However, relationships are in a constant state of adaptation and re-adaptation and every end stage (Performing) is the beginning of a new, Forming [a new, adapted, relationship] stage. I propose, therefore, that we call this The Conflict Ripple [with the emphasis being on the damping effect].

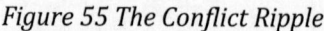

Figure 55 The Conflict Ripple

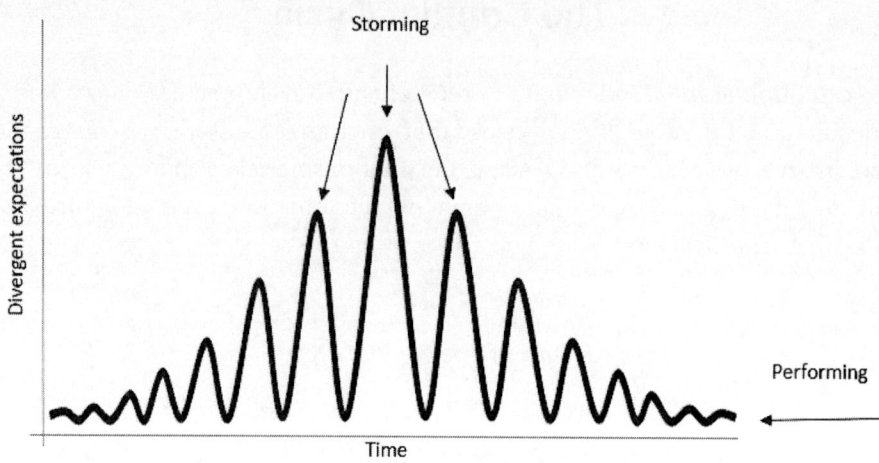

The shape of the 'ripple' reflects a trend. In the forming stage, we tend to have limited expectations. At this point, The Other is little more than a curiosity. As we begin to interpret the Other's behaviours, we begin to form an impression of The Other. This impression becomes the basis for our expectations. For example, if I happen to be walking along a beach in Baku and I see someone walking away from me, this would not be out of the ordinary. Now, if the person turns around and I see that he is wearing something with a Union Jack on it, this situation would arouse an expectation in me that he will be able to speak English. I may become curious and this emotion may lead me to seek to connect through this Common Element (§ 47 Common and Complementary Elements). This is a minor expectation [in this particular situation] and if it is not fulfilled, I will not have invested enough in the relationship for it to lead to significant conflict. The more we get to know each other, the more invested we tend to become in a relationship and the more severe the consequences of divergent expectations will become. This means that our reactions to conflicting situations will be more heated (emotional), as indicated by the increasing amplitude of the ripple in figure 55.

There comes a point in any relationship when the most major sources of potential conflicts are resolved and from there, newly emerging conflicts become less disruptive to the relationship. This is indicated by the 'damping' effect shown after the major peak in figure 55.

59.3
The Two Types of Conflict

59.3.1
Internal conflict

Usually, our inner Identities do not conflict with each other because they are context-dependent. For example, my Father Identity is not in conflict with my Husband Identity because they have different concerns and relate to different people. When we feel that the dominant Identity that emerges in a particular situation (to help us adapt to that situation) is not up to the task (i.e., we feel uncomfortable to a greater or lesser degree), we try to compensate by invoking more than one Identity for that particular situation, none of which are equal to the task in their own right. This is when internal conflicts can arise.

> *Once I went to a music concert* [at the Barbican Centre in London] *with my children. In the foyer, I bumped into a university colleague. My Father Identity was so focused on the situation that it did not give way to my Colleague Identity. As such, I missed some of the subtle cues that my colleague was giving that he was interested in getting to know the side of me that is interested in concerts and music. The interaction ended more abruptly than I would have liked and I felt that my response had been inept.*

59.3.2
External conflict

In the context of affinitology, external conflict is a mismatch between the expectations of The Self and The Other *in a particular situation*. In interpersonal relationships, the situation is often far more significant than we tend to appreciate. In other words, we tend to ignore the impact of the situation on our (and other people's) responses. The greater our internal conflict, the more likely we are to experience external conflict. If my Lover Identity and my Father Identity and my Husband Identity are battling it out inside my psyche, my wife's Identities would be at a loss as to which one should prevail to 'harmonize' the transactions or, to use Eric Berne's terminology, to respond with a *complementary transaction* (§ 73 Transactional Analysis).

59.3.3
Conflict Resolution

In most cases, conflict resolution begins with reframing (§ 63.1 Changing Beliefs). By asking ourselves a challenging question, we can often change the way we feel about a conflicting situation. The examples in § 63.1.1 (Meaning and Context Reframes) are there to help us see how this works.

Chapter 60

Abnormal Development

In § 58 (Post-Natal Development), we saw some examples of incidental influences on the Pactum. However, when other Identities or Nexuses begin to have a *significant* impact on a Pactum, then our perspective needs to change from mere influence to interference. As is often the case with most things in life, the boundary between influence and interference is blurred, grayscale being the norm (§ 25.3 Polar Bond: Partial Sharing).

It is tempting to want to take a legal perspective and to reduce the blurriness of the distinction by suggesting that, the more intentional an influence is, the more it veers towards interference. However, I am not convinced that this would be a particularly empowering approach because then there would be a risk of paying less attention to unintentional interference when, in practice, these may be far more significant and more deserving of our attention.

Interference is the primary focus in this chapter on 'abnormal development' because, the more a Nexus matures, the less vulnerable it becomes to interference. Conversely, the more a Nexus is affected by external influences before it matures, the more fragile it becomes. In other words,

---

**fragility is the most disempowering effect of 'abnormal development'
through interference (both in children and relationships).**

60.1
Label Fixation

According to Rumi, in order for us to see our 'clear and clean (pure)' essence, we must first clear our mind of all the labels (adjectives) that we attach to ourselves.

> *Once, a client who was in her thirties, came to me and told me about all the restrictions that her father was placing upon her. I asked her if she thought that the restrictions were reasonable. She said no. I asked her if she thought that her father thought that the restrictions were in her best interest and she said, no. I said,*
> *- "Why do you think that he is imposing such restrictions on you?"*
> *- "For his own benefit (convenience, reputation and ego); definitely not for the benefit of his children."*
> *- "Why do you put up with such restrictions?"*
> *- "Well, he is my father and I don't want to upset him."*
> *- "Are you financially dependent on him?"*
> *- "No."*
> *- "Would you care if a stranger were upset by your being independent?"*
> *- "Of course not."*
> *- "So, why do you care if your father gets upset?"*
> *- "Because he is my father."*
> *- "What is a father?"*
> *- "Isn't that a somewhat obvious question?"*
> *- "OK, let me put it this way, is a biological father the only kind of father that can exist?"*
> *- "Well, no."*

I then went on to explain that her main problem was that she was confusing the different meanings of the word father [Actually, as a noun, there are at least fourteen definitions of 'father']. From a physiological perspective, a man's role as a 'father' ends at conception. His biological role continues only if his actions serve an evolutionary purpose. What this means is that after conception, a man can choose whether or not to put the welfare of his children before his own. Whenever he does so, at that moment, his true Father Identity is active and he is a father. Whenever he does not put the welfare of his children before his own, then he is not being a father. A Father-Child relationship (Pactum) is only possible when one of the Identities in the Pactum (i.e., The Self or The Other) is a Father Identity (male bestower of security) and its counterpart is a Child

Identity (seeker of security). Of course, a prerequisite for being able to do what a Father does, is being physically and psychologically healthy. In short, a biological father, looking after his own self-interests is using the Father label as a means to an end; he is not being a Father, unless the welfare of his offspring is the intention behind his apparent self-interest. Think of it this way, "A father is someone who *does* what a father *does*". A father's post-adolescence equivalent is a mentor or a role model.

> *I then asked my client if she had people who were supportive of her when she needed it and she said, "Yes". I asked her whether she had or could find mentors and role models and she said, "Yes". I then said, "Has your issue been resolved?" and she said, "Yes." In a tone that I took to mean, "I think I am beginning to understand and, given time to think it over, I think I can change the quality of our relationship to a more empowering one."* [You might be thinking, "Bijan, how did you read all that into a simple yes?" And I would boast that this is the power of rapport, being attuned to non-verbal cues and experience.]

60.2

Interference

Broadly, interference is unsolicited interjection or intervention. However, we do not interpret all such actions as interference. When we appreciate such actions, we reframe it as a 'contribution' or 'positive input' or a 'suggestion'. Notice that the difference is only in how we interpret the intention or the outcome. This is related to our discussion about Trust (§ 53) and the Atasinex Cluster (§ 33).

In § 20 (Language and Levels of Persuasion), I said that the more 'persuasive' language patterns become, the more they limit choice, and by extension, freedom and I referred to this as a type of interference. More broadly,

---

interference is any action that affects our decision-making processes.

If and interjection or intervention does not lead to a change in the subject's decision-making processes, then we don't tend to consider it to be interference. Furthermore, we only tend to resent interference when it is intended to limit our options. In this section, our primary focus is on the kind of interference that affects a Nexus.

60.3
Relationship Interference

Whose relationship is it anyway?

> *Sometimes clients come to me and say, "Doctor, I want to encourage my partner to come to see you. Then you can tell me about your impressions and whether you think we are a good match."*
>
> *My first reaction is to say something like, "Just as my conversations with you are completely confidential, my conversations with anyone else who comes to see me is also completely confidential." They then say, "But doc, I don't want you to tell me what he says, I just want you to tell me about your impressions of him." Then I explain, "It is not my impressions that matter. I may see a guy and consider him to be a saint, but if you tell me that there are things about this person that irritate you, then, it is those impressions that matter in your relationship with that person."*

Interference can be accidental or intentional. Interference is not inherently empowering or disempowering. It can disempower the Nexus despite benevolent intentions and it can empower the Nexus despite malevolent intentions.

As we repeatedly encounter in this course, people are only bound by the laws of Newtonian physics when choice, or consciousness (§ 35.11), is not involved. In other words, the effect of any phenomenon on our relationships is not determined by the phenomenon itself, it is determined by how The Self and The Other *react* to the situation.

We can think of it like this. A metal, mixed with another metal can result in something more valuable, an alloy or less valuable, an impure metal. The effect, and the subsequent value, depends on the properties of the metal, the nature of the additive, the conditions under which they are mixed and, crucially, the perspective of the observer (§ 33 Atasinex Cluster). Take iron and carbon for example. Depending on their proportions, the conditions of their reaction (think interaction), such as temperature, and the presence of other substances, we can end up with sooty iron, various types of cast iron or stainless steel, each of which are more or less valuable depending on the situation.

60.3.1
Intra-Bondle interference

It is possible for my Father relationship with my daughter to interfere with my Friend relationship with her. Becoming, and remaining (§ 16.2 Mindfulness and Conscious Gratitude), aware of this distinction can be very empowering because it will allow me to decide which relationship has priority. For example, I often tell my clients that, where child rearing is concerned, **being respected is more important** [mutually empowering] **than being liked**. This concept can be a little confusing at first, so let me explain it in the context of an anecdote.

> *One day, my daughter, who was about nine at the time, was sitting on a chair sulking. Her mother and her brother were also in the room. I can't remember why, but I remember her shouting, "I don't like daddy." I turned to her and said, "My role here is not to be liked. My role here is to make sure that you do what is best for you." I could see the process of her inner transformation in her various facial expressions and body language. Let me try to put what I think was going on in her mind into words:*
>
> "I know that everyone wants to be liked and I said that I don't like daddy to emotionally bribe him to do something to make it up to me (so that he would become liked again) but instead, he is willing to make the sacrifice of not being liked to make sure that I do what is best for me. That means that he has principles and I respect that."

Notice that, here, there are two Individuals (my daughter and I). Two of the Identities within each of these Individuals are in two different relationships with each other, i.e., have formed two separate Pacta [see figures 49 and 50 in (§ 58.3 Bilateral Influences)]. In one Pactum, my Father Identity and my daughter's Child Identity have created a Father-Daughter Nexus and in another Pactum, my Friend Identity and my daughter's Friend Identity have created a Friends Nexus. Being aware of this helps us to prevent one Pactum from interfering with (becoming polluted by) another. In my case, in most situations where there is a potential conflict of interest between what a father would say or do and what a friend would say or do, my Father Identity takes precedence over my Friend Identity. To put it another way, "As a matter of principle, I will not relinquish my role as a father (authority/support) to maintain my role as a friend (peer)". See also § 64.7 (Hierarchy of Values).

[I tend to take the results of personality tests with a pinch of salt because it is easy to fall into the trap of believing that we 'are' what a test says that we are, at which point confirmation bias (§ 33.8) kicks in and we eventually mould ourselves into that belief, losing part of our adaptability and, by extension, part of our soul, by which I mean, consciousness (§ 35.11), that is, the degree to which we have choice (§ 49.4 Degrees of Freedom). Having said that, what I said in the above paragraph reminded me of a personality test that I once took. The results of the test came back saying that I have a 'Guardian' Personality. I could relate to that quite well, except that, when I took the test sometime later, my result was different. Astrologists would put it down to me being a Gemini. Psychologists might be tempted to say that I have some sort of 'Multiple Personality Disorder'. I call it being human ;-)]

Let's take this one step at a time. Figure 56 is a variation on the diagram in figure 49 (§ 58.3).

Figure 56 Two independent Pacta between two individuals (Omniselves)

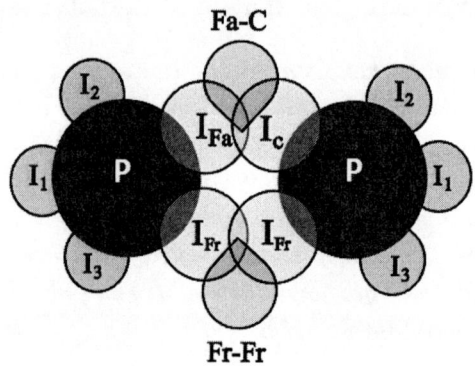

For illustrative purposes, figure 56 depicts two independent[1] Nexuses, a Father-Child Nexus and a Friends Nexus between the same two Individuals (Omniselves).

[1] [Just like adiabatic systems and ideal gases (**§ 58.2 Good Vibrations**), the idea that these two Nexuses can be completely independent of each other is both too idealistic and too simplistic. Nevertheless, simplistic and idealistic approaches can be useful starting points for teaching purposes, as long as we make it clear that they need to be tweaked for real-world (practical) applications.]

Let's now use the Father-Child Nexus as our reference relationship. To be congruent with the above anecdote, we can narrow this to my relationship with my daughter, making it a Father-Daughter Nexus. This is depicted in figure 57 and labelled as R1 (the reference relationship).

Figure 57 Diagram Representing the 'Reference Pactum'
in a Multi-Nexus Relationship

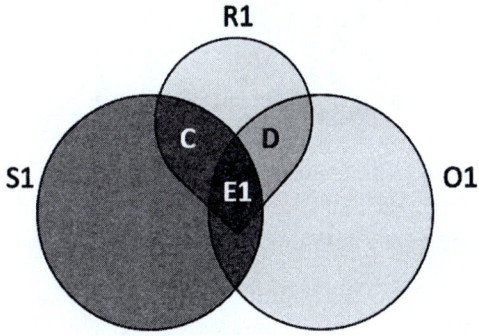

Key:

Circle S1 (The Self): My Father Identity ($\equiv I_{Fa}$ in figure 56)

Circle O1 (The Other): My daughter's Child Identity ($\equiv I_c$ in figure 56)

Piriform R1 (The Nexus): Our Father-Child Nexus ($\equiv Fa\text{-}C$ in figure 56)

Region E1 (The Interdependence Zone): Those aspects of The Self, The Other and the situation (that we are aware of) that are conducive to a 'Father-Daughter' SMER.

[Note that my father Identity believes that being 'liked' is not a prerequisite for a father-daughter SMER, whereas being respected is. I am not denying that being liked can be a bonus, but not at the expense of losing respectability.]

Figure 58 Diagram Representing the 'Second Pactum'
in a Multi-Nexus Relationship

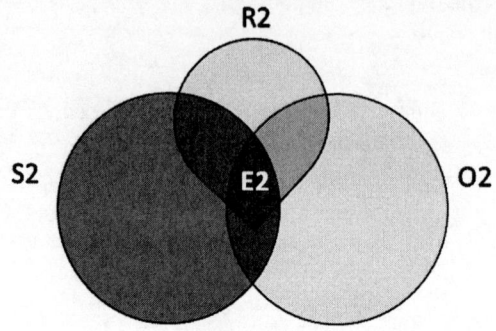

Key:

Circle S1 (The Self): My Friend Identity ($\equiv$ I$_{Fr}$ in figure 56)

Circle O1 (The Other): My daughter's Friend Identity ($\equiv$ I$_{Fr}$ in figure 56)

Piriform R2 (The Nexus): Our Friend-Friend (Friends) Nexus ($\equiv$ Fa-C in figure 56)

Region E2 (The Interdependence Zone): Those aspects of The Self, The Other and the situation (that we are aware of) that are conducive to a Friends SMER.

Figure 59 Diagram Representing the Potential Zones of Interference between two Nexuses in a Multi-Nexus Relationship

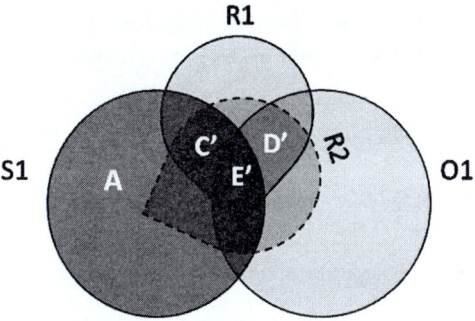

In theory, the Friend-Friend Nexus (R2) can interfere with all seven zones of the Father-Child Pactum. However, in this case, only its possible effects on parts of the Interdependence Region (C', D' and E')[3] is of practical relevance[4].

---

[3] [For those of you who notice things like this, yes, the diagram does not show that, theoretically, there are aspects of Zone E' that cannot potentially affect (or be affected by) R2, in the same way that regions C' and D' are sunsets of regions C and D (figure 57). In other words, E' is a subset of E1 (E' ⊆ E). What I mean is that the R2 region has only partially covered the other Zones, but, if I wanted to be accurate, it would have to only partially cover the E' too, to do this, I would need to show a hole in the piriform representing R2']

[4] [Because, R2 intersect S1 (R2 ∩ S1) and R2 ∩ O1 already exist as part of the Friends Pactum, R2 ∩ F is not within The Self or The Other's locus of control and R2 ∩ G is unrealised potential. R2 ∩ A is where me and my daughter's 'Friend-Friend' relationship can be affected by, or can affect, The Independent Self (those aspects of me that is not related to my 'Father-Child' relationship with my daughter)]

60.3.2
Inter-Pactal Interference

Once, in a question-and-answer session in one of my seminars, a lady said, "My daughter does not have a good relationship with her father, what should I do?" And I said, "Do not interfere." I told her that the way she asked the question suggested that she considers it her responsibility to interfere.

I then went on to explain that unsolicited interference is often more disempowering than it is helpful. This can happen for two reasons: self-referential assumptions and 'relationship derailment'.

[From Eric Berne's (§ 73 Transactional Analysis) perspective, the urge to interfere can be related to what he calls 'life scripts'. A life script, similar to a movie script, consists of a plot and characters that need to be present for the plot (the script-writer's life trajectory) to go according to plan. The life script writer then writes a character role for himself in that script and plays the role of that character at every opportunity. The urge to interfere can be related to a common character that we often script for ourselves; 'The Saviour'.]

Self-Referential Assumptions

Some years ago, I set up a chemical manufacturing company specialising in environmentally friendly solutions. I was responsible for research, development and manufacturing and my business partner was responsible for public relations and marketing. I gave my business partner the formula and showed him how to make one of the products, so that if I were indisposed for any reason, he could fulfil any orders. The first time he tried it, he called me to say that he had followed the instructions exactly, but the formulation was not working. When I went to see him, I asked him to show me what he had done and he had followed my instructions accurately, but the formula wasn't as effective as it was when I made it. Someone suggested to my business partner that it shouldn't matter who does it, if the instructions are complete, the result should be the same and that this meant that I was deliberately withholding vital information. I went through the motions of making the formulation again and paid particular attention to what I may have missed in my instructions. At the time, I had spent several thousand hours, either in a laboratory or in a kitchen, experimenting with chemicals. I cannot remember exactly what the problem was, but I think it had to do with the nuances of how the mixture was stirred.

It is like the difference between a novice and a seasoned driver, driving a manual transmission car. An experienced driver becomes sensitive to the sound of the engine and does not rely on a rev counter for deciding when to change gear. Similarly, when looking at a chemical formulation, the shimmering patterns in the water, its flow properties, how slippery it feels to touch, the patterns of bubbles that are formed and many other such subtle clues, provide valuable information about the formulation's quality and what needs to be done to adjust for any deviations from the set standards.

So, what does all this have to do with unsolicited advice? We make a huge number of assumptions every time we give advice. These are what I call **self-referential assumptions**, that is, they are based on the overarching assumption that **the person I'm giving advice to is like me** which would mean that he has similar beliefs, values, skills, experiences, intentions and, as such, he or she

a) can be creative in when, where and how to use that advice and

b) can adapt the advice to fit the particular circumstances.

Going back to the chemical example, a formulation may be sensitive to the hardness of the water (or 'room temperature') that is used as the main vehicle. Someone who does not know that this can be an important variable, may wonder why, when they make the solution in London, they get a different result to when they make the solution in Paris.

Similarly, when we give unsolicited (or even solicited) advice, a) we are often unaware of how much we are assuming (§ 33 Atasinex Cluster) and b) our advice may cause more harm than good (§ 5.2 Symptomatic versus Root Treatment).

Relationship Derailment and Salvage Operations

Disagreement and contention are often necessary steps in the development of SMER (§ 59 Affinito-Adolescence). Interference, especially unsolicited interference, can derail the natural process of conflict resolution. Conflict resolution is not simply a matter of reaching a compromise (§ 47.2.2 Opposites Attract) or putting aside our differences for the sake of a greater goal. This type of approach to conflict resolution stems from outcome-oriented thinking which often fails to appreciate the benefits of experience which we have discussed in § 8 (What If) and § 44 (Locus of Control) and § 42 (The Anatomy of Identity).

The process of conflict resolution is not merely a means to an end, it is also about discovering the methods of conflict resolution that work more efficiently and effectively for the Identities involved. In the words of Marshall McLuhan,

---

"The Medium is the Message."

It took a while for me to get my head around this concept. At first, I remember thinking, how can the car be the destination or how can what I write on be the meaning of what I write? And then it clicked.

In the absence of a destination, a car can still have meaning; a meaning that is independent of the destination. A car can be used as a medium for making a statement about its owner's values which may be status, the environment, speed, excitement, safety, simplicity, family, culture or preservation. It can also make a statement about the owner's interests, such as racing, the opposite sex, transport and art.

Similarly, *the way in which* we air our disputes, disagreements or dissatisfaction, convey messages beyond the utterances that are exchanged. Tone, volume, speed, gestures, eye contact and so on do not simply enhance communication, they, a) Change the meaning of the communication and, b) convey extra information that have little to do with what is being said. Without the verbal and non-verbal information that is conveyed through the spontaneous process of conflict resolution, the next stage in the process of relationship development; Norming (§ 59.1.3) would suffer because it would fail to take into account the crucial information that the natural process of conflict resolution would have drawn out.

Sometimes we interject in other people's quarrels with the notion that conflicts can be resolved by simply agreeing to disagree. This is like a track athlete's coach saying to the 400m runner, "Look, your goal is to get back to the starting line, but you are here already so why waste your energy? Just throw up your fists and shout, 'yes!' and that will be the end of it."

When two people do not go through the process that allows them to *arrive at* a mutual understanding, this leaves a gap in The Self and The Other's understanding of each other. This can have a negative impact on the future performance of the Pactum. One of the most important of such understandings is how the other party responds in conflict situations and to various approaches that could be used to resolve such conflict.

Imagine what might have happened if I had advised the lady at the seminar that, for example, she needed to talk to the father and to tell him that his daughter is going through a difficult phase and that he should be more understanding. Here are some of the thoughts that may race through my mind if I were the father:

1. What is the nature of this difficult phase (emotional, hormonal, social, academic, physical)?
2. When did this phase start and when will it end?
3. Is it typical of a girl her age to be going through such a phase?
4. Is there anything I can do to help her to transition through this phase more easily?
5. What are the typical behavioural changes and challenges for someone going through such a phase?
6. How long does such a phase typically last?
7. Is it typical for such a phase to selectively affect a girl's relationship with one of her parents only?
8. Should I confirm the mother's assertion with my daughter? (If I do, my daughter may either resent the implication or it may affect her relationship with her mother negatively because it would have meant a breach of confidence on her mother's part.)
9. Should I relinquish my authority/support on the basis that my daughter is going through a phase? (Should I change who I am because of it? Would that not leave my daughter feeling more vulnerable because she would feel that the people she relies on for support are not stable?)
10. Etc.

A similar set of questions would arise if I were to give any other kind of advice to the mother. As the person giving the advice, I may have experience and strategies for dealing with any of the questions or complications that may arise, but someone without the requisite background or ability to offer ongoing support is unlikely to be able to handle any complications (deviations from expectations) that will, most likely, arise. Any such advice would also be out of context because I would not know the subtleties of the communication and intentions. For example, one of the parties may be invoking psychological defence mechanisms (§ 79), in which case, taking what is being communicated at face value would be to misconstrue the person's veiled intentions. In short, when we intervene, interfere or offer unsolicited advice about how to resolve a conflict in someone else's relationship, we deny The Self and The Other the opportunity to learn about each other's conflict resolution processes. In other words,

---

> *How* **we solve a problem is just as important as
> the final resolution of the conflict.**

At this point, you may well be thinking, "But Bijan, what if the relationship is on the verge of breaking up? Shouldn't we at least try to help?" Here, the primary assumption is that the two people in the relationship are not entertaining the idea that a different relationship, or not being in this kind of relationship, would be more empowering. Their psychological defence mechanisms (§ 79) may prevent them from being able to be honest with themselves let alone with us. For example, someone may complain about how she is treated by her husband, but the problem may be that she is seriously contemplating another relationship. She may not tell us that part of the equation and the more we try to help her resolve her relationship with her husband, the more she is likely to try to avoid or resist our interventions. Alternatively, she may listen to what we say and nod in acknowledgement without having any intention of acting on that advice (or even hearing the advice she is thinking about something else) because she appreciates what you are trying to do but knows that, since you do not have the full information, your advice will not be appropriate.

Secondly, what makes us think that if, through our intervention, the relationship is resolved, it will be a more empowering relationship than an alternative relationship that would have developed to fill the gap had we not intervened? Sometimes, it is more mutually empowering to end a disempowering relationship.

"But Bijan, you said it yourself that relationships are what we live for and that without relationships we would die. Aren't you going back on your word here?

Because if relationships are so important, shouldn't we do our best to keep our relationships and to help other people keep theirs?"

"Yes." I would say, and this reminds me of something that I heard Professor Mostafa Mostafavi, a professor of mycology, say in his inaugural speech at a University in Iran, back in 1997. Here it is in English,

---

"There is a common misconception that some mushrooms are not edible. All mushrooms are edible, but some of them, only once."

Mostafa Mostafavi

Not everything that can be eaten is food. Similarly, not every relationship nourishes our soul [don't ask me to explain what I think a 'soul' is (here). Think of it as a figure of speech (for now)].

60.3.3
Offering Help without 'Interference'

"Bijan?" I hear you say in a seductive tone that suggests that you want something. "Yeees?" I would reply in a tone that lets you know that I know that your Child ego state (§ 73 Transactional Analysis) wants to ask for my permission. "Isn't there *any* way that we can help people with their relationships without interfering?" I hear you plea.

I absolutely understand the frustration of watching people being in conflict and being forbidden from barging in to put a stop to what is clearly a misunderstanding. It fills us with a myriad of feelings including helplessness, anger, sympathy, wastefulness and pity, contempt (both for ourselves and for what we consider to be 'squabbling' parties). And I have good news for you. There is a way that we can help people resolve their relationships without interfering *in the relationship itself.*

If we focus people's attentions on what they want, then they can judge the value of their relationships in relation to what they want.

For example, if our friend has a dispute with his work colleague, rather than saying anything about the work colleague, we can say, "Think of where you want to be in 5 years' time. What would that future look like?" The next question would be, "What do you think would be the best way of thinking about your current relationships that would move you towards that future in the most enjoyable way?" Here's a breakdown of what we are doing here:

1. By asking the person to think about their future, we are disassociating them from the present (feelings, state, concerns).

2. A question forces our mind to contemplate an answer and changes our focus away from our present concerns (§ 15.1 The Power of Questions).

3. Returning to the question of relationships from a 'future perspective' allows the person to place their current relationships in a new context. And as we encounter many times throughout this course, the context or situation changes meaning and evokes different Identities.

4. Talking about relationships in general and not about a specific relationship, allows our friend to see the bigger picture in the present moment. That is, the relationship where I have a conflict is one of many relationships that I have and, therefore, is not as big a deal as it would be if I were totally dependent on that relationship. This is related to the concept of independence (§ 23.2 The Road to Interdependence).

5. By focusing on your friend and her wants and needs, you are empowering your relationship with her.

6. By not reminding your friend of his conflicts you are avoiding the possibility that he may transfer those problems onto you, which may negatively affect your relationship with him.

7. By not giving direct advice, you are not allowing your Parent ego state to affect your relationship and this reduces the chances of your friend's Child ego state from resisting you. In other words, try to keep the conversation Adult-Adult (§ 73 Transactional Analysis).

Unit 14

Genetics of Relationships

[Based on an Images by Gordon Johnson from Pixabay]

For a bond (a relationship) to form, each of the individuals involved must have the capability to bond. In chemistry, this capability is afforded by the electrons in each atom's outer shell. In multicellular organisms, each cell can relate (have a relationship with) other cells by communicating (sending and receiving) messages. Each message is sent via chemical messengers and received via receptors (recognition sites for each of those messages) on the cell's surface. The important point here is that a cell cannot receive a message if it does not have a receptor (on its surface) for relaying that message (to its interior). This means that the extent to which a cell can communicate depends on the chemicals that it can send out (secrete), but more importantly, by the number and types of receptors on the cell's surface.

You may have noticed that I just sneakily implied that it is more important to be able to receive messages than to send them. My studies of physiology and pharmacology have led me to conclude that differentiated cells are capable of recognising more chemicals (have a wider range of receptors on their surface) than they are capable of secreting (producing and releasing) chemicals into their outer environment. Throughout our lives, from birth to death, we are able to perceive (and understand) far more than we are able to express. A child learning to speak can understand complex sentences before she can string three or four words together. Throughout the ages, ancient wisdom and modern experts have been telling us that it is more important to listen than to speak in various forms [e.g., "Seek first to understand then to be understood" or "you have two eras and one mouth, use them in that proportion"].

You may be wondering, "What has all this got to do with genetics and relationships?" That is a great question; thank you for asking. Bear with me for a little longer and it shall be revealed.

Chapter 61

Genetics

What factors give relationships the potential to become what they can become? Genes are about potential and genetics is about how that potential becomes manifest. This manifestation (expression) is a function of the environment. We may have the potential for developing magnificent romantic relationships, but if the environment does not lead to the manifestation of such potential, then we will not realise what we have been endowed with. So, what are the equivalent to genes in interpersonal relationships? I propose that,

> **Beliefs are the affinitological equivalent to genes.**

In other words, it is our beliefs that determine our aptitude and consequently, the extent to which our relationships can become SMERs. Like faulty genes, maladaptive beliefs can have disempowering effects on our relationships. (§ 62.4 Beliefs as Affinitological Genes)

61.1
Genes as Potential

Genes give us potential (possibilities). A 'potential' is a skill set, such as the potential to see, hear, feel, move, digest, defend ourselves against bacterial invasion and a myriad of others. I call them potentials because any skill set remains dormant until the conditions for it to manifest are satisfied.

I may be genetically endowed to become a world class tennis player. However, if I never see a tennis racket, that potential cannot manifest itself. Similarly, I may have the potential to see, but if I don't open my eyes or if I am in total darkness, that potential will not manifest; which means that I might just as well be blind (not have the skill set to see). I hear some of you saying, "But Bijan, what about effort? Doesn't becoming a world class tennis player depend on dedication and practice?"

"Yes!" I would reply, "Dedication and practice are *necessary, but insufficient* conditions for becoming a world class tennis player." Therefore, we need dedication and practice *and at least one other thing* and I am going to suggest that there is *only* one other condition that needs to be satisfied for a person to be able to become a world-class tennis player: **a favourable physiological makeup**. That's where genes come in.

[You might protest and say, "But Bijan, what about a tennis racket, tennis courts, a partner (to play tennis with), time, money and so on?" And I would say that those have already been taken care of in the first criterion, 'dedication and *practice'* because without the resources that you have just listed, there could be no practice. "What about a coach?", you might say. And I would say that that's where the dedication part comes in; if you are dedicated enough you would try to acquire the services of a coach which is related to our discussion about 'the hard way' and 'the easy way' in § 2.2 (What is the key to empowering and satisfying relationships?)]

An example of how genes can provide us with a favourable physiological makeup is this: We have two types of skeletal muscle cells; Type I (slow-twitch) and Type II (fast-twitch). Depending on the proportion of these types of cells in our body, we will be better at endurance tasks (such as running a marathon) or at short-term power tasks (such as short-distance sprinting) respectively. Studies have shown that through 'dedication and practice', we can change the proportion of these types of fibres by up to 30%. However, 45% of the variation is genetic. This means that if you are born with 30% Type II cells in your skeletal muscles, with 'dedication and practice' you can increase these to up to 60%. After all that effort, your endurance level will be on par with someone who is born with 60% Type II cells [Assuming that these do not atrophy through not being pushed I don't know of any studies that have investigated it from that angle].

A similar pattern applies across other potentials. For example, I have a five-degree squint in my right eye. This means that it takes me longer to read (or to follow a ball) because when following words on a page, I don't just move my eyes, I move my head too (albeit almost imperceptibly nowadays). This means that in spite of my love of reading, I am a slow reader.

[Until not very long ago, I used to think of this as a handicap and thinking about it reminds me of a scene in the movie Amadeus in which the character, Salieri says, "All I ever wanted was to sing to God. He gave me that longing and then made me mute. Why? Tell me that. If he didn't want me to praise him with music, why implant the desire like a lust in my body? And then deny me the talent?"]

My squint put me at a disadvantage in exams (amongst other things). I talk about factors that affect academic 'performance' in § 5.4.1 (Ability, Performance and Attainment). The point is that we need both *the potential* (genes) and *the opportunity* (environment) for our skill sets to manifest (express).

We tend to talk about opportunities as if they are like Frisbees or balls that we can simply lunge our hands out and grab before they fly past and out of reach. However, the opportunities that I am talking about here are not necessarily outside of us. Whether or not we see opportunities in the environment depends on how we 'choose' to perceive and interpret what goes on around us. We discuss this in more detail in § 44 (Locus of Control).

Perhaps counterintuitively, our 'potentials' can be disempowering as well as empowering depending on when and/or where they become manifest. For example, a powerful memory is empowering when we want to learn from our experiences but can be debilitating if we cannot let go of the past. A high proportion of fast-twitch muscle cells is empowering when running away from a grizzly bear, but this can be disempowering when we need to trek across a desert to find water.

What does all this have to do with relationships? Well, let's see. Is there anything of a non-physical nature that we can consider to limit or enhance our social skill sets? I propose that this is what our beliefs do. In other words, what genes do for our bodies, beliefs do for our minds in general, and interpersonal relationships in particular.

So, what insights can we gain from the science of genetics in our quest to develop mutually satisfying and empowering relationships (SMERs)? If we have the potential and the right environment, we can create The Third Entity. If we don't have the potential, no environment will allow us to do that. The good news is that, unlike genetic potential, creating high quality relationships can be learnt; beliefs can be changed (§ 63.1 Changing Beliefs).

Once we have *acquired* our relationship-building skill set (the potential), it can only be realised (expressed), if we are in the right environment, including being with someone who can bring out that potential; has Common and Complementary Elements (§ 47).

61.2
Genes and Receptors

Genetics is about how cells make proteins and why. These proteins have three main functions,

a) As enzymes, proteins can regulate chemical reactions, that is, everything that the body does at the molecular level.

b) As building materials, proteins are the primary constituents of our muscles, hairs and memories.

c) As receptors, proteins are the ports/gateways that enable each and every cell to become aware of its environment [what to notice/recognise and react to] and for it to communicate (coordinate) with other cells [so as to know what to do and when].

In this section, our focus is on the last function of proteins; as receptors [if you are into electronics, think 'transducer'. If you are into computers, think 'interface' or 'port'. If you are into languages, think 'definition']. From an affinitological perspective, the critical questions are, "What determines what a Pactum senses, that is, what is it sensitive to (pays greater attention to) and why?" And "What are the consequences of this sensitivity?" Which ultimately boils down to, "How does this affect this particular relationship?"

I propose that, in terms of our interpersonal relationships, our values are the affinitological equivalents to physiological receptors (§ 64.4 Values as Receptors). Without values, there can be no Common or Complementary Elements (§ 47) that can be communicated and, without communication (Unit 16: Physiology of Relationships), there can be no SMER (§ 2.1 What is a SMER?).

Chapter 62

Beliefs and Decision-Making

62.1
Beliefs

Before delving deeper into what a belief is, here, I propose that,

> **A belief is a unit of thought.**

Our beliefs change our perception and, consequently, our interpretation of reality (§ 33.2 Perception and § 33.7.1 Expectations and Belief). My interpretation of reality is based on what I can perceive through my senses, my imagination and collective consensus (Social Construction). In other words, beliefs change *what is* into *what I think it is*. Note that we can never know 'what is' (the truth about a phenomenon). We can only *create* a belief in ourselves [or adopt someone else's belief about it] as to what it means (or can mean) to us. In other words,

> **beliefs turn truth into our 'reality'.**

The Truth is unknowable, but reality is 'derivable' based on available evidence. This means that each person's reality is unique and may be closer or further away from the 'truth' than someone else's reality. Conflicts arise when we set our own reality as a standard against which to judge other people's realities.

[To get a handle on this, ask yourself, "Why do I believe that grass is green?" If our perception of colour were not based on the three types of cones in our retina and, if it extended beyond the narrow 400-800nm wavelengths, would our reality still be the same?]

We can categorise beliefs into two types depending on their source,

a) Reasoned beliefs (based on personal experience) and,

b) Acquired beliefs (based on what other people have told us).

[I am tempted to introduce a third kind of belief that I would call consolidated beliefs, resulting from our attempts to reduce cognitive dissonance by using our imagination to harmonise reasoned and acquired beliefs. But I shall leave that discussion for another time and place.]

The line between reasoned and acquired beliefs is not clear cut. That is, we cannot easily identify whether a belief is reasoned or acquired. This is because our reasoning is based largely on information that we acquire from others. Therefore, I may think that I have reached a logical conclusion for myself, but often fail to notice that my *premises* are based on what I have gleaned from others. Another characteristic of beliefs is that they are self-reinforcing, that is,

---

Our beliefs have prejudice built into them.

This is known as *confirmation bias* (§ 33.8). Being unaware of this (and other cognitive biases) often leads to disempowered or disempowering decision-making and, in our case, relationships (including interpersonal ones).

62.1.1
What is a Belief

In § 42 (The Anatomy of Identity) I said that beliefs are cause-and-effect associations. That is, **a belief is an 'if-then' association.** If I do this, I will feel pleasure. If I do that, I will feel pain. We can rephrase beliefs such as 'I can do this' in if-then terms; 'If I try, then I will succeed'.

For those things that we have little experience of, a more empowering belief may be, 'I won't know whether or not I can succeed until I try' which can be rephrased as, 'If I try this, then I will know whether or not I will succeed.'

**Beliefs don't simply *represent* skill sets,
beliefs *are* skill sets in themselves.**

In other words, my beliefs don't just *tell* me what I can or cannot do; they *determine* what I can and cannot do.

[Notice the similarities here between the generally perceived function of language (communication) and the more fundamental function of language (programming) – Unit 3 (The Power of Language)]

"But Bijan, what if I believe in angels? Where is the cause-and-effect association in that?" I hear someone ask and since 'belief' is a pivotal concept in affinitology, I feel that I should not leave a question like that hanging.

I have pointed out elsewhere in this course that a definition of anything can either be descriptive or functional (§ 21.1 What is a Relationship?). A functional definition implies cause-and-effect. If something does something, it does it *to* something, otherwise, in practical terms it is irrelevant until it does. For example, you may argue that a comet moving through space is doing something, but it is not doing it *to* anything. [Unlike a table, if you look up the definition of a comet in a dictionary, you will only find 'descriptive' definitions (this is what a comet *is* not this is what a comet *does*]. And my point is that, unless that comet is observed, at which point it starts doing something (at least to the observer), it is irrelevant as far as any belief about it is concerned.

So, what does any of this have to do with angels? Well, like a table, angels can have both descriptive and functional definitions; this is what an angel *is* (what it looks like and how it behaves) and this is what an angel *does* (brings messages from God). If, when I say, "I believe in angels" I am thinking about the functional definition, then what I am saying is that an angel *causes* a message to be delivered from God [or to be more precise, an angel *mediates* messages from god; mediating means being a part of the cause].

If believing or not believing in angels has no effect on me whatsoever, then the belief is irrelevant. On the other hand, if the belief *does* have an effect on me, then there is a concealed (implied) cause-and-effect relationship in the descriptive definition of an angel too. For example, "An angel is a concept that makes (causes) me to feel more secure in that it reinforces my belief in (or facilitates my relationship with) a God."

"So, Bijan, what does all this talk about angels have to do with interpersonal relationships?" I hear some of you asking. Well, let's begin by considering the effect of believing or not believing in angels from an affinitological perspective. Imagine a scenario where Alex meets a seemingly angelic person and she asks him whether or not he believes in angels? He might then consider the possible effect of his response on the direction of the potential relationship; "How do I believe my beliefs about angels could affect the potential trajectory of the relationship?"

[Now Alex is thinking about his beliefs about his beliefs; this is called metacognition; a very interesting topic that is beyond the scope of this book. Incidentally, in the above example, Alex is also thinking about how he can manipulate this situation to his advantage, and in doing so, he is falling into the 'game-playing' (lack of sincerity) trap (§ 45 To Play or Not to Play)].

You see, all beliefs *are* about cause and their effect, even ones like believing in angels that don't, at first, appear to be. In the final analysis, facts are indistinguishable from beliefs. Yes, that's right; facts are not as robust as our security-seeking limbic system would like us to believe (rely upon). Facts are opinions supported by evidence (or social consensus) that are congruent with an individual's ways of thinking (other sets of beliefs). This is another way of saying,

---

Objectivity is collective subjectivity.

Beliefs cannot be proven

We cannot prove a cause-and-effect; we can only demonstrate it repeatedly [This is related to Hume's problem of induction. I encourage you to look it up]. If I believe in something that I have not deduced for myself, then I have deduced (decided) that there is value in believing in what someone else has suggested.

> **The value of believing in something that I have not experienced personally is in facilitating connecting with other people.**

In other words, the belief can be used to instigate or maintain a relationship:
- "Hey Joe, did you know that comets are a sign of good luck?"
- "So, I have heard."
- "I hear that there is a comet passing by tonight. Do you fancy walking up the hill with me to take a look at it?" ☺

62.1.2
Belief versus Perception

Perception is based on direct (sensory) experience. The colour green is not something that I believe in, it is something that I perceive. What I might believe in is that others perceive the colour green in the same way that I do. I might also believe that the label 'green' is an accurate representation of what I am perceiving.

[In reality, one of the things that this perception depends on is the language that we speak. In some languages, there is only one word for both green and blue. This is related to our discussion in Unit 3 (The Power of Language) where I explain language is not merely a means of communication, it also programs the way we perceive].

62.2
Genes and Belief Cycles

Our beliefs affect our values, [I hesitate to use the word 'dictate' (§ 40.2 Behaviourism versus Humanism)] our values affect our emotions, our emotions inform our attitudes, our attitudes affect our decisions, our decisions determine our (re)actions, our actions cause results. The consequences of those results on our psyche (sense of self) depend on our beliefs, creating an upward, a downward or a meandering spiral. Figure 60 depicts how genes and beliefs can lead to similar spiral patterns.

Figure 60 From Potential To Expression:
Genes and Beliefs (can) follow the same spiral patterns

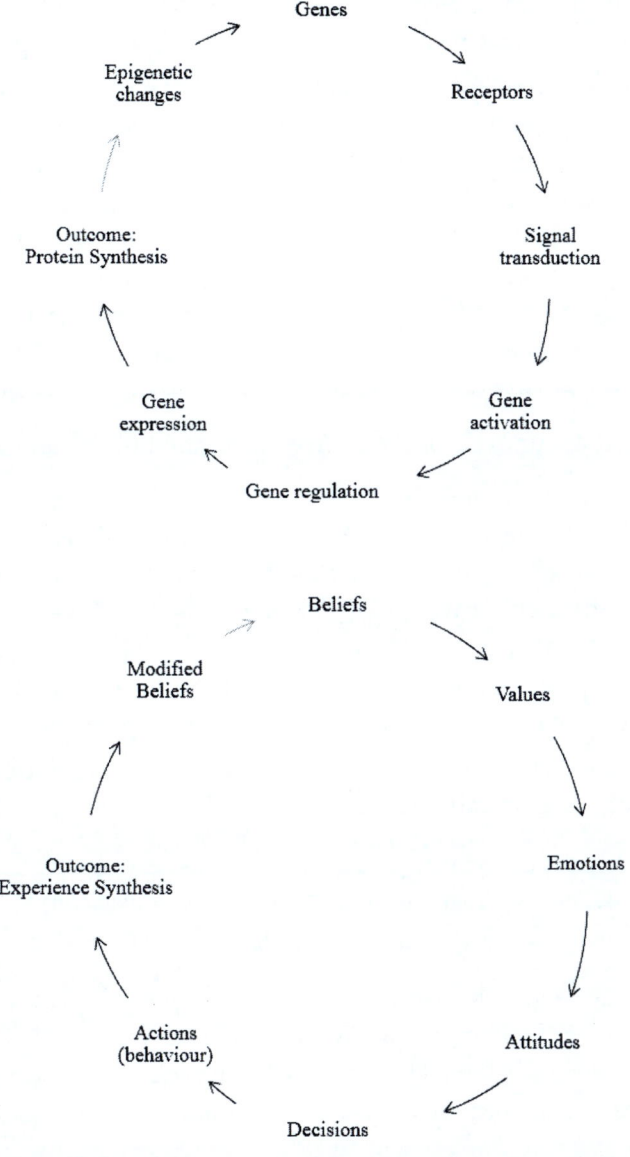

62.3
Beliefs, Genes and Decision-Making

We discuss the practical aspects of the process of decision-making in § 72. In this section, our focus is on the belief-related factors that affect our decision-making.

In § 26.2 (Characteristics of Living Systems), I proposed that the primary indicator of consciousness is the ability to exercise choice, i.e., the ability to decide. Clearly, without an implied goal or purpose, the idea of making decisions would be meaningless. Afterall, why would any conscious being spend energy on making a decision if that decision doesn't move it closer to something that it wants or away from something that it does not want? This implies that,

---

consciousness is necessarily goal-directed.

It also means that our decisions stem from (and are directed and informed by) our goals.

Goals are things (achievements) that we want to move towards. The prospect of achieving such goals must be attractive to us, otherwise we would not want to move towards them. It would be obvious to say (but I will say it anyway) that only things that appear to be attractive to us, attract us. Things (whatever they may be) appear to be attractive to us only if our beliefs (whether conscious or subconscious) lead us to conclude that they have some value.

In short, our goals stem from our values and our values stem from our beliefs which ultimately direct and guide our decisions.

Beliefs → Values → Goals → Options → Decision(s)

[For "→" read 'lead to']

Another way of saying this is that, unless we believe in *something*, we cannot have any values and without values, we cannot have any goals [if nothing is valuable, what is the point of pursuing anything?]. Therefore, without goals, consciousness becomes irrelevant; our behaviour becomes reactive rather than proactive. In other words,

---

Consciousness (decision-making) is predicated upon beliefs

Beliefs do not need to be congruent with reality. If they were, they would not be 'beliefs', they would be 'reality'. Beliefs, and by extension, consciousness is about the processes through which living beings fill in the gaps in their knowledge. Or, more succinctly,

---

Beliefs are about things that we do not know.

Decision-making is the attempt to make logical connection between our beliefs in order to predict an outcome that takes us closer to the achievement of our goals (§ 66 Goals). And this process is involved at all levels within affinitological organisations, beginning with The Self and The Other and extending to The Nexus, the Pactum, The Bondle and beyond (§ 32 Extended Relationships, Communities and Beyond), § 36 Levels of Organisation and § 90 Fractals). The implication here is that each of these structures is a semi-autonomous conscious system. I say *Semi*-autonomous because each of the component structures of an affinitological system, whatever its level of organisation (§ 36), is part of a symbiotic relationship (§ 31 Symbiosis).

Affinitological decision-making can occur at two levels, cognitive and emotional. **When beliefs are linked to emotions, they become attitudes** (§ 65 Attitudes).

62.4
Beliefs as Affinitological Genes

Like genes, beliefs are about *potential*. They can affect us in one of two ways; they can either bestow potential or inhibit potential. Like genes, beliefs only affect us when environmental conditions 'activate' them. I may believe that spiders are scary, but if I am not in the presence of a spider (or am not being reminded of one), that belief (and potential for reacting to it with fear) remains dormant (unexpressed).

Our beliefs determine what we can and cannot do by mediating how we interpret and, therefore, understand our external world.

When my son and daughter were of primary school age, I used to take them to various events on the London Underground. There was always a race between them to see who could get to sit on the last seat in a row of seats or between me and the other sibling; they did not want to sit next to a stranger. I used to tell them that 'a stranger is a friend you haven't got to know yet.' I discuss this example in a different context in § 18 (Art or Science).

> **It is not beliefs (genes) that make SMERs possible, it is the actions that are instigated through beliefs (how the gene is expressed).**

Like genes, beliefs need the right conditions to manifest. The belief that 'a stranger is a friend you have not got to know yet' is redundant when one is taking a shower at home.

Like genes, beliefs can be empowering or disempowering. The belief that 'a stranger is a friend you haven't got to know yet' is empowering in the context of, "When you are being supervised by daddy, you can use this opportunity of being in a safe environment to expand your comfort zone." However, such a belief can become disempowering in the context of someone standing near the school gates, looking around cautiously and saying, "Hey little girl, would you like to stroke my puppy."

Faulty beliefs (and genes) are those that are disempowering because they are not adaptive enough to *the context*; they manifest inappropriately.

62.5
The Three Levels of Belief

Three hierarchical beliefs are necessary for us to be motivated to be proactive in any endeavour, including forming and maintaining any kind of interpersonal relationship. These beliefs are determined by our answers to three questions I call each of them a Belief Level (BL):

- Belief Level 1 (BL1): Is it possible? (Possibility)
- Belief Level 2 (BL2): Can I make it happen? (Self-confidence)
- Belief Level 3 (BL3): Is it worth the effort? (Priority)

We need to be able to convince ourselves that our answer is "Yes" to all three questions before we are motivated enough to take action proactively. We need to bear in mind that, as I keep pointing out, few things in life are pure black or white [a quantum is a good candidate for being one of the exceptions to this rule]. As such, our answers (and feelings towards) each of these questions lie on a spectrum. So, when I say that we need to answer 'Yes' to each of these questions, what I am really saying is that,

> **our level of agreement with the premise of each of these questions must be beyond a certain *threshold* (tipping point).**

Belief Level 1: Possibility

Taking the first step towards any goal (§ 66), including initiating any kind of relationship, depends on the extent to which we believe in the possibility (our assessment of the probability) that **it *can* happen**, this can lie anywhere along the following spectrum

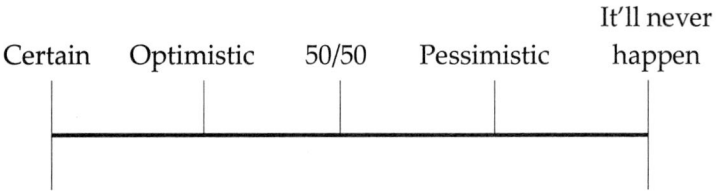

Note that these evaluations are subjective and are based on our personal experience and what we have come to accept from what other people impart to us (through their words or actions). This reminds me of the Frog Race Story.

The Frog Race Story

Once upon a time, a group of small frogs decided to organise a race to see who could reach the top of a high tower first. A large crowd had come to watch.

The race began…

Early on, some of the frogs lost their grip and fell off the wall of the tower. It was becoming apparent to the spectators that no one was going to win the race and so they started to shout out things like, "get back down here, you're not going to make it, so don't embarrass yourselves." and "It can't be done." and "Give it up before you hurt yourselves."

More and more frogs began to fall.

The crowd continued to shout, "It's too difficult! No one will make it!"

More frogs kept falling off, except one who wouldn't give up. He reached the top of the tower.

When he came back down, people were all gathered around and someone asked, "How did you manage to do that when everyone else failed?"

The little frog looked at him intently and started to make gestures in sign language.

The more we entertain the possibility of something being possible and the less we are distracted by those who do not share our belief, the more motivated we will be. This motivation is mediated by the value that we assign to the outcome. Note that there is a self-reinforcing process at work here:

> The more we believe in the possibility of a valuable outcome, the more effort we put into achieving that outcome. And the more effort we put into anything, the more invested we become in it (the more valuable it becomes to us) and the more valuable it becomes, the more effort we put into achieving it. This also applies to our efforts in establishing and maintaining SMERs. See also Unit 23 (Mechanics of relationships).

BL1 Example: It is impossible

If I believe that something is impossible, I can either choose to a) forget it or b) to fantasize about what would happen if it were possible. In either case, I would not take any direct action towards making it happen, although, if I fantasize about it, I can take action towards making *something* happen, such as writing a novel or a story about what might have happened, if it were possible.

Note that here, we are talking about a 'belief' that something is impossible. The belief may be true, or it may be false. If something is, in fact, impossible and I believe it to be possible, then, depending on my level of motivation (§ 93.1 Motivation and Motivational Energy), I may take some kind of action towards its achievement. Even though such action may not result in the outcome that I want (after all, it is impossible), any action that I do take will have an impact in that it is likely to change the course of history in some way [I say this because I believe that Sensitive Dependence on Initial Conditions applies to everything that we do (§ 90 Fractals)].

From an affinitological perspective, this means that,

> **if we believe that a certain type of relationship is impossible, we are unlikely to take any action that could move us in the direction of such a relationship.**

62.5.3
Belief Level 2: Self-Confidence

Once we have determined our belief about how possible something is, in order to be motivated enough to take action, we need to believe in our own ability to make it happen. Self-confidence only becomes relevant at this point (§ 40 Self-Esteem and Self Confidence).

BL2 Example 1
It is possible, but I cannot do it

What can we do if we are bounded by such a belief? Here are some possible reactions.

Forget it: The outcome of choosing to "forget it", will be the same as believing that it is impossible (as above).

Jealousy: An alternative response to this belief would be to feel jealous. We compare and contrast jealousy and envy and their possible consequences in § 87.4 (Autoimmune Responses and Diseases).

Self-resentment: One of the feelings that can result from believing that something is possible, but *I* can't do it, is self-indignation or self-resentment. We can respond to this feeling in several ways. We can turn the feeling inwards, which could lead us down the path of spiralling low self-esteem, or we can turn it outwards and project it onto The Others in our Pacta (§ 79 Psychological Defence Mechanisms). In both cases, our existing relationships are likely to suffer (reduced SMER). The feeling of jealousy can also be a by-product of self-resentment.

"Why me?" is also a common reaction to this belief. We explore how questions beginning with 'why' are usually detrimental to our mental and social health and what we can do about it in Exercise 3 (Exploring the disempowering effects of 'why') in § 11.1 (Why Can Seriously Damage Our Health).

Acceptance is another way in which we can deal with this belief. This is when we say to ourselves, "OK, I will not dwell on this anymore, I will change the direction of my thoughts and will start to think about something that I believe that I *can* do".

BL2 Example 2
I would do it if I knew how to deal with the possible consequences

This is the 'what if' syndrome that we discussed in § 8 (What If). Here are some of the possible reactions to this belief.

'Forget it': See above.

Lament: A consequence of lament is for us to approach relationships with a victim (self-pity) orientation. This leads us to attract predators or saviours.

[For more information, I suggest adding "Games People Play" by Eric Berne to your reading list. I mention this book in § 45 (**To Play or Not to Play**). The midnote in § 60.3.2 (**Inter-Pactal Interference Self-Referential Assumptions**) is also relevant.]

Research (AKA due diligence), is a proactive reaction to such a belief which helps us take positive action towards achieving our goal.

Procrastinate.

Procrastination

Procrastination is a common problem and it tends to become more prevalent when we are faced with the 'what if' syndrome (§ 8). This has several possible consequences.

We could continue to be productive in other areas of our lives and brush aside the niggling thought that something needs to be resolved until time resolves the issue for us by making it 'no longer relevant'. This is probably the best possible outcome of procrastination. However, the issue often comes back to haunt us in the form of 'I wish I had done something about it at the time' or 'I wonder what would have happened if...'. If our life takes a meaningful and fulfilling trajectory, such feelings tend to be fleeting and will not disrupt the normal flow of our lives. However, if we hit a period of 'slump' then these feelings can become obsessive, stacking one on top of another, and will prevent us from being able to take action to take us out of that slump. That is one of the junctures at which many people choose to seek my advice.

Procrastination can have more direct effects on our lives in that we can feel paralysed. On the one hand, we feel guilty about not doing it and on the other, the thought that 'I ought to be doing it' prevents us from doing anything else that could be useful. This is when, as we try to escape by doing something mindless like pretending to watch television or eating when we are not hungry or drinking to escape our conflicting thoughts and emotions, Brian Tracy's words keep circling inside our heads; 'swallow the frog, swallow the frog …'. This is another juncture at which people choose to come to me for help.

The thought that we may not be able to cope or deal with the consequences is not the only reason that we procrastinate. We also procrastinate when we cannot decide on our priorities. That is, when we have a decision-making problem. "Do it anyway" (or "just do it") is a piece of advice that has found great appeal, at least in theory. As my clients frequently demonstrate, however, in the light of the 'what if' syndrome, this is not as easy as it sounds. For example, if you live somewhere where 'losing everything' doesn't mean losing your life (or right to live) [you will still have the minimum required for survival and growth], then you are much more empowered in terms of your ability to take risks. Similarly, if 'losing everything' doesn't mean losing your mind because you have a robust sense of self because you are less dependent on SRC (§ 39) then it is more likely for you to decide to 'do it anyway'.

Another factor that can influence our confidence in taking risks is social capital. Being able to rely on friends and family for one or more of physical, social, financial, emotional and intellectual support can make the difference between saying, 'let's take the risk' and 'let's not'. If we move to this position, then we have already decided where we stand in relation to Belief Level 3; "Is it worth the effort?".

BL2 Example 3
I can cope with whatever happens

If I adopt the belief that I can cope with whatever happens, this allows me to go directly to Belief Level 3; "Is it worth the effort?"

62.5.4
Belief Level 3: Opportunity Cost
(Is it worth the effort?)

I will only need to consider my beliefs about a situation at this level after I have decided that what I want to achieve is possible and that I have the ability to do something about making it happen. This reminds me of the Serenity Prayer.

The Serenity Prayer
Dear Lord,
Grant me the serenity to accept the things I cannot change,
The courage to change the things I can,
And the wisdom to know the difference.

In addition to believing that it can be done and that I can do it, I would also need to consider the outcome (in our case, instigating or maintaining a relationship) to be more valuable than if we were to expend that energy pursuing an alternative endeavour. The last is what in economics is referred to as, opportunity cost. In other words, "What opportunities am I willing to lose in order to pursue this opportunity?" And this brings us to what I call **the first law of decision making**:

In every decision that we make,
we lose many things in order to get some things.

Whether or not I believe something is worth doing depends on my hierarchy of values (§ 64.7), which determines my priorities.

The following examples illustrate how beliefs at this level, and our *choice of reaction* to them, can affect our existing or potential relationships.

BL3 Example 1: It's not worth doing

No matter how competent we believe ourselves to be at being able to achieve some outcome (in our case, instigating and maintaining a relationship), we will not do it if we do not think that it is worth doing, that is, if it is not our priority. Whether or not achieving a particular outcome is a priority for us is determined by our perceived needs, values and alternatives.

BL3 Example 2: It may be worth doing

If I believe that, a) something can be done and that, b) I can do something about making it happen and c) decide that such an endeavour has its merits, then we enter a new level of decision-making. This time, the decision is to resolve this conflict: "Do I move the priority of this action up to 'It is definitely worth doing' or do I move it down to 'It is definitely not worth doing.' We can also decide to postpone or delegate the decision. I can only think of two possible reasons for postponing a decision:

a) I need more information
b) I need to consider this under different circumstances [I am too busy right now or it is too noisy in here or I can't concentrate at the moment]

When it comes to interpersonal relationships, we can delegate the decision, but we cannot delegate the action (of connecting) [no one else can connect my Identity (The Self) with The Other's Identity without my involvement]. I can tell someone to gather information about The Other, but I cannot expect anyone to be in a relationship with someone on my behalf. To put it another way,

---

I can delegate a responsibility, but I cannot delegate a relationship.

BL3 Example 3: It is definitely worth doing

At this point, we are clear about our values and our needs (this may or may not be at a conscious level) and we will have resolved any conflicts between this and other opportunities. We can react to this situation in one of two ways (by making one of two decisions).

Go for it. By this I mean that we can act somewhat on impulse and do the 'first' (first most appropriate) thing that comes to mind (talk, wink, call, etc). This is where we begin to instigate a new Nexus (§ 56.1 Fertilisation: Pactum Formation).

Plan for it. This is when we take action in Zone C (§ 56.3.1 Gestation), such as order some flowers, fill out an application form, pick up a pen to write a letter or install a social networking app.

62.5.5

The Importance of the Three Levels of Belief

Belief change is a prerequisite for behaviour change. We will not change the way we do things unless we are motivated to do so and we will not be motivated to do so unless we think differently (change our beliefs) about what that change means. Often my clients say to me, "But that can't be done." At this point, I take them through the following steps.

> I ask: Has no one else ever done it?
> Answer: Yes, they have.
> - So, it *can* be done.
> - OK, it can be done, but *I* can't do it.
> - So, what you are saying is that you don't *know how* to do it.
> - Yes.
> - So,

'It can't be done' means, "I don't know how to do it, *yet*."

The process of belief change (as in the above example) is called 'reframing'. This is what we shall turn our attention to next (§ 63 Epigenetics of Relationships).

Chapter 63

Epigenetics of Relationships

In the mid-1980s, I was conducting research into why those working in cotton processing factories develop a certain type of asthma, known as byssinosis. At the time, I was also interested in evolutionary theory and felt that something didn't make sense in Darwin's theory of evolution.

The part that didn't make sense to me was the idea of randomness. According to Darwinian theory, when cells divide, especially when gametes are formed, random 'mistakes' happen in the copying of the DNA and that leads to the next generation being different. If that difference happens to help the organism survive better, then the next generation is empowered and if it happens to be detrimental to the organism's survival, that version of the randomly changed DNA and its associated genes will die off. This process is called 'natural selection'. This means that the organism and its experiences do not help the next generation survive, unless that experience is passed on through some form of culture. I had numerous problems with this theory most of which would be resolved if this idea of randomness was taken out of the equation. At the time, I veered towards Lamarckian (acquired characteristics) theory of evolution. Then, I came across a finding in a piece of research that provided the evidence I was looking for. To quote:

> "Workers whose fathers had a history of exposure to flax dust were more resistant to the development of the disease than those with fathers without such a history. It may be interesting to stress that most of the fathers, if not all of them, had a history of considerable exposure before their marriage."
>
> [Source: Noweir, M. H., Amine, E. K., & Osman, H. A. (1975). Epidemiological investigation of the role of family susceptibility and occupational and family histories in the development of byssinosis among workers exposed to flax dust. *Occupational and Environmental Medicine, 32*(4), 297-301.]

This indicated that Lamarck may have been right [our current understanding of epigenetics suggests that he was, at least partially, right]. Why was this important? Because it provided a genetic (father-offspring) link that showed that fathers (at least) pass on genetic information to their offspring that enable them to survive (adapt) better to their environment. At the time, I took this to mean that we are able to auto-splice our genes so that we pass on a different genetic code to our children. In other words, what we think of as 'random' mutation is not so random.

Later [I think it came to the fore sometime in the 90s], it was discovered that 'heritable changes in gene function' can occur which 'cannot be explained by changes in DNA sequence'. How is that possible? Well, it has been found that our cells play a little trick where they switch certain sections of the DNA (genes) on and off by attaching little 'bookmarks' to them. [The implications are enormous, but this is not the time and place to go into the details (keep an eye on introducingaffinitology.com)]

"So, Bijan, what has all this got to do with improving the quality of our relationships?" I hear you asking (again). Bear with me as I show you how we can take these understandings and apply them to create affinitological theories and frameworks.

Beliefs are like genotypes and the behaviour that ensues are like phenotypes. See § 62.4 (Beliefs as Affinitological Genes). Unlike [what is currently believed about] biological genes, we can change our affinitological genotypes by changing our beliefs. Looking to nature to see what genes and, by extension, beliefs, are capable of doing, we see that,

- There are genes that code for proteins that create structure (anatomy and histology).

- There are other genes that code for proteins that provide infrastructure (Physiology).

- Other genes that code for factors (enzymes) that regulate the dynamics of the system (laws, regulations, policies and procedures).

Despite the exponential advances that we have made in the past few decades, we are still in the early stages of exploring what exactly our bodies are capable of, especially in terms of changing our genes, including which genes we can turn on and off and how we do it. At this stage, what we know is that genetic changes can be passed on to the next generation, at least in some form.

Lamentably, I believe that there is also a certain amount of dogma in our beliefs about genes and what our bodies can and cannot do with them. For example, the current view amongst the scientific community is that now that we can explain, through epigenetic theory (switching genes on and off) how acquired characteristics are passed on from one generation to another, we can stick to our original notion that changes in the actual nucleic acid sequence of our DNA are outside of our bodies' control and that genetic mutations are random. But I am still not comfortable with that notion. Let me explain why.

The current COVID-19 epidemic has made us, the public, more acutely aware of how microorganisms in our environment are constantly changing and evolving. This means that their DNA sequence is changing (whether randomly or not). However, back in the early 1980s, when I became interested in evolutionary biology, and even before reading the Noweir *et. al.* paper mentioned above, I was not convinced by the prevailing theory that inter-generational genetic variations are random. My contention was that, in order to fight these ever-changing organisms, our immune system needs to first, recognize them as being alien and second, create target-specific antibodies (protein traps) for them. We need DNA to make proteins. If our DNA sequence is fixed, we can only make a fixed number of proteins. This means that we will not be able to make new proteins to fight newly emerging strains of parasites. It seems to me that, if that were the case, we would have become extinct millennia ago. There has to be a mechanism for our bodies to splice DNA and recombine it in a way that will make a protein (antibody) that is specific to the newly evolving threats that emerge in our environment.

This dogma, that the DNA sequence cannot be purposefully changed by our bodies (§ 35.11 Consciousness), has led to the proposal that our DNA contains a database of antibodies and the reason we can fight new strains of bacteria, fungi, protozoa and viruses is that evolution (those random mistakes we talked about earlier) has provided us with so many existing templates that it enables us to cope with all the existing and emerging strains of parasites. Forgive me if I consider this to be incredulous.

Whilst epigenetics is the 'safer' way (provides the lowest risk-to-benefit ratio) for passing on what we learn about what our bodies' need to adapt from one generation to another, it is my belief that, in time, we will discover that those changes in DNA sequence that we call mutations are also not as random as we think. OK, now that I have got that off my chest, let's see how we can apply various concepts from the science of genetics to improving our interpersonal relationships.

An epigenetic belief change is one that renders a belief's phenotype (resultant behaviour) to be more suited to a particular situation. For example, in some societies, smiling 'too much' is taken to indicate 'dullness of mind' or not giving life the serious attention that it deserves. Let's call this belief, the do-not-smile belief (DNSB). If this individual moves to a society where smiling is an indication of openness, then a belief change is required for the person to adapt to the new society (otherwise he may be perceived as being unapproachable). Let's call the new belief smile-to-connect belief (STCB). If this individual moves back and forth between two societies, then he will need to switch between these two beliefs by either switching on DNSB and switching off STCB or vice versa. This is what I mean by epigenetic belief change (it does not impact Core Values (§ 29.4.1), such as sincerity and respect).

63.1
Changing Beliefs (Reframing)

Beliefs can be changed by a process called reframing. There are two types of reframing; a meaning reframe and a context reframe. Both of these involve changes in our perceptions.

63.1.1
Meaning and Context Reframes

An example of a meaning reframe

When I was young, I once picked up a cockroach, held it steady in the palm of my hand, showed it to my mother and said (in Persian), "Mum look how ugly this thing is." She looked at it and said, "On the contrary, look at its beautiful shiny wings, its intricate shape and its delicate legs."

I still remember the profound effect that this simple encounter had on me. It was as if I could sense the neuro-connections changing in my head and could feel the effects of those changes resonating throughout my body [of course, I did not know anything about neurones or resonance at the time; I can only express that experience in those terms in retrospect]. I also suddenly remembered something that I had heard, but had not paid much attention to, because I had not understood it [this is related to confirmation bias (§ 33.8)] which was, "Beauty is in the eyes of the beholder." This is how a meaning reframe works; same context, different meaning.

An example of a context reframe

The only thing that I remember from the 1973 film, Papillon, is a scene where a man was so hungry that he was catching cockroaches and eating them.

Why did I choose to share that nugget with you? Because the more emotive something is, the more memorable it becomes. More pertinently, in the context of starvation, a cockroach *means* food, whereas in the context of a modern hospital, it *means* vermin.

Comparison of context and meaning reframes

Notice that in both cases, the reframe is a change in *meaning* (and perception). However, in the first case a change in context is not required; that is, it is a purely meaning reframe and in the second example, a change in context is required for the meaning to change.

[Therefore, strictly speaking, they are both 'meaning' reframes, so perhaps it would be more accurate to call one of them a 'context-independent reframe' and the other a 'context-dependent reframe' but experience has shown that where language is concerned, we incline more towards short and ambiguous than long and unambiguous. It seems to me that it would be worth doing some research to see which one has a greater impact on our cognitive load (§ 72.5 Cognitive Load and Heuristics) and biases.]

63.1.2
Factors Affecting Belief Change

The ease with which we can change a belief depends on the strength of our emotional association (attachment) to that belief. It also depends on whether or not that belief is a part of a *belief set*. This reminds me of the proverb, "You can't break a stick in a bundle." [fans of Star Trek may recognise that as a quote from 'Scotty' in Star Trek Beyond]

The more meaning I attach to a belief and the more I associate that meaning to my sense of Identity, the more emotive and, as such, the more entrenched, that belief will be.

Beliefs can be changed directly by providing evidence to the contrary. This is where the sequence that will ultimately lead to belief change is instigated at the *intellectual* level. Here, the probability of success depends on at least four factors:

a) the validity (believability) of the new evidence,
b) the relative strength of the emotional associations that accompany the existing and the new beliefs,
c) the strength (potential impact) of the new evidence and
d) the frequency with which we encounter the new evidence.

Beliefs can also be changed covertly by approaching the process from an emotional angle. If, contrary to my belief that a particular situation will be painful, I experience pleasure, then I am likely to sever the link between that belief and the negative emotion.

If beliefs are a part of a *belief set*, then the task of belief change becomes more complicated. It would be like trying to disassemble a Jenga tower one block at a time. Trying to do it at random can have disastrous consequences. Similarly, to try to build a belief set without careful consideration of the structural congruity of the set can also have deleterious consequences. In fact,

> **many of the inner conflicts that disempower us and sabotage our relationships stem from incongruent belief sets.**

We adopt beliefs because we assume (§ 33 Atasinex Cluster) that those beliefs serve (empower) us. I am more likely to be motivated to change my beliefs about something if I foresee (assume) that the prospective new belief is more likely to empower me.

Adopting other people's beliefs 'lock, stock and barrel', so to speak, is unlikely to feel (or appear) empowering because beliefs need to be internalised (owned) to be empowering and they are unlikely to be internalised if we do not arrive at the conclusions through our own cognitive processes or experiences (§ 60.3.2 Inter-Pactal Interference).

63.2
Beliefs and Conflict

Conflicts (internal and external) are indicators that a belief change is called for. The challenge is that the conflict, and the associated disempowering feelings that we experience, are outcomes whereas the beliefs that get us there are processes. I feel that an explanation is in order here.

Earlier, I defined beliefs as "if-then statements that we live by". A conflict is where the output of two of these 'if-then' processes clash. For example, consider the following two beliefs:

Belief 1: "If he is alluring, then attempt to connect."

Belief 2: "If already committed to someone else, then do not attempt to connect."

Both beliefs are internally congruent [they do not conflict with themselves in the way that, for example, oxymorons do]. However, the output/outcome of each these beliefs can result in conflict if he is alluring and one is committed to someone else. To change either of these beliefs is to decide that the belief itself is faulty (it does not have internal congruity) which would be false; we would be throwing the baby out with the bathwater, so to speak.

[Note that this would be equivalent to an organism deciding to throw away one of its genes because it manifested inappropriately. Based on what I think I understand about how evolution works, evolution is not about mere adaptation, it is about increasing our repertoire of adaptive capabilities (§ 35.12.2 Repertoire). This means that, rather than throwing genes away when our immediate environment no longer has any use for them, we archive them (switch them off). This is what the new science of epigenetics is beginning to reveal to us.]

Here are some of the ways in which we can try to resolve such a conflict:

1. Make Belief 2 irrelevant by refusing to commit.
2. Prevent Belief 1 from manifesting by reframing it at Belief Level 3 (§ 62.5 The Three Levels of Belief) by changing its value to "It is not worth it".
3. Change perception (premise) to make Belief 1 irrelevant, "He is not alluring".
4. Change interpretation to make the premise (the 'if' part of the 'if then' clause) false, "She only appears to be alluring, but the reality is different."
5. Introduce a new belief, the outcome of which takes priority over Belief 2; "Hedonism takes precedence because life is too short."
6. Introduce a new belief, the outcome of which takes priority over Belief 1; "My current commitment takes precedence over potential new connections" (because my current commitment is based on a spiritual connection whereas the new potential connection is based on carnal values).

[Whilst writing point 6, above, Carmina Burana, by Carl Orff, came to mind and I just thought I would share that moment with you ;-)]

Of course, there are many other ways of dealing with such conflicts. However, I think that the above examples are enough to demonstrate the point.

Notice that we have not factored morality into this equation at all. Here, our discussion is not about 'right' and 'wrong' [see also § 3.5 Good or Bad], it is about resolving our inner conflicts. I often tell my clients that,

---

Our mind prefers to believe a lie than to be in conflict.

63.2.1
Some Major sources of Conflict

I have found that one of the most prevalent and disempowering errors that we make is to confuse means with ends. Similar concepts that come to my mind that are often confused [insufficient attention is paid to their distinctions] and which can, and often do, lead to conflicts of various kinds include:

- Form and function
- Action and intention
- Fact, opinion and theory
- Attachment and dependence
- Love and lust
- Sexual and sensual
- Ability and attainment
- Information, knowledge, skill and wisdom
- Food and nutrition
- Price and value
- Respiration and breathing
- Mathematics and arithmetic
- Want and need
- Remembering and understanding
- Process and outcome

[I shall endeavour to expound on these elsewhere. Keep an eye on introducingaffinitology.com]

Chapter 64

Values

64.1

What are Values?

Values emerge through prioritisation of beliefs. The moment we decide that one of our beliefs is more important than another, we create a 'value system' for ourselves. In other words, values are beliefs about beliefs (§ 64.4 Values as Receptors). This means that values only matter when there is a conflict in our beliefs, i.e., when we need to decide which belief is more important. Depending on the situation, different beliefs will come into play. It is these situation-dependent beliefs that create the potential for conflicts that need to be resolved through prioritisation (evaluation). This makes our values situation-dependent, although, by definition, our Core Values (Principles) are less labile than our Identity-based values (§ 29.4 The Omniself).

64.2

The Purpose of Values

Values serve the following purposes. They,

a) provide benchmarks against which we judge what is important and what is not in any particular situation,

b) reduce cognitive load by providing shortcuts to help us make decisions faster (§ 72.5 Cognitive Load and Heuristics),

c) provide anchors to give us a sense of who we are; I am the sum of what I value,

d) determine which of the myriad of environmental (and mental) stimuli that we receive through our senses and from our thoughts, reach our consciousness (we become aware of).

64.3
Values are Comparative

There are no absolute values; values have no meaning in isolation. You could think of them as being like transitive verbs, they need an object and a context to make sense.

You may say, "But Bijan, nothing makes sense out of context." And I would agree. However, some verbs have an intrinsic context; the context is already in the verb. For example, I am hungry does not need any more context or explanation. On the other hand, the verb 'send' needs an object AND a context. If I were to say to you, "I sent", that would be an incomplete sentence and you would not expect that to be the end of my 'transaction' (§ 73 Transactional Analysis). If I say, "I sent Jack", that *would* be a complete sentence, but it would not be much more helpful unless the context were provided by a question like, "Who did you send?" or if it were followed by a phrase like "to fetch a pale of water." Our values are similar. They only have meaning in context, that is to say; they are relative. This means that,

---

Nothing has intrinsic value. Value is created through comparison.

We can also look at values from a decision-making perspective and say that values are only invoked at a point where a decision needs to be made. Another way of looking at this is to say that our values only matter in the context of answering a question related to a decision that we need to make. In general terms, that question is,

---

"Which do I value more, the sum of what I stand to lose or the sum of what I stand to gain?"

64.4
Values as Receptors

For something to have value, we must believe in it first. Therefore, values are a subset of beliefs; they are beliefs about beliefs. If we consider beliefs to be the affinitological equivalent to genes, then what is the physiological equivalent to values?

One of the most important functions of genes is to code for receptors on the surface of cells. These receptors determine what each cell is sensitive to. The vital importance of this becomes clear when we remember that sensitivity is one of the criteria that we use to 'define' life (§ 26.2 Characteristics of Living Systems). In terms of our non-physical (spiritual) life, including our relationships,

> **Our values determine our sensitivity
> to practically all aspects of our lives.**

Therefore, we can think of each value as the equivalent of a receptor. To wit, our values determine what we are sensitive to and what we are not. Each value is the product of a single, or a set of, belief(s); just as, receptors are the product of genes. Note that values are both Identity- and context-dependent.

We pass on our biological genes through sexual intercourse. Beliefs are passed on through social intercourse.

Beliefs are modified by experience along the same lines as gene expression is mediated by the environment.

Receptors are specialised proteins on the surface of every cell that inform it of what is going on outside of it and what the cell should do about it. Receptors also give organisms the potential to be sensitive to certain stimuli* in their environment. Receptors on sensory nerve cells have been compared to transducers, converting any number of energies (sound, heat, light, pressure, etc.) from the environment into action potentials (nerve impulses).

* [For the philosophers amongst you, yes, I appreciate the logical incongruity her, in order to be a stimulus, the potential needs to have been realised.]

Different types of cells have different receptors, just as different peoples have different values. The same receptor can exist on more than one type of cell. However, different cells, or more accurately, different groups of cells (tissues) respond differently to the stimulation of the *same* receptor. Similarly, different peoples can have common values, but may respond differently to situations where those values become relevant. I say people$\underline{s}$ because culture (social influences) is probably the most instrumental factor in determining our values, especially those values that affect our interpersonal relationships. This is the main tenet of social constructionism [I encourage you to look it up].

The importance we attach to something determines its value; our values are those aspects of each dimension of human experience (§ 48-50) that we believe deserve more of our attention (§ 93.1 Motivation and Motivational Energy).

64.5

The Nature and Types of Values

Like the notion of love, the word 'values' is used so broadly that the qualitative and quantitative differences in their meanings in different contexts often eludes us. This can deprive us from appreciating subtle, or sometimes even glaring, differences between one set of values and another. For example, I can say, "I value my freedom" and "I value my job." A visiting alien would be forgiven for concluding that these two concepts carry equal weight in my decision-making process.

64.5.1

Principles and Expediencies

Although there is probably a relationship between my job and my sense of freedom, I would argue that, when I say, "I value my job" I am talking about a different type of value compared with when I say, "I value my freedom." Freedom is a core value; a **principle** I live by. Unless I live my job [it is not something that I do, it is who I am; I would feel incomplete without it], my job is an **expediency**; a means through which I (only partly) fulfil my need for a sense of freedom. We could think of expediencies as those things that have contextual or temporary value; they are usually a means to an end. This is what Abraham Maslow's hierarchy of needs proposes; as one level of needs becomes satisfied, it is no longer a motivator [which, in practice, tends to mean that we start to take it for granted and begin to appreciate (value) it less]. In contrast, some of my values form the basis on which I define who I am; my Identity [in any particular situation]. These Identities are held together (harmonised/unified) by still other values that are common to all our 'True' Identities. I have called these our 'Core Values' or Principles (§ 29.4.1 Identities, Core Values and Principles). In § 25.3 (Polar Bond: Partial Sharing), I explained how we have a tendency to impose blackness and whiteness by drawing arbitrary lines somewhere along what is essentially a spectrum (Figure 3).

You could, of course, point out that, since all values lie along a spectrum of 'something to avoid like the plague' to 'something to die for', by suggesting that we classify values into the two categories of Principles and Expediencies, I, myself, am not immune to imposing categories on what is, in essence, a continuum. Whilst I would concede that I, too, am prone such an error, in the following section, I hope to exonerate myself from this accusation in this specific instance by arguing that there are discernible characteristics that categorically differentiate Principles from Expediencies.

64.5.2
Expediencies versus Principles

Our principles (core values) are those sensitivities that remain stable across our different Identities. Our other (non-core) values are about what we think is important (expedient) in a specific situation. Our principles are, therefore, about who we perceive ourselves to be at our core. These are the beliefs that give us a sense of at-one-ness, of being a single entity, of being who I am, of being *me*.

You might say, "Yes Bijan, all that sounds plausible in theory but, how can I distinguish an Expediency from a Principle?" And my response would be, "I am glad you are thinking this through, it makes me feel as if what I am saying has the potential to make a difference and I thank you for that." I would then go on to explain that there are two ways in which we can ascertain how close a value is to the core of our being. [And the astute amongst you would say, "Hey Bijan, it looks like you have gone back on your word and are talking in 'grayscales' again." And I would thank you for that observation and say, "Old habits die hard."] One way is through its robustness. Our non-core values can change from situation to situation, whereas our principles do not. Here is an example to put the cat amongst the pigeons.

If I purport that I value life as a matter of principle, then the situation is irrelevant and I would abhor killing for whatever reason. Upholding such a principle, I would declare myself a conscientious objector to war and accept a court-martial rather than to agree to be drafted and to be ordered to kill in the name of my country. This is what my chemistry teacher, the late Phillips Harris did when he was called to National Service. After the court ruled in his favour, the court stated [this is from memory, so it may not be precise], **"We do not understand his arguments but we have no doubt about the strength of his conviction."**

This brings us to the second way in which we can determine how close a value is to the core of our being; the strength of our emotional reaction to it, especially to its violation. The stronger we feel about something, the more value it has for us. Now, here is an important point. Since one of our psychological defence mechanisms (§ 79) is emotional detachment, if upholding one of our principles becomes so difficult (threatening) that we emotionally detach ourselves from it, one of the major consequences is a very deep sense of loss. This is because, it is not simply a matter of losing an Identity and replacing it with another one, it is about losing one's essence; that which holds my Identities together and gives me a sense of being whole (wholesomeness).

Trying to change our Principles feels like we are shaking the very foundation of who we are. To use an organisational metaphor, the management may decide to change strategies or review policies and the way in which they are implemented and, as long as the core of the organisation remains intact, stakeholders will go along with it. However, if management decides to change what the organisation stands for, then, although robots may comply, conscious beings within the organisation will begin to re-evaluate their purpose for being there.

We can think of non-core values (expediencies), as being like the branches and leaves of a tree. Our core values (Principles) are like the trunk of the tree. The trunk is a conduit through which the branches and leaves are nourished (§ 26.2.6 Nutrition) from the roots.

For example, one of my core values is 'respect'. How do I know this? Because, whenever I interpret something as being disrespectful, I sense a negative emotional reaction (typically, anger, guilt or pity) permeating through my body irrespective of the Identity that may be active at the time.

Another one of my core values is 'growth'. This one affects the decision-making process of all of my Identities. Trying to put the feeling into words, I would say that it is as if I weigh my options against a single reference question, "Will this decision yield the highest dividend in terms of growth?". If the decision is being made by my Teacher Identity, then the question becomes, "Will this decision yield the highest dividend in terms of my students' growth?". When my Father Identity is deciding, the question becomes, "Will this decision yield the highest dividend in terms of my child's growth?" And when faced with a decision relating to business, my entrepreneur Identity bases its decision primarily on the question, "Will this decision yield the highest dividends in terms of the growth of the business?"

In retrospect, my focus on growth has not always led to the most empowering choices. This is because core values do not simply provide direction, they also act as heuristics (§ 72.5 Cognitive Load and Heuristics).

To help us understand Core Values better, let me offer you another example. If you were to ask me to name one of my mother's core values, I would say Survival. In fact, one of her mottos is, "Survival before progress", which makes sense. In practice, this means that she takes the idea of health (looking after one's body) very seriously. In contrast, I have often taken survival for granted and focused on progress instead. I would suggest that her second core value is service; given a choice between doing something that will benefit herself and benefit someone else, she will choose the latter, on one condition: That it does not conflict with her survival value. And this brings us to another important consideration; values are hierarchical.

64.6

Hierarchy of Values

Suppose that one of my values is that 'friends should always be there for each other' and another value is that 'I have a responsibility for my son's welfare'. Both values are potentials that only manifest themselves (are activated) when the relevant situation arises.

If I am reading a book and my friend calls me to ask for my help with a project, the first value is stimulated/triggered/activated [think receptor activation] and results in my putting down my book and going over to my friend's place. Similarly, if I am reading a book and I hear my son scream, the second value is activated and I put down my book and rush over to help him.

In both of the above cases, even though I might believe that reading a book is a valuable pastime, the new situation invokes my critical faculties to assess the importance of my values relative to each other. My value hierarchy determines which of those values I choose to act upon. As the number of options that arise in a particular situation increase, the likelihood of my values conflicting (competing) with each other increases and the hierarchy of values becomes more complex. This brings us to the crux of the matter.

> **Our hierarchy of values can be a critical determinant of
> the quality of our interpersonal relationships.**

For example, let's imagine that, as I am reading my book, my friend calls me to ask for help and I tell him that I will come over straight away and then, as I hang up, my son screams and I spend the next few hours tending to his needs and completely forget the promise I made to my friend. When I realise this and I call him to explain, I trust (§ 53) that my friend (§ 92.8 Friendship) would not feel undervalued.

But what if two friends ask me for help at the same time? Whomever I choose to help, I risk disappointing the other. This is a situation where, if I'm not careful, my psychological defence mechanisms could kick in (for example, I could be tempted to lie or make excuses) and that could be very detrimental to my relationships. I explain the nature of psychological defence mechanisms and how they affect our relationships in § 79.

64.7

Values and Attention

At any one moment, in every decision that we make, we are making a choice; a choice based on values. The more important something is to us, the more resources (attention) we devote to it. Yes, that's right; attention is the key.

Attention is not necessarily conscious, but *conscious* attention is the key to *purposeful* change and improvement.

Being intrinsically hierarchical, no two values are identical; if they were, it would be impossible for us to make decisions. In situations where we perceive two values to be identical (usually when we are too emotionally or cognitively compromised [e.g., distracted or overwhelmed] to be able to ascertain the relative importance of each value), we tend to either defer the decision to someone else, toss a coin or defer the decision to a later time. See also 'Procrastination' in § 62.5.2 (Belief Level 2: Self-Confidence).

Sometimes we pay less attention to things that are more important to us. One reason for this is overwhelm. When too many thoughts vie for our attention, we often try to relieve ourselves of some of them by taking a shortcut; we delegate some decisions to our limbic system (emotional centres).

The limbic system tends to prioritise the urgent (immediate/short-term) over the more important, but long-term. It prioritises survival over progress. Therefore, we can choose to hand over our value judgements to our emotions knowing that the decision will be in favour of short-term survival. Alternatively, we can imprint our long-term or more wide-ranging values onto our emotions so that our emotions become aligned with our values. This is how attitudes are created. We explore attitudes in more detail in § 65 (Attitudes).

64.8
The Origin of Values

So where do our values come from? That's a great question; let's explore that a bit. You have probably heard of the parable of the Elephant in the Darkness. I think it is relevant to all types of research and so I translated it from the original Persian and put it before the main text of my PhD thesis. Here it is:

The Elephant in the Darkness

An elephant had been brought
To a house in a remote place
The house was too dark to see the creature
Many people had gathered in the darkness
As it was not possible to catch sight of the creature
People tried to understand the creature through touch
One who touched the trunk
Said that the creature is like a water pipe
On touching the ears another said
I envisage an elephant to be like a fan
Another who felt the legs of the elephant
Said that an elephant is like a pillar
Another touched the back of the elephant and said
The creature was more like a thrown
So it continued
Whosoever touched a part
Built up his own picture of the animal
As the interpretations were all different
One label the animal, D
Another, A
Had there been a candle in each person's palm
All differences would have parted from their discussion.

- Masnavi of Rumi Book III, Story V
(Translated by the author)

If ten people walked into the room and nine of them touch the elephant's ear and one of them touches the elephant's leg, nine out of ten people would concur that an elephant is like a fan and might even ridicule the one who says that an elephant is like a pillar. Experiments by Solomon Asch have demonstrated that in such cases about 70% of those people who are in the minority (of one) would go with the majority view. And, of course, the extent to which we deny our own senses is a measure of our self-confidence (§ 40.4), that is, trust in what our own senses are telling us.

Imagine a scenario where there are ten people in a society, nine of whom are blind. The seeing person then becomes an authority on what is what. Now if the ten people walk into the dark room where the Elephant is kept and the seeing man (who does not have any advantages over the others in this situation) were to touch the ears of the elephant and declare that an elephant is like a fan, whilst everyone else touches other parts of the elephant, then everyone else is likely to concede to the opinion of the 'authority' on the basis that he has higher powers. If one of the nine were to say, "OK, so we might be blind but why should there be such a divergence of opinion on this amongst the rest of us?" He might well be told not to question authority.

The above examples demonstrate two sources of our values; individual authority and social consensus. The examples also alert us to beware that neither of these sources are absolute.

64.9

Values and Perfectionism

So, what is a humble perfectionist looking for absolute answers to do? The first thing to recognise is that perfectionism is itself a value system and its roots (premises) are far from perfect. We can't even define 'perfection' in any concrete sense, so how can we aspire to achieve it? Even if we could define what perfect is, it is inherently unachievable. The reason is that the effort-outcome relationship is not linear. Let me explain.

Imagine that you know nothing about a particular subject, let's say, nutrigenomics, and you have a week to study for an exam in the subject. What is the likelihood that you will be able to achieve a score of 5%? Now imagine that you have studied the subject for three years and you know that if you took the exam now, you could get 95%. The exam is in a week. What is the likelihood that you could increase your score to 100% in one week? Notice that in this example, if the relationship were linear, you would say to yourself, "OK, so I have scored 5% in one week, I should be able to score 100% in 20 weeks (less than 5 months)." But that's not the way it works, as I am about to explain.

[Note that I have oversimplified this scenario by making many assumptions about the extent to which we are in control of our exam results (§ 5.4.1 Ability, Performance and Attainment)]

What I hope the following will help you to see is that, the more we improve, the more effort is required to make further improvements. It is sometimes called the law of diminishing returns. It has also been referred to as the 20-80 (or 80-20) rule. I prefer to think of it as an *asymptotic relationship*. Let me show you what this looks like on a graph. I had some fun with an online graphing tool (desmos.com) to marry the idea of the 20-80 rule with an asymptotic relationship. You can see from the graph that when about 80% of the work requires 20% of the effort, then 50% of the work requires around 9% of the effort, so you could also call it the 9-50 rule (or the 13-60 rule).

Figure 61 The Relationship between Effort and Result

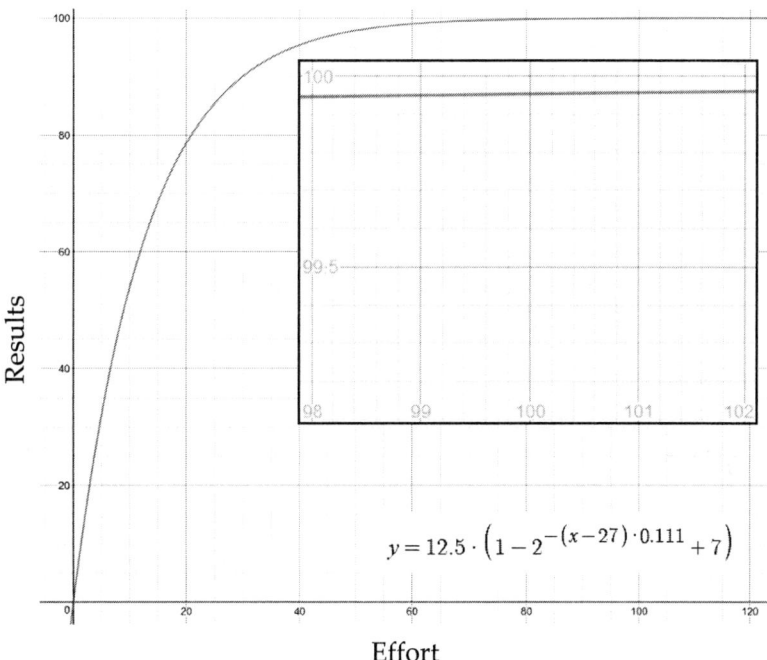

$$y = 12.5 \cdot \left(1 - 2^{-(x-27) \cdot 0.111} + 7\right)$$

Effort

In the inset, I have zoomed in on the top right of the graph because this is where you can see the problem with being a perfectionist: In an asymptotic relationship, no matter how much effort you put in, the result will never be perfect (100%).

Actually, this is an optimistic graph because it assumes that our perfectionist will continue to aim for perfection with the same vigour, in spite of seeing diminishing returns (less improvement with more effort). In reality, this does not happen. At some point, a perfectionist becomes self-critical, thinking that the diminishing return is a reflection on some kind of inadequacy in her. Since perfection is the aim, anything below that is 'not good enough'. And nothing batters our self-esteem (§ 40.3) more than constantly believing that we are not good enough.

64.10
Values and Culture

The effects of society's culture on the values, and the consequent behaviour, of its members was studied extensively by Geert Hofstede [Look up Hofstede's cultural dimensions theory]. Here, I simply want to point out that our values are heavily influenced by those around us. Accordingly, the people around us (our cultural environment) affect what we are sensitive to, and what we are desensitised against (§ 81 Emotional Allergens and Hypersensitivity). See also § 32.4 (Collective Identity)

64.11
Values and Self-Confidence

Authority and social consensus are the most pervasive sources of our value systems. However, as our awareness and self-confidence develop, we begin to decide our priorities (what is more important and what is less important) for ourselves, based on our own emotional and intellectual feedback. In doing so, our values become more idiosyncratic (cannot be generalised from me to other people).

Abandoning the crowd's values and developing our own individual set of values go hand in hand with self-confidence (§ 40.4). This can create its own problems. Self-confident people tend to carry more authority. "So, what's the problem with that?" You might be wondering. In addition to the problem that I indicated about the seeing man in the dark room with the elephant (§ 64.9 The Origin of Values), people who lack self-confidence, as well as young people who are still unsure of their sense of Identity, are prone to adopting the value systems of those who appear self-confident and authoritative. However, a value system, no matter how firmly believed by an individual or how empowering it is for that individual, is not necessarily empowering for others who may adopt it arbitrarily. A person who arrives at a value system through their own experience and judgement is like an engineer who builds a bicycle. The engineer is in a better position to know more about the possibilities and the limitations of the bicycle and can also modify the specifications of the bicycle to suit different conditions (racing bike, mountain bike, road bike, track bike, touring bike, etc). A person who is not aware of these distinctions may use a bicycle under conditions that it was not designed for, and this could cause injury to himself or others. Similarly, adopting the values of others, without the prerequisite experience can have detrimental consequences. We explore this in more detail § 60.3.2 (Inter-Pactal Interference).

Dimensions of Values

The following is adapted from The Theory of Basic Human Values, developed by Shalom H. Schwartz. Values have been extensively studied and, using Factor Analysis around, ten overlapping 'Basic human values' have been identified. These fit into a kind of circle. And a circle, being two dimensional, can be defined mathematically along two axes. Most of our values can be placed somewhere along these two axes or dimensions. These are shown in figure 62.

Figure 62
The Two Principle Values Dimensions

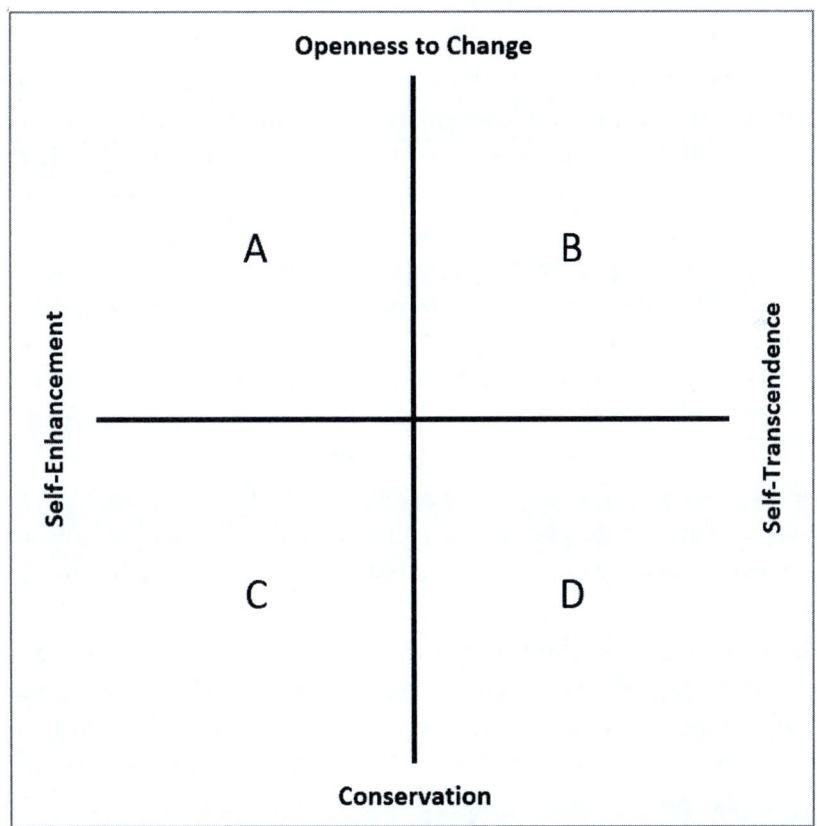

Let us begin by considering the vertical axis; the stability-change dimension.

To someone who values stability, change means instability, uncertainty and danger whereas, to someone who values change, it means growth, adventure and excitement. Conversely, to someone who values change, stability means stagnation and boredom whereas, to someone who values stability, it means predictability and security.

Imagine that your partner's values fall within quadrant C of the graph and you ask, "What shall we do this evening?" A response consistent with that may be, "Let's cuddle up together in front of the TV set" or something like that. With someone whose values fit within quadrant D, an answer may be something like, "Let's invite some friends round and sit around the television." Someone whose values fit within quadrant A might say, "Let's set off on an adventure together". And, if the person's values fall within quadrant B, you might hear, "Let's get together with some friends and go on some kind of adventure." These examples are, of course, gross generalisations and gross simplifications, but like post-Impressionist paintings, they still convey a discernible sense of the scene (intended message).

People's tolerance of variation along each of these value dimensions differ. Some people may be equally comfortable with either a spur of the moment adventure with lots of people or sitting quietly and reading a book by themselves. Others may be more inclined towards one or other end of this continuum. In addition, the degree to which our emotions and activities are inclined towards any part of this graph, as well as our tolerance levels, depend on both the situation and on which of our Identities is dominant at the time (§ 29.4 The Omniself). Note that, although the dominant Identity at the time may make the decision, other Identities may then take over at various times. For example, my Father Identity may decide that, right now, security is more important than adventure and, therefore, may decide against going bungee jumping ("I need to preserve myself for the benefit of my kids"). Having decided to play it safe and to go camping with the family instead, my Gregarious Identity may take over and decide to invite five other families to come with us.

At first glance, it may appear that relationships will work better if the values of The Self and The Other are within the same quadrant. However, whether or not incompatible values strengthen or weaken relationships depends on the type of relationship (§ 92 Relationship Frameworks) and many other factors that contribute to the formation and maintenance of that particular Nexus (§ 47 Common and Complementary Elements).

64.13
Values, Decision-Making and a Sense of Guilt

We discuss decision-making in more detail in § 72. Here, I simply want to point out that our values do not simply *guide* our decisions, they *dictate* our decisions. I say this because, if we fail to comply with our values, then we punish ourselves; this punishment being in the form of a sense of guilt or remorse.

One of the practical problems with the feeling of guilt or remorse is that, since we consider it as some kind of 'punishment', a part of us feels that we have 'paid our dues' and are, therefore, exonerated from taking any further action to change ourselves so as to, a) mitigate the detrimental effects of our actions and, b) make the effort to change our behaviour so as to reduce the possibility that we make the same 'mistake' again. In other words,

---

we often use the feeling of guilt to justify to ourselves why we do not need to change.

64.14
Complementary and Conflicting Values

Earlier (§ 64.6.1 Expediencies versus Principles), I cited 'survival' and 'service' as examples of two core values that co-exist within a single individual. These are complementary values. That is, in most situations, they are not in conflict with each other; service to others can complement, rather than compete with, survival. I also mentioned that 'respect' is one of my Core Values. This Value is complementary to many other values, such as achievement, benevolence, autonomy and universalism. As such, acting on these Values need not be in conflict with 'respect'. 'Respect' infers freedom and acceptance and, in doing so, implies trust; trust in people's ability to adapt harmoniously.

Power (as in dominion), on the other hand, is based on the premise of distrust, "I cannot trust people to act in ways that serve our mutual interest and, therefore, I must seize power (control their actions)."

[I wander if you notice the implicit sense of insecurity in this way of thinking. It also has another implication; separateness and potential isolation because, clearly, I cannot feel a part of what I seek to be superior to. This will make more sense in the context of our discussion about psychological defence mechanisms (§ 79).]

This notion of power is, therefore, in conflict with the concept of respect. The two cannot co-exist as core values within a single individual without conflict.

Authority (as in competence, not rank) is an alternative to power that is not in conflict with respect. Here is a story to demonstrate this.

In around 2008, I attended a talk by Professor Sugata Mitra at the Institute of Education, University of London, where he described an experiment he had carried out in India. He explains what he did in his January 2018 TED Talk. Here is a transcript of his introduction to that talk:

> "Eighteen years ago, I conducted a small experiment in Delhi. There was an underprivileged community in Kalkaji. There were a lot of children there. In those days, there were many children who had never seen a computer, never heard of the internet. So, I thought what will happen if I give them a computer? So in a wall we made a slot, like an ATM machine and fixed a computer in it. In a few hours, I saw that the children were surfing the net. People said, "They don't know English, so how are they surfing?" I said, "I do not have any idea." After two days, they had downloaded and installed a game and were playing!"

One of the things that Professor Mitra shared with us at the talk that I attended was that,

> *at one point, an eight your old girl was at the workstation and a bully pushed her out of the way (Note: Power, no respect). **Soon, he realised that he was not able to do anything with the terminal and let the girl continue to do what she was doing.***

The girl did not have 'Power' (as in dominion) but did have authority (in this situation) which 'demanded' respect.

64.15

Values and Innocence

I have a hypothesis that what we perceive as 'innocence' is inversely related to the formation of our values. In other words, since our sense of 'right' and 'wrong' emerges from our value systems, in the absence of such beliefs, the idea of intentionality becomes meaningless; we act on instinct. This is because we are not judging what we are doing against some standard to determine its rightness or wrongness. This reminds me of a Persian proverb that says, "A scorpion's sting is not through grievance, it is decreed by its immutable essence." [Translation (and poetic licence) by yours truly].

Chapter 65

Attitudes

Although the word attitude is very familiar to us and there are plenty of research and academic papers that investigate this construct, definitions of 'attitude' are quite diverse and tend to be somewhat vague. However, there is consensus on one aspect of attitudes; they are 'formed'. That is to say, attitudes are acquired; we are not born with them. It is also obvious that our attitudes are related to our perceptions; how we perceive something.

When we are studying attitudes, what we are looking for (measuring) are positive or negative feelings towards some 'thing'. This 'thing' may be an object, an abstract concept (such as 'communism' or 'mathematics' for example) or a certain person or group.

So, now we know (have decided) three things about attitudes. They are acquired, they are related to our perceptions and they are related to our feelings towards a particular concept or thing. But, for it to become a construct that we can work with scientifically, we need to have a better 'handle' on what we are dealing with.

As scientists, we tend to avoid what I would call 'wet fish' ideas. Concepts that are too slippery to hold on to. The reason that attitudes can be, and are, studied extensively scientifically, is because we believe that the construct is robust (it is practically applicable, reproducible and can predict behaviour).

OK, so now we have found a way of measuring 'something' that can predict behaviour. But, whilst it is related to our perceptions and our feelings, we still need a model or, more precisely, a theoretical framework where the concept of attitude can fit in nicely without disrupting anything else that we have decided that we know about the mind. On the one hand, attitudes are like decisions because we are deciding whether we like something or not. On the other hand, we tend to think of emotions (§ 51.2 Affect, Feelings and Emotions) as being distinct from cognition (thoughts and thinking).

Research has shown that we cannot make decisions without emotional involvement at some level (usually at the final level; just before we take action). In other words, we act through our emotions and in order to be able to act, our cognitive faculties need to convince our emotional centres. Yes, it is as if our 'higher' faculties has to constantly negotiate with an often stubborn child for us to be able to do anything (§ 51.3.2 Feelings trump logic).

So, where do attitudes come into all this? I am coming to that, but bear with me as I explain a little more so that we can put the final verdict (conclusion) into a more meaningful context.

To survive, organisms need to be very energy conscious. We try to minimise the amount of energy (effort) we use in our quest for acquiring whatever we want. Thinking is very energy-intensive. That is why most of us rarely think. We either use heuristics (mental shortcuts) or habits (§ 68.5 Habits) or delegate the thinking to other people. It is also why most of us tend to like computers and the television so much. [Despite the fact that they distort reality and tend to make us lazy (unappreciative of our own abilities) but that is a discussion for another time and place (keep an eye on introducingaffinitology.com.]

So, what we have so far is this. We need to think in order to make decisions and our decisions are linked to our beliefs (§ 62.1). But we cannot act on those decisions unless our emotions get involved; our cognitively approved decisions need to be ratified by our emotions (§ 51.3.2 Feelings trump logic).

There is evidence that the processes involved in our emotional reactions, just before commands are sent through our peripheral nervous system, that is, just before we *act*, are very similar to our cognitive processes (thinking).

[Some authorities have argued that the distinction between emotions and cognition is a fallacy. Others have heavily criticized such claims saying that they are based on broadening of the meaning of the word 'cognition' so as to make it so inclusive as to blur real distinctions. If you are interested in this, look up the phrase 'cognitive theories of emotion'.]

These two processes are designed [for want of a better word I am not going to get into the 'intelligent design' argument here] to complement each other. That being the case, emotional processing is also energy-intensive and it would not be surprising to find the equivalent of heuristics for emotional processes. That's where attitudes come in. Whilst making decisions, including reacting to our environment, there is a constant back-and-forth loop between our thoughts and our emotions. It would be very convenient if the emotional faculties did not need to process each thought from scratch. In other words, it would save a lot of processing if our mind could say, "If this thought, then that emotion." And this is what I suggest attitudes are. In other words,

---

Attitudes are beliefs that are linked directly to emotions.

65.1
Attitudes as Reflexes

I propose that an attitude is the psychological (or, in the case of those attitudes that affect our relationships, affinitological) equivalent to a physiological reflex action. emotional responses to stimuli that allow for the use of more rapid and less energy-intensive pathways than our more diligent decision-making processes.

Chapter 66

Goals

There is an old adage that says, "If you don't know where you're going, you will probably end up somewhere else." This is a paradoxical statement, of course. Perhaps it would be more meaningful to say, "If you don't know where you're going, you shouldn't mind where you end up." This is an approach that we can take if we put ourselves in, what I call, Explorer Mode. In fact, there are all kinds of modes that we can put ourselves into. To use an aircraft analogy, we can, for example, put ourselves into Autopilot (habit) Mode, Cruise (flow) Mode or into Manual (thinking mode).

The important point here is that, in our relationships, we are interacting with other people's Modes as well. For example, in an interview situation, one party could be in Growth Mode (I am keeping my eye open for new opportunities) and the other in Survival Mode (I need someone to fill this position right now).

The Self has goals, the Other has goals, the Nexus has goals and the Pactum has goals. In this section, I am going to talk about goals from the perspective of individual Identities; The Self and The Other.

I cannot think of anything that we say or do that does not imply a goal; an outcome, something to be achieved. Every noun that has a functional definition (§ 21.1 What is a Relationship?) and sentences that contain words like 'want' and 'should' and 'could' carry with them the idea of a goal. Words such as 'choice' [and concepts contingent on choice, such as decision and freedom] also imply goals in their essence because if I have no goals, the idea of choice becomes meaningless; if it is not relevant to any goal of mine, then any choice that I appear to be making will be completely random [if there is such a thing, but let's not go down that slippery path today].

Where conscious beings are concerned, even inaction implies a goal. Since conscious beings have a choice as to whether or not to take action, the choice not to act can be expressed in terms of goals. For example, I choose not to act because my goal is to avoid the consequences of that action as I perceive, predict or expect them (§ 33 Atasinex Cluster).

We instinctively know that everything we do is goal-oriented. You can probably remember times when someone asked you something like, "Why did you do that?" At times like these, we are much more likely to say, "I don't know" than we are to say, "For no reason at all." In other words, "I believe that there was a goal, but I am not conscious of it." From time to time, you may hear someone say, "For the hell of it", I suggest that this is an alternative expression for "I don't know" or "I cannot articulate the reason". It could also be a Psychological Defence Mechanism (§ 79), "I do not wish to tell you my reasons." It does not mean that there was no goal.

66.1
Goals, Expectations and Purpose

Expectation is implied in the notion of goal; without expectations, goals would be meaningless. Expectations are rooted in beliefs and beliefs are rooted in assumptions. Hence, all of our goals are based on conjecture. This gives us another reason for not becoming too attached to outcomes and focusing on enjoying the journey (§ 6-11). This is what I tell my clients:

The purpose of a goal is to give us an impetus to move, to grow, to create, in short; to avoid stagnation.

66.2
Dimensions of goals

66.2.1
Consciousness dimension

Our goals can lie along a continuum from being fully conscious (focused, well thought out and deliberate) to fully unconscious (I have no idea why I did that). A subconscious act would be where I act without thinking but, if someone asked me why I did that, I would know.

You may remember our discussion about consciousness in § 35.11 and ask, "Can there be non-conscious goals?" I suggest that, unless, at least, some level of consciousness or potential for conscious choice is present, we can consider our behaviour to be 'fully reactive'. This means that what we are doing is not instigated or directed by any of our Identities. There being no choice, the behaviour is somehow forced upon us. In this case, our behaviour is no different from the behaviour of a Newton's cradle; governed only by the laws of Newtonian physics.

Note that if someone puts a gun to my head and tells me to do something, I still have a choice. However, if someone or something pushes me beyond the abilities of my muscles to resist that movement, then my behaviour (beyond what I can resist) is non-conscious [Here, I do not mean conscious as in 'aware', I mean conscious as in 'able to exercise choice' (§ 35.11 Consciousness)]. Therefore, what I am saying here is that, if a behaviour is non-conscious, it is at an inanimate level which then becomes a simple cause-and-effect relationship.

66.2.2
Direction of Goals (Goals as Vectors)

Goals can be directed inwards (within the Self) or outwards (beyond the Self). We could think of this as being two directions (back and forth or positive and negative) along the same dimension. However, I think it would be more productive to think of them as two separate positive dimensions that we can consider to be independent of (perpendicular to) each other. We can now think of each goal as a vector along two dimensions; The Self and 'Beyond the Self'. The latter can be anything such as a person (e.g., The Other in a Pactum), a cause (e.g., Global Warming) or a group (e.g., a competing team).

Vectors have two properties, a direction and a length (strength/intensity). Let's see what happens when we look at goals from this perspective. Figure 64 shows eight ways in which our goals can affect ourselves or others.

Figure 63 Goal Effects (Vectors) representing
the effects of goals along two dimensions

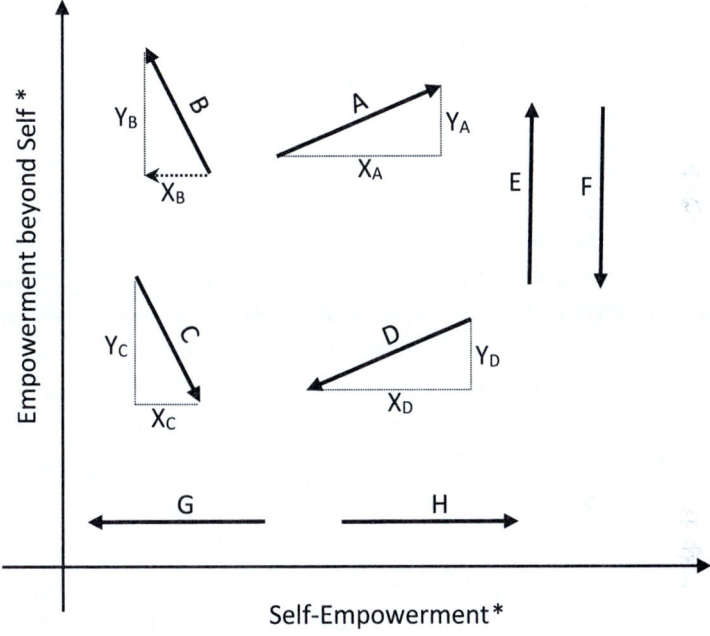

* The empowerment can be along any of the dimensions of human experience (see text)

Goal Effect A (Win-Win)

Let's assume that the X and Y axes in figure 64 represent empowerment along the Financial Dimension. And we are looking at a situation where I contract Sam to do a job that I have negotiated with a client. Vector A represents such a scenario. Let's also assume that my net income from that job is $500,000 whilst the net income of Sam, who carried out the work, is $200,000. X_A (the Self component of vector A) shows the extent to which I am empowered financially by this goal and Y_A (the Beyond Self component of vector A) shows how much Sam is empowered financially by this goal. This is a win-win situation, **even though it is not 50:50.**

Goal Effect B (Lose-Win)

Let's, now, redraw the graph with each of the axes representing The Social Dimension.

Now imagine that I, the negotiator of the above contract, found the negotiations to be very stressful whilst Sam thoroughly enjoyed carrying out the job. This is represented by Vector B. Here, the Self component of the emotional dimension of the Goal (X_B) is negative whilst the 'beyond self' component (Y_B) is positive. In other words, Sam has been emotionally empowered by this goal and I have been emotionally disempowered. And the vector shows by how much [We are, of course, assuming that these are reliably measurable, but it demonstrates the concept].

Goal Effect C (Win-Lose)

Let's redraw the graph again where, this time, the axes represent The Social Dimension. Now imagine that, whilst negotiating the contract, I make some good friends/contacts, then the goal will have empowered me socially. If, meanwhile, Sam misses out on some opportunities to make or maintain relationships (such as at a social or business event) and the job does not offer any compensatory social benefits (no one new to meet and no opportunities to improve existing relationships), then, from a social perspective, Sam will have been disempowered. Vector C is a representation of such a situation.

Goal Effect D (Lose-Lose)

Let's, now, redefine the axes to represent the Family Dimension. If, in negotiating and carrying out the contract, both Sam and I end up missing out on opportunities to see our children perform in a school play, then we both lose something along the family dimension (vector D) [as depicted in the graph, I seem to be losing more, for some reason].

Goal Effect E (Neutral-Win)

Suppose that vector E represents the extent of empowerment along the cultural dimension as it pertains to The Self (X axis) and The Other (Y axis). Let's assume that the contract is negotiated in London, but is to be carried out in Iran. This gives Sam the opportunity to meet Iranian people and to learn about Persian culture. Vector E shows that this experience has a positive cultural influence on Sam (broadens Sam's cultural horizons) leaving me unaffected. This is an example of a neutral-win situation.

Goal Effect F (Neutral-Lose)

If vector F were to represent the physiological dimension, then, if the job to be carried out is dangerous, involving being exposed to poisonous substances, for example, then Sam is likely to be disempowered whilst I remain unaffected. From a physiological perspective, this would be a neutral-lose outcome.

Goal Effect G (Lose-Neutral)

Similarly, ff the negotiations mean that I miss out on a family reunion, then, along the **family dimension**, the goal will have been disempowering to me, leaving Sam unaffected. This is depicted by Vector G.

Goal Effect H (Win-Neutral)

If negotiating this contract gives me opportunities to scale my business, then this goal will benefit me along the **occupational dimension**, Sam being unaffected. This is represented by Vector H.

66.2.3
Temporal dimension

Goals may be immediate, short-term, medium term or long-term. At another level, we can conceptualise these in terms of actions, procedures, policies and strategies. From a different perspective, we can see these as 'levels of urgency'. I am not going to elaborate on these here, but I just wanted to make you aware of this aspect of goals.

66.2.4
Hierarchy of Goals and Sanity

Goals are directly linked to our needs and our values, both of which are hierarchical. In other words, at any given moment, our goals depend on our priorities.

The most important aspect of our priorities is that they affect what we focus our attention on and consequently, how we structure our time.

In every decision that we make (and we make thousands of decisions every day), we are prioritising one goal over a myriad of others. Such severe competition for our mental and physical resources can be a recipe for insanity. And the more complicated our lives become, the more we teeter on the edge of insanity. Sadly, we are increasingly spending more time on 'the other side' as we fail to adjust for the disempowering choices that we make.

SMERs can help us to mentally highlight our higher goals so that we can prioritise our options accordingly. In other words, we need empowering relationships to avoid going insane and this is one of the criteria by which we can judge whether a particular relationship is empowering or not;

"Is this relationship making me feel more in control and focused on my higher goals?"

66.2.5
What is Sanity?

Good question. Here is my definition of sanity:

> **Sanity is the extent to which our mental image of reality is congruent with reality itself.**

We are all more or less insane. That is to say, we are either on 'this side of' (closer to) reality or 'the other side of' (beyond) reality. The 'more or less' part can be along one of four dimensions;

a) Frequency (how often we cross over to 'the other side')
b) Duration (how much time we spend on 'the other side')
c) Intensity (how fervently we embrace being on 'the other side')
d) Quality (what it feels like to be on 'the other side')

Note that, once again, I am saying that something is not as black and white as we imply when we use a word (in this case, sanity) in everyday language. Sanity is, of course, a huge topic (and a can of worms). At this point, all I want to do is to provide a frame of reference so as to be able to discuss the link between goals and sanity.

There are many other intricately interconnected factors in the machinery that manages the extent of our sanity, but that is a discussion best left for another time and place. I will close this topic by sharing with you my own framework for understanding insanity. To me,

> **insanity (insane) is not something that we *are*, it is a place that we *go to*.**

There are many reasons why we might go to any place such as; to escape, to explore, to enjoy or to find. Sometimes we unwittingly wander aimlessly and find ourselves in unfamiliar territory (a mental territory that conflicts with reality). How we deal with that will also determine the extent of our sanity. You may find it useful to compare my definition of sanity here with my definition of mental illness in § 86 (What is Mental Illness?).

Unit 15

Relationship Maintenance

(Homeostasis)

Relationship homeostasis is about how relationships keep their inner environments to within optimal parameters. In practice, this means asking, "What can I do to ensure that any one of my relationships doesn't get too hot, too cold, too tight, too loose, too deep, too shallow, too isolated, too open, and so on?" The answer is that we rely on *feedback loops*. That is what we are going to explore in more detail in this section.

---

homeostasis (n.)

"tendency toward stability among interdependent elements," 1926, from **homeo-** "similar to" + **stasis** "a standing still." Related: *Homeostatic*.

[source: etymonline.com]

Chapter 67

Feedback loops

We can summarise everything that we do and we are [because, in the final analysis, we are (our consciousness is expressed through) what we do or don't do] as consisting of four components; input, process, output and feedback. A feedback loop is when information about the output of a system is used to control either something about the input or something about the process.

Figure 64 - A simple representation of a feedback loop

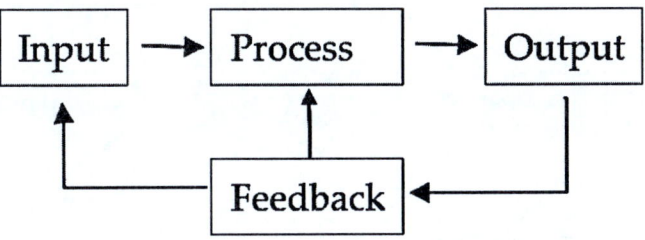

67.1
Homeostasis in relationships

Figure 65 extends the concept of feedback loops to Affinitological processes.

Figure 65 Homeostasis in relationships (from the perspective of The Self)

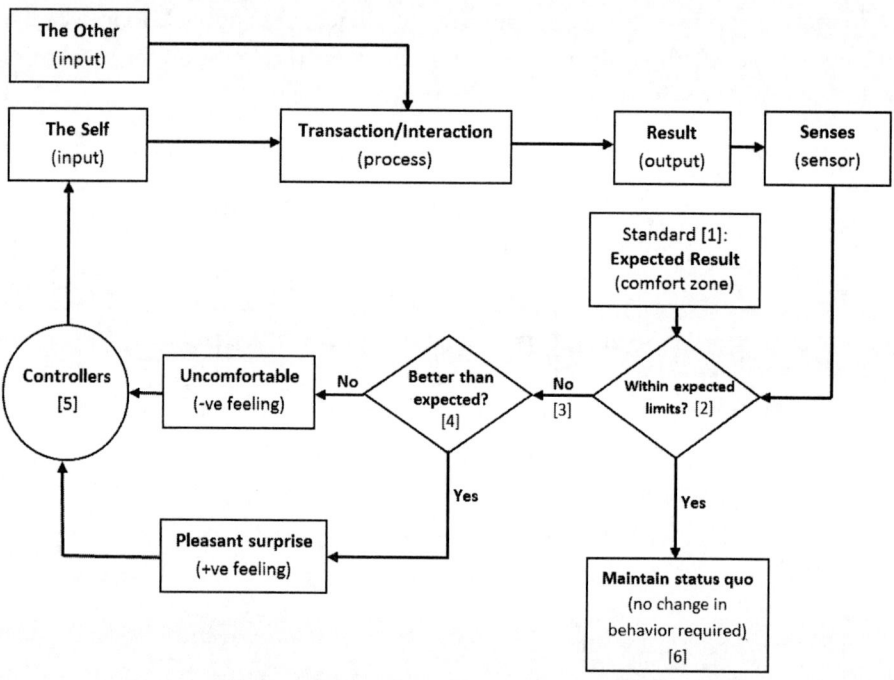

67.2
Explanation of Figure 66

In the following discourse, the numbers in the square brackets refer to the relevant sections in figure 66.

Our expectations [1] are pivotal in the quality of our relationships and their trajectory since, following every transaction or interaction, we compare the signals that we receive from our senses with our expectations.

[Note that I am not using the word 'pivotal' to merely stress the importance of expectation. I am using it as an accurate metaphor in that *everything* that we do and feel (even the feeling of tiredness in our muscles) is based on (pivots around) our expectations and not on physical reality. Everything. (§ 33 The Atasinex Cluster)]

Our 'comfort zone' is the region that lies between the 'expected limits'; our tolerance levels [2]. Something beyond our comfort zone can be 'too good' as well as 'too bad' [3]. Although I have suggested that we feel 'uncomfortable' when something is worse than we expect, whether or not we can say that surprise (pleasant or otherwise) is 'uncomfortable' depends on our definition of 'comfort' [4]. It is not uncommon to hear of people dying of a heart attack on hearing 'good' news.

[You may, somewhat cynically, argue that these people may have faked being 'pleasantly' surprised when in fact they had wished for some other scenario, however, it is clear that being surprised, even pleasantly, does put pressure on our physiology including increased heart rate and change in breathing pattern.]

Feedback systems consist of three main components; sensing something about the output, comparing that against some standard and a control mechanism to change something about the input or the process if necessary. In our case, the 'Controllers' [5] control our emotions and our behaviours, hopefully, in ways that promote SMERs.

Appreciating the Expected

Although, in classic feedback systems, the output is ignored when it is within expected limits [6], I suggest that, if we do that in our interpersonal relationships, we miss many opportunities to strengthen or maintain the relationship and if we miss too many of these, in the end, it can lead to complacency and the withering away of the relationship. Let me explain.

When parents come to see me for advice about how to control their children's behaviour, I explain to them that, to children (and to adults who are dependent on others) any attention is better than no attention at all. Therefore, if they do not receive praise for what they do 'right', they will seek attention by doing something 'wrong'. [If you are interested in this, it is called negative reinforcement. I encourage you to do your own research on it.] One of the problems that we, as parents, often encounter is that we expect children to do what is 'right' and punish them for doing what is 'wrong'. We tend to do this in our other interpersonal relationships too. This is how the early excitement of meeting someone wanes as familiarity grows. There is a way of preventing this; it is called **appreciation** (§ 51.7.5 Gratitude).

[The words 'right' and 'wrong' are in quotation marks to highlight my aversion to their use. § 39 (Social Ranking Criteria) and § 73 (Transactional Analysis). I am using them here because they are common 'Parent-Speak'.]

Cultivating the habit of appreciation can help improve and maintain our relationships at peak, or closer to peak, levels. Appreciation is like saying, "I am glad you are who you are". That is, "I do not need you to do anything unexpected (different) for me to be glad that you exist". Similarly, if we reward our children for what they do 'right', which is, in fact, most of the time, then *not praising* or giving them attention is enough of a 'punishment'. This was brought home to me when,

> *One day, when my daughter was three years old, she turned away from me, walked towards her mother, spontaneously burst into tears and whimpered, "Daddy doesn't love me anymore." In a very concerned voice, her mother asked her why she thought that and she said, "Because he doesn't say 'well done' to me anymore." I don't know whether or not the frequency with which I had been saying 'well done' to her had diminished, but her expression of that sentiment was illuminating.*

In short, not mere appreciation, but *expression of appreciation* is the antidote to complacency and taking each other for granted.

Finally, expressing appreciation is not merely for The Other's benefit. It establishes a separate line of communication between the two hemispheres of our brains that reinforces the signals that are exchanged between them through the *corpus callosum*. I believe it is also the main mechanism through which journaling and talking about our problems exert their therapeutic effects.

[I find this very interesting and I must force myself not to be detracted off the main topic. I intend to talk about this in more detail elsewhere. Meanwhile, if you are interested, I suggest you search the internet for 'split brain experiments']

Chapter 68

Tolerance and Comfort Zones

68.1

Tolerance

The word tolerance has different meanings in different disciplines. For affinitological purposes, I suggest we apply the term in its Engineering sense to mean acceptable limits, that is, our comfort zones. In pathology, these acceptable limits are indicated on lab reports as 'Normal Range'. See figure 66.

Figure 66 Sample Lab report showing tolerance levels (Normal Range)

COMPLETE BLOOD COUNT

Test Name	Result	Normal Range	Units
Hemoglobin	12	11.0 – 16.0	g/dL
RBC	3.3	3.5-5.50	10^6/uL
HCT	36	37.0-50.0	%
MCV	83	82-95	fl
MCH	28	27-31	pg
MCHC	33	32.0-36.0	g/dL
RDW-CV	12	11.5-14.5	%
RDW-SD	44	35-56	fl
WBC	6.7	4.5-11	10^3/uL
NEU%	60	40-70	%
LYM%	30	20-45	%
MON%	8	2-10	%
EOS%	2	1-6	%
BAS%	0	0-2	%
LYM#	2	1.5-4.0	10^3/uL
GRA#	4.7	2.0-7.5	10^3/uL
PLT	256	150-450	10^3/uL
ESR	2	Up to 15	mm/hr

Source: https://upload.wikimedia.org/wikipedia/commons/4/44/GNU_Health_lab_report_sample.png

68.2
Elastic Limit

Any material [Yes, even diamond, but I suggest you visualise a spring] can be bent, contracted and expanded, *up to a point*, without affecting its basic structure (integrity). Before this point, when the pressures are released, it will return to its default position. However, if pushed *beyond* this point, known as its **elastic limit**, its structure will change permanently so that when the forces are removed, it will not revert to its previous state.

We (people) can be surprisingly flexible. However, we have our elastic limits too. When the forces acting upon us (whether these be social, emotional, intellectual, physical or whatever) push us beyond our 'elastic limit', our *situational* change in behaviour (contingent response) becomes a change in our *attitude* (default response). One name for this way of changing attitudes is *acclimatisation* (§ 68.5 Habits). We discuss and explore attitudes in more detail in § 65 (Attitudes). There is a practical lesson for therapists here:

> **If we want the effects of our interventions to last for longer than the immediate period after the intervention, we need to push the client beyond his or her 'elastic limit' for that behaviour.**

"But Bijan," you might say, "How do I know what each person's elastic limit for a particular behaviour in a particular situation is?" And my response would be; nobody knows, not me, not you and not even the client; calibration is required. Notice that I did not say, we need to calibrate; I said, calibration is required.

[The use of the passive voice in science is very convenient indeed. In earlier periods, it was used to talk about effects (observations of changes) when we did not know what caused the effect. For example, if I report that, "The needle was deflected", I am released from explaining what deflected the needle, but I can, nevertheless, report my observation in the hope that someone will pick up from where I left off and eventually find out what caused the needle to be deflected.]

In most cases, the client is the best person to do the calibration. Every calibration requires a point of reference. This could be a starting point or an endpoint, but would need to be described *in measurable terms*. The practical question here would then be, "Has there been any change in my comfort zone?"

68.3
Comfort Zones

There are three components to each of our comfort zones; sensitivity, interpretation and reaction. These roughly map onto the three factor or ABC (Affect, Behaviour, Cognition) model of Personality Psychology. Actually, the logical order would be Cognition→ Affect → Behaviour, that is, we perceive first, then we interpret (and attach value) which the 'affects' us and then we act on that feeling (show emotion) and behave accordingly. We explore this in more detail in § 51.2 (Affect, Feeling and Emotion).

Not surprisingly, sensitivity is about how sensitive we are to a 'trigger' within a specific environment (§ 64.4 Values as Receptors). A trigger is something that starts a chain reaction within our psyche that leads us to break our routine, veering our thinking (beginning with attention) and, consequently, our behaviour into a different direction. It is a matter of perception (an aspect of cognition).

With the above explanations in mind, we can expand our comfort zones by,

a)   Reducing our sensitivity by reframing our values.

b)   Changing our perspective (leading to a change in interpretation)

c)   Resisting the urge to reaction to our feelings. When feelings are kept in check so that they do not become emotions, they are easier to control.

68.4
Examples of Homeostatic Factors

For us to be able to say that something is excessive (too something) we need to specify benchmarks [Statistically, these are called confidence intervals] and a tolerance level. This would be a calibrated range (§ 10 The First Step) for each Individual (Omniself), Identity or group so as to provide benchmarks for comparison.

Personal Space

With reference to a review of a 2017 research article by Sorokowska et al, Rachel Hosie of the Independent newspaper writes,

> "If you've ever lived or travelled abroad and felt uncomfortable at the frequent invasions of your personal space, you are, most probably, British. According to a new study, Brits like to keep a metre from a stranger, 80cm from an acquaintance and just over 50cm from an intimate or close friend. This is in contrast to Argentinians who keep a 76cm distance for a stranger, 59cm for an acquaintance and 40cm for a friend. The results of the study suggest that cultural differences could result in misconceived rudeness."

[Note that reported research findings tend to sound much more clear-cut than they actually are. In this case, we have no idea of the range (confidence intervals) so, although the comfortable distance may be one meter for the average Brit, there is no such thing as an average Brit ('average' is a statistical construct). Therefore, if you are British and prefer to keep strangers at least two arm lengths away from you or if you don't mind someone standing two handspans away from you, you are still a 'normal' Brit. Also, in most cases, the circumstances are undoubtedly much more important than cultural background. Compare, for example, a situation where the stranger is in a secluded park with one where he is at a peace rally convention. Or the difference between when the stranger is same sex or opposite sex. In spite of these limitations, however, we can use the figure of one metre as a guide; a point of reference.]

If we use a distance of one metre for Brits as a benchmark and add our own arbitrary confidence interval of around 60cm then, if you are British and you see a stranger who shows signs of discomfort when you get closer than two metres from each other, what might you think to yourself? Depending on your level of self-esteem, you might think something like, "I wonder what's wrong with me?" or "I wonder what's wrong with him/her?"

If closer than 40cm is too close and 2m is too far away, what is the optimal range of distances that one needs to be from the 'average' Brit for it to be conducive to instigating a respectful relationship? This *range* is what I mean by tolerance level.

Of course, these numbers are averages and they vary from individual to individual and from situation to situation. So, what do we do when we are faced with situations where we do not know what level of personal space a person is comfortable with? We do what we tend to do intuitively; we calibrate. We begin by maintaining a distance that we, ourselves are comfortable with (or have found to be generally non-threatening or too distant) and lean in or out gradually and watch for the other person's physical reaction and adjust accordingly. Becoming adept at this requires practice.

The take-away lesson is that every aspect (Unit 11 Dimensions of Human Experience) of interpersonal relationships has an optimal level and a tolerance level (normal range) and that, if we allow any aspect of our relationship to go beyond that range, we risk putting a strain on the relationship.

Incidentally, here is an interesting angle on the subject of personal space. Based on their research findings, William J. Ickinger and Sandra Morris (2003), related our level of need for personal space to how secure we feel. They concluded that,

> **"Interpersonal distance is not generally manipulated actively to influence others but that greater distance is used as a defence against perceived negative characteristics of others."**

We explore Psychological Defence Mechanisms in greater depth in § 79).

Tone of voice

Tone is a very powerful aspect of communication. Tones can convey anything from lust to disgust, amour to angst, supportiveness to superiority and patronage to patronization.

Tolerance limits for tone vary from individual to individual and from culture to culture and depend on factors including aural sensitivity, childhood environments and self-concept.

The important point here is that tone can be a critical factor in making or breaking relationships. And it behoves us to be extra sensitive to it. Tones send signals regarding the kind of relationship that we intend to instigate. The effect of tone can be modified by other non-verbal cues.

Just imagine the potential change in the dynamics of a job interview if one were to say, in a seductive tone, "I am *reeaally* interested in (you taking up) this position." [For extra effect, you could imagine this being accompanied by a lowering of volume (more about this later), a barely noticeable change in the stress on the word 'position', narrowing of the eyes, a barely noticeable smile and one slightly raised eyebrow ;-)]

Volume of speech

As any experienced classroom teacher can tell you, volume of speech is a critical tool in keeping control of a classroom. Too loud and you are shouting, which signals to children that you have lost control and too quiet and you are too timid which tells children that they can walk all over you, in a manner of speaking.

Silence

Silence is a powerful moderator of relationships and can have both empowering and disempowering effects on the Pactum depending on the situation and circumstances. This is another topic that needs to be expounded upon elsewhere [keep an eye on introducingaffinitology.com].

Push or Pull

This may conjure up images of a tug of war, but I would rather you thought of it as a balance of forces, as in the equilibrium that creates stability. I have borrowed the terminology from Michael Cope's book, "The Seven Cs of Consulting" in which he talks about a 'push-pull relationship', the 'Push' being the extent to which the pressure is on you (The Self) to maintain the relationship [This is presented by Cope in the context of the extent to which the pressure is on you to sell your idea] and the 'Pull' is how keen The Other is on maintaining the relationship. Remember that it is *the situation* that determines where on the Push-Pull spectrum we are and what needs to be done to strengthen the relationship.

Known-Unknown

Another factor that Mr. Cope talks about in his book is the Known-Unknown dimension which basically means how far along the desired type of relationship we are. We already have many things in common, even before we are introduced (§ 47 Common and Complementary Elements)). More specifically, this may be because we have a mutual friend, have a mutual interest or have met at a location that is significant to both of us.

The next stage is to see if each of us is interested in what the other person wants from a potential relationship. The more we can find out about each other, the more we can move towards the 'known' end of the scale and the easier it will be to build the relationship along different dimensions (§ 48-50). See also 'Scenario 1' in § 52.4.3 (Focus and Situationality).

This is obviously linked to the idea of trust (§ 53). The more we feel that we know someone the more we trust our 'instincts' in relation to The Other.

Eye Contact

Again, depending on the situation, too much eye contact can feel intrusive (creepy even) and too little eye contact can appear (or indeed, be) evasive or dismissive.

Eye contact is not simply quantitative, that is, it is not merely about how long we look into a person's eye for; it also has qualitative components. The level of tension in the various muscles around the eye conveys meaning. I am confident that you can tell the difference between a disapproving glare and an enchanted gaze. The former may be more appropriate when chastising a child but would not be apposite when you disapprove of being stopped by a police officer at a checkpoint when you are in a hurry, neither would an enchanted gaze.

Personal Questions
(Sex, nationality, religion, income, past, family)

Clearly, what is or is not appropriate depends on the situation. If in a bank a teller were to ask, "What is your mother's maiden name?" we are unlikely to interpret that as being too intrusive, but we would consider the same question, asked by someone we may have just met at a scientific conference to be too personal to be appropriate. Unless, of course, it happens to be at a nameology or a numerology conference.

The 'Comfort Zone' Test

I had some fun imagining the practical outcome of some research that led to the development of a 'comfort zone test' (similar to the blood test results in Figure 66) for each of our current or potential relationships and decided to share it with you. For example, some entries in the 'comfort zone test' for an interviewer-interviewee Pactum may look like the following table.

Table A - Part of Mr. John Doe's Interviewee Identity Comfort Zone Test results

Test Name	Result *	Normal Range	Units
Eye contact duration (whilst listening) Male Female	<2 L	3-10	Seconds
Eye contact duration (whilst speaking) Male Female	<2 L	3-10	Seconds
Eye contact frequency (whilst listening) Male Female	50 L	60-80 60-80	% %
Eye contact frequency (whilst speaking) Male Female	70 H	40-60 40-60	% %
Closed posture	80 H	<30	(% total time)
Open posture	10 L	45-75	(% total time)
...			

* L= Too low H= Too high

68.5
Habits

In medical science, homeostasis is controlled by the autonomic nervous system. And, in many ways, we are not conscious of our comfort zones (tolerance limits) until *after* we respond to their violation. In other words, our reactions to our tolerance limits are unconscious, that is to say, habitual.

In § 62.1.1 (What is a Belief) I proposed that "Beliefs are a set of 'if-then' statements that we live by". Here, I propose that our habits are a subset of our beliefs. Let me clarify.

Habits are behaviours that stem from certain types of beliefs. What makes these beliefs different from other types of beliefs is that the beliefs have become so deep rooted in our subconscious that we have become oblivious (desensitized) to their existence.

"Beliefs about what, Bijan?" A belief that something specific (predictable) will happen if I behave in a specific way in response to a particular stimulus. For example, before opening this book (assuming that you are holding a physical copy in your hand), most of you will have automatically; as a matter of habit, held the book with its spine facing left. Why? Because you *believe* that the first page of the book is on top when the spine is on the left. In other words,

---

A habit is a belief that when something happens (stimulus), I do not need to think about what to do about it, I simply behave in the predetermined way that I have done in the past (response) and the outcome (a reward) will be as it has 'always' been.

Habits, like other heuristics (§ 72.5 Cognitive Load and Heuristics), are energy-saving devices. They enable us to do things without thinking about them. They reduce our cognitive load. Because thinking is very energy consuming (Unit 22: § 93-95 Thermodynamics of Relationships).

We can think of habits as being the behavioural equivalent of the autonomic nervous system because they regulate our behaviour unconsciously.

Chapter 69

Divergence (Drifting Apart)

Much of what I am about to say here will sound familiar to those of you who are conversant with the theory of evolution.

Divergence means moving in different directions (and away from each other). Divergence is not necessarily physical. It can be across any of the dimensions of human experience (§ 48-50). It is most noticeable when The Self and The Other are close, physically, cognitively (intellectually), emotionally, morally, etc. That assertion, in itself, is not very earth shattering because, obviously, the closer things are to us, the more we notice them. Except that, sometimes, the opposite happens; overexposure leads to desensitization.

69.1
Causes of divergence

Why do people 'drift' apart? This can be the subject for a series of extended research studies. Here, I am only going to try to scratch the surface.

69.1.1
Over-familiarity

What causes it

Overfamiliarity results from a cognitive bias. It occurs by a mechanism through which we create a heuristic, the purpose of which is to free up our mental resources in our constant quest to grow; learn, develop and expand our comfort zones. Rereading that, it sounds a bit 'heavy', so let me simplify.

One of the principles by which our mind and body operates is **economy**. That is, we try to get the most by doing the least. Looking at this from a different angle, it's the principle of frugality; that is, not being wasteful. But we should not confuse frugality with being miserly. From a certain perspective, these last two are opposites. Being miserly is about keeping it to yourself once you acquire it whereas being frugal is not taking it all for yourself but letting other people have a chance to use that resource too. So, where am I going with this?

The less familiar something is to us, the more we try to understand it (the more curious we are about it; "Is it safe? Is it useful?"). Of course, that is only one of the factors in our motivation to try to understand something. Another factor is how interesting it is to us. That is, the less familiar and the more interesting we find something, the more we try to understand it. Other factors are also involved. For example, the more we find something to have potential for our growth or safety, the more interested we become in it. Similarly, the more we feel that something might be a threat, the more attention (§ 33 Atasinex Cluster) we allocate to it. The more we think we understand something, the less we tend to allocate our (attentional) energy to it; because our energy is limited and we try to budget that energy optimally. This is as true for us as it is for fruit flies. It is just that fruit flies have fewer items (sensory inputs and potential decisions) to budget for.

With regards to frugality, nature does make an exception; reproduction. Organisms try to eat efficiently, move efficiently, digest efficiently, breathe efficiently and so on, but when it comes to reproduction, it appears that mother nature 'lets rip' so to speak; producing billions of pollens, millions of sperm, thousands of seeds and dozens of offspring. Our psychological overemphasis on the concept of sex attests to the disproportionate attention (§ 93.1 Motivation and Motivational Energy) that we pay to [and energy that we spend on] it, even when it does not appear to serve any reproductive purpose. In other words, we seem to be wired to be seemingly wasteful where our reproductive faculties are concerned.

[I could go on to compare the disproportionate amount of resources that nature spends on reproduction with the disproportionate amount of resources that some governments spend on destruction (so-called defence), but I will refrain from doing that. This reminds me of a Persian proverb: "To the wise, a pointing finger is enough of a sign, but to the unwise, a minaret is not a big enough sign."]

So, what does all this have to do with overfamiliarity and divergence? Well, it's all about where our attention goes. With our limited energy resources, we need to decide, consciously or subconsciously (§ 35.11 Consciousness), where our attention should flow. The more we spend on one thing, such as reproduction, the less we can spend on another, such as growth, be it physical, affinitological, social, emotional, ethical or whatever.

Overfamiliarity occurs when we decide that we know enough about something or someone that we can reduce the amount of attention (§ 93.1 Motivation and Motivational Energy) we allocate to it, or in our case, to The Other.

"But Bijan, what you are saying is simply familiarity, so what do you mean by **over**familiarity?" and I would say, well spotted. The difference between familiarity and overfamiliarity, as with most such things, is not in the concept, it is in the context. When something is familiar, we notice it, but are not surprised by it. Overfamiliarity is when we fail to notice something. In essence, it becomes unimportant to us. This only happens when the purpose that it served becomes redundant or when other priorities smother its importance.

How it happens

The more repetitive something becomes, the more predictable it becomes. And the more predictable something (or someone) becomes, the fewer attentional resources we allocate to him.

When we become 'too familiar' [for 'too' read disempoweringly] with someone (not in the sense of being 'imposing' but in the sense of thinking that we know enough about them), then our reactions to (and interactions with) that person become routine; repetitive, unexciting. In essence, this means that we do not expect to learn anything new through our interactions with that person and, most detrimental of all, we begin to take that person for granted. This is the beginning of a relationship becoming, at best, dormant (neutral) and at worst, stale (disempowering). I say dormant and not dead because I don't believe that relationships ever die, but they can, and often do, metamorphose into something different [I appreciate that this requires more explanation, however, it is beyond the scope of our objectives here. I shall endeavour to expound on this idea elsewhere (keep an eye on introducingaffinitology.com)]. Once two people interact, that interaction creates a permanent connection. We may not even remember the person's face or name, but we will remember the connection (or its impact) in some way. The more emotionally charged a relationship is, the stronger the link.

How to mitigate against overfamiliarity

As a reader, my first question might be, "Why would we want to mitigate against it?" If we consciously 'decide' to let ourselves drift apart because we are pursuing a more 'important' goal (§ 72 Decision-Making), then, of course, there is no reason to concern ourselves with how to mitigate against drifting apart. The problem occurs when, one day we wake up and say to ourselves, "I wish I had taken better care of that relationship." Or from now on, "I wish I had taken better care of that Nexus."

The way to mitigate against overfamiliarity is by developing our ability to spot the difference between familiarity and overfamiliarity. As I mentioned earlier, the difference is in the context.

From an affinitological perspective, familiarity is not about how well I think I know someone, it is about how confident I feel about the reaction that I will get from that person in response to a transaction (§ 73 Transactional Analysis). This is an important distinction. Overfamiliarity happens when we become too confident about what something means including, who someone is, their role in our life, how they will behave in a given situation and so on.

There are two ways of approaching the question of how we might mitigate against overfamiliarity; either from the perspective of The Self or The Other.

Firstly, I can ask, "What can I do to reduce my chances of behaving in ways that could lead The Other to think that I have become less interesting (worthy of attention)?" Secondly, I can ask, "What can I do to reduce my chances of behaving in ways that I will begin to find The Other less interesting (worthy of attention)?" Note that in both cases, I am asking, "What can I do to reduce my chances of behaving in ways that can lead to us drifting apart?" Here is a soundbite that answers all three questions:

Plan to break routine.

Let's elaborate on that a little. Anything we don't plan, we leave to chance. When we don't plan, we fall into certain habits. Sometimes, these habits are conducive to maintaining the quality of a relationship. However, in most cases, they are not (because they are more likely to lead to overfamiliarity).

Conscious attention (§ 16.2 Mindfulness and Conscious Gratitude) is the antidote to overfamiliarity. This requires that we break with routine. Breaking with routine requires awareness. Hopefully, we are now more aware ;-)

Planning to be unpredictable

This may sound like an oxymoron so let me explain. The planning part is about managing (putting aside) time, and the unpredictable part is about changing our default or habitual behaviour in a particular situation.

There are two ways in which we can change our behaviour; we can deliberately choose to do something out of the ordinary, by which I do not mean doing something irrational or unconventional, just doing something that we do not normally do is enough. Or we can act on impulse (be spontaneous). To plan to do this, we can set aside moments during each day when we do something to make ourselves aware of the routine or structure that we are behaving within (constrained by). All we need is that momentary awareness. Routines are, by their nature, subconscious (§ 35.11 Consciousness). Once we direct our attention to the routine, that is, bring them into our conscious awareness, we will tend to (spontaneously) break that routine in some way. At that point we can 'decide' what to do. As soon as we decide, even if it is what we would have done previously as part of the subconscious routine, it is no longer a routine in the habitual sense; it becomes conscious choice.

69.1.2
Isolation

Isolation is one of the core stages in Darwin's theory of evolution. It is a necessary step for the development of new species. It is also a core mechanism through which people can drift apart.

[My reference to evolutionary theory is to point out that, although isolation may, initially, be distressing (through a feeling of loss), in the long run (or in the grand scheme of things), it can be empowering in providing us with novel adaptive strategies.]

Which of the following idioms do you think is more accurate; "Absence makes the heart grow fonder" or "Out of sight, out of mind"? I am confident that you will be able to guess my answer by now:

It depends on the *situation*.

What causes isolation?

There are two possible mechanisms for Isolation: problems with instigating a connection (§ 35.1 Embryology of Relationships) and divergence (drifting apart). In this section, our focus is on the latter.

We can feel emotionally isolated, intellectually isolated, physically isolated, morally isolated or isolated along any of the other dimensions of human experience (Unit 11: § 48-50). If either of the Identities within a Pactum (The Self or The Other) feel isolated along any dimension, this can have knock-on effects on the quality of the Nexus across other dimensions too.

One possible reason for isolation is that the Complementary or Common Elements (§ 47) that led to the creation of the Nexus are no longer relevant. This is easier to conceive for a Neighbours Nexus than it is for a Friends Nexus (§ 92 Relationship Frameworks). If neighbours move then, obviously, they are no longer neighbours (I cannot ask him to keep an eye out for prowlers whilst I am away). However, if a Friends Nexus has also formed, then, one would expect that aspect of the relationship to persist in spite of the distance. If it does not, then at least one of the Friend Identities was a false one (§ 38 Personas).

[Note that the individual may not have been consciously aware that she was creating the 'Friends' nexus through a False Identity].

Friendship is probably the most enduring of Relationship Frameworks (§ 92). Nevertheless, isolation can affect the quality of a Friends Nexus to different extents depending on the nature of the isolation. More specifically, the endurance of a Friends Nexus following isolation will depend on The Self or The Other's *expectations* within that particular Friends Relationship Framework (§ 92 Relationship Frameworks).

For example, my intellectual and emotional connection with my cousin Hamid was so robust that we reconnected through a telephone call after twenty years of having been out of touch and resumed from exactly where we had left off, beginning with a three-hour conversation. Where this does not happen, we need to focus on The Self and The Others' *expectations* and the roots of such expectations (cf. Unit 7 Atasinex Cluster and § 79 Psychological Defence Mechanisms).

How it happens

Isolation can happen for many reasons.

Physical isolation can happen due to emigration or for occupational reasons (e.g., soldier or seafarer).

Emotional isolation can occur through stress, depression, overwhelm or (as is becoming increasingly the case in our electronically, so-called 'connected' world) distraction.

Social Isolation can occur through immigration, loss of self-confidence or self-esteem, for financial reasons or through overwhelm. Paradoxically, social networking apps often cause social isolation [because they are often used as a screen to hide behind, think superficiality].

Intellectual isolation is more likely to occur when The Self and The Other's personalities lie at different positions along the 'Openness to Experience' personality dimension (§ 50.9 Temperament and Personality Dimensions). The reason for this is that a person who scores 'higher' on the Openness to Experience scale would tend to place greater value on change, growth and learning whilst a person who scores 'low' on this scale is more likely to place greater emphasis on (equally important) values such as security and stability (§ 34.1.2 Values). As time goes by, the Identity who values change will change more than the Identity who values stability. Eventually they reach a point where, at the intellectual level, the Nexus shrinks to a point where the interdependence disappears. Note that other dimensions may, at least initially, be unaffected. For example, at an emotional level, the two people may still love each other very much, it is just that they no longer feel able to provide for each other's intellectual needs, such as, for example, when one needs confirmation and the other needs stimulation (§ 64.13 Dimensions of Values).

How to mitigate against isolation

How we mitigate against isolation depends on the nature of the Nexus and the relevant dimension of human experience (Unit 11: § 48-50). It may seem difficult to contemplate how we can mitigate against the effects of physical isolation or emotional isolation that can occur through depression. One way is by creating multiple Nexuses with each of the Individuals (Omniselves) with whom we interact. In other words, we need not put all our proverbial eggs in one basket. More importantly, if one of those Nexuses is a Friend Nexus (§ 92 Relationship Frameworks), then the relationship becomes less conditional and, as such, levels of expectations are reduced [in theory ;-)] making the relationship more enduring.

What to do when it happens

If a Nexus breaks down and The Self and The Other become isolated, then each Identity may be reabsorbed into the Omniself [in rodents, some foetuses are reabsorbed before they reach full term, presumably because they are somehow recognised as not being able to prosper after birth]. Alternatively, each Identity could find another counterpart to establish a similar Nexus to replace the one that has been lost/severed.

[In chemical reactions (§ 25 Relationships as Chemical Bonds), when bonds break, often, very reactive 'free radicals' are created. These are very transient species because they do not remain unbonded for long (they become less 'discriminating' about 'who' they bond with, as long as it makes them 'feel' more stable – the idiom, "on the rebound" comes to mind).]

It is also possible for the energies allotted to the lost Nexus to be channelled into developing other Nexuses with the same Individual through other Identities. For example, if I appreciate a collaborator's Core Values and the Collaborators Nexus breaks down for some reason (end of contract for example), a link with that person (Omniself) can be maintained through the establishment or maintenance of a Colleagues Nexus or a Sports Fans Nexus (§ 92 Relationship Frameworks).

69.1.3

Selective Adaptation

When the physical, emotional, intellectual, moral, social or other aspects of the environment change, necessitating different adaptive responses from each of the three constituent parts of the Pactum, each of the The Self, The Other and the Nexus may adapt in different ways. Whilst independent, such adaptive reactions can have three possible consequences. They can be,

a) harmonious, maintaining the integrity of the Pactum,
b) in conflict, leading to storming (§ 58.1 Stages of Relationship Development)
c) Disruptive, leading to a dysfunctional or non-functional Nexus,

What causes selective adaptation?

Selective adaptation occurs when a change in circumstances makes the maintenance of the previous Nexus untenable. For example, my colleague may be my peer and our primary Nexus may be a Mutual Employee (Employees) Nexus. If my colleague is then promoted to become my supervisor, then the Peer-Peer (Peers) Nexus becomes redundant and a new Nexus, Supervisor-Supervisee Nexus is created.

How it happens

We selectively adapt to changes to our circumstances that we deem to be outside of our Circle of Influence (§ 44.4). Otherwise, we tend to adapt the environment in ways that reduce our need to adapt to the environment (§ 44 Locus of Control).

How to mitigate against it

The best way to create a robust Nexus; one that is resilient to changes in circumstances that are outside of our circle of influence, is to establish a Friends Nexus (§ 91.8 Friendship), at least as a secondary Nexus.

You may well ask, "But Bijan, are you telling us to hedge our bets and create a Friends Nexus as a backup? Isn't that contrary to the spirit of friendship? Can a Friends Nexus be 'secondary' to another Nexus within a Multi-Nexus relationship (§ 58.3)?" And I would say, it all depends on our intentions.

For example, if I want to maintain my relationship with my children after they become independent, I need to establish and nourish a Friends Nexus with them. However, the Father-Child Nexus will need to remain dominant whilst they are still dependent upon that particular Nexus.

What to do when it happens

When a relationship diverges through selective adaptation, then an occasional reminder of 'the relationship that was' can serve as a seed for the development of a different relationship, such as Friendship (§ 91.8); if the motivation is there.

69.1.4
Differential Experiences

When Individuals live through different experiences, their perspectives and, sometimes, their Core Values change. Such changes in perspective can either empower or disempower the Nexus. Empowerment can occur through the creation of Complementary Elements (§ 46.2) or resolvable conflicts (§ 51.8 Stages of Relationship Development). Disempowerment can occur through drifting apart (§ 68 Divergence) or through unresolved conflicts (§ 86 What can go wrong).

How it happens

Here is an example of how this could happen. Consider The Self and The Other in a Spouses relationship where one partner goes out and works and the other stays at home. This can create a Dependent-Independent Nexus (§ 23 Two Types of Relationship) along several dimensions, including the financial and the social dimensions. In this case, as the working partner develops new insights through new experiences, he develops different expectations that are alien to the partner who does not have those experiences.

[This is why those who work within the pornography industry can rarely form stable romantic relationships with those who do not (so, I have heard).]

How to mitigate against it

Where possible, enter relationships (create Nexuses) where both parties have and can share their experiences in a meaningful (mutually relatable) way.

What to do when it happens

Creating dependence creates responsibility. I consider it immoral for someone to make someone else dependent upon them and then to withdraw that support unilaterally.

[Unfortunately, this is what I believe the education system tends to do with us. We expect our children to give us at least twelve years of the most golden years of their lives, during which time we only teach them how to be dependent on those who may need people with their knowledge or skills. We then unleash these young adults into society without the requisite financial or social skills and expect them to become 'independent'.]

Just like with addicts, an effective way to end such a relationship is through phased withdrawal during which we help that particular aspect of the person (that Identity; The Other) to become independent.

What shall we do if we *are* The Other, that is, if we are the one who is leaning on someone who then withdraws their support? In many cases, we look for another support along that particular dimension. If we have daddy issues, we look for daddy substitutes. If we have emotional support issues, we look for others who can offer us emotional support and so on. The danger here is that by doing these, we leave ourselves vulnerable to abuse because social predators tend to be on the lookout for the, however subtle, signs of the kind of desperation that we tend to exhibit. An example is what is colloquially referred to as being 'on the rebound'.

> *Once, a lady came to me to ask for advice regarding job seeking and interview technique. She had plenty of skills and experience. What she lacked was self-esteem. I simply needed to help her through a simple reframe; "You are not just the interviewee; you are also the interviewer. The organisation who is calling you to interview also needs to convince you that they are worthy of having you as an employee." In our next session, she told me that one of the early questions that she was asked by the interviewing panel was inappropriate (too personal) and she decided at that point that she would not want to work for that company.*

In short, the solution is to do what any self-respecting addict (dependent person) would do; seek to 'kick the habit' (of putting yourself in a situation where you are dependent). For example, if our dependence is along the financial dimension, we need to learn entrepreneurialism and look for opportunities to offer our services on our own terms.

"But Bijan, a recurring theme in what you have been saying is that we are all dependent upon each other. And now you are espousing that we should become independent. That does not fit." I hear you say. And my response would be that there seems to be a misunderstanding here. I am not saying be a table without legs, I am saying be a table with more than three legs, strategically arranged so that if you lose a leg, you will still be able to function as a table until that leg (relationship) is repaired or replaced. If you need a father figure, have a few father figures and not just one, because that leaves you open to exploitation. If you are employed, make sure that you are employable elsewhere (or have other sources of income), otherwise you become open to exploitation and so on.

Unit 16

Physiology of Relationships

[Image by Gerd Altmann from Pixabay.
Source: https://pixabay.com/illustrations/connection-fractal-neural-pathways-647217/]

Chapter 70

What is Physiology?

Physiology is about how the various components [tissues and organs] of the body [the things we identify and label in Histology and Anatomy] interact with each other. Life is a dynamic, and adaptive, process; unless the different parts of the body let each other 'know' about what their situation is, and what state they are in, the body cannot work as a unit. In short,

> **Physiology is about how the various parts of the body *communicate* with each other.**

We have covered different aspects of the physiology of relationships in other sections of this course as summarized in Table 9.

Table 9 Selected sections related to the Physiology of Relationships

In section,	we explore the affinitological equivalent to,
Unit 3: 12-20 (The Power of Language)	Intercellular 'signalling'
§ 33 (Atasinex Cluster)	Intracellular signal processing
§ 64 (Values)	Receptors
§ 53 (Trust)	Immune tolerance
§ 65 (Attitudes)	Reflexes

In this section, our focus is on the following three areas of Affinito-physiology;

a) Defining Normal
b) Decision-Making and
c) Transactional Analysis.

Affinitological Communication

Our physiology is about chemical signals that are passed to and from cells, either directly, through interstitial space, or indirectly through other cells, mainly nerve cells or hormones.

As I have mentioned elsewhere in this course (§ 56.2 When Does a Relationship Begin?), you and I are currently in a relationship. Our relationship consists of my, primarily, Teacher Identity, your, primarily, Learner Identity [I presume] and The Third Entity that is created through this connection; our Teacher-Learner Nexus. **This Nexus is created through the medium of language.** We have explored language in some detail in Unit 3 (§ 12-20 The Power of Language). In this section, I want to draw your attention to the role of language and other 'signals' in the creation and maintenance of SMERs.

In interpersonal relationships, verbal and non-verbal signals are equivalent to chemical signals between cells and consist of words, facial expressions, stance, gait, gaze, tone, volume, body position, makeup, clothes, accessories, hand gestures and, when in close proximity, pheromones. The last is a powerful signal that we have least control over and which cannot be replaced or be compensated for [as yet] through virtual communication.

Thinking

The Identities within an Omniself (§ 29.4) can communicate with each other. We call this thinking (§ 73 Transactional Analysis). For example, my Teacher Identity may be negotiating with my Author Identity about what to say in this book and how to say it.

Intra-Bondle Communication

Intra-Bondle communication is when the Identities that are communicating with each other are a part of a Bondle (§ 22.4). For example, when my Father (nurturing) Identity is communicating with my son's Child (nurtured) Identity [Not to be confused with the Parent and Child ego states of Transactional Analysis (§ 73)]. My Father Identity could also decide to address my son's Learner Identity by asking, "Do you need any help with your mathematics homework?" Note that such a question can emanate from other Identities within my Omniself, such as my Friend or Teacher Identity. Each of these will lead to a different type of Nexus based on different Relationship Frameworks. Each of these Nexuses will have different dynamics due to differences in each Identity's values (§ 64.6 Principles and Expediencies), intentions and expectations (§ 33 Atasinex Cluster).

Inter-Bondle Communication

If I (my Omniself) were to speak to a counsellor about my marriage, then part of the Pactum that houses my wife and I's Spouses Nexus, namely, my Spouse Identity, is communicating with the Pactum that houses our Counsellor-Client Nexus through my Client Identity. This is an example of two Pacta connecting with each other. In this case, my Identity in the Marriage Pactum is connecting with the Counsellor Identity of the counsellor through the Counsellor-Client Nexus.

Figure 9A Representation of Inter-Pactal Communication (see figure 9)

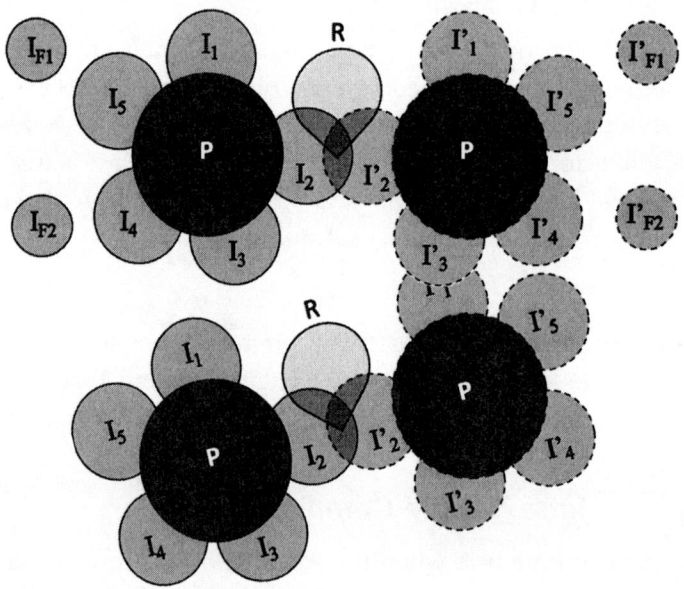

Chapter 71

What is Normal?

The difference between physiology and pathology (Unit 19: Pathology and Therapeutics of Relationships) boils down to our understanding of what is 'normal' and what is not. Therefore, it is crucial that we clarify this before we continue. The idea of 'normal' can arouse different emotions in different contexts. Here is an example.

> *Some years ago, I went to a therapist. I told him that prior to the age of forty, I had not experienced any sort of depression and that everything had been a challenge and exciting and that, even when I had been worried about how to make ends meet, I had been upbeat and optimistic. He told me that this was not normal and that I was just beginning to understand the realities of life and that I should learn to accept that depression is just a part of everyday life. So, I decided that that should be the end of that particular relationship because I wasn't interested in being 'normal', I was interested in getting back to my natural 'abnormal' state.*

Most of the time, when we say 'normal', what we really mean is 'close to average'

The further something, including a Relationship Framework (§ 92), deviates [think Standard Deviation] from the 'norm' (average), the more abnormal and, therefore, deviant ('bad') we tend to consider it to be. This idea is closely related to the beginning of our discussion in § 39.1 (SRC are Binary). As such, I am going to take the liberty of repeating that section here.

"In every 'normal' population (and being normal is 'good') half of the people will always be *below* average (that's 'bad') and half will always be *above* average (that's 'good'). This is true for any 'normal' population. In a 'normal' population of geniuses, half of them will be above average (more worthy) geniuses (that's 'good') and half of them will be below average (less worthy) geniuses (that's 'bad'). Similarly, in a population of morons, half of them will be above average ('better') morons (that's 'good') and half of them will be below average ('worse') morons (that's 'bad'). This is what 'groupthink' does to us."

Before we can discuss what is and is not a 'normal' relationship, we need to be clear about what we mean by normal. Otherwise, we leave our relationships (and ourselves) open to misinterpretation which is one of the main causes of both affinito-physiological impairment and structural damage. In § 61.1.1 (What is a Belief), I explained the difference between functional and descriptive definitions. However, some words have become so pervasive that they also require situational definitions. The word 'normal' is one such word. Love is another one that we shall explore elsewhere [keep an eye on Introducingaffinitology.com].

Normal vs Nominal

The distinction between normal and nominal is an important one. Normal is a statistical construct, it is about what is generally *observed* and nominal is a criterion that is *chosen* deliberately. It is likely that the nominal standard is based on a statistical norm, but it need not be [for the astute amongst you, yes, this paragraph also appears in § 35.6 (Pathology)].

Normal as Adaptive

It is normal for people to behave in different ways in different situations. These behaviours may be considered abnormal in other situations. For example, it is normal for an infection to be accompanied by a fever, but it is not abnormal if an infection is not accompanied by a fever.

Normal as Functional

"Despite a few bumps and bruises the car is working normally." Although this may be the mechanic's or the Mechanic Identity's prospective, the young driver seeking to make an impression may think differently. Because normal for him would mean fit for his purposes, namely, making a 'good' impression.

Normal as Average

This is related to the idea of comfort zones (§ 68). For example, we could say that an IQ within two standard deviations of the mean is normal. However, this is a descriptive definition and someone with a functional orientation may well ask, normal for what?

Normal as a Statistical Distribution

From a statistical point of view, normal is everything that lies under a normal distribution curve; from the smallest to the largest. You might ask, "But Bijan, if the entire sample population is normal, doesn't that make the word redundant?" And I would say, No. Because, from a statistical perspective, it is the shape of the curve (distribution) that determines whether a population is normal or not. In other words, in statistics, normal is a kind of distribution and anyone interpreting such distributions should not, in theory, make judgements about individual points within that distribution.

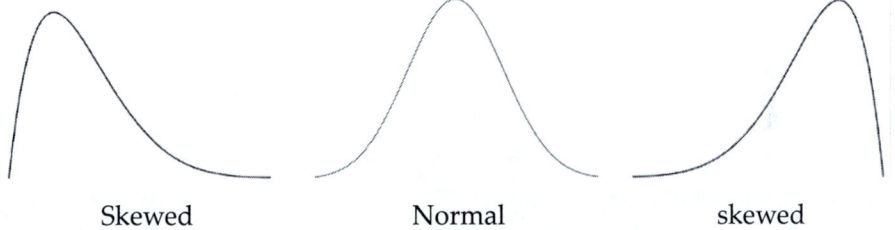

Skewed   Normal   skewed

Normal as Expectation

If something is expected, we do not tend to think of it as being abnormal. An exception might be a weather prediction; "We are expecting a storm tomorrow, which is abnormal for this time of year".

We also communicate our expectations by using the words 'usual' and 'unusual'. When we say, for example, that it is unusual for someone in England not to speak in English, what we are saying is that, if we were to pick someone walking the streets of England at random, we would not expect them not to speak English. However, if we did meet such an individual, the situation might be unusual, but the person would not be abnormal.

Notice the relationship between 'normal as expectation', here, and 'normal as statistical', above. When we apply statistical analysis using our innate abilities, we call it expectation and when we use mathematical models, we call it extrapolation. Also notice that, as I pointed out in the 'Normal as Statistics' section, and demonstrated through the English speaker example in the above paragraph, just because something is very unusual, it does not mean that it is 'abnormal'.

Normal as a Consensus

I think of this as a collective 'should'. In one society, it is normal to eat with a knife and fork and, in another society, it is normal to eat with chopsticks and in another society, it is normal to eat with your hands.

Normal as a Feeling

There are many words that indicate some kind of tension (muscle tone) in our body; what we call feelings (§ 51.2 Affect, Feelings and Emotions). Here, I am going to use the feeling of surprise as an example.

Compare the following questions.

1. If something is surprising, is it normal?
2. If I'm surprised by something, is it normal?

The first question is more abstract than the second. The first question has two components (or elements); the something and its effect. The second question has three components, me, the something, and its effect on me. And the more components we have the more opportunities there are for combinations and permutations. For example, the second question can be interpreted in one of two ways,

a. Is the 'something' normal?
b. Am 'I' normal to feel that way (be surprised)?
c.

Normal as Tribal

The word normal can be used to create (unduly highlight) distinctions between people, creating division in the process, e.g., "This is normal for our group, clan, tribe, society, culture, etc."

[Note that distinctions are not necessarily divisive; sometimes that can create opportunities for connection through Complementary Elements (§ 47.2). They only become divisive when placed in the context of conflict, rather than cooperation.]

Normal as an Attentional Phenomenon

This is related to the idea of desensitisation (§ 81 Emotional Allergens and Hypersensitivity). The more experienced we become, the fewer things surprise us. We become desensitized. And the things we become desensitized to become a normal part of life. This means that if we are exposed to something often enough, it becomes normal. We no longer question it. We are no longer intrigued by it. We are no longer curious about it. In short, we tend to ignore it.

A Normal Life

Based on what we have discussed in this section, you won't be surprised if I tell you that my mind recoils every time I hear someone say something like, "I just want a normal life." Because the sentence conveys almost nothing about what the person wants, but tells me much about the roots of their problem, namely, vagueness (lack of clarity).

Vagueness is paralysing. It paralyses thought and action and leads to both personal and social disempowerment.

Physiology is about communication and, therefore, from an affinitological perspective, especially from the point of view of creating and maintaining SMERs, vagueness impairs our ability to create and maintain healthy relationships because the Pactum will be physiologically impaired (Unit 16: Physiology of Relationships).

Incidentally [or perhaps, not so incidentally], wanting an 'extraordinary' life creates the same problem because unless we are clear about what we mean by 'ordinary', extraordinary is practically meaningless.

Normal Physiology

Bearing in mind our discussion about the various ways in which the word normal can be interpreted, talking about 'normal' in the context of physiology can become problematic. I could attempt to offer a functional definition and a descriptive definition. However, as our discussion so far in this section indicates, neither definition would be entirely satisfactory. In other words, the problem is not with physiology; it is with the way in which the meaning of the word normal has mutated throughout the development of language. Given its potential complications, I propose using my favourite alternatives to normal and abnormal; empowering and disempowering (§ 3.5 Good or Bad?).

Normal as Isotonic

Finally, you may have heard of the phrase, 'normal saline'. In this context, 'normal' means that the salt solution has the same osmotic potential as blood serum (it is not too 'thick' or too 'thin' to force water in or out across membranes).

Summary of "What is Normal?"

What I hope you will appreciate from this section is that interpersonal problems can arise when we do not think through the words that we use (§ 15 The Power of Specialised Language).

Imagine a scenario where you do not know Alex and you hear someone say, "Alex is not normal". What effect would that have on your perception of Alex and, more importantly, your initial interaction - think 'primacy effect'. Now that we know that there are many ways in which the word 'normal' can be interpreted, hopefully, we will be more hesitant in jumping to conclusions (§ 72.5 Cognitive Load and Heuristics).

[I would have liked for us to explored this and some of the other cognitive biases that can have a critical effect on our relationships in this course, but, alas, it will have to wait for some other time. Meanwhile, I encourage you to use what I have said here as a seed and to look up 'primacy effect' and 'recency effect' on the internet.]

Unlike the way we sometimes think about it, anatomy is not strictly about what is where; it is about structure, that is what is where *in relation to everything else* within the holon (§ 36.9 Holons). Physiology, on the other hand, is about what does what. It is about process.

The two most important processes in interpersonal relationships [we could say, affinito-physiological concerns] are,

a) what we decide to do and,

b) how we do it.

Here, I am going to explain a little bit about decision-making and then use one of my favourite models, Transactional Analysis (§ 73); to explain how we can improve how we interact, so as to empower the Nexus and the Pactum to create SMERs (§ 2.1 What is a SMER?).

Chapter 72

Decision-Making

We looked at the relationship between our beliefs and decision-making in § 62. In this section, we elaborate on the concept of decision-making.

In § 58.2 (Good Vibrations), I used the analogy of action potentials to demonstrate that, in dynamic equilibria, there is a constant expenditure of energy as the body strives to maintain muscle tone. I also said that this is a consequence of having choice (§ 35.11.1 Defining Consciousness). Similarly, our relationships, being conscious (able to exercise choice), are in a constant state of vibration.

I propose that our decisions are the equivalent of physiological action potentials. We make thousands of decisions every day and, each decision that we make changes the initial conditions of the system in, albeit minute, ways. Nevertheless, every single decision that we make, alters the trajectory of our lives in general and our relationships in particular in profound ways. How? Through a principle known as 'Sensitive Dependence on Initial Conditions' (AKA the 'Butterfly Effect') see § 90 (Fractals).

I appreciate that grasping the depth of this phenomenon can make us feel quite uncomfortable because it could mean,

a) We do not have as much control over the consequences of our actions as we [are led to] believe,

b) We need to be impossibly super-diligent to make sure that we take every possible consequence into consideration before making the 'smallest' of decisions and,

c) [potentially most disturbing of all] Throw out the notion of responsibility and adopt a completely external locus of control (§ 44).

None of these options seem very satisfactory (reassuring). So, let me reassure you by reminding you of what we talked about in § 40.2 (Behaviourism versus Humanism). Chaos theory is about Newtonian interactions (no consciousness or choice assumed). In every decision that we make, there are many aspects of that decision, including its consequences, that we have no control over. However, we do have control over what we do and what we *think* will happen if we do it. We can also *observe* the consequences of our actions and *adjust* accordingly.

72.1
What is a decision?

Simply put, a decision is the *resolution* of an option or a set of options. In other words,

---

where there are options, there is a decision to be made

As the word resolution implies, decision-making is a *response* to the emergence of a *conflict*. This makes decision-making tantamount to conflict resolution. However, we tend to see conflict resolution as more of *a process* than decision-making, which we tend to think of as *an event*.

[It may help us to become more aware of the degree of control that we can have over our decision-making process by changing the narrative of decision-making from "I made a decision" to "I went through the process of making a decision."]

We discuss conflict resolution in more detail in § 59.3.3 (Conflict and Conflict Resolution). Meanwhile we explore the 'event' perspective (decision-making) here.

72.2
Options, Choices and Decision Types

An option is any situation in which we can exercise choice. Choices can be grouped into five categories that I have called, the five types of decision. We can decide to,

1. Start doing something
2. Stop doing something
3. Do more of something
4. Do less of something
5. Change the way we are doing what we are doing

The first four decisions are quantitative (about how much) and the last is qualitative (about what and how).

These decision types also apply to any relationship situation. Awareness of these five 'options' help to veer our minds away from binary thinking, such as a relationship either works or doesn't work or that I have two options, to stay or to go. Only the first two types of decision are binary (either this or that). Where relationships are concerned, the other three types of decision are fluid and adaptable (*negotiable* and *renegotiable*).

72.3
The First Law of Decision-Making

Let me begin by telling you a story.

The Story of the 'Unsuccessful' Doctor

One day, a doctor went to a psychologist and said, "I am not a successful person, I want you to help me to become successful." The psychologist asked, "In what areas of your life are you successful?" and the doctor said, "Look, I just told you; I am not successful." So, the psychologist asked the doctor to tell him a little bit about himself. The doctor said that he lived with his wife and two children. The psychologist then asked the doctor whether he had any hobbies or interests outside of work and the doctor said, "Yes, I have a garden and I enjoy gardening in my spare time." The psychologist asked him whether he had any problems with his relationships such as with his wife and his children and the doctor said no. The psychologist then said, "Well, you seem to be successful enough in your family life." And the doctor said, "No, you don't understand. There is a doctor on the other side of the street and he earns three times more than me and I want to be successful like him." So, the psychologist asked, "What is the other doctor's relationship with his wife and children like?" and the doctor said, "Well, his wife and children have left him." The psychologist then asked, "What are the other doctor's hobbies and interests?" to which the doctor replied, "He doesn't have any because he works from early in the morning until late at night." Then the psychologist asked, "Are you willing to give up your family and your hobbies to triple your income?"

This story demonstrates what I call *the first law of decision-making*:

**In every decision that we make,
we lose many things in order to get some things.**

It may seem unfair that we lose so many things.

In my therapy sessions, this is what I tell my clients, "When I decided to spend this time to be at your service, I decided to not do a lot of things including, not to read a book, not to play with my children, not to go out with my wife, not to go for a walk, not to have a bath, not to eat something, not to write something and many other activities that I could be engaged in. These are opportunities that I chose to forfeit to be here with you (economists call them opportunity costs). However, after I have made my choice, if I think about them for even one second, not only will I not get them, I will also lose the second that I could be here, in the present, with you."

A lady I know used to buy something and then she would look through catalogues to see if it was cheaper anywhere. This is one of the best formulae I have come across for throwing one's life and sanity away, not to mention the sanity of those around.

We need to be able to let go of some of the things that we want so that we can pursue other things that we want. This is what the doctor story, above, demonstrates. Notice that the conflict can be in different aspects of our lives (Unit 11: Dimensions of Human Experience). In the doctor's case, the family and recreational dimensions were in conflict with the financial dimension.

In terms of our interpersonal relationships, we need to get into the habit of considering, anticipating and noticing the effects of our numerous daily decisions on the quality of each of our Nexuses by asking,

1. To what extent has this decision the potential to empower or disempower the Nexus?
2. If this decision is in conflict with another Nexus, how resilient are each of those Nexuses to the consequences of this decision?
3. To what extent is it possible to compensate for any detrimental effects that this decision may have on each Nexus.

72.4
Fear and Decision-Making

In § 51.8.11 (Fear), I defined fear as the perception of impending loss. My 'First law of decision-making', above, shows how the idea of loss is implicit in every decision that we make. This is why decision-making is often difficult, especially when the decision that we need to make is not about whether to start or stop doing something, but about whether to start or stop doing something *else*, that is, when I need to make a *choice* **about what to lose** to gain something else.

[Elsewhere (§ 35.11 Consciousness), I have argued that consciousness is the ability to choose; going with the flow or being spontaneous is easier - requires less energy (Unit 22: Thermodynamics of Relationships). This is because not resisting the status quo creates entropy (§ 95 Entropy) whereas decision-making is an attempt to create relative order from relative disorder (negative entropy). This idea was espoused by Erwin Schrodinger, the esteemed physicist and one of the pioneers of quantum physics. What I take this to mean is that conscious beings bring order to disorder through making decisions. In other words, when we are not making decisions, (consciously, subconsciously or unconsciously), we are being non-conscious (§ 35.11 Consciousness).]

72.5
Cognitive Load and Heuristics

Decision-making [exercising choice] is the final stage of thinking before we take action (or not). The preceding steps are perception, analysis, interpretation, evaluation and expectation (§ 33 Atasinex Cluster).

Thinking is very energy-intensive (§ 93-95 Thermodynamics of Relationships). This energy must come from somewhere. For us to think (perceive, analyse, interpret and make decisions), we need to divert energy resources from other systems in the body, such as the immune system or the digestive system. Part of us; the less evolved limbic system, is content with mere survival. It thinks like this, "In a similar situation, whatever I did before must have been good enough because I am still here to tell the tale. Therefore, I do not need to think too much about what to do in this situation, I will just do what I did before." The fundamental assumption here (§ 33.4 Assumptions), of course, is that the circumstances are sufficiently similar for me to get at least an equally satisfactory outcome from repeating my previous behaviour. This leads to a host of cognitive biases including, familiarity principle, confirmation bias (§ 33.8), anchoring bias, illusory truth effect, omission bias and fluency heuristic.

A heuristic is when our mind tries to conserve energy by minimising (bypassing) the thinking process, especially, the decision-making part. If we feel that the situation is favourable; we have enough resources, such as food, time, social support and safety, we allow ourselves more time to evaluate the circumstances. If, on the other hand, we feel depleted or overwhelmed, then we are much more likely to resort to heuristics.

We can think of cognitive load as the number of items waiting in line to be evaluated so that we can make a decision about them. The greater our cognitive load, at any one time, the more we resort to heuristics to avoid depleting our precious energy resources. The concept of 'the number of items' is important here because, as far as the mind is concerned, an 'item' is not a 'bit' of information (to use computing parlance), it can be a category or 'chunk' of information, such as a 'byte', a 'sector' or even a whole 'drive'. Each category, then acts as its own heuristic, carrying with it all the cognitive biases it entails. [This reminds me of the Rumi quotation in § 60.1 (Label Fixation) and § 40.3 (Self-Esteem).]

Attitudes (§ 65) are the emotional counterparts to heuristics.

72.6
Decision-Making and Witchcraft

This is probably highly off topic, but I found it fascinating and decided to share it with you [just in case it is not quite as off topic as it appears ;-)].

I once asked Dr Bahman Rahimian, who has researched witchcraft, whether he could explain what exactly happens to someone who is, supposedly, bewitched (is under a spell) and his explanation was the most clear and concise that I have ever heard. He said [in Persian], "The bewitched person's decision-making process is disrupted."

I find this fascinating because it establishes a connection between decision-making, choice and consciousness (§ 35.11) and highlights the many ways in which steps leading to a decision can be manipulated (§ 33 Atasinex Cluster).

Chapter 73

Transactional Analysis

73.1
What is Thinking?

When I am trying to explain Transactional Analysis to my clients, I begin with a story like this.

> *Imagine that one day I say to myself, "I want a new mobile (cell phone)" and then the following conversation ensues inside my head:*
> *- But you already have a mobile.*
> *- Yes, but this one is getting old.*
> *- But it's still working isn't it.*
> *- But it doesn't look good in front of my clients.*
> *- But you are not here to impress your clients with the quality of your mobile phone.*
> *- But it could affect the way they see me and therefore, my impact.*
> *- Ok, if that is your argument, let's examine the pros and cons of buying a new mobile.*

I then tell my clients that the process I just described is me 'thinking'. In other words, thinking is an internal dialogue; it is me talking to myself. But if there is only one of me, then I can only give a sermon. For a dialogue, there needs to be more than one 'person' (entity) inside my head. So, how many of us are there?

This is not a new problem. The 14th century Persian mystic, Hafez of Shiraz, put it like this,

---

"I know not who is inside of this exhausted heart of mine, for I am silent and he is throwing a tantrum."

Hafez of Shiraz
[Author's translation]

In the early 20th century Sigmund Freud put forward the idea of the three agents of the psyche which he called the Id, the Ego and the Superego. In the 1960s, Eric Berne put forward his three ego states model which was very well received by the psychology profession and gave birth to a new school of therapy; Transactional Analysis (TA).

Like Freud, Eric Berne proposed that there are three entities within our psyche, but Berne's entities, which he called 'ego states', are somewhat different from Freud's. Eric Berne called his three entities, The Parent, The Adult and The Child.

The Child ego state is the emotional component of our psyche; it *feels* and it 'knows' what it wants, what it doesn't want, what it likes and what it doesn't like. The Adult ego state is the analytical [cognitive/thinking] component of our psyche. It focuses on, and tries to determine, the pros and cons of the situation.

Unlike The Adult and The Child which exist within us at birth and develop from there, The Parent ego state is about our *acquired* beliefs. It is formed from different aspects of different worldviews that we put together based on what we glean from other people. In other words, The Parent ego state is composed of conclusions that we accept from others without having taken the time, or having had the requisite experience, to reach for ourselves. [I think of the Parent ego state as an advocate for the external sources of our heuristics.] It often results in binary thinking which condenses our judgements of an action or a decision as being either wrong or right, good or bad, should or shouldn't (§ 39.1 SRC are Binary).

Although Eric Berne applied his model primarily to interactions between people, as the above example demonstrates, it can also be applied to thinking. Let's re-examine what is happening in my head when I am thinking about buying a mobile from a TA perspective.

Child: I want a new mobile. [Want]

Parent: But you already have a mobile. [Shouldn't (it is wrong to) Waste]

Adult: Yes, but this one is getting old. [This is The Adult appealing on behalf of The Child. We can also think of it as the Child speaking 'through' the Adult what, in TA, is called Adult-Child Contamination. The unadulterated Adult would say something like, "This one is no longer fit for purpose."]

Parent: But it's still working isn't it. [Adult-Parent Contamination: I am not convinced that it is not wasting/overindulgence.]

Adult: But it doesn't look good in front of my clients. [Adult-Child Contamination]

Parent: But you are not here to impress your clients with the quality of your mobile phone. [Adult-Parent Contamination]

Adult: But it could affect the way they see me and therefore, my impact. [Adult-Child Contamination]

Adult: Ok, if that is your argument, let's examine the pros and cons of buying a new mobile. [Adult-Parent Contamination]

Adult: How much is it going to cost?

Adult: How much is it going to benefit (the Client/the Practice)?

The point is that, once the child has expressed its desire, the Adult and The Parent try to work together (or battle it out) to determine, a) whether or not what the child desires is to its advantage and, b) what the most appropriate (safest and/or most efficient) way of achieving that goal is (§ 66 Goals).

In the final analysis, the job of The Adult and The Parent ego states is to convince The Child.

If the Child is not convinced by the other two ego states' arguments to 'change its mind', The Child will do what it wants.

This is related to the research I mentioned in § 51.3.2 (Feelings Trump Logic) that shows that we cannot make decisions without some kind of emotional involvement. In other words, emotions (especially those that pertain to our Child ego state) are the final ratifiers of any decision that we make.

73.2

Thinking Together?

After I explain the three ego states in the context of thinking, I demonstrate how this can be extended to interpersonal relationships. I do this through another story.

> *Imagine that, one morning, I say to my wife, "Have you seen my keys?"*
> *And she says to me, "You haven't lost your keys again, have you?" or*
> *"You really should be more careful about where you put your keys."*

[Note that in this example, 'my wife' represents what, in affinitology, we are calling, The Other (§ 22.1)].

We now know that, from a Transactional Analysis perspective, there are three of her and three of me talking to each other. This is depicted in the following diagram.

Figure 67 An Interaction from a TA perspective

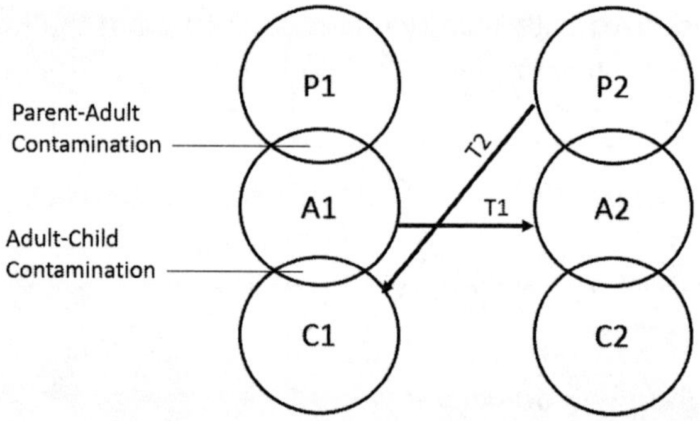

"Have you seen my keys?" is a prompt for a response. In TA, this is called a *transactional stimulus*, depicted as T1 in Figure 67. Here, my Adult ego state (A1) is addressing her Adult ego state (A2). Instead of responding through her Adult ego state [This would be what in TA is called a 'complementary transaction'], her *transactional response* is through her Parent ego state (P2), addressing my Child (C1) ego state [This is called a 'crossed transaction'].

What do you think is likely to happen if this were a conversation involving six friends talking in a group? A1 may well turn to P2 and say, "I wasn't talking to you; I was talking to A2 so why did you butt in?" And C1 may say, "What are you laying into (chastising) me for; I didn't say anything?" I imagine the different ego states in each of us react in a similar way.

At this point, I go on to explain to my clients that the chances are that, if I were to ask my wife some other question such as, "What's for breakfast?" She might well turn around and say, "Can't you make breakfast for yourself for a change?" If this happens, it wouldn't surprise me because her Parent ego state is likely to be dominant at that particular time and place and whatever I say [whichever of her ego states I address], she would probably respond through her Parent ego state. Being aware of this, it is probably best that I do not aggravate the situation. Here, the best strategy would, probably, be to avoid confrontation.

Let's now assume that I come home in the evening and find her sitting in the living room, reading a book. I ask her, "What are you reading?" And she says, "Oh, on my way home I passed this bookshop and I saw this book that looked interesting…" Since she responded to me through her Adult ego state, her Adult is now 'available for comment'. So, I may say, "I am wondering why you reacted so severely to my question about my keys this morning." And she may respond with statements such as, "Oh I was feeling irritable because I hadn't slept well." Or, "I was preoccupied because an inspector was due to visit our premises at work." Or "I was in a hurry because I was going to be late for work."

[Notice that I did not say, "Why did you…? Because that is reminiscent of how our parents talked to us when we were kids and if we are not alert to this, it might stimulate her Parent or Child to respond. Instead, I framed it in the context of something that I am simply thinking about; "I am wondering…". Her Adult ego state realizes that this is a transactional stimulus requiring a transactional response]

Now remember what I said about our Parent ego state being our primary source of heuristics [decision-making (and judgmental) shortcuts]. We use heuristics when we want to save or conserve our energy [Energy is the relationship between mass, distance, direction and time (§ 92-94 Thermodynamics of Relationships) and therefore, when I say 'save energy', saving time is a part of it].

In the first example (because I had not slept well), what she is saying is, "I did not have enough energy to think things through and resorted to something I knew that would get you off my back." That is, "I was avoiding the responsibility of having to think about where your keys might be." [This is related to our discussion about the three most energy consuming processes in our bodies (§ 94 Energy Balance)].

In the second example (I was preoccupied), her response again indicates that she was trying to avoid thinking, but this time the reason is overwhelm; she is devoting her mental energies to avoiding possible problems with the inspection.

In the third example (I was in a hurry), her reason [for not allowing the adult ego state to respond] was time limitations; she did not have the time to think things through.

Note that in all these cases, The Other has the potential to respond in a manner that is empowering for the relationship.

Here, I venture to suggest that, with regards to SMERs (§ 2.1), the majority of our interpersonal problems stem from a lack of resources (time, energy and focus) [note the implication of 'situationality' (§ 52.4.3 Focus and Situationality) here] not from a lack of knowledge. In other words, given enough time to think, we instinctively [and/or through experience and reasoning (common sense)] know how to respond to people in a way that can strengthen the Nexus.

One way of mitigating against the 'resource' problem is to think things through when we *do* have the resources and then practice to respond empoweringly until it becomes a habit; rather like an actor practicing his role.

"But Bijan, isn't that like suggesting that I should practice to give ready-made answers without thinking about what the person has said?" And I would say, yes and no. We can remove the negative connotations associated with 'ready-made' by reframing it as 'well-thought-through' (§ 63.1 Changing Beliefs: Reframing). We can also remove the idea of 'without thinking about what the person has said' by reframing it as 'without having to think too much about how *I* respond to what the other person has said.' In other words, it is not about the extent to which I value (pay attention to) the transactional stimulus (§ 72.3), it is about how I can make my response most efficient.

73.3

Transactions, Interactions and Social Intercourse

In Transactional Analysis, a unit of communication (what Eric Berne social intercourse) is called a *transaction*. There are two types of transaction, a (transactional) stimulus and a (transactional) response. An *interaction* is a pair of such transactions.

Breaking interpersonal communication into units, has similar advantages and disadvantages of thinking about matter in terms of atoms and thinking about organisms in terms of cells.

73.4

A Quick Overview of TA in the Context of Affinitology

Applying a Transactional Analysis perspective to affinitology, we see that when, through an interaction, we create a SMER (§ 2.1), we expand our thinking capacity from three units (a Parent, an Adult and a Child) to six units (two Parents, two Adults and two Children). But the difference is not merely arithmetic; as I keep repeating, 'The whole is more than the sum of its parts'. Table 10 shows thoughts and their corresponding goals for each of the three ego states. Note that this applies separately to each of the Identities within the Omniself (§ 29.4).

Table 10 An Identity from the Perspective of Ego States

Ego State	Thought	goal/payoff
Parent	I should	Approval
Adult	I need	Resolution
Child	I want	Satisfaction

The Hidden Observer	I am	Harmony/Atonement*

* See § 7.1 You make me want to be a better Man

Thinking of ourselves (our psyches) as consisting of a multitude of Identities, each comprised of three ego states can give us a very fragmented view of ourselves. This, sadly, is the price we pay for gaining a scientific (analytical/reductionist) understanding of the world around us. That is why we also need an artistic (holistic) perspective to ameliorate the potential negative impacts that a purely scientific view may bestow upon us. See § 9.1 (Science as an Art) and § 18 (Art or Science). This reminds me of the following anecdote.

> *Once, many years ago, I met an eye surgeon in Vancouver. He told me that when he looks at eyes, what he sees is a collection of cells and tissues and muscles and that he did not feel the same sense of awe that others feel when they talk about the beauty that they see in other people's eyes.*

This encounter left a lasting impression on me for several reasons. My own experiences of dissection (as a pharmacologist) *increased* my appreciation of the interconnectedness of all things and the value of connection and connectedness, rather than diminish it; to reiterate, "The whole is more than the sum of its parts." This means that there is something in the whole, in this case, an eye in context, that is absent from a disembodied, sliced or otherwise cannibalized eye.

> **The beauty is in the part that becomes absent when the whole is reduced.**

But the most heart-breaking part of the encounter with the surgeon was how a potentially empowering experience (one that could help him appreciate eyes even more) had been interpreted (§ 33 Atasinex Cluster) in such a way as to deprive him of appreciating one of the most magnificent works of nature.

In table 10, I have added a spaced row at the bottom where I have suggested that there is a coordinating entity whose mission is to ensure that the other parts of our psyche work in harmony. I have talked about this 'Hidden Observer' in § 6 (Know Thyself), § 37.9.1 (The Decision Ratifier), § 38.2 (Persona versus Self-Deception) and § 78 (Active Protection: Immune Response).

73.5
Only a Peep through a Keyhole

Although what I have explained about Transactional Analysis in this section distils its basic principles, I don't think that it does justice to the spirit of the field. I shall endeavour to expound on these concepts in more detail at some other time and place [keep an eye on introducingaffinitology.com]. Meanwhile I encourage you to delve into this topic for yourselves. Here is a teaser to whet your appetite. Eric Berne says that our need to communicate is fundamentally a substitute for our need to continue to be "stroked" after infancy, when we stopped being physically caressed by our carers. This means that, every time we acknowledge someone, such as saying "hello", we have stroked them in some way and when they respond, they are stroking us back. This brings us to the notion of reciprocity.

73.6
Reciprocity

We are social animals, which means that we are hard-wired to connect with other people; our mental health (§ 86 What is Mental Illness?) depends on it (§ 86 What is Mental Illness?). There are plenty of words that allude to this, including, obligation, guilt, debt, promise, agreement, indebtedness, gratitude, appreciation and acknowledgement. This means that, in a healthy relationship, there is a *response* to every *transaction*, turning it into an *interaction*. What these words also imply is the idea of a 'proportional response' [I do not mean this in its military sense]. Oftentimes, conflicts arise in relationships (between The Self and The Other) because of a mismatch between the perceived value of a transaction and what is, therefore, a proportional response for that transaction.

This topic can be the basis of many a research program, but here, I simply wanted to alert you to it as a factor that needs to be taken into account in any Nexus aspiring to become a SMER (§ 2.1).

Unit 17

Pharmacology of

Relationships

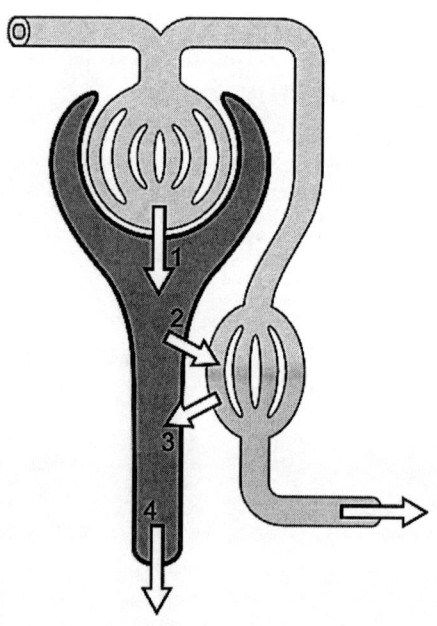

Source (before modification):
https://commons.wikimedia.org/wiki/File:Physiology_of_Nephron.png

Chapter 74

Introduction to Affinito-Pharmacology

Pharmacology is the study of the interaction between the body and chemical substances that enter it from outside. There are two main perspectives from which we can view this; what those chemicals do to the body and what the body does to those chemicals; pharmacodynamics and pharmacokinetics respectively.

Consider a situation where our prevailing emotional state is one where our physiology is in harmony with its environment *at that instant and in that situation*. This is our 'steady state' condition at the time.[1] An external stimulus or an internal stimulus (thought) is needed to change this state. We can look at this stimulus from a pharmacological perspective; as being like a foreign substance entering the body.

[1] [From a Newtonian physics perspective, this 'steady state' is like saying, "An object will continue to move in a straight line and at constant speed, unless it is acted upon by an external force." This assumes that there are no 'internal' forces that can change the speed or trajectory of the object, such as a booster rocket]

Psychologically, we can look at this from two perspectives; what the stimulus does to our psyche and what our psyche does with the stimulus. I propose that we call the former, 'psychodynamics' [not to be confused with 'psychodynamic therapy'], and the latter, 'psychokinetics'.

Organisms interact with their environment at two levels: physical level and chemical level.

At the physical level we are dealing with the body as a whole, objects, people in the environment and the interaction between the two [the last falls within the realms of behavioural science and ergonomics].

At the chemical level, organisms are a complex mixture of chemicals; a 'chemical soup'. From this perspective, the environment is also a mixture of chemicals. What the organism does with its own chemicals falls within the realm of physiology. What it does with the chemicals that enter from outside falls within the realm of pharmacokinetics. How the organism is *affected* by external chemicals that can affect it (xenobiotic agents) falls within the realm of pharmacodynamics. Having said that, what the body does to chemicals [e.g., metabolise; produce metabolites] affects what the chemicals do to the body (and vice versa). This is why pharmacodynamics and pharmacokinetics are part of the same discipline; pharmacology.

Applying these understandings to affinitology, the pharmacology of relationships also consists of two areas; affinitodynamics and affinitokinetics.

[Actually, I am not too happy with the naming of these because they do not indicate that they are about the study of 'external' factors that can influence the Nexus and the Pactum. I am still thinking about this. Here are some of the candidates I am considering; affinitoxenodynamics and affinitoxenokinetics, xenodynamics and xenokinetics, affinitoexodynamics and affinitoexokinetics, exokinetics and exodynamics, ...]

Affinitodynamics is about those aspects of relationships that are affected by external circumstances, especially other relationships such as how the mother-in-law or The Other's ex can affect a Nexus (§ 58.2 Good Vibrations).

Affinitokinetics is about how our relationships affect other people and other relationships, such as how the Nexus (or the unique features of the Pactum) affects the 'mother-in-law' or The Other's ex.

Note that we are not talking about how individuals affect individuals; that would fall within the realms of relationship formation and development (Unit 12: Embryology of Relationships), growth (Unit 13: Paediatrics of Relationships), maintenance (§ 35.5 Homeostasis) and so on.

---

affinitopharmacology is about how relationships affect relationships.

Another important point to realise is that Individuals (§ 29.4 The Omniself) cannot affect relationships directly. Individuals can only affect relationships if they form a Nexus (however precarious) with The Pactum (§ 22.3).

Here, our focus is primarily on the pharmacodynamics of relationships.

74.1

Pharmacodynamics of Relationships

The focus of our discussion so far in this discourse has been on why and how people interact with each other and the remarkable consequences of such interactions. Our treatment of the subject has been limited to the confines of the Nexus and the Pactum, that is, two Identities forming a single bond. However, to paraphrase a famous adage, 'no Nexus is an island'. As part of a single, mind-blowingly interconnected system, each and all relationships affect the whole system, and thus, each other, in some way. Perhaps lamentably, we are only equipped to consider localised and [in the grand scheme of things, almost instantaneous] short-term effects.

Chemical bonds resonate. And so do relationships (§ 58.2 Good Vibrations). These resonances may or may not be 'on the same wavelength'. Wavelengths and resonance are properties and characteristics of *waves*. When two waves collide, they cause constructive or destructive interference. Resonance can occur if the waves have the same wavelength.

[For the sake of completeness, resonance is a special form of constructive interference, not that I'm being pedantic or anything, I just don't want to confuse the curious or to exasperate the expert.]

In § 58.2 (Good Vibrations), we saw how the addition of other bonds to already bonded atoms can have significant effects on the existing bond. Similarly, other relationships (Nexuses) can influence our relationships. These effects can be empowering or disempowering.

We need to have indicators (signs) that help us recognise the potential effects of another Nexus at an early stage. We can begin with the question, "How might this Nexus be affected by the presence of another Nexus?" To answer this, we need to focus on what is holding this Nexus together, that is, "What are the foundations on which this Nexus is based?" and, "What are its potential vulnerabilities?" We cover the first question in § 47 (Common and Complementary Elements).

74.1.1
Relationship Vulnerabilities

Like our bodies, a Pactum can be vulnerable from the inside (prone to imbalances) or vulnerable from the outside (prone to interference). Pharmacology (and affinitopharmacology) is primarily concerned with the latter. Of course, for any external substance or stimulus to cause harm to the body or a Pactum, it will need to cause some kind of imbalance in the system and this blurs the boundaries between physiology and pharmacology.

Vulnerability is unavoidable

The maintenance and growth of any dynamic system requires input. Input implies a portal; a means through which things can enter the system. And, whenever we have a mechanism for something to enter the system, be it our body, one of our relationships, an organisation or a computer program, we run the risk of letting in unwanted and potentially disempowering agents. To minimise potential damage, we need to have safeguards. The primary requirement for establishing a safeguard against the abuse (or the potential abuse) of the portal is awareness (sensitivity); if I cannot distinguish between food and poison, I cannot protect my body from poisons. Similarly, if I cannot discriminate between facts and opinions, I run the risk of basing my decisions on inaccurate or false information. At this point, it might be useful for me to remind you that,

> **it is relationships that interfere with relationships; not individuals.**

[This reminds me of a stanza from one of the odes of Hafez of Shiraz that has become an idiom in Persian,

I shall complain no more about strangers,	من از بیگانگان دیگر ننالم،
For, whatever was done to me, was done by the familiar [one].	که با من هر چه کرد آن آشنا کرد.

Note that Hafiz's poems have mystical interpretations (hence the "[one]" qualifier that I incorporated into the translation), but, as in our case here, they can often be applied to more mundane situations.]

Factors that increase vulnerability

Several factors can make a Nexus vulnerable to outside interference, including,

a) Insufficient trust
b) Situationality
c) A utilitarian perspective

Insufficient Trust

In § 2.1.2 (What is Satisfying?), I implied that we cannot have a SMER (§ 2.1) without Trust. We cover the notion of trust in detail in § 53 (Trust). The purpose of this section is to briefly highlight the consequences of insufficient trust from the point of view that it makes our relationships vulnerable to outside influences, especially interference (§ 60.2).

> **The level of trust in a relationship determines the extent to which others can influence that relationship.**

This is partly related to the relationship's gestation period (§ 56.3.1); the longer a relationship can remain isolated, the less likely it is for the development of trust to be disrupted by other people's expectations, especially their self-referential judgements (§ 60.3.2 Inter-Pactal Interference). The more trust there is between The Self and The Other, the less vulnerable the Nexus becomes to interference.

Utilitarian Perspective

In § 21.3 (Exchange versus Flow) and § 21.2 (Identity and Vocabulary), we touched upon the Social Exchange Theory of interpersonal relationships. From this point of view, we only instigate relationships if there is something in it for us. This would make our relationship conditional on something 'better' not coming along.

There is nothing inherently disempowering about such a relationship except that it would make any current Relationship Framework (§ 92), consistently have a temporary feel to it; I am only in this relationship until (for as long as) I get what I want out of it. If such an intention is not made explicit and The Self perceives there to be a utilitarian motive (and hence, deception) in The Other, an atmosphere of distrust is created.

Situationality

In § 52.4.3 (Focus and Situationality), we looked at situation-dependence from the perspective of Nexus formation. In other sections of this book, we have seen how the dynamics of relationships can be influenced by a change in the situation. In some cases, a change in the situation causes a Nexus to 'take a back seat' whilst another relationship is in progress, without being affected by the interruption. At other times, a change in circumstances (§ 14.3 Situation vs Circumstance) can infringe upon the nature and quality of an existing Nexus (§ 58 Post-Natal Development).

The extent to which 'insufficient trust' and a 'utilitarian perspective' can derail a relationship depends on how situation-dependent the relationship is. Another way of looking at this is to say that, the point at which trust becomes 'insufficient' or the perspective of The Other is perceived to be 'utilitarian enough' to jeopardise the integrity of the relationship depends on the extent to which the Nexus relies on the situation to manifest. For example, a Friends Nexus can manifest in a wider variety of situations than a Buyer-Seller Nexus. Also, a relationship that is evoked and nurtured by a home environment usually involves greater levels of expectation than one that is manifested in a social club environment. Whilst higher expectations increase the chances for 'storming', the home environment can also lead to more opportunities for 'norming' (§ 59.1 Stages of Relationship Development).

Chapter 75

Toxicology of Relationships

Just like organisms, relationships can be poisoned too. Toxicology is about trying to answer the following questions,

a) What is a poison? (Definition and classification)
b) Where can poisons come from? (Aetiology)
c) How do poisons affect the body*? (Pharmacodynamics and Pathology)
d) How does the body* handle them? (Pharmacokinetics)
e) What can therapists do about them? (Clinical practice)

> * For *affinito*toxicology, replace the word 'body' with 'Nexus'.

75.1

Poisons, Toxins and Venoms

A poison is any substance that can disrupt homeostasis. Notice the connection with Pathology, being the study of disruptions in homeostasis (Unit 19: Pathology and Therapeutics of Relationships).

In broader terms, we can say that a poison is any factor or phenomenon that can disrupt normal operations or routines (of an organism, an Individual, a Nexus, a Pactum or an organisation) to its detriment. Borrowing metaphors from computing, these can be 'bugs' or 'viruses'. We discuss viruses in the context of relationships in § 36 (Levels of organisation).

The difference between a poison and a toxin is not in what it does, but in where it comes from. When a potentially disruptive agent is made by a living organism, we call it a toxin. Similarly, the difference between a toxin and a venom is not in what it does but in the intention behind its production. A venom is made by its producer with the 'intention' of causing harm, either as a defence mechanism or as a means of immobilising prey. I am now about to make a bold statement.

There is no such thing as a poisonous substance.

What makes something poisonous is its dose. This is in line with a consistent theme within this book that a) there are few or no absolutes, grayscale being the norm and b) meaning is derived from the situation or context.

The same argument applies to medicines. There is no such thing as a medicinal substance. If someone is dehydrated, then water is a medicine, but in the case of hyperhydration (drinking too much water) water becomes a poison.

Dose is not the only factor that determines whether or not a substance is poisonous. Different systems (Individuals, Identities, organisms, relationships, organisations, Societies, etc. - (§ 90 Fractals)) have different capacities that determine how, and the extent to which, they can deal with poisons. For example, there are differences in the pattern of absorption, distribution, transport, metabolism and excretion between different individuals and ethnicities (§ 47 Overview of Affinito-Immunology). Similar differences exist in the way in which relationships are affected by potentially harmful elements (thoughts, messages, opinions or other internal and external influences).

In § 57.5 (The Exo-Nexus), we looked at the possible effects of other relationships on an existing Nexus. Here we consider Exo-Nexuses from the point of view of their potential disruptive influences. Before another Individual or, more specifically, another Identity, can affect a Nexus (negatively or positively), The Self or The Other must have some kind of relationship with that Identity. That is, there needs to be an existing Nexus between the influencing Identity and one of the Identities within the Pactum.

You might say, "But Bijan, in that case, the chemical analogy breaks down here because particles (especially free radicals) can collide with a molecule and cause a bond to break; there being no prior bond between the reactants and the products." I would thank you for taking such an integrative approach to this course and point out that, although this is congruent with what we are taught about chemical reactions at school, it is not entirely accurate.

Before continuing with our chemical analogy, I feel I had better clarify something. The potentially disruptive Nexus need not be a previously established one. If a stranger, Ali, walks into a room when Sam and Alex are having a conversation and Alex momentarily loses concentration [which could lead to misunderstandings because she may miss an important qualifier in something that Sam is saying], the reason for the distraction cannot be attributed entirely to Ali or to Alex. There is a momentary connection between Ali and Alex. You might say, "But Bijan, none of Ali's Identities have engaged with Alex, so there is no relationship yet." And this brings us back to our chemical analogy. See also § 56.2 (When does a Relationship Begin?). Atoms and molecules are colliding all the time, but relatively few of those collisions lead to a chemical reaction (the breaking and forming of bonds). Some chemical species, notably noble or, so-called, inert gases, hardly ever cause any bonds to break when they collide with a molecule. The reason for this is that chemical bonds are created by charged particles (electrons). This charge is a field which can affect nearby objects, if those objects are (or can become) suitably charged. Noble gases are not 'suitably' charged. But when a suitably charged atom or molecule gets close enough to be within the field of influence of another, it will exert an effect on the existing bond, usually weakening it. If a collision is successful, a bond breaks and each of the moieties [chemical species] that were attached to each other become available for creating another bond with a suitably matched partner (another moiety).

What this chemical analogy can tell us about interpersonal relationships is that, for another Identity (including a stranger) to have the potential to influence a Nexus, the incoming Identity would need to have the *potential* [akin to a charge on a chemical species, but in the case of Interpersonal relationships, this would be Common or Complementary Elements (§ 47)] to form a Nexus of some kind with one of the Identities in the Pactum. Let's look at an example.

If I am negotiating the purchase of a house will a seller and I see an old colleague of mine, one of three things can happen; I can

    a) Ignore my colleague and continue with the negotiations,

    b) Signal an acknowledgement to my colleague without breaking negotiations,

    c) Break off negotiations *temporarily* (and signal to The Seller that 'I' The Buyer Identity will be back soon) in order to allow for my Colleague Identity to take over,

    d) Break off negotiations, focus on my colleague and not indicate or return to the negotiation.

Meanwhile, my colleague also has a choice as to how to act; she can,

    e) Ignore me (so as not to interrupt my current Nexus),

    f) Signal acknowledgement (to indicate that she does not want/intend to interrupt),

    g) Come over and greet me (interrupting the conversation),

    h) Come over and 'force' me to abandon my existing conversation (either by changing the subject or by taking me aside or away).

If my Buyer Identity reacts to seeing my colleague in a way that is detrimental to this particular Buyer-Seller Nexus, then my colleague's presence will have had a 'toxic' (disruptive) influence on that Nexus.

If my colleague reacts to seeing me in a way that is *potentially* detrimental to the negotiations, then my colleague's presence is *potentially* poisonous (depending on how immune/vulnerable the Buyer-Seller Nexus is to the stimulus). If either Identity in the Nexus react in such a way that it negatively impacts the negotiations (e.g., take offence), then the presence of my colleague *will* have had a poisonous influence on the Buyer-Seller Nexus. Notice that it is the mental and behavioural *reactions* of the Identities forming the Pactum that determine the effect of the exogenous relationship, the Exo-Nexus (§ 58.5).

If my colleague deliberately wanted to disrupt that particular Nexus, then his actions could be said to be affinitologically venomous.

Unit 18

Affinito-Immunology

(Immunology of Relationships)

Source (before modification):
https://en.wikipedia.org/wiki/T_helper_cell#/media/File:Activation_of_T_and_B_cells.png]

Chapter 76

Overview of Affinito-Immunology

If a Nexus can react to an Exo-Nexus (§ 58.5) in ways that are conducive to its wellbeing, then it is well-equipped to handle the external influence. See the Buyer-Seller Nexus example in § 75.1 (Poisons, Toxins and Venoms).

In medicine, words and phrases such as immunity and immune response are reserved for the body's reactions to large proteins, invading microorganisms and misbehaving cells. Small exogenous chemicals (xenobiotics) do not tend to activate our immune system unless they cause damage to our cells. If they do, then our immune system will be activated to decommission the affected *cells*. This usually happens when poisons, toxins and venoms enter the bloodstream *directly* (through cuts or bites or stings or through natural pores in the skin).

When we ingest potentially damaging chemicals, the first mode of defence is absorption [the body can prevent potentially harmful substances from being absorbed through the walls of the gastrointestinal tract]. If the substance is absorbed, our second line of defence is the liver where the poison is metabolised and, hopefully, detoxified. Both absorption and metabolism vary between individuals. They can be quite idiosyncratic, in fact. This has given rise to the fledgeling field of personalized or precision medicine. From an affinitological perspective, we may be able to find equivalents to these biological concepts, but I am going to leave that kind of detail for consideration at some other time in the future ['lifespan permitting', as they say in Iran].

Relationships can become resistant or resilient to outside influences in three ways; toughness, flexibility and active protection. Affinito-immunology is about the last of these. However, to put the subject into a wider context, I shall briefly discuss the other two first.

Chapter 77

Toughness & Flexibility

I lost touch with one of my cousins when I was in my early twenties. We used to be close. Twenty years later, I found out he was in Sweden and acquired his telephone number. I called him on his birthday ...

Toughness can be thought of as impermeability; the nexus is so strong that it does not bend to outside pressure or influence (including the passage of time). In a SMER, this can happen through unwavering trust and/or effective communication.

Bonds between two carbon atoms tend to be strong. One of the reasons for this is that the electrons (the things being shared) are close to the nucleus (think Core Values: § 29.4.1). This is what makes diamond so tough. This does not mean that diamond is indestructible, it simply means that much more effort is required to break its bonds than most other types of bond.

Flexible objects bend to pressure, but do not lose their integrity; when the pressure is off, they resume their original shape. Bonds between hydrogen and oxygen are flexible. In water, for example, hydrogen atoms attach and detach at the drop of a proverbial hat. Whether we think of it as fickleness, promiscuity or freedom, the characteristics of the substance that they form; water, is defined by such behaviour. In other words, it is the fickleness of its O-H bonds that make water what it is, giving it its life-supporting, or should I say, life bestowing, properties. Water can change its shape to fit into any container without losing its integrity. This is related to our discussion in § 39.6 (SRC are Unstable at the Individual Level), where I made a distinction between molecules and their colligative properties.

Immunology is about the body's reaction to exogenous substances and affinito-immunology is about the Nexus' reaction to exogenous relationships (Exo-Nexuses) that could have potentially disruptive or unbalancing (disempowering) effects on the Nexus. Note that, here, we are veering away from the behaviour of individual Identities and Pacta (atoms and molecules) in vacuo and beginning to enter the realm of 'intermolecular' interactions.

[However, strictly speaking, to talk about the equivalent of colligative properties in the context of social interactions, we would need to have large enough numbers for the group to exhibit behaviours that cannot be defined in terms of single Identities or Pacta. We discuss this in § 32 (Extended relationships). The important point here is the idea that, in spite of the labels, the concepts of Individual, Pactum, community, society and crowd lie along a continuum (§ 25.3 Polar Bond: Partial Sharing)]

In affinitological terms, the flexibility of a Nexus boils down to **tolerance** (§ 67 Tolerance and Comfort Zones). The more disruption a Nexus can tolerate, the more flexible it is. This disruption may be spatial (physical distance), temporal (time apart), social (others diverting our attention away) or individual (having other things on our minds).

> *... When my cousin answered the phone after us not having heard from each other for twenty years, we simply picked up from where we had left off. Time and distance had not changed the core quality of our relationship.*

Chapter 78

Active Protection

(Immune Response)

Toughness and flexibility are passive processes by which I mean that the Nexus does not need to *decide* what to do about the outside influences. In Active Protection, The Self and The Other implement specific strategies, whether planned or impromptu, in order to ensure the integrity of the Nexus. This means that anything that a Pactum does, or can do [as opposed to ignores or tolerates] in order to preserve its integrity can be thought of as an immune response and the processes that enable it to do that constitute its immune system. There are specialised cells in our bodies for doing these things.

Our immune system protects us from most external threats, that is, anything that can cause cell or tissue damage that can lead to a disruption of homeostasis (§ 35.5), including parasites and poisons. It also protects us from internal threats, such as apoptosis (cell death/suicide) and cells that are in the wrong place at the wrong time or doing the wrong thing (such as cancer cells). In this context, wrong means anything that is not conducive to the common good; the collective, the whole, the entire body that we call an organism. See also § 36 (Levels of organisation).

The equivalent of active protection appears to exist at the most basic levels of organisation. The simplest level that has its own internal security systems is probably the cell.

[If you are interested, one such protective system is called "Endoplasmic-reticulum-associated protein degradation". It is like a quality control system that makes sure that the outputs of the cell are of a prerequisite quality, otherwise, like contaminated food, or faulty car parts, it could damage the system (think organism or population) that it is serving. If this particular security mechanism in cells fails, it can lead to diseases such as Parkinson's disease and cystic fibrosis].

The structure that we call an 'organism' is a collection of interacting cells, made possible through intercellular communication. The integrity of these structures is entrusted primarily to self-organisation (§ 92: Relationships as Self-Organising Systems) and then to the immune system. The structure that we call humanity is made possible through the interaction of cultures and subcultures.

[Notice that I am saying 'cultures' and not 'nations' because people are brought together by culture, but separated by national boundaries. We could start getting into the argument that it is the very separation of cultures that create cultures remember Darwin (§ 69.1.2 Isolation). We could also have a debate about how cultures can be divisive or that national boundaries prevent cultural aggression. Another argument could be that national boundaries facilitate 'safe' cultural exchange. And all of these would be valid up to a point. I just noticed that this is becoming a rather long ramble, so let's leave it at that for now.]

Between the structures that are made possible by intercellular communication (organisms) and the structures that are made possible by intercultural communication (humanity), there is a structure that we call society (§ 36 Levels of organisation). This is a collection of interacting Identities made possible through interpersonal communication. The question that arises is this, "What is responsible for the integrity of cultures?" I propose that every Identity is a cultural unit. In addition, since multiple Identities coexist within each individual, something within each individual is responsible for maintaining its integrity.

[I have given some thought to the nature of that 'something' and have some tentative hypotheses based on some of the research that has emerged from the field of hypnosis. So, alas, this is another discussion which will have to be postponed to some other time and place (keep an eye on introducingaffinitology.com). But if you are really interested, it is related to the Hidden Observer theory of Ernest Hilgard.]

Culture emerges through a collection of interpersonal relationships (Nexuses) similar to the way in which molecules are created by the joining of three or more atoms. In other words, a connection between two Identities creates a Pactum. A collection of Pacta can (and most often do) lead to the creation/emergence of a culture. When cultures emerge, they seem to bring with them mechanisms for defending themselves against annihilation. We can begin our search for understanding the nature of these subcultural defence mechanisms by looking at the work of Henri Tajfel and his colleagues that has come to be known as the Minimal Group Paradigm. Research in this area has shone some interesting lights on the roots of prejudice. From this perspective, we can see that there can be an upside to prejudice; it is there to preserve the integrity of a subculture.

[I have made a distinction between 'group' and 'subculture' here because a group refers to a collection of organisms we call individuals, but a subculture comprises a collection of Identities. That is to say that, each individual can be a member of different subcultures at different times and places (§ 32 Extended Relationships).]

Prejudice is a concept that can help us understand why and how the immune system can be a double-edged sword. Trying to preserve internal integrity can sometimes be in conflict with maintaining the organism's healthy external connections. This pattern is observed at different levels of organisation (§ 36), including at the organism level (think autoimmune diseases and allergies), at the subcultural level (think prejudice) and at the cultural level (think fascism).

Table 11 shows six levels of organisation along with their respective Active Protection (security) systems. The corresponding security system for each level is indicated in column three.

Table 11
Comparison of security systems at different levels of organisation

Discipline (Level)	Process	Security Systems	Examples
Cytology	**Intra**cellular processes	? (No name that I know of)	Endoplasmic-reticulum-associated protein degradation
Physiology	**Inter**cellular processes	Immune System	Immunoglobulins
Individual/ Identity	Psychological processes	Psychological Defence Mechanisms	Denial, deception, aggression, justification
Affinitology *	**Interpersonal relationships**	**Affinito-immunology or Pactum Defence Mechanisms (proposed here)**	**See § 80**
Sociology	Cultural norms	Rituals and taboos	Ostracization
National	National Politics	National Security organisations	Police, Army, Judicial system
International	International treaties	International Security organisations	Interpol, United Nations

[* Proposed here as a new discipline]

At the individual Identity level, our Psychological Defence Mechanisms (§ 79) act like an immune system in that their function is to defend our Identity from feeling threatened (anxiety and other unpleasant emotions). These PDMs can become barriers to the establishment of SMERs (§ 2.1 What is a SMER?). In order for The Self or The Other to invoke defence mechanisms to protect a Nexus, each Identity will need to extend its sense of self to include the rest of the Pactum. We explore this in more detail in § 80 (Relationship (Pactum) Defence Mechanisms).

Chapter 79

Psychological (Identity) Defence Mechanisms (PDMs)

"Bijan, shouldn't that be 'defense'?" I hear some of you asking. Well, that depends on which version of English you incline towards. In this instance, there is some reason in the seeming madness of British English. Words like defence and practice are spelt with a 'c' when they represent a noun and are spelt with an 's' when they represent a verb. In English, we can take a noun and put it before another noun and turn the first one into an adjective (e.g., 'spider man', as compared with 'man spider'). We cannot do that with a verb. However, just to confuse matters, we can turn verbs into nouns (and vice versa) by simply changing the sentence structure (e.g., 'his book' and 'book him'). In our case, the word 'defence' as used here, is adjective (repurposed noun) for 'mechanisms' and some of us 'boomers', as my son occasionally calls me, still adhere to these archaic, but reasoned, practices.

Psychological Defence Mechanisms (PDMs) are techniques that we use to protect our self-concept. I cannot see how a *healthy* relationship can be created or maintained without healthy self-concepts. See also § 29.6 (Aspects of The Self). PDMs protect our sense of Identity and can, therefore, be thought of as immune systems for each of our Identities. Yes, that's right. I am suggesting that for each Identity that we create within our psyche, we have a different protective strategy; we use different PDMs. The strategy that I use to protect my Father Identity is different to the one that I use to defend my Psychologist Identity and so on.

79.1
What is a Self (an Ego)?

Here, I am not adhering to the strict Freudian definition of 'ego'. The way in which I am using the word is probably closer to a construct that in psychology is referred to as self-concept or self-image. Here, by 'ego' I mean the entity that is responsible for the creation and management of the 'amalgam', a coherent collection of Identities (§ 37.7 The Emergence of Identity).

My ego is the part of me that builds a picture that I think of as me, my self-image. It is the part of me that distinguishes between 'me' and 'not me' (other).

Sometimes, it leads me to believe that 'I' am more deserving than other people (vanity). Sometimes it leads me to believe that 'I' am less deserving than other people (timidity [low self-esteem]). My ego gives me my sense of Identity and my sense of individuality. The ego is where our 'pride' resides. It is the part of us that gets offended when someone says something that doesn't match the picture that we have of ourselves in that situation. Another way of putting this is to say that, if someone asked you, "Who are you?" your answer would come from the content of your ego. And, of course, your answer would be different depending on which one of your Identities is dominant (is at the podium) at the time (§ 27.1 'Who' is a Fluid Concept: Situational).

We are born with physical needs. Our egos emerge in response to those physical needs and then take on a character of their own, a character that becomes independent of (sets itself aside from) those physical needs. Another way of looking at this is that our egos expand our perception of need to beyond the physical/physiological. I propose that the catalyst for this dissociation is other people. In other words,

---

Our sense of self, our ego, is socially induced.

Notice that I am not saying "socially constructed". Social construction is when we create a new phenomenon in conjunction with others. What I am proposing here is that our ego (sense of self) is created by something within our own psyche to distinguish us from others.

Here, I propose that our egos emerge, not to create, but to circumvent social barriers to connection. As such, our egos signal our uniqueness to ourselves and to others with a view to creating opportunities for connection through Complementary Elements (§ 47.2). Ironically, the same phenomenon often leads to thoughts and actions that have the opposite effect.

[The image of a lump of putty just came into my mind. Without an ego, we (our consciousness) would be an integral (amorphous) part, and indistinguishable from the whole lump of putty. If we now break a piece off, we can shape it into something different and then use it as a 'building block' to build structures that we might not be able to create with the original single lump.]

You might well ask, "But Bijan, if connecting is such a fundamental aspect of our lives, why would society put up barriers to such connection?" Well, here is my hypothesis. In primitive societies, basic rules were put in place to bring order into the emerging conglomerates of people so as to create structure by prohibiting random connections. Structures such as class hierarchies, caste, roles, ranks, sex and age) [I propose that this is a consequence of Dunbar's number and the 'magic number of short-term memory (7±2). I shall not dwell on these here, but I encourage you to look them up].

This eventually led to the emergence of a sense of self; the 'I' who has to adapt (comply with the rules) to be allowed to join the 'not I' which is the collective. See also § 32 (Extended Relationships: Communities and Crowds).

79.2
Ego is Anticipatory

Crucially, our psychological needs are in anticipation of our physical needs, they are not a reaction to our physical needs. Let me clarify that point because it is important. In § 33 (Atasinex Cluster) I said that our expectations, which are determined by our assumptions, have a huge impact on every aspect of our lives. This includes what we expect of others and what we expect them to expect of us; all of which, of course, strongly influence the quality of our relationships.

Part of the function of the ego is to manage our expectations. However, it is not a perfect system and, quite often, our predictions and reality do not match up. The way our ego manages such errors of judgement, that is, the effect that such errors have on our sense of Identity, determines whether we develop healthy an empowering self-concept (§ 40 Self-Esteem and Self-Confidence) or develop an external locus of control (§ 44) and think of ourselves as being at the mercy of kismet.

[Some commentators suggest that what Admiral Nelson actually said to Sir Thomas Hardy at the Battle of Trafalgar was not 'kiss me Hardy, but 'kismet, Hardy'. One could argue that this was a manifestation of Nelson's psychological defence mechanisms kicking in whereby he absolves himself of responsibility in preparation for facing whatever might come next].

If we do not have any physical needs and we do not anticipate having any physical needs in the future, then the ego would become redundant. Unfortunately, when the time is right for that to happen [albeit temporarily], the ego invents problems so as to be a solution for them (lamentably, this is a common survival mechanism, not just for egos, but for Identities, Individuals, ranks, communities and societies).

79.3
PDMs and Mental Health

Before we continue our discussion about Psychological Defence Mechanisms, here is how I have defined mental health my definition of mental illness in § 86 (What is Mental Illness?).

> **Mental illness is a chronic feeling of discontentment when there is no immediate physical threat.**

In modern times, for the vast majority of us, there's little chance that our health and safety is under *immediate* threat. Compare that with the amount of time that we spend being dissatisfied. The more we are dissatisfied when there is no immediate physical threat, the greater is our degree of mental illness. In such cases, our thoughts and feelings cause a fight or flight response in our body, but this response is based on what is happening inside our mind and not on any immediate external threat. This means that what our mind is doing is inappropriate for the situation we are in. Our mind puts our body into a state of stress when there is nothing tangible to fight, or to run away from. This is a mental problem because, clearly, it is not a physical (survival) issue. We explore this in more detail in Unit 19 (Pathology of Relationships).

A baby *learns* to anticipate his carer's 'love and attention' in response to its cry. Initially, this love and attention means food, warmth and security; in short, comfort. Later, our mind discards with the original *source* of this association and associates 'love and attention' with 'comfort' in the absence of physiological needs. When the ego takes this one step further and associates the *absence* of 'love and attention' with *discomfort*, even though what it is seeking is not related to its physical needs, that is when the seeds of mental illness are sewn. [The ideas in this paragraph were inspired by the works of Eric Berne.]

With that clarified, for the rest of this section, I am going to try to put the above into context.

79.4
The Purpose of
Psychological Defence Mechanisms

The notion of purpose has been called into question. This stems from a purely materialistic perspective where it is argued that, since everything flows through a cascade of action and reaction, purposefulness is an illusion. In place of the word 'purpose', I would have preferred to have used the equivalent to a Persian word that I could not find a translation for in English. The Persian word, *khāstgāh* consists of the stem *khāst* meaning 'want' and the suffix *-gāh* which is used to denote a 'set place' as in 'base'. For example, *ist* means 'stop' and *istgāh* means 'station' (literally, a 'place/base for stopping'). I would translate *khāstgāh* as 'the place where desire makes its home' which could also be interpreted as 'the source of desire'. It is one of my favourite (non-translatable) Persian words because it reflects the intention to pinpoint the root of our desires and, to me, this is a prompt for us to try to determine the root of our value systems.

The 'purpose' of PDMs boils down to one thing: Fear of being judged. Another way of saying this is that we use PDMs to avoid threats to our sense of Identity whichever Identity is active at the time (§ 29.4 The Omniself). Therefore,

> **Anything that is done to avoid being judged is a**
> **Psychological Defence Mechanism.**

Note that often, the entity doing the judging is another aspect of ourselves; a different Identity within us may be doing the judging. In other words, we can resort to PDMs to escape feelings such as guilt or remorse, as well as to avoid alienation.

Like physical shields, PDMs are barriers that we put up to protect ourselves against what we perceive to be threats to our ego. I say perceive because nothing can damage our ego if we do not allow it to. Egos are not physical entities that can be literally attacked and damaged. Any 'attack' would need to pass through our cognitive faculties first (§ 33 Atasinex Cluster). For example, if someone were to say to me, "Oh, you are such an idiot", I would have to somehow process and accept that statement before taking offence to it, otherwise it would just be meaningless or irrelevant vibrations going through the air and being picked up by my ear drums.

Let's do a thought experiment to demonstrate this.

Exercise 23 What is it inside us that takes offence?

1. Imagine that you hear one of your colleagues saying to you, "You are such an idiot." How would you feel and react?
2. Now, imagine that you turn around and realise that it was the parrot in the corner of the room that said that. How would you feel and react this time?

The differences in our feelings and reactions to these two (and similar) scenarios demonstrate clearly that it is cognition (§ 33 Atasinex Cluster) that is responsible for our feelings and reactions (response) and not the sensory input (stimulus) *per se*.

79.5
The Main Effect of Psychological Defence Mechanisms

Ultimately, the effect of PDMs is to keep people a metaphorical 'safe distance' away from us. The primitive reasoning behind them can be summarised as, "If I keep people away from me, they can't hurt me." I say primitive because the primitive part of our brain is more concerned with survival than with growth (§ 11 The Therapeutic Effects of Awareness) and whilst, in most cases, its effect is to reduce the risks to the structural integrity of our psyche, it can, at times, be counterproductive since it is not adaptive, that is, open to change, which is, of course, necessary for growth.

From an affinitological perspective, PDMs create barriers that obstruct the development of SMERs. For the rest of this section, we will concentrate on exploring the structure and dynamics of PDMs.

79.5.1
Aetiology of Psychological Defence Mechanisms

Once, mummy gave little Sam an apple. Sam took the apple and went out to play. A few moments later, Sam came back and said, "Mummy, I gave my apple to the boy next door." And mummy said, "Well done, my dear, that is very generous of you." Meanwhile, Sam's uncle overhears the conversation and says, "You shouldn't be such a pushover. Others should be giving you their apple, not taking yours."

It is not just little Sam who is confused. Society bombards each of us with contradictory expectations everyday of our lives. How we deal with such contradictions affects our self-esteem, self-confidence, the quality of our relationships and, ultimately, our wellbeing. Let's try to imagine how little Sam may try to make sense of what has just happened.

As it stands, little Sam has a problem. If he chooses to give, he is a pushover and if he chooses not to give, he is not generous (he is a miser). Neither of these are endearing propositions.

Little Sam's physical security and psychological wellbeing depends on forming attachments with significant others. Sam may decide that he is more attached to mother and to 'side' with her. At this point, he has to decide how to deal with falling out of favour with uncle. Alternatively, Sam may decide that he likes the idea of keeping things for himself and, therefore, he may decide to agree with uncle. Now he needs to strain his little grey cells to work out how to deal with mother. One option is that, next time, he will eat the apple himself and tell mother that he gave it away. This kind of deception, intended to avoid falling out of favour with our significant others, is probably the most prevalent type of psychological defence mechanism, although it is not often listed as one.

You may ask, "How is deception a Psychological Defence Mechanism?" And I would firstly commend you for asking such a question. I would then go on to explain that the purpose of PDMs is to protect our ego or self-concept. One of the determinants of a healthy self-concept is integrity. The more integrity we have, the less vulnerable we feel.

One of the greatest threats to our integrity is doubt (§ 51.8.8). Other people's judgements can cause us to doubt ourselves, reducing our self-confidence (§ 40.4). When we use deception to avoid being judged, that is when it becomes a psychological defence mechanism.

If I don't feel conflicted inside (I have integrity), I am more likely to have a more empowering self-concept. We explore conflicts in more detail in § 48 (Conflicting

Elements), but briefly, conflicts can be between what I say, what I do, what I believe, what I want and, of course, what is. Any of these can potentially be in conflict with any of the other.

You may be thinking, "But Bijan, my biggest conflict is between what I want and what others expect of me." A quick reframe here can help us to recentre our locus of control (§ 44). Your conflict is not between what you want and what others expect of you, it is between what others expect of you and what you want others to expect of you (§ 44.5 Zone of Anxiety).

79.5.2
Speed of Response

One way of recognising (suspecting) that a PDM is in progress is by looking at people's speed of response. PDMs are emotion-laden responses and emotional responses operate on a different (generally faster) timeframe to cognitive responses. Therefore, one of the easiest indicators that a PDM has been activated is by noticing how quickly someone responds to something that is said to them. Of course, the speed of response is just one factor and needs to be considered in conjunction with other factors, including the nature of the response and the emotional charge of the response.

Taking too long (disproportionately long) to respond can also be a gauge that the response is intended as a PDM. This is, as always, situation-dependent. Since PDMs arise out of something that a person strongly identifies with, the more the stimulus (prompt or cue) is related to the person's sense of Identity, the more likely it is for a PDM to be invoked. When a response time is disproportionately long, then it may mean that the person is thinking to herself, "How should I respond to this situation without, a) disempowering the Nexus (e.g., being rude) and, b) exposing a potential vulnerability that I feel in this situation.

79.5.3
Examples of Psychological Defence Mechanisms

Dissociation: In dissociation, I remove myself (my conscious awareness) from the circumstances whereby my conscious thoughts are no longer focused on anything that may involve my being judged, either by myself (feeling of guilt) or by others (blame).

Denial: This is dissociation's psychological cousin. In this case, I refuse to make a logical association that will make me conscious of the reality of a situation, i.e., I create a different situation for myself (§ 14.3 Situation vs Circumstance).

Regression: This is saying to one's self, "I remember a time when I wasn't held responsible for anything. For example, if I broke something, my mother would say that it was her fault for giving me access to something that I was clearly not yet ready for. If I do the things that I did then, I will get the sympathetic reactions that I got then and I won't be judged in a way that would threaten my self-concept."

Acting out: This is when someone believes that she is more likely to be judged on the basis of her words and, therefore, takes the less-likely-to-be-judged route of acting out. Actually, we *do* tend to think of words as being more permanent than what happens in our environment, so it makes sense.

In short, anything that we do, whether consciously or not, to lessen the possible impact of being negatively judged is a PDM.

79.5.4
Blame

Blame is a diversion tactic (moves attention away from me); "You won't be thinking about judging me if your focus is on someone else."

I have singled out blame here because I consider it to be one of the more pernicious PDMs, not only in the way in which it can disrupt our own relationships, it also has ripple effects throughout society. "Whose fault was it?" is, in my opinion, a far too common question. It reminds me of the following quote from the movie, Take the Lead:

> **"Even if you find somewhere to place the blame,
> it doesn't make the problem go away."**

If someone makes a mistake, by blaming them, we are questioning their intention. Our intention is intertwined with our sense of Identity (§ 29.4 The Omniself). This is why PDMs are very sensitive to (readily evoked by) blame. This makes blame counterproductive. Blame makes the problem more difficult to resolve because the person who probably knows most about the situation is also the person who is being blamed. This means that,

> the person who is most likely to be able to resolve the situation is the person who is being 'provoked' to psychologically remove himself or herself from the situation.

Therefore, in our pursuit of SMERs, we need to endeavour to purge our mind from blame mentality.

We cannot simply pull a belief out of our system. Even if we could, another 'weed' would take its place. We need to consciously replace that belief with a more empowering one. The first rule is that the new belief cannot be too conflicting with the old one otherwise it will encounter resistance (we are more likely to want to keep what is familiar to us). Let's look at possible workarounds. There are two alternative perspectives that we could consider,

a) No one is to blame and

b) Everyone's to blame.

Let's consider each of these in turn and see what the possible consequences of each of these perspectives could be as compared with the 'regular' blame perspective.

No one is to blame

How do we deal with earthquakes? We first run away from them and then, when the danger has passed, we rush back to see what we can salvage. During this time, our minds are entirely focused on operational procedures, that is, what can be done; more specifically, "What can I do?" Compare that with what we do when we suspect human error or foul play? We expend a significant portion of our resources into trying to find out who did it. Those resources could have been 'better' [more effectively, efficiently, empoweringly, usefully] spent mitigating the consequences of what has happened. You might argue, "Oh, but the guilty party will get away and may do it again." When a thought like that infects our mind, we can exercise this simple reframe(§ 63.1 Changing Beliefs: Reframing):

> **"This is not a criminal we are talking about; we are talking about our friends and colleagues or our potential friends and colleagues."**

There are two possible reasons for no one accepting responsibility (hence the need for pointing the finger):

a) No one feels responsible or

b) The last person in the chain of events that led to the event in question believes that the consequences of accepting responsibility are likely to be too disempowering and not worth it. (§ 62.5 The Three Levels of Belief)

In the vast majority of cases, the consequences are not physical, they are sociopsychological by which I mean, psychological effects that are primarily mediated through social needs.

Everyone is to blame

'A chain is as strong as its weakest link' so the saying goes. We tend to think of the person who makes a mistake as the weak link. We could also blame the maker of the chain for creating a weak link. Also, if all the links are not made from the same material, then the adjoining link could have unevenness which can gradually erode the link next to it making it more prone to malfunction. If the chain snaps and part of it goes flying through the air, it might hit a piece of glass. The glass breaks. Here's a quiz for you.

Which one of the following statements is true:

1. The glass broke because part of the chain hit the glass with sufficient impact to break it; it was the chain fragment's fault.
2. The glass broke because it was too weak to withstand the impact of the part of the chain that flew off to hit it; It was the fault of the glass for being too weak.
3. The glass broke because of the weakest link in the chain; it was the link's fault.
4. The glass broke because the link next to the weakest link had an uneven surface and eroded the one next to it until it became the weakest link; it was the broken link's neighbouring link's fault.
5. The glass broke because the chain-maker made a low-quality chain.; it was the chain-maker's fault.
6. The glass broke because the person using the chain didn't know how to use the right tool for the right job; it was the chain user's fault.
7. The glass broke because the teacher or carer of the user or maker of the chain did not teach him how to use or make the chain properly; it was the instructor's fault.

8. The glass broke because the user of the chain was temporarily distracted by an image that reminded him of an old flame; it was the fault of that image for being in the wrong place at the wrong time.
9. One or more of the above
10. None of the above: The glass broke because chains are chains and they sometimes break and when they break, they sometimes fly into glass and break them too.

To what extent does whether we answer 9 or 10 affect the approach that we take to resolving the problem (mitigating the consequences by fixing the broken glass)? The question I am asking here is, "Does trying to find (or pointing out) the culprit help us fix the glass?"

You could say, "Yes Bijan, we can make him pay for it." But here is the problem with that. If the person who we blame accepts responsibility, then he will want to volunteer to pay for it. If he does not, then he either does not feel responsible or considers the price that he would have to pay to be too high. Either way, trying to cajole him into paying will, inevitably lead to resentment. And since it is our friends and colleagues - or potential friends and colleagues (§18.1 A Stranger is a Friend You Haven't Got to Know Yet) - that we are talking about here, we really need to ask ourselves, "Which is more important, compassion or the broken glass?" Of course, if your answer is, "In this case, the glass", then you are bound by your values to do what you believe is right and I cannot argue against that. For my own perspective see § 51.7.4 (Empathy and Compassion)

We shall pick up our discussion of PDMs again in § 19 (Pathology and Therapeutics of Relationships) where we look at how PDMs can harm the Nexus and, consequently, the Pactum. Also, in § 73 (Transactional Analysis) we look at ways in which we can communicate with people in ways that minimize the chances of invoking Psychological Defence Mechanisms.

79.6

PDM Summary

To summarise, PDMs are concerned with maintaining the overall integrity of our ego (self-concept), *one Identity at a time* (§ 29.4 The Omniself). However, defending an Identity too vehemently can lead to us erecting too many barriers for a SMER to develop. In other words, protecting our ego (or any of the Identities that comprise it) can come at a great cost. We will explore the down sides of PDMs in § 87.4 (Autoimmune diseases).

Chapter 80

Relationship (Pactum) Defence Mechanisms (RDMs)

The title of this section looks a little awkward because, although I would have preferred to have called the concept, Pactum Defence Mechanisms, we would not have been able to distinguish its acronym from Psychological Defence Mechanisms.

The main difference between a PDM and an RDM is that the former is focused on preventing psychological damage (loss of integrity) to an Identity whereas the latter is concerned with preventing damage to the Nexus. The more The Self identifies with The Other in the Pactum, the more The Other and the Nexus become a part of The Self's Identity.

Like PDMs, RDMs have their pros and cons. On the one hand, they can protect a relationship from being disempowered in some way. They can also isolate the Nexus and prevent healthy Inter-Nexus interactions. Let's look at a few examples.

When we feel a possible threat to a relationship, what do we do? When we say things like, don't you talk to/about *my* friend (*my* spouse, *my* colleague, *my* car, *my* house, etc.) in that way, it is the word 'my' that indicates that the object of the sentence is an extension of the self. The other person or object has become a part of me. I no longer perceive them as being separate from me.

Here are a few indicators of RDMs. Like PDMs, depending on the situation they can either be empowering or disempowering.

- Interjecting to speak on the other's behalf
- Ignoring accusations or negative comments about the other
- Defending the other against accusations or negative comments
- Warning the other about accusations on negative comments
- Invoking psychological defence mechanisms by proxy to defend the other such as denial, justification.

This was a very short chapter because much of what needs to be said about defence mechanisms in general has already been covered in § 79 (Psychological Defence Mechanisms).

Chapter 81
Emotional Allergens and Hypersensitivity

Our reactions to challenges to our beliefs depend on the extent to which we identify with that belief. If I said to you that I believe the world is "a flat disc balanced on the backs of four elephants which in turn stand on the back of a giant turtle" [with thanks to Terry Pratchett (1948-2015)], how would you react? I doubt it would affect your life or interrupt your flow to any degree of significance. I also doubt that you would start to try to think of ways to convince me otherwise. That's because that image doesn't strike a chord with anything that you have identified yourself with.

How about this one, "School is a twelve-year jail sentence where bad habits are the only curriculum truly learned." [John Taylor Gatto, *Dumbing Us Down: The Hidden Curriculum of Compulsory Schooling*]. In a typical conversation, it is very unlikely that your emotional reaction to this sentence will be the same as to the previous one.

Both of the above sentences can be challenging to our beliefs. However, one of them strikes a chord and the other doesn't. Why is that? The more we identify with a phenomenon or a concept (idea, notion, belief, point of view, etc.), the more sensitive we become to it. Becoming sensitive means that our nervous system becomes primed to noticing it (§ 64.4 Values as Receptors). This means that the percept is more likely to attract our attention. See also § 33 (Atasinex Cluster) and Unit 22 (Thermodynamics of Relationships).

Hypersensitivity (too much sensitivity) means being 'disproportionately' sensitive which means that the sensitivity, usually a requirement and an indicator of life (§ 26.2 Characteristics of Living Systems), becomes disempowering. When being sensitive to what someone else says disempowers us, that sensitivity becomes an ailment that needs to be treated. Desensitisation is a common method used in medicine to treat allergies (hypersensitivity).

From a medical standpoint, we don't yet know enough about how we become hypersensitive to devise methods for preventing it and so, we focus on either desensitising the person (through 'allergen immunotherapy') or alleviating the symptoms (with things like antihistamines or corticosteroids).

I venture to propose that the roots of our psychological hypersensitivities are easier to determine and, therefore, we can aim to treat the cause. The good news is that self-awareness is itself therapeutic (§ 11 The Therapeutic Effects of Awareness). Self-awareness begins with a question (§ 15.1 The Power of Questions). Here is an exercise for you to try.

Exercise 24 The Effect of not Taking it Personally

Remember a time when, on reflection, your reaction was too hasty.

1. What stimulus prompted you to react in that way?
2. What aspect of your identity (what you identify with) did you feel was threatened?
3. What effect did that reaction have on the quality of your relationship *at that moment*?
4. Was defending that aspect of your ego worth the effect it had on your relationship at the time?
5. How would you have responded if you had not taken what was said personally?
6. If you had not taken it personally, would you have thought less of yourself?
7. If you had not been so sensitive to the situation would others have thought less of you (especially in the long run)?
8. What insights did you gain from doing (not just reading) this exercise?

The culture that we identify with (our Cultural Identity) is one of those associations that can make us 'allergic' to other people. There are many ways in which we can express or imply the idea, "Not one of us". Such notions make us more sensitive than is affinitologically healthy; they actively prevent us from connecting to a whole host of beautiful people.

[My Medical Scientist Identity wants to call this 'Culture-Induced Atopy' (CIA), but the Social Scientist Identity in me thinks 'Socially Constructed Aversive Reaction' (SCAR) is more appropriate.]

Lamentably, this reminds me of the way in which allergies to pollen restrict the extent to which sufferers can experience the beauties of spring.

In Unit 19 (Pathology and Therapeutics of Relationships), we explore this and other, emotional allergens from a different practical perspective.

Unit 19

Pathology of Relationships

Pathology is partly about what *can* go wrong, but mainly about what *has* gone wrong. And what *can* go wrong, which informs prevention and diagnosis, is informed by what *has* gone wrong.

Semantics aside, there are certain patterns in what can go wrong; themes that run through trouble spots in relationships (and living systems in general). In this section, we are going to take a look at some of these.

[Image by Tumisu from Pixabay.
Source: https://pixabay.com/illustrations/divorce-separation-argument-dispute-2437969/]

Chapter 82
Imbalance

In therapeutics, we often hear talk about the cause of a medical problem being an 'imbalance'. Imbalance can either be caused by malfunctions within the system or disruption of homeostasis (§ 35.5) from outside the system. In the latter case, when we restore the balance, we call it 'adaptation' or 'healing', when we haven't restored the imbalance yet, we call it 'disease' and when we fail to restore the imbalance, we call it 'chronic injury'.

When, in our attempts to restore the balance in one part of the system, we disrupt other systems within the body, it is called things like complications, intolerance, allergy and side-effects, all of which point to the body's inability to cope with (respond appropriately to) the new situation, i.e., maladaptation. Autoimmune diseases are a form of maladaptation. We need equivalent affinitological terms for when, in our attempts to restore the balance in one part of a social system (including a Pactum), we disrupt other systems within society. I propose the word 'derangement'.

[The implication is that communities and, by extension, societies, can also become deranged when they are faced with influences that they are unable to cope with.]

In medical pathology, everything that can go wrong in the body can be classified into two categories; structural damage and physiological impairment. You might be wondering, "What about infections?" Well, infections can cause problems either by causing structural damage, or physiological impairment. They do this either directly by hijacking the body's own cells (e.g., viruses) or indirectly, such as by mobilising or immobilising the body's immune system. This is similar to the way in which mobilizing an army affects the fabric of society, causing what we might call 'social inflammation' in some parts and 'social atrophy' in other parts.

Although, for simplicity, I have divided the factors that can disrupt living systems into two categories (structural damage and physiological impairment), this reductionist approach is more a heuristic and a learning aid than an accurate representation of reality because, as I frequently point out, grayscale is the norm (§ 25.3 Polar Bond: Partial Sharing). In this case, for example, structural damage can cause physiological impairment; damage to a cardiac (heart) muscle disrupts the flow of nutrients and hormonal communication. Conversely, problems with communication systems within the body (nervous, hormonal, interstitial or lymphatic) can lead to tissue damage and organ failure. Let's see how we can apply these understandings to relationships.

Chapter 83

Structural Damage

The three main structures that make up a relationship (a Pactum) are The Self, The Other and The Nexus. Damage to each of these 'structures' can have a detrimental impact on our relationships.

Structural damage to organisms can happen through trauma, obstruction, displacement and rupture and usually results from external influences. Likewise, structural damage to relationships can occur when external factors interfere with the normal functioning of relationships. These include factors related to career, family, time, society, environment, finances and distractions. I would say that the last item on this list is the most prevalent cause of disruption to relationships. Distractions are cases when The Self and/or The Other is paying attention (§ 33.3) to things that are less important, urgent or valuable than the relationship in question.

83.1
Preventing Structural Damage

83.1.1
Mindfulness

Sages throughout the ages have grappled with the idea of restoring balance [in our case, the balance between what can be done and what is most important in maintaining SMERs] and have presented many solutions, such as yoga, prayer and meditation. The spirit of these teachings can be summarised in the word mindfulness. Mindfulness is the antidote to distraction and its disempowering effects on our relationships. In its essence, mindfulness is focusing on the 'here and now' rather than 'why' (§ 11.1 Why Can Seriously Damage Our Health) and 'what if' (§ 8 What If).

83.1.2
Active Trust Building

Another way of preventing structural damage to our relationships is what I am calling 'active trust building'. This means that, rather than expecting The Other to trust us (§ 53 Trust), and being offended when he does not, we open up, i.e., make ourselves vulnerable (§ 79.5.1 Aetiology of Psychological Defence Mechanisms).

For example, consider a situation where, in a Romantic Partners Pactum, I decide to keep my mobile phone locked and private because I believe that privacy is a personal right. Even if I respect my partner's right to the same, the act of locking and protecting my mobile phone can be interpreted as keeping a secret, i.e., being reticent (cagey) as opposed to exercising my personal right. And the idea of keeping secrets is indicative of a lack of trust. So, what do I do? Do I act in accordance with my belief that privacy is a personal right or with my belief that keeping secrets is a sign of lack of trust (§ 53 Trust)? A way around this apparent dilemma is to reframe at least one of the beliefs (§ 63.1 Changing Beliefs: Reframing). Here is a possible reframe of "privacy is a personal right":

> **"Trusting others to respect my privacy is a sign of respect."**

"I trust that my privacy will not be invaded and do not need to actively protect my privacy from my partner." AND "If, by not guarding my privacy, one of my vulnerabilities is exposed, I trust that my partner will, a) not judge me and b) shield me against the possible negative consequences of that weakness."

And here is a possible reframe for "keeping secrets is a sign of lack of trust":

"Keeping secrets can be a Pactum Defence Mechanism" (§ 80)

"I trust that my partner will not act in a way that will be deliberately detrimental to our Nexus, and, if she is keeping secrets, it is with the intention of protecting or strengthening the relationship. I, therefore, will not invade her privacy for fear of exposing vulnerabilities that could be to the detriment of our relationship."

You might ask, "How can keeping secrets strengthen the relationship, Bijan?" I would say, "How about a surprise Birthday party?" Notice that the assumption here is that the relationship is founded on trust, that is, a person is innocent until proven otherwise and, therefore, since I do not have any reason to suspect otherwise, I am not going to investigate. The point here is that,

---

**trust does not negate due diligence and
due diligence does not imply the presumption of guilt.**

Another way of active trust building is by being seen to invoke Pactum Defence Mechanisms (§ 79). For example, if you see someone doing or saying things that could be to the possible detriment of the Nexus, you can alert The Other in the Pactum to the threat and reassure The Other that your side of the relationship is not vulnerable to it.

83.2
Treating Structural Damage to the Pactum

In terms of the structure of the Pactum, anything that disempowers The Self, The Other or the Nexus can be 'structural damage'. Here, I am going to talk about one of the most prevalent of these, damaged self-confidence.

83.2.1
Damaged Self-Confidence

Along with self-esteem (§ 40.3), self-confidence (§ 40.4) is one of the pillars of mental health. A stumbling block that I often need to remove before I can begin to tackle the problem of self-confidence is the way in which the idea is framed in everyday language. Let me illustrate.

In everyday speech we talk about building a car and building self-confidence. Using the verb 'build' for both of these processes masks a fundamental difference between them. Becoming aware of this linguistic sleight of hand is crucial because otherwise we are thrown off track regarding what we need to do in order to help someone become more confident.

When we build a car, we must first make the parts and then put those parts together in accordance with our design schematics. Thinking about confidence in terms of something that needs to be built makes us look at the problem from the wrong direction. We are already born with self-confidence. Unfortunately, this innate tendency is eroded by the conflicts that are imposed on us, primarily by Society (§ 79.5.1 Aetiology of Psychological Defence Mechanisms and § 39 Social Ranking Criteria). So, we don't need to *build* confidence in people, we need to restore, or better still, *unmask* or reveal their self-confidence to them.

You could argue that, since their confidence has been taken away, it needs to be rebuilt. However, even in those who think that they have no self-confidence, we find that their self-confidence waxes and wanes depending on the context and my argument is that this is because in different contexts our self-confidence is masked to a greater or lesser degree. Hence it is already there; it does not need to be 'built'.

As young children, we have no problems in believing in ourselves and that we can do whatever anybody else can do. That is why children try to mimic others; if we didn't have the self-confidence (belief) that we can do whatever other people can do, we wouldn't even try. As we grow older, however, Society imposes its, often conflicting, expectations and values upon us (§ 79.5.1 Aetiology of Psychological Defence Mechanisms). These conflicting ideas are almost always intangible and abstract, leaving us with no objective criteria against which to evaluate society's judgements on us. Let's look at some of the factors that create conflicts within us thereby eroding our self-confidence. If I were a betting man [I have done on occasion], I would bet that,

> **false comparisons are the biggest culprits in obscuring self-confidence.**

False comparisons are so endemic in our Society that we rarely notice them. It may seem obvious, but I will it anyway (because it brings it into our conscious awareness): comparison is the source of bias. I would even go as far as to argue that there cannot be comparison without some level of bias. Yet, every noun and every adjective in every language forces us to make comparisons, irrespective of whether or not that comparison is relevant to the situation. And since knowledge is not possible without some frame of reference (something to compare with), we can hardly escape the conclusion that all knowledge is inherently biased. We could call that, *'Original Spin'* (§ 39.7 Social Ranking Criteria Summary).

There are many examples that demonstrate our biases in the visual domain (e.g., figure 68), but it is not limited to vision.

Figure 68 An example of a cognitive bias in the visual domain

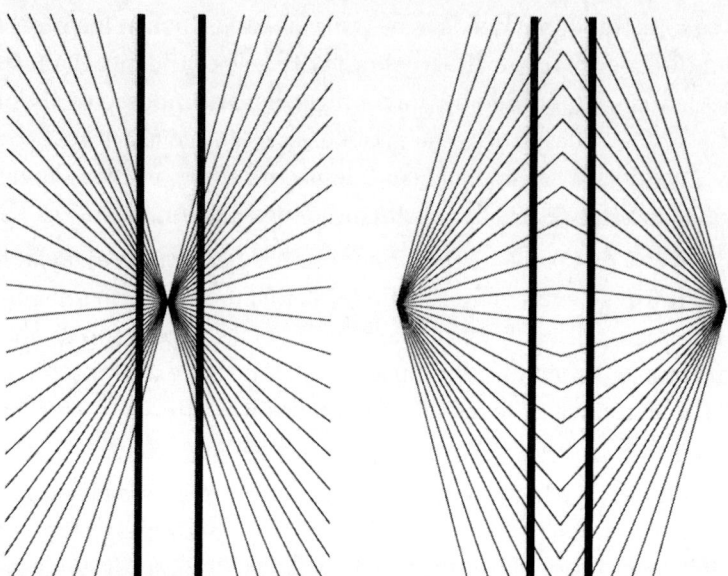

All of our senses and our cognitions (intellect, thoughts, conclusions, beliefs, perspectives, values, etc.) are susceptible to bias. Let me correct that; cognition is not merely susceptible to, but is, by necessity, biased.

Not tiptoeing around that fact that all of our perception is inherently biased can be very empowering (after the initial shock wears off). Accepting that fact may initially dent our self-confidence (or even shatter it if we really grasp the depth of the issue), but once we come to terms with it, we become much more tolerant of our fellow humans' flaws.

Our intellect also buckles under the strain of too many comparisons; we begin to rely on heuristics (§ 72.5 Cognitive Load and Heuristics). Let me illustrate the effect of this, pervasive, false comparison on our self-confidence and self-esteem through an anecdote.

A few years ago, I had a 16-year-old client who had been at the top of her class ever since she could remember. She had even won medals at the International Chemistry Olympiad and aspired to become a pharmacist. She was referred to me by her teacher because after a particular exam, she had dropped in rank from 1st to 2nd in her class and after that, she had lost interest in her studies...

In this case, my therapeutic technique was guided by Attribution Theory (§ 43). My young client's problem was that she had been led to believe that whether or not she was number one in class was entirely up to her. Either her own effort or her own aptitude or both; and nothing else. In other words, she attributed all of her success or failure to herself and none of it to her environment. In my decades of teaching, I had found this to be a very common problem.

Society leads us to believe that our children's examination attainment is down to only two factors; the child's aptitude and the child's effort or persistence (§ 39 Social Ranking Criteria). Whilst certain echelons of society may be beneficiaries of inequalities and, therefore, seek to create or maintain such inequality, Society as a whole is averse to it because the perception of inequality leads to social disorder (i.e., everyone's disempowerment).

[Note that we are not talking about 'inherent' inequalities, i.e., the differences that make us unique (§ 39.6 SRC are Unstable at the Individual Level). It is the perception of deliberately imposed (Manmade/artificial) inequality that we tend to be hostile towards)]

Promoting the idea that children's aptitude and effort are the only factors that affect their examination performance helps to maintain a semblance of equality; it dissuades individuals from looking for sources of variations in students' attainment elsewhere. However, the reality can be very surprising. I discuss this in more detail elsewhere [keep an eye on introducingaffinitology.com].

...I showed my young client evidence that demonstrate how some of the factors at play in determining students' examination results can hardly be conceived or predicted under normal circumstances. One of these was the finding that the proportion of male to female students in a class has a positive impact on boys' attainment in mathematics but has a negative impact on boys' attainment in English.

In short, I managed to convince her that, whilst it is empowering to hold oneself responsible for one's *actions*, it is disempowering to hold oneself responsible for the *final outcome* because there are far too many factors at play that we do not have control over. I did this through techniques that included a combination of *life as a journey* (§ 6-11 The Journey) and *zone of anxiety* (§ 44.5 Zone of Anxiety) approaches. I met her serendipitously a few years later and she told me that she was studying pharmacy at university.

Another factor that can severely undermine our self-confidence is thought patterns that are stuck-in-the-past. Our self-concept and our self-confidence depend on how we appraise our performance from one time frame to the next. If my experiences tell me that I am capable, or that I am improving, then I become more self-confident and develop a more robust self-esteem. This is related to the question that I asked elsewhere in this course, "Does measuring my weight affect how much weight I lose?" (§ 10.2 How do you track progress?)

Opportunities for developing our self-confidence and self-esteem lie in the future. Being stuck in the past, i.e., being preoccupied with our memories, blind us to the opportunities that lie in the opposite direction: the future. To resolve issues like this, we can use a combination of techniques including mindfulness, thought observation and what I call the '*zone of anxiety awareness* technique'.

Fear of not being able to cope with the consequences is a self-confidence issue that is very detrimental to our self-esteem. To resolve this, we can use a combination of techniques including the *life is a journey technique* and the *I can cope with anything technique*.

Another issue that can knock our self-confidence is what I call '*misunderstanding love*'. There is so much that I want to discuss about the notion of love that it is beyond the scope of this discourse. I shall, however, endeavour to explore love with you in detail elsewhere [keep an eye on introducingaffinitology.com].

[I initially intended to include more detail about the techniques that I have mentioned above in this book. However, in consideration of space limitations, I shall endeavour to make them available elsewhere (keep an eye on introducingaffinitology.com).

Structural Damage at the Nexus Level

Whilst vulnerabilities in The Self or The Other can threaten the integrity of the Nexus, there are times when the Nexus can be vulnerable despite the robustness of the Identities that comprise the Pactum. This can happen because,

a) Although The Self or The Other could, potentially, do something to prevent damage to the Nexus, they are either,

    i) Oblivious to their own potential or

    ii) Oblivious to the needs of the Nexus (leading to the expenditure of motivational energy (§ 93.1) elsewhere

b) External factors; physical or social barriers to the kind of communication required for that particular Relationship Framework, can lead to the erosion of the Pactum. Distance is an obvious example.

Chapter 84

Physiological Impairment

[Initially, I intended this to be a much longer chapter but, in the light of the fact that the book is already quite long, I decided to settle for simply highlighting the main points for now (keep an eye on introducingaffinitology.com).]

Physiological impairment is basically related to communication problems within the body, where cells fail to send and receive messages or, more commonly, the right messages are not sent at the right time to the right places. The main effect of this kind of problem is the 'imbalance' referred to earlier leading to disruption in homeostasis (§ 35.5).

Like its physiological counterpart, the most important factor that can disrupt relationship homeostasis is inefficient or inappropriate communication (§ 47.1.1 Common Language). The most pervasive factors causing communication problems are Psychological Defence Mechanisms (§ 79). Another factor that can cause problems in relationships from within is distrust (§ 53 Trust).

Some words have a greater potential for destabilising relationships. It behoves us to minimise their use (i.e., where possible, replace them with more empowering words). These include,

- **Why:** Exercise 2 (§ 11 The Therapeutic Effects of Awareness)
- **Good/Bad:** Binary thinking (§ 3.5 Good or Bad?)
- **Better/Worse:** Comparative/Competitive (§ 39.4 SRC Embody Elitism and Competition)
- **Maybe:** Indecisive (§ 51.8.7 Indecision)
- **Must/Should:** Parent ego state (§ 73 Transactional Analysis and § 20 Language and Levels of Persuasion)
- **Should:** Incites the feeling of guilt (§ 64.14 Values, Decision-Making and a Sense of Guilt and § 79.4 The Purpose of Psychological Defence Mechanisms)

Chapter 85

Affinito-Parasitology

Relationships can become infected. This means that an outside agent can *actively* damage (impair) the strength and effectiveness of The Nexus. Agents that cause infections vary in their degree of complexity. Biologically, viruses, bacteria, protozoa, fungi, small insects and helminths (worms) cover almost all of them. From an evolutionary perspective, as parasites evolve, there is a shift in the degree to which the parasitic agent takes in proportion to how much it gives. This shifts the relationship along a spectrum from being entirely parasitic towards becoming more mutualistic.

In terms of relationships, we are talking about the extent to which an external agent takes from (and disrupts) the Nexus. Various aspects of The Self, The Other or Exo-Identities (§ 58.1 Core Values Probing) can be vectors in the parasite's lifecycle.

85.1
Tapeworms in context

In § 31 (Symbiosis) we looked at the different ways in which organisms can interact with each other. From an evolutionary perspective, the relationship between a parasite and its host goes through a similar process to that described in § 35.2 (Paediatrics of Relationships), namely, forming, storming, norming and performing.

Forming: Inexperienced parasites (latecomers to the scene in evolutionary terms) take what they need without any consideration of their effect on their hosts.

Storming: Such parasites tend to kill their host because they have not yet adapted enough to optimise their harvest.

Norming: As parasites become more seasoned (evolved), they become less debilitating to their host. The most seasoned parasites 'learn' to maximise their yield with minimal damage to their host (commensalistic symbiosis), although they don't confer any benefits either. Tapeworms are of this ilk. They live in the intestines with the host hardly being aware that they are there. In evolutionary terms, tapeworms appear to have been with us for a very long time. [Incidentally, in sociological terms, this reminds me of the trend from slavery to suffocating taxation to 'free' social and medical care.]

In theory, for a host not to be harmed by a commensalistic parasite, it would have to produce more than it needs for its own survival and growth. A question would then arise as to why an organism would produce more than it needs and wouldn't such inefficiency have detrimental effects on its evolutionary progress? From one perspective, producing more than its need can be seen as a kind of insurance policy in case of famine. [This would suggest that, in case of famine (or malnutrition), a tapeworm would become a liability for its host.] Another reason would be to compensate for what parasites take from it.

Performing: As the relationship matures (over many generations), hosts begin to develop mechanisms to take advantage of the parasite too, eventually turning the relationship into a mutualistic one. An example of such a mutualistic relationship is the one between animals and fruit trees. The tree discourages us from eating its vital organs (its leaves), and rewards us for carrying its seeds far from its roots so that its offspring do not compete for the same patch of soil as itself, by providing animals with fruit.

The same applies to affinitology. A parasitic relationship is one where one **social entity** (Individual, Identity, Pactum or society) takes from another such entity, without conferring commensurate benefits (directly or indirectly) to the host. Examples of parasitic relationships include theft, extortion, coercion, slavery, colonisation, neocolonialism and any other activities that are detrimental to the growth, maintenance or contribution of another **social entity** (§ 32 Extended Relationships: Communities and Beyond).

85.2
Affinitological Viral Infections

In § 36.1 (Viruses), I proposed that from an affinitological perspective, we can think of viruses as faulty information that is fed into a relationship to serve someone else's agenda to the detriment of a relationship. Note that a piece of information need not be 'false' to be detrimental to a relationship. It may be,

a) Open to misinterpretation
b) Incomplete
c) Inappropriate
d) A cause of misdirection

Chapter 86

What is Mental Illness?

What is mental illness? The answer you will get depends on who you ask. Here's my definition of mental illness:

> **Mental illness is a chronic feeling of discontentment when there is no immediate physical threat.**

The reasoning behind this is quite simple; if it does not originate in the body, then it must come from the mind. This definition also points to another crucial characteristic of mental illness; it does not manifest through cognition. In other words, since it is our emotions that dictate our decisions (§ 51.3.2 Feelings Trump Logic) and, therefore, our actions (behaviour), unless the thought leads to an emotion that is maladaptive, it cannot be considered as mental illness.

> *Many years ago, when I was teaching in a school, I walked into the staff room just as one of the teachers was saying, "It is the thought that counts. The thought reveals the person." I have no idea what the conversation was about, but my immediate response was to Say, "That's interesting. I always thought that the job of the mind is to consider every possibility, but not to act on all of them."*

If you ask the pharmaceutical industry, they would tell you that mental illness is an imbalance in the neurotransmitters in the brain. If you ask behaviourists, they would tell you that it is mental conditioning that causes abnormal behaviour (§ 71 What is Normal?). At this point the statistician might intervene and ask, what exactly is abnormal and where does one draw the line? Meanwhile, an evolutionary biologist would say that we should be talking about adaptive and maladaptive behaviour rather than normal and abnormal. And then, Jiddu Krishnamurti, a contemporary Indian Philosopher, could come along and say, "**It is not a sign of good mental health to be well adjusted to a profoundly sick society**".

So, what does one do when one is born into a 'profoundly sick society'? Well, it appears that most of us become mentally ill (e.g., depressed, stressed, frustrated, aggressive, deceitful, reclusive and competitive instead of co-operative). Most of us don't recognise these as signs of mental illness in ourselves because being mentally ill has become the norm. What is this norm?

The norm is simply what most of us do. It is a statistical construct (whether we are conscious of it being so or not). It does not inherently say anything about morality, right or wrong, good or bad or anything like that. Most of us simply infer these value judgements by assuming that if most people do it, think it or value it, it is more valuable ('better').

So, what is the 'normal' reaction when dealing with a 'profoundly sick society'? What do most of us do about it? We resort to Psychological Defence Mechanisms (§ 79).

86.1
The Feeling of Insecurity

Once again, time and space limitations curb my enthusiasm for delving deeper into an important aspect of ourselves; one which plays a crucial role in preventing us from creating SMERs, namely, the feeling of insecurity. Here, I simply want to plant some seeds of curiosity and introspection [and, perhaps, some healthy controversy].

If thoughts do not translate into feelings, they do not cause maladaptive behaviour and, therefore, do not result in mental illness, or problems with our interpersonal relationships. I propose that the feeling of insecurity is the most prevalent and pervasive cause of mental problems which also, through the invocation of psychological defence mechanisms (§ 79), leads to our inability to create SMERs. Although I am very tempted to devote a separate chapter to this, my arguments in support of what I have just said will have to wait for another time and place [keep an eye on introducingaffinitology.com].

Chapter 87
What can go wrong?

87.1
What is right?

Before we can discuss what is wrong, we need to be able to define what is right. However, in pathology there is no absolute right or wrong. And talking about right or wrong in general is unhelpful anyway (§ 39.1 SRC are Binary). In this context, it is more helpful to talk about adaptive and maladaptive which we shall use in the context of this chapter. In other contexts, I suggest we replace the words 'right' and 'wrong' with empowering and disempowering (§ 3.5 Good or Bad?).

As I have mentioned elsewhere (§ 10 The First Step), before we can proceed with any kind of scientific investigation, we need to be specific about what we mean by adaptive or maladaptive in the context of relationships.

The idea of adaptation is made up of several other concepts, including organism, environment and adapt. The last is about change which brings time into the equation.

With regards to time, we can take a snapshot of the state of a relationship at any specific moment. We cannot, however, take a snapshot of 'adaptation' because adaptation is a process.

Since we have defined pathology in terms of adaptation, when we apply the idea of pathology to relationships, we automatically invoke the idea of change and with it, time. We, therefore, need reference points and yardsticks (standards) by which to judge what is adaptive and what is maladaptive (§ 68 Tolerance and Comfort Zones).

Every measuring device needs to be calibrated before it can be used (§ 10 The First Step). This is because each relationship has its own unique characteristics and we need to know what the optimum conditions are for that specific relationship. This is no easy task, but we need to start somewhere. After calibration, we need criteria by which to judge how far the relationship is from its optimal conditions.

If you are with me so far that's great but if it is getting a little too complicated don't worry. It will begin to make more sense as I put these ideas into practical everyday contexts through examples and anecdotes.

87.2

Conflict as an Indicator of Relationship Pathology

Since every relationship is unique, how do we gauge what is pathological and what is not for that specific relationship?

The single most important indicator of the health of any relationship can be summarised in one word: conflict. Conflict between The Self and The Other and conflict within The Self and within The Other. Having said that, we also need to bear in mind that,

---

not all conflicts are disempowering.
Often, conflict is a necessary step to the development of SMERs.
(§ 59.2 The Conflict Cycle)

We have looked at Conflict from various perspectives in different sections of this book, including in

§ 33.7.3 (Expectation and Conflict: Divergent Expectations)
§ 48 (Conflicting Elements)
§ 59.2 (The Conflict Cycle)
§ 63.2 (Beliefs and Conflict)
§ 64.15 (Complementary and Conflicting Values)

In this section, we explore conflict from the point of view of how they can be potentially disempowering for relationships.

I am going to go out on a limb here and boldly state that **conflict is the root of** *all of our problems;* conflicts between, and within, our thoughts, emotions and behaviours. As simple as that sounds, what makes it difficult for people (us) to change, and for therapists to help them change, is identifying what is in conflict with what (diagnosis). Only then can we identify the roots of those conflicts (cause or causes) so that, finally, we can find ways of aligning those elements so that they won't be in conflict anymore (treatment).

Do you remember the story of the doctor who thought that he was not successful? (Unit 11: Dimensions of human experience)

> **We make thousands of decisions every day. And every decision that we make is an exercise in conflict resolution.**

One of the most encountered, and most problematic, conflicts in relationships is, "The classical dilemma between the head and the heart." [As Chris de Burgh puts it in his song, 'The Head and the Heart']

> *Once a client came to me and, after much deliberation, the problem could be summarised as this, "One guy is stable and makes me feel secure. The other guy is spontaneous and makes me feel excited. I want both."*

Affinitological thinking, as described in this book, can help us resolve such dilemmas. For example, we can begin to talk about invoking different Identities with different Values in different situations creating different Nexuses in ways that will minimise interference. We can also look at the different dimensions of each relationship (Unit 11: Dimensions of Human Experience) so that we can create situational barriers to interference and conflict.

In the final analysis, to resolve conflicts, we need to understand the decision-making process. Although we have discussed decision-making in several places in this book, it is a topic that is beyond the scope of this already extensive, introductory course [keep an eye on introducingaffinitology.com]. Meanwhile, look carefully through the following partial list of factors that can cause inner conflicts.

Table 12 Potentially conflicting factors within The Self

The Self's		
Achievement	Behaviours	Beliefs
Expectations	Experiences	Feelings
Needs	Values	Wants

Taking the first item from the list, you can see that my 'achievements' can be in conflict with any of the other eight items. It can also be in conflict with itself because, for example, I can go to a playground fare and play a game of trying to throw hoops around poles and I can get very different results on each attempt (similar behaviour, similar beliefs, similar expectations, similar experiences, similar feelings, similar needs, similar values, similar wants, *different results*).

Here's another example. If I feel that I have worked really hard but have little to show for it, my behaviour is in conflict with my (expected) achievement. This is, of course, mediated by my beliefs. If I believe that the amount of work that

I have put into something *should* have produced better results, there will be conflict between my behaviour and my achievement and my expectations and the beliefs that led to those expectations - but let's keep things simple here, after all, this course is only meant to be an overview.

At the individual level, each of the examples on the list in Table 12 can be in conflict with any of the other eight items. Similarly, in a Pactum, each of these factors can potentially create a conflict within the Nexus. Looking at the factors across from each other can give us a clearer view of the situation (Figure 13). Each factor can be common, complementary (§ 47 Common and Complementary Elements) or in conflict with each other, either in specific situations (at the Identity level), or as a matter of principle (at the Core Values level).

Table 13
Examples of Potentially conflicting factors between The Self and The Other

The Self's	The Other's
Achievement	Achievement
Expectations	Expectations
Needs	Needs
Behaviours	Behaviours
Experiences	Experiences
Values	Values
Beliefs	Beliefs
Feelings	Feelings
Wants	Wants

When we consider these potential causes of conflict in the context of relationships, even when we limit the possibilities to these nine factors only, with nine areas of potential inner conflict and nine areas of conflict within The Other in the relationship there is a plethora of opportunity, or potential, for conflicts to arise. It is no wonder then that we experience so many ups and downs in our relationships, romantic, professional, family or otherwise.

[If the social scientist in you is saying that this is too simplistic because each factor can have a mediating effect on other conflicts, I agree with you but not introducing this complication still allows me to get the point across.]

The thousands of decisions that we make every day (consciously and subconsciously) are all exercises in conflict resolution. I intend to explore this idea in more detail in a separate course [keep an eye on introducingaffinitology.com].

Each conflict pair has its own dynamics and results in a unique set of physiological reactions that we call feelings.

Another insightful take away lesson from this is that it would be short-sighted to expect other people not to be conflicted when so often, we, ourselves, are.

Along with the complexity and confusion that all this may cause, comes a feeling of liberation knowing that we are not alone and that relationships are not simple and, therefore, if it's not working, there's nothing wrong with us, we just need more knowledge and practice. So, let's carry on.

What all this makes clear, so far, is that a major step towards building mutually empowering and satisfying relationships (§ 2.1 What is a SMER) is learning how to resolve our *own* inner conflicts. When we fail to notice our own *internal* conflicts, or when we externalise them by blaming other people (§ 79.5.4 Blame), we are not psychologically ready to experience magnificent relationships.

One problem with not being ready to receive or experience something is that we won't even recognize it when we do get it.

Here's a story to illustrate this.

> *When my daughter was six and my son was four, their grandmother wrapped up some money for them for Christmas. My daughter opened her package first and finding a couple of notes of large denomination inside expressed her pleasure and excitement in a manner not atypical of six-year-olds. A few parcels later, my son opened his present from grandma. It looked just like the present that his sister had received. With a nonchalant expression, he turned to his sister and gave her the banknotes and said, "Here Ariana, you can have these as you seem to like them so much."*

The moral of this story is that,

---

we cannot fully appreciate what we do not fully understand.

Relationships are no different.

87.3

Conflict Diagnosis

The single most important determinant of the effectiveness of therapy (chosen solution to a problem) is diagnosis. Therefore, the most important question here becomes, "How do we identify a conflict or, hopefully, a potential conflict within a relationship?"

From an affinitological perspective, we can think of conflict as a source of imbalance (§ 82 Imbalance).

Every conflict is different in its quality, but all conflicts have two quantitative dimensions; severity and frequency (§ 49.3 Depth and Breadth).

Fortunately, there is a simple indicator of whether or not there is a conflict or impending conflict within a relationship, which I shall demonstrate through the following exercise.

Exercise 25 How to Identify potential conflicts within a relationship

1. Think of a relationship (Pactum) that you are currently a part of.
2. Begin a sentence with, "I wish…" and complete it [Just in case you missed it; it must have something to do with the relationship ☺]
3. What is it about the relationship that you think could be better that prompted you to think that wish?

You have just identified a potential source of conflict in that Nexus. Why? Because it indicates there is something about the relationship that is not entirely fulfilling and, if the situation arises for that aspect of your psyche to be satisfied, you may be tempted to seek that which is missing from this relationship from another relationship *at the detriment of this one.*

87.4
Autoimmune Responses and Diseases

Autoimmune responses are where the body's immune system,

a) Fails to differentiate between the body's own tissues and those of an invading organism and attacks and destroys or disrupts its own tissues or processes.

b) Overreacts to a minor problem. Think of it as being like sending in the army because there has been a break in at a local store.

Autoimmune *responses* become autoimmune *diseases*, when the immune response against the body's own tissues results in serious disruption of homeostasis (§ 35.5), either through structural damage (§ 83) or physiological impairment (§ 84).

From an affinitological perspective, this is when factors that are supposed to safeguard a relationship actively interfere with it. For example, *too much or too little* trust (§ 53), jealousy (§ 51.8.12 Jealousy and Envy), communication (§ 12), PDMs (§ 79) or RDMs (§ 80).

You might be wondering why I have indicated that too little Jealousy can be detrimental to some relationships. This depends on the specific Relationship Framework (§ 92). In § 51.8.12 (Jealousy and Envy), I pointed out that some people consider jealousy to be a sign of love [I would prefer to see it as an indication of commitment, because love is something else]. In such cases, the Nexus can become vulnerable if one partner does not believe in Jealousy. I shall endeavour to expound on this idea elsewhere [Keep an eye on introducingaffinitology.com].

87.5
Immune Deficiency and Other Immune Disorders

The flip side of an oversensitive or over eager defence system is an apathetic one. This is called 'immune deficiency', such as in a situation where The Other in a Spouses Pactum does not support the Business Partner Nexus of The Self's Omniself, thus putting financial strain on the Spouses Pactum.

These are, of course, seedling ideas and need to be developed further. However, taking our cues from physiology can provide us with some of the tools that we need to create better (more empowering) roadmaps towards SMERs.

Unit 20

Therapeutics of Relationships

Image by wollyvonwolleroy from Pixabay

Chapter 88

How to fix things when they go wrong

What is the **most significant barrier** to SMERs? **Communication**. In short, the answer to the problem, "How to fix relationships when they go wrong" is,

---
Fix Communication

This works at every level of organisation (§ 36) from the cell to humankind (§ 90 Fractals).

Communication problems underlie every medical problem that exists. [I say this in spite of having an aversion to sweeping statements]. In other words, for a medical problem to occur, intercellular communication must be impaired in some way; either through physiological impairment or structural damage. Such impairment affects health by disrupting both homeostasis and adaptation.

I believe that, we have all the necessary resources to resolve almost any problem that may arise if communication is not disrupted or can be restored. Remember the 'first law of satisfactory relationships' (§ 28).

We have explored different aspects of communication, as it pertains to interpersonal relationships, in various parts of this book. In this section, I want to provide you with a summary, along with cross-references to help you navigate this aspect of relationships.

Communication is about information exchange.

It is a process. As such, it requires some kind of input and leads to some form of output.

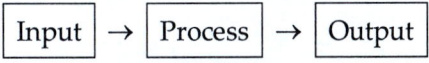

$$\boxed{\text{Input}} \rightarrow \boxed{\text{Process}} \rightarrow \boxed{\text{Output}}$$

Looking at any process or phenomenon from this perspective is a 'systems approach' (§ 67 Feedback Loops).

88.1

Factors Affecting Internal Communication

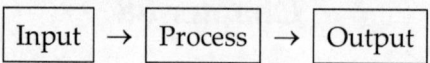

Internal Communication can be at the Identity level, the Omniself level, or the Pactum level. At the Identity and Omniself levels, internal communication is about the process of thinking.

Input

Obviously, before we can exchange information, we need to have some. This input can be sensory information received directly through experience or indirectly through others (§ 39 Social Ranking Criteria). We can process this information (think about it) immediately (short-term memory) or later, through our long-term memory.

We can classify information into two types, theoretical and practical. I define theoretical information as fact or fiction that we can memorise, but cannot implement (do anything with). I can think of two reasons for wanting to exchange this kind of information: as a means, or as an end in itself. Theoretical information is exchanged as a means when The Self believes that The Other can make practical use of it. Although the information itself may be practically useless, being something that can be communicated means that it can be used to attract attention (§ 55 Taxis). Once a connection has been instigated, more useful communication can ensue.

There is a third and a fourth reason for imparting non-useful information; entertainment (no educational value) and misdirection (sinister intent). Since this course is about SMERs (§ 2.1), I shall not elaborate on these here.

Process

In this book we have explored the thinking process from various perspectives, including transactional analysis (§ 73), Atasinex Cluster (§ 33), decision-making (§ 72), self-esteem and self-confidence (§ 40), consciousness (§ 35.11) and locus of control (§ 44).

Output

The output of the process of thinking can be a change in focus (§ 33.3 Attention), assumptions (§ 33.4), beliefs (§ 62.1), values (§ 64), state (§ 51.5.1 Feelings and States), feelings (§ 51 The Emotional Dimension), behaviour (§ 73 Transactional Analysis) or simply a delay in response (§ 79.5.2 Speed of response).

Internal Communication at the Pactum level

At the Pactum level, internal communication is about what happens in Zone E, Interdependence Zone (§ 56.3 Differentiation and Gestation) and involves communication between The Self and The Other (§ 73 Transactional Analysis).

88.2
External Communication

Here, the same systems approach applies as with Internal Communication.

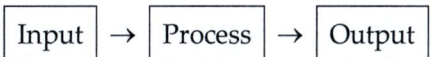

$$\boxed{\text{Input}} \rightarrow \boxed{\text{Process}} \rightarrow \boxed{\text{Output}}$$

What constitutes internal or external communication is a matter of perspective. When my Teacher Identity is talking with my Father Identity, at the Omniself level, I am talking to myself. However, at the Identity level, two separate entities are talking to each other.

In some cultures, when two people want to marry, two families talk to each other. In this case, conversation within the members of each family is internal (within-family) communication and when members from different families talk to each other, that is external communication (at the family level). If these two families, let's call them A and B, are from the same tribe and they go to negotiate a trade agreement with two families, C and D, from another tribe, then, communication between either A or B with either C or D will be 'external' and communication between A and B or C and D will be 'internal' (at the tribal level).

88.3
Social Identity Theory

We can relate our discussion in this section to Social Identity Theory. In § 78 (Active Protection), we came across the minimal group paradigm. In their research on in-group and out-group ('us' and 'them') behaviour, Henri Tajfel and colleagues found that, when opportunities exist for people to be categorised on the basis of the most trivial of criteria (even by something as trivial as tossing a coin), people tend to allocate resources in favour of their own group; often very slightly (low effect size), but to a (statistically) significant extent.

It seems to me that there is scope here for applying these concepts to such affinitological constructs as Identities within an Omniself and other holons (§ 36.9), including those mentioned in § 36 (Levels of Organisation) and § 90 (Fractals). Like the naming of colours, which blind us (literally/practically) to the variety of colours that can be available to us (§ 12 Communication), even the designation of False and True Identity that proposed in Unit 9 (Identities, Roles and Personas) may be more of a grayscale (§ 25.3 Polar Bond: Partial Sharing). However, through a slight of mind, we can categorise these Identities (into True and False, for example) and use them to torture ourselves through the inner conflicts that these groupings create within us.

[I feel I am getting a little carried away here, so, having hopefully planted some seeds of curiosity, I shall stop here. Meanwhile, this leads us seamlessly to our next topic; Diversification and Speciation of Relationships].

Unit 21

Diversification and

Speciation of Relationships

[Image by Gerd Altmann from Pixabay.
Source: https://pixabay.com/illustrations/woman-face-photomontage-faces-789146/]

Chapter 89

Evolution Through Relationships

Why are relationships so important to us? As always, the answer we get depends on who we ask. From an anatomical perspective, because by the time our brain matures, it would be too big for the skull to pass through the mother's pelvis. Accordingly, human babies are born with immature brains. As such, unlike other animals, humans require long periods of nurturing. This leads to a long period of childhood dependence and makes us wired to bond.

Economic theories focus on 'resources' and suggest that we connect because we are interdependent, like a pride of lions who are more likely to catch prey if they work together.

My own, personal, perspective is that each level of connection is preparation for the next step in evolution. Protons and neutrons connect to make diverse atoms. Atoms connect to make diverse molecules. Molecules connect to make diverse eukaryotic cells. Eukaryotic cells connect to make diverse prokaryotic cells. Prokaryotic cells connect to make diverse organisms. Organisms connect to make ecosystems. Extending this line of progression, when our beliefs, habits and values facilitate the establishment and maintenance of healthy relationships (§ 2.1 SMERs), they pave the way for the emergence of a superorganism, in the same way that billions of amoeba-like units, called cells, emerge into the variety of life that we see around us, including humans.

We are wired for clustering into groups. It's what attracts us to crowds, flags and ideologies. In fact, research findings in individual psychology are seldom applicable to crowd behaviour because crowds, or even simpler groups, have dynamics that lead to people behaving in very different ways than they would as individuals (see anecdote in § 32.2 Communities).

Since, through connections, we are constantly evolving, that is, pushing the boundaries of possibility, conflicts are inevitable, i.e., relationships create conflicts as well as alleviating them. The upside of this is that, if a relationship isn't perfect, it doesn't mean that it is unnatural; it simply means that it's evolving (§ 7.1 You make me want to be a better Man).

On the other hand, we also seem to have a need to maintain a sense of individuality and there seems to be conflict here and raises the question, "In order to evolve, must we lose our sense of being an individual?" I am going to explore this question through embryology; the study of how a single fertilised cell becomes a whole human being.

Very quickly after a fertilised cell begins to divide, the cells begin to differentiate. They all begin with the same capabilities, *but their environment causes them to specialise*. In doing so, they group together as different tissues and organs, but each cell retains its multi-potential (undifferentiated) roots in the form of the genetic information inside its nucleus.

Using embryology as a metaphor, or what I prefer to think of as a 'fractal blueprint' (§ 90 Fractals), what gives each of us our sense of individuality is partly genetic but, for the most part, it is social. Some social systems are better at creating and maintaining social cohesion than others. [I was going to elaborate on this but decided to leave that for another time and place. Keep an eye on introducingaffinitology.com]

> *Many years ago, I heard a speech by a young lady who had gone to Africa to be a teacher. She told us that, at first, she couldn't tell the children apart. She was the only white person in the village. When, a few months later, a Caucasian friend went to visit her, the kids rushed over to her friend and talked to her as if she was their teacher. She told us, "My friend doesn't look anything like me." It's not that the two were not different, it was just that the kids didn't know what to look for to recognise those differences.*

Compare that with our earliest experiences of looking at cells. As children, we are usually introduced to cells through observing onion skin under a microscope.

> *Once, I was holding a small child in my arms and, as we were walking, she pointed at various objects and made a noise and I would tell her what it was. At one point, she pointed at a Sycamore tree and I said, that's a tree. She then pointed at a wall and then at a car (or something) and then at a pine tree and, again, I said, that's a tree. Later, she pointed at a Cypress tree and, again, I said, that's a tree. What I wasn't aware of at the time, was that I was depriving this baby of the pleasures of seeing the beauty inherent in the individuality of each tree. By labelling them with the same name, I was stripping each tree from what made it unique. This is, in fact, what was done to me too. When I see a weeping willow, it's a 'tree'.*

> **This is also what we do when we teach our children that there are only seven colours in the rainbow; <u>we reduce our sensory acuity</u>.**

If you ask me a question like, what colour was her dress, I might say, "Oh, it was green." And if you said, what shade of green, I would have difficulty in *remembering* (not merely articulating) because the label condenses all greens into one colour. Similarly, when we are first introduced to cells, what we see is rows of 'cells' and what is pointed out is what they have in common; a cell wall and a nucleus. If our attention were drawn to them, we would also notice that each cell is slightly different in its size, shape, the location of its organelles and so on.

Cells are individuals. And it is my belief that individual cells make individual decisions that affect the whole organism in the way that individual people make individual choices that affect the whole 'organism'. See § 36 (Levels of Organisation) and § 90 (Fractals).

Chapter 90

Fractals

When we first encounter the word fractal and do an internet search for it, we might be a little intimidated by, a) its apparent complexity and b) that there are, look out, 'equations' involved. However, **fractals are simple ideas with complicated consequences**; somewhat like throwing a snowball down a hill where there might be a road at the bottom of the hill with lots of cars going passed. The act of throwing the snowball is simple enough, but the consequences can be overwhelming; if we stop to consider them. Let's look at an example.

We can take a straight line and do something simple to it (figure 69). Here, I have decided to bend it somewhere in the middle. This gives us two new lines. We can do the same thing to these lines, giving us four new lines to work with. If we keep doing this over many iterations (repetitions), we will end up with an intricate and elaborate pattern like the one you see in Step 4 of figure 69.

You can try it for yourself through the following url:
http://www.shodor.org/master/fractal/software/Snowflake.html

Figure 69 Simple rule to complex pattern

Step 1 Take a straight line   Step 2 Bend it

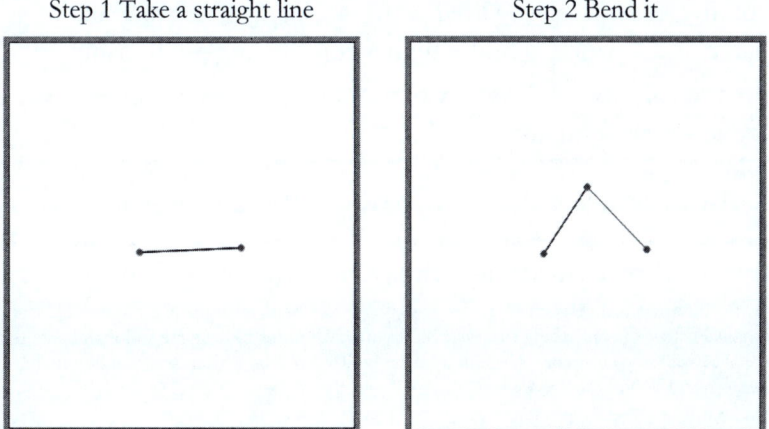

Step 3 Repeat for each new line   Step 4 Continue for 6 more steps

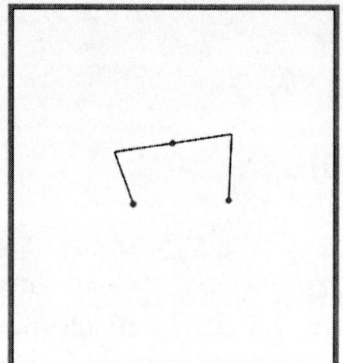   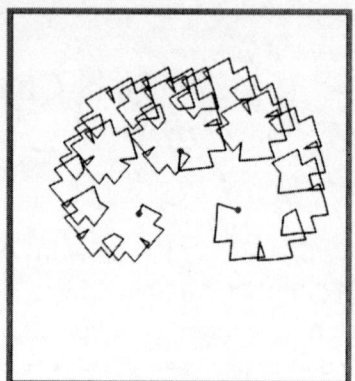

Even though the pattern is complicated, the rules that gave rise to that pattern are simple. This is probably the biggest insight that knowledge of fractals [and chaos theory] endows us with.

[If you are interested in this subject, here are a few other words and phrases for you to explore: Turing Machine, Cellular Automaton, Conway's Game of Life, Langton's ant, Sensitive Dependence on Initial Conditions (the Butterfly Effect), Chaos Theory.]

When we begin to recognise them, we see fractals everywhere; from the shapes of leaves and trees to geological formations and to trends in violence throughout history [Thanks to Stephen Pinker's TED Talk entitled 'The Surprising Decline in Violence' for that insight].

We can think of interpersonal relationships in the same way. They are intricate and elaborate too, however, they are made up of a series of simple rules repeated. We can observe patterns emerging in relationships as they progress (develop), that is, as the number of interactions increase. The quality and quantity of each interaction can lead to the development and maintenance of a SMER or it can lead to a 'downward spiral' culminating in, at best, no relationship and at worst, a mutually disempowering relationship.

The primary rule for all relationships, not just interpersonal ones, can be summarised in one sentence:

To connect, something must have an effect on something else.

This 'something' can be material, such as an electron or abstract, such as an idea.

[Ultimately, for interpersonal relationships, the 'something else' is perception (§ 33 Atasinex Cluster). What I have just implied is that the only thing that we need to affect in order to instigate and maintain a relationship is The Other's perception. This reminds me of a stanza by Rumi, "Oh brother, you are all thought, the rest of you is mere flesh and bone." (My translation)]

The effect can be unidirectional (one way) or bidirectional; unidimensional or multidimensional. When it is unidirectional, we call it an interaction and when it is bidirectional, we call it a transaction (§ 73 Transactional Analysis). The transaction can involve giving, taking, sharing or exchanging. This is how,

---

atoms give rise to molecules to RNA to DNA to viruses to bacteria to amoebae to tissues to organs to organ systems to organisms to herds and tribes to societies to nations to Humankind.

(§ 36 Levels of Organisation)

What is happening at each stage? The *total surface area* (cf. § 25.1 Atomic and Molecular Orbitals) of each new unit (§ 36.9 Holons) increases, providing greater opportunities to connect or interact with its environment, especially other connectable units. This, in turn, provides greater opportunity for information exchange. As the organism's capacity for storing and using information increases, it acquires a greater repertoire of behavioural strategies through increased choice.

Figure 70 shows a fractal pattern that I found on the internet.

Figure 70 A Four Branch Fractal Pattern

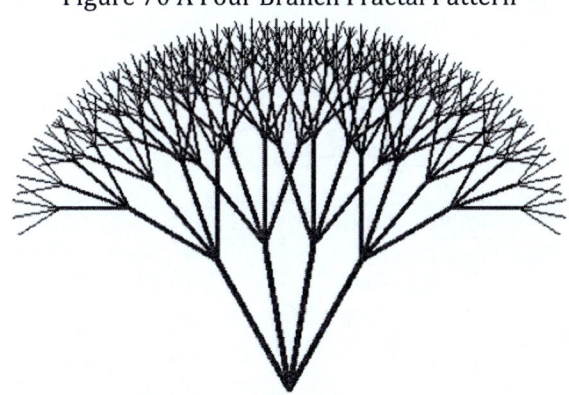

[Source: http://ccgi.jkhudson.plus.com/logoweb/learnlogo/logotree.php]

In Figure 71, I have shown correlates between the chemical analogy, the biological analogy and affinitology. Figure 72 shows how this structure can be represented as a fractal pattern .

Figure 71 The relationship between the chemical analogy, the biological analogy and Affinitology

Fractal Level (Tentative)		
Chemical	**Biomedical**	**Affinitological**
Proton Number	Codon	Concept
Outer electrons	Gene	Belief (Gestalt)
Impurity	Virus	False [potentially disempowering] Belief
Electron Density	Receptors	Values
Atom	Cell	Identity
Moiety	Tissue	Individual
Bond	Intercellular junction	Nexus
Molecule	Organ	Pactum / Bondle
Compound	Organ System	Community
Mixture	Organism	Society
Colligative properties	Species(?)	Culture
Materials	Ecosystems	Humankind

Figure 72 A fractal view of evolution

Electron
Bond
Functional Group
Molecule
Compound
Mixture*

Cell
Interstitial space/synapse
Tissue
Organ
Organ system
Organism*†

Identity
Omniself
Nexus
Pactum
Social group (sub-culture)
Nation/culture/religion/...
Humankind†

* The mixture becomes the basic unit of a new entity (the organism)

† The organism becomes the basic unit of a new entity, Humankind

The main idea that I want us to take away from this section is that,

> **many of the problems that we encounter in our interpersonal relationships arise because we are too caught up in the complicated fractal patterns to see the simple rules that govern them.**

Chapter 91

Relationships as Self-Organizing Systems

Here are two variations on the definition of Self-Organisation:

1) **Self-organization is the appearance of structure or pattern without an external agent imposing it.**

2) **Self-organization is the spontaneous emergence of global coherence out of local interactions.**

How can order emerge from chaos? What you need is a simple set of rules that describes what each element in the system should do when it encounters another element.

[Remember our definition of a relationship (§ 21.1 What is a Relationship?); "When a change in one system causes a change in another, then the two systems are related."]

Let's look at an example. Consider the football industry. It is huge, it is sophisticated, it is organised and it is global. But what is football? It is a set of rules that can be printed on the back of a postage stamp.

["The most words on a postage stamp is 1969, and was achieved by the United Nations Postal Administration (USA) in New York, New York, USA, on 20 October 2017. The record-breaking stamp features the entire text of the Universal Declaration of Human Rights and its pre-amble in French."]

[Source: http://www.guinnessworldrecords.com]

On close examination, the complexities, the (relative) order and the beauty of our entire universe seem to be governed by just a few universal laws and elements. In § 90 (Fractals), we saw how simple rules can lead to complicated patterns. In the late 1960s, John Conway began to look for simple rules that could simulate 'life'. Here is a direct quote from Wikipedia,

"Conway chose his rules carefully, after considerable experimentation, to meet these criteria:
There should be no explosive growth.
There should exist small initial patterns with chaotic, unpredictable outcomes.
There should be potential for von Neumann universal constructors.
The rules should be as simple as possible, whilst adhering to the above constraints.
The game made its first public appearance in the October 1970 issue of Scientific American, in Martin Gardner's "Mathematical Games" column. Theoretically, the Game of Life has the power of a universal Turing machine: anything that can be computed algorithmically can be computed within the Game of Life. Gardner wrote, "Because of Life's analogies with the rise, fall and alterations of a society of living organisms, it belongs to a growing class of what are called 'simulation games' (games that resemble real-life processes)."

In an article entitled, *The Science of Self-Organisation and Adaptivity*, Francis Heylighen writes:

> "The different studies which we reviewed have uncovered a number of fundamental traits or "signatures", that distinguish self-organizing systems from the more traditional mechanical systems studied in physics and engineering. Some of these traits, such as the absence of centralized control, are shared by all self-organizing systems, and can therefore be viewed as part of what defines them. Other traits, such as continual adaptation to a changing environment, will only be exhibited by the more complex systems, distinguishing for example an ecosystem from a mere process of crystallization."
>
> [Source: Heylighen, F. (2001). The science of self-organisation and adaptivity. The encyclopedia of life support systems, 5(3), 253-280.]

Given the points made in this and the previous chapter (Fractals), I put together a few tentative rules for creating SMERs (§ 2.1). It is not exhaustive and the 'rules' do not have a consistent structure, but we need to start from somewhere. I hope that, together, we can build a more empowering set. I don't need anything as big as the back of a postage stamp to write down what I consider to be the **rules for self-organizing relationships**. Here they are.

- If it hurts, avoid
- If it's pleasurable repeat
- If there is conflict, resolve if possible, otherwise avoid
- If it's uncertain communicate
- If you want, say
- If you need, say
- If you get, thank
- If you can, do
- If you can't, be honest
- If you don't get, accept
- If you don't agree, explain
- If there's doubt, clarify
- If you fail and it's worth it, try again
- If a thought begins with "Why", change it to "How can I?"
- If the result did not match your intention and someone was disempowered by it, apologise and try to compensate

Chapter 92
Relationship Frameworks

I was fortunate enough to have access to, and be interested in, computers in the late seventies, early eighties, when personal computers where just being introduced to the mainstream market. Often, my friends would say to me, "Bijan, I want to buy a computer, what should I buy?" And my answer was, "If I were to say to you, I want to buy a car, what should I buy? what would you tell me." Invariably, the answer was, "That depends on what you want to do with it." And I did not need to say, "Exactly."

I think you can see where I am going with this; "Why should relationships be any different?" We define cars and bicycles (and even spoons and knives) based on what we intend to do with them. Would it not be helpful to have a similar classification for our relationships? This is the main intention of this section. I have called the different 'types' of relationship, Relationship Frameworks. The differences between them reflect,

a)   The nature (characteristics) of the Identities involved
b)   The nature of the Nexus that emerges through those identities.

92.1
Marriage

Sometimes, clients ask me how they would know whether or not they are ready for marriage. My response is, "Do you think you are ready for divorce?" I then explain that if the relationship is to be a SMER, that is, where the main purpose is mutual empowerment and not exploitation or subservience, then, one is only ready for marriage when one is ready for divorce.

You may say, as some of my clients do, "But Bijan, isn't that counter to the spirit of marriage? After all, if I say to myself, OK, well, if we don't get along, then we'll just go our separate ways, doesn't that make us more likely to give up if there is tension (as there is in any relationship)? I mean, if we feel that there is no turning back, wouldn't we try harder to resolve our differences?" I would argue that, if we feel that there is no turning back, we are more likely to take the relationship for granted. In other words, believing that our partner is always going to be there gives us less of an incentive to maintain the quality of the relationship. It is also more likely for us to see the relationship from a materialistic perspective; he is mine (and I have the papers to prove it).

"Hey, Bijan, would anyone who thinks like that ever get married?" You might well ask. Yes, because nowadays, especially in societies where women can be financially independent of men, love is rarely a reason for getting married. Other reasons include,

- Financial (e.g., tax incentives or financial security),
- Strategic (socioeconomic or political manoeuvring),
- Sociocultural (peer pressure, tradition),
- Religious beliefs,
- Reassurance (I can hold you accountable) and,
- Control (now I've got you where I want you).

  [From Eric Berne's Book, *Games People Play*]

You might say, "But Bijan, that's a very cynical view of the 'great institution of marriage', isn't it?" And I would say that using words such as 'great' and 'institution' confirm my suspicions that you are trying to subtly harass me into confirming your point of view, otherwise, you would come to me with more solid arguments than mere rhetoric. Secondly, I am not being cynical, I am being practical. In no way do I judge people based on their choice of Relationship Framework; that would be both disempowering for all concerned and hypocritical. What I am saying is that,

---

considering the possibility of divorce when we contemplate marriage is an effective way to becoming aware of our reasons for tying the knot.

Speaking of knots, on my bookshelf, I have a book that is all about knots. Some knots are strong when they are tied, but can be untied easily. Others, once tied, cannot be untied easily. Some knots are tied for their aesthetic value only (such as a bow tie), others for functionality. We are, of course, at liberty to tie any kind of knot we want, but my personal view is that a safety belt without a release button is a noose and can be very dangerous, especially just after an accident. Note that, just because I click my seat belt on it doesn't mean that I expect to be involved in an accident. Similarly, just because I sign a prenuptial agreement, it does not mean that I expect there to be trouble ahead. However, not designing a release button into a marriage contract (or any mental image of the future) is not preparing for contingencies which may be beyond our control.

Marriage is not an extension of a romantic relationship. Marriage is not an extension of friendship. Marriage has both implicit and explicit contractual obligations. It is not a spontaneous emergent relationship. It's a relationship with a predefined template and the stipulations of the contract are both enforced and reinforced by Society. In addition to the melodrama associated with getting married, including weddings and receptions and gifts and rings and so on, being a contract, especially a written one, Society (§ 39 Social Ranking Criteria) considers it to be its right to interfere. This is not the case with friendship. The treatment of the 'joining together' of two people in this way is rooted in our ancestors' tribal mentality because it was important for them to keep control of the gene pool. The contractual obligations imposed by marriage allowed Society to keep track of pedigree.

When you get married you tell Society that your partner is 'off the market' or 'off limits' which makes the phrase 'open marriage' and oxymoron. Open 'relationships', on the other hand, are a different matter.

Marriage, in addition to defining and limiting sexual partners, imposes and implies other commitments, obligations, expectations and even protocols. Being society's business, marital disputes become legal disputes. Society has also provided a 'get-out clause' called divorce with its own rules and regulations. From a legal point of view, marriage ties people together both financially and in terms of their responsibilities towards any children.

Reasons for getting married fall into two broad categories; security and Society. Here are a few alternative ways in which a marriage contract can be conceptualised by each of the parties contemplating it:

- We must get married because I want your children.
- I want to get married because I don't want to lose you.
- I want to make our relationship official
- I want to cement our relationship
- I agree to look after your kids if you agree to look after me
- I want our relationship to be exclusive
- I want our relationship to be legally recognized
- I want to spend the rest of my life with you
- I want to get the family off my back
- I want financial security
- I want my children to have your surname
- I want our families to be united
- I want a wedding

This section is not intended to be a comprehensive treatise on marriage. I may expound on these ideas elsewhere at some point in the future.

92.2
Boyfriend/girlfriend

The pivotal concept around which this Relationship Framework is centred is 'physical touch'. It can be a social concept, like marriage (keep your hands off). Or it can be an Intra-Pactum understanding (§ 70.1 Affinitological Communication). If the concept of boyfriend or girlfriend is understood as being an agreement between 'us' (and it is no one else's business), then being a boyfriend or girlfriend can have different meanings, as agreed between the parties. Here are some examples (more than one can apply).

- I agree to keep my hands off other sexual interests
- I promise that my priority will be to spend time with you when I am not committed elsewhere
- I promise to be available to spend time with you whenever you need me
- I promise to be available to give you emotional support whenever you need me.

92.3
Fiancé

When two people become 'engaged', they agree to announce to Society that they are seriously contemplating marriage. This Relationship Framework has many of the features of marriage, especially the involvement of Society. It is akin to 'try before you buy'. It means that society stops asking questions like, "Why are those two spending so much time together."

92.4
Significant Other

I think of a 'Significant Other' as the person that one likes to spend most of his spare time with. Although the term carries a sexual connotation [almost everything can, and sadly, often is, perverted to give it a sexual slant], child psychologists use it to also mean, 'those people who have the greatest influence on a child's psychological development'. My Significant Other can be

- Someone I like to spend most of my spare time with
- Someone I think of as my primary role model
- My first port of call when I need advice
- Someone who brings me the greatest comfort when I am distressed

92.5
Parent-Child

A parent child *interaction* can occur at the ego state level (§ 73 Transactional Analysis), the Identity level or at the Individual (§ 29.4 The Omniself) level. Relationship *Frameworks* are only instigated at the Identity level.

At the ego state level, a Parent-Child interaction can occur within any Relationship Framework. However, it may be more empowering in a Mentor-Mentee Framework than, for example, a Buyer-Seller Framework, where it can be construed as being patronising.

At the Identity level, a healthy Parent-Child Relationship *Framework* is established when a 'nurturing' Identity interacts with an 'Identity that seeks to be nurtured. Having said that, a parent or guardian can interact with a child through any number of Identities. The specific Relationship Framework depends on the Identities that are interacting in a specific time and situation. For example, when my daughter asks me to help her with a mathematics problem, my Father Identity gives way to my Teacher Identity who then communicates with my daughter's Learner Identity. Similarly, if she asks me a philosophical question, our Philosopher Identities come to the fore leading to the emergence of a Philosophers Nexus and Pactum.

92.6
Teacher-Student

A Teacher-Student type of *interaction* does not necessarily mean a Teacher-Student Relationship *Framework*. A Teacher-Student Nexus only emerges when a Teacher Identity in one Individual (Omniself) interacts with a Student Identity in another Individual. This Nexus is created primarily through three sets of complementary elements (§ 47 Common and Complementary Elements),

a) I know something that I am willing to teach you

b) I want to learn that which you know

c) We are both willing to abide by the protocols congruent with our respective roles; Teacher and Student respectively.

92.7
Partnership

In a partnership, two Identities from two Individuals join forces (knowledge, skills and experience) to accomplish something that neither party could achieve by themselves. Such a Nexus is held together primarily by a common goal.

92.8
Friendship

For the purposes of this course, I have defined the word 'relationship' in its broadest sense, that is, as two systems that can affect each other in some way (§ 21.1 What is a Relationship?). Therefore, an employer and an employee, the soldier and his commander, a seller and a customer, a lawyer and her client, and so on, are all in some kind of relationship. These examples involve contractual (explicit or implicit) expectations in which there are well-defined roles and payoffs.

Friendships, on the other hand, are emotional attachments between two individuals outside of specific social roles or purely contractual obligations. In its purest form, this kind of relationship can be summarised in the following dialogue:

> The Self: "I like you for who you are. That is, with no expectation of material or emotional reciprocation."
> The Other: "The feeling is mutual."

Implicit in the idea of friendship is mutual independence (§ 23.2 The Road to Interdependence). That is, I don't strictly need you but I like it when you're around. This means that, for this kind of relationship framework to ensue, the two Identities involved would need to be socially and financially independent of each other. Note that this does not apply to the Omniselves that the Identities are a part of. For example, if my employer and I establish a Friends Nexus through our Respective Friends Identities, in theory, my commitment to him does not interfere with our Employee-Employer Nexus (§ 58.3 Multi-Nexus Relationships). In practice, most friendships are not as pure as that and are tainted with expectations, that is to say, some kind of trade-off is involved.

Trust is implicit in this kind of relationship (your being around is not going to affect me disempoweringly in any way). In other words, you don't expect me to sacrifice one of my higher values for a lower one (§ 64.7 Hierarchy of Values).

Back in 1981, I was browsing the shelves of a bookshop in Barnsley in West Yorkshire when I came across a small book called The Rubaiyat of Omar Khayyam. I had enjoyed reading the work in its original Persian, but I didn't feel that the popular 1859 translation by Edward Fitzgerald did it Justice. Omar Khayyam, whilst poetic, is quite blunt in the way in which he delivers his message whereas Fitzgerald has imbued his translations with Victorian sentimentality.

The translation I saw in the bookshop was different. It was a collaborative work between a British Scholar of Persian and a poet [I did not know that at the time]. It was not only true to the spirit of the original text, it also included footnotes describing the cultural, historical, social and political background that helped the reader to connect more personally with the intentions of Omar Khayyam himself. I became a fan of the authors. At this point the seed of a relationship was sewn. This was one-way of course as they had no idea that I existed.

On an impulse, I picked up my pen and wrote a letter to the publishers thanking the authors for their commendable translation. Shortly afterwards, I received a letter from one of the authors, Peter Avery [later to become Sir Peter Avery], who turned out to be the head of Persian Studies at Cambridge University. In his letter, thanking me for my comments, he invited me to be his guest at Cambridge University. I called him on the telephone (there were no mobile phones or internet back then) and arranged to meet him in Cambridge. We met and we talked. At that point the relationship changed from me being an unknown admirer to me becoming a known admirer. After that, I visited Peter regularly and we followed each other's progress with interest. We had become friends. To me,

> **the defining factor that distinguishes a friendship from other types of Nexus is that any sense of obligation is self-imposed.**

The people I call my friends never say (and I never say to them) things like, "Why didn't you return my calls?" [unless it is in the context of 'I was concerned about you' because, as I have highlighted above, in an unadulterated friendship, any sense of obligation is self-imposed (not obtained through seeking to induce a sense of guilt)]. We trust each other's intentions (§ 53 Trust). In other words, implicit in a 'pure' Friends Nexus is this, "You don't need to explain, I trust you".

As I mentioned earlier, for friendship not to be tainted with expectations, the two parties need to be independent of each other; they are not in a relationship because they need to be, they are friends because they want to be. In a situation like that it is much easier to trust people because you have 'nothing' to lose.

Of course, you might argue that where there is nothing to be lost the idea of trust is meaningless. So, let me clarify. If you trust someone who you believe to be a friend and that trust is betrayed, you will lose that friendship and that is, of course, lamentable, but your life will not fall apart unless that friendship is tainted with some kind of dependence. In that case, it was either a contractual relationship masquerading as friendship or there were, in fact, two parallel relationships, a contractual one and friendship and the former has interfered with the latter (§ 60.3.2 Inter-Pactal Interference).

Consider a scenario where I have a good friend and we decide to set up a business together. The relationship now expands to include four Identities: Friend 1, Friend 2, Business Partner 1 and Business Partner 2. My Business Partner Identity has different expectations from my Friend Identity. If I get into an argument with my business partner regarding matters to do with the business, I am arguing with my business partner and not with my friend. If I then ask my friend to come to dinner and he refuses because of the arguments that we had about business matters, this is what I mean by a friendship being tainted. The exception to this is where The Self or The Other's Core Values (Principles) are violated (§ 58.4 Multi-Nexus Breakdown).

What I have just described is similar to crossed transactions in Transactional Analysis (§ 73). Here, I have applied it to a broader range of 'selves' than Eric Berne's three ego states.

92.9
Other Relationship Frameworks

We could apply the same treatment to other Relationship Frameworks (Soulmates, Family Members, Colleagues, etc.), but I think that for the purposes of this book, the above examples are enough to lay the foundations.

Part 4
The Physics of
Relationships

[Image by mohamed Hassan from Pixabay.
Source: https://pixabay.com/illustrations/bridge-businessman-concept-running-2892681/]

Unit 22

Thermodynamics of

Relationships

[As I was thinking about this section, my mind continuously probed ideas that related to Newtonian physics, mechanics and engineering. It began to link the notions of mass, length, time, direction, speed, acceleration, force, force fields, momentum and the like to cognition, affect, motivation, attention, desire, consciousness and so on. At one point, I became apprehensive; it seemed that it was becoming too diverse and too complex for what I am trying to achieve at this juncture. Then, the acronym KISS popped into my head. As many of you probably know, KISS stands for "Keep It Simple, Slick". That inspiring thought made me cut a large chunk out of here and to create an outline for a separate volume incorporating the Thermodynamics of Relationships. See § 98 **(Preview of Volume Two)**]

Thermodynamics means 'movement of heat'. In practice, it is applied to any kind of energy and not just heat.

[source: https://commons.wikimedia.org/wiki/File:Microscale_heterogeneity_in_the_ocean.jpg]

Chapter 93

Energy

We tend to use the word 'energy' liberally in our everyday language and we assume that everyone understands it in the same way. I am not going to make that assumption here.

Energy is about change and potential for change. More accurately, it describes how much *change* is happening or can happen. You might ask, "Change in what?" The answer is, change in the relationship between mass, distance, time and direction.

> **If the relationship between mass, distance, time and direction changes, energy is converted/transferred from one form to another.**

["What about charge?", I hear some of you thinking. Charge is a field, like gravity and, in the final analysis, fields (potential forces) only become relevant when they affect (act on) something (mass), to move (distance, time) or change direction].

Although we talk about energy *conversion*, it is more accurate to say energy *transfer*. One advantage of thinking about energy in terms of transfer rather than conversion is that we can extend our reach to other disciplines beyond physics and begin to shake hands with Economics and Accounting.

As your accountant friend will tell you, when keeping track of money, what we are really doing is keeping track of *transfers* from one account into another. To make sure that we do not lose track of the money along the way, we use a system called double-entry book keeping. In this system, we note how much we take out of one account and we must enter the same amount into the receiving account. When we try to do that in physics, we invariably find that less money (energy) goes into the receiving account than comes out of the donating account. We call this 'embezzled' amount of energy, entropy (§ 95).

Staying with our accounting metaphor for a moment, what is an account? It is a label that we attach to money that we allocate. If I allocate the money to John, the account is likely to be called something that points to John. If the money is allocated for household expenses, then the account is likely to be called something that points to household expenses. Where energy is concerned, these different accounts from which energy is transferred to and fro are called 'types' of energy (heat, sound, chemical, nuclear, potential, kinetic, etc.).

Since I am using money as an analogy for energy, it seems appropriate for us to stop, for a moment, to consider what money is.

"What is money?"

As always, the answer depends on who you ask. Here is my personal definition of money: Money is a measure of the value of people's time [This is as far as I will go here because a full explanation of this needs at least another book. However, for those of you who are interested in exploring this topic in more detail, I intend to write about it elsewhere; keep an eye on introducingaffinitology.com]. This means that whenever we buy something, we are, ultimately buying other people's time [nature provides everything else that goes into buying that product or service for free]. And what do we want to buy people's time for? One of two things only; their body or their mind. With their minds, people can imagine things and with their bodies they can make (or break) things. In other words, people make change happen and money is a means of directing what changes people make happen.

The important point is that money is not the change itself, it is a *means*; a means of acquiring resources (in this case, human) to effect change. Similarly, energy is like an account and the money in that account is the amount of change (influence) that it can 'buy' *under the right conditions*.

For example, the energy stored in a chemical bond (deposited in that particular bond's account) can only be transferred (withdrawn) if there is a collision (an interaction). If a transfer goes from any kind of energy account (such as a 'chemical bond' account) into a 'heat account' then we talk about that energy being *released*. From an accounting point of view, money that is *released* is still assigned to an account; this time to a 'current' (able to flow) account [think liquidity]. Heat is like an energy current account. It is not as tied up as capital or deposit accounts. This is why the discipline is called Thermodynamics (the movement of heat).

To wrap up this section, energy is not a thing; it is a label that we attach to an account that contains something that is a measure of value (like money). So, if money is a measure of the value of people's time, what is its equivalent for energy? Energy can (has the potential to) 'buy' the resources necessary to make things happen to Mass, Length, Time and Direction. Therefore,

---

energy is the universal currency for effecting (causing) change.

Like money, we can look at energy from different perspectives, and the more of these perspectives we see, the closer we get to that most elusive of all things; truth. Here is another useful perspective,

---

If there is a change somewhere, then there must be a change somewhere else that compensates for it. Energy is that compensatory mechanism.

If that sounds a bit heavy, bear with me; it will get easier, especially as we begin to describe it in terms of our interpersonal relationships. Another way of conceptualising energy is to say,

---

whenever there is a change of any kind, energy is converted (transferred) from one form (account) to another.

That is to say, since there is no change without movement, whenever something starts to move, stops moving, changes speed or changes direction, these are compensated for by a change in energy somewhere else; something else starts moving, stops moving, changes speed or changes direction.

93.1
Motivation and Motivational Energy

All processes, relationships included, require expenditure of energy. Living systems need to decide what to allocate their limited energy resources to, and how much energy to allocate.

[Note that making decisions, itself, requires energy (look up decision-fatigue). So, we need to decide how much energy we expend thinking about what to do with the energy that we have. It is like deciding how much 'time' we spend in board meetings (thinking), as opposed to spending that 'time' to get things done (taking action).]

Earlier, I said that we can think of energy as currency and the different types of energy as different accounts into which that money can be deposited. In § 58.2 (Good Vibrations), I explained the difference between static equilibria and dynamic equilibria and said that dynamic equilibria need energy simply to maintain their balance. I then related that concept to relationships, explaining that our relationships are also in dynamic equilibrium. This means that energy is not only transferred (required) when relationships (bonds) are formed or when they break, energy is also required to maintain relationships, that is, to prevent them from drifting or flying apart (§ 69 Divergence: Drifting Apart).

Here, I am proposing that we can conceive of a new type of energy account [in addition to light, heat, sound, nuclear, electrical, etc.] that I am calling Motivational Energy. The various forms of Motivational Energy are created from four components. We can think of them as psychological counterparts to mass, length, time and direction. These are,

a) Cognitive: How we interpret whatever it is that we are focusing on
b) Dimensional (Domain of desire): Material, social, sensual, sexual, etc.
c) Temporal: When, how often and for how long.
d) Attentional: What we are paying attention to (focusing on)

We explore the first two of these in § 33 (Atasinex Cluster) and the third in Unit 11 (Dimensions of Human Experience).

We have already noted that energy is derived from the relationship between mass, length, time and direction. For affinitological purposes, I propose that we can reframe the cognitive aspect of relationships as the substantive (mass) component of motivational energy, attention as its directional component and dimension as its length (spatial) component.

93.2

Manifestations of Motivational Energy

Expenditure of motivational energy manifests itself in some physical form; a change in the relationship between mass, distance, time and direction. Here are five ways through which Motivational Energy can be transferred; they are not mutually exclusive:

- Words spoken
- Objects exchanged
- Time devoted
- Service provided
- Touch

[These seem to correspond to the 'five love languages' proposed by Gary Chapman.]

Chapter 94

Energy Balance

Someone once told me that whenever she became irritable whilst on a drive to somewhere, her husband would pull over at the nearest shop and would buy her something to eat, commenting, "I thought you are probably hungry."

Everything we do requires energy. This energy comes directly from what we ingest. All of the processes that our body and mind must perform for us to be alive (MRS GREN), be conscious (able to exercise choice), be human (seeking to become a better Man) be unique (do the things that only we can do) require the energy that what we ingest provides.

Once food has been processed to provide us with the energy reserves that we need to function, it is essential that these energy resources be *managed effectively*. Like any other organisation, resources must be distributed in accordance with the energy requirements for each process (no less and no more). Some processes in our bodies are more energy intensive than others. What I have said in this paragraph is not in dispute.

What I am about to say is based more on experience and intuition than on direct scientific research and may, therefore, spark some controversy, which I would welcome - because controversy fuels debate and debate attracts resources for research and research leads to greater understanding and, of course, more controversy. That is the nature of knowledge:

> **the more we know the more we become aware of the extent of our ignorance**

I propose that, when we are not in a 'fight or flight' state, there are three energy-intensive processes in our body that are in competition with each other; the digestive system, the immune system and the frontal lobe; the thinking system (Figure 73).

Figure 73 Three Competing Energy-Intensive Bodily Systems

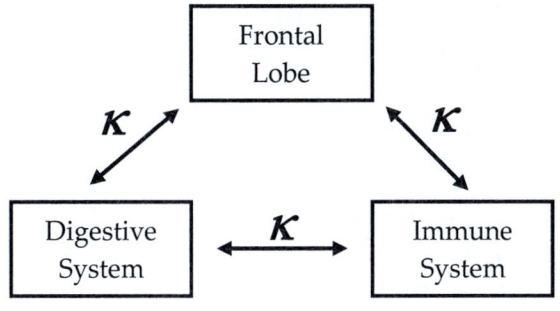

κ = is in competition with

[I could not find a symbol to mean 'is in competition with' and decided that, given the pervasiveness of this concept, it would be useful to have one. Close competitors were cf. (compare) and vs. (contrast), but neither of them seemed satisfactory to me. So, I appropriated the Greek letter κ (kappa) for this purpose.]

Depending on the circumstances, such as during vigorous exercise, other systems, including the cardiovascular and pulmonary systems, may become energy-intensive. Normally, however, as your accountant friend might say, the energy requirements of these systems are more like 'fixed costs' (expenses that do not vary (significantly) as a function of the normal activity of a business). Ordinarily, the three systems that I have shown in Figure 73 are like 'variable costs' (costs that change as the quantity of the goods or service that a business produces changes). Let me elaborate.

94.1

Energy and Glucose

How and when we eat affect our relationships. I am not just talking about the bonding effect of eating together, which is quite strong by the way. Here, I am talking about the energy balance in our bodies and how this affects the ways in which we interact with people.

Digestive System κ (is in competition with) Immune System

Certain illnesses, such as bacterial infections, cause us to lose our appetite as energy is diverted from our digestive system to our immune system.

It is well documented that there is a link between obesity and autoimmune diseases. Here is what I propose as part of the mechanism for this. A digestive system that works more than is healthy, takes the extra energy that it needs from the immune system. This leads to immune system related disorders, including immune suppression [like workers going on strike because they are underpaid] and autoimmune diseases [Think mutiny].

Frontal Lobe κ Digestive System

When we are digesting food, energy is diverted away from the frontal lobe, which also makes us less able to think clearly; we become drowsy. Conversely, it is my hypothesis (guess) that when we eat too much, we also become slightly immune compromised. [I have already pointed to the link between obesity and autoimmune diseases, above (Digestive System κ Immune System)]. You may have noticed that, when we are concentrating hard on learning something, or on solving a difficult problem, we forget about food. This is because our body knows that it needs to prioritise energy usage. As such, when we eat, we feel drowsy and are unable to think clearly maintain our focus on the task (and people) at hand.

Frontal Lobe κ Immune System

Using our frontal lobe too much can make us ill because less energy will be available for our immune system. This makes us more prone to becoming immune compromised. Conversely, when we are fighting infection, or when our immune system is otherwise activated, our cognitive faculties are compromised and the quality of our decision-making suffers. In § 38.3 (Alternatives to Personas), I mentioned that, when I catch a cold, I rarely have the typical symptoms [fever, runny or stuffy nose or headaches or itchy eyes, etc.]. The main thing that alerts me to it is that I begin to feel drowsy (lethargic) and unable to concentrate well.

Frontal Lobe and Fatigue

What this means is that, when we are digesting, or when we are fighting infection, energy is diverted away from our rational, energy-intensive, decision-making centres and we lose the ability to analyse the situation as accurately as before and we become more cautious which means that fatigue sets in earlier; we feel less motivated.

Interestingly, research has shown that we feel fatigued long before there is any risk of cellular stress, meaning that fatigue is a mental state and not a physical one. In other words, when we are feeling fatigue, it is our mind and not our body that is telling us to slow down.

94.2
The Frontal Lobe and Emotional Control

The Frontal Lobe is responsible for regulating our emotions, amongst other things. Here is what Wikipedia says about the function of the Frontal Lobe:

> "The Frontal Lobe plays a large role in voluntary movement. It houses the primary motor cortex which regulates activities like walking.
> The function of the Frontal Lobe involves the ability to project future consequences resulting from current actions, the choice between good and bad actions (or better and best) (also known as conscience), the override and suppression of socially unacceptable responses, and the determination of similarities and differences between things or events.
> The Frontal Lobe also plays an important part in integrating longer non-task-based memories stored across the brain. These are often memories associated with emotions derived from input from the brain's limbic system. The Frontal Lobe modifies those emotions to generally fit socially acceptable norms."

It is hard to be objective when our Frontal Lobe is compromised and we are "High on Emotion" [to quote from the lyrics of a Chris De Burgh song]. The trick is to have enough of a light on in our Frontal Lobe to be able to recognise that emotions have taken control and to have had enough practice to take the control back, if we decide that it is to our advantage to do so. However, the Frontal Lobe needs a lot of energy to do its job. When other body systems need energy, the Frontal Lobe loses its grip on our emotional centres. It becomes less competent at mediating between our experiences and our emotions. When the Frontal Lobe is compromised, our emotional processes take over and we become more impulsive; less rational.

There is plenty of scope here for research into the relationship between the immune system, the frontal lobe, the digestive system, emotional control, decision-making and our interpersonal relationships.

Sometimes being with other people feels draining and at other times it feels satisfying (nourishing). We can explain these feelings through our discussions about energy and emotions. Here are some examples.

Resistance

Resisting means opposing a force. Active resistance (§ 58.2 Good Vibrations) requires energy. This energy comes from the glucose that we derive from the food that we eat. In interpersonal relationships, resistance stems from a feeling of vulnerability; a feeling that if I don't have my guards up, then I am likely to lose more than I am likely to gain. This means that resistance is a psychological defence mechanism (§ 79). Since in this course, our primary concern is with SMERs, our discussion is centred around normal (§ 71 What is Normal?) human interactions which means that we are not talking about fear of violence or things like that. There are two types of active resistance; active avoidance and Persona.

Avoidance

The difference between active and passive avoidance is that in the latter, we simply remove ourselves from the situation. In this case, as they say in Iran, we 'rub out the question' then the question is no longer there for us to worry about. This solves the immediate problem, the uncomfortable feeling, but it does not 'resolve' the issue, the reason for avoiding the situation in the first place. In active avoidance, we remain in the social situation that is making us feel uncomfortable, but we avoid certain types of interaction, for example by, not answering certain questions, changing the subject or being aloof.

Persona

A much more common method of resistance is pretence. That is, we create a false Identity (§ 38 Personas) and interact with people through it. The problem with a false Identity is that, to our collection of real Identities, it is an outsider and they tend to want to reject its presence. In other words, we would prefer to be genuine. The energy that is required to maintain a persona is, therefore, used mainly to resist its rejection by our real selves (Identities). If we have sufficient energy resources, that is, if we have not eaten too much, are not hungry, tired, preoccupied or fighting a disease, a persona can survive for several days or maybe even weeks. However, it is rare for us to remain in a situation when we are not hungry, not tired, not overeaten, not preoccupied and not fighting a disease for more than a few days. This is why sometimes, early impressions are positive, but later, we see 'another side' to people.

Chapter 95

Entropy

Emergence is something out of nothing
Entropy is nothing out of something

Most of us know about the first law of thermodynamics in one way or another; 'energy is never lost; it is always converted from one form to another'. There is a similar law called the law of conservation of mass; in any closed system, the total amount of matter remains constant; it may be converted from one form to another, but it is never lost [Well, this is what we used to teach our kids at school until Albert said E=MC ^{2}. And in 1981, a group called Landscape sang a song about it called, 'Einstein a go-go'].

Now, we can think of mass as a form of highly condensed energy and we call the first law of thermodynamics, the law of conservation of mass-energy which says that mass and/or energy is never lost, it is converted from one form to another. Well, I am glad we sorted that one out. Or did we? Because there is this niggling matter of entropy.

95.1
What is entropy?

[Bear with me and you will soon find out what all this has to do with relationships; I haven't gone off the rails, although it may appear that way at the moment.]

Entropy is a gap between what we think should happen in theory and what happens in practice. In theory, energy is converted (§ 93 Energy) from one form to another without any of it being lost in the process. In practice that never happens. We always get less energy after conversion than we had before it converted. So, where does it go? We have absolutely no idea. But to make our observations fit our theories, we created this concept of phantom energy that we call entropy [because it has a nice scientific ring to it and it makes us think that we know what we're talking about]. So, now we can say that when energy is converted from one form to another, and we don't see as much of it after conversion, it is not that the energy is lost; it has turned into phantom energy called entropy.

The concept of entropy emerged (in the 19th Century) from studies of heat loss and, whenever we are dealing with heat, we measure temperature. This is why, in practice, the 'embezzled' energy that we call entropy is defined as a function of temperature. In other words, we calculate the energy loss by multiplying the fiddle factor by temperature to derive the embezzled energy [Energy loss divided by temperature equals change in entropy].

In academic parlance, we call this sort of thing a 'fiddle factor'. It is some extra term (piece of an equation) that we add to a mathematical model that makes the data fit the theory. This is not entirely redundant because often, we find a practical explanation that helps us to understand the world around us better. Sadly, the best that we have come up with to explain entropy is that it is a measure of the 'degree of disorder' in a system. To make this explanation work, we need to define a new kind of energy [which I haven't heard of yet]. Let me explain.

We have already said that energy can convert (be transferred) from one form to another. At school we needed to memorize a list of forms of energy; kinetic energy, sound energy, electrical energy, chemical energy, heat energy and atomic energy [Looking through Wikipedia it seems that they've added a few others since my days in school]. But I see no sign of 'disorder energy' [I could, of course, suppose that entropy is it]. Nevertheless, this is an interesting notion that we can use in our discussion about relationships. Intrigued? I hope so.

The idea of something disappearing into nothingness is uncomfortable for scientists, hence the invocation of the concept of entropy [This being 'something' rather than nothing]. The idea of something emerging out of nothing is even more uncomfortable for them [I could have said for 'us' but I am siding with my non-scientist Identities for now (§ 29.4 The Omniself)]. But this is, in effect what I have proposed as a basis for affinitology:

---

when two people begin to interact, a relationship (Nexus) emerges, i.e., an entity 'appears from nowhere' and takes on an Identity of its own.

Furthermore, this relationship is, in part, independent of the two identities that led to the creation of that relationship - See figure 36 in § 56.3 (Differentiation and Gestation).

95.2
Entropy and Emergence

Emergence is the counterpart to entropy.

Whilst entropy can be thought of as the 'disappearance' of energy (nothing from something), emergence is the opposite; it is the creation of something from nothing. This notion of a process that is the opposite of entropy has been called 'negentropy'. The word 'syntropy' has also been proposed. I postulate that emergence, negentropy, syntropy and relationships also converge onto 'love' and that we can define love in terms of affinitological thermodynamics and energetics. However, that is beyond the scope of this course. [Keep an eye on introducingaffinitology.com]

Unit 23

Mechanics of Relationships

(Affinito-Mechanics)

Here is how mechanics is defined on Wikipedia:

> "Mechanics is that area of science concerned with the behaviour of physical bodies when subjected to forces or displacements, and the subsequent effects of the bodies on their environment."

We can derive an equivalent description for affinito-mechanics thus:

> "Affinitomechanics is that area of science concerned with the behaviour of Identities and Nexuses when subjected to motivational forces and the subsequent effects of those phenomena on their environment."

There are many words that we already use in our everyday language to describe various aspects of relationships that are borrowed from mechanics; words such as stress, strain and pressure. Thus far, these terms have been used metaphorically. What if we could devise more literal definitions for such words so that we could apply the language of mathematics to them? This is what I propose to spark in this section.

When we talk about stress, strain and pressure metaphorically, we usually apply them to cognitive and emotional processes within individuals; "They are stressed", "She is under pressure", "He is buckling under the strain of the job". We also talk about relationships in such terms, such as when we talk about something putting a 'strain on the marriage' or about 'peer pressure'.

Chapter 96

Directionality of Relationships

One of the central tenets of mechanics is the idea of direction. Direction is what changes the abstract notion of numbers (scalars) into the more practical concept of vectors. Here, I have outlined my thoughts about how we can apply this to relationships.

Based on our working definition of a relationship (§ 21.1 What is a Relationship?), there is a relationship between two people when a change in some aspect of one person causes a change in some aspect of another. For example, a lady taking her clothes off, an environmental change, may cause an emotional change in a man standing nearby. If the lady is by a waterfall in the woods and the man is an ornithologist who happened to be looking at some blue tits when the lady happened to enter his field of view, then the relationship is unidirectional (only one party is affected) and cross-dimensional (an environmental change causes an emotional change). This is depicted in figure 74.

Figure 74 - A Cross-Dimensional Unidirectional Change

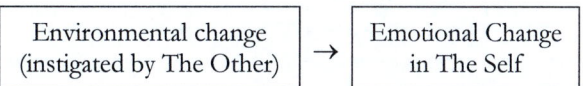

If the two people in the above example were in the same hotel room and the man picking up his binoculars to look for birds leads the other to do the same, that would constitute a unidimensional relationship because a change in the *behaviour* of one causes a change in the *behaviour* of the other, that is, the change occurs along the same dimension of human experience, as depicted in figure 75.

Figure 75 A unidimensional unidirectional change

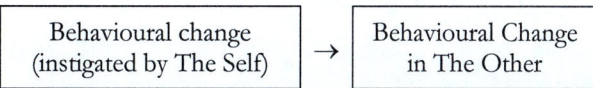

If, in the second scenario, above, the woman picking up her binoculars causes a deep sense of appreciation to sweep through the man, then the relationship is bidirectional; a change in one person leads to a change in another which leads to a change in the first. Here, the first 'connection' is unidimensional (behaviour-behaviour) and the second connection is cross-dimensional (behaviour-emotion). This is depicted in figure 76.

Figure 76 A multidimensional bidirectional change

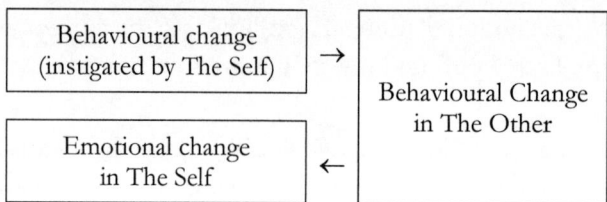

If now, the man turns to the woman and says, "I really appreciate you being here" and she responds sincerely with, "Me too", then this last connection is mutual (bidirectional AND along the same dimension); mutual appreciation (figure 78)

Figure 77 A unidimensional bidirectional change

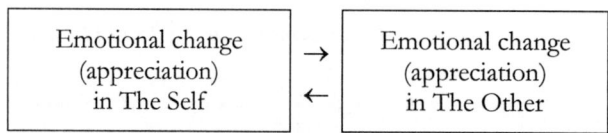

Actually, this diagram isn't quite right (but sufficient for illustrative purposes) because it implies that the feeling of appreciation in one party is causing the feeling of appreciation in the other party and this will lead to a spiralling loop. However, whilst the expression of appreciation by The Self may lead The Other, either to notice (realise) her own appreciation of the situation or to express it, it is more likely that they are both appreciating being in the same situation together. This is expressed well by the following quote from the author of 'The Little Prince'. You may remember having seen this before in § 25.4 (Dative Bond: Give and Share).

> **"Love does not consist of gazing at each other, but in looking outward together in the same direction."**
>
> - Antoine de Saint Exupéry

An interaction, that is, a pair of transactions (§ 73 Transactional Analysis) can be 'reciprocal' or 'antagonistic'. A transaction is antagonistic when a response is not conducive to strengthening the connection (empowering the relationship). An example would be if in response to "I really appreciate you being here", the lady had responded by saying, "Well, if you appreciated me being here, you wouldn't be looking elsewhere all the time." This is what, in Transactional Analysis (§ 73), we would call a 'crossed transaction'.

In summary, a relationship can be one-way; unidirectional, or two-way (bidirectional). The changes in the parties involved may be unidimensional; along the same dimension of human experience (§ 48-50); or cross-dimensional.

Chapter 97

Pressure, Stress and Strain

Compare the following two equations:

$$\text{Pressure, } p = \frac{\text{Force}}{\text{Area}} \qquad \text{Stress, } \sigma = \frac{\text{Force}}{\text{Area}}$$

Both pressure and stress are measured in pascals. If we are measuring the same things (force and area), and deriving the same units (pascals), why are we calling them by different names? Imagine that you are standing on a platform, looking at a train coming towards you. What you will experience is a train approaching the platform. Now, imagine that you are a passenger on that train. This time, what you will experience is that the platform is approaching the train.

[I hear some of you saying, "Yes, yes, of course, this is basic relativity, everyone knows that." And all I ask is that you bear with me for a moment.]

Similarly, if I tie a rock to the end of a rope and start to spin it round, from my point of view, it feels as if the rock is trying to *pull away* from me (the centre). We call this centrifugal [(trying to') 'escape' (think fugitive) from the center] force. However, from the rock's point of view (if it had one), I am preventing it from pulling away, that is to say, I am *pulling it back* (towards the center). We call that centripetal force. According to physicists, the rock would be right, the direction of the force is *towards the centre*. What these examples demonstrate is that our perception depends on our point of reference.

As with the train and the rock examples, pressure and stress are about looking at the same phenomenon from different perspectives. When an elephant puts one of its feet on the ground, the elephant's foot exerts 'pressure' whilst the ground under its foot experiences 'stress'. In other words, pressure is about what the environment does and stress is about how the object responds [think Newton: equal and opposite]. This is like the difference between pharmacodynamics and pharmacokinetics (Unit 17: Pharmacology of Relationships).

The difference between mechanical stress and affinitological stress is in *choice* (§ 35.11 Consciousness and § 40.2 Behaviourism vs. Humanism). A conscious organism can choose how to *respond* to emotional or cognitive pressure [It is limited in its choice of how it responds to physical pressure since that is determined by the laws of physics].

Chapter 98

Every Ending is a New Beginning

Throughout this course, we have borrowed terminology and concepts from already well-established scientific disciplines and we have seen how they can be applied to help us develop theoretical frameworks and concepts that can help us to improve the quality of our interpersonal relationships.

I hope that, in addition to having planted the seeds of a new academic discipline, this course will have provided us with practical frameworks for developing empowering strategies for improving our interpersonal relationships.

As I pointed out elsewhere in this book, I have had to self-regulate my enthusiasm for writing more in this volume with a view to continuing our discussions in a second volume. As such, the final section (Unit 23) on the mechanics of relationships is not as well-developed as the previous units. Think of it as a foot in the doorway to the second volume. As a taster, there now follows a preview of what I have in mind for inclusion in the second volume.

Part 5
The Next Leg of the Journey

[Image by GraphicMama-team from Pixabay.
Source: https://pixabay.com/vectors/man-map-smile-world-travel-1597963/]

Preview of Volume two

There are many other topics that I wanted to include in this volume. However, as the work began to expand, I decided to leave some of it for a second volume. In this section, I simply want to let you know what I intend to include in the next volume.

The Evolution of Relationships

Based on our current understanding of interpersonal relationships, can we map a historical path and extrapolate possible trajectories for more evolved (empowered) relationships and, consequently, societies?

Love and Unification

According to the venerable Persian Mystics, there is a strong relationship between love and unification (joining to become one with the divine). This idea is, of course, not limited to Greater Iran. Many scholars, including the illustrious Erich Fromm, have also alluded to it. In the next (or another) volume, I hope to elaborate on the relationship between love and unification from different perspectives.

Beyond Satisfaction

What if we could reach a stage where our goals were no longer dictated by our needs? What if we no longer strive to acquire anything (wealth, friends, love, health, etc.)? Would there still be something in life that would bring us joy?

Relationship Engineering

Relationship Engineering is about how we can further apply our understanding of mass, length, time, distance, direction, energy, force, pressure, stress, strain, etc. to improving the quality of our interpersonal relationships.

How to Influence People

There are two facets to influencing people: one sinister and one benevolent. Actually, as I hope we have come to understand on this journey together, it is not as black and white as that. It would be more accurate to say that there are two extremes of influence along a spectrum ranging from most sinister to most benevolent. Teachers, spiritual guides, parents, civic leaders, motivational speakers, psychotherapists, lawyers, salespersons, comedians, con artists, beggars, advertisers, journalists, politicians, social predators, extortionists, drug dealers, cult leaders and other manipulative individuals are all influencers. The differences are in intentions, outcomes and methods.

In the next volume, I intend to develop these ideas further with a view to developing a framework whereby we can mutually empower each other through well-intentioned influence and without triggering our psychological defence mechanisms.

Psychology of Relationships

Anatomy is about what and where, physiology is about how and psychology is about why. There are many theories about why organisms do what they do and the answers always depend on the context. The most popular scientific theories, including evolution, are based on adaptation and survival.

The psychology of relationships can be considered at five levels;

  - The Individual (Omniself) level
  - The Identity (The Self and The Other) level
  - The Nexus level,
  - The Pactum level,
  - The Bondle level.

At each level, the primary question will focus on why. However, as I have argued elsewhere (§ 11.1 Why Can Seriously Damage Our Health), the word 'why' often creates more problems than it solves and, as such, I prefer to replace it with 'impetus'. That is, what is the impetus (or motivation) for,

  a) An Individual to create multiple Identities?
  b) Each Identity to create a Nexus?
  c) Each Identity to maintain (remain part of) a specific Pactum?
  d) Individuals to behave in ways that they would not in isolation?

The one-word answer to every one of these questions, I would posit, is 'empowerment'.

Ideas as Living Systems

It is my belief that ideas also behave as living systems in that they 'strive to survive'. In other words, each level of empowerment tries to build on the previous level and to do so, it must ensure the survival of the existing structures. What I am sharing with you here are my initial thoughts on this topic. It still needs to be nurtured and developed.

Epidemiology of Relationships

Epidemiology is primarily concerned with 'risk factors' and how to mitigate against them. From an affinitological perspective, these can be classified into two broad categories:

1. Factors that can potentially disempower the individuals comprising the relationship; 'The Self' or 'The Other'
2. Factors that disempower The Nexus.

More Thermodynamics

As I was pondering the potential for applying thermodynamic principles to interpersonal relationships, I picked out an aging book on thermodynamics from my bookshelf and flicked through it. The possibilities seem endless and very alluring.

Imagine being able to transform our current knowledge of interpersonal relationships, which I currently consider to be akin to ancient alchemy, into the equivalent of modern chemistry and beyond. We can consider the affinitological equivalents to force, distance, acceleration, energy, etc. Let's look at a few thermodynamic concepts that we could extend to affinitology.

Dynamic Equilibrium

A steady state that all relationships tend towards. When the equilibrium is disturbed, Identities' (The Self and The Other's) beliefs and values will tend toward a direction that restores the equilibrium.

Heat Capacity

The amount of Motivational Energy required to raise the resonance level (§ 58.2 Good Vibrations) of a Nexus by one (to be defined) level.

Enthalpy of Formation

The elements involved in forming a bond are only 'motivated' to do so if they become more stable than they would be if they did not form the bond [as is often the case, there are exceptions.].

Imagine being stressed. What do we usually do to feel better? In our quest to relieve our anxiety, we often look at what we can 'take' to calm us down; we even talk about 'taking it out on someone' [we can think of this as an 'endothermic' turn of phrase)]. Other ways that we seek to 'take', in the hope that it will calm us down, is acquiring things (e.g., retail therapy). Now, imagine what happens when someone says something or does something that calms you down. One of the first things that we do is to emit a sigh of relief. We can think of this sigh as 'letting it out' [exothermic]. When chemical bonds form, they too, 'let out' energy, usually in the form of heat which, in that case, is called the enthalpy (heat) of formation.

The more stable we become (secure we feel), the less we need to 'take' and, in the process of changing (becoming more stable), we let go of the things that we used to hold on to in order to make us feel more secure; we either throw them away or give them away. This is like bond making, which is usually exothermic (gives out energy/resources).

I hear some of you saying, "But Bijan, the process of getting married can be very expensive. Isn't that the same as energy consuming?" At which point I would remind you that we are not talking about material things here. We are talking about [for want of a better word] the soul. If the marriage, or any SMER, does what it is supposed to do, then The Self and The Other will be more 'emotionally' stable. During the marriage (bonding) process we often talk about the bride and the groom looking 'radiant', giving out rays (of hope, enthusiasm, love, etc.).

Enthalpy of Dissociation

Breaking chemical bonds (§ 25 Relationships as Chemical Bonds) is like trying to pull two magnets apart. It requires energy. A relationship breakup is similarly energy consuming; requires sufficient motivational energy to overcome the resistance that the Nexus puts up.

You see, sometimes, when The Self and The Other are motivated to break the relationship, the Nexus itself resists. Remember that the Nexus is a separate entity which has influence beyond The Self and The Other (see figure 36).

I hope, lifespan permitting, to include these and other concepts (such as catalysis, heats of reaction, equilibrium constant and bond strengths) in the next (or another) volume. [There's a lot to be done and there's a lot of fun to be had doing it.]

Therapeutic Applications of Affinitology

As I mentioned in the introduction to this volume, when I embarked upon this project, I intended to write a book to accompany a course. It was meant to be primarily a book of practical techniques. Having transformed itself [notice the dissociation ;-)] into a primarily theoretical discourse, in the next volume, I hope to advance more clinical and real-world applications of the ideas explicated here to help readers (and myself) use these models to improve our interpersonal relationships at every level (of organisation).

Differential Diagnosis of Affinitological Diseases

I originally wanted to include a section on Differential Diagnosis in this book. However, I have postponed this for the next stage of this project.

Indexes

When I was compiling the subject index, I did not strictly adhere to the notion of 'subject' as in words that were directly pertinent to affinitology. What I had in mind can be better thought of as a 'pointer' index. Let me explain.

When I am trying to remember a topic in a book, I don't always remember the most relevant words. Sometimes, I remember a random word that was mentioned around the place where I saw something of interest. For example, in the following index, you will find an entry for the word sausage. In § 23, I wanted to show that the concept of interpersonal relationships is a subset of all relationships and that if we understand the rules that govern relationships in general, then we will be in a better position to determine whether or not our fundamental approach to our interpersonal relationships is empowering. To this end, I compared our relationship with other people with our relationship to a sausage. This word is not central to any of the themes in this book, however, it is likely to stand out in our mind. We may want to draw on the information in § 23, but all that comes to mind is the word 'sausage' and since this word is included in the index, this makes our task easier.

On the other hand, highly related words such as relationship, Identity and Nexus do not appear in this index because they are too frequent for a page listing to be of practical value.

SUBJECT INDEX

H

I

O

W

X

Y

NAME INDEX

INDEX OF ORGANISATIONS

INDEX OF PLACE NAMES

MENTIONED MUSICAL WORKS

INDEX OF MOVIES (FILMS)

Glossary

Affinitology The study of interpersonal relationship from the point of view that there are many identities within each Individual and that the connection (a **Nexus**) is a separate entity that emerges when two people interact with each other.

Atasinex Cluster An acronym for the sequence of processes that lead from sensory input to our value judgements.

attention → assumptions → interpretation → expectations

Bondle A unit consisting of two Omniselves connected through one or more Nexuses.

Common Elements Shared factors that attract two Identities to each other, such as common goals or common beliefs.

Complementary Elements Factors that attract two Identities to each other because they are different, but lead to mutual empowerment.

Core Values = Principles The values that are shared by all of the 'True Identities' within an Omniself.

Exo-Nexus A Nexus outside the pactum that has the potential to influence the Pactum.

Identity The sum total of everything that affects a self's value judgements in a particular situation. In any particular situation, my Identity is made up of everything that I identify with at that moment.

Nexus = The Third Entity The connection (Common and Complementary Elements) that hold two Identities together.

Omniself = Individual A collection of the Identities (selves) that coexist within an individual physical body.

Pactum A unit consisting of two Identities connected through a Nexus.

Persona = False Identity An Identity within an Omniself that does not share the Omniself's Core Values.

Personette A set of Identities and their associated Core Values in an Individual who has more than one set of Core Values (because they are incongruent with each other).

Sculpturism The world view that society is a living sculpture and each of us is a creative element within that sculpture through a mechanism of self-organisation.

SMER Satisfying and mutually empowering relationship.

Superself A unit consisting of several Identities from different Individuals held together by a set of common beliefs and Core Values.

Epilogue

We are the continuation, not the culmination, of life on earth and our relationships are the mechanism through which we evolve. The nature and quality of the relationships that we are able to establish and maintain are the primary indicators of our contribution to our own evolution.

> **"And the end of all our exploring will be to arrive where we started and know the place for the first time."**
> - T. S. Eliot